Luminos is the Open Access monograph publishing program from UC Press. Luminos provides a framework for preserving and reinvigorating monograph publishing for the future and increases the reach and visibility of important scholarly work. Titles published in the UC Press Luminos model are published with the same high standards for selection, peer review, production, and marketing as those in our traditional program. www.luminosoa.org

The publisher and the University of California Press Foundation
gratefully acknowledge the generous support of the
Robert and Meryl Selig Endowment Fund in Film Studies,
established in memory of Robert W. Selig.

Global Movie Magazine Networks

Global Movie Magazine Networks

Edited by

Eric Hoyt and Kelley Conway

UNIVERSITY OF CALIFORNIA PRESS

University of California Press
Oakland, California

© 2024 by The Regents of the University of California

This work is licensed under a Creative Commons CC BY-NC-SA license.
To view a copy of the license, visit http://creativecommons.org/licenses.

Suggested citation: Hoyt, E. and Conway, K. (Eds.). *Global Movie Magazine
Networks*. Oakland: University of California Press, 2024. DOI: https://doi.org/
10.1525/luminos.212

Library of Congress Cataloging-in-Publication Data

Names: Hoyt, Eric, editor. | Conway, Kelley, 1963– editor.
Title: Global movie magazine networks / edited by Eric Hoyt and
    Kelley Conway.
Description: Oakland, California : University of California Press, [2024] |
    Includes bibliographical references and index.
Identifiers: LCCN 2024010108 (print) | LCCN 2024010109 (ebook) |
    ISBN 9780520402768 (paperback) | ISBN 9780520402775 (ebook)
Subjects: LCSH: Motion pictures—Periodicals—History—20th century.
    Classification: LCC PN1993 .G56 2024 (print) | LCC PN1993 (ebook) |
    DDC 791.4305—dc23/eng/20240325

LC record available at https://lccn.loc.gov/2024010108
LC ebook record available at https://lccn.loc.gov/2024010109

33   32   31   30   29   28   27   26   25   24
10   9   8   7   6   5   4   3   2   1

For Vance Kepley

CONTENTS

List of Figures and Tables   *x*

Acknowledgments   *xiii*

Introduction: Building and Analyzing Movie Magazine Networks   *1*
     Eric Hoyt and Kelley Conway

SECTION ONE: HYBRID JOURNALS

1. From Paris to the World: *Pour Vous* and French Film Culture, 1928–1940   *25*
     Eric Smoodin

2. *Filmindia* and Its Publics: Magazine Culture, the Expert, and the Industry   *37*
     Darshana Sreedhar Mini

3. The Popular Media Boom and Cultural Politics in South Korea (1956–1971): The Case of a "Photographic" Magazine, *The Delight* (*Myŏngnang*)   *57*
     Chung-kang Kim

4. Compilation, Collage, and Film Publishing in 1950s–1960s Iran: *Setāreh-ye Sinemā* (*Cinema Star*)   *71*
     Babak Tabarraee and Kaveh Askari

5. Syndicated Sunday Movie Sections: The Highest-Circulation Fan Magazines (You've Never Heard Of)   *86*
     Paul S. Moore

6. Cine-News, Paper Cinema, and Film Periodicals as Intermedial
Encounters   107
Belinda Qian He

SECTION TWO: FILM CULTURES, CRITICS, AND CIRCUITS

7. Latin American Cine Club Magazines: Nodes in Mid-century Networks
of Film Culture   131
Rielle Navitski

8. Hands-On Cinema: *Film und Lichtbild* (1912–1914) and the Promise
of Amateur Science   145
Michael Cowan

9. *Cinéma* and the Vitality of Mid-century French Film Culture   163
Kelley Conway

10. African Film Criticism in the Colonial Capital, 1957–1967   184
Rachel Gabara

11. Japan's Post-1968: *Kikan firumu, Shinema 69*, and *Eiga hihyō*   202
Naoki Yamamoto

12. *Film Appreciation*: The Steady Rear Guard of Taiwanese Film Culture   219
James Udden

SECTION THREE: INTERMEDIARIES OF STATE, REGION, AND MEDIA

13. *Kino*: The Cinema Weekly of Stalin's Times   235
Maria Belodubrovskaya

14. *Cine-Mundial*: Transatlantic and Hemispheric Cultural Circuits   248
Laura Isabel Serna

15. *Radiolandia*, Fan Magazines, and Stardom in 1930s and 1940s Argentina   262
Nicolas Poppe

16. The Illustrated Popular Film Magazine *Neue Filmwelt* (1947–1953):
A Complex Stimulator of a New German Film Culture   277
Vincent Fröhlich

SECTION FOUR: DATA, CURATION, AND HISTORIOGRAPHY

17. Chronicling a National History: Hye Bossin's *Canadian Film Weekly*
and *Year Book*   301
Paul S. Moore

18. Cinema Theaters from Within: *Giornale dello Spettacolo*'s Success, Longevity, and Data Abundance *316*

 Daniela Treveri Gennari

19. Searching for Similarity: Computational Analysis and the US Film Industry Trade Press of the Early 1920s *330*

 Eric Hoyt, Ben Pettis, Lesley Stevenson, and Sam Hansen

20. Provenance of Early Chinese Movie Publications *347*

 Emilie Yueh-yu Yeh and Darrell William Davis

Appendix: Magazines Available Online in the Media History Digital Library *369*
Contributor Bios *377*
Index *381*

LIST OF FIGURES AND TABLES

FIGURES

0.1. Cover of *filmindia*, May 1938   2

0.2. Pete Harrison featured in *filmindia*, May 1938   3

0.3. Olivia de Havilland on the front cover of *Empresario Internacional*, 1941   12

1.1. First issue of *Pour Vous*, November 22, 1928   27

1.2. Final issue of *Pour Vous*, June 5, 1940   33

2.1. G.I.P. Railway advertisement, *filmindia*, March 1941   44

2.2. Columns addressing sexual health and pleasure, *filmindia*, June 1941   45

2.3. Cover of *filmindia* featuring Bombay Famous Cine Labs, February 1941   46

2.4. Panama cigarettes advertisement on the cover of *filmindia*, April 1946   47

2.5. Advertisement for Dharma Patni, *filmindia*, January 1941   49

3.1. *The Delight*, March 1957   60

3.2. *The Delight*, October 1956   61

3.3. *The Delight*, August 1958   62

3.4. *The Delight*, August 1960   63

3.5. *The Delight*, December 1961   66

4.1. *Tufān dar shahr-e mā* (*Storm in Our City*, Samuel Khachikian, 1958)   74

4.2. Competitions for readers in *Setāreh-ye Sinemā*   77

4.3. Lana Turner on the cover of *Setāreh-ye Sinemā*, March 21, 1959   78

4.4. Alfred Hitchcock in an illustration for *I Confess* (1953)
in *Setāreh-ye Sinemā*, January 12, 1955   79

5.1. Mary Pickford rotogravure supplement, *Chicago Tribune*,
February 28, 1915   90

5.2. *Motion-Play Magazine* rotogravure supplement, *The Indianapolis Sunday Star*, November 20, 1921   *93*

5.3. *Screen & Radio Weekly* supplement, *Detroit Free Press*, May 27, 1934   *96*

5.4. Grace Wilcox, "Hollywood Reporter," *Detroit Free Press*, May 27, 1934   *98*

5.5. *Screen & Radio Weekly* supplement, *South Bend Tribune*, June 25, 1939   *100*

6.1. Illustration of "The Future Kingdom of Silver (Screen)," *Movie Pictorial (Dianying huabao)*, 1943   *108*

6.2. "Fragments of Anita Louise's Life," two-page spread in *Movie News Weekly* (*Dianying xinwen*), 1939   *116*

6.3. "Illustrated Pictures: The Dawn," in *Picture News (Dianying zazhi)*, 1948   *118*

6.4. Film stills from *Yan Ruisheng* (1921) in *Shibao Weekly Pictorial (Shibao tuhua zhoukan)*, 1921   *119*

7.1. Covers of *Film, Séptimo Arte,* and *Tiempo de Cine* in the 1950s and 1960s   *134*

7.2. Cover of the first issue of *Tiempo de Cine*, August 1960   *136*

8.1. *Film und Lichtbild*, front cover, January 1913   *146*

8.2. *Kosmos Handweiser für Naturfreunde*, title page, 1912   *152*

8.3. "The Electric Human," illustration from Hanns Günther, *Experimentierbuch für die Jugend*, 1912   *156*

9.1. *Cinéma 57* cover featuring Jean Gabin, March 1957   *164*

9.2. *Cinéma 57* table of contents, March 1957   *165*

9.3. *Cinéma 59* statement about the phrase "New Wave" and the film *Hiroshima, mon amour*, July 1959   *173*

9.4. Emmanuelle Riva in *Hiroshima, mon amour*, pictured in *Cinéma 59*, July 1959   *174*

10.1. Paulin Soumanou Vieyra and the African Cinema Group   *186*

10.2. "Cinema and Africa" special issue of *La Vie Africaine*, June 1961   *189*

10.3. "Cinema Brings People Together; It Is Universal," *La Vie Africaine*, June 1961   *192*

10.4. "Africa to the Rescue of Western Cinema?," *L'Afrique Actuelle*, February 1967   *193*

10.5. *Écrans d'Afrique/African Screen*, 1994   *196*

11.1. Cover of *Kikan firumu*, March 1971   *206*

11.2. Cover of *Shinema 69*, January 1969   *207*

11.3. Cover of *Eiga hihyō* 4, August 1973   *209*

12.1. Kodak ad featuring cinematographer Mark Lee Ping-Bing, *Fa* issue 151, 2012   *225*

12.2. Cover design for *Fa* issue 120, 2004   *227*

13.1. *Kino* title graphics in the 1920s and 1930s   *242*

13.2. *Kino* title graphics in 1934, 1938, and 1941   *243*

14.1. Advertisement for Inter-Ocean Film Corporation, *Cine-Mundial*, November 1917   *251*

xii LIST OF FIGURES AND TABLES

14.2. Publicity photograph of Ramón Novarro, *Cine-Mundial*, March 1932 *252*

15.1. Advertisement for Floren Delbene's radio program in *Radiolandia*, April 1940 *263*

15.2. A short note in *Radiolandia*, December 1940 *270*

16.1. National focus in *Neue Filmwelt*, no. 1, 1947 *284*

16.2. Temporal direction in *Neue Filmwelt*, no. 1, 1947 *286*

16.3. Mentioned films by country, *Neue Filmwelt*, no. 1, 1947 *288*

16.4. Mentioned films by country and year of premiere, *Neue Filmwelt*, no. 1, 1947 *288*

16.5. *Neue Filmwelt*, no. 1, 1947, 4–5 *290*

16.6. Mentioned films by country, *Neue Filmwelt*, no. 12, 1953 *292*

16.7. *Neue Filmwelt*, no. 12, 1949, 18–19 *293*

17.1. Nameplate of *Canadian Film Weekly* *302*

17.2. Hye Bossin with his sister, Celia *305*

17.3. Hye Bossin, Ray Lewis, and Martin Quigley in *Motion Picture Herald*, September 1953 *306*

17.4. Hye Bossin receiving a citation for his historical writing, *Ottawa Journal*, November 1955 *309*

18.1. New theater profile in *Giornale dello Spettacolo*, May 1957 *321*

18.2. Borsa Film ad in *Giornale dello Spettacolo*, 1959 *323*

19.1. Advertisement for "Strongheart the Wonderdog in 'Brawn of the North,'" *Motion Picture News*, 1922 *342*

19.2. Cover of *Camera!* criticizing film schools, 1922 *343*

20.1. Title page, *On Photoplay* *352*

20.2. Bilingual glossary of film terms, *On Photoplay* *353*

20.3. Front cover, *The China Cinema Year Book 1927* *355*

20.4. Full-page advertisement for Peacock Motion Picture Corporation *360*

20.5. Cheng Shuren, Chen Dingxiu, and Gan Yazi *362*

TABLES

19.1. Corpus of Selected 1922 Trade Papers *333*

19.2. Top Volume Pairings Arranged by Set Distance *334*

A.1. Magazines Available Online in the Media History Digital Library *369*

ACKNOWLEDGMENTS

A magazine is a highly collaborative production, with contributions from writers, editors, designers, sponsors, and readers. The same is true for this book and its interconnected digital collections. They are the results of many years of cooperative work. We would like to thank the institutions and individuals that worked with us to make this all possible.

The publication of this book, as well our work in enhancing the database and global collections of the Media History Digital Library (MHDL), was enabled thanks to a Digital Extension Grant from the American Council of Learned Societies. We discuss the grant project more in the introduction and in a separate report. Here, we would like to thank the ACLS for their generous investment and believing that the MHDL was a project deserving of the resources to globalize, expand, and improve.

Of course, there would have been no project to expand upon without the strong foundation established by the MHDL's first decade of activity. Thank you to the MHDL's founding director, David Pierce, for his vision and tenacity in building the project and for his support of Eric leading it forward. Thanks also to Carl Hagenmaier, Wendy Hagenmaier, Charles Acland, Derek Long, Kit Hughes, Tony Tran, Kevin Ponto, Alex Peer, Edward Betts, Andy Myers, Joseph Pomp, and Anne Helen Petersen for their contributions to the development of Lantern and Arclight.

We also thank the heritage institutions that shared non-English-language and internationally published movie magazines with the MHDL. Thank you especially to La Cinémathèque française; Biblioteca Luigi Chiarini del Centro Sperimentale di Cinematografia; Museum of Modern Art Library; New York Public Library; and Library of Congress Motion Picture, Broadcasting, and Recorded Sound Division.

xiv ACKNOWLEDGMENTS

Those magazines are freely available online—and many are analyzed within this book—because of these institutions' generosity and commitment to accessibility. Our thanks also extend to the Internet Archive, which served as a vendor for past scanning and continues to host and preserve the MHDL's digital files.

The MHDL's operations have been financially supported by the contributions of many organizations and individuals. There are too many to name. Here, we would like to thank Matthew and Natalie Bernstein, George and Pamela Hamel, Kelly and Kimberly Kahl, Stephen P. Jarchow, Richard Koszarski, the Mary Pickford Foundation, California Digital Library, and Columbia University Library for their consistent and generous support. Grant funding from the American Council of Learned Societies, Institute of Museum and Library Services, National Endowment for the Humanities, and Social Sciences and Humanities Research Council of Canada has enabled significant enhancements to the MHDL's collections, capabilities, and platforms. Without the support of these sponsors, neither the MHDL nor this book would exist.

We received additional support within our extraordinary home institution, the University of Wisconsin–Madison. The Office of the Vice Chancellor for Research and Graduate Education, College of Letters & Science, Center for Interdisciplinary French Studies, Wisconsin Center for Film and Theater Research, and Communication Arts Partners all contributed substantial resources toward the production of this book and the ongoing success of the MHDL.

We are fortunate to work in UW-Madison's Department of Communication Arts with an outstanding group of colleagues. We would like to thank the Media and Cultural Studies and Film faculty, past and present—Jonathan Gray, Michele Hilmes, Derek Johnson, Lori Kido Lopez, Jason Kido Lopez, Jeremy Morris, Maria Belodubrovskaya, David Bordwell, Aaron Greer, Erik Gunneson, Lea Jacobs, Darshana Mini, JJ Murphy, Ben Singer, Jeff Smith, and Kristin Thompson—for the intellectual community that makes this work possible. We have dedicated this book to our emeritus colleague, Vance Kepley, an outstanding researcher and teacher of film history with a deep commitment to service and helping others. Thank you, Vance, for your leadership, generosity, and grace.

The staff at UW-Madison have played crucial roles in the success of the MHDL and completion of this book. Our database developer, Sam Hansen, dramatically enhanced the MHDL's data model and the user experience. Moreover, the efforts of the entire Wisconsin Center for Film and Theater Research team of staff—Sam, Mary Huelsbeck, Amanda Smith, and Matt St. John—have helped transform the MHDL into a far more sustainable digital project. Thanks also go to Pete Sengstock for keeping our servers running (and a million other things) and to Lynn Malone for her accounting superpowers. We are so lucky to work with all of you.

We also want to call attention to the graduate students, past and present, who have contributed immeasurably to the MHDL and this book. They include Kallan

Benjamin, John Bennett, JJ Bersch, Samantha Janes, Liz Kristan, Pauline Lampert, Maureen Mauk, Jacob Mertens, Kat Pan, Olivia Johnston Riley, Tom Welch, Lauren E. Wilks, and Zach Zahos. We would like to particularly acknowledge two graduate students, Ben Pettis and Lesley Stevenson, for their important contributions to this book and the larger project. Ben's initiative, insights, and programming skills were vital to improving the database and interface of Lantern and the MHDL. Lesley's attention to detail, communication skills, and copyediting savviness were essential to the final assembly of this manuscript. Thank you, Ben and Lesley. We could not have done this without you!

Beyond Madison, we are grateful to belong to a vibrant community of scholars working at the intersections of film history and the digital humanities. Thank you to members of the Global Cinema History Task Force: Kaveh Askari, Maria Belodubrovskaya, Michael Cowan, Darrell Davis, Vincent Fröhlich, Rachel Gabara, Daniela Treveri Gennari, Belinda Qian He, Chung-kang Kim, Darshana Mini, Paul S. Moore, Debashree Mukherjee, Rielle Navitski, Nicolas Poppe, Laura Isabel Serna, Eric Smoodin, James Udden, and Emilie Yeh. We would particularly like to acknowledge the partnership and contributions of the Recovering the US Hispanic Literary Heritage project team, led by Gabriela Baeza Ventura, Lorena Gauthereau, and Carolina A. Villarroel. Thanks also to Priya Jaikumar, Ellen Seiter, Elana Levine, Tami Williams, Allyson Nadia Field, Stephanie Sapienza, Dan Streible, Haidee Wasson, Peter Bloom, Mark Williams, Richard Abel, Scott Curtis, Ross Melnick, Jessica Leonora Whitehead, Gregory Waller, Barbara Klinger, Daniel Biltereyst, Lies Van de Vijver, Tamar Jeffers McDonald and Lies Lanckman, Nancy Friedland, and Charles Tepperman for support, feedback, and inspiration along the way.

In completing this book, it was a pleasure to work with the University of California Press, a publisher that shares our commitments to open access. Thank you to our editor, Raina Polivka, for her constructive ideas and skillfulness in guiding us through the process. We also wish to thank Kathryn Fuller-Seeley, Alastair Phillips, and an anonymous reader for constructive comments on an early version of the manuscript. This book is stronger because of you. Thanks also to Sam Warren, Francisco Reinking, Richard Earles, Joan Shapiro, and Teresa Iafolla for their important contributions to the book's production.

Finally, we would like to thank our families for their support of us throughout this journey. Eric thanks Emily, Arli, Liam, and Esme for their love, eccentricity, and creativity. Kelley is deeply grateful for the patience and love of Patrick, Sullivan, and Charlotte; she appreciates David Gardner, Bernard Bastide, and Richard Neupert for their advice, affection, and shared love of French film. Finally, we thank all of those who use the Media History Digital Library for the pleasure of it and/or to expand our understanding of film and film culture, periodicals, and the historical contexts from which they emerge.

Introduction

Building and Analyzing Movie Magazine Networks

Eric Hoyt and Kelley Conway

In a 1938 editorial entitled "The Brother Overseas," *filmindia* publisher Baburao Patel proudly announced that his Bombay-based magazine would now publish excerpts from America's top film reviewer. "As the most eminent critic in America, he is held in reverence by the producers and the cine goers in general," wrote Patel.[1] The critic in question did not write for *The New York Times, Los Angeles Times, Photoplay, Life,* or *Variety.* Instead, *filmindia's* brother overseas was Peter S. Harrison.

"Who doesn't know Mr. Pete Harrison?" asked Patel. It was meant to be a rhetorical question, but—if truthfully answered, then or now—the answer would be "most people." Harrison was not well known by the US public, but he occupied a unique niche within the film industry. For the previous two decades, he had been publishing *Harrison's Reports,* a weekly review service "free from the influence of film advertising." That distinguishing feature—no motion picture company advertising—was emphasized on the front page of every issue, right below the title.[2] One consequence was that subscriptions to *Harrison's Reports* cost substantially more than other, larger US film industry trade papers of the 1930s, such as *Motion Picture Herald* and *Boxoffice,* because Harrison's production and distribution costs could not be offset by ad revenue.[3]

While Patel trumpeted the advertising-free nature of *Harrison's Reports* as a sign of the critic's credibility, he downplayed the identity of its core audience: US exhibitors, especially small to midsized independent exhibitors, who loyally subscribed to *Harrison's Reports.* They read the paper for film reviews that they considered more trustworthy than those in the other papers, as well as for its fiery editorial page that validated their anger and resentments toward the major

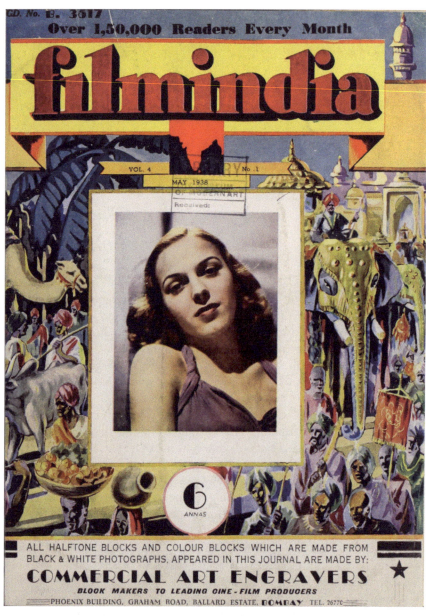

FIGURES 0.1 and 0.2. The May 1938 issue of *filmindia* proudly announced the contributions of Pete Harrison, who reviewed films for US exhibitors in his publication, *Harrison's Reports*.

movie companies. Contrary to Patel's claims, most US cine goers had never heard of Harrison, and most producers probably wished that they hadn't. Over the years, Harrison had developed the nickname "Poison Pete" for his reviews that poisoned the exhibition market for pictures that he panned, frequently on grounds that films were too salacious or downbeat.[4]

Mr. Pete Harrison, Editor, "Harrison's Reports" New York.

Feared and admired, this eminent critic provides a beacon light of guidance to thousands of exhibitors all over the world by his impartial and trenchant opinions on pictures and of men behind the American film industry.

When reprinted in the pages of *filmindia*, however, Harrison's words took on a new and different light—the opinions of America's most eminent critic, not "Poison Pete," the partisan warrior for independent exhibitors. Moreover, Patel's framing of Harrison as a critic revered both by moviegoers and by producers fit the hybrid nature and dual address of *filmindia* (see figures 0.1 and 0.2). Patel's *filmindia* was

4   INTRODUCTION

not alone in this regard. Whereas most US film publications of the 1930s could be neatly divided between the categories of "trade papers" and "fan magazines," the majority of film magazines published elsewhere in the world addressed both the industry and the public together. Hybridity was the norm, not the exception.

Harrison's words circulated beyond the US and India, too. In 1934, *Cinelandia*, a Spanish-language magazine published in California and distributed across Latin America, reported: "Las películas de los estudios de Artistas Unidos son las que más dinero han producido durante el año, según una estadística publicada en el 'Harrison's Reports'" (The pictures from the United Artists studio are the ones that have received the most money produced during the year, according to a statistic published in "Harrison's Reports").[5] Nine years later, *Cine-Mundial*—another Spanish-language film magazine published in the US—featured a quote from Harrison within an advertisement for *Los Tigres Voladores* (*The Flying Tigers*, 1943), distributed by Republic Pictures and starring John Wayne.[6] Like *filmindia*, *Cinelandia* and *Cine-Mundial* catered to industry members and film fans alike.

In other cases, Harrison functioned less as an eminent critic and more as an innovator and role model. Argentina's most important film industry trade paper, *Heraldo del cinematografista*, modeled its entire format on *Harrison's Reports*. Editor Chas de Cruz emphasized the independence and integrity of his trade paper, founded in 1931. He promised that *Heraldo del cinematografista* would be "a service of criticism, information and analysis, free from the influence of cin-ematographic advertising." Impressively, the Buenos Aires trade paper outlasted *Harrison's Reports* by nearly three decades, finally folding in 1988.[7]

How did a newsletter, narrowly pitched toward independent US exhibitors, become adapted and transformed for readers in Argentina and India? What industry practices, business needs, and audience demands explain the process of magazine networking and adaptation? And how did film journals in China, France, Iran, South Korea, and elsewhere position themselves as speaking to the industry, film fans, or both? These magazines communicated news and ideas about the movies and, in doing so, fostered the creation and spread of film cultures—communities, both imagined and real, invested in cinema's ability to entertain, educate, make money, bring people together, and/or be a great art form. How did that process play out in different times and places? And what did it mean?

The book that follows seeks to answer these questions, excavating and ana-lyzing the histories of film magazines published around the world. An edited collection featuring twenty chapters from leading film historians, *Global Movie Magazine Networks* explores the histories and connections across film journals published in countries such as Argentina, France, Italy, India, Germany, China, Iran, Russia, Mexico, and South Korea. While movie magazines are frequently cited as sources, they are far less often centered as the objects of study. By ana-lyzing specific magazines for their hybridity and heterogeneity and by situating these publications globally as part of an exchange of information and ideas about cinema, the contributing authors of *Global Movie Magazine Networks* collectively reframe and expand our understanding of historic movie magazines.

Moreover, the book is an expression of the collaborative processes needed to access and interpret these historical sources today. Our University of Wisconsin–Madison colleague Darshana Sreedhar Mini called our attention to the presence of P. S. Harrison within *filmindia*. Nicolas Poppe, a member of our wider research network, helped us understand the important influence of *Harrison's Reports* upon *Heraldo del cinematografista*. Eric Hoyt then brought in his own understanding of Harrison's niche and reputation within the US film industry's trade press. Collectively, we were able to recognize connections and meanings that individually we would have missed.

Additionally, the historical sources analyzed in support of this research were accessible thanks to collaborative digitization efforts. The Media History Digital Library (MHDL, https://mediahist.org) coordinated the scanning of *filmindia* from the Museum of Modern Art Library in 2014; *Harrison's Reports* from the collection of John McElwee in 2015; *Cine-Mundial* from the Library of Congress in 2013; and *Cinelandia* from the New York Public Library in 2022. Making those scans discoverable and searchable took additional steps. For each digitized volume, members of the MHDL team entered descriptive metadata, with required fields encompassing both familiar categories (e.g., "title" and "creator") and fields invisible to users yet necessary for our search engine to function (e.g., date expressed in time zone format, "1938–01–01T23:23:59Z"). The digital images and metadata were then uploaded together to the Internet Archive's servers, which applied optical character recognition (OCR) and generated derivative files, including JPEG2000, PDF, TXT, and XML formats. After the creation of the derivative files, the MHDL team ran Python scripts to index the digitized publications and make them searchable within Lantern, our search platform that connects the user to specific materials hosted by the Internet Archive. It is, finally, at that point that researchers can run full-text searches, browse the results, and locate sources that support or refute their arguments.

Here, we see the integration of research paradigms that are often distinguished as either basic or applied. Basic research pursues the advancement of knowledge without a specific utilization outcome in mind. Applied research is all about utilization outputs—building things that can be adopted and used. There are problems with these distinctions, of course, but the terms persist in the context of universities, funding agencies, and perceptions of research value. In our work, however, we have deliberately sought to blend basic and applied research frameworks. The critical and historical work of analyzing the magazines has developed alongside the practical work of identifying and scanning as many of the magazines as possible. The field of Film and Media Studies benefits from collaborating with archives and putting basic research on the histories of movie magazines into conversation with the applied research of digitization initiatives.

6   INTRODUCTION

In the remainder of this introduction, we will explore and reflect upon the integration of research approaches at the heart of this project, then explain the organization of the book and preview the chapters that follow. As a starting point, though, we might ask the question—why take movie magazines seriously at all?

BASIC RESEARCH: WHY STUDY GLOBAL MOVIE MAGAZINES?

When making the distinction between research paradigms, the term *pure research* is sometimes used synonymously with *basic research*. Yet designating anything related to movie magazines as "pure" feels almost farcical. These are publications that frequently take on a parasitic quality in relation to the industries they cover. Many of the magazines delight in gossip and salacious details. They report on activities that occur far beyond their pages, and they activate communities that ripple out even further. Movie magazines are many things, but they are not pure.

So, why take movie magazines seriously as objects of research? As film scholars Daniel Biltereyst and Lies Van de Vijver have argued, "movie magazines play an important role in re- or intermediating between the realm of cinema and the audience's everyday life, practices and imagination."[8] Movie magazines—whether trade papers, fan magazines, film society newsletters, scholarly publications, or some combination thereof—provide scholars an array of entry points into the history of both film and journalism. Magazines help us chart the release of films and gather evidence about their circulation and impact in particular places and times. Studying the paper trails left by fans and film societies in movie magazines helps us document the importance of film for specific audiences. With the help of digital search tools, we can chart the ebb and flow of attention paid to studios, guilds, distribution companies, film theaters and exhibition circuits, film festivals, and the work of individual producers, directors, craftspeople, and actors. The texts and images in magazines have long helped historians support their arguments about films, film culture, and film theory. And film periodicals have lives of their own. As analyses of our collection amply reveal, the magazines' graphic design, rubrics, and circulation—along with the composition and commitments of their editorial boards—reveal rhetorically and aestheticically rich modes of discourse, above and beyond the information such publications can provide about film.

Global Movie Magazine Networks engages with film periodicals in all the ways mentioned above and, more broadly, contributes to the disciplinary turn referred to as the "new cinema history"—an approach that emphasizes the value of investigating cinema's connection to industry and society, as well as its meaning in the lives of the people who have participated in its exhibition, circulation, and reception.[9] In the introduction to the edited collection *Looking Past the Screen*, film historian Eric Smoodin (whose chapter on the French magazine *Pour Vous* is part of this collection) has referred to this basic approach, with its emphasis on non-filmic primary sources, as "film scholarship without films." Smoodin's description fits this book as well, with its embrace of a mixed-methods approach to understanding the complex roles of periodicals in facilitating film cultures.[10]

Within the new cinema history research paradigm, there has been a small but growing area of scholarship focused on film periodicals. Hollywood fan magazines have received a significant amount of attention over the past two decades.[11] Hollywood trade papers are receiving more attention, too, with the publication of Hoyt's *Ink-Stained Hollywood: The Triumph of American Cinema's Trade Press* and earlier high-caliber articles by Kathryn Fuller-Seeley, Richard L. Stromgren, and Gregory A. Waller.[12] In contrast to these works of scholarship focused on fan magazines and trade papers in Hollywood, *Global Movie Magazine Networks* investigates the histories of motion picture periodicals primarily outside of the US context, blurring the fundamental categories of fan magazines and trade papers that have governed much of the Hollywood-oriented scholarship.

This book builds upon the 2020 volume *Mapping Movie Magazines: Digitization, Periodicals and Cinema History*, edited by Daniel Biltereyst and Lies Van de Vijver.[13] *Mapping Movie Magazines* is an important, agenda-setting collection that demonstrates the diversity in format and function of film publications while foregrounding their "intermediality"—that is, their connections between the worlds of film and print media, literature, photography, radio, television, and fashion. We, too, are keen to show that film magazines engage with multiple cultural realms and speak to a diverse readership. Like the research in *Mapping Movie Magazines*, our volume revels in the eclectic array of source material film periodicals offer, including editorials, fan letters, advice columns, film criticism, accounts of film society activities, and film trade statistics. A diverse set of publications and the rubrics contained within them allow scholars to create new knowledge about film industries, the discursive construction of directors and stars, fandom and cinephilia, and, more broadly, the relationships between film magazines and their political and social contexts.

Another collection of essays that has influenced our work is *Star Attractions: Twentieth-Century Movie Magazines and Global Fandom* (2019), a study of fan magazines edited by Tamar Jeffers McDonald and Lies Lanckman.[14] Presenting well-researched analyses of the editorial and aesthetic strategies of fan magazines from their emergence in the 1910s to the 1960s, the volume focuses on Hollywood fan magazines, but includes analyses of French, Malay, and Romanian periodicals as well. The authors reveal a wide array of discursive strategies in the advice columns, fan letters, articles, and ads, while challenging our assumptions about the homogeneity of fan magazines, gendered readership, and cinephilic hierarchies.

8   INTRODUCTION

The scholarship in both *Mapping Movie Magazines* and *Star Attractions* makes substantial use of the MHDL and other digital tools, using new methods for accessing material held in far-flung physical archives. With the use of digital tools, these volumes introduce exciting new methodologies for film periodical research, from the consultation of digitized fan letters to the study of circulation patterns via the use of online census records. Our volume is similarly invested in the use of digital tools to access and analyze film periodicals. Indeed, a major part of our project has been to work with libraries and archives to identify, scan, and render searchable new material for the MHDL. In addition to generating deeply researched case studies on exemplary yet often under-researched periodicals, we have sought to make possible a dramatic expansion of resources for future scholarship on global networks in film culture (a process described below, and in greater detail in our essay in the journal *NECSUS*).[15]

One of the most important characteristics of both *Mapping Movie Magazines* and *Star Attractions* is the effort to stretch beyond the handful of anglophone US magazines typically researched by film and media scholars. Both volumes contain important essays about non-US magazines, yet their overwhelming focus remains on North American and Western European publications. Indeed, the current scholarly map of movie magazines is incomplete and uneven. Although no single book can exhaustively cover all movie magazines across all times and places, we are pleased that the chapters that follow offer considerable attention to the film industries and cultures of Asia, Africa, and South America—as well as their connections with one another and the rest of the world. The result of our global ambition is an implicit decentering of anglophone film publications, but also a conception of global film culture as networked. Scholars in the humanities use the term *network* in a variety of ways. In our use, the term connotes both the broad community of researchers at work on the diffuse and diverse phenomenon of film periodicals and a body of scholarship on film magazines that reveals connections, relays, and echoes among publications from many different geographical contexts.

Given our volume's emphasis on the myriad ways in which periodicals traverse national borders, it is worth explaining in some detail our commitment to both national and transnational conceptions of film culture. In analyzing global movie magazines, we seek to bring a nuanced approach to questions related to the national, transnational, and global character of cinema. Many film scholars have argued persuasively in favor of a decisive move away from an old-fashioned "national" paradigm of film history in which ossified notions of national identity persist alongside a limited canon of allegedly representative films. Theoretical interventions on transnational historiography and case studies of transnational exchange can be found in *Cinema and Nation*, edited by Mette Hjort and Scott MacKenzie, and *World Cinemas, Transnational Perspectives*, edited by Nataša Ďurovičová and Kathleen Newman.[16] Another branch of productive work in transnational film studies consists of rethinking film movements. In *Global Art Cinema: New Theories and Histories*, editors Rosalind Galt and Karl Schoonover chart the "geopolitical intersections" of art cinema, demonstrating its centrality to global cinema since the 1970s.[17] Along these same lines, *Global Neorealism: The Transnational History of a Film Style*, edited by Saverio Giovacchini and Robert Sklar, examines the contours of neorealism beyond the borders of Italy, while James Tweedie considers the global reach of the French New Wave in *The Age of New Waves: Art Cinema and the Staging of Globalization*.[18] Mette Hjort, for her part, demonstrates the ongoing necessity of refining our concepts of national belonging in the context of globalization in *Small Nation, Global Cinema: The New Danish Cinema*.[19] *Transnational Cinema: The Film Reader*, edited by Elizabeth Ezra and Terry Rowden, demonstrates the diversity of traditions within nations *and* argues that the advent of digital technology and the forces of advanced capitalism have accelerated the flow of films across borders, resulting in a transnational and global cinema.[20] We share this impulse to retain, yet transform, the "national" lens in the investigation of transnational cinema.

To our minds, film scholarship benefits from an awareness of the transnational circulation of films and film periodicals as well as an awareness that the "national" as an historical category retains relevance. As a result, some essays in this volume argue for the specificity of film culture in particular national contexts, while others show how movie magazines participate in the transnational circulation of ideas, building hybrid film cultures. Maria Belodubrovskaya's essay on *Kino* and Vincent Fröhlich's essay on *Neue Filmwelt* reveal the complexity and specificity of film culture under Stalin in the Soviet Union and East Germany, respectively. Rielle Navitski's expansive analysis of Latin American cine club magazines finds a desire to strengthen local and regional film cultures, as well as an interest in the films and film theory emerging from other nations, reflected in the frequent publication of translations of articles from European and US journals.

Film magazines reflect the conditions of their national film industries and cultures, but they also cross national borders, circulating information about films and filmmakers, the challenges faced by film industries, and the sheer richness of film culture, inviting emulation and/or differentiation. In some cases, the magazines even entered into formal arrangements for sharing information. One example is P. S. Harrison's reviews and editorials that appeared in *filmindia*. Another example took place a decade earlier, and on a grander scale. In the late 1920s, the New York–based trade paper *The Film Daily* entered into a cooperative news-sharing agreement with three of its international peers: *The Daily Film Renter* (London), *Die Lichtbild-Bühne* (Berlin), and *La Cinématographie française* (Paris).[21] This international cooperative fell apart in the 1930s amid the pressures of the global financial depression and the growing nationalism, hostility, and anti-Semitism within Germany that led to World War II. But it is worth remembering that, roughly a century ago, film industry periodicals imagined and enacted a global network.

10   INTRODUCTION

What is required, and what does it mean, to excavate these and other publications and create new networks for the digital age?

APPLIED RESEARCH: GLOBALIZING
THE MEDIA HISTORY DIGITAL LIBRARY

Our digitization and network-building efforts emerged as extensions of our work on the MHDL (https://mediahist.org). As such, any discussion of our applied research efforts requires starting with the MHDL. Housed within the Wisconsin Center for Film and Theater Research, the MHDL is a collaborative initiative dedicated to digitizing books and magazines from the histories of film, broadcasting, and recorded sound for broad public access. The project depends upon the affordances of the internet—the great network of networks—and the digital preservation infrastructure of the Internet Archive. Since the launch of its first website in 2011 and search engine Lantern in 2013, the MHDL has transformed the study of film and broadcasting history, now offering broad public access to over three million pages of out-of-copyright books and magazines.[22]

Despite making a positive impact on the field, though, the MHDL was suffering in the late 2010s from gaps and weaknesses. Some shortcomings were technical in nature. One tradeoff of the MHDL's low overhead had been a data model that was decentralized and messy—a limitation that resulted in an inefficient workflow and, more problematically, broken links and missing thumbnails for our users. We needed to do the hard work of developing and implementing a new data model and user interface. Another area of weakness was the limited amount of digitized content published outside the United States and in languages other than English. We needed to build new partnerships that would enable us to digitize more international and non-English-language film magazines and better represent film history's global reach.

To address these shortcomings and enhance the MHDL, we applied to the American Council of Learned Societies (ACLS) Digital Extension Grant program, which was ideally suited for our project and needs. Supported by the Mellon Foundation, this ACLS program sought to take projects that were already doing good work and make them stronger, more effective, and more available to a broader public. After obtaining the grant in 2020, we were able to significantly improve our database and user interface—achieving a far more integrated, efficient, and sustainable data model, as well as a more stable and user-friendly public-facing design. The most ambitious component of our grant proposal, however, was to globalize the MHDL's collections. To achieve that goal, we assembled a Global Cinema History Task Force—a group of a dozen scholars who could identify important non-US film publications, investigate their locations and copyright statuses, and analyze the magazines for their historical significance (see the chapters that follow). The Task Force members possessed expertise in Portuguese, Spanish,

Mandarin, Japanese, Russian, French, Italian, German, and Hindi languages, cultures, and cinemas. Although we recognized that not all the works identified by Task Force members would be able to be scanned (for reasons of availability and copyright), we were confident that we would be able to add at least several international film magazines to the collection.

Within our research network, the Task Force members came to serve as crucial bridge nodes—connecting the MHDL to archives and libraries around the world. The Task Force mobilized their decades of pursuing basic research, and the relationships they had developed with librarians and archivists, toward helping the MHDL team achieve our applied research goals. Several Task Force members helped us obtain permission from libraries to obtain digital files of magazines that had already been scanned, and then put these digital copies through our post-production and indexing systems, making them accessible within the MHDL while including attribution to the original source. For example, Italian cinema scholar and Task Force member Daniela Treveri Gennari facilitated a productive collaboration between the MHDL and the Biblioteca Luigi Chiarini del Centro Sperimentale di Cinematografia. As a result, we were able to add six Italian film periodicals to the MHDL: *Lo schermo, Film d'oggi, Cinema illustrazione, Bianco e Nero, Star,* and *La critica cinematografica.* Emilie Yueh-yu Yeh, Belinda Qian He, and Darrell Davis all generously shared scanned Chinese movie magazine files with us. And Michael Cowan helped us add the German film industry's first two trade papers, *Der Kinematograph* and *Die Lichtbild-Bühne,* to the collections with the permission of the Mikrofilmarchiv der deutschsprachigen Presse. All in all, by utilizing the model of consent, file sharing, and post-production, we added hundreds of thousands of pages of non-English-language movie magazines to the MHDL.

Alongside the post-production and indexing of previously scanned magazines, we sought out new collaborative digitization arrangements with libraries and archives. Three of our Task Force members—Rielle Navitski, Laura Isabel Serna, and Nicolas Poppe—are experts in Latin American film history. They knew from their research that the New York Public Library (NYPL) held an impressive physical collection of Spanish-language movie magazines. We began talking with the staff in 2020 about ways we could work together to scan them once the library fully reopened after the COVID-19 shutdown. We identified three Spanish-language film magazines, all published within the US, as being out-of-copyright and excellent candidates for digitization: *Cinelandia* (1924–47), *Teatro al día* (1936–39), and *Empresario Internacional* (1940–41) (see figure 0.3). We made arrangements with the NYPL to scan all three magazines. We were also pleased to collaborate with the Cinémathèque française on the scanning of *Le Courrier cinématographique* (1911–37), an early and important French film industry trade paper.

By the end of the ACLS grant funding period, we had tripled the number of non-English-language digitized magazines within the MHDL's collections. This milestone was achieved through collaborations and the blend of basic research

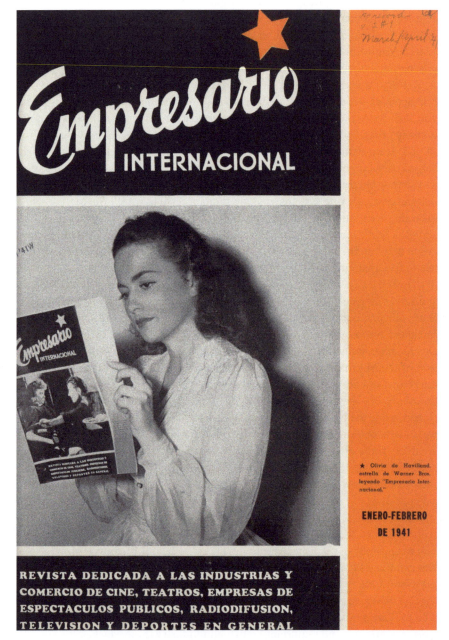

FIGURE 0.3. On the front cover of this 1941 issue of *Empresario Internacional*, scanned in cooperation with the New York Public Library, Olivia de Havilland poses with an earlier issue of the magazine featuring fellow Warner Bros. star Ida Lupino.

and applied research discussed earlier. In their chapters in this book, Daniela Treveri Gennari, Darrell Davis, and Emilie Yueh-yu Yeh share their work locating and scanning important publications from Italy, China, and Taiwan. Their experiences show the value of collaborative and hybrid research models. But they also serve as reminders of the uneven landscape of digital collections. Despite our best efforts, some nations and regions remain much better represented within the MHDL than others, and, even when they are represented, it's not always by the most influential or potentially revealing publications. This book, then, attempts to level the field by shedding light on magazines that are now freely available online, alongside magazines that are undigitized and difficult to access within the US. Whether utilizing digitized or paper-based sources, however, the book's authors always place the magazines they discuss within broader historical contexts and debates. In doing so, they generate new knowledge about dozens of significant movie magazines and model the possibilities for future research in this field.

BOOK STRUCTURE AND CHAPTER DESCRIPTIONS

The twenty chapters that follow offer a guide to significant global movie magazines, the process for researching them, and the histories they reveal. This book is not a complete and exhaustive catalog of every movie magazine ever published across world history. Such a project would require thousands of chapters given the sheer number of publications, many short lived (indeed, we could fill a multivolume anthology with film zines that published only a handful of issues). And, even if it were possible to generate a comprehensive encyclopedia of all international movie magazines, the end result would miss much of what the authors in this book show to be most fascinating and significant: the way the publications function as nodes—connecting industries, cinephilic communities, fans—and necessarily direct our attention to institutions and events that play out far beyond their pages. Thus, we have organized the chapters that follow into four sections, thematically grouped to highlight continuities and differences among the magazines and the communities to which they spoke, across time and space.

Section One: Hybrid Journals

One of the major findings of this book (and the theme of the first section of chapters) is that genre hybridity, in terms of both the content and readership of film magazines, was commonplace rather than exceptional. In earlier US-centered conceptions of film periodicals, scholars—ourselves included—have frequently emphasized distinctions between trade publications and fan magazines. When we explore movie magazines globally, however, those neat divisions fall away.

Eric Smoodin explores a magazine that responded to local, national, and international spheres in his chapter on *Pour Vous* (1928–40). Firmly rooted in Paris—the magazine systematically published a complete listing of films playing in the

14   INTRODUCTION

city by neighborhood and by theater each week—*Pour Vous* also covered trends in international cinema. The life of the magazine, Smoodin shows, was also intimately linked to the nation's technological and political culture, beginning in 1928 with the fraught shift from silent to sound cinema and ending in 1940 with the fall of the Third Republic and the fascist takeover of the country.

In her analysis of the daily trade paper *filmindia* (1935–85), Darshana Mini shows how editor Baburao Patel cultivated a heterogeneous readership that included exhibitors in search of information about Hollywood releases, fans craving tabloid coverage of their favorite stars, and cinephiles looking for film reviews. The magazine's identity was also "hybrid" in its pan-Indian and transnational readership, as well as in its contradictory discourses on nationalism and anticolonialism.

Other magazines derive their hybrid identity through attention to multiple forms of entertainment and through the need to please fans and government authorities alike. In her essay on the South Korean entertainment monthly *The Delight* (1956–92), Chung-kang Kim emphasizes the role of magazines in that nation's postwar drive for national reconstruction, economic development, and universal education. The magazine's success, she argues, depended heavily on its wide-ranging coverage of film, radio, music, theater, the popular novel, sports, and cartoon strips, as well as its capacity to satisfy the desires of its popular readership while also adhering to repressive government policies of the 1950s and '60s.

The Iranian magazine *Setāreh-ye Sinemā* (*Cinema Star*, 1954–present) is the focus of the essay by Kaveh Askari and Babak Tabarraee. Respected for its film reviews, the magazine was also criticized for its pinups and attention to low-budget genre films known as *filmfārsi*. Askari and Tabarraee describe the magazine's distinctive editorial voice, its collage aesthetic, and its commitment to film criticism and news about technology. Their essay reveals the tensions "between the critical reception of local productions and imports, and between popular fan service and the intellectual commitments of critics and filmmakers whose careers were incubated at the journal."

Paul Moore explores a different kind of hybridity in film journalism in his analysis of syndicated weekly film fan magazines distributed as supplements to Sunday newspapers in the United States. The supplements, which started in the teens and survived downturns in the circulation of freestanding magazines in the post-Depression era, circulated existing gossip columns, gravure portraits, serial stories, and local advertising.

Belinda Qian He sheds light on the intermedial and dynamic play between cinema and print media in her analysis of Chinese film publications.[23] Ranging from film journals, newsletters, and modernist literary magazines to glossy entertainment magazines and fanzines, these periodicals "defy simple differentiation and categorization, do more than cater to industry professionals and communities, and should not be viewed in isolation." Focusing on the use of still images in film magazines, and on the transformation of news into cinema, He demonstrates the necessity of considering both the material and discursive elements of film periodicals.

Section Two: Film Cultures, Critics, and Circuits

Movie magazines constitute global networks that participate in the construction of film cultures and the exchange of information and ideas about cinema. This section explores the transnational circulation of films and ideas between Latin America and Europe, the links between film culture and science, and the engagement with film history and contemporary film culture in France, Japan, and Taiwan.

Rielle Navitski explores the wave of film society magazines that appeared in Latin America from the late 1940s through the late 1960s. She focuses on publications such as Uruguay's *Cine Club* (1948–52) and Argentina's *Gente de Cine* (1951–57), revealing that they "sought to transcend the novelty-driven coverage of newspapers and fan magazines while serving as a point of contact between like-minded cinephiles at home and abroad." More broadly, Navitski points to the important role of film magazines in the circulation of global art cinema and the transnational fostering of cinephilia, as well as their transformations in the 1960s due to shifts in leftist political culture.

Michael Cowan invites us to think broadly about the "technologies, practices, and social imaginaries" with which cinema is associated in various eras. In his analysis of the German journal *Film und Lichtbild* (1912–14), Cowan explores the cultural links between cinema and amateur science. The journal rejected an alarmist stance on cinema, positioning film instead as a "new branch of optical technology" with educational, scientific, and amateur uses. *Film und Lichtbild*, he reveals, served as a nodal point within a larger network of readers interested in the scientific applications of cinema and other optical projection media.

Kelley Conway asserts the vitality and diversity of film culture in post–World War II France, focusing on *Cinéma*, the monthly magazine of the French Federation of Ciné-Clubs. The publication, which existed from 1954 to 1999, had multiple functions and audiences. It was committed to providing information about film history to the *animateurs* and members of its ciné-clubs, while also tracking the vicissitudes of the contemporary French film industry. Focusing on the 1950s, Conway excavates the magazine's month-by-month account of the New Wave as it emerged, as well as its sophisticated contributions to film historiography from figures such as Lotte Eisner and Georges Sadoul.

Rachel Gabara explores the birth of Black African and Black French–authored film history and criticism in her analysis of three publications: *Présence Africaine*, *La Vie Africaine*, and *L'Afrique actuelle*. These African-owned and Paris-based and -edited publications, studied here from 1957 to 1967, bridge the period just prior to and following the independence of France's African colonies. Gabara

16 INTRODUCTION

excavates the writing and editorial work of D'dée, the Paris-born son of Martinican parents who was a writer, artist, bebop dancer, and collaborator of Boris Vian. She also sheds new light on the early writings of Paulin Soumanou Vieyra, who would later be at the epicenter of Senegalese film and broadcasting. These publications covered the rare African films that already existed and called for the promotion and development of a truly African cinema.

Naoki Yamamoto analyzes the impact of three Japanese film journals—*Kikan firumu*, *Shinema 69*, and *Eiga hihyō*—during a turbulent period in Japanese politics and cinema in the late 1960s and early 1970s. The journals underwent a discursive shift, focusing on expanded cinema and video art, French post-structuralism, far-left radicalism, Third World politics, and a reconsideration of the auteur theory. Moving beyond the simple geopolitical divide between the West and the rest, Yamamoto shows that Japanese film journals of this period revitalized both film criticism and film theory and had a profound impact on the emergence of alternative cinema.

James Udden's analysis of the quarterly Taiwanese journal *Film Appreciation* (1983–present) reveals the constraints and possibilities experienced by a journal originating from a government-run film archive, the Taiwan Film and Audiovisual Institute (formerly the National Film Archive). While the journal did not participate in the robust debates around Taiwan's New Cinema movement found in other publications, its staying power and in-depth analyses—produced well after fiery debates had cooled—render it essential for scholars of Taiwanese cinema.

Section Three: Intermediaries of State, Region, and Media

This section foregrounds the multiple and occasionally contradictory positions film magazines hold regarding their relationship to state and region. Magazines can serve as the mouthpiece of a political regime, yet also convey concrete information about the workings of a film industry. Movie magazines can promote commercial goods, yet also serve as a vibrant meeting place for diasporic communities. And film magazines can promote national stars and films, yet influence international film culture.

Maria Belodubrovskaya focuses on a publication tightly linked to the state: the weekly Soviet newspaper *Kino* (1923–41). The mouthpiece of Soviet state cinema authorities, *Kino* always devoted at least one page in each issue to accounts of official government business. But its articles on feature-production planning and execution, distribution, and exhibition, and its screenplay drafts and proposals, provide an invaluable portrait of industry concerns and developments. An effort to fully digitize the newspaper for readers outside of Russia is underway. Belodubrovskaya reveals that *Kino* is a "rich and almost entirely unexplored repository of information on discourses, images, personalities, activities, institutions, and issues of the time" and "has the potential to generate many new research questions about both Russian culture and transnational cinema."

Laura Isabel Serna explores a film magazine's role in fostering mutually beneficial relationships between North and South America in her analysis of *Cine-Mundial* (1916–48), which was published in Spanish by New York's Chalmers Publishing Company. *Cine-Mundial* functioned as a "mouthpiece for a consumer culture based on the consumption of goods produced in the United States" but also intersected in surprising ways with the "transatlantic and hemispheric movement of intellectuals and journalists," providing a refuge and meeting point for members of the Spanish-language press in New York City.

The influence of movie magazines on the development of local film culture in the face of Hollywood competition is the subject of Nicolas Poppe's contribution. Focusing on *Radiolandia*, one of a constellation of new fan magazines in 1930s Argentina, Poppe explores how local stars of cinema and radio such as Floren Delbene came into focus and helped popularize Argentine cinema in the early sound period.

Vincent Fröhlich's analysis of an East German film magazine, the illustrated popular monthly *Neue Filmwelt* (1947–53), reveals the impact of political volatility on the life of a publication. Using quantitative and rhetorical analysis, Fröhlich shows how text and image work together, initially to remind readers of a positive pre–National Socialist German film culture and to celebrate the films of many national cinemas, before shifting decisively to Soviet propaganda, a celebration of Stalin, and an emphasis on films of the Eastern Bloc. Popular illustrated film magazines, Fröhlich argues, have been neglected by scholars but are fascinatingly "multimodal" and "polyphonic" in their discourse. With his mix of methodologies, including quantitative research, qualitative techniques, and data visualizations, Fröhlich's chapter also serves as a bridge to our final set of chapters.

Section Four: Data, Curation, and Historiography

The chapters in this final section reflect on the opportunities and challenges that digitization and digital tools pose for analyzing the magazines as historical sources.

The historically unequal relationship between media industries in adjacent nations can affect the availability of sources, as Paul Moore shows in his study of Canadian film journals. Canada's film trade news was routinely reported in US entertainment trade papers and, for those seeking information today on the history of the Canadian film industry, US sources are more accessible and searchable than Canadian sources. To research his essay for this collection, Moore sought access to *Canadian Film Weekly* at the HathiTrust Digital Library, a resource available to many university researchers in the US but geo-blocked to researchers in Canada. Moore explores the legacy of editor Hye Bossin, a staunch defender of the Canadian film industry, who was also beholden to the goodwill of Hollywood distributors for advertising revenue. As Moore reveals, Bossin was also the architect of an analog database: his *Year Book of the Canadian Motion Picture Industry* (1951–70) helped address the Canadian film industry's information management needs.

18 INTRODUCTION

Like Moore, Daniela Treveri Gennari explores the data available to researchers within film industry trade publications. She draws our attention to the recent digitization of a wide range of Italian popular movie magazines, as well as the omission of a key Italian trade paper, *Giornale dello Spettacolo*. The journal, a rich source of data on film distribution and exhibition in Italy, is so "granular" that "it has no equal across the rest of Europe." Treveri Gennari's essay invites readers to consider the vast number of primary sources, and information within them, that are underutilized even in the era of digitization.

Digitization and optical character recognition also transform magazines into completely different kinds of data that can be computationally analyzed. In "Searching for Similarity," coauthors Eric Hoyt, Ben Pettis, Lesley Stevenson, and Sam Hansen apply similarity detection algorithms to US film industry papers. During the 1920s, *Exhibitor's Trade Review, Exhibitors Herald, Moving Picture World*, and *Motion Picture News* all emphasized their distinctiveness, strenuously denying allegations that they all merely reprinted the same press releases. By applying computational methods to the digitized texts, we can see patterns of language reuse that allow us to read the trade papers—and trends within them—in new ways.

Finally, in their chapter on curating 1920s Chinese film history, Emilie Yuehyu Yeh and Darrell Davis write about the process of choosing and searching key sources in early Chinese-language film history while distinguishing between three distinct sources of film history: periodicals, catalogs, and book-length publications. The result is not a triumphant narrative, but a "partial, accidental, and provisional" account of "setbacks due to bureaucracy, the pandemic, and even avarice." Yeh and Davis's chapter is a reminder that many valuable primary sources remain offline to researchers.

To help guide readers toward the historic magazines that they can immediately access online, our book concludes with an appendix, rich in hyperlinks, listing the dozens of global movie magazines currently available within the MHDL. For each magazine, the appendix includes key metadata fields (e.g., title, publisher, nation/ location, date span, and more), as well as brief descriptions. Stable hyperlinks associated with each unique magazine point toward the corresponding MHDL catalog records, providing access to all of the digitized issues for a particular publication. The result is that the book ends with what we hope will be the beginning of countless new research projects.

A common thread across many of the chapters is the importance of understanding the magazines' materiality. Their size, weight, paper quality, and color tones demand our attention, alongside the manifestos, star profiles, and film reviews that more frequently capture the eyes of film historians. If digitization has the unfortunate effect of flattening those material traces, then we must also recognize the rich experiences that it opens up: new possibilities for juxtaposition, search, and access. When approached with curiosity and collaboration, our new network of digital connections draws our attention to figures like "The Brother

Overseas," aka "Poison Pete" Harrison, revealing the intellectual and cultural networks that were there all along.

NOTES

1. Baburao Patel, "The Brother Overseas," *filmindia*, May 1938, 1, https://lantern.mediahist.org/catalog/filmindia193804unse_0013.

2. The first issue of *Harrison's Reports* was published in the summer of 1919. P. S. Harrison, "To All Exhibitors," *Harrison's Reports*, July 5, 1919, 1.

3. Eric Hoyt, *Ink-Stained Hollywood: The Triumph of American Cinema's Trade Press* (Oakland: University of California Press, 2022), 92–98, https://doi.org/10.1525/luminos.122.

4. "Poison Pete" referenced in Arthur James, *Exhibitors Daily Review*, December 1, 1928, 1, https://lantern.mediahist.org/catalog/exhibio1exhi_0539.

5. Galo Pando, "Chismes y Cuentos," *Cinelandia*, September 1934, 55, https://lantern.mediahist.org/catalog/cinelandia-1934-09_0047.

6. "Los Tigres Voladores" [Advertisement], *Cine-Mundial*, March 1943, 92, https://lantern.mediahist.org/catalog/cinemundial28unse_0012.

7. *Harrison's Reports* published its final issue on September 1, 1962. D. Richard Baer, "Preface," *Harrison's Reports and Film Reviews, 1919–1922*, vol. 1 (Hollywood: Hollywood Film Archive, 1991), iv.

8. Daniel Bitereyst and Lies Van de Vijver, "Introduction: Movie Magazines, Digitization and New Cinema History," in *Mapping Movie Magazines: Digitization, Periodicals and Cinema History*, ed. Lies Van de Vijver and Daniel Bitereyst (London: Palgrave Macmillan, 2020), 2.

9. For more on new cinema history, see Daniel Bitereyst, Richard Maltby, and Philippe Meers, eds., *The Routledge Companion to New Cinema History* (New York: Routledge, 2019).

10. Eric Smoodin, "The History of Film History," in *Looking Past the Screen: Case Studies in American Film History*, ed. Jon Lewis and Eric Smoodin (Durham, NC: Duke University Press, 2007), 2.

11. Kathryn H. Fuller, *At the Picture Show: Small-Town Audiences and the Creation of Movie Fan Culture* (Charlottesville: University Press of Virginia, 2001); Anthony Slide, *Inside the Hollywood Fan Magazine* (Jackson: University Press of Mississippi, 2010); Tamar Jeffers McDonald and Lies Lanckman, eds., *Star Attractions: Twentieth-Century Movie Magazines and Global Fandom* (Iowa City: University of Iowa Press, 2019).

12. Hoyt, *Ink-Stained Hollywood*; Kathryn Fuller-Seeley, "'What the Picture Did for Me': Small Town Exhibitors and the Great Depression," in *Hollywood in the Neighborhood: Historical Case Studies of Local Moviegoing*, ed. Kathryn Fuller-Seeley (Berkeley: University of California Press, 2008), 186–207; Richard L. Stromgren, "The Moving Picture World of W. Stephen Bush," *Film History* 2, no. 1 (Winter 1988): 13–22; Gregory A. Waller, "Projecting the Promise of 16mm, 1935–1945," in *Useful Cinema*, ed. Charles R. Acland and Haidee Wasson (Durham, NC: Duke University Press Books, 2011), 125–48.

13. Bitereyst and Van de Vijver, "Introduction," 2.

14. Tamar Jeffers McDonald and Lies Lanckman, eds., *Star Attractions: Twentieth-Century Movie Magazines and Global Fandom* (Iowa City: University of Iowa Press, 2019).

15. Eric Hoyt and Kelley Conway, "Globalizing and Enhancing an Open Project: The Media History Digital Library in the 2020s," *NECSUS*, (Spring 2024), https://necsus-ejms.org/open-scholarship-a-portfolio-on-funding-globalising-and-enhancing/.

16. Mette Hjort and Scott MacKenzie, eds., *Cinema and Nation* (London: Routledge, 2000); Nataša Ďurovičová and Kathleen Newman, eds., *World Cinemas, Transnational Perspectives* (London: Routledge, 2010).

17. Rosalind Galt and Karl Schoonover, eds., *Global Art Cinema: New Theories and Histories* (Oxford: Oxford University Press, 2010).

20   INTRODUCTION

18. Saverio Giovacchini and Robert Sklar, eds., *Global Neorealism: The Transnational History of a Film Style* (Jackson: University Press of Mississippi, 2012); James Tweedie, *The Age of New Waves: Art Cinema and the Staging of Globalization* (New York: Oxford University Press, 2013).

19. Mette Hjort, *Small Nation, Global Cinema: The New Danish Cinema* (Minneapolis: University of Minnesota Press, 2005).

20. Elizabeth Ezra and Terry Rowden, eds., *Transnational Cinema: The Film Reader* (New York: Routledge, 2006).

21. James P. Cunningham, "Foreign Service," *The Film Daily*, April 7, 1929, 12, https://lantern.mediahist.org/catalog/filmdaily4748newy_0874.

22. For more on the development of Lantern and the Media History Digital Library, see Eric Hoyt, "Building a Lantern and Keeping It Burning," in *Applied Media Studies*, ed. Kirsten Ostherr (New York: Routledge, 2017): 238–50.

23. These periodicals include film trade journals; serial publications from film production companies; *wenyi* (letters and art) periodicals concerning cinema's connection to other arts and media such as drama, literature, opera, photography, broadcasting, and performing arts; and film-specific columns in newspapers.

BIBLIOGRAPHY
Books, Journal Articles, Dissertations, and Reports

Acland, Charles R., and Eric Hoyt, eds. *The Arclight Guidebook to Media History and the Digital Humanities.* Falmer, UK: REFRAME/Project Arclight, 2016. http://projectarclight.org/book.

Askari, Kaveh. *Relaying Cinema in Midcentury Iran: Material Cultures in Transit.* Oakland: University of California Press, 2022.

Baer, D. Richard. "Preface." In *Harrison's Reports and Film Reviews, 1919–1922, vol. 1.* Hollywood: Hollywood Film Archive, 1991.

Biltereyst, Daniel, Richard Maltby, and Philippe Meers, eds. *The Routledge Companion to New Cinema History.* New York: Routledge, 2019.

Biltereyst, Daniel, and Lies Van de Vijver. "Introduction: Movie Magazines, Digitization and New Cinema History." In *Mapping Movie Magazines: Digitization, Periodicals and Cinema History*, edited by Lies Van de Vijver and Daniel Biltereyst. London: Palgrave Macmillan, 2020.

Ďurovičová, Nataša, and Kathleen Newman, eds. *World Cinemas, Transnational Perspectives.* London: Routledge, 2010.

Ezra, Elizabeth, and Terry Rowden, eds. *Transnational Cinema: The Film Reader.* New York: Routledge, 2006.

Fuller, Kathryn H. *At the Picture Show: Small-Town Audiences and the Creation of Movie Fan Culture.* Charlottesville: University Press of Virginia, 2001.

Fuller-Seeley, Kathryn. "Dish Night at the Movies: Exhibitors and Female Audiences during the Great Depression." In *Looking Past the Screen: Case Studies in American Film History and Method*, edited by Jon Lewis and Eric Smoodin, 246–49. Durham, NC: Duke University Press, 2007.

Galt, Rosalind, and Karl Schoonover, eds. *Global Art Cinema: New Theories and Histories.* Oxford: Oxford University Press, 2010.

Giovacchini, Saverio, and Robert Sklar, eds. *Global Neorealism: The Transnational History of a Film Style.* Jackson: University Press of Mississippi, 2012.

Hjort, Mette. *Small Nation, Global Cinema: The New Danish Cinema.* Minneapolis: University of Minnesota Press, 2005.

Hjort, Mette, and Scott MacKenzie, eds. *Cinema and Nation.* London: Routeldge, 2000.

Hoyt, Eric. "Building a Lantern and Keeping It Burning." In *Applied Media Studies*, edited by Kirsten Ostherr, 238–50. New York: Routledge, 2017.

———. *Ink-Stained Hollywood: The Triumph of American Cinema's Trade Press*. Oakland: University of California Press, 2022. https://doi.org/10.1525/luminos.122.

Hoyt, Eric, and Kelley Conway. "Globalizing and Enhancing an Open Project: The Media History Digital Library in the 2020s." *NECSUS* (Spring 2024). https://necsus-ejms.org/open-scholarship-a-portfolio-on-funding-globalising-and-enhancing/.

McDonald, Tamar Jeffers, and Lies Lackman, eds. *Star Attractions: Twentieth-Century Movie Magazines and Global Fandom*. Iowa City: University of Iowa Press, 2019.

Salazkina, Masha. *World Socialist Cinema: Alliances, Affinities, and Solidarities in the Global Cold War*. Oakland: University of California Press, 2023. https://doi.org/10.1525/luminos.154.

Slide, Anthony. *Inside the Hollywood Fan Magazine*. Jackson: University Press of Mississippi, 2010.

Smoodin, Eric. "The History of Film History." In *Looking Past the Screen: Case Studies in American Film History*, edited by Jon Lewis and Eric Smoodin. Durham, NC: Duke University Press, 2007.

Stromgren, Richard L. "The Moving Picture World of W. Stephen Bush." *Film History* 2, no. 1 (Winter 1988): 13–22.

Sunya, Samhita. *Sirens of Modernity: World Cinema via Bombay*. Oakland: University of California Press, 2022. https://doi.org/10.1525/luminos.130.

Tweedie, James. *The Age of New Waves: Art Cinema and the Staging of Globalization*. New York: Oxford University Press, 2013.

Waller, Gregory A. "Imagining and Promoting the Small-Town Theater." *Cinema Journal* 44, no. 3 (2005): 3–19.

Film and Entertainment Industry Trade Papers

Bianco e Nero
Boxoffice
Cahiers du cinéma
Canadian Film Weekly
Cine Club
Cinelandia
Cinéma
Cinema illustrazione
Cine-Mundial
The Daily Film Renter
The Delight
Der Kinematograph
Die Lichtbild-Bühne
Eiga hihyō
Empresario Internacional
Exhibitors Herald
Exhibitor's Trade Review
Film Appreciation
The Film Daily
Film d'oggi
Film und Lichtbild
Gente de Cine
Giornale dello spettacolo
Harrison's Reports
Heraldo del cinematografista
Kikan firumu

22 INTRODUCTION

Kino
La Cinématographie française
La critica cinematografica
La Vie Africaine
Le Courrier cinématographique
Life
Lo schermo
Motion Picture Herald
Motion Picture News
Moving Picture World
Neue Filmwelt
Photoplay
Pour Vous
Présence Africaine
Radiolandia
Screen
Setāreh-ye Sinemā
Shinema 69
Star
Teatro al día
Variety

SECTION ONE

Hybrid Journals

1

From Paris to the World

Pour Vous *and French Film Culture, 1928–1940*

Eric Smoodin

The first issue of the weekly film tabloid *Pour Vous* appeared on November 22, 1928, at the beginning of the French cinema's transition to sound. The great star Gaby Morlay was featured on the cover, dressed as a ballet dancer in a scene from Jacques Feyder's newest film, *Les Nouveaux Messieurs* (1929). Without fail, every week, a new *Pour Vous* came out until June 5, 1940, the date of issue number 603. This one had another, lesser Gaby on the cover: Gaby Sylvia, advertised as "one of our young stars" (*nos jeunes vedettes*), who would go on to have a minor film career.[1] *Pour Vous* ceased publication quickly enough after that, with the French surrender to Germany and the Nazi occupation of Paris, but for those twelve years it may well have been the most important of all the country's myriad film journals that flourished during the era. Week after week, *Pour Vous* played a vital part in the very film history that it covered, as a link between French fans and the movies they went to see, between the film industry and French journalism, and between national cinema and the geopolitics of war.

These dozen years of publication were consequential ones for French cinema, and of course for France, beginning with the massive technological shift to recorded sound and ending with the fall of the Third Republic and the fascist takeover of the country. Nevertheless, *Pour Vous* hardly changed. It was always an oversized twelve by seventeen inches, usually with images of stars and sometimes with scenes from films on the front and on the back. Each *Pour Vous*, until the abbreviated, final edition, had sixteen pages, except for the typically expanded issues at Easter and Christmas. Page 15 always included a complete listing of all of the films playing in the French capital, by arrondissement and by cinema, although there seems to have been an international version that eliminated this purely local

26   CHAPTER 1

information in favor of more news stories about movies. The first issue cost 1.50 francs, and by the last one, the price had only increased to 1.75 francs, holding steady over that period at about the equivalent of five cents in US currency.

At first glance, *Pour Vous* may have seemed like something of a vanity project of newspaper entrepreneur Léon Bailby, who years before had taken control of one of the country's leading far-right dailies, *L'Intransigeant*. At least by the 1920s, however, Bailby seemed determined to expand his empire beyond politics and news, first to sports with the illustrated newspaper *Match L'Intran* in 1926, and then to movies with *Pour Vous* two years later.[2] Indeed, Bailby's interest in film was serious; he opened a cinema in Paris in 1930, the elegant Les Miracles in the second arrondissement. In spite of this link to France's far right, however, *Pour Vous* concerned itself mostly with aesthetic and industrial issues rather than ideological ones, ran profiles of major stars and reviews of new films, and reported on the international film scene, but always with Paris at the center of film culture.

A who's who of French cinema, arts, and letters made up the original fourteen-member editorial board of *Pour Vous*, all of them announced in the first issue. Screenwriter Alexandre Arnoux served as the editor-in-chief, and others included Pierre Bost, the prolific screenwriter and one of the villains in François Truffaut's *Cahiers du Cinéma* essay from 1954, "Une Certaine tendance du cinéma français";[3] writer and critic Blaise Cendrars, whose work would include his notes on the US film industry published in 1936 as *Hollywood, la Mecque du cinéma*; Jean Giraudoux, the novelist, playwright, and screenwriter (including for *Les Anges du péché*, Robert Bresson, 1943); Pierre Mac Orlan, who later wrote the screenplay for Marcel Carné's *Le Quai des brumes* (1938), with Jean Gabin and Michèle Morgan in her first starring vehicle; and René Clair, who even at the time was understood as one of the most important filmmakers in France and whose reputation would only be enhanced with *Sous les toits de Paris*, from 1930. As this list indicates, French cinephilia at the time was resolutely masculinist. Only one woman served on that first board of *Pour Vous* contributors, the avant-garde artist Marie Laurencin.[4]

To open the first edition, the board issued a direct statement to their readers, using the title itself—*Pour Vous* (*For You*)—to assert the audience they hoped to reach. "For you, who love cinema. . . . For you, who want honest criticism, lively reporting, authoritative information, beautiful photos of films and performers, and amusing gossip." Then, in an official statement of principles, they claimed that they would never run a single line of publicity, either obvious or disguised (a promise they kept), that *Pour Vous* would remain independent, and that it would speak freely about the cinema, its producers, actors, and financiers, especially about everything that might serve France and the film industry, without attachment or obligation.[5] Arnoux wrote the first article for *Pour Vous*, in which he told readers, "Finally, in London, I saw a talking film," *The Terror*, a 1928 Warner Bros. movie directed by Roy Del Ruth and starring May McAvoy. Arnoux found the effect of sound disconcerting, because, with the speaker in back of the screen, the voice

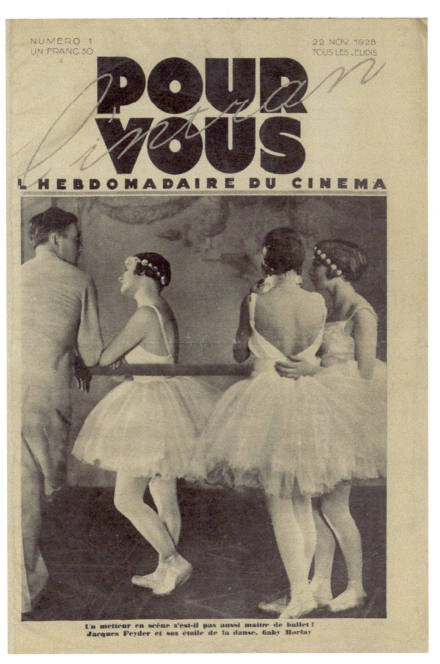

FIGURE 1.1. The first issue of *Pour Vous*, from November 22, 1928, with director Jacques Feyder and star Gaby Morlay on the cover.

28   CHAPTER 1

always came from the same place, regardless of where the actor might be on the screen. After that, the next articles, under the headline, "Always, Talking Films," acquainted readers with how these new movies were filmed and how the sound processes worked. As Arnoux wrote in his piece, "we are present either at a death or a birth," the end of cinema or the beginning of an important new art form.[6]

Pour Vous began, then, in its first edition by underscoring a decisive moment in film history. Twelve years later, in its last issue, a different, much more significant historical instance seems legible in *Pour Vous* mostly by its apparent absence. There is a brief update about current newsreels (*actualités*), showing the devastation of the war in Belgium, detailing a speech about the conflict by President Roosevelt, and discussing how images of war have become "etched" (*eaux-fortes*) for everyone in France. Then there is a review of an Italian film, *La Conquête de l'air* (*La conquista dell'aria*, Romolo Marcellini, 1939) that necessarily touches upon the military and airpower.[7] But otherwise, the stories might have appeared anytime during the run of *Pour Vous*. The tabloid told readers that "Joan Crawford Has Found a New Reason to Live," her six-year-old niece; that the French star June Preisser, newly arrived in Hollywood, had undertaken a rigorous physical fitness program, with photos of the star working out; that another actress, Annie Vernay, had learned to tap dance; featured a picture of Mickey Rooney attending a premiere with Diana Lewis, who recently had married the actor William Powell; and ran a photomontage of William Dieterle's newest film, *Quasimodo* (*The Hunchback of Notre Dame*, 1939).[8]

Really, though, the war might be seen everywhere in that issue of *Pour Vous*. The tabloid itself consisted of only nine pages, rather than the more typical sixteen, a result of the various and crushing shortages in Paris at the time, including the electricity required to run printing presses as well as the mobilization of thousands of professionals after the September 1939 beginning of the war. The listing of cinemas in Paris and the movies they showed required little more than a single column rather than an entire page, and there were just fewer than sixty cinemas open that week instead of the two hundred or so from twelve years earlier.[9] They showed a few new French films, such as *Le Café du port* (Jean Choux, 1940), but mostly there were US reissues, almost certainly because of a wartime decline in French production and distribution. These include Frank Capra's *L'Extravagant Monsieur Deeds* (*Mr. Deeds Goes to Town*, 1936) and *Vous ne l'emporterez pas avec vous* (*You Can't Take It with You*, 1938), as well as *Miss Catastrophe* (*There's Always a Woman*, Alexander Hall, 1938) and *Le Flambeau de la liberté* (*Let Freedom Ring*, Jack Conway, 1939). Much of the potential audience had already fled Paris, but those who remained fully understood that these diminished lists reflected the closing of so many businesses in Paris, including the cinema, because of the approach of the German army on the city.

During the twelve-year existence of *Pour Vous*, there were too many film journals, newspapers, and magazines in Paris to count with any accuracy. There were *Ciné Pour Tous*, *Ciné Revue*, *Ciné Miroir*, and *Ciné France*, among so many others. Some of them had fairly specialized interests, industrial or technological or simply telling the stories of new films. Paramount Pictures, the US movie studio, distributed its own journal in France, *Mon Film*, to advertise the movies that the company made in France—and in French—in the first years of the conversion to sound. But almost certainly, none of them was devoted to such an extraordinarily wide-ranging coverage of cinema, in Paris, in France, and in the rest of the world, as *Pour Vous*. In fact, this seems only fitting, given the similar, astonishing breadth of film culture at the time, in France generally and in the French capital in particular.

Throughout the 1930s, of course, films from all over the world played in Paris. Avant-garde films shared double bills with standard Hollywood movies, and films that blurred the lines between art cinema and commercial movies—the first Josef von Sternberg–Marlene Dietrich collaboration, *L'Ange bleu* (*The Blue Angel*, 1930), comes immediately to mind—had sensational runs at exclusive cinemas.[10] A vast ciné-club movement presented cinephiles as well as ordinary viewers with an incredible repertory of films, from the earliest Lumière films to German expressionism to British documentaries to Hollywood studio films and contemporary experimental movies (indeed, by 1940, the journal had formed its own ciné-club, Des Amis de *Pour Vous*).[11] No source typified these varied interests more than *Pour Vous*, and none of them added a more compelling context of film criticism and theory.

Over the decade, the writers there engaged in an ongoing debate about what constituted authorship in cinema, an argument that many film historians might think only began in the 1950s and '60s with the popularization of what came to be called the "auteur theory." In fact, *Pour Vous* insisted in December 1928 that *auteur* was indeed the correct term for a director, rather than the more technical *metteur-en-scène*.[12] The discussion continued a little more than a year later, in 1931, with "In Search of the Author" ("À la recherche de l'auteur") and then with an ongoing, multi-issue series in 1935, "Who Is the 'Author' of a Film?" ("Qui est l'auteur' d'un film?"), with various directors and screenwriters—Jacques Feyder, Abel Gance, Charles Spaak, and others—weighing in.[13]

During the same period, *Pour Vous* consistently took film aesthetics very seriously and always devoted ample space to discussions of art cinema. At the beginning of the sound era, for instance, in December 1928, editors asked the composer Georges Auric, known for his work with Jean Cocteau and Erik Satie, among other experimental artists, for his opinion on "The Future of Music in the Sound Film." The same issue featured a review of a cinema rather than a film, this one the Filmarte in Hollywood, which specialized in avant-garde movies.[14] But *Pour Vous* did not simply take an art-for-art's-sake view of motion pictures and understood, instead, the political implications of both cinema and national cinema industries. With the development of fascism in Germany, *Pour Vous* kept close tabs on the cinema there, running a piece by film critic Nino Frank "On Avant-Garde Cinema

30   CHAPTER 1

in Germany" in June 1937, for example, and then, that same year, asking Belgian journalist Denis Marion to report on the state of German cinema "After Three Years of National Socialism."[15]

Marion's analysis of Nazism's impact on film appeared in the same issue of *Pour Vous* as a brief article on "Masculine Sex Appeal" that included a two-page photo montage of such stars as Clark Gable, Maurice Chevalier, Gary Cooper, Charles Boyer, and Jean-Pierre Aumont, among others. There were also beauty tips, including tutorials on "How to Fight Against a Double-Chin" and "the importance of the proper application of eyebrow pencil," as well as a showcase of the décor in Claudette Colbert's Hollywood home.[16] Reports like these would have been absolutely familiar to readers of *Pour Vous*. The periodical always emphasized fashion and beauty advice, along with further inquiries into male sex appeal—for instance, 1935's "How Do You Prefer Them? Shaven, or with Beards and Mustaches?" featured two photos each of James Cagney, Cary Grant, Fernand Gravey, and other actors, without any facial hair and also with Van Dyke beards or pencil mustaches.[17]

There seem to be no circulation statistics available, but at the very least *Pour Vous* clearly imagined its readership in the widest possible terms. Issues provided subscription prices, which might vary by location, with standard fees for "France and the colonies," and reduced fees elsewhere, with such countries and regions listed as South Africa, Central America, Albania, Bulgaria, Canada, the Belgian Congo, Turkey, and the USSR.[18] In addition to this apparent global audience, *Pour Vous* seemed broadly to understand a readership that ranged from cinephiles, probably male to match the editorial board, with an interest in film authorship and the avant-garde, to Siegfried Kracauer's disparaged category of little shopgirls who only wanted to gaze at pictures of actors and aspire to the beauty of famous actresses.[19] In this, *Pour Vous* occupied a particular place among the film periodicals of the era. There were some, like *Ciné-Liberté*, with exclusively highminded concerns about film, politics, and art. Still others took film very seriously but tended not to pose abstract questions about such topics as the status of the director as author. In 1937, for instance, in one example among many, *Ciné-France* referred to director Marc Allégret as merely the "cinematic" author of the film *Gribouille* (1937), and assured readers that "the real author" was Marcel Achard, who had written the story on which the film was based, as well as the screenplay. Still other periodicals avoided these discussions altogether and catered their content to the "average" viewer, as with the prominent contests in *Mon Film* that asked fans to vote on the "king" and "queen" of movies.[20]

Pour Vous reported extensively on French film but always also provided readers an expansive sense of film culture. There was, of course, a great deal of coverage of the Hollywood films that played so frequently in France, but *Pour Vous* also understood the cinema as a global phenomenon, whether or not films from different countries might have an international reach. Various issues included the column "From around the world . . ." (*Du monde entier . . .*), in which readers might learn about the films being made in Russia, Poland, Austria, or Egypt.[21] That column gave just brief snippets of information, but there were also more extended articles about filmmaking in other countries, as when one of the final issues (May 15, 1940) asked, "Where Is Italian Cinema?," providing precise information for the numbers of films produced in Italy, from twelve in 1930–31 to eighty-five just eight years later, and the progress of the industry.[22] Lo Duca, one of the women who wrote frequently for *Pour Vous*, planned this as the first in a series of articles covering not just Italy but Sweden, Finland, Latvia, and other countries, necessarily cut short by the surrender to Germany the following month. These proposed pieces, however, would have followed in a long tradition in *Pour Vous* of documenting foreign practices, as well as examining US and European attempts to depict other cultures.

In 1937, for instance, *Pour Vous* highlighted "China and Japan in the Cinema," with stories about the movies being made there and also those from Hollywood, France, and Russia that attempted to represent the people from those countries. *Pour Vous* began by celebrating the accomplishment of Cecil B. DeMille's *Forfaiture* (*The Cheat*, 1915), which had an astonishing success in France and made Japanese actor Sessue Hayakawa an international star. But the article also understood some far more recent films precisely as damaging cultural appropriations, complaining that Sidney Franklin's *Visages d'Orient* (*The Good Earth*, 1937) "had nothing Chinese" in its characterizations, while Max Ophüls's *Yoshiwara* (1937) seemed "miserable" as a movie about Japan, with the filmmakers not taking the time to "bother to verify the accuracy of the most elementary facts."[23]

An article like this one, in fact, magnifies all of the complexities of *Pour Vous*, a journal so different from most of the others while still, often despite its best efforts, connected to the ideological issues of the period. "China and Japan in the Cinema" was written by Titaÿna, the pseudonym for the French journalist, filmmaker, and travel writer Élisabeth Sauvy. While we might admire her efforts to deconstruct the racism of Western cinema, we need also to keep in mind that Titaÿna herself made travel films that engaged in the same practices, for instance *Chez les mangeurs d'hommes* (1931), an apparent documentary, later revealed to be a hoax, about cannibals on the Pacific island of Malakula.[24]

Despite the apparent attempts of *Pour Vous* to separate itself from the far-right politics of *L'Intransigeant*, the editorial board seemingly had no problem working with Titaÿna, herself a fascist who became an active collaborator during World War II, shifting from critiques of US and European cinema to anti-Semitic articles for the Nazis occupying Paris.[25] *Pour Vous* frequently featured Titaÿna during the 1930s until the beginning of the war, at least as late as February 1940, acknowledging her activities at Parisian ciné-clubs, interviewing her for her thoughts about documentary films, or publishing her articles, which might range from fairly conventional film reviews to pieces that perhaps hint at her future activities. In December 1931, she wrote, "Do French Actors Have the Right to Act in Anti-French Films?" Titaÿna even questioned the nationality of those apparently French performers

32   CHAPTER 1

who worked in Hollywood in movies that made the French seem ridiculous. Fifi D'Orsay, for instance, a Canadian, was not French at all, and had never set foot in France, while Lily Damita was only "half French."[26] These apparently benign assertions of nationality and measurements of national belonging would become much more ominous in just a few years, given Titaÿna's admiration of Nazism. Looking backwards, then, just as World War II might best be "seen" in that last issue of *Pour Vous* through its apparent absence, so too might the politics of founder Léon Bailby, given voice by such writers as Titaÿna, appear just in traces throughout the existence of the journal.

The final issues of *Pour Vous* invoke the cinematic losses of the war years, themselves indicative of the devastation of the surrender to Germany in June 1940 and the subsequent violence of the occupation of France. *Pour Vous* occasionally mentioned the war directly. In the issue of May 8, 1940, for example, the correspondent Gaston Bénac wrote from Amsterdam about French films in Scandinavia, shown "under German bombs."[27] Over a map of Denmark, Norway, and Sweden, the article detailed the comforts of French cinema and French stars for those countries under aerial assault. In many of these final editions, however, there are articles that indicate the war that had begun a few months before, but only when viewed retrospectively, knowing what we now know about the last few weeks before the surrender and the three years of German occupation.

In early May 1940, anticipating the Hollywood films coming to France, the journal offered articles about *Autant en emporte le vent* (*Gone with the Wind*, 1939) concerning Margaret Mitchell, the author of the novel, and Olivia de Havilland (Melanie in the movie) and her increasingly serious relationship with James Stewart. *Pour Vous* also typically ran a column called "A Film in Twelve Images," with photos from movies about to be released in Paris. In the issue of May 1, 1940, that film was Ernst Lubitsch's *Ninotchka* (1939). For May 22, it was *Hollywood Cavalcade* (Irving Cummings, 1939), with Alice Faye and Don Ameche. For May 29, *Pour Vous* featured *Il épouse sa femme* (*He Married His Wife*, Roy Del Ruth, 1940), with Joel McCrea, and then, as noted above, the film for June 5 was *Quasimodo*.[28]

None of those movies were shown in Paris, or in the rest of occupied France, until well after the August 1944 liberation, because the Germans quickly banned US films after taking control of the city. These articles and photos stand not so much as the buildup to premieres of popular films, as *Pour Vous* may have meant them, but as tangible evidence of the losses and disruptions of war. *Pour Vous* would also be one of those casualties, ceasing publication around the time of the surrender, as did a number of other film periodicals. The Germans published their own film magazines to take their place, most notably the weekly *Ciné-Mondial*, a title—*Film World*—that perhaps indicated a view quite different from that of *Pour Vous*. Even a film magazine, then, seemed to signify fascism's global desires, as opposed to the more intimate aspirations of *Pour Vous*, a periodical with an international scope but the very title of which seemed directed at the individual reader, the film fan

FIGURE 1.2. A victim of the Nazi occupation of Paris, *Pour Vous* ceased publication with the issue of June 5, 1940.

34   CHAPTER 1

or serious cineaste, rather than a global audience. The Nazis, of course, seized all aspects of cinema in France, not just film journalism but also production and exhibition, the demise of *Pour Vous* serving as just one more sign of the absolute shift in Parisian and French film culture marked by the German invasion.

NOTES

1. "Notre couverture: Gaby Sylvia," *Pour Vous*, June 5, 1940, 2.

2. The website for the Bibliothèque nationale, *Gallica*, provides a nearly complete run of *Match L'Intran*, from 1926 to 1938, at https://gallica.bnf.fr/ark:/12148/cb32812178x/date&rk = 21459;2 (accessed March 19, 2021).

3. Truffaut wrote of Bost and his writing partner Jean Aurenche that "they are the authors of *frankly* anti-clerical films" (emphasis in original). Of their adaptations, he wrote, "Talent, to be sure, is not a function of fidelity, but I consider an adaptation of value only when written by a *man of the cinema* [emphasis in original]. Aurenche and Bost are essentially literary men and I reproach them here for being contemptuous of the cinema by underestimating it." See "A Certain Tendency of the French Cinema," uncredited translator, in *Movies and Methods: An Anthology*, ed. Bill Nichols (Berkeley: University of California Press, 1976), 224–37. Quotations come from pages 226–27, although criticism of Aurenche and Bost can be found throughout the essay.

4. *Pour Vous*, November 22, 1928, 3.

5. The first statement is on page 2 of the first issue of *Pour Vous*, November 22, 1928; the more official statement of principles is on page 3.

6. Alexandre Arnoux, "J'ai vu, enfin, à Londres un film parlant," *Pour Vous*, November 22, 1928, 3; Edmond Gréville, "Toujours les films parlants... Comment on les tourne," and G. Clairière, "Comment on les fabrique," *Pour Vous*, November 22, 1928, 4.

7. Jean Laury, "Actualités," and R.R., "*Vaincre*: Un film de Service Cinématographique de l'Armée"; Lo Duca, "Un film français, un film anglaise, un film italien: *La Conquête de l'air*," *Pour Vous*, June 5, 1940, 2, 3.

8. In the issue of June 5, 1940, see "Joan Crawford a trouvé une nouvelle raison de vivre," 4–5; "June Preisser fait sa culture physique," 6; "Anne Vernay fait des claquettes," 7; "Mickey Rooney avant et après...," 4; "Un film en douze images: *Quasimodo*, film de William Dieterle," 8.

9. "Programes des salles Parisiennes," *Pour Vous*, June 5, 1940, 2.

10. *L'Ange bleu* ran at the Ursulines cinema in Paris for practically all of 1931. See Eric Smoodin, *Paris in the Dark: Going to the Movies in the City of Light, 1930–1950* (Durham, NC: Duke University Press, 2020), 66.

11. For information about the club Des Amis de *Pour Vous*, see, for example, the film listings in *Pour Vous*, May 22, 1940, 15.

12. "Ne dites plus 'metteur en scène,' dites 'auteur,'" *Pour Vous*, December 6, 1928, 3.

13. Lucien Wahl, "À la recherche de l'auteur: il n'y a que des cas d'espèce," *Pour Vous*, June 11, 1931, 2; "Qui est 'l'auteur' d'un film?," *Pour Vous*, August 29, 1935, 2; September 5, 1935, 2; September 12, 1935, 2.

14. In the issue of *Pour Vous* from December 6, 1928, see Georges Auric, "L'Avenir musical du film sonore," 3; JVB, "Il y eut, à Hollywood, une salle d'avant-garde," 10.

15. Nino Frank, "Sur le cinéma d'avant-garde allemand," *Pour Vous*, June 3, 1937, 11; Denis Marion, "Où en est le film allemande après trois ans de national-socialisme," *Pour Vous*, January 21, 1937, 12.

16. See the issue of *Pour Vous* from January 21, 1937: Natalie Pilenko, "Sex-appeal masculin," 9–10; Gisèle de Biezville, "Sourgils et double menton," 13; MB, "Claudette Colbert et son décor," 15.

17. Doringe, "Comment les préférez-vous? Rasés? Ou avec la barbe et les moustaches?," *Pour Vous*, September 5, 1935, 8–9.

FROM PARIS TO THE WORLD 35

18. See, for example, the subscription notice in the issue from September 5, 1935, 2.

19. Kracauer originally wrote about shopgirls at the movies in 1927 in articles for the *Frankfurter Zeitung*. They would be reprinted as "The Little Shopgirls Go to the Movies," in *The Mass Ornament*, trans. Thomas Y. Levin (Cambridge, MA: Harvard University Press, 1995), 291–306.

20. "*La Dame de Malacca*, de Marc Allégret," *Ciné-France*, October 8, 1937, 6. See the issue of *Mon Film* from July 11, 1930, that announced the two winners of a poll of movie fans: "Maurice Chevalier et Marie Bell sont élus Roi et Reine de cinema français 1930," 9.

21. These were precisely the countries covered in "Du monde entier . . ." in the issue of *Pour Vous* from December 5, 1929, 10.

22. Lo Duca, "Où en est le cinéma italien," *Pour Vous*, May 15, 1940, 12. For other analyses of foreign cinemas, see J.V-B and Philippe Vloelberghs, "Du monde entier: l'activité du cinéma belge," February 25, 1932, 10; and Émile Vuillemoz, "Le cinéma en URSS," *Pour Vous*, October 29, 1936, 2.

23. Titaÿna, "Chine et Japon au cinéma," *Pour Vous*, September 9, 1937, 8–9.

24. For a discussion of *Chez les mangeurs d'hommes*, see Emilie de Brigard, "The History of Ethnographic Film," in *Toward a Science of Man: Essays in the History of Anthropology*, ed. Timothy H. Thoreson (Paris: Mouton, 1975), 42.

25. For Titaÿna's various activities, see Benoît Heimermann's biography, *Titaÿna: L'aventurière des années folles* (Paris: Flammarion, 1994). See also Hugo DeBlock, *Artifak: Cultural Revival, Tourism, and the Recrafting of History in Vanuatu* (New York: Berghahn Books, 2019), 164–94; Mary Lynn Stewart, *Gender, Generation, and Journalism in France, 1910–1940* (Montreal: McGill-Queen's University Press, 2018), 97–120.

26. L'Opérateur, "Sept tours de manivelle," *Pour Vous*, February 13, 1940, 2; Doringe, "*Pour Vous* au micro," *Pour Vous*, February 22, 1930, 13; R-E.-Bré, "Si vous aimez le documentaire, dites-nous . . . ," *Pour Vous*, May 28, 1931, 3; Titaÿna and Lucien Wahl, "Murnau évoque dans *Tabou* . . . la poésie des îles du Sud," *Pour Vous*, June 18, 1931, 8–9; Titaÿna, "Les acteurs français ont-ils le droit d'interpréter des films antifrançais?," *Pour Vous*, December 17, 1931, 3.

27. Gaston Bénac, "Sous les bombes Allemandes: Les films français dans les pays du nord," *Pour Vous*, May 8, 1940, 3.

28. G. Charensol, "Margaret Mitchell et les périls de la gloire," *Pour Vous*, May 1, 1940, 7; E.D., "Jim Stewart épousera-t-il Mélanie—Olivia DeHavilland?," *Pour Vous*, May 1, 1940, 7; "Un film en douze images: *Ninotchka*, film de Ernst Lubitsch," *Pour Vous*, May 1, 1940, 14; "Un film en douze images: *Hollywood Cavalcade*, film de Irving Cummings," *Pour Vous*, May 22, 1940, 14; "Un film en douze images: *Il épouse sa femme*, film de Roy Del Ruth," *Pour Vous*, May 29, 1949, 14.

PUBLICATIONS REFERENCED

Ciné France
Ciné-Liberté
Ciné Miroir
Ciné-Mondial
Ciné Pour Tous
Ciné Revue
Frankfurter Zeitung
L'Intransigeant
The Mass Ornament
Match L'Intran
Mon Film
Pour Vous

BIBLIOGRAPHY

de Brigard, Emilie. "The History of Ethnographic Film." In *Toward a Science of Man: Essays in the History of Anthropology*, edited by Timothy H. Thoreson. Paris: Mouton, 1975.

DeBlock, Hugo. *Artifak: Cultural Revival, Tourism, and the Recrafting of History in Vanuatu*. New York: Berghahn Books, 2019.

Heimermann, Benoît. *Titaÿna: L'aventurière des années folles*. Paris: Flammarion, 1994.

Kracauer, Siegfried. *The Mass Ornament*. Translated by Thomas Y. Levin. Cambridge, MA: Harvard University Press, 1995.

Smoodin, Eric. *Paris in the Dark: Going to the Movies in the City of Light, 1930–1950*. Durham, NC: Duke University Press, 2020.

Stewart, Mary Lynn. *Gender, Generation, and Journalism in France, 1910–1940*. Montreal: McGill-Queen's University Press, 2018.

Truffaut, François. "A Certain Tendency of the French Cinema." Uncredited translator. In *Movies and Methods: An Anthology*, edited by Bill Nichols, 224–37. Berkeley: University of California Press, 1976.

2

Filmindia and Its Publics

Magazine Culture, the Expert, and the Industry

Darshana Sreedhar Mini

In a 1947 review of V. Shantaram's *Shakuntala*, the first film produced in India and commercially released in the United States, *The Film Daily* reviewer Jayashree writes how Indian film culture for the West was mediated via *filmindia*—"a sort of Bombay version of The Hollywood Reporter [. . .] frequently impassioned, vehement, and funny."[1] While *The Hollywood Reporter* began as a daily trade periodical in the 1930s capitalizing on W. R. Wilkerson's "Tradeviews" as a main attraction, *filmindia*'s popularity was shouldered by its editor Baburao Patel, renowned for his powerful control over Indian film journalism in the 1940s and '50s. *Filmindia* was established in 1935, and in 1939, Patel, alongside K. A. Abbas, brought together film journalists as a collective to form the Film Journalists Association of India. Until the 1960s, Patel's residence, "Girnar" in Pali Hills, and his office in the Mubarak building on Apollo Street in Bombay became a stronghold of influence in Indian cinema, bringing tabloid-style information about stars, trade news, and film reviews under one umbrella.

In its early days, *filmindia*'s business potential was integrally connected to the film production enterprise. This was the time when Pune-based Prabhat Film Company was garnering a lot of popularity and success with films such as *Amrit Manthan* (V. Shantaram, 1934), *Sant Tukaram* (V. Shantaram, 1936), and *Amar Jyoti* (V. Shantaram, 1936). This led Prabhat to expand its operations through three sister concerns: Famous Pictures as the sole distribution agency; B.B. Samant & Company, in charge of the printing and production of publicity material; and New Jack Printing Press, which printed posters and pamphlets.[2] Financial support for *filmindia* comprised a combination of contributions from D. N. Parker, who owned New Jack Printing Press, and advertisement revenue from Prabhat

Film Company publicity, which gave it an initial foothold.[3] *Filmindia* was initially edited by D. N. Parker and B. B. Samant, but the job went to Baburao Patel when he was invited by Parker to take over the day-to-day operations. Despite his lack of formal education, Patel was an avid reader and had a gift with words. He started his career at the trilingual film magazine *Cinema Samachar* in 1926, and he had an entrepreneurial spirit that led him to buy the Urdu magazine *Karwan* after *filmindia* started to gain profits.[4] He also had a background in film production and dabbled as a script writer and director for films such as *Kismet* (1929), *Sati Mahananda* (1933), and *Chand Ka Tukda* (1933–35). While Patel initially handled most columns, *filmindia* soon became a family business when his wife Sushila Rani started to pen several popular columns, including "Bombay Calling," which she wrote under the pseudonym Judas, who, as the preface put it, was "a man who knows his job." After 1961, *filmindia* became a political magazine, under the new title *Mother India*. After Patel's death in 1982, Rani ran the periodical until it was shut down in 1985.

Starting with Patel's own position as an "expert," and through an examination of advertisements, trade discourses, and columns, I discuss Patel's strategies for carving out a heterogeneous readership base of upwardly mobile, financially well-off patrons, female readers, and cinephiles who were excited by the affordances and cosmopolitan potentialities of the medium. More than just a lifestyle or entertainment magazine, *filmindia* became a mediator between the film industry and the public—a *trade journal* in the truest sense of the term. Further, I also examine how, in its later phase, *filmindia*'s cosmopolitan veneer began to peel off with Patel increasingly turning towards right-wing rhetoric.

FORM AND CONTENT

Filmindia was printed on art-quality paper, featured hand-painted front covers that doubled as advertisements, and interspersed film production details with columns that catered to astrology and palmistry. It had content for all kinds of readers—from cinephiles, to prospective filmmakers, to casual readers—and brought together "varied formats, styles, and story types."[5] *Filmindia* was known for its resplendent cover images. For instance, the hand-painted front cover of the inaugural issue in April 1935 had a box image of actress Nalini Tarkhad (who starred in Shantaram's film *Chandrasena*) at the center, and elephants and Indian street scenes as its backdrop. The front cover also prominently displays the price of the issue, "4 annas," and the details of D. B. Neroy, a block maker from the New Jack Press who helped with transferring the work to the printed page. The details that went into the cover image—from scenic wonders and elephant processions to the center image of Tarkhad and details of the block maker—encapsulate how the journal's mode of production was addressed alongside the distinct Indian sensibility that *filmindia* provided for the reader. In the editorial, Baburao Patel underscores the journal's stated commitment to Indian cinema, writing that *film-india* emerged from the aspiration "to create new readers for Indian pictures . . . representative of Indian culture and tradition."[6]

This urge for an Indian contribution to film journalism seeped into the way *filmindia* addressed accountability in filmic representations and challenged the institutional practices followed by Hollywood and British films that relegated Indian lives by resorting to stereotypes. This can be seen in the campaign mooted by *filmindia* against anti-India representations in Empire films. While Patel fought for representations that would veer away from colonial visualizations of India as a series of timeless images, the April 1935 cover features images of Maharajas, caparisoned elephants, and snake charmers. As iconic images that emplaced India as an exotic space, the images partook in the way mysticism was used to enwrap colonized spaces as discrete units to be consumed by the West. Part and parcel of the magazine's colonial imagery were the images of actresses whose details were presented in the editorial page under the heading "girl on the cover." In addition to elaborate imagery, in 1937 the covers began boasting of monthly readership figures ("over 1,25,000 readers every month," equivalent to 125,000) to showcase the growing popularity of the subscription base. The cover image and illustrations designed by the painter Sambanand Monappa Pandit draw heavily from the calendar art tradition of painters such as Raja Ravi Verma, who popularized images of gods as realistic renderings. Pandit started off painting MGM showcards in Bombay's Metro Studio before he turned to designing publicity posters for *Bhabi* (Franz Osten, 1938) and subsequently took up advertising for Prabhat Studios.[7] If the cover images contributed to the popularity of *filmindia* and allowed for an aesthetic continuity with the preexisting calendar art tradition, from the 1950s onwards, the magazine drew on another visual tradition, the cartoon, for its column "Questions and Answers." One of the cartoonists who freelanced for them was Bal Thackeray, who subsequently floated Shiv Sena, a right-wing Marathi political party, in 1966.

Although *filmindia* was about the film industry in India, Hollywood's presence was marked through columns such as "Harrison's Reports," which featured reviews by Philadelphia-based film reviewer P. S. Harrison. Such columns were meant exclusively to provide exhibitors with information about unreleased films so they could make decisions about programming and potential profits. As Eric Hoyt argues, "Harrison's Reports" were promoted as observations that were free from the influence of film advertising.[8] Such distancing from purported conflicts of interest uniquely favored *filmindia*'s positioning as a serious platform for gauging potential gains and risks entailed in committing to projects. The "advance publication" strategy allowed *filmindia* to perform the role of a trade journal that catered to exhibitors and distributors as much as to cinephiles. In fact, in response to a writer's query on why *filmindia* published "foreign content," Patel responded that the periodical's focus on Indian cinema did not exclude attention to foreign films, which, according to him, were very much a part of Indian film culture.[9]

In fact, the journal addressed many types of viewers simultaneously. A typical *filmindia* issue in the late 1930s contained the editorial, "Bombay Calling," "Editor's Mail," "News from Across," "Round the Town," "Studio Close-Ups," "Foreign Pictures of the Month," and "Howlers for the Month." Such columns addressed a mix of topics framed somewhere between fact and fiction, gossip, and hearsay, which excited and attracted readers. The column "Round the Town" imagined its target constituency as the "average cine-goer and the exhibitor," and included technical details that were of importance to the exhibitor which could also interest the casual reader. "Round the Town" featured a range of material, including credits, listings of films' Bombay distributors, performance commentary, suggestions for successful publicity strategies, and "box office value," which offered tips on marketing specific films. Running up to five pages, the "Editor's Mail" section had questions ranging from queries about actresses and their offscreen lives to advice about acting schools and film industry careers. Some regular readers wrote in asking for the editor's advice about career prospects in the film industry, to which, in one instance, Patel responded: "If you are reading 'filmindia' your training has already begun . . . [T]he primary qualifications are: a good education, tact, and commonsense."[10] Letters submitted to this section were considered for a contest in which the best letters were awarded cash prizes. Such participatory readership strategies were in tune with the global film magazine ethos that allowed cinephile letter writers to emerge as a community.[11] It is interesting to note that Patel's trajectory and *filmindia*'s columns draw heavily from *The Hollywood Reporter*, which also made similar attempts to showcase the production schedules of studios through snapshots of the films at different stages of production.

THE CRITIC AS CULTURAL EXPERT

One of *filmindia*'s most distinctive discursive projects was the elevation of the film critic as a professional. The expert emerges through the relationship forged between experts and nonexperts as well as in the attribution by others. It also accrues from the socialization and membership that is cultivated through professional exchanges. In a 1941 issue of the journal, Patel asserted his position as a film critic by stating that "my opinion is based on experience and given as a bonafide criticism of a picture released for public approval."[12] This posturing is crucial, considering that *filmindia*'s role as a power broker was widely acknowledged, and it was believed to have had the potential to make and break careers. This kind of posturing can be seen in special features such as "Confessions of Rita Carlyle: Down South with Baburao Patel," which was written by Patel's secretary Rita Carlyle, detailing their trip to Madras.[13] Alongside diary-like coverage of visits organized by the South Indian Chamber of Commerce, readers were provided a glimpse of the life of a film journal editor. Patel's carefully crafted persona in *filmindia*'s columns and articles includes information on his private life; he addresses his female fans, whom he claims have been writing love letters to him, by stating his married status (despite the fact that there were rumors of him having love interests elsewhere). These rumors were widely known in the film circles and elevated his profile as a film critic who could rise up to the status of a celebrity by constantly peddling gossip and news stories pertaining to his personal affairs and actively contributing to speculative narratives centered around his life. While he promoted professionalism and expertise as defining aspects of a film critic, he was also the willing subject and purveyor of celebrity gossip. Under Patel's leadership, the film critic acquired the patina of a professional in an expanding and complex industry, but also that of a celebrity, capable of eliciting romantic interest and circulating gossip. In many ways, Patel's posturing as a jack-of-all-trades shared similarity with W. R. Wilkerson's self-assuredness and authority as an expert with something to say about every topic.[14]

A different dimension of this expertise can be seen in Patel's five-month trip to Hollywood in 1939. Periodicals such as *The Film Daily* reported in 1939 that Patel was visiting in his official capacity as a member of the Central Board of Governors of the Indian Motion Picture Congress. His expertise as a commentator on the Indian film industry was acknowledged in his speech, in which he talked about the future of Indian exhibition and distribution markets with the outbreak of the war.[15] Patel sent regular dispatches from Budapest, Berlin, Rome, and Los Angeles, giving detailed accounts of his experiences meeting film personalities. One of the crucial tasks he aimed to achieve in the tour was to convey the need to avoid unwarranted stereotyping of India. The trip to the US included a meeting with the members of the Hays office, which showcases *filmindia*'s praxis-driven imperative to resolve issues through deliberation. The meetings involved him expressing his discomfort with the way Hollywood represented India and the need to make amends through careful and proactive ways to understand the local realities of filmmaking in colonies.[16]

This effort to demonstrate the problematics behind representations pertaining to Hollywood can be seen in the move by Patel in 1939 when he commissioned a guest column from K. A. Abbas, a film critic who worked for the *Bombay Chronicle*. Abbas, who was in the same bandwagon as Patel in his critique of the Orientalist portrayals by the West, went on to demonstrate the problematic nature of representations of Indian lives in films such as *Gunga Din* (George Stevens, 1939), which he saw as an imperialistic worldview that posited Indians as barbarians.[17] In his preface to the article, Patel situated Abbas's firsthand knowledge of the film, stating that Abbas had seen the shooting script of *Gunga Din* during his Hollywood visit and had interacted with the RKO studio personnel, which made him qualified to write on the subject. In the course of the article, Abbas referred to the tradition followed in Hollywood of contacting the British embassy, which then would provide an expert who could guide the studio as an advisor. The expert figure who was in a position to advise the studio in most instances was someone who had some experience in British India but was bereft of any holistic understanding of either Indian cinema or culture in general. Thus, the category of the "insider" was constructed by colonial institutions to justify colonial knowledge production that suited white settlers and to mine and extract selectively from cultures of the colonies. The basis of *filmindia*'s charge against the use of Westerners as experts was the fact that their association with India was at best marginal or touristy. Thus, *filmindia* also questioned the way Hollywood research teams procured the services of British functionaries who had partaken in the colonial enterprise as beacons of insider knowledge of Indian culture.

Another instance in which *filmindia* highlighted the arbitrary way contracts were delegated to British filmmakers under the guise of public programming was its critique of the British policy of bringing in an outsider to render services as an expert. In the articles published in the 1940s, *filmindia* engaged with policy-level lapses on the part of the government bodies that sabotaged the prospects of the local film industry. In a series of articles published in 1941, Patel critiqued the arbitrary ways in which director of information Claude Scott was mismanaging the commissioning of 16mm British propaganda films to boost war efforts. Highlighting the waste of resources and money this entailed, Patel writes about how the money spent on ineffectively made propaganda films could ideally have been directed at supporting the Indian film industry.[18] This was also the time when British documentary filmmaker Alexander Shaw was appointed as head of production of the Film Advisory Board. While acknowledging Shaw's potential as a documentary filmmaker, *filmindia* railed against the way he was handpicked for the job, as he lacked an understanding of local realities, making him most undeserving of the job compared to many qualified Indians who were not considered for the position.[19]

Keeping up with the policy of allowing a space for hearing from the people at the receiving end of the attacks, *filmindia* also commissioned a special article by Shaw titled "Propaganda as Documentary," the main point of which was to showcase what constituted a film text as propaganda; according to Shaw, all films have an underlying propagandistic tendency, as they inevitably foreground hidden messages through persuasion.[20] Thus, it ultimately boiled down to the conditions of reception that contributed to the mobilizing of efforts to build consensus around certain issues that might not work under a different set of circumstances. The articles published on the propaganda films created immediate impact and Reginald Maxwell, the home member of the government of India, had to respond to the allegations at the Central Assembly. Needless to say, *filmindia* reproduced the transcript of the hearing in their next issue as a veritable example to showcase the stakes film journalism could have in dictating policy and outlining corrective measures.[21]

In the examples above, we can observe *filmindia*'s deeply wedged position that coalesced (sometimes contradictory) forces of nationalist overtures and anticolonial sentiments. On the one hand, as a proponent of protectionist practices, *filmindia* mobilized support to advocate for protectionist measures to safeguard the Indian film industry from being taken over by foreign companies. Whether it was the Shaw controversy or the propaganda films commissioned by Scott, the main line of attack by *filmindia* was that the local film industry didn't benefit at all from any of the commissions. On the other hand, *filmindia* was at the forefront in supporting British war efforts during World War II and allowed free advertisements for Defend India flags to collect money for the Royal Air Force. But this support for the British didn't stop Patel from writing against how the government was arm-twisting the Defense of India rules that were in vogue to prevent dissent against war efforts, to get back at him for his critique against the arbitrary actions of the Film Advisory Board. In his own defense, Patel wrote, "I am a militant nationalist," and that he wanted Britain to win the war.[22]

LIFESTYLES AND AUDIENCES

While film reviews in the 1930s were also covered in Urdu periodicals such as *Afaq, Mussawar,* and *Director, filmindia*'s novelty was its combination of the lifestyle magazine format with film content. *Filmindia* offered broad coverage including film posters, publicity stills, beauty columns, advertisements, film reviews, features on film-related technical equipment, technical institutes providing courses on radio and cinema, and columns like "Bombay Calling" that narrated inside stories of film production and the lives of stars. Advertisements by Bombay Telephone and G.I.P. Railway's All India Tour were very much part of the periodical, as were advertisements for household products like talcum powder, silk sarees, and soap. Apart from advertisements related to film equipment and publicity posters, *filmindia* also featured advertisements related to sexual health, including remedies for beautifying breasts and delayed menstruation, tonics for sexual vigor for men, and coital techniques that were available only for married couples who would have to provide a bona fide certificate to avail themselves of such products and services.[23]

SUBSCRIPTION AND ADVERTISING

In the 1940s, *filmindia* started to feature hand-drawn sketches as advertisements outlining facilities such as film laboratories—for example, Bombay's Famous Cine Laboratory was featured on its cover, showcasing a bird's-eye view of its different departments and services.[24] *Filmindia*'s inland subscription rate in 1941 was eight rupees, which rose to twenty-four rupees in 1948, and there were options to pay in British shillings as well. Advertisement rates in 1948 varied from 400 rupees for a full page inside or 210 rupees for a half page inside, to 1,000 rupees for its first cover. In the 1940s, Ranjit Cinetone bought the back-cover advertisement for their films on a long-term contract. The importance of advertisement revenue

FIGURE 2.1. G.I.P. Railway advertisement, *filmindia*, March 1941.

was addressed head-on by Patel, as evidenced by a statement in a 1941 issue that claimed that, without advertisements, it would be impossible to give readers "a profusely illustrated and well got up magazine every month at a small price of eight annas."[25]

The appeal of advertisements in *filmindia* bespeaks the readership constituency that was imagined both by its columns and by its advertisers. While in the 1940s

FIGURE 2.2. Columns addressing sexual health and pleasure, *filmindia*, June 1941.

and '50s film posters on the cover doubled as advertisements, there were also times when merchandise advertisements made it to the cover. A good example is the Panama cigarettes cover-page advertisement that appeared in different versions throughout 1946. The timing of the advertisement on the cover also coincided with Golden Tobacco Company's (manufacturer of Panama cigarettes) self-promotion as the "first cigarette made with Indian capital."[26] Technically speaking, it was not

FIGURE 2.3. Front cover of *filmindia* featuring Bombay Famous Cine Labs, February 1941.

the first Indian company to venture into the cigarette business—Gauhar be Baha, a local brand manufactured by Bukhsh Ellahie & Co., was the first to enter into cigarette manufacturing, in 1885.[27] But the advertising strategies that Golden Tobacco resorted to in featuring regular cover-page advertisements in *filmindia* reflected its efforts to occupy the status of a local brand. Just as *filmindia* was promoted as

FIGURE 2.4. Panama cigarettes advertisement on the cover of *filmindia*, April 1946.

an Indian iteration of film journalism, the wares publicized in the magazine also responded to popular audience/consumer expectations by stating their strategic brand image upfront.

Such advertisements can give us a sense of the target audiences imagined by Patel. This can also be extended to the advertisement of films. For instance, *Duniya*

48   CHAPTER 2

Kya Hai (G. P. Pawar, 1938), which was adapted from Tolstoy's *Resurrection* and starred Lalita Pawar, was advertised as "running to packaged cosmopolitan audiences."[28] This reference to a "cosmopolitan audience" testifies to the expectations that an English-speaking constituency fired by aspirations for upward mobility were ideal viewers of social films that demanded intellectual engagement. In fact, Patel was quite proactive when it came to discerning *filmindia*'s readership. To carve out an engaging readership whose expertise could be mobilized through the columns, *filmindia* came out with a "Reader's Research Questionnaire in 1941," which asked readers to partake in the task of improving the monthly by expressing their concerns and suggestions for improvement. The winners of the best suggestions were offered free subscriptions to the periodical.

The pan-Indian and transnational readership of *filmindia* was addressed right from its inaugural issue, in which there was a concerted effort to mobilize readership beyond the Bombay Province. This is indicative of the responses that appear in "Editor's Mail." In one of the queries on what the film industry has done towards the development of vernaculars, Patel casually responded that "even people from the South have started talking Hindi."[29] While one could read this as a statement that reflects the growing subscription base of *filmindia*, it also meant that the film culture of the rest of India was deemed important enough only when it intersected directly with Bombay cinema, either production-wise or through distribution networks. Occasionally, one can see advertisements for films released in South India, as in the case of the Telegu film *Dharma Patni* (P. Pullaiah, 1941) made by Famous Films at Shalini Cinetone Kolhapur, based on the work of Marathi writer Vishnu Sakharam Khandekar.[30]

In subsequent years, the vast reach of its patron base was recognized in the "Editor's Mail" column, which featured letters sent from Fiji, Ghana, South Africa, Kenya, and the Persian Gulf. This segment was expanded to a readers' forum titled "Woes and Echoes" in the late 1940s; upon selection for publication, letter writers were paid for their contribution. The interactive space offered through rewards and benefits made the readers' forum function as sample research to study the reading practices of the community. It also uplifted *filmindia* as a serious publication that was constantly looking for improvements based on the feedback received from its readers and thereby acting as a mediator between the film industry and the readership base. This was seen in the issue-driven campaigns initiated by *filmindia*, which were put before the readers as "impact reports" tracking the development of cases such as the controversies around the formation of the Film Advisory Board (1941), the Iraq agitation (1939), or the issue of anti-India representations in foreign films. In the case of what was subsequently referred to in the film journals of the time as the Iraq agitation, *filmindia* published a series of reports in support of the release of the film *Punjab Mail* (Homi Wadia, 1939)—starring Fearless Nadia—which was initially banned in Baghdad. *Filmindia*'s mission to garner support from other news portals was successful, and the magazine ceded its efforts to

FIGURE 2.5. Advertisement for *Dharma Patni* in *filmindia*, January 1941, upon its release by Andhra Desa—one of the few instances in which a film released for South Indian markets was announced in *filmindia*. The title of the film appears in Telugu in the top right corner.

50   CHAPTER 2

government-mediated deputation headed by G. F. Reardon, the chief of British Distributors, India, to negotiate on behalf of the Indian producers whose films were banned in Iraq. When the ban was lifted and *Punjab Mail* was released, a copy of the telegram sent from Baghdad thanking *filmindia* was published as a note of gratitude.[31]

The transnational aspects of its patron base were consciously woven into the way *filmindia* structured its columns. The column "At Home and Abroad," started in the mid-1940s, brought national and international news together, giving wide coverage of film industries based in Madras and Calcutta, alongside news from the USSR and Hollywood. Debashree Mukherjee locates the role of the film critic as a commentator in the context of the emergence of film journalism as a specialized trade in Bombay.[32] As Mukherjee notes, *filmindia* tried to frame its contribution by engaging with the cinematic publics around it and thereby define what film journalism could become by initiating change in industry patterns. It is in this context that Patel's response to readers' queries about film reviews published in other newspapers of the time should be read. To a disgruntled reader who expressed disappointment in the reviews that appeared in *The Times of India*, an English-language newspaper, Patel responded that as the employee of a commercial newspaper relying on advertisements, the critic had restrictions that placed their job in jeopardy; he states, "the best thing for a film fan to do is not to be guided by these reviews as the paper doesn't boast of any specialization in this particular job."[33] Occasionally, letters were published critiquing the editor's take on a film, offering a different perspective. In one letter, one Debi Singh from Durban wanted the voice of the fan to be inserted as a crucial way of gauging the film's success, writing: "To the director it is the opinion of the ordinary cinema-goer which matters more than that of the high-brow and pedantic critic . . . it's not the review in a film journal that makes a picture-goer decide to see or not see a picture; it is the comment of his fellow film fan who has already seen the picture."[34]

FILM CRITICISM AND THE FILM TRADE

Patel shared a conflicted relationship with the film industry. On the one hand, he attempted to distance himself from the industry to avoid *filmindia* being perceived as a vehicle for unconditional praise of films. This was despite the fact that while managing *filmindia* as an editor, Patel himself went on to direct films such as *Draupadi* (1945) and *Gwalan* (1946), both starring Sushila Rani. This was not an anomaly, as Ray Lewis, editor of *Canadian Moving Picture Digest*, had also ventured into the exhibition business, inviting a lot of criticism.[35] Patel's caustic, sharp comments on the industry, production process, and film reviews made the monthly distinct from other film-related columns covered in the newspapers and magazines of the time. On the other hand, there were also times when he aligned himself with the film industry as its representative. In addressing a reception held by the Film Artistes' Association of India in 1941, he called for a united front, calling himself a "spokesperson of the industry."[36] Patel's writing also showed sympathies for the working class. The reports on accidents happening in cinema-halls were part of the series of articles that Patel wrote on labor conditions in the film industry. In February 1950, in an article directly addressed to the health minister Rajkumari Amrit Kaur, Patel detailed the condition of defunct electrical installations and safety concerns that could endanger the lives of filmgoers.[37] Another article explored the conditions of labor of cinema operators and their long, fourteen-plus-hour workdays in unfavorable conditions, as for instance projectionists who worked in unventilated booths.[38]

Simultaneously, we see gestures in *filmindia* that highlight a critical distance from the film industry on the part of the critic, in order to offer honest reviews undiluted by commercial interests. In his review of *Afsar*, after warning the readers to avoid the film, Patel goes on to reveal the fact that the film has been publicized in *filmindia*. He further states that he decided to publish a negative review despite the producer spending around 3,200 rupees on publicity.[39] Needless to say, there were concerns and rebuttals to such strategies from people who were mentioned in the columns, some of which were even published by *filmindia* in an attempt to offer a different perspective. For instance, when he was accused of blackmailing producers at a hearing of the Film Enquiry Committee in Bombay in 1950, Patel came up with an article titled "Am I a Blackmailer?" He circulated a question to all leading producers, including Chuni Lall, managing director of Filmistan Studios and president of the Indian Motion Picture Association—"Have I at any time during your association with you ever asked you for any blackmail money threatening a bad review or an adverse comment on your picture if such a demand was not complied with?"[40] He also published in *filmindia* the letters written by producers who testified in favor of him and sent these to the Film Enquiry Committee as evidence of his good standing.[41] *Filmindia* also gave actors a chance to respond to the allegations through columns; actress Snehapradha Pradhan responded to a reader who countered her previous article, and she used it to clarify and elucidate her stance as a career woman.[42]

Filmindia also catered directly to the filmmaking constituency, both current and prospective, who were updated on the technical infrastructures that came with the market for imported film equipment, including sound projectors such as Micron XIB and RCA Photophone sound equipment, speaker systems like Itec's "The Voice of the Theatre" and the "Lansing Shearer Horn Sound System," and cameras such as Cine-Kodak, among others. There were also regular advertisements by Gramophone record companies on their latest offerings. One of the strategies used in the advertisement for cine-equipment was to collate the testimonies by different studios on their experience using these machineries. Despite being staged and commissioned with possible payment from the product manufacturers, such testimonies gave readers an overarching picture of the landscape of film production and updates on the studios that were embracing new technologies.

Filmindia columns were also central to the creation of public discussion about film culture and policy. Patel lobbied for strict standards and fair conditions for film censorship. *Filmindia*'s official policy on censorship was that objectionable material that impacted the taste and morality of the readers should be cleansed, while censors should behave like friendly and ethical guardians rather than despots.[43] One of the sections that started to appear in the late 1940s was the detailed list of cuts recommended by the Bombay censor, alongside the objections and the length of each cut. In this way, *filmindia* also functioned as a government gazette, by including details of government circulars related to the film industry, updates about film employee strikes, and notifications on the appointment of government nominees to the censor board committees, among others.

MOTHER INDIA AND THE TURN TO THE RIGHT

Film reviews in *filmindia* were often very acerbic. While it was reflective of Patel's personality and showcased his assertiveness in running the periodical, it was a masculine performance peppered by jocular remarks mixed with anti-Muslim and sexist jokes.[44] The Urdu writer Saadat Hasan Manto defined Patel's style as an "inimitable sense of humor, often barbed," which, when combined with a "guy assertiveness about his writing," deteriorated when *filmindia* became politicized.[45] Patel's Hindutva leanings and anti-Muslim sentiments became much more strongly pronounced when *filmindia* was converted to a new political journal called *Mother India* in 1965.

In fact, we can see traces of this political edge from the late 1940s and 1950s onwards when *filmindia* began including sharp critiques of Jawaharlal Nehru, alleging neglect of the Hindu communities and what he thought to be the government's attempt to play the secular card. Such right-leaning political commentary was evident in *filmindia*'s reports from 1947–48 in the context of the partition. Patel's editorials dealt with partition as an emotional issue and squarely blamed Pakistan for the bloodshed. In the editorial for the January 1948 issue, Patel blamed Jinnah as the "biggest criminal of history" and mourned the Indian film industry's loss of Karachi and Lahore, which were key film markets.[46] Another instance that showcases such tendencies in *filmindia* is Patel's review of *Arzoo* (Shahid Lateef, 1950), a film dealing with Hindu marriage. Titled "The Lateefs Make a Mess of *Arzoo*: Distortions of Hindu Married Life," Patel takes offense at the way Lateef and his scriptwriter-wife Ismat Chugtai use the plotline, which showcases a married Hindu woman pining for her lover after marriage. Patel's contention was that Hindu marriage was a "sacred bond inviolable through births to come . . . [and] once a Hindu woman marries, she is expected to identify herself with her husband completely mentally, physically, and spiritually."[47]

In the post-partition period, *filmindia* expanded its range beyond just film, with one 1948 job advertisement requesting applications for editorial staff and writers specializing in subjects as varied as history, medicine, international affairs, sociology, sport, music, and human relations.[48] In 1960, *filmindia* published an announcement asking readers for suggestions for a name change reflecting its focus on "political commentary, views on many national problems of the day," and the fact that it "no longer deals film reviews and film industry exclusively."[49] After its conversion to *Mother India* in 1967, the price per issue became one rupee, with an Inland edition for three rupees and a Foreign edition for six shillings, and it started to be printed on newsprint, as opposed to the art paper that had been associated with *filmindia*. Hindu mythologicals like Ramayana began to be featured in *Mother India*'s content, alongside a profusion of anti-Muslim articles. Patel's Hindutva leanings became clear when, in 1967, he contested Lok Sabha elections supported by Jan Sangh, the party that preceded Bharatiya Janata Party. Notably, Patel was also jailed in 1975 during the National Emergency for his anti-Congress content.

CONCLUSION

Filmindia is one of the few early Indian film magazines that is easily accessible in digital form. The journal's availability in the Media History Digital Library is a rarity; film periodicals from the 1930s and '40s are often dispersed, fragmented, in archives and personal collections. Digitization efforts to preserve archival material mean bringing the dispersed sources to a centralized data base, while acknowledging that what has been preserved is fragmentary at best. Did Patel at any point think of *filmindia* as an archivable or collectible item shedding light on the history of the 1940s and '50s?

In *filmindia* we can, in fact, see a keen interest in cultivating in its readers a taste for archival material. From 1941 onwards, regular advertisements appeared in the periodical announcing that the old issues were available for the reader to buy in bound format.[50] The popularity of this format was reified in the October 1941 issue that announced that bound copies had all been sold, and purchasers were requested not to remit money, as no more copies were available. The film critic K. A. Abbas also wrote about the pervasive presence of *filmindia* as a popular entertainment magazine, a fact that he noticed during his travels throughout the country, even in rural outskirts that didn't have basic amenities. For instance, in a 1941 issue of *filmindia*, Abbas recounted how he watched a film in a tin shack in Panipat, and of his visit to an adjoining juice stall which had paper cuttings and photos of stars from *filmindia* decorating the wall.[51] Secondhand issues of *filmindia* were bought by the shop owner from Delhi to capitalize on the proximity that he shared with the cinema hall, whose patrons were part of his clientele as well. Thus, while it is true that *filmindia* catered to a cosmopolitan audience,

54   CHAPTER 2

Abbas demystifies the perception that *filmindia* catered to *only* this segment of readership. Instead, *filmindia* catered to casual readers, diasporic audiences, filmmakers, and technicians, as well as a range of other readers. Or, as Abbas puts it, *filmindia*'s constituency included "intellectuals," the "semi-literate," "school-boys," and "professors," as well as those on the lookout for erotic thrills.[52]

NOTES

1. Jayashree, "Shakuntala," *The Film Daily* 7, no. 2 (October–December 1947), 5.

2. Saadat Hasan Manto, *Stars from Another Sky: The Bombay Film World of the 1940s*, trans. Khalid Hasan (New Delhi: Penguin Books, 1998), 182–83.

3. Sidharth Bhatia, *The Patels of filmindia: Pioneers of Indian Film Journalism* (Mumbai: Indus Source Books, 2015), 11.

4. Sidharth Bhatia, "'Most Wretched, Boring and Amateurish Hotch-Potch': Meet Baburao Patel, Pioneering Film Journalist," *Scroll*, June 13, 2015, https://scroll.in/article/733935/most-wretched-boring-and-amateurish-hotch-potch-meet-baburao-patel-pioneering-film-journalist.

5. Daniel Biltereyst and Lies Van de Vijver, "Introduction: Movie Magazines, Digitization and New Cinema History," in *Mapping Movie Magazines: Digitization, Periodicals and Cinema History*, ed. Daniel Biltereyst and Lies Van de Vijver (London: Palgrave Macmillan, 2020), 1–8.

6. *Filmindia*, May 1935, 3.

7. Bhatia, *The Patels of filmindia*, 91.

8. Eric Hoyt, *Ink-Stained Hollywood: The Triumph of American Cinema's Trade Press* (Oakland: University of California Press, 2022), https://doi.org/10.1525/luminos.122.

9. "The Editor's Mail," *filmindia*, April 1941, 17.

10. "The Editor's Mail," *filmindia*, May 1938, 35.

11. Biltereyst and de Vijver, "Introduction," 8.

12. K. Chengalrayan of Elfin Talkies, "Claiming Damages," *filmindia*, April 1941, 50.

13. Miss Rita Carlyle, "Confessions of Miss Rita Carlyle: Down South with Baburao Patel," *filmindia*, March 1941, 21–30.

14. Hoyt, *Ink-Stained Hollywood*.

15. "Coming and Going," *The Film Daily* 7, no. 6 (August 29, 1939), 2; "The Week in Review," *The Film Daily* 7, no. 6 (September 11, 1939), 6.

16. "Indian Pix Industry Talks about U.S. Boycott," *The Film Daily* 7, no. 5 (March 7, 1939), 1, 14.

17. K. A. Abbas, "'Gunga Din' Another Scandalously Anti-Indian Picture!," *filmindia*, February 1939, 26–31.

18. "A Sly Scheme of Wasting Money," *filmindia*, January 1941, 3–4.

19. "Agreeable Alex, The Mystery Man of Films—Old Stan's New Weekly," *filmindia*, January 1941, 45. For an extensive account of Shaw's films made in India, see Ravi Vasudevan, "A British Documentary Film-Maker's Encounter with Empire: The Case of Alexander Shaw, 1938–42," *Historical Journal of Film, Radio and Television* 38, no. 4 (2018): 743–61.

20. "Propaganda as Documentary," *filmindia*, February 1941, 68.

21. "Filmindia in the Central Assembly: Home Member Severely Heckled about Film Advisory Board Affairs," *filmindia*, April 1941, 51.

22. *Filmindia*, February 1941, 15.

23. *Filmindia*, June 1941, 32–33.

24. *Filmindia*, February 1941.

25. *Filmindia*, July 1941, 17.

26. Kathinka Singa-Kerkhoff, "Wooing Indians with New Smokes: Cigarette and Bidi Advertising in British India," in *Globalising Everyday Consumption in India: History and Ethnography*, ed. Bhaswati Bhattacharya and Henrike Donner (London: Routledge, 2021).

27. Projit. B. Mukharji, "The First Cigarette," *Calcutta by Gaslight* (blog), August 9, 2018. https://web.sas.upenn.edu/mukharji/2018/08/09/bukhsh-ellahie-co/.

28. *Filmindia*, December 1937.

29. The Editor's Mail," *filmindia*, May 1938, 37.

30. *Filmindia*, January 1941, 44.

31. *Filmindia*, January 1941.

32. Debashree Mukherjee, "Creating Cinema's Reading Publics: The Emergence of Film Journalism in Bombay," in *No Limits: Studies of Media from India*, ed. Ravi Sundaram (New Delhi: Oxford University Press, 2013), 165–98.

33. "The Editor's Mail," *filmindia*, January 1941, 19.

34. Debi Singh, "*Shantaram* May Not Be Great but—Don't Bother with Realism," *filmindia*, May 1941, 25.

35. Jessica L. Whitehead, Louis Pelletier, and Paul S. Moore, "'The Girl Friend in Canada': Ray Lewis and Canadian Moving Picture Digest (1915–1957)," in *Mapping Movie Magazines: Digitization, Periodicals, and Cinema History*, ed. Daniel Biltereyst and Lies Van de Vijver (London: Palgrave Macmillan, 2020), 127–52.

36. "Born Slaves but Let Us Not Die as Slaves!," *filmindia*, November 1941, 23–27.

37. "An Appeal to Amrit Kaur," *filmindia*, February 1948, 9.

38. "Slow Death for Film Operators," *filmindia*, May 1938, 4.

39. "Avoid Afsar on Health Grounds: Filmgoers File Out Poorer and Wiser," *filmindia*, cited in Bhatia, *The Patels of filmindia*, 119.

40. "Am I a Blackmailer? Leading Producers of India Answer This Question," *filmindia*, May 1950, 47–48.

41. "Am I a Blackmailer."

42. Snehaprabha Pradhan, "A Mere Actress Replies Back," *filmindia*, May 1941, 27.

43. "Wanted Censorship—Not Persecution!," *filmindia*, May 1948, 3–5.

44. C. Yamini Krishna and Emilia Teles Da Silva, "Construction of Indian Femininity and Masculinity in *Filmindia* Magazine 1946–1948," *South Asian Popular Culture* 13, no. 3 (2015): 183–98.

45. Manto, *Stars from Another Sky*, 183.

46. *Filmindia*, January 1948, 4.

47. Bhatia, *The Patels of filmindia*, 114.

48. *Filmindia*, June 1948, 4.

49. Bhatia, *The Patels of filmindia*, 69.

50. *Filmindia*, June 1941, 27.

51. K. Ahmed Abbas, "Ahmed Abbas Condemns 'Filmindia': Unmerciful Criticism of Baburao Patel," *filmindia*, July 1941, 37–41.

52. Abbas, "Ahmed Abbas Condemns 'Filmindia.'"

PUBLICATIONS REFERENCED

Afaq
Bombay Chronicle
Canadian Moving Picture Digest
Cinema Samachar
Director

56   CHAPTER 2

The Film Daily
filmindia
The Hollywood Reporter
Karwan
Mother India (formerly *filmindia*)
Mussawar
The Times of India

BIBLIOGRAPHY

Bhatia, Sidharth. *The Patels of filmindia: Pioneers of Indian Film Journalism.* Mumbai: Indus Source Books, 2015.

———. "'Most Wretched, Boring and Amateurish Hotch-Potch': Meet Baburao Patel, Pioneering Film Journalist." *Scroll*, June 13, 2015. https://scroll.in/article/733935/most-wretched-boring-and-amateurish-hotch-potch-meet-baburao-patel-pioneering-film-journalist.

Biltereyst, Daniel, and Lies Van de Vijver. "Introduction: Movie Magazines, Digitization, and New Cinema History." In *Mapping Movie Magazines: Digitization, Periodicals, and Cinema History*, edited by Daniel Biltereyst and Lies Van de Vijver, 1–8. London: Palgrave Macmillan, 2020.

Hoyt, Eric. *Ink-Stained Hollywood: The Triumph of American Cinema's Trade Press.* Oakland: University of California Press, 2022, https://doi.org/10.1525/luminos.122.

Krishna, C. Yamini, and Emilia Teles Da Silva. "Construction of Indian Femininity and Masculinity in *filmindia* magazine 1946–1948." *South Asian Popular Culture* 13, no. 3 (2015): 183–98.

Manto, Saadat Hasan. *Stars from Another Sky: The Bombay Film World of the 1940s.* Translated by Khalid Hasan. New Delhi: Penguin Books, 1998

Mukharji, Projit. B. "The First Cigarette." *Calcutta by Gaslight* (blog), August 9, 2018. https://web.sas.upenn.edu/mukharji/2018/08/09/bukhsh-ellahie-co/.

Mukherjee, Debashree. "Creating Cinema's Reading Publics: The Emergence of Film Journalism in Bombay." In *No Limits: Studies of Media from India*, edited by Ravi Sundaram, 165–98. New Delhi: Oxford University Press, 2013.

Singa-Kerkhoff, Kathinka. "Wooing Indians with New Smokes: Cigarette and Bidi Advertising in British India." In *Globalising Everyday Consumption in India: History and Ethnography*, edited by Bhaswati Bhattacharya and Henrike Donner, 98–120. London: Routledge, 2021.

Vasudevan, Ravi. "A British Documentary Film-Maker's Encounter with Empire: The Case of Alexander Shaw, 1938–42." *Historical Journal of Film, Radio and Television* 38, no. 4 (2018): 743–61.

Whitehead, Jessica L., Louis Pelletier, and Paul S. Moore. "'The Girl Friend in Canada': Ray Lewis and *Canadian Moving Picture Digest* (1915–1957)." In *Mapping Movie Magazines: Digitization, Periodicals, and Cinema History*, edited by Daniel Biltereyst and Lies Van de Vijver, 127–52. London: Palgrave Macmillan, 2020.

3

The Popular Media Boom and Cultural Politics in South Korea (1956–1971)

The Case of a "Photographic" Magazine, The Delight (Myŏngnang)

Chung-kang Kim

Sometimes history is ironic, in that great devastation provokes an equally great desire and zeal for life amongst individuals and the population at large. The Korean War (1950–53), one of the most destructive wars of the twentieth century, offers an instructive example of this, as this period of devastating conflict none-theless also saw the remarkable growth of the national publishing industry. Even during the war itself, and despite the fact that most of the Korean peninsula was occupied by North Korea in the early stage of the war, numerous significant South Korean modern magazines published their first issues from two unoccupied cities, Taegu and Pusan.[1] Then, after the war, the popular enthusiasm for new forms of mass media was further maximized within the South Korean government's drive for the national reconstruction and subsequent mass movement toward economic development. Although poverty-stricken South Korea would not fully recover economically, from the 1950s onward, national reconstruction proceeded steadily, step by step over the next decades, and the media was a key part of this.

To take one example, the publishing industry thrived on an unprecedented level during the 1950s. By the end of the decade, around 180 new magazines had been launched in the valid expectation of a greatly increased readership, as the government initiated a Five-Year Plan for Compulsory Education (Ŭimu kyo-yuk wansŏng o gaenyŏn kaehwŏek, 1954–58). The illiteracy rate of South Koreans decreased roughly from 87 percent in 1948 to 4.1 percent by 1958.[2] Following this immense rise in literacy, which resulted from the new universal education system, the growth of the publishing market was drastic. Magazines became accordingly diversified into subject categories such as literature, cinema, and general enter-tainment that catered to groups such as women, children, students, intellectuals, and so on.

58   CHAPTER 3

Film magazines were also published on a massive scale during the post–Korean War period. Fourteen such magazines began publication in the mid-1950s, but most had financial difficulties and soon went into bankruptcy. The two major film magazines that survived during this period were *Cinema World* (*Yŏnghwa segye*, 1954–64) and *International Film* (*Kukche yŏnghwa*, 1955–80), though both had to halt publication in the 1960s.[3] One reason for the rapid closure of so many film magazines in this new national publishing market was probably a failure in their marketing strategy, particularly with regard to maintaining a broad readership. In comparison, the most commercially successful publishing ventures were entertainment magazines. The popularity of the entertainment magazine genre can be attributed to the publications' intermedial content, which covered cinema, radio, popular novels, music, theater, sports, and cartoon strips. This diversity helped them obtain and maintain a wide readership.

To investigate this publishing boom and the ways in which it ties into the wider political and cultural climate of the period, this chapter explores one such monthly magazine, titled *The Delight*. *The Delight* published its first issue in January 1956 and continued until February 1992.[4] Early in its life, the magazine branded itself as a "photographic magazine (*ponŭn chapchi*)," offering something different from other "reading magazines" through its new visual designs and editorial perspectives.[5] What *The Delight* primarily relied on in making its visual content as a photographic magazine more alluring was a focus on showcasing photos and illustrations related to cinema, movie stars, popular songs, and singers. Roughly one-quarter of the magazine was filled with images of renowned movie stars and singers. In scanning through extant copies of the publication today, it is hard to find a page that does not include an image of some kind. Like the US movie fan magazine *Photoplay*, it contained a profusion of adverts and publicity photos of movie stars alongside stories about their private lives. *The Delight* was also comparable to the Japanese monthly entertainment magazine *Heibon*,[6] in that it contained many supplemental illustrations and photos which could serve as pullout posters for readers. This visually oriented strategy of *The Delight* resulted in expanded sales of seventy thousand copies a month,[7] and the publication soon became listed as one of the top three magazines of the late 1950s. However, by the late 1960s, weekly magazines had taken over the mainstream and replaced the commercially prestigious status of monthly publications such as *The Delight*.

During its period of success, while the magazine was considered morally suspect for its sensationalist "yellow journalism" based on excessive sexual content and titillating photographic images of female bodies, it also paradoxically functioned as a platform for political messages from the military government. In this sense, the significance of *The Delight* resided not only in its commercial achievement but in its ability to balance risqué content with the propagation of authoritarian government politics. By exploring the editorial approaches, design, commercial strategies, and cultural and political content of *The Delight* from its first issue in 1956 until 1971, I will argue that *The Delight* was a success precisely because it catered both to the desires of the popular readership and to the repressive government policies of 1950–60s South Korea, and I will show how this was achieved.

THE DELIGHT, A NEW ENTERTAINMENT MAGAZINE

In 1950s South Korea, there were five major publishing companies, each of which owned several magazine brands: the Hope Company (*Hŭimangsa*), the New Sun Company (*Sint'aeyangsa*), the Academy Company (*Hakwŏnsa*), the Thought Company (*Sasanggyesa*), and Samjungdang. These magazine brands had relatively long lives compared to those published in the late 1940s, when most magazine companies ceased publishing after just a few months and went bankrupt. One major reason for the short life span of these publications in the 1940s was the low literacy rate amongst the general population. But after the drastic increase in literacy during the mid-1950s, the publishing market became an enticing prospect for investors, and business boomed.

The average price for each magazine issue varied from 200 hwan to 400 hwan, cheaper than the cost of a cinema ticket, which was around 4,000 hwan. The previously mentioned five major publishing companies strategically aimed their publications at different types of readers. The Thought Company targeted school-teachers and intellectuals, while the Academy Company targeted middle and high school students. The Hope Company issued *The Hope* as a generalist magazine which dealt with many different issues for adult readers. Samjungdang published Korea's first entertainment magazine, *Arirang*, in March 1955. This publication proved to be highly marketable, and the number of monthly issues of *Arirang* reached around 90,000 in 1955, the highest circulation achieved by any magazine at the time.[8]

The New Sun Company entered the entertainment magazine industry as a late-comer and launched *The Delight* in January 1956.[9] To compete with similar magazines like *Arirang*, the editor of *The Delight* highlighted that this new publication would be a *photographic* magazine, writing in the October 1956 issue that it would be distinctive precisely because it was a "photographic magazine. . . . This is what we pursue. Our magazine will go beyond the usual pattern of dry, small-print [and present instead a] broad outlook [for which] we changed the design to a 4x6 format."[10] The four-by-six-inch format meant that the standard page size was larger than in other magazines and could incorporate a larger size of photographs and bigger styles of font and typeface. This editorial strategy clearly indicates what the magazine's focus was and how it sought to make a difference visually. As displayed in figure 3.1, the March 1957 issue of *The Delight* included large-scale photographic images of Hollywood star Marilyn Monroe. The title of the article is "The Life of Marilyn Monroe through Photographs," and this type of pictorially and photo-graphically based content doubtlessly made the journal more attractive to readers

FIGURE 3.1. *The Delight*, March 1957.

who had only just learned how to read. In the editorial of the November 1956 issue, the editor wrote that *The Delight* was based on a "7S policy." This policy represented the subjects of "Sex, Story, Star, Screen, Sports, Studio, [and] Stage" as those that the magazine was primarily going to cover.[11] By including a wide variety of popular culture as its focus, the "7S policy" targeted a general body of popular readership, while the sensationalist component of the approach was also designed to further attract random casual consumers.

Among the parallel forms of popular media, *The Delight* depended for a large portion of its content on cinema, and many of the photographs in the magazine were still images or posters from films. Within postwar South Korea, the film industry grew rapidly thanks to systematic financial assistance by the government, resulting in the industry achieving something of a golden age.[12] Moreover, due to South Korea's frontline situation within the Cold War and the related massive influx of US culture, Hollywood films and stars were clearly also a primary interest of the magazine. In this respect, images from both South Korean and Hollywood films filled an overwhelming portion of space within *The Delight*. As exemplified in figure 3.2—a photographic montage from a "special report on kiss scenes in film" in the issue of October 1956—using images taken from scenes within Hollywood films was both an efficient way to highlight the goal of making a photographic magazine and a way to sensationally stimulate the interests of readers.

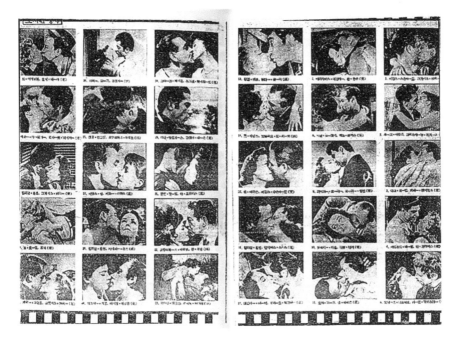

FIGURE 3.2. *The Delight*, October 1956.

Regarding the use of images from foreign films, it is hard to imagine that the New Sun Company obtained permission for the use of these images from production companies outside Korea, because there was a very weak concept of copyright at the time. In the August 1958 issue, *The Delight* published images of foreign model Judy Rawling almost naked (see figure 3.3). It indicated that these specific images were copied from the US magazine *Glamour*. This was a very exceptional note because most images of foreign actors and actresses were used without any such special note. This inclusion was probably also made to avoid censorship, by showing that a famous US magazine had also published the images. As such, most illustrations and images from Western films must have been used without permission, and this part of the magazine could be regarded as a simple pirated translation of foreign magazines.[13]

Despite this lack of originality, *The Delight* nonetheless attempted to forge a distinct visual identity through montages, as exemplified in figure 3.4. Alongside these "manually" designed composite photographic tableaux, the magazine staff also concocted interesting stories to complement the images. The example in figure 3.4 served as the introduction to actress Kim Hye-chŏng, one of the sex symbols of South Korean cinema, and the accompanying montage was designed to highlight the private space of Kim and her famous beautiful legs by showing how she wore her stockings. Sometimes the stories were based on actual interviews,

62   CHAPTER 3

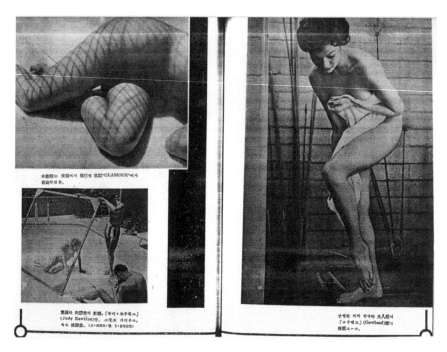

FIGURE 3.3. *The Delight*, August 1958.

yet it seems that many stories were created by reporters or other writers who simply invented narratives to fit the images. Considering the fact that most of the people who could make magazines were mostly educated during the Japanese colonial period, there is a high possibility that *The Delight* used Japanese entertainment magazines such as *Heibon* as its template, which had a similar manually made visual editorial strategy.[14]

The magazine also provided popular music scores with lyrics, which was unusual in comparison to other magazines. In the April 1958 issue, for instance, *The Delight* even distributed a free bonus book that contained one hundred scores of popular songs.[15] Cartoons appeared quite often in *The Delight*, which was related to the rising consumption of this media form nationally, as there were no comic magazines or graphic novels separately published at this time. Cartoons often served to summarize the story lines of films recently released, a visual and narrative approach to previewing and reviewing the latest movies which might have been helpful for readers and specific fans of cinema. The magazine also contained many images from sporting events, including scenes from the Olympic games or boxing matches, which were the most popular sports at the time. Popular stage performances such as *yŏsŏng kukgŭk* (all-female popular performances) or *akgŭk* (revues) were also showcased in the publication.[16] Through this diverse focus, the magazine used numerous parallel forms of popular media and

FIGURE 3.4. *The Delight*, August 1960.

entertainment culture to fill its pages and provided a boost to the overall economy of popular culture consumption through its wide circulation.

The most popular section, however, was probably that which contained images of movie stars and popular singers, featuring private background stories, interviews, and gossip. These details about the stars and their experiences of marriage, love, divorce, and scandal were for most readers the highlight of the magazine, just as such contents were for consumers of the magazine *Photoplay*. The degree to which the private life of the stars was exposed was quite astounding. For instance, in the July 1965 issue, *The Delight* wrote a ten-page exposition of the life story of actress T'ae Hyŏn-sil. This story was not just about her career, as a substantial portion was given over to describing her complicated love life and history of boyfriends, in which the names, jobs, and even educational backgrounds of these men were revealed.[17] In the same issue, another article, entitled "Grading a Star's Sex Life," divided Korean actresses into three grades, and gave individual comments about how much sex appeal each woman had. Revealing the private stories of the stars or exploiting female stars' sexuality was a shameless marketing strategy used regularly by *The Delight*. The details contained within such revelations became increasingly salacious by the late 1960s, to the degree that *The Delight* received a warning from the National Ethics Committee for Magazines in 1970.[18]

64   CHAPTER 3

Another interesting aspect of *The Delight* was that it functioned as a social network, akin to contemporary social media. In the early stages of the publication's life, there was only a small "letters" section that contained readers' opinions and their expressions of gratitude to the magazine. As time went on, participation by *The Delight* readers in creating content increased immensely. For instance, in the earlier issues, there was a section called "The Delight Post," which enabled readers to share their postal addresses, exchange letters, and look for "true friendship, brotherhood, and sisterhood."[19] It is notable in this regard that the specific words for "sister" (*nuna*) or "brother" (*oppa*) appeared quite often in this section, as readers searched for companionship and attempted to forge pseudo-family relationships. These letters were from all different regions of the nation, and the people who wrote them ranged from high school or college students to soldiers to salarymen and so forth.[20] In response, starting with the October 1960 issue, *The Delight* officially made a "Reader's Card" to systematize official feedback to the readers and increase audience interaction. For instance, if a reader asked about the address of a certain actor or actress in the card, the editorial office replied with this information directly by publishing the information in the next issue. Certainly, it would seem there was no concept of the right to privacy for celebrities at this time. But in this way, ordinary people were able to form a collective culture through and within the magazine, and for audiences this constituted an astonishingly modern and new way of social communication.

This practice of two-way communication extended to another section in the magazine, which was titled the "Counseling Center." Here, the readers posed their own personal questions to a celebrity and received advice. The questions asked were often very provocative, and within this section readers were able to find out what certain celebrities thought about risqué issues. For instance, one reader asked if it was okay that she rejected her boyfriend's suggestion to go to a hotel together, and the magazine answered that it was the virtue of a virgin to reject such a request from a boyfriend.[21] In addition, this kind of advice was a way to form discourse on certain moral issues and could function as a method of discipline for readers. By encouraging the participation of readers through these methods, the magazine could attract and sustain wider audiences. It also became a unique social space within the popular media, one through which we can see how the emerging desires of the audience and cultural production intersected.

THE DELIGHT AS A PLATFORM
FOR POLITICAL PROPAGANDA

Like many entertainment magazines, *The Delight* concerned itself primarily with commercial and audience growth. But when certain political issues became central to Korean society, the magazine also extended its commentary to politics. For example, when the April Revolution occurred in 1960,[22] the magazine reported on this mass demonstration of people who rose up against the Syngman Rhee government (1948–60) and explained in detail what happened during the event.[23] Some of these articles emphasized the things that Korean people should do in the face of such turmoil, while others highlighted the changes made through the revolution and introduced the leading figures in the new political landscape.[24] This political section became increasingly serious over the years, and reports on social change became longer and more in depth with the establishment of Park Chung Hee's military dictatorship in 1961.

Immediately after the military coup staged by Park Chung Hee, *The Delight* began to publish the new president's "Revolution Promise."[25] This "promise" contained the slogans that Park himself had pledged to Koreans with his ascension to power, and it was defined by the following commitments: (1) to intensify anticommunism; (2) to follow the political direction of the United Nations, United States, and other allied nations; (3) to rectify corrupt social customs; (4) to establish a full economic plan to resolve the poverty of Koreans; (5) to unite the nation; and (6) to dedicate ourselves to our nation. This promise was often featured in *The Delight*, sometimes with all six slogans printed on one page and sometimes spread across six pages. In terms of design, the graphic approach to formatting the promise was comparable to that used for a commercial advertisement. Also, using its platform as a "photographic magazine," *The Delight* was able to effectively display how Park's so-called revolution was well underway.[26] The photographic images displayed in the magazine often pointedly emphasized the "cooperation of all the nation" towards development and reconstruction, and interestingly this was very similar to the Japanese government's use of media platforms during the Asia-Pacific War to emphasize national unity (see figure 3.5).

In this respect, it is notable that the title of the magazine, "delight," had been used as a political slogan during the Asia-Pacific War to promote the sound and healthy minds of Korean people by the Japanese colonial government.[27] This word was therefore resurrected in postwar South Korean society, and it is possible that the political value of this slogan was deliberately utilized by the Park Chung Hee dictatorship. Many scholars have pointed out the similarities between Japanese fascism and the Park government,[28] and it is not difficult to imagine that the Korean dictatorial regime would similarly use all available media to propagate the ideology of the state. Regarding the political tone of the magazine, some scholars have also argued that in contrast to the 1950s' liberal conception of *The Delight*, the magazine became conservative and lost it vibrancy under military rule.[29] Some have asserted that, even though the dictatorship used the magazine to convey direct political messages, normal people also continued to utilize its space to express their own desires.[30] What we can say with certainty is that the display of such political messages offered a way to avoid total censorship[31] and maintain a limited freedom to express the desires of the people.

One of *The Delight*'s most interesting aspects with respect to censorship was its bold focus on overt sexual content. As mentioned previously, the magazine often used salacious stories to attract readers. But when the Park Chung Hee

FIGURE 3.5. *The Delight*, December 1961.

government started a campaign to regulate the "sound and healthy" sexual life of the citizenry, the magazine also began to publish reports more in line with the government perspective. For instance, in the March 1961 issue, *The Delight* contained an article about the Kinsey Reports, which exemplified how this new medical knowledge about sex could still be sensationalized as a topic to attract readers. These types of reports combining medical and scientific knowledge about sex increased drastically in the mid-1960s under the repressive military regime. For example, the magazine discussed specific ways to use various tools for contraception, the "anatomy of bodies," and medical knowledge about orgasms. The March 1971 issue included a medical report that mechanically explained the details of the female orgasm, saying that it is "due to the congestion of the blood and release of the muscle."[32] When such medical or physiological content appeared in the magazine, it was labeled "sex medical" or "sex science" reports. While these reports did indeed provide a medical or scientific analysis of sex, they obviously also attracted the general reader and reflected readers' desire to satisfy their secret interests in the biological and physiological details of sex.

Kim Chi-yŏng has argued that the presentation of this medical and scientific knowledge came from an entirely male-centric perspective and was therefore repressive to women and their bodies, reflecting the oppressive patriarchal ideology of the Park government.[33] While this notion has great validity, it is nonetheless

THE POPULAR MEDIA BOOM IN SOUTH KOREA   67

interesting that the bodies of men were also presented in a standardized way for readers, and that male sexual functions were also medically explained.[34] Similarly, the drastic increase in advertisements for supplements to increase male sexual strength and for procedures to enlarge the penis also show that the new scientific knowledge on sex was used to regulate and subjectify both genders, although women were undoubtedly prone to suffer more punitive moral and social judgment in relation to their use of this information and their sexual activities. Perhaps most significantly, this body of scientific knowledge functioned primarily not as a useful resource of knowledge in itself but as a way to discipline the bodies and private lives of the population. In this regard, Michel Foucault noted that the disciplinary discourse on sex and sexuality has increased in relation to the expansion of medical and scientific knowledge in modern society.[35] Here, this new professional knowledge was likewise utilized to help extend state control of the general population living mundane lives in South Korea. However, we cannot deny that this modern knowledge about sex was also simply of great interest to the readers of magazines as intriguing and disposable content.

This chapter has explored one of the most popular entertainment magazines of 1950s and 1960s South Korea, *The Delight*. With the print industry boom in the aftermath of the Korean War, *The Delight* paved a unique path within popular magazine culture. Through its innovative design, focus on visual novelty, and sensational photographs and stories, the magazine attempted to meet the rising interest in the latest popular culture. The magazine also offered a space for individual communication, as within and through it people could exchange ideas and personal stories and make social connections. It was also a didactic space providing socially useful modern knowledge, moral guidance, and even political propaganda, although it remains an open question if this government messaging within the magazine served to significantly discipline and regulate the lives and minds of audiences. What can be stated with more certainty is that *The Delight* offers historians a fantastic window into the past, one through which we can see how a multitude of desires, interests, and politics regularly intersected in relation to the construction of postwar South Korean pop culture.

NOTES

1. According to Yi Pong-bŏm, nearly twenty significant magazines, including *Sasanggye*, *Hŭimang*, and *Hagwŏn*, published their first issues during the war in Taegu and Pusan. Yi Pong-bŏm, "Magazine Journalism and Literature during the 1950s: Focusing on Popular Magazines," *Sanghŏ hakbo* 30 (2010), 400.

2. Yi, "Magazine Journalism and Literature," 422.

3. *Cinema World* halted publication permanently in 1964. *International Film* halted publication in 1964 and resumed in 1968. The titles of other film magazines include *Theater/Film* (*Yŏn'gŭk yŏnghwa*), *Modern Cinema* (*Hyŏndae yŏnghwa*), *Monthly Film* (*Wŏlgan yŏnghwa*), *Film Art* (*Yesul yŏnghwa*), *Film and Television Art* (*Yŏnghwa TV yesul*), *Korea Cinema*, *Film Magazine* (*Yŏnghwa chapchi*), *Film*

68   CHAPTER 3

and Entertainment (*Yŏnghwa yŏn'ye*), *Silver Screen, Scenario Art* (*Sinario munye*), *Cinema World* (*Yŏnghwagye*), and *Movie/Theater Fan* (*Yŏn'gŭkpaen*).

4. *The Delight* stopped publication in the 1980s by the order of the government when the new military regime led by Chun Doo Hwan came to power. But it resumed publication in February 1988 when Chun stepped down from the presidency following the success of the democracy movement in 1987.

5. The concept of the "photographic magazine" comes directly from the Japanese monthly entertainment magazine *Heibon*. *Heibon* had the same marketing strategy, focused on the photographic aspect of the magazine. This strategy could be comparable to US magazines such as *Look* and *Life*, which heavily used photography as the main feature of the publication to support as wide a readership as possible. However, while the US journals *Life* and *Look* used original photographs created by professional photographers, most of the visual images used in *The Delight* were gathered and re-edited from external already published sources, though some photographs seem to have been taken by staff working for the magazine.

6. *Heibon* focused mostly on the cinema, popular songs, and stars. It was a top popular magazine in 1950s and '60s Japan. See Sakamoto Hiroshi, *The Era of Ordinary: The Popular Entertainment Magazine of the 1950s* (Kyoto: Showadang, 2008). I appreciate Professor Ji Hee Jung at the Institute for Japanese Studies, Seoul National University, for introducing me to this important magazine of Japan.

7. "Autumn without Books," *Kyŏnghyang Shinmun*, October 24, 1957.

8. Yi, "Magazine Journalism and Literature," 417.

9. Before the publication of *The Delight*, the New Sun Company published *The New Sun* (*Sint'aeyang*) in 1952, and *The True Story* (*Silhwa*) in 1953. Compared to lucrative publications such as *The True Story* and *The Delight, The New Sun* was relatively serious and, as such, always had to confront a financial deficit.

10. *The Delight*, October 1956, 180.

11. *The Delight*, November 1956, 184.

12. The formation of the South Korean Golden Age of Cinema was a huge trend during the 1950s–60s in South Korea, parallel to the New Wave movement in Europe. See Nancy Abelmann and Kathleen McHugh, eds., *South Korean Golden Age Melodrama: Gender, Genre, and National Cinema* (Detroit: Wayne State University Press, 2005).

13. *The Delight*, August 1958.

14. After Korean liberation from Japan (1945), the diplomatic relationship between South Korea and Japan was halted until 1965, when the Normalization Act was passed. Even after normalization, Japanese culture, including film, novels, music, and other types of popular culture, could not be officially introduced in South Korea until the 1990s. However, Japanese magazines and films were smuggled into the country. Many Koreans copied the contents and the style of Japanese magazines and films. The editorial style and marketing strategy of *The Delight* are strikingly similar to the Japanese magazine *Heibon*.

15. *The Delight*, April 1958.

16. There were also serious artistic theater performances in South Korea, but it is notable that *The Delight* never wrote anything about these.

17. "All about This Actress," *The Delight*, July 1965.

18. "The Committee Gave Warning to Seven Monthly Magazines," *Maeil Kyŏngje*, February 27, 1970.

19. *The Delight*, October 1956.

20. Kim Yŏn-suk argues that this search for pseudo-family was a postwar cultural phenomenon that reflected the common desire to search for alternative forms of family after many people lost their close relatives during the Korean War. Kim Yŏn-suk, "An Epic on the Post-war Individual Relationships from the Viewpoint of the Pop Magazine *Myŏngnang*," *The Journal of Popular Narrative* 22, no. 2 (2016).

21. *The Delight*, January 1964, 261.

22. The April Revolution was the first mass civil demonstration in South Korea. It occurred when angry students and citizens rose up against the corruption perpetrated by the Syngman Rhee government and specifically Rhee's reelection in 1960. In response, Rhee stepped down and a new democratic government was established. This lasted until 1961 and the establishment of the Park Chung Hee military regime.

23. Articles about the April Revolution began to appear in the magazine from the July 1960 issue onward. Since it took a certain amount of time to publish the magazine, there were some delays in reporting on contemporaneous social issues, and usually it took two months for new social issues to appear in the monthly magazines. As such, this report on the April Revolution appeared two months after the event, in the July issue.

24. Many examples are found within the September issue in 1960.

25. *The Delight*, October 1961, 120.

26. *The Delight*, December 1961.

27. Yi Chu-ra, "Cheerful Citizens Who Poked Fun at the National Ideology," *Kaenyŏm kwa sot'ong*, vol. 20, 90–92.

28. On the direct lineage between the Japanese puppet state of Manchukuo and the South Korean dictatorship under Park Chung Hee, see, for example, Han Suk-Jung, "The Suppression and Recall of Colonial Memory: Manchukuo and the Cold War in the Two Koreas," in *Mass Dictatorship and Memory as Ever Present Past*, ed. Jie-Hyun Lim (London: Palgrave Macmillan, 2014).

29. Kim Chi-yŏng, "The Cultural Politics and Historical Transition of the Emotional Constitution of 'Gaiety,'" Ŏmunnonjip 78 (2016).

30. Yi Chu-ra, "Cheerful Citizens."

31. Chung-kang Kim, "Nation, Subculture, and Queer Representation: The Film Male Kisaeng and the Politics of Gender and Sexuality in 1960s South Korea," *Journal of the History of Sexuality* 24, no. 3 (September 2015).

32. *The Delight*, March 1971, 184.

33. Kim Chi-yŏng, "Sexuality over the Boundaries and Extension of Modern Knowledge Power: A Study on the Discourse of Sexuality in the Korean Yellow Journal of the 1960s," *Studies of Women's Literature* 45 (2018).

34. Chung-kang Kim, "Frustrated 'Masculinity': Sex Movie, Sexual Impotence, and the Discourses of Medical Cure (1967–1974)," *Yŏksamunjeyŏn'gu* 40, 2018.

35. Michel Foucault, *The History of Sexuality, vol. 1: An Introduction* (New York: Vintage, 1990), 4–13.

PUBLICATIONS REFERENCED

Arirang
Cinema World (*Yŏnghwa segye*)
The Delight
Film and Entertainment (*Yŏnghwa yŏnye*)
Film and Television Art (*Yŏnghwa TV yesul*)
Film Art (*Yesul yŏnghwa*)
Glamour
Heibon
The Hope
International Film (*Kukche yŏnghwa*)
Korea Cinema
Film Magazine (*Yŏnghwa chapchi*)

70   CHAPTER 3

Life
Look
Modern Cinema (Hyŏndae yŏnghwa)
Monthly Film (Wŏlgan yŏnghwa)
Movie/Theater Fan (Yŏngŭkpaen)
The New Sun (Sint'aeyang)
On Cinema (Yŏnghwagye)
Photoplay
Scenario Art (Sinario munye)
Silver Screen
Theater/Film (Yŏngŭk yŏnghwa)
The True Story (Silhwa)

BIBLIOGRAPHY

Abelmann, Nancy, and Kathleen McHugh, eds. *South Korean Golden Age Melodrama: Gender, Genre, and National Cinema.* Detroit: Wayne State University Press, 2005.

"The Committee Gave Warning to Seven Monthly Magazines." *Maeil Kyŏngje*, February 27, 1970.

Foucault, Michel. *The History of Sexuality, vol. 1: An Introduction.* New York: Vintage, 1990.

Han Suk-Jung. "The Suppression and Recall of Colonial Memory: Manchukuo and the Cold War in the Two Koreas." In *Mass Dictatorship and Memory as Ever Present Past*, edited by Jie-Hyun Lim. London: Palgrave Macmillan, 2014.

Kim Chi-yŏng. "The Cultural Politics and Historical Transition of the Emotional Constitution of 'gaiety.'" Ŏmunnonjip 78 (2016).

——. "Sexuality over the Boundaries and Extension of Modern Knowledge Power: A Study on the Discourse of Sexuality in the Korean Yellow Journal of the 1960s." *Studies of Women's Literature* 45 (2018).

Kim Chung-kang. "Frustrated 'Masculinity': Sex Movie, Sexual Impotence, and the Discourses of Medical Cure (1967–1974)." *Yŏksamunjeyŏn'gu* 40 (2018).

——. "Nation, Subculture, and Queer Representation: The Film *Male Kisaeng* and the Politics of Gender and Sexuality in 1960s South Korea." *Journal of the History of Sexuality* 24, no. 3 (September 2015).

Kim Yŏn-suk. "An Epic on the Post-war Individual Relationships from the Viewpoint of the Pop Magazine *Myŏngnang*." *Taejung sŏsa yŏn'gu* 22, no. 2 (2016).

Sakamoto, Hiroshi. *The Era of Ordinary: The Popular Entertainment Magazine of the 1950s.* Kyoto: Showadang, 2008.

Yi Chu-ra. "Cheerful Citizens Who Poked Fun at the National Ideology." *Kaenyŏm kwa sot'ong* 20 (2017).

Yi Pong-bŏm. "Magazine Journalism and Literature during the 1950s: Focusing on Popular Magazines." *Sanghŏ hakbo* 30 (2010).

4

Compilation, Collage, and Film Publishing in 1950s–1960s Iran

Setāreh-ye Sinemā (Cinema Star)

Babak Tabarraee and Kaveh Askari

Massoud Mehrabi, the licensee and managing director of *Film Monthly*—the longest-running film journal in postrevolutionary Iran—posted this comment on Instagram in 2018, less than two years before he passed away: "In *Film* [*Monthly*], we wanted to journey beyond Sohrab Shahid Sales and Parviz Kimiavi and [their] *A Simple Event* [1973] and *P for Pelican* [1972]. The path was too steep, however, and we fell into a valley. Now we've reached *Los Angeles–Tehran* [Tina Pakravan, 2018] and *Centipede* [Abolhassan Davoodi, 2018]. The ghost of *Setāreh-ye Sinemā* (*Cinema Star*) always returns to brazenly claim its due."[1] We cannot ask Mehrabi what he meant by this evocation of a periodical that, while long out of print and not easily accessible, still haunts film intellectuals and fans. And yet, his self-deprecating tone toward the status of his own influential magazine alongside *Setāreh-ye Sinemā* provides an example of Iranians' love-hate relationship with many aspects of their film industry, including its trade press.

Both of these publications have enjoyed a faithful readership. Their reviews were written by some of the most revered film critics in the country, and their translations have ensured an ongoing engagement among Persian speakers with important intellectual traditions in film theory and criticism from around the world. *Setāreh-ye Sinemā*, in particular, was sometimes pitched by its former staff as the closest Iranian publication to the ambitions of *Sight and Sound, Movie*, or *Cahiers du cinéma*.[2] This status has been partially intensified by a postrevolutionary generation of cinephiles who could not access it due to the Islamic Republic's strict laws about media related to the prerevolution film industry.[3] At the same time, both magazines have been continually criticized for their policies: *Film Monthly* for its politically conservative approach that has ensured the magazine's

CHAPTER 4

ongoing run and *Setāreh-ye Sinema* for the pulpy associations with pinups and the cheaply made Iranian popular films, known as *filmfārsi*, that have presented a challenge for those primarily interested in its highbrow currents. This chapter sits with the many contradictions of *Setāreh-ye Sinemā* in all of their vitality. We argue for a reevaluation of a magazine which, during its run of 1,067 issues over twenty-five years (encompassing the conflicting views of various editorial boards), proved to be neither an exclusively elitist platform for promoting festival favorites like Shahid Sales and Kimiavi nor merely a collection of lurid promotions of the Iranian popular cinema and cheap imports.[4] *Setāreh-ye Sinemā*, promoted by its first editorial board as "the most beautiful and original cinema magazine in the Middle East," was ambivalent in its forms of cinephilia.[5]

Our essay tracks the origins of the journal in 1954 out of a collaboration of a group of young film writers and the owner of a newsstand across the street from the famous Metropole cinema in Tehran. It points out the tumultuous editorial shifts as the journal increased its circulation, production values, and frequency to a weekly staple available at kiosks around major cinemas. Key topics include the place of the trade press within the Iranian film industry, *Setāreh-ye Sinemā*'s relation to other periodicals in Iran, and the collage style of its layout, design, and featured translations. The long life of the journal tracks precisely those tensions signaled by Mehrabi: between the critical reception of local productions and imports, and between popular fan service and the intellectual commitments of critics and filmmakers whose careers were incubated at the journal.

Between the release of the first Iranian feature in 1933 and the first issue of *Setāreh-ye Sinemā* twenty years later, only thirty Iranian films were exhibited in the country, and fewer than ten film-specific periodicals were launched and shortly died.[6] The industry was emergent in the early 1950s, but studios still had to contend with a lack of infrastructure and cinematic training.[7] Fledgling and fragile, they faced stiff competition with the stream of foreign movies dubbed into Persian in Iranian, Egyptian, and Italian studios since 1946.[8] As a result, those publications that served as the promotional material for the newly established studios faced significant obstacles.[9] It also took time for audiences to warm to the idea of making space for imported entertainment in the well-respected realm of print publication.

Setāreh-ye Sinemā arrived at a time when the demand for the ancillary services to support the economic aspects of both productions and imports had increased. The number of Iranian productions increased dramatically in the 1950s. More dubbing studios were founded in Tehran, the government offered low-interest loans and tax exemptions for building new movie theaters in provinces, and a national plan for eradicating illiteracy began, all around the same time.[10] In addition to this auspicious atmosphere, *Setāreh-ye Sinemā* benefited from a sizable investment by its founder, Paruir Galestian, as well as a brigade of young cinephiles who had gained experience in previous film journals, especially *Jahān-e Sinemā* (*The World of Cinema*) and *Sinemā Teātr* (*Cinema & Theater*).[11] Film historian Jamal

Omid—who was one of the numerous editors-in-chief of *Setāreh-ye Sinemā* in different periods—quotes the first editor of the journal on how Galestian, the owner of a kiosk/bookshop that had become the regular hangout of Tehran's cinephiles, invested 300,000 rials (roughly $3,300) in the magazine.[12] It was indeed, for a venture of this kind, "an enormous capital investment."[13] This combination of experience and enthusiasm guaranteed the continuation of the magazine's publication for at least about a decade before any significant reorganizing.[14]

But success and stature were two separate issues. Writing on cinema fared much better when it was relegated to a subsection of a broad cultural magazine. For this reason, while it was unrivaled as a cinema journal in its early years, *Setāreh-ye Sinemā* took a while to gain favor among the country's intelligentsia. Despite the illiteracy of much of the country up until mid-century, Persian periodicals were popular and influential after World War II.[15] In the twelve years between the Allied occupation of Iran in 1941 and Mohammad Reza Shah's 1953 coup d'état, for example, a total of 2,682 new titles were introduced to the country—most of which were driven by political partisanship.[16] Even during the politically dark period following the coup, many activists used the platform of periodicals for expressing their frustration with the failure of constitutional ideals.[17] As a result, a variety of literary publications by progressive forces formed a line of cultural resistance. That is, not only did they take on the political *estebdād* (tyranny), they also railed against cultural *ebtezāl* (vulgarity).[18] Just as the efforts to welcome films into museums elsewhere brought cultural legitimacy to the medium, it was the occasional cinema sections of arts and culture journals that rendered cinema worthy of debate among the intellectuals—even as many film critics wrote for both types of publications.

This condescending attitude toward journals focused exclusively on cinema was established in the 1950s, and it still exerted influence on film journalism and scholarship produced more than a generation later. Mehrabi, for example, elaborates on it in his influential book on the history of Iranian cinema, first published in 1984. He derides the "clamor of star-making and dream-selling in the vulgar and content-less cinema journals" such as *Setāreh-ye Sinemā* in contrast to the cinema pages of intellectual journals like *Ferdowsi, Rowshanfekr, Sadaf, Negin*, and *Sokhan*, which "mostly analyzed foreign films and belittled *filmfārsi*."[19] Such an assessment gestures back to divisions set up by readers and critics themselves in the publications of the 1950s. We can even see these tensions between cultural publications and cinema publications fictionalized in such films as *Tufān dar shahr-e mā* (*Storm in Our City*, Samuel Khachikian, 1958). In a scene designed to distinguish the naivete of Pari from her older brother Saeed (who works in publishing), Pari stands in front of cutout magazine portraits of Elizabeth Taylor and other stars while Saeed reads *Rowshanfekr* (*Intellectual*) on the other side of the room.

As with so many public debates about cinema's increasing prominence, the emergent film publishing scene in Iran took on much of the labor of assuaging

FIGURE 4.1. High and low—from *Tufān dar shahr-e mā* (*Storm in Our City*, Samuel Khachikian, 1958).

suspicions about the medium's status as art and as a force for social betterment.[20] In order to avoid assumptions about the medium as a depoliticized distraction, the editorial boards of film journals initially made efforts to promote cinema as a novel technological invention with economic and educational value. This fostered ambivalent messaging. Editorial teams were often compelled to pay lip service to values of social uplift while focusing on material that did not necessarily reflect such an educational mission. The opening editorial of the first journal in Iran devoted wholly to the cinema, *Sinemā va Namāyeshāt* (*Cinema and Spectacle*, published in August 1930), claimed that the aim of the publication was the "progress and development of this noble technology and industry in Iran." Cinema, according to the writers of *Sinemā va Namāyeshāt*, was an "important agent of social life and a foundation for the edification of the society's ethics." And yet, the majority of the contents of the first of its total of two issues were about the appearance of Mary Pickford, the private life of Lili Damita, and the biography of Mabel Normand.[21] This introduction of grand intentions while obsessively publishing pictures and snippets on US and European stars continued in subsequent magazines such as *Hollywood*, whose first editorial (July 1943) discussed World War II while dedicating much of its pages to Hedy Lamarr, Deanna Durbin, and Greta Garbo.[22]

This tactic for negotiating the disparate concerns of the country's intelligentsia and its growing population of moviegoers is evident from *Setāreh-ye Sinemā*'s first issue as well. In the magazine's opening editorial, "The Way Forward," the editorial board introduces the target audience of the magazine as those "who want to see cinema as it should be, not as it is."[23] Rather than merely paying attention to the actors or copying the taste of US magazines, the writers claimed, *Setāreh-ye Sinemā* aimed to foreground "proper and educational criticism" centering on "the subject or content of the film."[24] The emphasis of this editorial is on a conception of film art as tied to technological progress and social significance. Only some of the articles bore authors' names (a practice of semi-obscure authorship that continued for years). Those articles that were signed by their authors tended to align with an agenda of social responsibility or technological development. They included, in the first issue, an article on "the new techniques of cinema," introducing Cinerama, 3-D, and Cinemascope; an article on "the role of music in narrative films"; and two pages of reviews on respected foreign films screened in Tehran over the previous two weeks. The bulk of the magazine's items, however, covered rumors about Hollywood stars or celebrations of the high-grossing movies and highest-paid actors. Thirty-five of the overall forty-two images of the issue are reprinted illustrations of non-Iranian movie stars, including two small photos and a large cover photo of Ava Gardner.

The editors did recognize that they needed to walk a fine line in their coverage of the forms of celebrity, the market successes, and the capital-intensive technologies of Hollywood and European commercial cinemas. The magazine continually qualified its choices even as the enthusiasm of its fan service continued apace. Even in the first issue, "The Way Forward" acknowledges a "contrast" between the general policy of the magazine and "what is now available [in the magazine itself]." The authors justify this "ostensible" contrast by stating that their objective in introducing foreign films and stressing their stars is to increase the knowledge of their readers about the films they are actually watching and to help those who want to take up the profession of acting. "That we talk more about Hollywood products should not give the impression that *Setāreh-ye Sinemā* is a Hollywoodography," the writers stress. Their rationale is that it would be naive to ignore the fact that "95% of the films screened in Iranian theaters are of this type."[25] Indeed, the majority of the items in the twenty-four pages of the first issue (counting the front and back covers) are about US and European filmmakers, companies, and stars, while fewer than four pages cover the topics related to Iranian cinema.[26] In the decades that followed, however, many changes occurred in the management, editors-in-chief, policies, staff, format, and organization of the magazine's contents. Therefore, a thorough analysis of *Setāreh-ye Sinemā* would require distinguishing the different periods of the magazine. Just like the evolving meanings of cinema in the country, the identity of this cinema magazine was rarely immune to change.

The paradoxical policies and materials of the magazine are represented in both its design and its content. The composition of *Setāreh-ye Sinemā* in its first several years was a labor of compilation. Reprinted posters, celebrity news, translated interviews, and specs for new devices accompanied the critical writing. At times,

76   CHAPTER 4

the discussion feels rather personal. Directors and producers in Iran aired the minutiae of their feuds over multiple issues, often with a level of detail that must have been challenging to follow for readers without a professional stake in studio politics. This eclecticism is part of the reason it is difficult to categorize the magazine as primarily serving one sector. If the assembled contents are any indication, the magazine served a diverse readership that included fans, critical cinephiles, exhibitors, and other tradespeople. The editors referred to the magazine as a trade paper, giving space for technical discussions and allowing producers and directors serialized columns to discuss the state of the industry.[27] But the magazine also spoke directly to those interested in celebrity news. It made space for young fans to write in and provided them film trivia, crossword puzzles, and color portraits of stars.[28]

The world of the magazine was intertwined with the world of collectible print imagery circulating around the globe. The editors sourced material from film magazines as well as from the publicity material that was shipped along with the secondhand film prints destined for theaters. Warner Bros. distribution records, for example, indicate packages of posters, one-sheets, and press booklets sent from the Rome office (a key intermediary) to Iran, and we see these exact images for Warner's films reproduced in the magazine.[29] In many instances, an image of a globally recognizable actor is cut from studio publicity materials and pasted into an article, with scissor marks visible along the outline of the actor. In others, images were retouched, as in the 1959 Iranian New Year special issue, which features Lana Turner on the cover. The retouched cover included a generous addition of dark ink, which made her eyebrows heavier and extended the line of her eyes to correspond with Tehran fashion trends at the time.[30]

Such tactics of compilation and revision are of interest to current media historians tracking the flows of print media as material culture, and they were also of interest to the readers themselves. In the early years, the magazine dutifully responded to readers' letters that expressed curiosity about the magazine's sources. For example, in the third issue, the editors let one reader know that a key illustration was taken from *Clubman*, a British men's magazine.[31] They encouraged another reader to consider the images published in the magazine as comparable to posters and star photos that could be purchased à la carte in bookshops.[32] The magazine had partly grown out of Galestian's newsstand business, after all. Not only did the writing styles offer a little of everything, but the publishers also enclosed popular items from the newsstand within its binding and instructed readers to extract these valuable objects at home. The editors and publishers paid careful attention to the ways the magazine served audiences through its material presentation—including audiences disinclined or unable to read its criticism.

The news itself, the editors were happy to reveal, was compiled from a variety of film magazines from abroad. Some of it was direct translation in which the original author was credited. Other pieces condensed longer articles from French or English into Persian without translating them in their entirety and sometimes

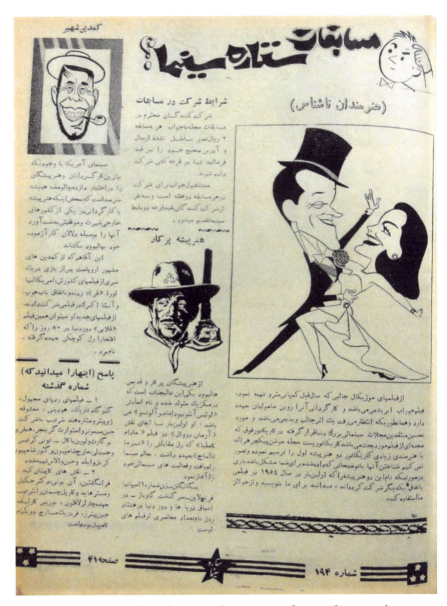

FIGURE 4.2. An example of *Setāreh-ye Sinemā*'s competitions for its readers: guess the names of these actors and win movie tickets.

without crediting the authors. This compilation strategy was prominent in the early years, but it continued even after the magazine became established. BBC critics such as Gordon Gow featured in these translations, which were often serialized over multiple issues.[33] The magazine incorporated serious criticism but hedged its bets with fan service. This strategy contrasted with that of short-lived highbrow

FIGURE 4.3. The Iranianization of foreign stars: Lana Turner on the cover of *Setāreh-ye Sinemā* issue 204, March 21, 1959.

magazines like *Honar va Sinemā* (*Art and Cinema*), which published a translation of Eisenstein's "Dickens, Griffith, and the Film Today" in its first issue.[34] By around 1960, the magazine had enlisted foreign correspondents to glean stories from the burgeoning auteurist film cultures in Europe: Bahman Farmanara from the UK, Kamran Shirdel from Italy, and Hajir Dariush from France.[35] All three of these foreign correspondents went on, after returning to Iran, to become major figures of the Iranian new wave and the festival scene of the 1970s.

This auteurist turn was not, however, a decisive break with previous editorial strategies. The magazine had carried regular director features long before it turned its attention to new waves. The coverage of Alfred Hitchcock offers one example. While Hitchcock was not the only prominent director in the 1950s issues of the journal, his interviews, the coverage of his films, and critics' engagement with those films do stand out. In the period from the first issue of the journal to 1960, every one of his new releases was advertised and reviewed. Photographs and illustrations of Hitchcock's face appear with frequency, sometimes cut and pasted onto posters or lobby cards reduced on the page so that taglines, exhibition information, and praise for the actors could be oriented in Persian text surrounding the original English text of the graphic. In one "photo corner" feature of the journal printed alongside an interview about *I Confess* (1953), Hitchcock's face is pasted over Montgomery Clift's belly, emerging from the layout of the original source poster in a sort of collage cameo, and in an advertisement for *The Wrong Man* (1956), the illustration combines a scene from the film with a production photo of the director with his arm extended. Suggestive of an act of conjuring, a dark cloud extends from the director's hand and envelops Henry Fonda's head and torso, superimposed over a police lineup.[36] Amid this steady stream of advertising and critical publicity that showcased Hitchcock as a public figure in

FIGURE 4.4. One of many disembodied Hitchcock cutouts, presented here in the "photo corner" illustration for *I Confess* (1953) in *Setāreh-ye Sinemā* issue 24, January 12, 1955.

the Iranian press, translations of interviews with the director were published, as were translations of synopses and original story material for films including *Rear Window* (1954) and *The Wrong Man*.[37] *Vertigo* (1958) received special treatment, with portions of Boileau-Narcejac's original source novel, *D'entre les morts*, translated and serialized in seven installments over two months beginning in July 1958.[38]

80   CHAPTER 4

In the pages of *Setāreh-ye Sinemā*, then, Iran's Hitchcock was pieced together through the sustained intellectual labor of editors, translators, critics, and graphic designers. They used the director's name as one way to frame prestige and aesthetic sophistication. Much of this critical discussion from the 1950s often took on effusive tones. This was the case for most of the writing on figures whose names had global currency, but Hitchcock's releases had an advantage in their ready-made publicity. "Undisputed master" accompanied the director's name in article titles and advertisements alike.[39] Some of *Setāreh-ye Sinemā*'s excessive praise might rightfully appear disingenuous or thin—it certainly did to some critics at the time and was, in fact, a topic of continual debate in the pages of the magazine. Critics were ever ready to call out their peers' puff pieces, and the magazine made room for rowdy disagreement. The debates around this collage approach to auteurism looked ahead to the focused auteurism in intellectual circles of the late 1960s, in which critics translated canonical pieces from *Cahiers du cinéma* and *Movie*.[40] Regardless of which side a critic may have taken in these discussions, such positions constituted the labor through which the magazine helped to build and manage cinema audiences. Reviews and advertisements occupied publication space alongside longer translations of interviews in which Hitchcock discussed the production context of his films, his relationship to art cinema, or the difference between mystery and suspense.[41] To understand the splashy celebrations of a global name as fundamentally distinct from more discerning forms of director-centered critical labor might overlook their interconnected functions in film publishing in 1950s Iran.

A pattern emerged in some of these debates between two forms of critical prestige: a tradition of film criticism concerned with social uplift met an emergent interest in cinema aesthetics. Such tensions have accompanied the medium of cinema since the origins of the feature film, with US organizations like the National Board of Review advocating aesthetic, not moral, censorship in the 1910s.[42] Certain genres and directors that engaged darker themes challenged straight moral or educational criteria of value. The crime thriller, particularly in its morbid postwar varieties, was less amenable than other genres to narratives of cinema as a vehicle for social uplift. It thus gave cinephile writers in Iran an opportunity to distinguish their work from that of other cultural critics who may have been less concerned with the possibilities of cinema as a medium of modern aesthetics. Cultural critics warning of the moral dangers of the crime film were, of course, common almost everywhere. Their work spanned the US press discussing its own national products, French writing on the crime film as a threat to versions of national culture, and worries by British colonial powers that US crime films would undermine their legitimacy among moviegoers in the colonies. What is worth stressing in this case is the way that film critics writing about crime thrillers in *Setāreh-ye Sinemā* saw debates about aesthetic or social criticism in local terms.

"A Little Bit about the History of the Crime Film," from 1956, offers an extensive discussion of the filmography of artistically notable noir directors and actors of the postwar period, but the material is framed by a partial turn away from censorship based on the perceived social value of films. The author discusses the "misconception that crime films cause moral decadence and corruption among viewers" as an idea that is "prevalent in improving countries (for example, our own) where it is applied with even greater dogmatism."[43] Whereas in "prominent countries of the world such as the US, UK, France, and Italy, crime films are not only marketable, they receive a surprisingly warm welcome."[44] In order to understand these films as artistic achievements evidenced by their ability to circulate and gain international attention, the author brackets questions of morality and social uplift in favor of questions of aesthetics. It is this turn toward style, in which aesthetic sophistication peels away from fears of social decay, that makes it possible to understand the appeal of postwar crime thrillers, which "have emerged from their dry and monotonous past to become an international phenomenon."[45] The issues of transnationalism appear here in the context of an essay that seeks, if not to eschew questions of uplift entirely, to switch over to aesthetic questions central to a definition of the medium. The crime film attracted those interested in the aesthetics of the medium. It placed questions of aesthetic value on the table for cultural critics in the habit of discussing the medium of cinema in terms of its social value. The critical life of Hitchcock and other stylists of foreign crime thrillers provide context for markers of prestige. *Setāreh-ye Sinemā*'s preoccupations demonstrate the global currency of the crime thriller and its stars for an emergent industry hard at work establishing codes of authorship and a sense of the aesthetic traditions of the medium.

Setāreh-ye Sinema's ambivalent policies, rowdy public feuds, and long-term material history continue to attract new generations of Iranian film scholars. While awards from international film festivals, the ever-politicized nature of film criticism inside Iran, and the continuous celebration of Iranian auteurs in the academy in the US and Europe have positioned textual (auteurist or symptomatic) analyses of Iranian films as a dominant tradition in the field, recent years have seen a wave of attempts to reroute such traditions. Partly influenced by the introduction of new cinema histories and partly as a result of the digital accessibility of many Iranian films and print sources, some scholars have considered cinema in Iran from the point of view of its transnational connections, its foreign and local distribution networks, its commercial productions, and the reception of those productions by both fans and critics. Widening their scope with the help of digital tools to incorporate not only the new wave or art films but a range of popular, marginalized, cultified, and detested products of Iranian media culture, these scholars have found a new appreciation for magazines such as *Setāreh-ye Sinema*. The magazine now presents itself as more than a symptom—as evidence of either uplift or vulgarity, depending on the critic. As narrow evaluative impulses reveal themselves to be part of a long intellectual history to which the magazine itself belongs, it can serve as a fresh primary source. The magazine that started at a city-center newsstand, a relay point for print sources, is now freely available at another relay point online. Its searchability has already started to change the habits and expectations

82   CHAPTER 4

of researchers in the field. Maybe now, seven decades after the publication of its first issue, the heterogeneous mixture of carnivalesque fan service and studied auteurism that was the very foundation of *Setāreh-ye Sinema* can offer leverage in the effort to overturn received ideas about the cinema of Iran.

NOTES

1. Massoud Mehrabi, Instagram post published on November 24, 2018, https://www.instagram.com/p/Bqkım-WFNmR/ (accessed January 8, 2021).

2. In 2013, well-known critic Parviz Davai, who was one of the staff members of *Setāreh-ye Sinema* in the 1950s, recalled in a newspaper piece how they would translate many influential essays and interviews originally published in *Cahiers, Movie*, and *Sight and Sound*. See Parviz Davai, "From a Letter: Us and *Cahiers du cinéma*," *Shargh Newspaper* no. 1788, July 22, 2013, 7.

3. To this date, Iranian cinema is not taught at Iranian universities, nearly all prerevolutionary films are banned from distribution, and the print copies of old film journals are sold only in the underground market of vintage book sellers.

4. The regular issues of the magazine were published in its continuous biweekly and weekly formats until 1978. Moreover, close to twenty special issues were published by the same publication in the format of monthlies and annuals.

5. *Setāreh-ye Sinemā*, no. 2, 12 Esfand 1332 (March 3, 1954).

6. Some of the most important titles of these journals include *Hollywood* (1943, thirty-three issues), *Film* (1951, fourteen issues), *Jahān-e Sinemā* (1952, nineteen issues), *Setāregān-e Sinemā* (1952, one issue), and *Sinemā Teātr* (1952, six issues overall including its third issue under the title *Setāregān-e Sinemā Teātr*). See Abdolhamid Shoai Tehrani, "Film Journals, from the Beginning until Now," in *An Analytical History of One Hundred Years of the Iranian Cinema*, ed. Gh. Heidary, 155–74 (Tehran: Cultural Research Bureau, 2000), 155–58; Jamal Omid, *History of Iranian Cinema, vol. 1: 1900–1978* (Tehran: Rowzaneh, 1995), 893–904; and Hosein Giti, *Iranian Cinema Press* (Tehran: Kabutar, 2016), 19–47.

7. The first official college of dramatic arts was not established until 1964. Therefore, most of the technical aspects of filmmaking were learned through various phases of apprenticeship and trial and error. Moreover, the cinematic infrastructure in the country was poor and outdated. See Fereydun Jeyrani, "The Fifties, a New Birth," in *An Analytical History of One Hundred Years of the Iranian Cinema*, ed. Gh. Heidary, 63–78 (Tehran: Cultural Research Bureau, 2000), 77–78.

8. In 1954, for example, 239 foreign films were screened in the country. Jeyrani, "The Fifties," 72.

9. Some of these studio publications included *Iran Film* for Sherkat-e Iran (1944, six issues), *'Ālam-e Honar* (The World of Art) for Pars Film (1951–52, seventeen issues), and *'Ālam-e Sinemā* (The World of Cinema) for Studio Alborz (1951, two issues).

10. Abbas Baharlu. *Iranian Filmography*, Vol. 1 (Tehran: Kabutar, 2016), 11–12. Jeyrani, "The Fifties," 72; "Film and Cinema in Iran and Abroad," *Nāmeh-ye otāq-e bāzargāni* no. 76 (January 1959), 31–36.

11. See Giti, *Iranian Cinema Press*, 49.

12. Born in the city of Qazvin in 1923 and raised in the city of Masjed Soleyman, Paruir Galestian moved to Tehran after finishing high school in 1942 and owned a magazine kiosk on Lalezar Street. The dollar rate of his investment is the authors' estimate based on the exchange rate of about 90 rials per dollar at the end of the Iranian year 1332 (early 1954). See Research Group of the Iranian Museum of Cinema, *Armenians and Iranian Cinema* (Tehran: Museum of Cinema and Rowzaneh Kar Publication, 2004), 99; and Hosein Montazeri and Hosein Rahbarian, "The Ups and Downs of the Dollar Exchange Rate in Dr. Mosaddeq's Cabinet (1951–1953)," *Jādu-ye eqtesād*, last modified May 9, 2015, http://economagic.blog.ir/1394/02/19/.

13. Omid, *History of Iranian Cinema*, 904.

14. In 1962, Galestian sold the license of the magazine due to financial hardship. However, he regained it after about six months in March 1963. See Giti, *Iranian Cinema Press*, 51–52.

15. According to the first-ever overall census of Iran in 1956, only 22.2 percent of men and 7.3 percent of women among the Iranians (a total population of 18,954,704) knew how to read and write. See "1956 Census: The Whole Country," *Statistical Center of Iran*, https://web.archive.org/web/20210518144040/https://ssis.sci.org.ir/ (accessed January 10, 2021).

16. "Presses in Iran," *Encyclopedia of the World of Islam*, https://rch.ac.ir/article/details?id=9621 (accessed January 10, 2021).

17. Afshin Matin-Asgari, "The Pahlavi Era Iranian Modernity in Global Context," in *The Oxford Handbook of Iranian History*, ed. Touraj Daryaee (published online in September 2012), https://doi.org/10.1093/oxfordhb/9780199732159.013.0016.

18. Ali Gheissari, *Iranian Intellectuals in the Twentieth Century* (Austin: University of Texas Press, 1997), 78–82.

19. Massoud Mehrabi, *History of Iranian Cinema from the Beginning until 1979*, 2nd ed. (Tehran: Film, 1987), 535, 557.

20. In *Iranian Cosmopolitanism*, Golbarg Rekabtalaei traces the elites' attitude toward cinema until the 1979 revolution. In her first chapter, she investigates the efforts of "the cosmopolitan intellectuals and the elite" of early twentieth-century Iran for promoting the educational and scientific values of cinema. The bleak intellectual atmosphere of the postcoup period, however, did not allow for a widespread acceptance of narrative features as a valid form of cultural expression by the elites of the time, "who either encouraged the blossoming of a high art or opted for a more pious lifestyle." Golbarg Rekabtalaei, *Iranian Cosmopolitanism: A Cinematic History* (Cambridge: Cambridge University Press, 2019), 25, 156.

21. Behzad Rahimian, "Present Perfect: The Old Dossier of *Majalleh-ye Sinemā va Namāyeshāt*," *Film*, no. 53 (September 1987), 92–93.

22. Omid, *History of Iranian Cinema*, 895–96.

23. Editorial Board, "The Way Forward," *Setāreh-ye Sinemā*, no. 1 (February 17, 1954), 2.

24. Editorial Board, "The Way Forward," 2.

25. Editorial Board, "The Way Forward," 23.

26. These include the editorial (pp. 2 and 23), an interview with an Iranian actor (8), and a report on an Iranian production studio (16–17).

27. "Letters to the Editor" *Setāreh-ye Sinemā*, no. 2, 12 Esfand 1332 (March 3, 1954), 19. It should be noted that the dates of the second and third issue were misprinted in the magazine. We have used the correct dates in this essay.

28. "*Setāreh-ye Sinemā*'s competitions," *Setāreh-ye Sinemā*, no. 194, 21 Dey 1337 (January 11, 1959), 41.

29. Warner Bros. Collection, University of Southern California, Iran Correspondence, box 2.

30. *Setāreh-ye Sinemā*, no. 204: New Year Special Issue, 30 Esfand 1337 (March 21, 1959), cover page. This illustration is discussed in Kaveh Askari, *Relaying Cinema in Midcentury Iran: Material Cultures in Transit* (Oakland: University of California Press, 2022).

31. "Letters to the Editor," *Setāreh-ye Sinemā* 3, 26 Esfand 1332 (March 17, 1954), 18.

32. Ibid.

33. For example, an excerpted translation of a Gordon Gow essay named *Ostādān-e jenāyat* (Masters of Crime) was serialized over three consecutive issues beginning with *Setāreh-ye Sinemā*, no. 184, 11 Aban 1337 (November 2, 1958), 20.

34. *Honar va Sinemā*, Nowruz 1340 (March 1961).

35. Ahmad Talebinezhad, *The Book of the New Wave* (Tehran: Cheshmeh, 2018), 98.

36. The image of the gestating cameo appeared in a translated interview with the director about *I Confess* in *Setāreh-ye Sinemā*, no. 24, 22 Dey 1333 (January 12, 1955), 12–13. The magic hand of the

84   CHAPTER 4

director appeared in an ad for the film's premiere at the Cinema Rex in *Setāreh-ye Sinemā*, no. 148, 20 Bahman 1336 (February 9, 1958), 31. The first appears to have been assembled for the journal, while the second appears to have been an imported illustration (possibly illustrated in Italy where much of the export publicity to the Middle East was created) selected for the journal and reproduced unaltered.

37. A synopsis for *Rear Window* or *Window Facing the Garden* (both titles were used for the film), translated by "Bahram," appeared in *Setāreh-ye Sinemā*, no. 34, 31 Khordad 1334 (June 22, 1956), 34–38. A serialized version of excerpts from the *Life* magazine true crime source for *The Wrong Man*, translated into Persian by Jahangir Afshari, appeared in six issues beginning with *"The Wrong Man (Mard-e 'Avazi*)," *Setāreh-ye Sinemā*, no. 117, 2 Tir 1336 (June 23, 1957), 28–29. It is a full translation of Herbert Brean, "A Case of Identity," *Life* (June 29, 1953), 97–107.

38. The first issue of the *Vertigo* (*Sargijeh*) serialization is in *Setāreh-ye Sinemā*, no. 170, 29 Tir 1337 (July 20, 1958), 28–29.

39. "Alfred Hitchcock, the Artist and Undisputed Master of Crime Films," *Setāreh-ye Sinemā*, no. 9, 27 Tir 1333 (July 18, 1954), 9.

40. For example, the critic who translated a number of Hitchcock articles on spectatorship, Hajir Dariush, was by the following decade making films associated with the New Wave and taking on leadership roles in the Tehran Film Festival and the National Iranian Radio and Television Corporation.

41. See, for example, "I Make Suspense Films Not Mystery Films," *Setāreh-ye Sinemā*, no. 24, 22 Dey 1333 (January 12, 1955), 12–13.

42. The National Board of Review started out as the National Board of Censorship but clarified its emphasis on the artistic quality of motion pictures in the mid-1910s. This goal was made clear in the board's early publication *Exceptional Photoplays*.

43. *Setāreh-ye Sinemā*, no. 90, 11 Azar 1335 (December 2, 1956), 12.

44. Ibid.

45. Ibid., 13.

PUBLICATIONS REFERENCED

'Ālam-e Honar
'Ālam-e Sinemā
Cahiers du cinéma
Clubman
Ferdowsi
Film
Film Monthly
Hollywood
Honar va Sinemā (Art and Cinema)
Iran Film
Jahān-e Sinemā (The World of Cinema)
Life
Movie
Nāmeh-ye otāq-e bāzargāni
Negin
Rowshanfekr
Sadaf
Setāregān-e Sinemā
Setāreh-ye Sinemā
Shargh Newspaper

Sight and Sound
Sinemā Teātr (Cinema & Theater)
Sinemā va Namāyeshāt (Cinema and Spectacle)
Sokhan

BIBLIOGRAPHY

Baharlu, Abbas. *Iranian Filmography*, Vol. 1. Tehran: Kabutar, 2016.

Gheissari, Ali. *Iranian Intellectuals in the Twentieth Century*. Austin: University of Texas Press, 1997.

Giti, Hosein. *Iranian Cinema Press*. Tehran: Kabutar, 2016.

Jeyrani, Fereydun. "The Fifties, a New Birth." In *An Analytical History of One Hundred Years of the Iranian Cinema*, edited by Gh. Heidary, 63–78. Tehran: Cultural Research Bureau, 2000.

Matin-Asgari, Afshin. "The Pahlavi Era Iranian Modernity in Global Context." In *The Oxford Handbook of Iranian History*, edited by Touraj Daryaee. Published online September 2012. https://doi.org/10.1093/oxfordhb/9780199732159.013.0016.

Mehrabi, Massoud. *History of Iranian Cinema from the Beginning until 1979*, 2nd ed. Tehran: Film, 1987.

Omid, Jamal. *History of Iranian Cinema, vol. 1: 1900–1978*. Tehran: Rowzaneh, 1995.

"Presses in Iran." In *Encyclopedia of the World of Islam*, https://rch.ac.ir/article/details?id=9621 (accessed January 10, 2021).

Rekabtalaei, Golbarg. *Iranian Cosmopolitanism: A Cinematic History*. Cambridge: Cambridge University Press, 2019.

Research Group of the Iranian Museum of Cinema. *Armenians and Iranian Cinema*. Tehran: Museum of Cinema and Rowzaneh Kar Publication, 2004.

Shoai Tehrani, Abdolhamid. "Film Journals, from the Beginning until Now." In *An Analytical History of One Hundred Years of the Iranian Cinema*, edited by Gh. Heidary, 155–74. Tehran: Cultural Research Bureau, 2000.

Talebinezhad, Ahmad. *The Book of the New Wave*. Tehran: Cheshmeh, 2018.

5

Syndicated Sunday Movie Sections

The Highest-Circulation Fan Magazines (You've Never Heard Of)

Paul S. Moore

What were the highest-circulation American movie fan magazines?

The answer depends on how you define a magazine. Frequency matters, and a magazine is generally neither a daily newspaper nor an annual yearbook. Illustration and layout matter, too, although the boundary can be blurred for periodicals that are better classified as journals or bulletins. A magazine certainly needs to have at least metropolitan reach in readership, not a purely local scope, although there are examples of neighborhood movie theater programs that looked and felt like fan magazines and contained a magazine's worth of boilerplate news and gossip. The Media History Digital Library (MHDL) includes all of these, as well as many other film publications such as pressbooks and catalogs that sit in between the seriality of periodicals and the uniqueness of archival documents. As the MHDL has grown, hybrid forms and unusual publication formats have been folded into the searchable mix among better-known titles. The globalization of collections has led to gathering examples of film publications that reflect the unique circumstances of their production across time and space, a key theme of this very book. But forgotten and liminal movie magazines exist at the very heart of Hollywood, too.

One such class of US movie magazine was weekly film fan magazines distributed as supplements to Sunday newspapers. These were not merely sections of the paper but had the form and feel of magazines, with their own mastheads and editors, printed tabloid or quarto-sized on fine paper in lithograph or in halftone color. At least one was also sold and distributed on newsstands by itself; at least one was listed under "motion pictures" in the class publications in the *N. W. Ayer and Son's American Newspaper Annual and Directory*; at least one was often quoted in 1930s Hollywood movie ads and cited by later movie star biographers. Two were syndicated to multiple Sunday papers circulated simultaneously on a national scale, and, summing circulations of newspapers known to have concurrently carried these supplements, I propose they were the highest-circulation movie magazines of their days. One printed more than a million and a half copies weekly for several years in the late 1930s, more than any other fan magazine ever did (although you've probably never heard of it, and fan magazine scholarship has almost entirely ignored it).[1]

Sunday newspaper supplements have a curious history distinct from the daily paper—a central concern of my book with Sandra Gabriele, *The Sunday Paper: A Media History*.[2] For mere pennies, an American Sunday edition was "more than a newspaper and better than a magazine."[3] The word *better* flagged how turn-of-the-century newspapers were competing with magazines, movies, and other media for the mass public's imagination, but *more* signaled how the Sunday paper provided an excess in both form and content beyond weekday news reading, incorporating an experience (or several at once) more akin to the weekly or monthly routines of magazines. "Instead of paying twenty-five cents for a magazine, ten cents for a comic weekly and five cents for a newspaper, making a total of forty cents in all," explained the leading New York paper, "get the three combined for five cents in *The Sunday World*."[4] The Sunday paper truly had an ability to mobilize all the new forms of media, and modernity itself, as it unfolded. This chapter weighs its intersection with movie magazines.

In the 1890s, many US newspapers began to include lithographed posters and song sheets in their Sunday editions, as well as printed items like cardboard or paper cutout toys and fashion dolls. In the first years of the 1900s, syndicated color funny pages and fine paperbound and stapled syndicated magazines became a standard weekly part of dozens of metropolitan Sunday papers. In the 1920s and '30s, some of these newspaper supplements became movie fan magazines, as I will shortly recount in detail. Those of us who specialize in cinema's use of newspaper publicity, like myself and Richard Abel, have not engaged much with scholars from fan studies who know movie magazines best and who have in turn steered clear of Sunday magazine supplements.[5] This has left a small but important class of newspaper-magazines neglected. These were not simply bannered pages or sections of the paper; these were true magazines with their own titles that contained much more than Hollywood gossip columns and local theater advertising. Let me be clear: my point is to bring awareness to them, not to overinflate their significance. There are few enough examples of this hybrid, intermedial form—both fan magazine and newspaper section—that each one had its own unique relation to Hollywood and therefore only an idiosyncratic relation to the well-known canonical list of fan magazines. Nonetheless, they merit greater familiarity *as fan magazines*, and this brief overview flags them for inclusion in

88   CHAPTER 5

the genre as important supplements to the periodicals catalogued and collected by the MHDL.

Hollywood studios, local movie theaters, and newspapers were tightly bound by mutually beneficial publicity and advertising. Expanded entertainment reporting increased news circulation in tandem with the popularity of moviegoing. Sometimes, in the pursuit of greater circulation, journalists and publishers would cross the line into muckraking celebrity gossip or moral castigation against the movies. One such moment in 1934, discussed in some detail below, spurred entire cities' exhibitors to boycott newspapers by withdrawing their advertising columns. Even in that exceptional case, however, theater owners had to weigh losses ascribed to public distaste for scandal against slowed box office due to missing advertising columns. As I have chronicled elsewhere, newspapers' movie directories followed a "paternal logic of mass consumption," providing a degree of "insurance against time wasted at a disappointing show."[6]

Between 1910 and 1914, the film business forged key partnerships with newspapers that were as important as the emerging class of fan magazines for the establishment of the industry. Movie news became an especially prominent and enduring part of the Sunday paper, where syndicated supplements allowed advertising campaigns and illustrated features to reach the entire national market. Such facets of fan magazines as motion picture stories, gossip columns, photos of film scenes, and posters of movie stars also became regular Sunday newspaper content. By November 1911, the *Cleveland Leader* had started a bannered page of news of "Photo-Plays and Players," edited by Ralph Stoddard, while a column "In the Moving Picture World" was pseudonymously penned by the Reel Observer (Gene Morgan) in the *Chicago Tribune*.[7] But the novelty was not limited to major metropolitan locations. A few months earlier in September 1911, Benjamin S. Gross, a budding local journalist for the *News* in Birmingham, Alabama (later radio editor at the *New York Daily News*), was briefly granted space for a weekly "Motion Picture Department." His columns stemmed from experience writing scenarios for Edison, Vitagraph, and Biograph, drawing upon insiders' knowledge that allowed him an unusually early use of the phrase "picture gossip" as the hook for his readers.[8]

Women film journalists were perhaps even more common, as Richard Abel's *Movie Mavens* compiles. An early example was Gertrude M. Price's column "The Movies" for the Scripps-McRae League of newspapers beginning in November 1912.[9] Price's expertise provided newspaper readers, who were also moviegoers, with the knowledge they needed to become *expert* moviegoers, skilled enthusiasts: "Read the first 'movie' story in today's paper—and keep your eyes open right along for the appearance of Your Favorites."[10] The call to read about the movies *first* in the paper before going to see them would be the central trope of metropolitan newspapers' embrace of the film industry. The link between newspapers' film columns and "movie-struck girls" was entrenched in 1914 when serial film stories began.[11] First to have wide syndication was Thanhouser Film Corporation's

Adventures of Kathlyn, accompanied by stories in a wide swath of newspapers across North America: the *Chicago Tribune, New York Sun*, and dozens of others in smaller markets.[12] By the end of 1914, hardly any metropolitan newspaper on the continent remained on the sidelines for the serial film craze in its first few faddish years.

In exactly these years, North American Sunday newspapers began also to include rotogravure sections of high-quality, full-toned photographs printed on high-gloss magazine paper. The public of film fans couldn't get enough pictures of its movie stars, and movie star photographs were as central to rotogravure sections as any other kind of picture, but the new printing technique was often used to circulate souvenir posters of movie stars, too. For a few months starting in February 1915, the *Chicago Tribune* offered "two big smashes," pairing an eight-page tabloid rotogravure weekly with a keepsake, "a photograph of one of the greatest motion picture stars, printed on the same Rotogravure Press, but printed by itself, on special paper, ready for framing."[13] Francis X. Bushman and Mary Pickford were among the first portraits (see figure 5.1). In June 1916, the *Milwaukee Sentinel*, for example, offered a poster of Theda Bara: "8 by 11 inches in size, loose in the folds of an inside section. . . . You can frame them and have a gallery of beautiful young women of the screen."[14] In May 1917, the *Chicago Tribune* again turned to movie stars as an anchor for its rotogravure section, where one full-page photograph of Charlie Chaplin filled the back page of the supplement, doubling as a poster. It proclaimed, "The movie stars are coming! . . . The movie stars will come to you— regularly, each Sunday—in your own home . . . handsome rotogravure portraits of your own movie favorites."[15]

To respond to the demands of newspaper-reading fans, between 1915 and 1917, several newspapers expanded their movie news and publicity to create special Sunday sections, heavily illustrated with magazine-style covers.[16] These supplements typically collected existing gossip columns, gravure portraits, serial stories, and local advertising, and were sometimes formatted tabloid-size to create a magazine experience. The *New York Evening Mail* began publishing the *Motion Picture Mail* in September 1915, "a Real Live Motion Picture Magazine . . . News pictures from all corners of the early by 'movie men.' Personalities of producers, stars, and writers. Up to the minute news about the moving picture world."[17] Since the *Mail* did not publish a Sunday edition, the movie magazine was offered at an extra cost of five cents with *any* daily edition of the paper. The additional cost permitted relatively lavish use of rotogravure process for the entire publication. "The New Photogravure *Motion Picture Mail* surpasses everything in beauty and news. Soft, brilliant, novel. Out to-morrow. Full-page portraits of beautiful motion picture stars, character pictures, personalities, and interesting special articles about the people of the films."[18]

Other papers followed the lead with free Sunday movie magazine supplements, sometimes in color, sometimes tabloid size. In Cleveland, the "Motion Picture

90   CHAPTER 5

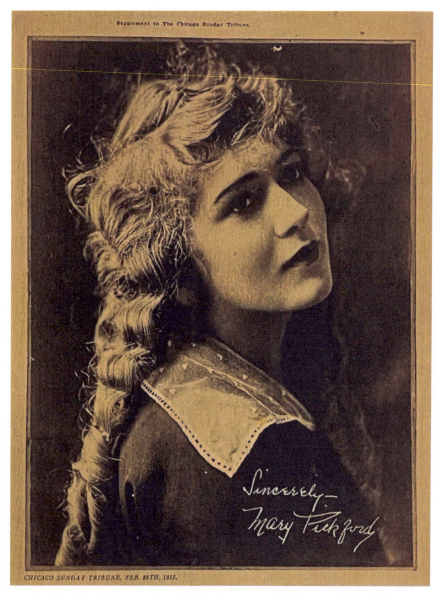

FIGURE 5.1. Mary Pickford rotogravure supplement, *Chicago Tribune*, February 28, 1915.

Leader" was a "magazine supplement to the *Leader* devoted entirely to the movies and movie people."[19] In Chicago, Louella Parsons's gossip columns anchored the *Herald*'s eight-page tabloid "Motion Pictures" magazine.[20] Publicity in St. Louis showed "Virginia Pearson, the famous motion picture star, reading her favorite newspaper, the Sunday *Globe-Democrat*. She likes it best because of the wonderful pictures, bright stories, and up-to-the-minute news of the film world."[21] In New Orleans, the "Moving Picture Item," circulated free with the Sunday *Item*, spanned "8 Pages—56 Columns—Beautiful Pictures of Stars—ALL the Screen News and Views—Local & National."[22] In the smaller city of Dayton, Ohio, Mabel Brown Martin edited the tabloid supplement "Motion Picture News," included with the *News*, mixing the "latest developments, present activities and future events" both nationally and locally.[23] This garnered appreciation from a national film trade paper, which marveled at the "eight-page motion picture supplement issued Sundays by the *Dayton News*. An entire section devoted to nothing but picture news and advertising. Do you get that? And in a city by no means one of the country's largest."[24]

To be clear, general-interest magazine supplements had been offered in many Sunday papers for more than two decades already. Magazines of various sorts and sizes had been folded into the sections of North American Sunday newspapers since 1890, when the *New York Morning Journal* began including a quarto-size "complete novel" insert. Throughout the 1890s, all variety of "Junior Journal" and "Comic Weekly" supplements were inserted in metropolitan Sunday papers in more than a dozen cities across the US. By the late 1890s, several New York newspapers—the *Times*, the *Tribune*, the *Mail and Express*—began inserting "true" magazine supplements, stapled and printed in halftone on fine paper. Syndicated versions of these Sunday magazines proliferated between 1903 and 1912, so that nearly every major paper in the US (and not a few minor papers) offered a weekly magazine free with the purchase of every weekend edition. The first syndicated version, Associated Sunday Magazines, was published by Joseph P. Knapp's American Lithographic Company, which dominated the market in color printing after amalgamating competitors in the 1890s. Identical magazines, exactly alike except for the mastheads of the papers, were inserted into the *Boston Post*, the *St. Louis Republic*, and a dozen others. Combined circulation exceeded four million copies weekly in 1907, about four times more copies than even the most popular magazines of the day. Syndicated magazines (and their advertisers) had the potential to reach every home in the US, almost simultaneously, every weekend, approximating the immediacy and range of later network radio broadcasting—at least on Sunday mornings.

Given the flurry of activity with rotogravure sections, movie magazine supplements, and syndicated moving picture stories, somebody was bound to attempt a combination of all those features—a syndicated, rotogravure Sunday fan magazine supplement. The new venture came in 1920 with *Motion-Play Magazine*, an expanded, syndicated expansion of a movie-themed rotogravure section that originated at the *Philadelphia Record* in 1919. It was, as stated in *Printer's Ink*, "The First Rotogravure Section With an Idea! The *Philadelphia Record Motion-Play Magazine*. A complete magazine devoted exclusively to pictures and news of screen players and plays. In rich sepia rotogravure."[25] While relatively short lived (the movie features were folded into a general magazine in 1922), the magazine was a partnership between the Alco Gravure Company and distributor National Gravure Circuit Inc., which was soon reorganized as the Gravure Service Corporation.[26] As its name indicates, "A.L. Co." Gravure was yet another outgrowth of the American Lithographic Company, which was never too far off stage when novelty Sunday supplements were introduced. The venture followed its forays into poster art supplements and magazine sections. This specific division was headed by G. H. Buek, who had pioneered cutout paper-doll supplements back in 1895. Alco Gravure were printers of magazines such as *Woman's Home Companion* and rotogravure sections such as that in the *Indianapolis Star* (figure 5.2).

Motion-Play Magazine was one of many magazines for movie fans, but this one was unique by virtue of being a newspaper supplement distributed free with such Sunday papers as the *Washington Herald* and the *Indianapolis Star*, along with a half-dozen others in the Midwest and Northeast. Alco Gravure took the established *Motion-Play Magazine* from the *Philadelphia Record* and sold it wholesale as a syndicated supplement to papers of relatively modest circulation in midsize cities that could not otherwise afford to print their own pictorial section. In 1920, the hook of a movie fan magazine was a bonus novelty for news publishers to attract new readers—especially for papers in second-tier cities that did not already have a glossy entertainment section. Syndication tapped into economies of scale and lowered costs to make a glossy entertainment section affordable, licensing big-city metropolitan content and form with the added bonus of nationally networked advertising reach. A trade ad in *Editor and Publisher* suggested that local papers should "add the strength of Gravure, the recognized Circulation Builder, to your Sunday Edition. . . . The *Motion-Play Magazine*, used by Seven Big Newspapers for over seven months is an eight-page tabloid printed in Rotogravure."[27] By 1920, movies were a major draw for mass readership and *Motion-Play* provided what the public wanted: "Its general make-up insures popular reading reception because it features Motion Pictures, Plays, Stars and Fashions—a combination of editorial subjects that appeal to the majority. Eighteen Million tickets sold daily to Motion Picture Fans."[28]

Motion-Play had a fair amount of advertising—a total of about one of its eight pages—and the company attempted to appeal to makers of national products, as if they would be purchasing a spot in a syndicated magazine rather than a single newspaper: "Rotogravure sections of newspapers give national advertisers the equivalent of magazine attention value and fine printing, with the flexibility of usage, timeliness, dealer influence and local concentration of newspapers—at the lowest cost."[29] Circulation reached nearly six hundred thousand by the end of 1921.[30] While this was a modest result compared to syndicated color comics, it gave *Motion-Play* a higher circulation than any fan magazine in the 1920s. In terms of its format, *Motion-Play* was comparable to a tabloid rotogravure section, a step beyond the earlier movie star posters rather than a fulsome magazine. Its slim

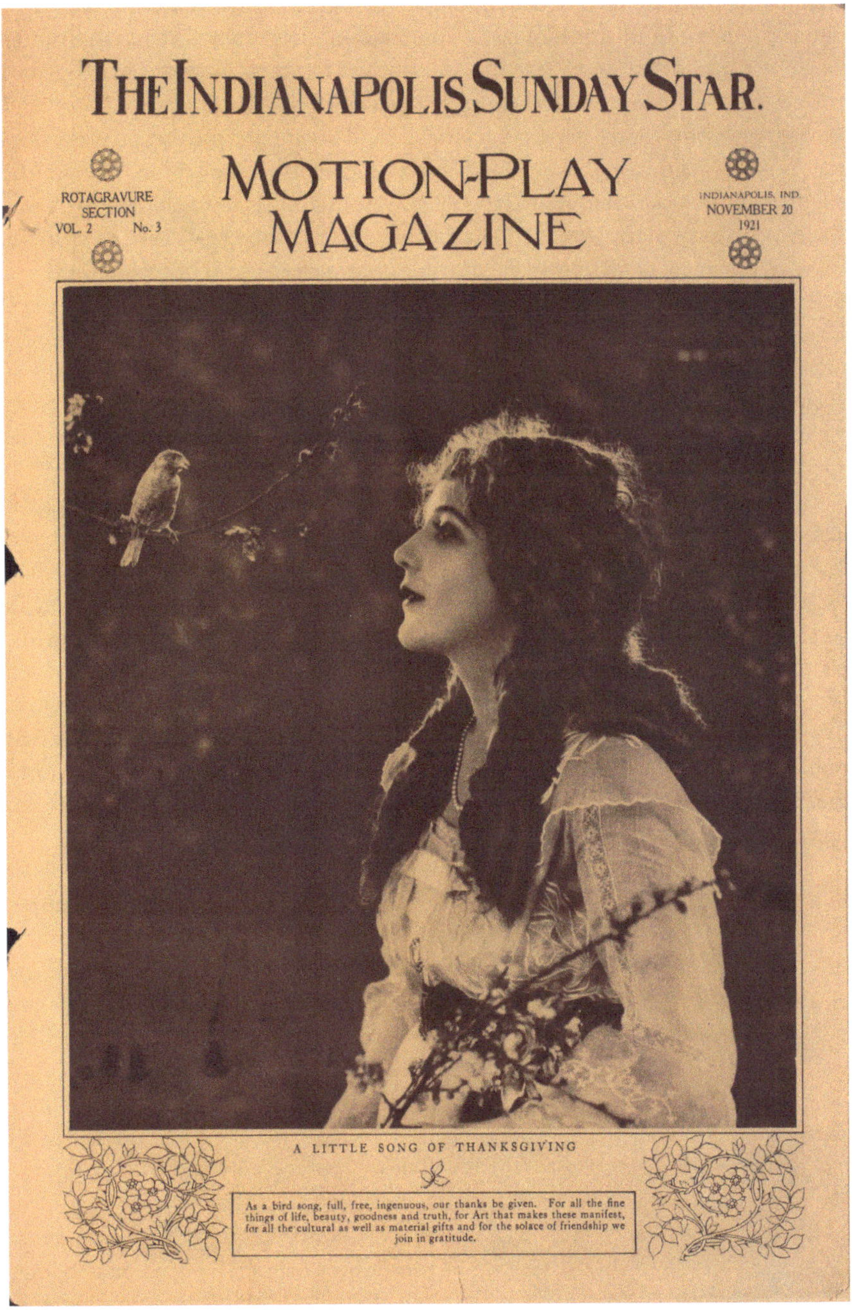
THE INDIANAPOLIS SUNDAY STAR.

ROTAGRAVURE SECTION
VOL. 2 No. 3

MOTION-PLAY MAGAZINE

INDIANAPOLIS, IND.
NOVEMBER 20
1921

A LITTLE SONG OF THANKSGIVING

As a bird song, full, free, ingenuous, our thanks be given. For all the fine things of life, beauty, goodness and truth, for Art that makes these manifest, for all the cultural as well as material gifts and for the solace of friendship we join in gratitude.

FIGURE 5.2. *Motion-Play Magazine* rotogravure supplement, *The Indianapolis Sunday Star*, November 20, 1921.

eight pages certainly did not require staples or a glued spine. Nonetheless, its layout and content fit the form of other fan magazines of its day—a full-page poster cover of a movie star and other "portraits of the foremost cinema stars, together with interesting gossip about them and their work."[31]

Motion-Play was presented as "a complete and fascinating moving picture entertainment" in its own right, intended "for all members of the family."[32] When the supplement was launched in Indianapolis, Washington, and Omaha, the logic was spelled out for newspaper readers, asking them to think of themselves as part of the mass of moviegoers nationwide. "Are you a star gazer?—in other words, are you one of approximately 35,000,000 movie lovers who are said to live in the United States?"[33] In Omaha, as in Indianapolis and Washington, DC, Sunday papers would offer "a delightful treat, a special surprise, a novel innovation . . . in a series of specially photographed views, enlivened by scintillating captions . . . scenes from all the newest film productions with special personal glimpses of the home life, social activities and daily diversions of famous stars and near-stars of Filmland."[34]

Just as *Motion-Play* ended its run, the *Los Angeles Times* launched another pictorial, tabloid-size newspaper-magazine to corral its existing film industry material and expand its coverage to take stewardship of news about Hollywood, published close to home. In June 1923, the *Times* announced the *Pre-View* was coming, a weekly tabloid magazine that "will deal with motion pictures, Los Angeles's greatest industry, in a manner never before attempted by any magazine or newspaper. The *Pre-View*, which will be printed in rotogravure, will present an authoritative digest of the activities of the motion-picture producers here, and will be the first publication of its kind issued in the place where 90 per cent of all motion pictures are made. The *Pre-View* will be profusely illustrated and will be designed to inform and interest producers, exhibitors, exchanges and film patrons everywhere."[35]

The *Times* defended the new venture for "departing somewhat from the sphere of a newspaper" and explained away potential allegations of veering into puffery by explaining how a Los Angeles–based film magazine was "part of its obligation of service to the public, not only of Los Angeles and the Southwest, but to the entire country. There are scores of film magazines, but 90 per cent of them are published in New York," whereas the *Pre-View* would be written and edited in Hollywood by Hallett Abend, "intimately associated with the industry [but] who is not of it. Mr. Abend's reviews of forthcoming releases will be written with the single purpose of telling the truth, expertly seen. In the end, it is the truth, uncolored by any extraneous consideration, which will best serve the public, the exhibitor, the producer, the actor and the industry as a whole."[36]

The *Pre-View* "weekly film magazine section" was sold on its own for ten cents on newsstands, or included for free to subscribers of the *Times*, a smart option given the likely appeal to such a wide swath of public, business, and film industry players across Los Angeles.[37] It was issued every Wednesday for its first two years, becoming a Sunday broadsheet rotogravure section in 1925 that lasted until 1932.

"Printed in the film capital of the world, the *Pre-View* is unique among newspaper supplements, furnishing a weekly pictorial trip through the strange and fascinating realm of screenland," the *Times* said in its announcement.[38] The *Pre-View* was such a success for the *Times* that it created a hefty souvenir special edition, *Annual Pre-View of the Motion Picture Industry*, in 1927.[39] The *Annual Pre-View* actually continued for many years as a special supplement to the *Times*, edited by Edwin Shallert for its entire quarter-century existence.[40]

Another byline in the *Los Angeles Times* in the 1920s was that of Grace Wilcox, an occasional writer of features who was also connected to Hollywood players. She had spent time in the 1910s working in the publicity departments at Mutual and Universal, then wrote for the *Los Angeles Express* in the late 1910s, *It Magazine* in the early 1920s, and the *Los Angeles Times* in the late 1920s, and again turned attention to the movies in the late 1920s, writing screenplays for Anna May Wong. It was newsworthy in May 1929 that Wilcox was in Europe with Wong when Wilcox's husband, financier George Dietz, died back in California.[41] Born Edith Grace Wilcox and raised in Michigan, her bylines also often used her married name, Edith Dietz. She kept ties to Michigan, and her brother-in-law, Douglas Martin, was editor of the Sunday feature section at the *Detroit Free Press* in the 1930s.[42] This laid the groundwork for Wilcox to front another nationally syndicated movie fan newspaper-magazine.

Screen & Radio Weekly was launched by the *Detroit Free Press* in April 1934 and published until 1940. The sixteen-page tabloid magazine was printed in bold color blocking, featuring rainbow-bright portraits of movie stars on its front and back covers (see figure 5.3). There are indications it was available as a magazine in its own right, not only as a newspaper supplement. The first issues initially indicated that the magazine was available separately for "five cents on all news stands. Free with every *Sunday Free Press*." The Sunday supplement offered "tasty morsels of Hollywood gossip, fashions from movieland and inside stories of radio and screen. . . . To each reader will be given an intimate study of the famous stars that grace America's screen, radio personalities that provide entertainment daily."[43] The weekly supplement was packed with illustrated features about movies and radio and all the entertainment stars of the 1930s. This Sunday movie fan magazine supplement was soon syndicated to dozens more newspapers across the entire United States.[44] Standardized advertising accompanied each paper's launch of the new feature, repeating the publicity lines first published in Detroit in April 1934: "Popping over with hot news snatched from in front of the whirring cameras of Hollywood and the buzzing microphones of radioland, this new Screen and Radio Weekly will give you a week-end of gala reading enjoyment. Not just 'another section,' but a full size tabloid in brilliant colors and breezy pictorial, FREE with your *Sunday Free Press*," or *Sunday Oakland Tribune*, or *Sunday Democrat and Chronicle*, or whichever location the novelty began in, separated by months and thousands of miles across the entire United States.[45]

FIGURE 5.3. *Screen & Radio Weekly* supplement, *Detroit Free Press*, May 27, 1934.

Over its six years of publication,[46] *Screen & Radio Weekly* was included in at least thirty-two papers, at least fifteen concurrently in 1937.[47] I estimate that its circulation approached 1.5 million copies weekly at the time, higher than *Photoplay*'s mid-1950s watermark of 1.4 million.[48] The *Detroit Free Press* itself boasted this claim to celebrate the magazine's first anniversary. Alongside quotes from congratulatory telegrams from Mae West, Clark Gable, Marlene Dietrich, James Cagney, and others, *Screen & Radio Weekly* was described as "an infant publication [that] has become the lustiest 'adult' of its kind on the American continent, for during the three hundred and sixty-five days of its existence, it has been honored with the Largest Circulation of Any Similar Publication in the United States."[49]

Douglas Martin was editor and Grace Wilcox, his recently widowed sister-in-law, penned the main gossip column, "Hollywood Reporter" (apparently no relation to the fledgling magazine of the same name). Just before the first issue circulated with the *Detroit Free Press*, Wilcox introduced herself to readers as being from Michigan herself, noting that she "went to school and college there and think of it always as my home. Hollywood is my second home, and will never be anything more."[50] She explained how all the big Hollywood studios were excited for the new magazine. "The opinion I hear expressed on every side is—'A Sunday screen and radio magazine in colors—what a swell idea. It's funny no one ever thought of that before.' . . . After all, you see, it isn't every screen magazine that starts with a circulation of a quarter of a million as ours does."[51] Wilcox also colorfully boasted how she was personally welcomed—in the Hollywood cliché—to do lunch. "The studios take good care of your correspondent. . . . And how they feed me. It's nothing for me to consume three luncheons a day; one at 11:30 at Paramount, another at RKO-Radio at 1:30, a snack at 3 at M-G-M's restaurant and a substantial high tea with English kippers in Fox's Café de Paris at 5 o'clock."[52]

The Sunday fan magazine promoted itself as "written in newsy, breezy style by writers who are behind the scenes in Hollywood and the big radio studios."[53] Besides the regular gossip column and features by Grace Wilcox (also writing weekly stories under her married name, Edith Dietz), the early years of *Screen & Radio Weekly* had a radio column, "They Tell Me," by Bernes Robert (succeeded by Jack Sher's "New York Reporter" in 1937), "Previews of the New Films" by Whitney Williams (replaced by Clarke Wales's "Reviews of the New Films" in 1936), a page of "Fashions" by Sara Day, and a page on "Beauty" by Grace Grandville. Like a miniature, weekly capsule of "Entertainment Plus," the magazine promised "a parade of loveliness in portraits of lavish color, latest fashions. Home decorations and beauty talks by stars."[54]

Another near-weekly reporter in the magazine's first year was Douglas W. Churchill, formerly a contemporary of Wilcox's in Los Angeles with the *Illustrated Daily News*. In September 1934, Churchill became Hollywood correspondent for the *New York Times*, but his gig for the *Detroit Free Press* began earlier that year, in May, from nearly the first issue of *Screen & Radio Weekly*. But the highlight of every issue was Wilcox's "Hollywood Reporter" gossip column, "a sparkling page of last-minute news from the capital of filmland . . . as colorful as it is interesting and authentic."[55] The subtitle of Wilcox's column seemed to counter aspersions of salacious or prurient gossip with the notably defensive tagline, "Personal But Not Confidential," which was kept for its entire six-year run (see figure 5.4).

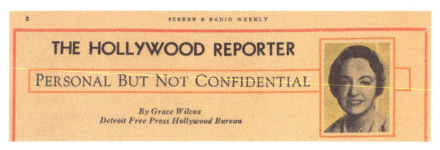

FIGURE 5.4. Grace Wilcox, "Hollywood Reporter," *Detroit Free Press*, May 27, 1934.

Within a few months, other newspapers around the country began including copies of the color fan magazine with their own mastheads printed on the cover. To do this, the *Detroit Free Press* partnered with the Des Moines Register and Tribune Syndicate.[56] Out of its Midwest headquarters, the *Register and Tribune* had begun selling packages of comic strips, news pictures, and illustrated features in the 1920s, and was already largely focused on syndicating color comics and rotogravure material.[57] *Editor and Publisher* explained at the time how "increased demand for comic and magazine sections, both in color and black on white, has been tremendous.... Comic sections have risen from the class of non-revenue producing newspaper supplements until today they produce a very sizable revenue because of the success of color advertising."[58] The economic constraints of the Great Depression, it was noted, meant "smaller home budgets for entertainment purposes and ... greater demand for features and comics in Sunday issues."[59] Since 1930, the Register and Tribune Syndicate, in particular, had introduced three new comic pages and a photo service for rotogravure sections as well as *Screen & Radio Weekly*, "which has put on thousands of circulation for its originator, *The Detroit Free Press*, and for other papers from coast to coast."[60]

Indeed, *Screen & Radio Weekly* was just one of two Hollywood-focused syndicated features launched by the Iowa syndicate at the same time in 1934. The Des Moines paper's own Sunday magazine editor, Vernon Pope, had reportedly gained access to multiple studios' historic photo files, under the pretense of writing a nostalgic look back at the history of movie stars and moviemaking. Instead, when the series began in the July 1934 pictorial section, it had the lascivious heading "Hollywood Unvarnished" or "Hollywood Unmasked."[61] The double-page layout was widely syndicated in major Sunday rotogravure sections across the country in the fall of 1934: "Pictures the Stars Don't Want Published!"[62] Instead of paying homage to the movies, the feature focused on unflattering pictures, gossip about divorce, and revealing how the magic of makeup, sets, and trick photography covered up flaws and created fantasies. "Does your favorite Hollywood Star have ... a double chin? bow legs? flat chest? ... the truth without bunk from Hollywood publicity agents."[63]

If the intent was to piggyback on the escalating controversy surrounding the introduction of the Production Code at the time, "Hollywood Unvarnished" backfired for many of the papers that ran it. In some local newspaper markets, the column sparked hostility from exhibitors, who organized boycotts and pulled advertising from the *Boston Globe* and led a protest against the *Kansas City Journal-Post*.[64] The fiasco allowed the competing *Kansas City Star* to announce "a policy of cooperation with the industry," starting its own syndicated feature, "Unreeling Hollywood," which celebrated the fantasy of the movies rather than unmasking it.[65] The acrimony between the studios, exhibitors, and various local papers did not quickly subside and spearheaded exhibitors' local protests against unflattering news and scandal columns. Writing for *Editor and Publisher*, Douglas Churchill reported in 1935 how Sidney Skolsky's "Hollywood" column in the *New York Daily News* was accused of having "destroyed the illusion of the screen," leading to advertising boycotts in Boston and Detroit against other papers printing it. According to Churchill, the film industry had determined in 1934 "to impose censorship on news emanating from Hollywood[,] . . . the lid was clamped on fan magazines and since then no stories have appeared without submission to and approval by studios."[66] Against the "anti-press faction [who] have consistently argued that the credentials of those who treat the business with candor should be revoked," Churchill held up the success story of his own alma mater, *Screen & Radio Weekly*: "The nation's readers have an acute interest in the cinema. . . . It is now being syndicated to a score of papers," and had helped the *Detroit Free Press* increase Sunday circulation by forty-four thousand—perhaps 20 percent or more.[67] "Hollywood recognizes and is liberal in praising this act for it is declared that it has not only been good for the paper but has stimulated interest in pictures and theatre attendance," Churchill wrote.[68] Of course, Churchill himself had been a weekly contributor to *Screen & Radio Weekly* for that entire first year—and a big part of its success, although he did not mention it in the article; only his current position at the *New York Times* was noted under his byline.

Many early syndicated versions of *Screen & Radio Weekly* followed a week behind the Detroit "original" version, but, when the *Rochester Democrat and Chronicle* added the supplement in April 1935, it was day-and-date identical with that of the *Free Press*, as were those of later adopters like the *Miami Herald*. Some syndicated publishers of *Screen & Radio Weekly* adapted the material—and even the format—to fit their own local purposes. The *Oakland Tribune* was an early adopter in November 1934 but spotlighted its own film correspondent, Wood Soanes, while the *Atlanta Constitution* featured its crossword and bridge columns in the magazine. The *Brooklyn Times-Union* and *South Bend Tribune*, on the other hand, had only eight-page abridged copies instead of the full sixteen-page *Free Press* version (see figure 5.5). The *Dayton Herald* issued it on Wednesdays as a "Mid-Week Screen and Radio Magazine."[69] Some of the papers used its content for weekly programs on radio stations they owned and operated—these included

100   CHAPTER 5

FIGURE 5.5. *Screen & Radio Weekly* supplement, *South Bend Tribune*, June 25, 1939.

WTMJ, the *Milwaukee Journal* station, and the *Oakland Tribune*'s KLX.[70] In Oakland, the *Tribune*'s adapted version of the supplement even had its radio page authored under the pseudonym "K. L. Ecksan."

But why would 1934 be a good moment to start a newspaper-based fan magazine in the first place? To start, as is well known, the Hays Office Production

Code had finally settled into its oversight of risqué content by 1934, after the first few notorious years of talking pictures known as the "pre-code" era.[71] Specific to fan magazines, a slump in circulation had taken hold with the Great Depression. For example, there was a turn to cheaper titles distributed through five-and-dime stores instead of costly subscriptions—the ten-cent upstart *Modern Screen* had just overtaken the "thoroughly middle-class" twenty-five-cent *Photoplay* as the highest-circulation fan magazine.[72] *Screen & Radio Weekly* also began the same time as the *Hollywood Reporter* spotlighted the "flop" of subscriptions and ad sales in fan magazines generally. As Tamar Jeffers McDonald notes, the *Hollywood Reporter*'s "Reviewing the Fan Mags" column had just declared falling circulation was because a "low level" of gossip-mongering was the standard roster.[73] True enough, when the same syndicate that distributed *Screen & Radio Weekly* concurrently launched its own tawdry series, "Hollywood Unvarnished," it backfired, as I reviewed above. Perhaps the *Detroit Free Press* thought its color magazine would attract major brand advertisers? Early issues had half-page ads from Lever Brothers for Rinso and Lifebuoy, but later issues of *Screen & Radio Weekly* ended up practically ad-free except for small items on its fan mail page. Certainly, an important factor was the Depression, which had eaten into household budgets, both for going out to the movies and for buying magazines—a cheap, free Sunday supplement would have seemed a bargain to provide a glimpse at the movie stars, even compared to one of the new cheaper, dime-priced fan magazines.

Let me briefly revisit my opening question to conclude: Does *Screen & Radio Weekly* fall within the definition of a magazine? Is it more than a newspaper section? In Tim Holmes's efforts at "mapping the magazine," he relies on the distinction that "the unique function of magazines, rather than newspapers or the broadcast media, [is] to bring high-value interpretive information to specifically defined yet national audiences."[74] For Holmes, "a magazine will always target a precisely defined group of readers and will base its content on the needs, desires, hopes and fears of that defined group, thus creating a bond of trust with their readerships."[75] Within that definition, the Sunday movie fan newspaper supplement was indeed a magazine precisely because its focus was the stars of screen and radio—not a collection of topical miscellany and general interest, nor an entertainment section with local advertising and a directory of nearby showtimes. The hybrid form and distribution—a magazine on its own, but normally circulated only with the paper—is a useful case to illustrate the need to interrogate accepted categories for our units of methodological analysis as media historians. Print ephemera and periodicals exist in a wide variety, sometimes resisting neat categorization into the usual pigeonholes. While the typical boundaries among journal, magazine, and newspaper are reliable, they are always contextual categories without firm ontological distinctions. In that sense, valorizing the newspaper fan supplement as also a magazine is a step toward justifying a swath of other print forms of periodicals in the MHDL. Yearbooks, newsletters, catalogs, annuals,

102   CHAPTER 5

pressbooks, circulars, pamphlets—all of those forms sit in the gray zone outside the clear definitions of magazines and books. None would be classified in an archive as a unique, one-of-a-kind document, even if only a single copy remained. Unsurprisingly, the MHDL already includes all of these, and more.

NOTES

1. Derek Long and Eric Hoyt, "Data on Media Publications, 1900–1960," compiled from selected classified listings of the American Newspaper Annual and Directory (Philadelphia: N.W. Ayer & Son), archive.org/details/ayermediadata.

2. Paul [S.] Moore and Sandra Gabriele, *The Sunday Paper: A Media History* (Urbana: University of Illinois Press, 2022).

3. "The Literary Features," *Chicago Inter-Ocean*, October 31, 1891, 12.

4. "The Sunday World," *New York World*, August 8, 1896, 16.

5. Richard Abel, *Menus for Movieland: Newspapers and the Emergence of American Film Culture, 1913–1916* (Berkeley: University of California Press, 2015); Paul S. Moore, "Subscribing to Publicity: Syndicated Newspaper Features for Moviegoing in North America, 1911–15," *Early Popular Visual Culture* 12, no. 2 (2014): 260–73.

6. Paul S. Moore, "'It Pays to Plan 'Em': The Newspaper Movie Directory and the Paternal Logic of Mass Consumption," in *Companion to New Cinema History*, ed. Daniel Biltereyst, Richard Maltby, and Philippe Meers, 365–77 (New York: Routledge, 2019).

7. Richard Abel, *Americanizing the Movies and Movie-Mad Audiences, 1910–1914* (Berkeley: University of California Press, 2006).

8. Benjamin S. Gross, "Motion Picture Department," *Birmingham News*, September 9, 1911, 15; September 23, 1911, 15; and September 23, 1911, 14. "Bright Birmingham Boy," *Birmingham News*, July 8, 1911, 12, which claimed "he has made some hundreds of dollars writing moving picture stories for the Edison, Vitagraph and Biograph company." See also "Ben Gross, Radio-TV's Best Ear, Dead at 87," *New York Daily News*, August 15, 1979, 47.

9. Abel, *Americanizing the Movies*, 223–26; Duane C. S. Stoltzfus, *Freedom from Advertising: E. W. Scripps's Chicago Experiment* (Urbana: University of Illinois Press, 2007). See also Richard Abel, ed., *Movie Mavens: US Newspaper Women Take on the Movies, 1914–1923* (Urbana: University of Illinois Press, 2021).

10. "Oh, There's That Smiley Golden-Haired Girl Again," *Sacramento (CA) Star*, November 18, 1912, 1, and others.

11. Shelley Stamp, *Movie-Struck Girls: Women and Motion Picture Culture after the Nickelodeon* (Princeton, NJ: Princeton University Press, 2000).

12. Ilka Brasch, *Operational Detection: Film Serials and the American Cinema, 1910–1940* (Amsterdam: Amsterdam University Press, 2018); Josh Lambert, "Wait for the Next Pictures: Intertextuality and Cliffhanger Continuity in Early Cinema and Comic Strips," *Cinema Journal* 48, no. 2 (2009): 3–25. Of course, radio serials continued in similar fashion in later years. Anne F. MacLennan, "Women, Radio, and the Depression: A 'Captive' Audience from Households to Story Time and Serials," *Women's Studies* 37, no. 6 (2008): 616–33. See also Roger Hagedorn, "Doubtless to Be Continued: A Brief History of Serial Narrative," in Robert C. Allen, ed., *To Be Continued . . . : Soap Operas around the World*, 27–48 (New York: Routledge, 1995).

13. "Two Big Smashes," *Chicago Tribune*, February 28, 1915, 12.

14. See regional promotion for the Sunday *Milwaukee Sentinel*—for example, "A Gallery of Beautiful Young Women of the Screen," *Wisconsin State Journal* (Madison), June 22, 1916, 7.

15. "The Movie Stars Are Coming!," *Chicago Tribune*, May 20, 1917, VII–11.

16. Abel, *Menus for Movieland*, 246–56.

17. "Motion Picture Mail," *New York Sun*, September 6, 1915, 9.

18. "Motion Picture Mail," *New York Sun*, November 12, 1915, 9.

19. Ad for "The Cleveland Sunday Leader," *Sandusky Star*, November 24, 1916, 2.

20. Louella O. Parsons, "Girls Win Screen Place and Big Future as Film Contenders," *Chicago Herald*, Motion Pictures, October 8, 1916, VII–1.

21. "Here Is Virginia Pearson," *St. Louis Globe-Democrat*, May 2, 1916, 10; "The World a Movie Pageant," *St. Louis Globe-Democrat*, Motion Picture Section, May 7, 1916, 1.

22. "The Moving Picture Item," *New Orleans Item*, October 29, 1916, II–16.

23. "Motion Picture News," *Dayton News*, November 26, 1915, 26.

24. "News' Enterprise Commented on by Big Eastern Publication," *Dayton News*, December 22, 1915, 8, quoting "Live Wire Exhibitors," *Motion Picture News*, December 25, 1915, 73.

25. "The Philadelphia Record," *Printers' Ink*, May 1, 1919, 115.

26. "Rotogravure Companies Merge," *Editor and Publisher*, June 26, 1920, 18. The restructuring of the company sparked a lawsuit by the advertising manager, working on commission. See Lynn S. Abbott, Respondent, v. National Gravure Circuit, Inc., Gravure Service Corporation and Alco Gravure Printing Company, Appellants. Appelate Division of the Supreme Court of New York, First Division, February 10, 1922.

27. "The Motion-Play Magazine," *Editor and Publisher*, April 30, 1921, 80.

28. Ibid.

29. "Motion-Play Magazine," *Printers' Ink*, February 16, 1922, 142.

30. "Motion-Play Magazine," *Printers' Ink*, December 8, 1921, 138.

31. "Gaze upon Stars in Sunday Star's Movie Supplement," *Indianapolis Star*, October 26, 1920.

32. "Something Very Special," *Indianapolis Star*, October 24, 1920, 12; also *Omaha World-Herald*, October 31, 1920, E-9; *Washington Herald*, November 8, 1920, 6.

33. "Gaze upon Stars in Sunday Star's Movie Supplement," *Indianapolis Star*, October 26, 1920.

34. "Something Very Special," *Indianapolis Star*, October 24, 1920, 12; also *Omaha World-Herald*, October 31, 1920, E-9; *Washington Herald*, November 8, 1920, 6.

35. "The 'Pre-View' Coming," *Los Angeles Times*, June 24, 1923, 1.

36. "The Pre-View Announcement," *Los Angeles Times, Pre-View Magazine*, July 18, 1923, 3. Hallett Abend became Shanghai correspondent of the *New York Times* in 1927 and spent more than a decade in China as a reporter.

37. "The 'Pre-View' Out Tomorrow," *Los Angeles Times*, July 17, 1923, 17.

38. "Announcement, a Greater Pre-View!," *Los Angeles Times, Pre-View Magazine*, July 22, 1925, 11.

39. "Has the Motion Picture Created a Universal Language?," *Los Angeles Times, Pre-View Section*, April 3, 1927, 6.

40. Edwin Schallert, "Golden Film Era Recalled," *Los Angeles Times*, January 4, 1958, III–3.

41. "Dietz Rites Delayed," *Los Angeles Times*, May 18, 1929, II–2.

42. "Husband Dies While Wife on Trip Abroad," *Benton Harbor (MI) Herald-Palladium*, May 21, 1929, 4.

43. "Sunday D. & C. Readers Given New Feature," *Rochester Democrat and Chronicle*, April 12, 1935, 20.

44. "12 Newspapers Now Using Screen-Radio Supplement," *Film Daily*, October 25, 1934, 10.

45. "Here It Is!," *Detroit Free Press*, April 27, 1934, 9; "Here It Is!," *Oakland Tribune*, October 24, 1934, 11; "Here It Is!," *Rochester Democrat and Chronicle*, April 15, 1935, 6.

46. Edwin Fisher Forbes, "Newspapers: Detroit," *Writer's Digest*, July 1940, 36.

47. "Radio Publicity Still Shut Out of Most Dailies; Columns Only Chance," *Variety*, March 2, 1938, 30.

48. My best estimate summed Sunday circulations from the 1934 to 1939 Ayer & Son's *Annual* for newspapers I had confirmed were syndicating copies of *Screen & Radio Weekly*. This sum reaches a maximum in January 1937. For circulations of *Photoplay* and other movie fan magazines, see Long and Hoyt, "Data on Media Publications, 1900–1960."

49. "1st Birthday," *Detroit Free Press*, April 28, 1935, 2.

50. "Goes behind Scenes in Filmland," *Detroit Free Press*, April 28, 1934, 3.

51. Ibid.

52. Ibid.

53. "Who Are Radio's Four Matinee Idols?," *South Bend Tribune*, December 3, 1936, 12.

54. "Here It Is!," *Atlanta Constitution*, November 10, 1935, 4.

55. "Bing Crosby, His Life Story," *Detroit Free Press*, May 5, 1934, 8.

56. "Has Screen-Radio Weekly," *Editor and Publisher*, July 21, 1934, 25.

57. "Doc Sure Pop: A Screamingly Funny New Comic Strip with a Strong Localized Classified-Advertising-Building Appeal," *Editor and Publisher*, November 11, 1922, 22; "New Colored Comic Page," *Editor and Publisher*, October 29, 1932, 60.

58. "Big Demand for Sunday Feature Copy," *Editor and Publisher*, March 28, 1936, 7.

59. Ibid.

60. Advertising for the Des Moines Register and Tribune Syndicate, *Editor and Publisher*, April 25, 1936, 79.

61. "Exhibitors Aroused by 'Expose' of Hollywood," *Motion Picture Herald*, January 12, 1935, 9.

62. "Hollywood Unmasked," *Chicago Daily News*, July 26, 1934, 21; "Hollywood Unvarnished (in The Detroit News)," *Port Huron (MI) Times-Herald*, July 27, 1934, 4.

63. "Hollywood Unvarnsihed," *St. Louis Globe-Democrat*, September 23, 1934, C–12.

64. "Won't Sue in K.C. Crusade on 'Indecency,'" *Motion Picture Daily*, August 31, 1934, 8.

65. "Al Firestone, "Film Stills Write World Scenario," *Motion Picture Herald*, May 18, 1935, 52.

66. Douglas W. Churchill, "Hollywood Fighting Picture Censors, Gags Candid Press Critics," *Editor and Publisher*, August 10, 1935, 5.

67. Circulation of the Sunday *Detroit Free Press* was 228,678 around 1925 (the closest year to 1934 I could confirm), according to the 1925 *American Newspaper Annual and Directory* (Philadelphia, N. W. Ayer & Son, 1925), 485.

68. Churchill, "Hollywood Fighting Picture Censors," 5.

69. "New Supplement Part of *The Herald* Every Wednesday," *Dayton Herald*, July 20, 1934, 21.

70. George A. Brandenburg, "Radio Rendering Valuable Aid in Circulation Promotion Work," *Editor and Publisher*, October 9, 1937, 9; "KLX Highlights," *Oakland Tribune*, November 22, 1934, 12.

71. Richard Maltby, "The Genesis of the Production Code," *Quarterly Review of Film and Video* 15, no. 4 (1995): 5–32.

72. "Big Fan Magazine Drop," *Hollywood Reporter*, May 25, 1933, 1; Sarah Polley, "A Spectrum of Individuals: U.S. Fan Magazine Circulation Figures from 1914 to 1965," in *Star Attractions: Twentieth-Century Movie Magazines and Global Fandom*, ed. Tamar Jeffers McDonald and Lies Lanckman, 61–80 (Iowa City: University of Iowa Press, 2019). On the contrast between *Photoplay* and the cheap alternatives, see Anne Helen Petersen, "The Politics of Fan Magazine Research," *In Media Res*, November 13, 2013, http://mediacommons.org/imr/2013/11/04/politics-fan-magazine-research.

73. Tamar Jeffers McDonald, "Reviewing Reviewing the Fan Mags," *Film History* 28, no. 4 (2016): 29–57.

74. David Abrahamson, "The Bright New-Media Future for Magazines," *Magazine Matter: Newsletter of the AEJMC Magazine Division*, Summer 1996, 1, as cited in Tim Holmes, "Mapping the Magazine: An Introduction," *Journalism Studies* 8, no. 4 (2007): 510–21.

75. Holmes, "Mapping the Magazine," 514.

PUBLICATIONS REFERENCED

Atlanta Constitution (Screen & Radio Weekly)
Birmingham (AL) News
Boston Globe
Boston Post

Brooklyn Times-Union (Screen & Radio Weekly)
Chicago Examiner
Chicago Record-Herald
Chicago Tribune
Cleveland Leader
Dayton (OH) News (Screen & Radio Weekly)
Detroit Free Press (Screen & Radio Weekly)
Hollywood Reporter
Indianapolis Star (Motion-Play Magazine)
It Magazine
Kansas City Journal-Post
Kansas City Star
Los Angeles Express
Los Angeles lllustrated Daily News
Los Angeles Times (Pre-View)
New Orleans Item
New York Daily News
New York Evening Mail
New York Mail and Express
New York Morning Journal
New York Sun
New York Times
New York Tribune
New York World
N. W. Ayer and Son's American Newspaper Annual and Directory
Milwaukee Journal (Screen & Radio Weekly)
Modern Screen
Motion Picture Mail (New York Mail and Express)
Motion-Play Magazine (ALCo Gravure/Gravure Service Corp.)
Oakland Tribune (Screen & Radio Weekly)
Philadelphia Record (Motion-Play Magazine)
Photoplay
Pre-View (Los Angeles Times)
Rochester Democrat and Chronicle (Screen & Radio Weekly)
Screen and Radio Weekly (Des Moines Register and Tribune Syndicate)
South Bend Tribune (Screen & Radio Weekly)
St. Louis Globe-Democrat
St. Louis Republic
Washington Herald (Motion-Play Magazine)

BIBLIOGRAPHY

Abel, Richard. *Americanizing the Movies and Movie-Mad Audiences, 1910–1914*. Berkeley: University of California Press, 2006.

———. *Menus for Movieland: Newspapers and the Emergence of American Film Culture, 1913–1916*. Berkeley: University of California Press, 2015.

———, ed. *Movie Mavens: US Newspaper Women Take on the Movies, 1914–1923*. Urbana: University of Illinois Press, 2021.

Abrahamson, David. "The Bright New-Media Future for Magazines." *Magazine Matter: Newsletter of the AEJMC Magazine Division*, Summer 1996, 1.

Brandenburg, George A. "Radio Rendering Valuable Aid in Circulation Promotion Work." *Editor and Publisher*, October 9, 1937, 9.

Brasch, Ilka. *Operational Detection: Film Serials and the American Cinema, 1910–1940*. Amsterdam: Amsterdam University Press, 2018.

Churchill, Douglas W. "Hollywood Fighting Picture Censors, Gags Candid Press Critics." *Editor and Publisher*, August 10, 1935, 5.

Forbes, Edwin Fisher. "Newspapers: Detroit." *Writer's Digest*, July 1940, 36.

Hagedorn, Roger. "Doubtless to Be Continued: A Brief History of Serial Narrative." In *To Be Continued . . . : Soap Operas around the World*, edited by Robert C. Allen, 27–48. New York: Routledge, 1995.

Holmes, Tim. "Mapping the Magazine: An Introduction." *Journalism Studies* 8, no. 4 (2007): 510–21.

Jeffers McDonald, Tamar. "Reviewing Reviewing the Fan Mags." *Film History* 28, no. 4 (2016): 29–57.

Lambert, Josh. "Wait for the Next Pictures: Intertextuality and Cliffhanger Continuity in Early Cinema and Comic Strips." *Cinema Journal* 48, no. 2 (2009): 3–25.

MacLennan, Anne F. "Women, Radio, and the Depression: A 'Captive' Audience from Households to Story Time and Serials." *Women's Studies* 37, no. 6 (2008): 616–33.

Maltby, Richard. "The Genesis of the Production Code." *Quarterly Review of Film and Video* 15, no. 4 (1995): 5–32.

Moore, Paul S. "'It Pays to Plan 'Em': The Newspaper Movie Directory and the Paternal Logic of Mass Consumption." In *Companion to New Cinema History*, edited by Daniel Biltereyst, Richard Maltby, and Philippe Meers, 365–77. New York: Routledge, 2019.

———. "Subscribing to Publicity: Syndicated Newspaper Features for Moviegoing in North America, 1911–15." *Early Popular Visual Culture* 12, no. 2 (2014): 260–73.

Moore, Paul [S.], and Sandra Gabriele. *The Sunday Paper: A Media History*. Urbana: University of Illinois Press, 2022.

Polley, Sarah. "A Spectrum of Individuals: U.S. Fan Magazine Circulation Figures from 1914 to 1965." In *Star Attractions: Twentieth-Century Movie Magazines and Global Fandom*, edited by Tamar Jeffers McDonald and Lies Lanckman, 61–80. Iowa City: University of Iowa Press, 2019.

Stamp, Shelley. *Movie-Struck Girls: Women and Motion Picture Culture after the Nickelodeon*. Princeton, NJ: Princeton University Press, 2000.

Stoltzfus, Duane C. S. *Freedom from Advertising: E. W. Scripps's Chicago Experiment*. Urbana: University of Illinois Press, 2007.

6

Cine-News, Paper Cinema, and Film Periodicals as Intermedial Encounters

Belinda Qian He

A hand-drawn sketch titled "The Future Kingdom of Silver (Screen)" depicts people flocking to the "Movie Theater for Today's News." The caption accompanying this scene declares, "Cinema replaced newspapers; all the news that happened yesterday will be seen in cinema today" (figure 6.1).[1] This utopian vision of cinema's capabilities was portrayed in a 1943 issue of the Chinese periodical *Movie Pictorial* (*Dianying huabao* 電影畫報). The sketch highlights cinema's potential as an archival medium driven by instantaneousness and as infrastructure for news production and dissemination. It assumes that the use of moving images and the placement of those images in the public space of the movie theater represents an upgrade from newspapers. This moment, envisioned in the 1940s, can be seen as a foreshadowing of the rise of digital networked video, smartphone footage, and user-led journalism via social media in the internet age.

However, the irony lies in the irreplaceable role of print in the then ongoing reality and future history of cinema, as exemplified by this small episode within the landscape of movie magazines in Republican China. It is the very format—magazines as a platform—that enabled and facilitated the playful, metacinematic, and self-reflexive take on the tension between cinematic apparatus and print journalism.

Chinese terms such as *dianying zazhi* (lit., film magazines) and *dianying qikan* (lit., film periodicals) are used interchangeably to refer to a diverse and heterogeneous range of film-related publications spanning various genres. These publications include film trade journals, film studios' serial publications and publicity materials, news-oriented *huabao* (pictorial magazines) centered on the film industry, *wenyi* (letters and art) periodicals that explored the intersection of cinema

FIGURE 6.1. Binghua Gao, "Weilai de yingse guo [The Future Kingdom of Silver (Screen)]," *Movie Pictorial* (*Dianying huabao*), no. 5 (1943).

with other arts and media (drama, literature, opera, photography, broadcasting, and performing arts), and dedicated film-specific sections or columns within newspapers and tabloids. Accordingly, this chapter intentionally uses the concept of "film periodicals" for the wide spectrum of publications related to films (but not limited to trade papers) in China, which were released periodically (e.g., weekly, biweekly, or monthly).

This term, *film periodicals*, distinct from the more frequently used *movie magazines*, highlights the temporal organization and serial structure of the periodical media format, invoked issue after issue through the repetition of specific formal features. Many of these film periodicals—including film trade journals, promotional booklets and prints tied to certain film productions, fanzines, and technical magazines—complicate or unsettle the boundary between established genres in the global film industry and show business. They serve as platforms where the realms of cinema and print media converge, creating a space for the interaction of various media, such as literature, film, photography, *manhua* (Chinese-language comics), design, typography, radio, graphic art, and stage play. Editorials, news stories, columns, movie reviews, special sections of photographs or illustrations, fans' sketches, readers' letters and contributions, and a wealth of advertising are all assembled and published as one piece of miscellany in print. In some instances, the intersection of different media and art forms is readily evident from the titles of the periodicals. Notable examples include *Screen Stage Monthly* (*Dianying xiju* 電影戲劇), published by the Screen and Theater Press in Shanghai in 1936; *Movie & Dance News* (*Wuying xinwen* 舞影新聞), which existed from 1935 to 1938; *New Movie Songs* (*Dianying xinge ji* 電影新歌集), published between 1942 and 1948; and *Film and Radio* (*Dianying yu boyin* 電影與播音), also published between 1942 and 1948. In other instances, different periodicals shared the same title as they gained popularity: *Movie Pictorial* (*Dianying huabao* 電影畫報) and *Film News* (*Dianying xinwen* 電影新聞). Certain rhetorical naming strategies subtly addressed the centrality of cinema in cultural life by incorporating *yinmu* ("silver screen," referring to the cinema screen) or other terms with the connotation of *yin-*, like *Silver City* (*Yindu* 銀都, indicating the city of cinema), *Silver Screen Singing* (*Yinmu gesheng* 銀幕歌聲), or *Silver Flower Monthly* (*Yinhua ji* 銀花記). In addition to *ying* (shadow), Chinese film periodicals established the word *yin* (silver) as one of the most fitting metonyms of the cinematic medium and the film industry.

Many historians and scholars have utilized Chinese film periodicals as faithful historical sources in their footnotes, investigated specific types of periodicals as linchpins of urban modernity from a media history and industry studies perspective, or explored their cultural and political significance within the dominant vocabulary of imagined communities. However, limited attention has been given to the mediated nature and interconnectedness of such magazines. This chapter seeks to place these Chinese film periodicals within a broader media history framework, departing from the conventional text-centered approach and instead focusing on the *intermedial dynamic* at play. As a keyword and one of the most challenging concepts in the critical vocabulary of film and media studies, the term *intermediality* refers to a variety of things: the dynamic and ongoing nature of media; the crossings and transformations between two or more forms of media; the presence of media within and through other media; the coexistence of multiple media; or the convergences of different media systems and networks. The shared aspect of the term's different meanings pertains to the interconnectedness of various media and their potential to interact, to transition between one another, and to reside in-between. By highlighting the intermedial, this chapter aims to briefly explore and reveal the reciprocal relationship between cinema and print media, offering a potential direction for reflecting on the historiographic approach to global movie magazines. It suggests that Chinese film periodicals defy simple differentiation and categorization, do more than cater to industry professionals and communities, and should not be viewed in isolation. Instead, it is crucial to understand these periodicals, as Eric Hoyt notes, "in relation to one another and to various other players within the ecosystem of the film industry."[2] What I refer to as Chinese film periodicals is a diverse category of media artifacts and hybrid genres (ranging from film journals, newsletters, and modernist literary magazines to pulp and glossy entertainment magazines, movie swag, fanzines, and amateur periodicals) that are characterized by periodicity and a serial structure and that embody social engagement with cinema through print forms.

Furthermore, drawing on the critical approach to magazines and/as media proposed by scholars in modern periodical studies, this chapter foregrounds the importance of examining Chinese film periodicals in their entirety, including advertisements, design, and format, and seeing them as intermedial encounters within their material realities.[3] Despite the tendency of film scholars to prioritize cinema over print and moving images over still images, a productive exploration of film periodicals should recognize the equal significance of print media alongside the cinematic medium and the inherent interplay and dynamic not merely between the two but also among multiple media forms.[4] The picture shown in figure 6.1, which was printed on paper and concerned the fate of cinema, encapsulates three angles through which this chapter aims to explore Chinese movie magazines as intermedial encounters. These perspectives include, first, cinemascapes (centered on the production of what I call *cine-news*): modes of human and nonhuman encounters with cinema in which ongoing interactions in and with the material, industrial, sociocultural, and discursive environments of films occur across screen and page; second, the portable style of "paper cinema" largely involving an arrangement of still frames in print (whether film-strip sequences or serialized pictures), which echoes the grammar and rhythm of the cinematic; and, third, material intermediality as a mode of thinking about cinephilia.

CINEMASCAPE ACROSS SCREEN AND PAGE

Chinese film periodicals were both born out of and instrumental in shaping the central aspects of what are known as cinemascapes. *Cinemascape*, a term commonly used to describe the world of cinema, points to the expansive realm of film-related practices and discursive networks. Although likely taken for granted, it carries material significance and the potential to bridge the divides between the film industry, academia, the fan world, and everything in between. The multifaceted nature and richness of this term have made it particularly valuable in studies that explore non-Hollywood and Global South cinemas, allowing for a shift away from conventional perspectives on the film industry and specific national cinema frameworks.[5] I see cinemascapes as material, bodily, tangible, discursive, and mass-mediated all at once. On many occasions that shaped the Republican-era cinemascape, filmmakers, journalists, activists, fans, audiences, readers, producers, writers, critics, artists, and business owners engaged with each other through cinema and its paratextual world. Film periodicals were by no means decorative backdrops of the cinemascape; instead, they documented things, voices, images, offscreen events, and behind-the-scenes frameworks, as well as activated and materialized the interactions, debates, and connections that lay at the core of such encounters. To fully understand the role of film periodicals, it is essential to recognize two interrelated aspects of the cinemascape across the screen and the page: the *transformation* of news into cinema and the *generation* of news through cinema (or within the realm of cinema).

The emergence of homegrown film publications as periodicals in early 1920s China was historically rooted in a compelling intersection of early filmmaking, sensational journalism, and entertainment culture. On the one hand, many newspapers and periodicals, despite not being exclusively devoted to films at the time, acted as intermediaries between current events and the emerging medium of cinema. One notable example revolves around the real-life murder case of Yan Ruisheng, an employee of a foreign trading company in Shanghai, who killed a well-known courtesan named Wang Lianying. This case garnered significant public attention and received extensive serialized media coverage, followed by numerous copycat publications, stage performances such as "civilized plays" (*wenming xi* 文明戲), and appearances in entertainment venues, including amusement halls and storytelling courts.[6] The Shanghai Photoplay Society (*Zhongguo yingxi yanjiuhui* 中國影戲研究會), established in 1920 and renamed in May 1921 (*Zhongguo yingxi yanjiushe* 中國影戲研究社, hereafter referred to as "the Society," also see Chapter 20 in this volume), was one of the earliest organizations in China dedicated to film research, education, and filmmaking. Inspired by the real-life case of Yan Ruisheng, the Society produced the first Chinese-made feature-length film, *Yan Ruisheng* (阎瑞生, dir. Ren Pengnian, 1921), commissioning the Commercial Press's film department to do the filming.[7] Major newspapers and periodicals, such as *Shenbao, Xinwen bao*, and *Shibao*'s pictorial weekly (*Shibao tuhua zhoukan*), along with leading theater-sponsored ephemeral pamphlets, closely followed both the murder case and the film adaptation.[8] The film's popularity and unexpected success at the box office can be attributed to the media sensation surrounding the case and the way in which the worlds of theater, film, journalism, and reality coalesced.

One might find it challenging to differentiate between actual press photos, like the series of pictures taken at Yan Ruisheng's execution, and publicity for the film adaptation, which mainly consisted of selected sets of film stills pairing dramatic plot points with the display of major protagonists in a tableau-style setting

112   CHAPTER 6

(see figure 6.4).[9] The film *Yan Ruisheng* recalls one of the "two principal modes of staging cinematic spectacles of violence" in the context of early twentieth-century Mexico and Brazil, as noted by the film historian Rielle Navitski: films as "violent actualities," which recorded and reconstructed real-life violent events.[10] *Yan Ruisheng* shared several filmmaking techniques with the noted style in the Latin American case, including reenactment, location shooting, the appearance of participants or witnesses from the original incidents (or people who physically resembled them), and, in some cases, a combination of staged and unstaged footage. By reenacting the unpredictable occurrences of violence that eluded the camera's lens during the original event, the footage develops an ambiguous relationship with the topical event.[11] In the end, the Yan case thrived both as news and as cinematic event, both previously nonexistent entities, mutually shaping and transforming each other.

On the other hand, film periodicals increasingly turned into information factories and found a way to provide a logistical platform and exhibition space through which cinema itself became a source of news and topicality. In 1921, the Society founded the oldest surviving Chinese film periodical, the *Motion Picture Review* (*Yingxi zazhi* 影戲雜誌). During the period in which the *Motion Picture Review* was published and *Yan Ruisheng* was released, several other film periodicals made their debut. Notable among them are *Film Weekly* (*Dianying zhoukan* 電影周刊) and *Film Journal* (*Dianying zazhi* 電影雜誌), which were launched in Beijing in 1921 and 1922, respectively. Although both the Society and the *Motion Picture Review* were relatively short lived, many members of the Society and the magazine's editorial collective eventually became significant players in the Chinese film industry. The booming growth of film studios led to the proliferation of film news: magazines specifically centering on current trends in the film industry (including pictorials that capitalized on popular film celebrities) and newspaper columns dedicated to film-related topics. Because the early Chinese film periodicals primarily focused on foreign cinema and its cultural impact, everything, big and small, that occurred in the global entertainment industry (particularly Hollywood) on a daily basis became commodifiable, possessing exotic attraction and embodying the allure of foreignness and heterogeneity in modern urban life.

Among the earliest Chinese film periodicals, three distinct groups emerged, with loosely defined boundaries.[12] The first group consisted of film studio publicity materials, what scholars have considered "supplementary film publications" as opposed to major "public-oriented film periodicals." These publications were often attached to certain film projects and released either non-periodically as serialized booklets or as special issues.[13] For instance, first published in late 1922, *Morning Star* (*Chenxing* 晨星) was the first studio-sponsored trade publication focused on domestic film production, particularly the productions of Mingxing Film Company. Another influential example is *Movie Monthly* (*Dianying yuebao* 電影月報), published by Liu-He Film Company in Shanghai from April 1928 to September 1929. The second group comprised scholarly journals that fostered theoretical debates about cinema. Some of these periodicals were edited by individuals with leftist orientations: *Mingxing Monthly* (*Mingxing yuebao* 明星月報), *Stage and Screen* (*Wutai yinmu* 舞台銀幕), and *Film Art* (*Dianying yishu* 電影藝術), among others. However, *Modern Cinema* (*Xiandai dianying* 現代電影) stood out in resisting ideological imposition on cinema by political or moral interference. The third and largest group consisted of tabloid press publications that monetized the private lives of film stars and filmmakers. By 1935, more than two hundred film periodicals had been published and distributed in China. As documented in the *Complete Catalog of Chinese Modern Film Periodicals*, which is the most comprehensive collection of modern Chinese film journals, a total of 376 different film magazines were published and distributed before 1949.[14] Two particularly noteworthy and long-running cases that incorporated elements and styles from all three groups were the best-selling *Movietone* (*Diansheng* 電聲) and the longest-lasting film magazine before the founding of the People's Republic of China, *Chin Chin Screen* (*Qingqing dianying* 青青電影).[15]

Crucial to the spectrum of film periodicals was the mass production of what I refer to as *cine-news*—compilations of events, gossip, scandals, and seemingly unremarkable information from the realm of cinema, on and off the screen, skillfully crafted, invented, and reinvented as *news*. Cine-news became a prominent shared category of content in film periodicals, making them artifacts created, regulated, and tempered within a formal framework that repeated from the past and reconciled difference. A wide range of topics were covered in columns with names such as "Yingxun" (Film-News) or "Dazhong yingxun" (Film-News for the Masses), "Yingquan suoshi" (Fragmented Matters within the Filmmakers' Circle), "Yinhai xinwen" (News from "Silver-Ocean," namely, the film world), "Yihai jinshi ji" (Records of Current Affairs in the Art Scene), "Yingren miwenlu" (Catalog of Secret Tales about Film Stars), and more. This generic category purported to provide readers with comprehensive coverage of the film industry and associated fields, catering to their varied interests and promising that they were up to date with the latest happenings in the world of cinema. For example, the special section in *Chin Chin Screen*, titled "news from silver-ocean" as mentioned above, frequently featured a catalog of cine-news with identifiable names, presented in one-sentence form. The news items ranged from secrets about film crews and quotations from renowned directors like Fei Mu, to anecdotes about actor-actress romances, vivid details from the personal lives of stars, and tidbits that claimed to be funny facts from behind the scenes of films. Customized information, including mailing addresses, birthdays, and information about the personal belongings of stars (particularly popular actresses) were published in dedicated sections of the periodicals.[16] These sections were specifically designed to respond to readers' and movie fans' letters and to address their questions and requests (e.g., "Cinephile's Mailbox" in the periodical *Hollywood* and "Readers' Mailbox" in *Chin Chin Screen*). In this sense, the readers were allowed and invited to participate in the coproduction of cine-news within individual film periodicals, as well as in the circulation across different publications.

One of the intriguing categories of cine-news revolved around anecdotal details from the movie set. An example of such cine-news, which served as a selling point in one issue of *Chin Chin Screen*, was a report about the actress Chen Yanyan (a well-known star nicknamed "beautiful bird") experiencing her period on the set, causing distress to director Yang Xiaozhong.[17] Interestingly, special sections for cine-news in periodicals like *Movie Sketch* (*Dianying manhua* 電影漫畫) were given the name *yuejing*, a term that literally refers to the menstrual cycle in Chinese. The deliberate use of this term in the magazine aimed to play with the ambiguity of its double meanings: one as "period," with both feminized and sexual connotations, and the other rhetorically as "(news about cinema that comes) once a month."[18] Enabling multimedia strategies to entice readers and fans, the form of cine-news itself structured reader engagement by fueling the tabloidization of the female body and sexuality. These were just two episodes among many in which cine-news took shape as media artifacts that were not necessarily in the form of traditional press photos or textual reports. Rather, they operated through various other means and trivial details, such as the verbal, the rhetorical, the decorative, the typographic, and even as wordplay in a predigital form of clickbait.

By making something mundane and uneventful into something eye-catching, cine-news actively unsettled the line between tabloid, scandal, sensation, true crime, personal matters, and public affairs, as well as fact and fiction. As exemplified in the case of *Yan Ruisheng*, the interplay between news and cinema, facilitated by periodicals, established a recurring pattern in the creation of cine-news, which was later shared by many similar cases involving homicide, suicide, and scandals. In this pattern, real-life cases took on a new life on stage or screen and sparked controversies over violence, gender, criminal justice, and moral order. These scenarios—dramatic incidents about celebrities (especially film stars) involving violence, death, or legal processes followed by sensational journalistic engagement, media representation, and public debate—may be best seen in cases such as the suicides of the film stars Mao Jianpei, Ai Xia, and Ruan Lingyu in the 1930s.[19] After all, the captivating power of cine-news, which was no less significant than any other type of news produced and disseminated by conventional newspapers, lies in the blurred distinction between actuality and fiction, reality and fabrication.

PAPER CINEMA

Historically rooted in and stylistically intersecting with the print genre of pictorial magazine (*huabao*), Chinese film periodicals contested the long-standing word and image divide, and they need to be understood as existing at the center of "the pictorial turn" in early modern China.[20] Film periodicals arose not only *in* print, but *as* prints, the visuality and intermediality of which deserve more critical attention. One specific form of cine-news in Chinese film periodicals is characterized by keywords such as *zhishang yingyuan* (movie theater on paper), *zhangshang dianying* (cinema on hand), and *zhishang dianying* or *zhi dianying* (paper cinema). Shaping the dominant categories in periodicals, this type of cine-news utilizes still frames or images grouped together to establish connections, create contrasts, or build tension frame by frame. Examples can be found in periodicals like *Movietone, Starlight* (Xingguang 星光), and *Film News*, where "cinema" in printed format showcased the step-by-step creation of a six-minute scene over the span of nine weeks, presented a pictorial biography of movie fans, or documented the boudoirs of female stars, all as a series of pictures (see figure 6.2).[21] Whether through photomontage, film stills, or a more integrated approach that combines hand-drawn sketches, photography, and text, the pairing of the keywords *paper* and *cinema* highlights a fundamental reconfiguration of the printed page prompted by cinematic qualities such as elastic organization of time and space and an interplay between stillness and movement. In the paper cinema model, not only are the images interlinked and arranged in a sequential manner, but the captions, designed with specific fonts and styles, are meant to be read successively along with them. The one- or two-page spreads incorporate conventions of magazine layout and graphic design with the language of film and the spatial logic of editing (perhaps seen as *mise-en-page*), to encourage the reader's imagination of a narrative sequence.

Film periodicals were a defining site in which paper cinema, including a network of genres at the intersection of cinema, print, and other media, emerged in the 1920s and thrived throughout the twentieth century. The portable form of paper cinema, driven by the mutual embrace of genre varieties and media differences, materialized and popularized the fascination with and charm of cinema to varying degrees and from various perspectives. One of the subgenres within the network of paper cinema is *yingxi xiaoshuo* (lit., shadow-play fiction, or cine-fiction), which entails fictionalizing film narratives based on one's own perception and understanding after watching imported silent films. The genre could be understood as a unique or alternative personal cinephiliac archive. This genre was primarily developed by writers from the Mandarin Ducks and Butterflies School (*yuanyang hudie pai*) with the intention of introducing films to those who could not afford to watch the films themselves.[22] Other relatable subgenres included film-narrative introductions (*dianying benshi*), which were used during the filmmaking process to outline plot developments and often merged with other genres such as lyrics, novels, and comics, giving rise to new hybrid forms. Both film novels (*dianying xiaoshuo*), which were fictionalized adaptations or retellings of film storylines and cinematic illustrated storybooks (hereafter referred to as "cinematic *lianhuanhua*"), were genres prominently featured in film periodicals and enjoyed a hybridity formed from drawing on various other genres.[23] Film novels traversed the realms of movie reviews, novels, and film stills (in cases where

FIGURE 6.2. "Shenghuo pianduan anni tailuyi" [Fragments of Anita Louise's Life], *Movie News Weekly* (*Dianying xinwen*), no. 5 (1939): 114–15. Courtesy of the Media History Digital Library.

illustrations accompanied the text), resembling a form of (film) fanfiction, while cinematic *lianhuanhua* incorporated elements of montage, publicity stills, comic strips, poetry, photo stories, and illustrated literature.

Cinematic *lianhuanhua*, in particular, stood out as the most remarkable form of frame-by-frame storytelling in Chinese film periodicals, and the form resonates with David Campany's "paper cinema," a concept describing the format of film-strip sequences in print as a mix of instructional and captivating material for viewers.[24] Sometimes translated as "linked pictures," "comic books," "serial-picture stories," or "illustrated storybooks," *lianhuanhua*, a broader category of illustrated sequential images, can be traced back to the transnational "kaleidoscopic aesthetics" of the 1920s and '30s. It eventually became a popular format of pocket-size books enjoyed by readers of all ages in China during the twentieth century.[25] As both a subgroup of *lianhuanhua* and film spin-offs, cinematic *lianhuanhua* typically consists of a series of film stills accompanied by captions (see figure 6.3).[26] It is akin to a body of genres known as "photo-fiction," "photo-stills," "photo-novels," "found film stills," "photofilms," or "still films," among many others in anglophone and globally comparable contexts.[27]

The case of *Yan Ruisheng* displays the earliest Chinese cinematic *lianhuanhua* in relation to the film's transmedia iterations through film periodicals. Publicity stills of *Yan Ruisheng*, as previously mentioned, paired key scenes with the portrayal of major protagonists. Frame by frame, the actions frozen in stillness ranged from gatherings at the crime scene, to the flight, arrest, and interrogation of Yan, to the trial. The photographic form of the film scenes signaled the transformative power of cinematic vision and the photojournalistic quality of crime news, which promised to unveil an unjust reality inaccessible through other media. However, the final execution of Yan was not shown as part of the paper cinema in the periodical *Shibao*, perhaps because it was one of the film's biggest selling points and attractions, which needed to be rendered invisible to promote suspense. As an apparently incomplete narrative, the film stills make sense of an unrelieved desire, echoing the earlier call of the theatrical version of *Yan Ruisheng*: "Men, women, old and young" would have to come to the theater in order to "see the news" (*kan xinwen*), to see the topical event *anew* (the reenacted execution on the big screen), and to see the topicality of *the new* itself (in this case, a resolution through cinematic means).[28] Cinematic *lianhuanhua* should be recognized as a collaborative creation of cine-news by the filmmakers, the editors of the periodicals in which they were published, the readers, and the film audiences. It embodies the potential for interactive vernacularization of the paper cinema form within the serialized format of a publication. The images, mediated and re-mediated by the form of paper cinema, invite readers to engage in serialized and frame-by-frame (or shot-by-shot) interpretations of the polytextual surfaces presented in the periodicals.

Within the printed space, cinematic *lianhuanhua* frames itself into an illusion of seriality and continuity, despite its inherent discontinuity. Fundamentally a series of still frames, cinema materially unfolds on paper and is captured in selected, suspended, and curated moments. Through playing with the cinematic and responding to the dialectic between stillness and movement, film periodicals manipulated readers-cum-audiences' perception of time. There was always a promise of the incomplete and the discontinued beyond the frames of cinematic *lianhuanhua* and film periodicals. Readers were enticed to watch and experience the films that could come to life on the big screen. Film audiences revisited the films, animating a passion for cinema as things, as collectible, and as prints that preserve the potential to freeze time in passing. More broadly, cinematic *lianhuanhua* was an integral part of the temporal structure of Chinese film periodicals, what may be called *the politics of periodicity*, shaped by the issue numbering system, ongoing columns and sections, intervals created by special issues or bound volumes, and interrupted or unfinished publication cycles. Such a temporal structure evoked and manipulated a sense of pleasure and anticipation through the tension between serialized continuity, frozen duration, and limited yet capturable timeliness.

FIGURE 6.3. Ming Qi and Er' Dian, "Lianhuan tuhua: jiming zaokantian" [Illustrated Pictures: The Dawn], *Picture News* (*Dianying zazhi*), no. 13 (1948): unknown page number.

FIGURE 6.4. "The Film of Yan's Murder for Money," film stills from *Yan Ruisheng* (1921), published in *Shibao Weekly Pictorial* (*Shibao tuhua zhoukan*), no. 49 (1921): 3.

Cinematic *lianhuanhua* relocated the cinematic experience from the confines of the theater into various surrounding spaces and mediascapes. Through the workings of paper cinema, as exemplified by the instance of cinematic *lianhuanhua*, film periodicals served to create a paratextual world of cinema. With a wide variety of film-related materials and their in-between forms, ranging from film stills, production photos, movie posters, commercials, and booklets to manipulated photographs based on the film and so forth, the paratextual world of cinema

120   CHAPTER 6

points, as some scholars have suggested, to the "portability" of the film experience or the human encounter with fragments of cinema in daily life.[29] One may recall how Jean Cocteau created the scenario of his avant-garde film *The Blood of a Poet* (1930) in a way that visualizes a poet-director's mind through a frame-by-frame structure.[30] Corresponding to what Caetlin Benson-Allott calls "the stuff of spectatorship," the American book series "The Film Classics Library" bears a resemblance to Chinese cinematic *lianhuanhua* as it pioneered the use of film stills (or enlarged frames) and blow-up techniques to recreate popular films such as *Casablanca* in book form.[31] Likewise, the book fully illustrated with black-and-white scenes from D. W. Griffith's *The Battle at Elderbush Gulch* (1913); the pages from the flipbooks depicting Georges Méliès's lost films, which are considered "half book, half cinema"; and more intermedial artifacts that curate moments from film all speak to the old and new fascination with stilled movement. In addition to being present within film periodicals, the form of frame-by-frame still images as a series has found its way into literary works, tabloid stories, stage plays, and various popular prints and ephemeral artifacts that shape global film experiences outside the movie theater.

Indeed, throughout China's socialist era, the style of paper cinema continued to flourish in different genres and forms of public display, serving accusation and denunciation purposes. Land Reform exhibition catalogs that took the form of pamphlets, for instance, employed frame-by-frame flipping from left to right to shape the graphic and emotional flow. Dramatic crops and "zoom in" close-ups mobilized the page, as seen in printed materials or photographic catalogs of counterrevolutionary evidence. Cinematic *lianhuanhua*, whether in the form of pocket-size books or materials included in film periodicals, along with other types of prints such as slides, comic strips, posters, or one-page instruction manuals for films, became influential portable media, reshaping films (including some presumed to be pirated) and cinematic encounters in motion (see figures 6.3 and 6.4).

CODA: MATERIAL INTERMEDIALITY
AS A MODE OF THINKING

Film periodicals were both *new* media and a remediation of *old* media in their own time of emergence and proliferation in early twentieth-century China. As historical artifacts, they constituted and, in turn, were shaped by the cinemascape. Beyond just serially published collections of individual film-centered pieces, film periodicals emerged as film-inspired prints, objects, serial systems, trade networks, hybrid genres, and circulating media defined by their very periodical form and material intermediality. With the use of concepts such as "cinematic intermediality," "cinema between media," or "cinema by other means," scholarship has increasingly revisited and rethought cinema through the politics of *inter-*, namely, a passion for in-betweenness.[32] This ambitious approach leads to analysis of the multimedial components of cinema, the positioning of cinema across a variety of media and arts, and the tensions generated by media differences from within and in-between. As this chapter proposes, we need greater consciousness of intermediality, not merely in terms of metaphorical tool sets or symbolic economies, but as the center of material conditions that constitute what is encountered, perceived, described, relived, and imagined as the cinematic.

Material intermediality, in this regard, deserves to be an object of historical analysis as well as methodological inquiry in scholarship on global movie magazines. Cine-news and paper cinema in the Chinese context, as discussed above, were only two among many mundane and yet key aspects that shaped the intermediality of the periodicals' material realities, where a consistent interplay between cinema and print media occurred and thrived between and across space, screen, and page. Intermedial interplay, in this case, moves beyond the process whereby one medium embraces another; it benefits from blurred boundaries among cinema, print, and other media, but does not elevate one at the cost of the others. Many studies of periodicals "privileg[e] the story over the advertisement, the enduring over the fashionable, or, more broadly, the exceptional over the repetitive."[33] To recognize the ubiquity of cine-news as a product of mass mediation in and through the Chinese film periodicals helps to resist such an implicit hierarchy of content. Paying close attention to *paper cinema* as a format that is both Chinese and global, that is primarily associated with magazines as media, and that exists in a generic network formed at the intersection of cinema, print, and in-between forms invites potential methodological reflections on the study of film periodicals and archival work in general. To read film periodicals *forensically*, then, is a key mode of thinking about and working with the hidden material details of the subject matter and format, which are complex media artifacts in themselves. Far more than transparent repositories of historical information and ancillary records of cinema, periodicals must be regarded as primary materials and secondary sources simultaneously, with their mediated essence requiring clear recognition and contextualization. Given the technical challenges of rigorous fact-checking and limited access to multi-perspective archives, our task is not to distinguish fiction or exaggerated imagination from fact in film periodicals. Instead, our focus should be on tracking the curation of what is presented as fact (such as the category of cine-news) within and across the printed pages. It is necessary to consider what matters and what is excluded from mattering; the material mechanism of inclusion and exclusion should be at the core of our inquiry into the periodicals as media creation. In a way, film periodicals can be viewed as both the self-archive and autobiographic fiction of the cinemascape. As I have argued elsewhere, cinephilia is not the precursor or aftermath of filmmaking but the nonlinear, intertwined relationships among film production, distribution, circulation, and reception; in China, film periodicals have played a crucial role in developing the roundtable, notably as an intermedial genre by materializing live film discussions and their mediated documentation. This has been evident since the Republican era and the socialist period, and it remains relevant today.[34] Material intermediality gives us the very language and mindset through which we conceptualize cinephilia as a range of human encounters with cinema across time, space, and scale, as well as across print, audiovisual, electronic, and digital platforms.

Due to the limited scope of this chapter, the exploration of intermedial elements in Chinese film periodicals and their material complexities remains incomplete. Inspired by emerging studies driven by the "forensics of magazine materiality," what I provide in this chapter is a point of departure for envisioning how to locate global movie magazines as intermedia encounters in history. It entails understanding them as material objects, social practices, and a form of technology in transition. By committing to this approach, it becomes possible to imagine a comparative framework for discussing the unexpected and unlikely connections between film periodicals across borders, time, and regime. For example, one potential avenue may be to historicize the creation and material culture of *yingmi* (film fans, or cinephiles) in *Movietone* and *Mass Cinema* (or *Popular Cinema, dazhong dianying* 大眾電影). *Movietone* was one of the longest-running and most popular magazines in Republican China, while *Mass Cinema*, widely known and circulated, emerged during the socialist era with a focus on "cinema for the masses" as indicated in its title. Despite being produced under different political regimes, the two periodicals share a comparable mass appeal to the public interest. To conduct such archive-based comparisons, it is necessary to create and enact a meta-database in which film magazines, functioning fundamentally as a miscellany, network, and database themselves, can encounter and speak to one another in unexpected ways (as the still growing Media History Digital Library at the University of Wisconsin–Madison has done fruitfully).[35] The key method for exploring the very different film magazines beyond ideological binaries is to begin with a critical understanding of periodicals and the platforms in which they are (digitally) archived both *as*, and *in relation to*, media. An exciting opportunity awaits us: to dig into the materiality of print, cinema, and their relationships with other and different media forms and interlocking systems of mediation. In the meantime, it is more urgent than ever to approach and reflect on the role of the rapidly expanding digital archive itself as a multiauthored, crowdsourced media artifact, as well as a comprehensive system of material mediation.

NOTES

1. Binghua Gao, "Weilai de yingse guo" [The Future Kingdom of Silver Screen], *Dianying huabao (Movie Pictorial)*, no. 5 (1943). As documented in Paul Fonoroff's book (2018), there are eight kinds of film periodicals titled *dianying huabao*.

2. Eric Hoyt, *Ink-Stained Hollywood: The Triumph of American Cinema's Trade Press* (Oakland: University of California Press, 2022), 3, https://doi.org/10.1525/luminos.122.

3. Faye Hammill, Paul Hjartarson, and Hannah McGregor, eds., "Introducing Magazines and/as Media: The Aesthetics and Politics of Serial Form," *English Studies in Canada* 41, no. 1 (2015): 1–18; Faye Hammill, Paul Hjartarson, and Hannah McGregor, "Introduction: Magazines and/as Media: Periodical Studies and the Question of Disciplinarity," *The Journal of Modern Periodical Studies* 6, no. 2 (2015): iii–xiii.

CINE-NEWS, PAPER CINEMA, FILM PERIODICALS   123

4. I am inspired by and also share the view of a few exceptional historiographical examinations that still images are of no less significance than moving images; photography (or print) and cinema intersect with and mutually enrich each other. See Thomas Elsaesser, "The Architectural Postcard: Photography, Cinema, and Modernist Mass Media," *Grey Room*, no. 70 (2018): 80–101; Noam Elcott, "The Cinematic Imaginary and the Photographic Fact: Media as Models for 20th Century Art," *PhotoResearcher*, no. 29 (2018): 7–23; Belinda Qian He, "Socialist Multimedia Warfare: Cine-Exhibition of Class Struggle in 1960s China," *Grey Room* 89 (2022): 6–41.

5. For example, the term encompasses the multifaceted ways in which "films navigate the structures and pathways of society and the infrastructures of film production, distribution, exhibition and consumption." See Haseenah Ebrahim, "Traversing the Cinemascape of Contemporary South Africa: A Peripatetic Journey," *Black Camera* 9, no. 2 (2018): 197–215. For an exploration of cinemascape as key to a postnational critical praxis, see Ann Marie Stock, "Migrancy and the Latin American Cinemascape: Towards a Post-national Critical Praxis," *Revista Canadiense de Estudios Hispánicos* 20, no. 1 (1995): 19–30. An intriguing concept that echoes the idea of cinemascape is what Emilie Yueh-yu Yeh and Enoch Yee-lok Tam call "the movie field" (or "the early filmscape" as an evolving, cross-disciplinary terrain) in Republican China. As they argue, the formation of this movie field was highly associated with the unique position of "film literati" (*dianying wenren*) in bridging the filmic and literary fields. See Emilie Yueh-yu Yeh and Enoch Yee-lok Tam, "Forming the Movie Field: Film Literati in Republican China," in *Early Film Culture in Hong Kong, Taiwan, and Republican China: Kaleidoscopic Histories*, ed. Emilie Yueh-yu Yeh, 244–76 (Ann Arbor: University of Michigan Press, 2018).

6. Laikwan Pang offers a compelling discussion around the Lianying case in the theatrical world at the time. See Laikwan Pang, *The Distorting Mirror: Visual Modernity in China* (Honolulu: University of Hawai'i Press, 2007), 161–63.

7. The Chinese Film Research Society functioned primarily as a speculative company and was disbanded shortly after the production of *Yan Ruisheng*.

8. "Moubi Lianying an yaofan jiang chu sixing" 謀害蓮英案人犯將處死刑, *Xinwenbao*, November 19, 1920; "Moubi Lianying an yaofan yiding chu sixing" 謀害蓮英案人犯已定死刑, *Xinwenbao*, November 23, 1920.

9. "The Film of Yan's Murder for Money," *Shibao tuhua zhoukan* 49 (1921): 3; Hui Fang, "Yan ruisheng moucaihaiming zhi jieguo," 閻瑞生謀財害命之結果 [The Retributive Consequence of Yan Ruisheng, Who Murdered for Money], *Shibao tuhua zhoukan*, November 28, 1920, 4.

10. Rielle Navitski, *Public Spectacles of Violence: Sensational Cinema and Journalism in Early Twentieth-Century Mexico and Brazil* (Durham, NC: Duke University Press, 2017), 6.

11. Navitski, *Public Spectacles of Violence*.

12. Yingjin Zhang and Zhiwei Xiao, *Encyclopedia of Chinese Film* (London: Routledge, 1998), 271.

13. For scholarship that distinguishes "public-oriented film periodicals" produced relatively independently from "film's special publications" (*dianying tekan*) or "supplementary film publications" (*fushuxing dianying kanwu*), which were largely sponsored by leading studios and theaters, see Shanshan Ding, *Zhongguo dianying kanwu shigao* 中國電影刊物史稿：1921–1949 [A Historical Study of Chinese Cinema–Related Publications: from 1921 to 1949] (Beijing: Zhongguo dianying chubanshe, 2017), 74–146. Xiaoyu Xia's work in progress also touches on such special journals (tekan) associated with specific film productions as film-studio sponsored publications, as well as early Chinese cinema's intertwining with other media, such as typography. I am indebted to Xiaoyu Xia for her insights on "cine-bibliophilia," shared during the virtual roundtable event "A Deep Focus on Global Chinese Cinephilia," which I co-organized with Timmy Chen in April 2022, at the Center for Chinese Studies, University of California, Berkeley.

14. Shanghai Library, eds., *Zhongguo xiandai dianying qikan quanmu shuzhi* 中國現代電影期刊全目書志 [Complete Catalogue of Chinese Modern Film Periodicals] (Shanghai: Shanghai kexue jishu wenxian chubanshe, 2009). Another remarkable large-scale archiving and publication project about Chinese film periodicals is the "Compilation of Movies Magazines from the Republican Era," carried

124   CHAPTER 6

out by Shanghai Library, renowned for its extensive collection of over three hundred film periodicals from Republican China, and Chinese National Library Press. This compilation comprises seventy-three mainstream film periodicals from the 1920s to the 1940s in the Republican era, totaling 167 volumes. See Shanghai Library, *Minguo shiqi dianying zazhi huibian* 民國時期電影雜誌彙編 [Compilation of Movies Magazines from the Republican Era] (Beijing: Guojia tushuguan chubanshe, 2013).

15. *Chin Chin Screen* and *Movietone* are two of the major Chinese film periodicals documented in the China collection of the Media History Digital Library. See https://mediahistoryproject.org/collections/china/.

16. Examples include "Zuixin nannǚ mingxing zhuzhilu" 最新男女明星的住址錄 [A Catalogue of the Most Updated Male and Female Stars' Addresses], *Chin Chin Screen* (*Qingqing dianying*) 8, no. 21 (1939): 17; "Duzhe xinxiang nǚmingxing de dizhi" [Readers' Mailbox: Addresses of Female Stars], *Chin Chin Screen* (*Qingqing dianying*) 40 (1948): 3; "Yingmi xinxiang shengyu he dizhi" 影迷信箱：生日和地址 [Movie Fans' Mailbox: Birthdays and Addresses], *Haolaiwu* (Hollywood), no. 54 (1939): 23.

17. "Chen yanyan yuejing laichao jihuaile daoyan yangxiaozhong" 陳燕燕月經來潮急壞了導演楊小仲 [Chen Yanyan Got Her Period, Making Director Yang Xiaozhong Greatly Anxious], *Chin Chin Screen* (*Qingqing dianying*), no. 3 (1939): 9.

18. For one such example in the *yuejing* section, also about Chen Yanyan, see Bai Ding and Mei Zi, "Yuejing meiyuejian zhi dianying jingye chen yanyan zainanjing shengzi zhi chuanwen" 每月間之電影經也：陳燕燕在南京生子之傳聞 [Monthly Chronicle of Cine-News: Rumors of Chen Yanyan Giving Birth in Nanjing], *Movie Sketch* (*Dianying manhua*), no. 5 (1935).

19. For some of the most well-known cases, see Kristine Harris, "The New Woman Incident: Cinema, Scandal, and Spectacle in 1935 Shanghai," in *Transnational Chinese Cinemas: Identity, Nationhood, Gender*, ed. Sheldon Hsiao-peng Lu, 277–301 (Honolulu: University of Hawai'i Press, 1997); Bryna Goodman, "The New Woman Commits Suicide: The Press, Cultural Memory and the New Republic," *The Journal of Asian Studies* 64, no. 1 (2005): 67–101.

20. For discussions about "the pictorial turn," see Laikwan Pang, *The Distorting Mirror*; John A. Crespi, *Manhua Modernity: Chinese Culture and the Pictorial Turn* (Oakland: University of California Press, 2020).

21. Examples include Ming Li, "Chen yanyan guifang canguan ji" 陳燕燕閨房參觀記 [A Record of Visiting Chen Yanyan's Boudoir], *Chin Chin Screen* (*Qingqing dianying*), no. 6 (1937): 10; Unknown author, "Shenghuo pianduan anni tailuyi" 生活片段：安妮泰露薏絲 [Fragments of Anita Louise's Life], *Movie News Weekly* (*Dianying xinwen zhoukan*), no. 5 (1939): 114–15; Unknown author, "Zhishang dianying yinmu liufenzhong gongzuo jiuxingqi 紙上電影：銀幕六分鐘，工作九星期 [Cinema on Paper: Six Minutes Onscreen, Nine Weeks of Work Offscreen], *Starlight* (*Xingguang*), no. 17 (1946): 4–5.

22. For an exploration of *yingxi xiaoshuo*, see Shawn Shao, *Zhishang yinmu minchu de yingxi xiaoshuo* 紙上銀幕：民初的影戲小說 [The Silver Screen among Pages: A Study of Yingxi Fiction in Early Republican China] (Taipei: Xiuwei jingdian, 2017).

23. For examples of *dianying xiaoshuo* as a journalist's report that documented the story from the big screen, see Zhengqiu Zheng (jizhe), "Dianying xiaoshuo zimei hua" 電影小說：姊妹花 [Film Novel: The Sisters], *Xiaoshuo* (*Novels*), no. 1 (1934): 22–25. The list of film crew members of the narrated film is included alongside this piece of film novel.

24. See David Campany, *Photography and Cinema* (London: Reaktion Books, 2008), 66.

25. John C. Hwang, "Lien Huan Hua: Revolutionary Serial Pictures," in *Popular Media in China: Shaping New Cultural Patterns*, ed. Godwin C. Chu, 51–72 (Honolulu: University of Hawai'i Press, 1978); Julia F. Andrews, "Literature in Line: Picture Stories in the People's Republic of China," *Inks: Cartoon and Comic Art Studies* 4, no. 3 (1997), 17–32; Kuiyi Shen, "Lianhuanhua and Manhua—Picture Books and Comics in Old Shanghai," in *Illustrating Asia: Comics, Humor Magazines, and Picture Books*, ed. John A. Lent, 100–120 (Honolulu: University of Hawai'i Press, 2001); Jianing Yang,

"Hudong shuangsheng dianying yu lianhuanhua de kuameijie lüxing" 互動雙生：電影與連環畫的跨媒介旅行 [Interactive Twins: Cross-Media Travel between Films and Comics], *Movie Review (Dianying pingjie)*, no. 20 (2019): 75–81. About kaleidoscopic modernism, see Paul W. Ricketts, "Kaleidoscopic Modernisms: Montage Aesthetics in Shanghai and Tokyo Pictorials of the 1920s and 1930s," in *Liangyou, Kaleidoscopic Modernity and the Shanghai Global Metropolis, 1926–1945*, ed. Paul Pickowicz, Kuiyi Shen, and Yingjin Zhang, 15–44 (Leiden, The Netherlands: Brill, 2013).

26. For examples, see Ming Qi and Er' Dian, "Lianhuan tuhua: jiming zaokantian" 連環圖畫：雞鳴早看天 [Illustrated Pictures: The Dawn (1948)], *Picture News (Dianying zazhi)*, no. 13 (1948): unknown page number.

27. Raymond Bellour, "The Film Stilled," trans. Alison Rowe and Elisabeth Lyon, *Camera Obscura: A Journal of Feminism, Culture, and Media Studies* 1990 (24): 99–121; Margarita Tupitsyn, "Photo-Still versus Photo-Picture: The Politics of (de)Framing," *The Soviet Photograph, 1924–1937* (New Haven, CT: Yale University Press, 1996), 66–98.

28. "Hepingshe bianyan huazongli moushaan di xuanyan," *Xinwenbao*, November 25, 1920. The periodical *Laughter Stage (Xiaowutai* 笑舞台) made an explicit claim earlier about people's experience in the theater as *kan xinwen*, suggesting the beauty of theatrical experiences concerning news that mixes life as drama and drama as life.

29. For such insights, see Thomas Stubblefield, "Disassembling the Cinema: The Poster, the Film and In-Between," *Thresholds* 34 (2007): 84–88; Victor Burgin, *The Remembered Film* (London: Reaktion Books, 2004).

30. Jean Cocteau, *The Blood of a Poet: A Film*, trans. Lily Pons (New York: Bodley Press, 1949).

31. Richard J. Anobile, ed., *Michael Curtiz's Casablanca* (New York: Avon, 1974); Caetlin Benson-Allott, *The Stuff of Spectatorship: Material Cultures of Film and Television* (Oakland: University of California Press, 2021).

32. For example, see Jørgen Bruhn and Anne Gjelsvik, *Cinema between Media: An Intermediality Approach* (Edinburgh: Edinburgh University Press, 2018); Kim Knowles and Marion Schmid, *Cinematic Intermediality: Theory and Practice* (Edinburgh: Edinburgh University Press, 2021).

33. Hammill, Hjartarson, and McGregor, "Introduction: Magazines and/as Media: Periodical Studies and the Question of Disciplinarity," iv.

34. Belinda Qian He, "Cinema at the Table, Cinema as Roundtable," *Journal of Chinese Cinemas* 15, no. 2 (2021): 176–99.

35. Another noteworthy and growing database of Chinese periodicals, with some restrictions in both material and digital access, is housed in the Paul Kendel Fonoroff Collection for Chinese Film Studies at the University of California, Berkeley. The special collection contains 436 titles (5,901 issues in total) from China's pre-1950 era, including sixty titles not cited in the standard reference work *Complete Catalogue of Chinese Modern Film Periodicals*.

PUBLICATIONS REFERENCED

Chin Chin Screen (Qingqing dianying 青青電影)
Film and Radio (Dianying yu boyin 電影與播音)
Film Art (Dianying yishu 電影藝術)
Film Journal (Dianying zazhi 電影雜志)
Film News (Dianying xinwen 電影新聞)
Film Weekly (Dianying zhoukan 電影周刊)
Laughter Stage (Xiaowutai 笑舞台)
Mass Cinema (Dazhong dianying 大眾電影)
Mingxing Monthly (Mingxing yuebao 明星月報)
Modern Cinema (Xiandai dianying 現代電影)

126 CHAPTER 6

Morning Star (*Chenxing* 晨星)
Motion Picture Review (*Yingxi zazhi* 影戲雜志)
Movie & Dance News (*Wuying xinwen* 舞影新聞)
Movie Monthly (*Dianying yuebao* 電影月報)
Movie News Weekly (*Dianying xinwen* 電影新聞)
Movie Pictorial (*Dianying huabao* 電影畫報)
Movie Sketch (*Dianying manhua* 電影漫畫)
Movietone (*Diansheng* 電聲)
New Movie Songs (*Dianying xinge ji* 電影新歌集)
Screen Stage Monthly (*Dianying xiju* 電影戲劇)
Shenbao 申報
Shibao Pictorial Weekly (*Shibao tuhuazhoukan* 時報圖畫周刊)
Silver City (*Yindu* 銀都)
Silver Flower Monthly (*Yinhua ji* 銀花記)
Silver Screen Singing (*Yinmu gesheng* 銀幕歌聲)
Stage and Screen (*Wutai yinmu* 舞台銀幕)
Starlight (*Xingguang* 星光)
Xinwen bao 新聞報

BIBLIOGRAPHY

Bao, Weihong. *Fiery Cinema: The Emergence of an Affective Medium in China, 1915–1945.* Minneapolis: University of Minnesota Press, 2015.

Beeston, Alix, and Stefan Solomon. *Incomplete: The Feminist Possibilities of the Unfinished Film.* Oakland: University of California Press, 2023.

Benson-Allott, Caetlin. *The Stuff of Spectatorship: Material Cultures of Film and Television.* Oakland: University of California Press, 2021.

Bevan, Paul. *'Intoxicating Shanghai'—An Urban Montage: Art and Literature in Pictorial Magazines during Shanghai's Jazz Age.* Leiden, The Netherlands: Brill, 2020.

Braester, Yomi. "A Genealogy of Cinephilia in the Maoist Period." In *The Oxford Handbook of Chinese Cinemas,* edited by Carlos Rojas, 98–115. University of Oxford Press, 2013.

Bruhn, Jørgen, and Anne Gjelsvik. *Cinema between Media: An Intermediality Approach.* Edinburgh: Edinburgh University Press, 2018.

Ding, Shanshan. *Zhongguo dianying kanwu shigao* 中國電影刊物史稿：1921–1949 [*A Historical Study of Chinese Cinema-related Publications: from 1921 to 1949*]. Beijing: Zhongguo dianying chubanshe, 2017.

Fonoroff, Paul. *Chinese Movie Magazines: From Charlie Chaplin to Chairman Mao, 1921–1951.* Oakland: University of California Press, 2018.

Fu, Xiao, and Yao Wang. "Zhishang kan dianying xinzhongguo dianying lianhuanhua de meiti kaoguxue 紙上看電影：新中國電影連環畫的媒體考古學 ['Watching Films on Paper': A Media Archaeological Study of Film Picture-Story Book in People's Republic of China]." *Film Art (Dianying yishu)* 412, no. 5 (2023): 153–60.

Hammill, Faye, Paul Hjartarson, and Hannah McGregor. "Introduction: Magazines and/as Media: Periodical Studies and the Question of Disciplinarity." *The Journal of Modern Periodical Studies* 6, no. 2 (2015): iii–xiii.

He, Belinda Qian. "Socialist Multimedia Warfare: Cine-Exhibition of Class Struggle in 1960s China." *Grey Room* 89 (2022): 6–41.

Hockx, Michel, Joan Judge, and Barbara Mittler, eds. *Women and the Periodical Press in China's Long Twentieth Century: A Space of Their Own?* Cambridge: Cambridge University Press, 2018.

Hoyt, Eric. *Ink-Stained Hollywood: The Triumph of American Cinema's Trade Press*. Oakland: University of California Press, 2022, https://doi.org/10.1525/luminos.122.

Huang Xuelei. *Shanghai Filmmaking: Crossing Borders, Connecting to the Globe, 1922–1938*. Leiden, The Netherlands: Brill, 2014.

Judge, Joan. *Republican Lens: Gender, Visuality, and Experience in the Early Chinese Periodical Press*. Oakland: University of California Press, 2015.

Knowles, Kim, and Marion Schmid. *Cinematic Intermediality: Theory and Practice*. Edinburgh: Edinburgh University Press. 2021.

Macdonald, Sean. "Montage as Chinese: Modernism, the Avant-Garde, and the Strange Appropriation of China." *Modern Chinese Literature and Culture* 19, no. 2 (2007): 151–99.

Ricketts, Paul W. "Kaleidoscopic Modernisms: Montage Aesthetics in Shanghai and Tokyo Pictorials of the 1920s and 1930s." In *Liangyou, Kaleidoscopic Modernity and the Shanghai Global Metropolis, 1926–1945*, edited by Paul Pickowicz, Kuiyi Shen, and Yingjin Zhang, 15–44. Leiden, The Netherlands: Brill, 2013.

Shao, Shawn. *Zhishang yinmu minchu de yingxi xiaoshuo* 紙上銀幕：民初的影戲小說 [The Silver Screen among Pages: A Study of Yingxi Fiction in Early Republican China]. Taipei: Xiuwei jingdian, 2017.

Yang, Jianing. "Hudong shuangsheng dianying yu lianhuanhua de kuameijie lüxing" 互動雙生：電影與連環畫的跨媒介旅行 [Interactive Twins: Cross-Media Travel between Films and Comics]. *Movie Review (Dianying pingjie)*, no. 20 (2019): 75–81.

Yeh, Emilie Yueh-yu, and Enoch Yee-lok Tam. "Forming the Movie Field: Film Literati in Republican China." In *Early Film Culture in Hong Kong, Taiwan, and Republican China: Kaleidoscopic Histories*, edited by Emilie Yueh-yu Yeh, 244–76. Ann Arbor: University of Michigan Press, 2018.

Zhang, Zhen. *An Amorous History of the Silver Screen: Shanghai Cinema, 1896–1937*. Chicago: University of Chicago Press, 2005.

Zhou, Chenshu. *Cinema Off Screen: Moviegoing in Socialist China*. Oakland: University of California Press, 2021.

SECTION TWO

Film Cultures, Critics, and Circuits

7

Latin American Cine Club Magazines

Nodes in Mid-century Networks of Film Culture

Rielle Navitski

The inaugural issue of *Gente de Cine* (1951–57), published by the Buenos Aires film society of the same name, opened with a concise statement of purpose: "It was an urgent necessity for the Gente de Cine Club to have an organ of information and film criticism of a permanent nature that would be, at the same time, a means of bringing its members closer together."[1] This brief declaration encapsulates the shared ambitions of a wave of cine club magazines that appeared in Latin America from the late 1940s through the late 1960s. This moment was marked by art cinema's emergence as a concept and phenomenon and by the expansion of the region's urban middle classes, which fostered the growth of leisure practices that offered cultural prestige to the upwardly mobile. These publications sought to transcend the novelty-driven coverage of newspapers and fan magazines while serving as a point of contact between like-minded cinephiles at home and abroad. Offering an overview of Latin American cine club magazines, I focus on titles from the Río de la Plata region (Argentina and Uruguay), most available online from the Archivo Histórico de Revistas Argentinas (https://ahira.com.ar/) or Anáforas (https://anaforas.fic.edu.uy), a digital repository hosted by Uruguay's Universidad de la República.

As the film society movement expanded in post–World War II Latin America, cine clubs moved into publishing in order to extend the reach of their activities. Their periodicals developed a discourse on cinema that aspired to greater complexity, depth, and theoretical rigor than existing press coverage.[2] For instance, *Cine Club* (1948–52), published by the Cine Club del Uruguay, declared that it "seeks to fill an inexplicable gap created by the almost total absence in South America of any other publication dedicated to the study and research of cinematic questions."[3]

132   CHAPTER 7

Magazines complemented the screening and discussion of films that cine club leaders deemed aesthetically and historically significant, furthering efforts to foster a sophisticated and discerning film culture and ultimately improve the "quality" of film production, bringing cinema closer to its desired status as a legitimate art.

As signaled by *Gente de Cine*'s emphasis on its "permanent nature," film society magazines sought to offer lasting critical reflections and to give a more enduring character to the information contained in their screenings' ephemeral programs, even as they grappled with the difficulties of sustaining niche periodicals without the backing of major publishing houses. If programs prepped audiences to evaluate films in relation to a director's trajectory, a national cinema, or an artistic movement, magazines could add to this context with longer pieces or even supplant the program altogether.[4] Detailed filmographies compiled by film societies' leadership—a valuable resource for Spanish-speaking cinephiles of the period given the relative scarcity of specialized books—also appeared in both programs and magazines.

Despite their ambitions to serve as durable reference works, film society magazines struggled to maintain their continuity, to the extent that *Film*, a publication of Montevideo's Cine Universitario, listed "not to be an ephemeral magazine" as the first goal in its statement of purpose that appeared in the first issue.[5] Given that cine clubs were noncommercial in character—a stipulation of the national and international federations that regulated their activities, intended to allay commercial exhibitors' fears of competition[6]—their magazines usually lacked a strong financial foundation, although nearly all included advertisements to generate income beyond subscriptions and single-issue sales. Due to their specialized nature, their audience was inherently limited; yet, nevertheless, they circulated beyond the clubs' immediate membership. Film society magazines were sold in bookstores, in some cases on newsstands, and through the efforts of cinephiles who served as international distribution agents.[7] Furthermore, their contents were repurposed in other Latin American cine clubs' magazines and outside the region.[8]

As their circulation and reuse suggests, cine club publications fostered connections with a geographically dispersed network of film enthusiasts, even as they strengthened bonds among each organization's ranks with columns that allowed members to engage in dialogue via letters and film reviews. In addition to including columns on domestic and international cine club activities, magazines recruited foreign correspondents to report on local film scenes and international festivals. Cine club magazines also commonly published translated texts that had first appeared in French, Italian, British, and US publications. To expand members' access to international film criticism, the Buenos Aires magazine *Tiempo de Cine* (1960–68),[9] published by Cine Club Núcleo, even offered to broker subscriptions to *Cinema Nuovo* (Italy), *Cinéma 61* (France), and *Film Culture* (United States).[10] Cine club magazines also inventoried resources for film study through their commentary on specialized books and periodicals, which complemented film societies' efforts to create libraries for member consultation. Through engagement with their international counterparts, film society publications positioned themselves as cultural mediators, seeking to enrich the local level of discourse on cinema with insights from abroad.

LATIN AMERICAN CINE CLUB MAGAZINES: A PANORAMA

While cine clubs are typically understood as defined by their exhibition activities, the publication of specialized periodicals actually preceded the clubs' first screenings in a number of key cases. Indeed, the term *cine club* first gained public currency with the launch of French filmmaker and critic Louis Delluc's magazine *Le Journal du Ciné-club* in January 1920, six months before he organized the famous screening that marked the cine club's emergence as a social activity.[11] Suggesting how periodicals might effectively intervene in the public sphere when projecting films proved difficult, the Chaplin Club in Rio de Janeiro, one of Latin America's earliest film societies, initiated its activities with the publication of *O Fan* (1928–30). Beginning in August 1928, the magazine printed lectures delivered by club members—including vigorous defenses of silent cinema in the face of the transition to sound—alongside reviews of recent releases and other reflections.[12] *O Fan* quickly attracted attention from the local press, including the newspapers *O Globo* and *O Paiz*.[13] Yet, due to logistical challenges, the Chaplin Club would not show its first film until a January 1930 screening of *Die Büchse der Pandora* (*Pandora's Box*, Georg Wilhelm Pabst, 1929).[14]

Similarly, the creation of *Cine Club*, Latin America's earliest postwar film society magazine, was the first official act of the Cine Club del Uruguay in February 1948.[15] (Its debut session, featuring a reconstructed version of Abel Gance's *Napoléon* [1927], followed the next month.) Sharing its title with the magazine of the Fédération française des ciné-clubs (1947–54) and two periodicals published by film societies in Mexico City (1955–56) and Barranquilla, Colombia (1957–58), the Uruguayan *Cine Club* occupied one extreme of the broad range of production values among its counterparts. Duplicated by a club officer on a mimeograph machine, the first issue featured professionally printed photographs painstakingly glued into a hundred copies.[16] Since this approach proved impractical as the organization's membership expanded, the editors outsourced the printing to professionals, only to return to self-publication two years later after acquiring an offset machine.[17] The printing of the magazine's later iteration, *Cuadernos de Cine Club* (1961–67), was also done in house, making the Cine Club del Uruguay's publications the most literal manifestation of film enthusiasts' desires for an independent cinematic press.[18]

While the do-it-yourself methods of the Cine Club del Uruguay were unusual, its publications' limited scope and lack of visual polish were not. The Colombian

FIGURE 7.1. Color blocking in cine club magazines of the 1950s and 1960s: *Film*, *Séptimo Arte*, and *Tiempo de Cine*.

Cine Club resembled a film program with its compact measurements, although it included magazine-like features such as "Breviario del Séptimo Arte," a digest of film-related news. While most film society periodicals of the 1950s and '60s were closer to fan magazines in size—including the Uruguayan *Cine Club*, *Film*, and *Séptimo Arte* (1954–56), the short-lived magazine of Santiago de Chile's Cine Club Universitario—they were also characterized by brevity and graphic simplicity. All used simple layouts, typically with one or two columns, and were printed in black and white. Cover designs that combined photographs with bold blocks of a single color predominated in this period and remained prevalent through the 1960s (see figure 7.1). *Gente de Cine*, the most enduring cine club magazine of the 1950s, distinguished itself from its counterparts with its tabloid-size dimensions and newspaper-like layout.

There was also considerable overlap in film society periodicals' regular sections, a reflection of shared goals and close contact between organizations.[19] As noted above, these magazines extended the functions of the program with articles on directors and individual works; interviews with and writings by filmmakers; filmographies; and announcements of clubs' upcoming schedules. However, material with direct links to programming tended to diminish over time as publications took on a life of their own; for instance, *Gente de Cine* stopped including information on the club's future screenings in late 1952. Stand-alone articles on an eclectic range of topics—major developments of the 1950s and '60s like 3-D and widescreen, Italian neorealism, and new waves, along with broader issues like censorship and the relationship between film and other arts—were accompanied by explicitly topical columns. These included brief roundups of international happenings in the film world and more substantive updates on the national industry, in the case of Argentina, and on amateur filmmaking activities in Chile and Uruguay. Overall, cine club periodicals strove to stay abreast of recent developments—a challenge given the irregular intervals at which they often appeared—while offering a retrospective look at film history and theory. The Uruguayan *Cine Club* included an "Archivo" section that showcased works of early cinema, mimicking a similar feature of the Italian magazine *Bianco e Nero* (1937–present), while *Tiempo de Cine* published a column entitled "Tiempo de Biógrafo" (In the Time of the Biograph), which compiled commentary on cinema from newspapers of the 1920s.

During the 1960s, this balance of historical and contemporary topics shifted decisively towards the new as France's *nouvelle vague* and other young cinemas took critics and cinephiles by storm. As film culture became increasingly imbued with the leftist politics that energized the New Latin American Cinema movements of the 1960s, cine club magazines abandoned their precursors' treatment of aesthetics as an autonomous sphere disconnected from social issues. These 1960s publications also broke with the more conventional layouts of their precursors, utilizing splashy fonts, collage, multiple bright ink colors, and superimpositions of image and text (see figure 7.2). Key titles of the period include *Cuadernos de Cine Club* and *Nuevo Film* (1967–69), respectively reboots of *Cine Club* and *Film*. These two titles had been casualties of their editors' success; as contributors were recruited to work as film critics at major periodicals, they had less and less time to devote to cine club publications.[20] Magazines of the 1950s that survived into the next decade, such as *Revista de Cinema* (1954–64), based in Belo Horizonte, Brazil, were a rarity.[21] Entirely new titles include *Tiempo de Cine*, the Brazilian *Cineclube* (1960–67), and the Chilean *Cine Foro* (1964–66). The Peruvian magazine *Hablemos de Cine* (1965–85) also debuted in this period. While not officially a film society publication, its editors served as programmers for the Cine-Club de la Universidad Católica in Lima and the club kept the periodical financially solvent.[22]

Cine club magazines of the 1960s intensified their precursors' ambitions to make weighty contributions to film criticism. *Cuadernos de Cine Club* offered lengthy and highly polemical discussions of new waves and cinema's relationship to politics that irritated some local critics.[23] Originally conceived as a venue for monograph-length texts by club members, the magazine's issues regularly exceeded a hundred pages. With its strident tone and intellectualized approach— its title's similarity to *Cahiers du cinéma* was likely no coincidence[24]—*Cuadernos de Cine Club* reached a maximum circulation of fifteen hundred in 1963.[25] The print run of *Tiempo de Cine*, likely the most popular cine club magazine of the period, topped out at five thousand.[26]

The relatively small size of cine club periodicals' audience enabled, at least in theory, a sense of proximity between readers. At the same time, these publications sought to bring geographically distant cinephiles closer together through their circulation abroad and dispatches sent from overseas. The remainder of this essay maps how two groups of contributors beyond magazines' staff—readers/club members and foreign critics—participated in their efforts to foster film culture locally and internationally.

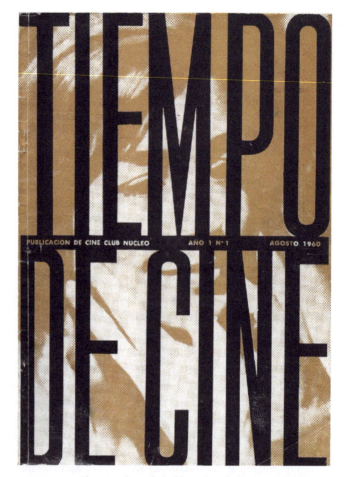

FIGURE 7.2. The 1960s brought bold graphic choices to cine club magazines, such as the cover of the inaugural August 1960 issue of *Tiempo de Cine*.

THE ACTIVE VIEWER/READER

The relationship between cine club publications and their readership was shaped by a paradox inherent to these organizations' mission in the late 1940s and '50s: to institute a rather elitist form of cinematic enjoyment on a mass scale. To achieve this goal, film enthusiasts solicited the active engagement of viewers, who had to be trained out of their presumably passive consumption of film's seductive pleasures. In the polarized Cold War moment, film reformers—often aligned with supranational organizations like the United Nations Educational, Scientific and Cultural Organization and the Office catholique international du cinéma—championed active spectatorship as a means of managing cinema's potent psychological, moral, and political effects.[27] If one could promote a critical mindset in spectators through post-screening discussions—a staple of cine clubs' practice, particularly in France, that was widely adopted as an ideal by their Latin American counterparts[28]—film society magazines extended these debates in their pages. Yet the organizations' structure inevitably imposed limits on the agency of rank-and-file members. A small leadership typically determined programming, and often complained of members' lack of receptivity to older or more challenging films.[29] For their part, cine club magazines explicitly opened up space for member/reader opinions, but often curtailed them in practice.

Like the post-screening discussion, reader contributions to film society magazines had French roots. When the Uruguayan *Cine Club* launched the section "Tribuna del Cine Club" (Cine Club Forum) in June 1950, its editors noted a precedent in the Fédération française des ciné-clubs' magazine of the same name. The section proved to be short lived, lasting only two issues before *Cine Club* went on hiatus during 1951. *Gente de Cine* featured a more lasting section with an almost identical title: "Tribuna de los socios," or "Members' Forum." After appearing in the club's programs, the column was transplanted to *Gente de Cine* in April 1951. Initially, it provided space for members to weigh in on past club screenings, but its scope quickly expanded. In September 1952, the magazine placed clear limits on reader contributions, claiming a need to maintain strong editorial control: "It has been decided we will not accept film reviews in this section, except when these—of an obviously polemical nature—render the inclusion of opinions other than those of the editorial board a matter of public interest. In this regard, we want to clarify that by no means are we restricting freedom of expression, but rather that we reserve for ourselves the review of new releases, a fundamental section for a film magazine."[30] If reader contributions had originally expanded on the post-screening discussion, they now encroached on territory that *Gente de Cine*'s editors were unwilling to cede. Some worked professionally as film critics, notably editor-in-chief Andrés José Rolando Fustiñana (Roland), and their livelihood depended on their role as arbiters of opinion. The often unfulfilled promise of reader participation persisted in film society magazines into the 1960s: *Tiempo de Cine* promised to devote space to reader letters in November 1960 and in February 1961, but only began to publish correspondence in 1963.[31]

While sections devoted to reader contributions failed to fulfill the promise of spirited debate between equals, they nonetheless led to memorable exchanges. One such dialogue, which unfolded in *Gente de Cine*, pitted a defense of "art for art's sake" against the imperative that films incorporate moral or social "messages." In a brief text published in October 1951, director Leopoldo Torre Nilsson rejects this latter idea, writing, "A film that proposes a message displeases like a sonnet whose last verse recommends a brand of cigarettes."[32] A lengthy response by writer Leo Sala, who introduces himself as a bookseller and frames his text as

138 CHAPTER 7

a tongue-in-check sales pitch, appeared in the following issue. Sala—who would become known for his film columns published in mass-circulation magazines starting in the late 1950s—recommends that Torre Nilsson acquire the complete works of Dostoevsky to familiarize himself with the Russian author's conviction that literature should serve the highest aims, namely religious salvation.[33] Noting that he was left cold by Torre Nilsson's short *El muro* (*The Wall*, 1947), which he describes as "perfect art and one of the purest things there has been in the history of cinema," Sala ironically states, "But I am just a bookseller, easily influenced by the renown of those celebrities who speak [here he quotes Torre Nilsson] 'with growing and terrifying naturalness' of messages in art."

Sala signals his inferior position in relation to Torre Nilsson within a hierarchy of cultural workers while nevertheless asserting his right to criticize the filmmaker's claims. In the letter's opening, Sala notes that in his profession "one in some way helps to 'distribute' culture" before going on to borrow the authority of a celebrated author to justify his subjective impressions. While Torre Nilsson was still early in his career in 1951—he had a single feature film credit, *El crimen de Oribe* (*The Crime of Oribe*, 1950), which he codirected with his father, Leopoldo Torres Ríos—Sala's text nevertheless feels daring given the divide separating filmmaker and spectator. In March 1952, Torre Nilsson renewed the polemic, suggesting his own reading list to Sala (namely, a critic who affirmed that Dostoevsky's merits were entirely separate from the moral lessons he sought to convey) and "congratulat[ing] him [Sala] for his resolution to keep selling books, for it seems it would be quite terrible if he resolved to write them."[34] Attacking Sala's erudition, Torre Nilsson reserves the role of cultural producer for himself.

As this example suggests, sections like the "Tribuna de los socios" opened space for member/reader reflections on film while simultaneously reinforcing the cultural authority of cine club organizers and filmmakers. Nevertheless, film society magazines proved somewhat insecure about their own critical clout given their generally dim view of the state of local discourse on cinema. As a result, cine club periodicals endeavored to connect their readers with a vibrant film culture always imagined as elsewhere.

COSMOPOLITAN HORIZONS

When the Uruguayan *Cine Club* resumed publication in June 1952 after a gap of more than a year, it announced a new program of activity with an international scope. Reflecting local intellectuals' perception that they inhabited the periphery of film culture, the editors affirmed: "The relative isolation in which our critics must work, distanced from the major centers of international opinion, and without possibilities of direct discussion, will motivate the inclusion in future issues of commissioned contributions from abroad, in order to facilitate the exchange and very necessary confrontation of ideas."[35] *Cine Club* ceased publication a year and a half later without bringing this goal to fruition beyond a few scattered articles.[36] Yet texts by foreign correspondents and works translated from European and US publications often dominated the pages of Latin American cine club magazines.

During the 1950s, articles from foreign magazines most often worked to contextualize cine club programming through interviews with directors, excerpts from their books and essays, and critics' reflections on individual films and filmmakers. Translation also played a key role in magazines' efforts to elevate discourse on cinema from subjective evaluation to theoretical reflection. Writings by Rudolf Arnheim and Vsevolod Pudovkin, now considered part of the canon of classical film theory, appeared alongside seminal texts for 1950s movements. Cesare Zavattini's "Alcune idee sul cinema" (Some Ideas on the Cinema), which articulated the ideals of Italian neorealism, was serialized in *Gente de Cine* in 1953; Alexandre Astruc's 1948 essay "The Birth of an Avant-Garde: *La caméra-stylo*," a precursor of the French *politique des auteurs*, was published in *Cuadernos de Cine* at the height of the *nouvelle vague* in the early 1960s.[37] Beginning in the 1960s, excerpts from film scripts, including Alain Resnais's *Hiroshima mon amour* (1959), Federico Fellini's *La dolce vita* (1960), and Jean-Luc Godard's *Vivre sa vie* (1961), began to appear as well, offering readers a glimpse into the production process.[38] Foreign periodicals and books also made their presence felt in bibliographic sections and citations in quasi-academic essays. Although cine club magazines borrowed from each other and from local publications, like the Uruguayan weekly *Marcha*, the bulk of their sources were European: *Sight and Sound* (1932–present) and *Sequence* (1947–52) from the UK; *Bianco e Nero* and *Cinema Nuovo* (1952–96) from Italy; and *Cine Club* (1947–66; the magazine was renamed in 1954 with a title that incorporated the current year, e.g., *Cinéma 61*), *L'Écran français* (1948–52), *Cahiers du cinéma* (1951–present), *Cinémonde* (1928–66), and *Revue du cinéma* (1928–48) from France. US publications such as *Films in Review* (1950–96) and Jonas and Adolfas Mekas's magazine *Film Culture* (1955–96) figure as sources more infrequently.

Beyond these links to international film culture mediated by print publications, Latin American cine club magazines drew heavily on the work of foreign correspondents. Periodicals took advantage of preplanned trips by editors that reflected the cosmopolitan yearnings and geographic mobility of film societies' largely upper-middle-class leadership. For instance, in 1952, *Film* announced that editors Giselda Zani and Julio Ponce de León would respectively send reports from the Venice film festival and the United States.[39] In other cases, editors relied on contacts abroad. Argentine and Uruguayan publications most often listed foreign correspondents across the Río de la Plata and across Brazil, with representatives from Bolivia, Chile, and Paraguay mentioned more rarely. Magazines' connections with Europe were especially robust, with the largest number of correspondents hailing from Southern European countries (Italy, Spain, Portugal, France). West Germany,

140   CHAPTER 7

the USSR, and Poland were represented less frequently. *Tiempo de Cine* had a particularly prominent lineup of foreign correspondents, including Italian Marxist critic Guido Aristarco; George N. Fenin, an editor of *Film Culture* with close links to the New American Cinema Group; and Jerzy Toeplitz, founder of Poland's Łódź Film School and longtime president of the Fédération internationale des archives du film.[40]

This cosmopolitanism became a target of criticism by the early 1960s as left-leaning intellectuals championed the quest for an "authentic" national culture in response to what was increasingly viewed as cultural colonization by the United States and Europe. Writing in *Cuadernos de Cine Club* in April 1963, Manuel Martínez Carril commented skeptically on *Tiempo de Cine*'s reliance on foreign contributors, who had penned almost 40 percent of the articles in the magazine's first twelve issues. The critic observed, "Each of these correspondents has a point of view shaped by a different milieu (New York, Paris, Italy, Montevideo) but does not represent an Argentine perspective. We want to know what they really think in Buenos Aires about various aspects of cinema."[41] Three years later, Martínez Carril acknowledged *Cuadernos de Cine Club*'s own role in this dynamic. In a retrospective look at Uruguayan film criticism, he reflected that "we were indiscriminately following *Cahiers, Sight and Sound* or any other foreign magazine."[42] More broadly, he noted a disconnect between film criticism and pressing social issues that enabled intellectuals to turn their back on the nation: "All the cinema that is seen and written about in Montevideo is foreign. Thus, for a generation of critics, writing about cinema is an understandable vocation because it avoids any reference to our own reality and because it works in favor of the culture of consumers that to some extent characterizes us. Watching and writing about foreign cinema allowed a generation to evade its responsibilities."[43] Viewed from the vantage point of the late 1960s, the efforts of film society magazines to open up international horizons to their readers read as a means of sidestepping social commitments, suggesting the intense politicization of Latin American film culture during the decade.

CONCLUSION

Working locally to expand its members' critical faculties (albeit within strict limits) while facilitating international connections, Latin American cine club periodicals embodied the contradictions of the organizations that created them. Through the early 1960s, cine clubs cultivated national film culture largely through exposure to European and US films and criticism, rather than through attention to domestic or regional film production, an approach reflected in the translations and reports from foreign correspondents that appeared in their magazines' pages. In a similarly counterintuitive way, these periodicals actively solicited reader opinions while jealously defending professional critics' and filmmakers' role as cultural arbiters. Cine club magazines thus registered the simultaneously elitist and democratizing impulses that pervaded the postwar film society movement in Latin America.

NOTES

1. "A los lectores," *Gente de Cine*, March 1951, 1. For a detailed look at this periodical, see Ana Broitman, "La cinefilia en la Argentina: cineclubes, crítica y revistas de cine en las décadas de 1950 y 1960" (PhD thesis, Universidad de Buenos Aires, 2020), 215–72. Broitman notes that prior to the launch of its magazine, the Gente de Cine club published a brief bulletin starting in 1945.

2. On the perceived flaws of local film criticism, see R.O., "Omisiones de la prensa nacional: la crítica cinematográfica," *Cine Club*, September 1949, 8; Ad-Hoc [pseud.], "Sin mala intención," *Gente de Cine*, May 1953, 3; and Homero Alsina Thevenet, "La cultura cinematográfica en el Uruguay: situación hasta la fecha," *Film*, November–December 1953, 28–32.

3. "Editorial," *Cine Club* (Montevideo, Uruguay), May 1949, 1.

4. Cine Universitario temporarily replaced its hand programs with *Film* in 1952. "La cultura cinematográfica (Uruguay 1952)," *Film*, December 1952, 32.

5. "Principio," *Film*, March 1952, 1.

6. Typically, film societies' noncommercial character was guaranteed by making screenings open only to members. These and similar conditions were enforced by the Fédération internationale des ciné-clubs and the Fédération internationale des archives du film, whose members provided cine clubs with many of their vintage prints.

7. For example, a list of bookstores that carried *Gente de Cine* appeared in the magazine. *Gente de Cine*, July 1953, 14. *Tiempo de Cine* was available at both bookstores and newsstands according to "Libros y revistas," *Cuadernos de Cine Club*, April 1963, 92.

8. For instance, in March 1951 *Gente de Cine* reproduced program notes on *Antoine et Antoinette* (Jacques Becker, 1947) that had appeared in a 1950 issue of *Cine Club*. A dossier on Alberto Cavalcânti that was published in *Film* in September 1953 was reprinted in English translation in *The Quarterly of Film Radio and Television*. See Emir Rodríguez Monegal, "Alberto Cavalcanti," *The Quarterly of Film Radio and Television* 9, no. 4 (Summer 1955): 341–58.

9. *Tiempo de Cine* is the most extensively studied of Latin American cine club magazines. See Daniela Kozak, *La mirada cinéfila: la modernización de la crítica en la revista* Tiempo de Cine (Mar del Plata, Argentina: 28 Festival Internacional de Cine de Mar del Plata, 2013); and Ana Broitman, "Aprender mirando: Los cineclubes y sus revistas como espacios de enseñanza-aprendizaje del cine en las décadas de los cincuenta y sesenta," *Toma Uno* 3 (2014): 233–45.

10. *Tiempo de Cine*, April–June 1961, 48.

11. Christophe Gauthier, *La passion du cinéma: cinéphiles, ciné-clubs et salles specialisées à Paris de 1920 à 1929* (Paris: Association Française de Recherche sur l'Histoire du Cinéma, 1999), 14.

12. The literature on the Chaplin Club is extensive; see, for example, Ismail Xavier, *Sétima arte, um culto moderno: o idealismo estético e o cinema* (São Paulo, Brazil: Editora Perspectiva, 1978), 199–263; Fabricio Felice Alves dos Santos, "A apoteose da imagem: cineclubismo e crítica cinematográfica no Chaplin Club" (master's thesis, Programa de Pós-graduação em Imagem e Som, Universidade Federal de São Carlos, 2012); Tatiana Heise and Andrew Tudor, "Constructing (Film) Art: Bourdieu's Field Model in a Comparative Context," *Cultural Sociology* 1, no. 2 (2007): 165–87.

13. "Nós, de novo," *O Fan*, October 1928, 1.

14. "Sessão especial do Chaplin-Club: apresentação de 'A Caixa de Pandora,'" *O Fan*, January 1930, 4.

15. Eugenio Hintz, *Algo para recordar: la verdadera historia del Cine Club del Uruguay* (Montevideo, Uruguay: Ediciones de la Plaza, 1998), 19. On *Cine Club* and other Uruguayan film society periodicals, see also Mariana Amieva, *De amores diversos: derivas de la cultura cinematográfica uruguaya (1944–1963)* (Quilmes, Argentina: Universidad Nacional de Quilmes, 2023).

142   CHAPTER 7

16. Hintz, *Algo para recordar*, 19–20.

17. Hintz, *Algo para recordar*, 31, 39.

18. *Cuadernos de Cine Club*, July 1962.

19. On the links between Argentine and Uruguayan cine clubs documented in *Gente de Cine*, see Ana Broitman, "'Por los cine-clubs': dinámicas de intercambio entre cineclubes argentinos y uruguayos en la revista *Gente de Cine*," *Revista Encuentros Latinoamericanos* 4, no. 2 (2020): 96–115.

20. M[anuel] Martínez Carril, "Chau a los súpercriticos," *Cuadernos de Cine Club*, December 1966, 17.

21. On this publication, see José Américo Ribeiro, *O cinema em Belo Horizonte: do cineclubismo à produção cinematográfica na década de 60* (Belo Horizonte, Brazil: Editora Universidade Federal de Minas Gerais, 1997), 63–93; and Mario Alves Coutinho and Paulo Augusto Gomes, eds., *Presença do CEC: 50 anos de cinema em Belo Horizonte* (Belo Horizonte, Brazil: Crisálida, 2001).

22. Jeffrey Middents, *Writing National Cinema: Film Journals and Film Culture in Peru* (Hanover, NH: Dartmouth College Press, 2009), 47, 49–50.

23. "La opinión ajena," *Cuadernos de Cine Club*, January 1963, 81–3. See also Martínez Carril, "Chau a los súpercriticos," 20.

24. Both *cahiers* and *cuadernos* translate to "notebooks."

25. *Cuadernos de Cine Club*, October 1963, 2.

26. Broitman, "Aprender mirando," 322.

27. See Zoë Druick, "UNESCO, Film, and Education: Mediating Postwar Paradigms of Communication," in *Useful Cinema*, ed. Charles Acland and Haidee Wasson, 81–102. The literature on the Office catholique international du cinéma is considerable; see, for example, Léo Bonneville, *Soixante-dix ans au service du cinéma et de l'audiovisuel* (Anjou, Québec: Editions Fides, 1998); Gaye Ortiz, "The Catholic Church and Its Attitude to Film as an Arbiter of Cultural Meaning," in *Mediating Religion: Conversations in Media, Religion, and Culture*, ed. Jolyon P. Mitchell and Sophia Marriage (London: T&T Clark, 2003), 179–88; Fernando Ramírez Llorens, "So Close to God, So Close to Hollywood: Catholics and the Cinema in Argentina," *Journal of Latin American Cultural Studies* 23, no. 4 (2014): 325–44.

28. Rielle Navitski, "The Cine Club de Colombia and Postwar Cinephilia in Latin America: Forging Transatlantic Networks, Schooling Local Audiences," *Historical Journal of Film, Radio and Television* 38, no. 4 (2018): 808–27.

29. Navitski, "The Cine Club de Colombia and Postwar Cinephilia in Latin America," 816.

30. "Tribuna de los socios," *Gente de Cine*, September 1952, 11.

31. "Miscelánea," *Tiempo de Cine*, November–December 1960, 24; "Espacio y *Tiempo de Cine*," *Tiempo de Cine*, February–March 1961, 36; "Cartas de los lectores," *Tiempo de Cine*, July 1963, 44.

32. Leopoldo Torre Nilsson, "Sobre el mensaje," *Gente de Cine*, October 1951, 2.

33. Leo Sala, "Cartas de un vendedor de libros al Sr. Leopoldo Torre Nilsson," *Gente de Cine*, November–December 1951, 10.

34. Leopoldo Torre Nilsson, "Tribuna de los socios," *Gente de Cine*, March–April 1952, 10. The debate continued in Pedro Barstz, "Crítica de la crítica del cine," *Gente de Cine*, February–March 1953, 4; and Leopoldo Torre Nilsson, "Mensaje y compromiso," *Gente de Cine*, August–September 1953, 1. On Sala's career, see Lelia González, "Leo Sala, la crítica como mediación," *Imagofagia* 5 (2012), http://asaeca.org/imagofagia/index.php/imagofagia/article/view/701.

35. "Punto crítico," *Cine Club* (Montevideo, Uruguay), June 1952, 1.

36. Eugenio Hintz, "Con Alexander Mackendrick en los estudios Ealing," *Cine Club*, December 1952, 14–15; see also a series of heated letters relating to Giselda Zani's participation in the 1952 FIAF conference, "Cartas," *Cine Club*, December 1953, 32–42.

37. Vsevolod Pudovkin, "Teatro y cine," *Gente de Cine*, July 1951, 7; Vsevolod Pudovkin, "Peculiaridades del material cinematográfico," *Séptimo Arte*, July–August 1956, 15–18; Rudolf Arnheim, "Film y realidad," *Cine Foro*, September–October 1964, n.p.; "Astruc: La caméra-stylo," *Cuadernos de Cine Club*, January 1963, 66–69; Zavattini's text appeared in *Gente de Cine* between May 1953 and November 1953.

LATIN AMERICAN CINE CLUB MAGAZINES   143

38. *Cuadernos de Cine Club*'s inaugural February 1961 issue, distributed to club members only, was devoted to *La dolce vita* and included a Spanish translation of the full script. Fragments also appeared in *Tiempo de Cine* in September, October, and November–December 1960. *Tiempo de Cine* published a scene from *Hiroshima mon amour* in August 1960, and *Cuadernos de Cine Club* dialogue from *Vivre sa vie* in April 1963.

39. *"Film* en el exterior," *Film*, August 1952, 30.

40. *Tiempo de Cine*, February–March 1961, 2.

41. M[anuel] M[ártinez] C[arril], "Libros-revistas," *Cuadernos de Cine Club*, April 1963, 92.

42. Martínez Carril, "Chau a los súpercriticos," 21.

43. Martínez Carril, "Chau a los súpercriticos," 19.

PUBLICATIONS REFERENCED

Bianco e Nero (Italy)
Cahiers du cinéma (France)
Cine Club (Colombia)
Cine Club (France), later *Cinéma 61*
Cine Club (Mexico)
Cine Club (Uruguay), later *Cuadernos de Cine Club*
Cine Foro (Chile)
Cineclub (Brazil)
Cinéma 61 (France), previously *Cine Club*
Cinema Nuovo (Italy)
Cinémonde (France)
Cuadernos de Cine Club (Uruguay), previously *Cine Club*
L'Écran français (France)
Film (Uruguay), later *Nuevo Film* (Uruguay)
Film Culture (United States)
Films in Review (United States)
Gente de Cine (Argentina)
Hablemos de Cine (Peru)
Le Journal du Ciné-club (France)
Marcha (Uruguay)
Nuevo Film (Uruguay), previously *Film*
O Fan (Brazil)
O Globo (Brazil)
O Paiz (Brazil)
The Quarterly of Film Radio and Television (United States)
Revista de Cinema (Brazil)
Revue du Cinéma (France)
Séptimo Arte (Chile)
Sequence (United Kingdom)
Sight and Sound (United Kingdom)
Tiempo de Cine (Argentina)

BIBLIOGRAPHY

Alves Coutinho, Mario, and Paulo Augusto Gomes, eds. *Presença do CEC: 50 anos de cinema em Belo Horizonte*. Belo Horizonte, Brazil: Crisálida, 2001.

144   CHAPTER 7

Alves dos Santos, Fabricio Felice. "A apoteose da imagem: cineclubismo e crítica cinematográfica no Chaplin Club." Master's thesis, Programa de Pós-graduação em Imagem e Som, Universidade Federal de São Carlos, 2012.

Américo Ribeiro, José. *O cinema em Belo Horizonte: do cineclubismo à produção cinematográfica na década de 60.* Belo Horizonte, Brazil: Editora Universidade Federal de Minas Gerais, 1997.

Amieva, Mariana. *De amores diversos: derivas de la cultura cinematográfica uruguaya (1944–1963).* Quilmes, Argentina: Universidad Nacional de Quilmes, 2023.

Bonneville, Léo. *Soixante-dix ans au service du cinéma et de l'audiovisuel.* Anjou, Québec: Editions Fides, 1998.

Broitman, Ana. "Aprender mirando: los cineclubes y sus revistas como espacios de enseñanza-aprendizaje del cine en las décadas de los cincuenta y sesenta." *Toma Uno* 3 (2014): 233–45.

———. "La cinefilia en la Argentina: cineclubes, crítica y revistas de cine en las décadas de 1950 y 1960." PhD thesis, Universidad de Buenos Aires, 2021.

———. "'Por los cine-clubs': dinámicas de intercambio entre cineclubes argentinos y uruguayos en la revista *Gente de Cine.*" *Revista Encuentros Latinoamericanos* 4, no. 2 (2020): 96–115.

Druick, Zoë. "UNESCO, Film, and Education: Mediating Postwar Paradigms of Communication." In *Useful Cinema*, edited by Charles Acland and Haidee Wasson, 81–102. Durham, NC: Duke University Press, 2011.

Gauthier, Christophe. *La passion du cinema: cinéphiles, ciné-clubs et salles specialisées à Paris de 1920 à 1929.* Paris: Association française de recherche sur l'histoire du cinéma, 1999.

González, Lelia. "Leo Sala, la crítica como mediación." *Imagofagia* 5 (2012). http://asaeca.org/imagofagia/index.php/imagofagia/article/view/701.

Heise, Tatiana, and Andrew Tudor. "Constructing (Film) Art: Bourdieu's Field Model in a Comparative Context." *Cultural Sociology* 1, no. 2 (2007): 165–87.

Hintz, Eugenio. *Algo para recordar: la verdadera historia del Cine Club del Uruguay.* Montevideo, Uruguay: Ediciones de la Plaza, 1998.

Kozak, Daniela. *La mirada cinéfila: la modernización de la crítica en la revista* Tiempo de Cine. Mar del Plata, Argentina: 28 Festival Internacional de Cine de Mar del Plata, 2013.

Middents, Jeffrey. *Writing National Cinema: Film Journals and Film Culture in Peru.* Hanover, NH: Dartmouth College Press, 2009.

Monegal, Emir Rodriguez. "Alberto Cavalcanti." *The Quarterly of Film Radio and Television* 9, no. 4 (Summer 1955): 341–58.

Navitski, Rielle. "The Cine Club de Colombia and Postwar Cinephilia in Latin America: Forging Transatlantic Networks, Schooling Local Audiences." *Historical Journal of Film, Radio and Television* 38, no. 4 (2018): 808–27.

Ortiz, Gaye. "The Catholic Church and Its Attitude to Film as an Arbiter of Cultural Meaning." In *Mediating Religion: Conversations in Media, Religion, and Culture*, edited by Jolyon P. Mitchell and Sophia Marriage, 179–88. London: T&T Clark, 2003.

Ramírez Llorens, Fernando. "So Close to God, So Close to Hollywood: Catholics and the Cinema in Argentina." *Journal of Latin American Cultural Studies* 23, no. 4 (2014): 325–44.

Xavier, Ismail. *Sétima arte, um culto moderno: o idealismo estético e o cinema.* São Paulo, Brazil: Editora Perspectiva, 1978.

8

Hands-On Cinema

Film und Lichtbild *(1912–1914) and the Promise of Amateur Science*

Michael Cowan

Studying early film journals can teach us much about the institutionalization of cinema and its attendant cultural claims, as well as the early history of institutions such as film criticism, film theory, arthouse cinema, and genres. But journal history can also help us understand when, how, and why more specialized communities of interest—educational, professional, political, and so on—came to see film and cinema as a matter of concern. That does not mean that we should take such groups' pronouncements at face value, since every constituency had vested interests in normative definitions of cinema (as art, as political "weapon," as national industry, etc.). But we can gain insight into questions such as why different communities turned to cinema when they did, what presuppositions they brought to bear upon it, what questions they looked for it to answer, and what potentials of cinema they helped to make intelligible.

In the German context, much has been written about the pioneering trade journals such as *Der Kinematograph* (founded in 1907 and usually considered the first German-language film journal) and *Die Lichtbild-Bühne* (1908),[1] as well as the role of film journals in the development of film criticism.[2] But we can also learn a lot from the more specialized publications—on educational film, amateur film, film technology, film and politics—that dotted the early film publishing scene. In this chapter, I examine the short-lived journal *Film und Lichtbild* (1912–14) as part of a broad-based "discovery" of film and cinema by amateur science communities in the early 1910s. Why, the chapter asks, did such groups come to see film as a sector important enough to merit an independent journal? What questions, preconceptions, and desires did they bring to it? What kind of "company"—to borrow a term from Greg Waller—did film keep in their publications?[3] That is, what other kinds of technologies, practices, and social imaginaries was cinema associated with in

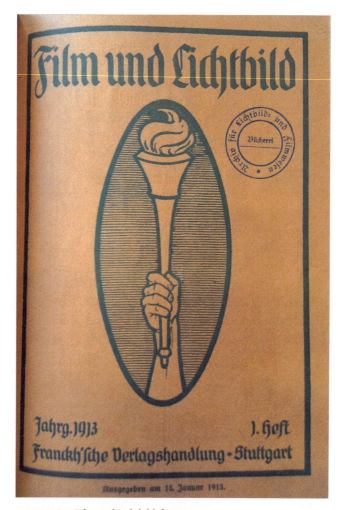

FIGURE 8.1. *Film und Lichtbild*, front cover, January 1913.

the journal's pages? And what does this tell us about the conception of cinema and its potentials being worked out here? Finally, what kind of readerly community did these journals imagine building around film as they understood it? As I will argue, to answer these questions, we need to approach a publication like *Film und Lichtbild* not only in the context of film publishing but also in the context of publishing in amateur science.

SCIENCE DISCOVERS CINEMA

Launched in July 1912 by the journalist Fritz (Friederich) Seitz from the popular science publishing house Franck'sche Verlag, *Film und Lichtbild* described its mission in its inaugural editorial as that of "fostering the undeniable advantages of cinematographic technology for various scientific fields."[4] This idea of cultivating film for science hardly arose in isolation, as the period just after 1910 was marked by a broad-based turn towards science and education in German film culture. Of course, "scientific" films had existed since the earliest days of the cinematograph, with precursors in lantern slides and chronophotography. But such films, often screened as part of a larger entertainment program, were not yet supported by a separate distribution infrastructure.[5] This began to change around 1910 with the rise of a wave of new journals dedicated to scientific and educational uses of cinema, including not only *Film und Lichtbild*, but also the Viennese *Kastalia* (founded in 1911), the Mönchen-Gladbach–based *Bild und Film* (founded in 1912), and several others. The launch of these publications coincided with the rise of other related (and often directly affiliated) initiatives, including the opening of special screening venues for educational cinema such as the Altonaer Lichtbildtheater in Hamburg, the Fata Morgana cinema in Dresden, and the Universum and Kosmos cinemas in Vienna;[6] the creation of specialized distribution networks for educational film, such as the Lichtbilderei GmbH in Mönchen-Gladbach (founded in 1912); and the first film societies dedicated to educational cinema, such as the Kastalia Gesellschaft in Vienna and the Kinematographische Studiengesellschaft in Berlin.[7]

To understand this upsurge in the promotion of scientific and educational film after 1910, we might begin by asking why the idea gained so much traction when it did. An obvious starting point is that these initiatives were inseparable from the well-known "cinema reform" movement, in which medical and juridical authorities such as Albert Hellwig characterized entertainment cinema (often with the derogatory term *Schundfilm* or "trash film") as a public health crisis and sought to curb its effects through state intervention. Cinema reform, in turn, can be understood only against the backdrop of the boom in entertainment movie houses around 1910, as cinema became increasingly viable as a middle-class leisure activity. As the most oft-repeated formulation of the time had it, cinemas were "popping up from the ground like mushrooms," and the reform movement was almost certainly driven in part by fears about their expansion from the lower-class peripheries into affluent urban districts.[8]

Since the rapid growth of movie theaters posed a direct form of competition for audiences, institutions of popular science felt cinema's newfound prominence in a particular way. For instance, the Berlin Urania Institute, Germany's most prominent public venue, founded in 1888 for popular science lectures, courses, and exhibitions, noted in its annual financial report for 1911: "The unprecedented increase in . . . movie houses in Berlin has exerted an adverse influence on our society's financial operations this year."[9] It is hardly a coincidence that the Urania first introduced films into their own scientific lecture series the following year (1912, the same year that *Film und Lichtbild* was founded).[10]

In some ways, as Frank Kessler and Sabine Lenk have argued, cinema reform and educational cinema were simply two sides of the same coin, since both sought

148   CHAPTER 8

to counter the increasing clout of entertainment cinema with more "edifying" uses.[11] Yet amateur science publications like *Film und Lichtbild* were also at pains to distinguish their mission from the alarmist stance associated with reformers. Thus, the journal's opening editorial from 1912 told readers in no uncertain terms that it would go beyond the tired reformist complaints about cinema's "harmful excesses" (*schädliche Auswüchse*) to focus on the beneficial potentials of cinematography, especially for science.[12] Hence, while a journal like *Film und Lichtbild* might have shared some of the reformers' misgivings about entertainment cinema, it wanted its approach understood differently: as an effort to establish and cultivate a genuine passion for "quality" film, understood here in scientific terms.

But perhaps we should turn the question about historical timing around and ask what exactly these groups were discovering in the cinema. As the title *Film und Lichtbild* (*Film and Photo/Slide Projection*) suggests, their understanding focused less on feature films for the big screen than on the broader world of optical projection media—an idea also borne out in the publication's opening editorial, which characterizes film as "a new branch of optical technology."[13] Accordingly, the journal ran not only articles on cinematography but also regular reports on amateur slide production, stereoscopic images, and related areas of still photographic media.[14] The majority of articles that did treat cinematography tended to explore its widest technological potentials, ranging from amateur cinema apparatuses to panoramic cinema for geography lessons, from cinematic shooting galleries for military training to so-called diaphragmatic projections for teaching planar geometry.[15] *Film und Lichtbild* was not alone here, as other journal titles (such as *Bild und Film*) suggest. The specialty cinemas, film clubs, and distribution networks mentioned above were also a case in point, as they never limited themselves to moving images but understood their remit to cover a broad range of optical media, focused in particular on the idea of the visual "lecture." The Lichtbilderei GmbH, for example, provided not only films but also complete audiovisual lectures, as well as projection apparatuses for slides and moving images.[16] Specialty cinemas were also being conceived in this hybrid manner, as Otto Theodor Stein wrote in another article for *Film und Lichtbild*: "My ideal cinema [Musterkino] would not be a pure movie theatre, but rather a kind of lecture space with a main stage and separate rooms for cinematographic lectures."[17]

One could interpret this "hybrid" understanding of cinema as a typical manifestation of early film culture, where slides and film still regularly shared the stage.[18] But more than other groups, scientific communities had good reason to cling to still images alongside film, since they offered a key means (alongside the speech of lecturers) for ensuring that moving images would serve the ends of knowledge transmission. Reports like the following, from *Film und Lichtbild* on a screening of deep-sea films by the Cologne Society of Natural Scientists, were numerous: "Since rapid moving images often leave no time for the recognition of details, the screening was preceded by slides, in which the lecturer could show audiences what to look for."[19] Similarly, in an article on film and statistics, Friederich Felix explained that "all rules of mnemotechnics fail when confronted with the speed of this type of visualization" and insisted on the "aid of still slides."[20] Something analogous was almost certainly at stake in the first Urania show to integrate film in late 1912, "Geheimnisse der belebten Natur" (Secrets of Living Nature), in which Dr. Wilhelm Berndt of the Berlin Zoological Institute showed a mix of films he himself had made and films borrowed from Jean Comandon and the Neue Photographische Gesellschaft. As Berndt recalled in an article for *Film und Lichtbild*, it was arduous work learning to present the films in such a way that "from this jumble of nearly indecipherable actions there could emerge a little drama . . . , in which biological comedy and tragedy could achieve clear expression."[21] This was achieved partly through the use of still images, as a separate report on Berndt's show for the journal explained: "[Dr. Berndt] explained the content of the films in advance, in a humorous and easily comprehensible manner, by means of spoken word and still images."[22] This emphasis on combining still and moving images also explains the keen interest these groups took in projectors that could be paused (a technology that was only just starting to become viable).[23]

Clearly, then, any understanding of this approach to cinema as a "new branch of optical technology" requires that we look back to the world of popular science from which it emerged. That field had been undergoing a pictorial turn for decades through illustrated publications, exhibitions, and slide lectures.[24] As the case of the Urania shows, cinema likely appeared as the next step in this process, albeit one that had to be approached with some care. This is, indeed, the way in which film was conceived in a journal like *Film und Lichtbild*: as an optical medium that was quickly becoming indispensable to both the practice and popularization of science.

SCIENTIFIC PUBLISHING

At the same time, the particular take on cinema espoused in *Film und Lichtbild* also speaks to more specific questions of science *publishing* and the way it conceived of its readerly communities. As print historians such as Ina Pfizer and Klaus Taschwer have shown, popular science literature experienced a boom in Germany starting around the turn of the twentieth century, when several major publishers shifted their focus from fiction to science and technology and numerous new popular science journals came on the scene.[25] This was, in part, a story of economics, as publishing houses discovered that the new demand for popular science offered a lucrative market niche and a new generation of science journalists emerged to meet the need. But that increased demand for popular science was itself driven by cultural factors, above all by the culture of "self-betterment" that arose in the late nineteenth century to fill the growing leisure time of the middle

150   CHAPTER 8

classes—particularly in the form of clubs and associations (*Vereine* in German), which provided a key terrain for traveling lecturers and to which so many of these journals sought to appeal.

The idea of popular science as a form of self-betterment also had deeper roots, stretching back at least to Alexander von Humboldt's sweeping *Kosmos. Entwurf einer physischen Weltbeschreibung* (*Cosmos: A Sketch of a Physical Description of the Universe*), which began as a series of public lectures at the University of Berlin (1827–28) before becoming one of the best-selling books of the nineteenth century and a staple of bourgeois self-instruction. The appeal of Humboldt's model resided largely in its promise to compensate for the increasing abstraction and specialization of scientific knowledge by offering an accessible overview, grounded in the first-person experience of the polymath author.[26] This promise helped to outline the horizon of expectation in which subsequent popular scientific groups would operate. Institutions such as the Urania (founded in 1888) sought explicitly to build on the Humboldtian model of making abstract scientific knowledge comprehensible and experiential for lay people. In this context, there was a strong emphasis on "visual education," but perhaps more broadly on *experiential* participation: the culture of amateur science thrived on the promise to allow audiences to experience science and research for themselves.

This is the context in which amateur scientific publishing took off, and the story of Franck'sche Verlag offers an insightful case study. Founded in 1822 as a landing place for fiction (including names like Wilhelm Hauff, E. T. A. Hoffmann, and Walter Scott), the press changed its remit shortly before 1900 to become one of the most successful publishers of popular science, home to many of the key authors in the field, such as Ernst Haeckel disciple Wilhelm Bölsche, Urania founder Max Wilhelm Meyer, and Raoul Heinrich Francé, a proponent of amateur microscopy.[27] Particularly influential, as Pfitzer has shown, was the publisher's flagship journal *Kosmos: Handweiser für Naturfreunde* (founded in 1904), which would remain in circulation until the end of the twentieth century. In their inaugural editorial, the editors of *Kosmos* (citing Humboldt as their model) characterized the journal as a space where readers could gain an accessible overview of scientific knowledge, despite the "unavoidable specialization" of current research. Just as importantly, they emphasized the importance of experiential learning and promised to help readers bridge expert knowledge and everyday experience through "participation in scientific research": either vicarious participation through the study of the journal's richly illustrated articles (which carefully translated expert knowledge into lay terms)[28] or more active participation by following the journal's lead to "undertake one's own observations." All of this, moreover, was framed as a means of self-betterment: "Research in natural sciences and the participation in such research through study . . . influence one's outlook on life and one's character, elevating thought to a higher level. Absorbing oneself in the natural sciences strengthens the intellect, the temperament and the will."[29]

Such work on the self would occur not only by reading the journal, but also through its supplemental publications, such as the series *Kosmos Bändchen* (*Kosmos Booklets*), in which prominent authors from the field covered topics ranging from planets to plants to microscopy to evolution in easily digestible, illustrated form. The Franck'sche publishing house also pioneered more experiential forms of hands-on knowledge acquisition, such as the Kosmos Baukasten, a kind of amateur laboratory allowing for experimentation with chemistry, electricity, microscopy, astronomy, wireless technology, and so on.

Moreover, like other journals published by Franck'sche Verlag (e.g., *Mikrokosmos*, launched in 1907 as a publication for the Mikrologische Gesellschaft, a club for amateur microscopy enthusiasts founded by Francé), *Kosmos* was directly linked to an amateur science society, the Kosmos Gesellschaft der Naturfreunde (Kosmos Society for Friends of Nature). The society not only provided a forum for the exchange of ideas and questions, but also organized various excursions and holiday courses for members and offered them means of acquiring affordable scientific equipment.[30] Here, amateur science publishing wasn't simply selling text but also the promise to make scientific knowledge experiential and thereby compensate for the increasing gulf between everyday experience and the abstractions of scientific knowledge.

FILM UND LICHTBILD: THE BIRTH OF AMATEUR FILM FROM AMATEUR SCIENCE

This is the context in which *Film und Lichtbild* was founded (just as *Kosmos* was reaching a circulation of one hundred thousand) to offer lay readers an insight into film and science.[31] Seitz, who had already served as an editor of *Kosmos* before launching the new film magazine, adopted many of the familiar strategies.[32] Like *Kosmos*, *Film und Lichtbild* was meant to be affordable, with subscription coupons from the first year offering readers "at least 10 richly illustrated issues for only 2 Marks" (around fifty cents at the time).[33] And it had an analogous mission, albeit at a smaller scale: namely, to offer readers an overview of the exploding field of scientific film and related optical technologies. Articles were organized most often by fields of application (biology, medicine, military science, ballistics, mathematics, geography, meteorology, visual statistics, traffic regulation, career aptitude, etc.) or by technologies and techniques (home cinema, stereoscopy, color cinematography, aerial cinematography, etc.). In addition to the articles themselves, there were numerous rubrics designed to help readers determine what was worth knowing or watching. Most prominent here was the monthly "List of Scientifically and Technologically Quality Films," which readers could consult when planning their own educational screenings.[34] Issues also contained more specific film reviews, reports on significant events, notes on new developments in the world of scientific or educational film,[35] descriptions of key figures,[36] and discussions of significant

Kosmos

Handweiser für Naturfreunde

und Zentralblatt für das
naturwissenschaftliche Bil‌-
dungs- und Sammelwesen

herausgegeben vom

Kosmos, Gesellschaft der Naturfreunde, Stuttgart

9. Jahrgang 1912

Franckh'sche Verlagshandlung in Stuttgart

FIGURE 8.2. *Kosmos Handweiser für Naturfreunde*, title page, 1912.

books and journals (including overviews of literature in other languages).[37] Like the writers for *Kosmos*, moreover, the authors for *Film und Lichtbild* consistently emphasized their ability to translate specialized research into easily comprehensible terms, with such phrases as "In accordance with the goals of the Franckh'sche publishing house, I have chosen a few texts here that make it easier for readers to work their way into this exciting material."[38] Many (if not most) articles were, in fact, summaries of longer key studies, presented in lay terms.[39]

The journal also encouraged readers to understand themselves as part of a self-conscious community with an interest in using optical technologies for scientific self-betterment. The opening editorial explicitly asked readers to "make contact with us and share their wishes."[40] The journal continued to solicit readers' participation, in particular through the letters column ("Briefkasten"), where readers could find answers to various queries (e.g., where to acquire high-quality educational film material, how to program educational film screenings, how to avoid flicker).[41] There were also regular invitations to readers to signal good films or suggest topics for coverage in the journal.[42]

Moreover, although *Film und Lichtbild* did not begin as the journal of a film club, it quickly attached itself to one when the Viennese Kinematographie Klub, founded in 1912 by schoolteacher and filmmaker Alto Arche, adopted the journal as its house publication in August 1913 and changed its name in the process to the Kosmos Klub für wissenschaftliche und künstleriche Kinematographie (Kosmos Club for Scientific and Artistic Cinematography). While the film club almost certainly chose its new name in emulation of the Kosmos Gesellschaft der Naturfreunde (with which it claimed to be affiliated),[43] the publishing house was also presumably happy to attach *Film und Lichtbild* to a prominent film club as a means of gaining dedicated readers. As the Kosmos film club explained in its inaugural statement printed in *Film und Lichtbild*, it sought to appeal not only to a small circle of filmmakers or cinemagoers, but "to every educated person who wishes to increase his knowledge in a vivid way [*in anschaulicher Weise*]" via optical technologies.[44] This remit was borne out by the group's member list, which included men and women from various areas of middle-class professional life: teachers and university lecturers (especially among the scientific governing committee), but also accountants and bank clerks; electricians, engineers, and architects; public officials and attorneys; hairdressers, tailors, and salespeople; as well as printers, artists, and theater set designers.[45]

What held this group together, I believe, was a familiarity with the ideals of popular science as a means of self-betterment—and the conviction that optical projection technologies had a role to play here. Indeed, the club's first report in *Film und Lichtbild* from 1913 sounds a note reminiscent of nothing so much as the opening editorial of the *Kosmos* science journal a decade earlier: "The development and spread of technology and natural sciences has provoked massive upheavals in every area of our cultural life in recent years. Dirigibles, airplanes, modern steamships, the feats of explorers in the North and South Pole, color photography, stereoscopic photography, and other arts are just a few examples from most recent memory. The goal of our club is to use the projected image [*Lichtbild*] to help audiences understand these scientific accomplishments, as well as the life and culture of our Earth."[46] To this end, the film club offered predrafted scientific lectures to its members and also teamed up with the publishing house to offer film equipment such as the "Kosmos Projektions-Apparat," which could be rented from the publisher for film and slide presentations in local associations. It even opened its own specialty theater in Vienna, the Kosmos Theater, which remained a specialty theater for film clubs into the late twentieth century.[47]

All of this suggests that *Film und Lichtbild* approached film as a medium of *experience*. On the one hand, film itself would help make science experiential, allowing viewers to participate vicariously in scientific research. Time and again, one encounters sentiments such as those of one writer who claimed that educational screenings can teach audiences "more than dozens of lectures and more than all books. They experience the nature of the ocean, of the Sahara Desert, of the primal forest, as if it were the result of their own research."[48] This promise of experiential "participation" in scientific research was one of the central tenets of the passion for cinema being developed in the pages of *Film und Lichtbild*, and one that it shared with other institutions of popular science film.

On the other hand, the journal's readers were encouraged, to the extent possible, to experience film technology for themselves: to get their hands on it and to see it as part of the remit of their various clubs and associations, whether this meant simply learning to run a projector or learning to produce films.[49] This objective was announced from the journal's inaugural editorial, which vowed to help enterprising readers gain access to "first-class cinematograph apparatuses, as well as valuable scientific and impeccable artistic films and slides"—a vow later realized when Franck'sche Verlag announced the founding of an "Office for First-Class Films and Slides," which also offered a projector for 147 Marks.[50] The remit was taken up again in the opening editorial for the second year, which explained: "*Film und Lichtbild* seeks to . . . spur readers on to their own experiments, to disseminate the foundational knowledge of cinematographic technology through the description of the most important apparatuses and how to operate them, and above all to offer practical tips for putting together popular scientific programs. . . . Our journal places great value on independent activity."[51] It was also the main point of a journal supplement launched in the second year entitled "Elektrotechnisches Beiheft" (Electro-Technical Supplement) with the tagline "Reports on the electro-technical features of cinema apparatuses and how to work them in easily understandable essays."[52] In this sense, the journal sought to do for cinema what amateur science had done for other scientific equipment, making it appear to be within everyone's grasp—even if most cinematic technology was unaffordable for the average reader. Here, cinema stood in the company not only of slides and related technologies, but also of scientific objects like telescopes and microscopes, as suggested vividly by the frequent appearance of the two side by side in the advertising pages of *Film und Lichtbild*.

This affinity with the instruments of amateur science also suggests that the editors of *Film und Lichtbild* understood the film culture they sought to promote as a culture of the *amateur* in a sense analogous to amateur science and its promise of participation. The journal ran numerous articles on "amateur cinema," a category that was only beginning to gain legibility as the obverse of cinema professionals,[53] in addition to reports on devices for home use, such as the Cinéphote apparatus for creating short animated family portraits,[54] the Salonkinematograph of Georges Bettini (which used glass slides not unlike Charles Urban's Spirograph to project moving images safely in the home),[55] and the Pathé KOK projector for home and schools, also known as "Kino in der Westentasche."[56] But more than a separate category of films or filmic apparatuses, the word *amateur* describes the broader horizon of expectation that writers for a journal like *Film und Lichtbild* brought to bear on cinema as such. Cinema appears, in the pages of the journal, as a sector full of promise for hands-on participation, one that, even as it was professionalizing, still held out the possibility for amateur involvement and even agency in the future of film.[57] In this way, these scientific film journals, like the early film clubs and specialty distributors with whom they collaborated, stood for a promise analogous to that of amateur science: that of humanizing a (technological) sector increasingly out of reach for ordinary people.[58]

This was, indeed, a promise that the writers for *Film und Lichtbild* knew well, as so many of them wrote amateur science publications with a similar thrust. Wilhelm Berndt, for example, in addition to lecturing at the Urania and contributing to journals such as *Film und Lichtbild*, also published books on the emerging practice of home aquariums.[59] Other writers, including Hanns Günther and Albert Neuburger, specialized in the genre of the Experimentierbuch (experiment book), with which young readers could emulate the work of professional laboratories in the amateur mode, with everything from electrical experiments to optical illusions to psychological tests to the fabrication of their own homemade color organs and spirit photographs.[60]

This world of amateur scientific participation shows us the kind of "company" that a journal like *Film und Lichtbild* kept beyond the world of film publishing, but it might also suggest one of the factors behind the early demise of these journals in the mid-1910s. The most immediate cause was, of course, the outbreak of World War I; although journals like *Film und Lichtbild* and *Bild und Film* tried to stay relevant by focusing articles on film's role in military mobilization, most of them folded by the end of 1914 due to financial difficulties. The fact that none of them was picked up again after 1918 might have something to do with the increasing professionalization of scientific film itself, its development into a distinct branch of a complexifying film industry. In the context of the Kulturfilm movement of the

FIGURE 8.3. "The Electric Human," illustration from Hanns Günther, *Experimentierbuch für die Jugend*, 1912.

1920s, science film production came increasingly to be understood as the purview of experts working in professional production units such as the UFA company's Kulturfilm department (inaugurated in 1918), in any of the new Kulturfilm studios that dotted the Weimar film scene (e.g., Deulig, founded in 1921), in companies specializing in production for schools and universities such as the Unterrichtsfilmgesellschaft GmbH (founded in 1921), or in well-funded institutes such as the Medizinisch-Kinematographisches Institut at the Berlin Charité hospital (founded in 1923).

Within this context, the few attempts to found new popular journals on film and science—such as *Film und Wissen* (1919–20)—were short lived.[61] And although Frank'sche Verlag would continue to offer films and slides through its aptly named Photokosmos department (founded in the early 1920s), it never launched another journal like *Film und Lichtbild*. Instead, "scientific film" and "amateur film" underwent a kind of functional differentiation in the publishing scene of the 1920s. For its part, scientific film migrated largely into the realm of specialized educational journals, such as the Berlin-based *Der Lehrfilm* (1921–26) or the Viennese journal *Das Bild im Dienst der Schule und Volksbildung* (1924–30, published by the Film and Image Syndicate of Viennese Teachers), as well as a few discipline-specific undertakings such as the *Programme der medizinischen Woche/Medizin und Film* (1924–30, published by the above-mentioned Unterrichtsfilmgesellschaft GmbH). The concept of "amateur film," on the other hand, also lived on, but took on a much narrower meaning in the pages of journals such as *Film für Alle* (1927–62). Here, as we know, amateur film was increasingly understood—in opposition to the professional work of the film industry—in the sense of home movies and small-gauge travel pictures, rather than a promise of cinema as such.

NOTES

1. For example, both titles have Wikipedia entries, and both merited entries in Richard Abel's *Encyclopedia of Early Cinema* (London: Routledge, 2010), 515, 553.

2. See, for example, Helmut Diederichs, *Anfänge deutscher Filmkritik* (Stuttgart, Germany: Verlag Robert Fischer und Uwe Wiedleroither, 1986); Matthias Frey, *Permanent Crisis of Film Criticism: The Anxiety of Authority* (Amsterdam: Amsterdam University Press, 2015), 81–101.

3. I borrow the idea of cinema's "company" from Greg Waller, "Beyond Fan Magazines and Trade Journals: Motion Picture Discourse in Periodicals of the 1910s," unpublished presentation at the Society of Cinema and Media Studies, April 1, 2016.

4. Opening editorial, *Film und Lichtbild* 1, no. 1 (1912), 1.

5. See, for example, Oliver Gaycken, *Devices of Curiosity: Early Cinema and Popular Science* (Oxford: Oxford University Press, 2015), 37–53, 125–28. This was precisely the situation these groups sought to change. For example, Wilhelm Berndt (a pioneer of film lectures at the Urania Institute, to whom I return below) stated in one article for *Film und Lichtbild*: "There can be no doubt that the method of weaving scientific film between marriage comedies and circus tricks . . . is the wrong one." Berndt, "Aus der Praxis der biologischen Kinematographie," *Film und Lichtbild* 2, no. 1 (2013), 4.

6. Such specialty cinemas—sometimes known as "Gemeindekinos" (municipal cinemas) since they were sometimes funded by local councils—were central to Kinoreform debates more broadly. For

158   CHAPTER 8

a book-length treatment of the problem, see Willi Warstat, *Kino und Gemeinde* (Mönchen-Gladbach, Germany: Volksverein Verlag, Lichtbühne-Bibliothek, 1913). See also Otto Theodor Stein, "Musterlichtbühnen. Ein Beitrag zur praktischen Kinoreform," *Film und Lichtbild* 2, no. 2 (1913), 19–22.

7. For a good discussion of the film societies of this period, see Otto Theodor Stein, *Kinematographische Studiengesellschaften, Film und Lichtbild* 2, no. 9–10 (1913), 139–42. This was also the period that saw the first major exhibitions on cinema such as Berlin Kino-Ausstellung of 1912. Guests of honor at this exhibition included the astronomer Friedrich Simon Archenhold (who would soon found the Cinematographic Study Society of Berlin), Franz Goerke (director of the Berlin Urania), and many others. The exhibition included displays of *Film und Lichtbild*, as well as the educational journals *Bild und Film* and *Lichtbildkunst*. For an English-language report, see "Berlin Cinematographic Congress and Exhibition," *Motography*, February 1, 1913, 81–82.

8. As leading cinema reformer Adolf Sellmann put it in an article for *Bild und Film*, "Probably no recent invention has stimulated so much discussion in the daily press and in daily conversation as the cinema. Everywhere new cinemas shoot up overnight like mushrooms. One can no longer even picture our big cities at night without the gleaming portals of the movie houses." Sellmann, "The Secret of the Cinema" (1912), cited in *The Promise of Cinema: German Film Theory 1907–1933*, ed. Anton Kaes et al. (Oakland: University of California Press, 2016), 31.

9. *Bericht des Vorstandes der Gesellschaft Urania für das Geschäftsjahr vom 1. April 1910 zum 31. März 1911* (Berlin: Urania, 1911), 5–6.

10. For records of the lectures, see *Gesellschaft Urania. Bericht des Vorstands für das Geschäftsjahr vom 1. April 1911 bis 31. März 1912* (Berlin: Urania, 1912), 5, 7.

11. Frank Kessler and Sabine Lenk, "The Kinoreformbewegung Revisited: Performing the Cinematograph as a Pedagogical Tool," in *Performing New Media, 1890–1915*, ed. Kaveh Askari et al. (Bloomington: Indiana University Press, 2014), 163–73.

12. Opening editorial, *Film und Lichtbild* 1, no. 1 (1912): 1. Other writers for the journal went further, with one stating: "It has become boring, really boring. For years, we have been hearing the same alarmist phrases about 'cinema as a public danger' repeated ad infinitum. Jurists and pedagogues vie to see who can produce the most damning judgments of cinema. State and local councils compete for the most punitive taxes and restrictive operating rules, designed to make life difficult all of the cinemas shooting out of the ground like mushrooms. . . . But the cinematograph is here. Despite all the efforts of its detractors and philistines, it will not disappear again, and every effort to eradicate it is wasted effort. . . . A genuine improvement of is achievable by working with competent experts of cinematography and not by excluding them, let alone going to battle against them." "'Der Worte sind genug gewechselt . . . ,'" *Film und Lichtbild* 2, no. 4 (1913), 65–66.

13. Opening editorial, *Film und Llichtbild* 1, no. 1 (2012), 1.

14. See, for example, Walter Böttger, "Stereoskopbilder," *Film und Lichtbild* 1, no. 5 (1912), 56–61; P. Langbein, "Ein Stereoskopbild des Mondes," *Film und Lichtbild* 2, no. 7 (1913), 106.

15. On panorama cinematography, see Hans Goetz, "Kinematographische Rundpanoramen," *Film und Lichtbild* 2, no. 3 (1913), 37–41. On the shooting galleries, see Richard Schuster, "Förderung der Schießausbildung durch die Kinematographie," *Film und Lichtbild* 1, no. 6 (1912), 79–83; Friedrich Felix, "Lebende Zielscheiben," *Film und Lichtbild* 3, no. 8 (1914), 121–22. On diaphragmatic projectors, see Erwin Papperitz, "Kinodiaphragmatische Projektionsapparate," *Bild und Film* 2, no. 2 (1913), 22–25; Otto Theodor Stein, "Kinodiaphragmatische Projektion von Prof. Dr. Papperitz," *Bild und Film* 1, no. 4 (2012), 94–95.

16. For slideshow categories, see Josef Weigl, "Die Lichtbilderei GmbH in M.Gladbach," *Bild und Film*, 1, no. 1 (1912), 9. For film categories, see "Die Filmverleih-Zentrale der 'Lichbilderei GmbH in M.Gladbach," *Bild und Film* 1, no. 1 (1912), 28.

17. Otto Theodor Stein, "Musterlichtbühnen: ein Beitrag zur praktischen Kinoreform," *Film und Lichtbild* 2, no. 2 (1913), 21.

18. See, for example, Janelle Blankenship, "To Alternate/To Attract: The Skladanowsky Experiment," *Cinema & Cie: International Film Studies Journal*, no. 9 (2007): 61–79.

19. Otto Janson, "Bilder aus dem Leben des Meeres im bewegten Lichtbild," *Film und Lichtbild* 2, no. 6 (1913), 99.

20. Friedrich Felix, "Statistische Lichtbilder,"*Film und Lichtbild* 1, no. 6 (2012), 83–84.

21. Wilhelm Berndt, "Höhere Tiere als Filmobjekte," *Film und Lichtbild* 2, no. 2 (1913), 30.

22. "Vermischtes," *Film und Lichtbild* 2, no. 1 (1913), 16.

23. Discussions of pausing mechanisms abound in *Film und Lichtbild*, as well as in other educational journals of this period. It is unclear how successful pausing mechanisms for school projectors were at this point, though one can find claims about pausable apparatuses. After encountering the Pathé KOK projector at the 1913 Kino-Kongress in Berlin, Friedrich Lambrecht reported on the apparatus as follows: "If one turns the motor off, everything continues working as before, but the filmstrip stands still, and the individual image can be used like a slide." Friedrich Lambrecht, "Vom Kinokongress und von der Kino-Ausstellung Berlin," *Film und Lichtbild* 2, no. 2 (1913), 26.

24. For an overview of the visual turn in popular nineteenth century science, see Bernard Lightman, *Victorian Popularizers of Science: Designing Nature for New Audiences* (Chicago: University of Chicago Press, 2009). For the importance of slide lectures and scientific photography in Germany, see especially Christian Joschke, *Les yeux de la nation. Photographie amateur et société dans l'Allemagne de Guillaume II (1888–1914)* (Dijon, France: Les Presses du réel, 2014), 201–27.

25. See Klaus Taschwer, "Vom Kosmos zur Wunderwelt: Über popularwissenschaftliche Magazine einst und jetzt," in *Öffentlische Wissenschaft: Neue Perspektiven der Vermittlung in der wissenschaftlichen Weiterbildung*, ed. Peter Faulstich, 80–81 (Bielefeld, Germany: Transcript, 2006); Ina Pfitzer, "Das 'Verlangen nach einer Bereicherung und Vertiefung wissenschaftlicher Kenntnisse'. Die Zeitschrift Kosmos. Handweiser für Naturfreunde—ein Beispiel erfolgreicher Leserbindung," in *Das bewegte Buch: Buchwesen und soziale, nationale und kulturelle Bewegungen um 1900*, ed. Mark Lehmstedt and Andreas Herzog, 349–68 (Wiesbaden, Germany: O. Harrassowitz, 1999).

26. In the introduction to the book, Humboldt returns repeatedly to the problem of scientific specialization and the promise to overcome the fragmentation of advanced knowledge through the identification of forces uniting the whole of the observable universe. At one point, for instance, we read: "[My object is to] prove how, without detriment to the stability of special studies, we may . . . arrive at a point of view from which all the organisms and forces of nature may be seen as one living active whole, animated by one sole impulse." Alexander von Humboldt, *Cosmos: A Sketch of the Physical Description of the Universe, vol. 1*, trans. E. C. Otté (London: Henry G. Bohn, 1864), 36.

27. See Pfitzer, "Die Zeitschift Kosmos," 350–352.

28. See Pfitzer, "Die Zeitschrift Kosmos," 360.

29. "Moderne Bildung," *Kosmos: Naturwissenschaftliche Literaturblatt* 1, no. 1 (1904), 1.

30. Pfitzer, "Die Zeitschrift Kosmos," 366.

31. On the circulation of *Kosmos*, see Pfitzer, "Die Zeitschrift Kosmos," 349.

32. On Seitz, see also "Nachlass Friederich Seitz (1890–1966)," Landesarchiv Baden-Würtemberg, n.d., https://www2.landesarchiv-bw.de/ofs21/olf/einfueh.php?bestand=6798.

33. Insert, *Film und Lichtbild* 1, no. 6 (1912), 84. As the quote suggests, images were also a key selling point, and most article headings included a note signaling the number of illustrations.

34. For the first such list, see *Film und Lichtbild* 1, no. 2 (2012), 16.

35. This occurred in particular in the section "Vermischtes" (Various). See, for example, *Film und Lichtbild* 2, no. 1 (2013), 14–15.

36. See, for example, Paul Liesegang, "Marey, der Begründer der modernen Kinematographie, "*Film und Lichtbild* 1, no. 6 (1912), 70–72.

37. See, for example, "Buchbesprechungen," *Film und Lichtbild* 1, no. 4 (1912), 48.

38. Walter Böttger, "Stereoskop-Bilder," 56. The quote also speaks to a pattern of articles referring to other publications of the Franck'sche Verlag, as when one writer began an article on stereoscopic images of planets with a reference to "the September 1912 issue of the *Kosmos Handweiser*." P. Langbein, "Das Saturn und seine Wiedergabe im Stereoskop und anderen optischen Instrumenten," *Film und Lichtbild* 2, no. 1 (1913), 8.

160   CHAPTER 8

39. For example, Bruno Glatzel's article on ballistics cinematography, published in 1913 in *Film und Lichtbild*, offered a more accessible summary of the explanations from his and Arthur Korn's *Handbuch der Phototelegraphie und Teleautographie* (1911) concerning the use of ultra-rapid spark flashes for ballistics photography and recycled the same illustrations. Glatzel thematizes the simplifying work of his article in several places, for example: "Ohne im Einzelnen auf die technische Anordnung einzugehen, mag hier nur so viel bemerkt werden, daß das Verfahren in sehr einfacher Weise gestattet, die Funkenfrequenz innerhalb der Grenzen von 200 und 100.000 zu verändern" [Without going into detail regarding the technological design, we can simply note here that the procedure makes it simple to change the frequency of sparks within a range of 200 to 100,000"]. Bruno Glatzel, "Über Geschoß-Kinematographie," *Film und Lichtbild* 2, no. 4 (1913), 57.

40. Opening editorial, *Film und Lichtbild* 1, no. 1 (1912), 1.

41. See, for example, "Briefkasten," *Film und Lichtbild* 2, no. 2 (1913), 34.

42. See, for example, "Zum Geleit," *Film und Lichtbild* 2, no. 1 (1913), n.p.; "An unsere Leser," *Film und Lichtbild* 2, no. 9/10 (1913), 137.

43. In a letter to the Lower Austrian Imperial Governor's Office (Staathalterei), which oversaw permits for voluntary associations in the region, Alto Arche stated that the Kosmos film club "maintains a business relationship with the Kosmos Gesellschaft der Naturfreunde." Alto Arche, letter to the KKNÖ Statthalterei, March 18, 1914, Vereinsakt for Kosmos Klub für wissenschaftliche und Künstlerische Kinematographie (Vienna: Vereinsarchiv: 1938), 473

44. "Mitteilungen des 'Kosmos' Klub für wissenschaftliche und künstlerische Kinematographie," *Film und Lichtbild* 2, no. 8 (1913), 121.

45. Member lists were regularly published in the group's newsletter (along with members' professions) in *Film und Lichtbild*. See, for example, "Mitteilungen des 'Kosmos' Klub für wissenschaftliche und künstlerische Kinematographie," *Film und Lichtbild* 2, no. 9 (1913), 138.

46. "Mitteilungen des 'Kosmos' Klub für wissenschaftliche und künstlerische Kinematographie," *Film und Lichtbild* 2, no. 8 (1913), 121.

47. For the Kosmos-Apparat, see insert, *Film und Lichtbild*, 1, no. 6 (1912), 84. For a history of the Kosmos Theater, see Peter Payer, *Das Kosmos-Kino: Lichtspiel zwischen Kunst und Kommerz* (Vienna: Verlag für Gesellschaftskritik, 1995).

48. Ernst Lorenzen, "Kinematographie und Schule," *Film und Lichtbild* 1, no. 3 (1912), 23. Elsewhere, another writer compared cinema to the Fröbel gifts used in education for hands-on knowledge acquisition. See Friedrich Lambrecht, "Handarbeiten im Lichtbilde," *Film und Lichtbild* 1, no. 5 (1912), 54.

49. Here, too, there was a direct affinity with slides. The journal ran an ongoing series on how to produce scientific slides starting in the second year. See Alfred Streißler, "Die Herstellung von Diapositiven," *Film und Lichtbild* 2 (1913), 41–43, 63–65, 98–100.

50. Opening editorial, *Film und Lichtbild* 1, no. 1 (1912), 1; *Film und Lichtbild* 2, no. 3 (1913), 50.

51. Opening editorial, *Film und Lichtbild* 2, no. 1 (1913), 1

52. The first supplement can be found in *Film und Lichtbild* 2, no. 1 (2013), 17–18. Hans Bourquin reported on devices for converting alternating current to direct current for the operation of projectors.

53. See Otto Theodor Stein, "Amateurkinematographie," *Film und Lichtbild* 2, no. 3 (1913), 36.

54. See Yvonne Montmollin, "Der Cinéphote," *Film und Lichtbild* 1, no. 3 (1912), 28

55. See Friedrich Felix, "Der Platten-Kinematograph Bettini," *Film und Lichtbild* 1, no. 5 (1912), 52–54; Stein, "Amateurkinematographie," 36.

56. See "Die Kino-Ausstellung in Wien," *Kastalia* 1, no. 4 (1912), 7.

57. That agency was conceptualized in particular in the idea that amateur filmmakers would help to create a stock of quality films to counter the "trash" of the film industry. See, for example, Otto Theodor Stein, "Der Lehrer als Photokinoamateur," *Film und Lichtbild* 2, no. 6 (2013), 93–94.

58. This was precisely the task that Stein assigned to the new wave of educationally inflected film societies. See Stein, "Kinematographische Studiengesellschaften," 140–41.

59. See Wilhelm Berndt. *Das Süß- und Seewasser-Aquarium: Seine Einrichtung und Seine Lebenswelt* (Leipzig, Germany: Theodor Thomas Verlag, 1911).

60. See Hanns Günther, *Experimentierbuch für die Jugend* (Nüremberg, Germany: Nister, 1912) and *Experimentierbuch für die Jungen* (Stuttgart, Germany: Franck'sche, 1922); Alfred Neuburger, *Ergötzliches Experimentierbuch* (Berlin: Ullstein, 1911), and *Ergötzliches Experimentierbuch* 2 (Berlin: Ullstein, 1925).

61. An arguable exception here was *Der Lehrfilm* (1920–26), published by the Lichtbild-Bühne Verlag as a supplement to the *Kinematographische Monatshefte*.

PUBLICATIONS REFERENCED

Bild und Film
Das Bild im Dienst der Schule und Volksbildung
Der Kinematograph
Der Lehrfilm
Die Lichtbild-Bühne
Film für Alle
Film und Lichtbild
Film und Wissen
Kastalia
Kinematographische Monatshefte
Kosmos Bändchen (Kosmos Booklets)
Kosmos: Handweiser der Naturfreunde
Lichtbildkunst
Medizin und Film
Mikrokosmos
Motography
Programme der medizinischen Woche

BIBLIOGRAPHY

Abel, Richard, ed. *Encyclopedia of Early Cinema*. New York: Routledge, 2010.

Bericht des Vorstandes der Gesellschaft Urania für das Geschäftsjahr vom 1. April 1910 zum 31. März 1911. Berlin: Urania, 1911.

Berndt, Wilhelm. *Das Süß- und Seewasser-Aquarium: Seine Einrichtung und Seine Lebenswelt*. Leipzig, Germany: Theodor Thomas Verlag, 1911.

Blankenship, Janelle. "To Alternate/To Attract: The Skladanowsky Experiment." *Cinema & Cie: International Film Studies Journal*, no. 9 (2007): 61–79.

Diederichs, Helmut. *Anfänge deutscher Filmkritik*. Stuttgart, Germany: Verlag Robert Fischer und Uwe Wiedleroither, 1986.

Frey, Matthias. *Permanent Crisis of Film Criticism: The Anxiety of Authority*. Amsterdam: Amsterdam University Press, 2015.

Gaycken, Oliver. *Devices of Curiosity: Early Cinema and Popular Science*. Oxford: Oxford University Press, 2015.

Gesellschaft Urania. Bericht des Vorstands für das Geschäftsjahr vom 1. April 1911 bis 31. März 1912. Berlin: Urania, 1912.

Günther, Hanns. *Experimentierbuch für die Jugend*. Nüremberg, Germany: Nister, 1912.

———. *Experimentierbuch für die Jungen*. Stuttgart, Germany: Franck'sche Verlag, 1922.

162　　CHAPTER 8

Humboldt, Alexander von. *Cosmos: A Sketch of the Physical Description of the Universe, vol. 1.* Translated by E. C. Otté. London: Henry G. Bohn, 1864.

Joschke, Christian. *Les yeux de la nation. Photographie amateur et société dans l'Allemagne de Guillaume II (1888–1914).* Dijon, France: Les Presses du réel, 2014.

Kaes, Anton, Nicholas Baer, and Michael Cowan, eds. *The Promise of Cinema: German Film Theory 1907–1933.* Oakland: University of California Press, 2016.

Kessler, Frank, and Sabine Lenk. "The Kinoreformbewegung Revisited: Performing the Cinematograph as a Pedagogical Tool." In *Performing New Media, 1890–1915,* edited by Kaveh Askari, Scott Curtis, Frank Gay, Louis Pelletier, Tami Wiliams, and Joshua Yumibe, 163–73. Bloomington: Indiana University Press, 2014.

Neuburger, Alfred. *Ergötzliches Experimentierbuch.* Berlin: Ullstein, 1911.

———. *Ergötzliches Experimentierbuch 2.* Berlin: Ullstein, 1925.

Payer, Peter. *Das Kosmos-Kino: Lichtspiel zwischen Kunst und Kommerz.* Vienna: Verlag für Gesellschaftskritik, 1995.

Pfitzer, Ina. "Das 'Verlangen nach einer Bereicherung und Vertiefung wissenschaftlicher Kenntnisse'. Die Zeitschrift Kosmos. Handweiser für Naturfreunde—ein Beispiel erfolgreicher Leserbindung." In *Das bewegte Buch: Buchwesen und soziale, nationale und kulturelle Bewegungen um 1900,* edited by Mark Lehmstedt and Andreas Herzog, 349–68. Wiesbaden: O. Harrassowitz, 1999.

Taschwer, Klaus. "Vom Kosmos zur Wunderwelt: Über popularwissenschaftliche Magazine einst und jetzt." In *Öffentliche Wissenschaft: Neue Perspektiven der Vermittlung in der wissenschaftlichen Weiterbildung,* edited by Peter Faulstich, 80–81. Bielefeld, Germany: Transcript, 2006.

Warstat, Willi. *Kino und Gemeinde.* Mönchen-Gladbach, Germany: Volksverein Verlag, Lichtbühne-Bibliothek, 1913.

9

Cinéma and the Vitality of Mid-century French Film Culture

Kelley Conway

In March 1957, *Cinéma 57* implicitly posed a question that reveals much about late-1950s film culture in France: Can a serious journal engage with actor Jean Gabin's love life *and* an anticolonial essay film by Chris Marker and Alain Resnais?[1] Absolutely, it turns out. Invested in both the *populaire* and the "elite," the issue contains both an installment of Gabin's autobiography and an excerpt of the script for *Les Statues meurent aussi* (*Statues Also Die*, 1953). The previous issue contains an essay by Marcel L'Herbier, then president of the film school Institut des hautes études cinématographiques (IDHEC), about the need to better educate film technicians, several articles about the work of Erich von Stroheim, an account of a workshop on Czech cinema, and a survey of thirty teenagers on their favorite films.[2] On the eve of the New Wave, the journal adroitly navigated fan culture, experimental documentary, trends in global cinema, the work of legendary auteurs, and film education, testifying with prescience to film's multiple cultural functions and pleasures. *Cinéma*, whose title shifted with each passing year (*Cinéma 56, Cinéma 57,* etc.), debuted in November 1954 and persisted until 1999. Launched ten months after the publication of François Truffaut's essay "A Certain Tendency of the French Cinema," the journal was less clubby and polemical than *Cahiers du cinéma* (1951–present), but shared many of its collaborators and goals.[3] A glimpse at even a small slice of the monthly journal's life in the latter half of the 1950s reflects the multifaceted nature of French film culture and the highly networked structure of institutional cinephilia at a moment of transition in French cinema.

When we think of 1950s French film culture, we tend to contemplate the activities of influential figures such as Truffaut, who wrote film criticism for multiple publications before becoming a film director; André Bazin, the critic and theorist

FIGURE 9.1. *Cinéma 57*, March 1957, front cover featuring Jean Gabin.

SOMMAIRE  MARS 1957

Le Cinéma Français

Jean Gabin raconte 2

« Les statues meurent aussi », commentaire intégral du film de A. Resnais et Chris Marker 13

Comment fut réalisé « Sous le manteau » 49

Hommage à Humphrey Bogart

Rien que l'homme 25

Le Cinéma dans le monde

Les bateaux de l'Enfer 28
L'Ogre d'Athènes a failli dévorer Nicos Koundouros 32
La bataille du jeune cinéma anglais 39

Les Métiers du Cinéma

L'image dépassée 53
Le Montage à l'I.D.H.E.C. .. 56

Le Cinéma dans la vie

Le cinéma et l'école 20
La Télévision américaine ou New-York contre Hollywood 62

Le guide du spectateur... p. 65

Films du mois. Une lettre d'Abel Gance.
Cinédisques. La Gazette des Ciné-Clubs.

TOUS DROITS DE REPRODUCTION INTERDITS POUR TOUS PAYS SAUF ACCORD PREALABLE AVEC L'ADMINISTRATION DE "CINEMA 57"

FIGURE 9.2. *Cinéma 57*, March 1957, table of contents.

celebrated for his theories of film realism; and Henri Langlois, who created the Cinémathèque française.[4] For the fullest understanding of this period, however, it pays to examine the cross-pollinated streams of the era's many vibrant publications and fora.[5] *Cinéma* emerged during a period of extraordinary institutional energy around film culture, whose elements include film festivals, the Cinémathèque française, the *ciné-club* network, and film journals. In 1947, the Cannes Film Festival finally materialized after its aborted 1939 launch, while the Tours International Festival of Short Films (Journées internationales du film de court-métrage de Tours) was born in 1955 with a prestigious inaugural jury that included Bazin, Abel Gance, Roger Leenhardt, and Francis Poulenc.[6] The now famous festival of animation, the Annecy International Animation Festival (Journées internationales du cinéma d'animation), officially launched in 1960 after several years in embryonic form. The Cinémathèque française, which had existed since 1936, became in the postwar period a "hive of cinema heritage . . . multiplying its programs, exhibitions, publications, courses, and lectures."[7] Ciné-clubs experienced an extraordinary resurgence in the postwar period, and became a veritable movement, one that was very different from its 1920s predecessors.

Bolstered by the new, postwar civic initiatives devoted to cultural democratization and adult education—Travail et culture (Work and Culture) and Peuple et culture (People and Culture)—ciné-clubs quickly developed their own framework in the form of federations.[8] By 1960, the federations oversaw approximately twelve thousand clubs throughout France. Figures familiar to us from their activity in other arenas of film culture—Langlois, Bazin, Truffaut, Jean Cocteau, and Jean Painlevé—were engaged in the formation of ciné-clubs in the immediate postwar period. At the end of the 1940s, for example, Cocteau and Bazin launched Objectif 49, the short-lived but influential club that called for a new avant-garde and cultivated a community of young cinephiles and critics.[9] In the immediate aftermath of the war, ciné-clubs expanded dramatically from their prewar incarnations, attracting members of diverse ages and socioeconomic milieux throughout France and its colonies and exposing viewers to a wider range of films from around the world.

Film journals, too, exerted a huge impact on film culture. Between 1950 and 1965, an astonishing 188 periodicals devoted to film were published in France.[10] The future New Wave directors at *Cahiers du cinéma* typically take center stage in any accounts of writing about film in the 1950s, but in fact a number of other notable journals were circulating in France.[11] *Cinéma* was launched by Pierre Billard (1922–2016), who served as editor-in-chief of the journal from 1954 to 1968. Billard is especially appreciated today for his wide-ranging history of French classical cinema.[12] When Billard launched *Cinéma*, he was already a respected and prolific film critic and, starting in 1952, a leader of one of the most important ciné-club federations, the French Ciné-Club Federation (Fédération française du ciné-club, or FFCC). In 1955, the FFCC had 205 clubs and 377,495 members.[13] *Cinéma* was the official journal of the FFCC, which, along with several other ciné-club federations, was a vital agent in film culture and, more broadly, the postwar proliferation of adult education opportunities in the arts.[14]

CINÉMA AND THE CINÉ-CLUB MOVEMENT

Cinéma's affiliation with the ciné-club movement was determinant. Indeed, the first three sentences in the journal's inaugural editorial state clearly the publication's expansive goals: "The renaissance and the continued expansion of the ciné-club movement constitute without doubt one of the significant events in French cinematic experience since the liberation. Until now, this movement lacked an organ that could further deepen and refresh its mission. This is the goal of CINEMA 55."[15] The journal further stated that it would rely on the FFCC network, be enriched by that organization's lengthy experience, and "extend to a wider audience the collective effort of reflection and criticism."[16] The emphasis here is on the creation of collective knowledge and a broader view of what is worthy of attention. *Cinéma* "will be interested in all of the cultural aspects of the production and diffusion of film as well as the history and aesthetics of film."[17] The journal was also, notably, invested in both exploring global cinema and supporting French cinema. It pledged to "report on worldwide film production" but would "follow closely the cinema of our country: artists and technicians will come into its columns to expose their reflections on their profession, their projects, and their problems. They will thus contribute to one of CINEMA 55's tasks: the defense and illustration of French cinema."[18] In its conclusion, the opening editorial imagines the journal not as a one-way channel of communication in which experts educate readers, but as a space for dialogue between ordinary viewers and specialists: "CINEMA 55, finally, will constitute a forum in which spectators and specialists will nourish a fruitful dialogue which will help us to better define and appreciate the reasons, both emotional and intellectual, behind cinephiles' love of cinema."[19] The goals of the journal were thus multiple: to draw on the knowledge and activities of France's vast ciné-club network, explore local and global cinema, provide a forum for technicians and artists working in the film industry, and launch discussions between specialists and nonspecialists on films, filmmakers, film history, aesthetics, and even the nature of cinephilia itself.

The first article published in *Cinéma 55*, by Jean Painlevé, was a fiery denunciation of mediocre documentary and a call for an expansion in ciné-club programming of one specific type of film: the industrial and scientific documentary. Celebrated for his documentaries about the natural world that are both serious scientific explorations and lyrical, inventive works, Painlevé had long been a defender of documentary's artistic, cultural, and educational value.[20] Through his membership in the Union mondiale du documentaire (World Documentary Union), created in 1947, and as a signatory of the 1953 manifesto of the Groupe des Trentes (Group of Thirty)—a collective formed to support short films—Painlevé

168   CHAPTER 9

was connected to multiple communities in French film culture, including the surrealists; documentary filmmakers Joris Ivens, Henri Storck, Paul Rotha, John Grierson, and Jean Grémillon; and archivist-programmers Iris Barry at the Museum of Modern Art and Henri Langlois at the Cinémathèque française.[21] In his article, Painlevé laments a degeneration in the quality of documentaries, a reduction in quality he believed had been sparked by television's mass production of documentaries and by those who simply wanted to take advantage of plentiful public subventions.[22] He expresses particular disdain for a recent wave of "pretentious" films about painting made by those he claimed knew nothing about art: "To be honest, there is nothing cheaper, in terms of production means and mental effort, than to light a painting, do a slow tracking close-up of a detail and sprinkle in some blandly flowery commentary by a narrator who deep down couldn't care less."[23] He is careful to exclude from his criticism of this group of films the short documentaries about art and artists made by Alain Resnais, expressing disdain instead for Luciano Emmer and Enrico Gras, Italian filmmakers who landed on an inexpensive formula for art historical documentaries in the 1930s and '40s—"as pretentious as they are worthless."

In his article, Painlevé did more than complain about documentaries he disliked; he also had a cause to promote. He was president of the FFCC from 1946 to 1956, and from his perch at the helm of this ciné-club federation he launched a call, in the first issue of *Cinéma*, for an expansion in ciné-club programming—arguing that in addition to the more typical ciné-club screenings of the documentaries he admired by Robert Flaherty, Joris Ivens, and Jean Vigo, viewers should have the chance to view programs of industrial and scientific documentaries.[24] Such programs, he asserts, could be offered three or four times per year, should feature the work of *chercheurs cinéastes* (researcher-filmmakers), and should be presented by the filmmakers or local specialists. Painlevé recommends the screening of specific industrial films, including those about the French national rail company, SNCF; the national electricity company, EDF; and the car manufacturer Renault. He also calls for programming of medical films and those made by biologists, zoologists, and astronomers. He recommends the work of, among others, Jean Comandon (1877–1970), the microbiologist and filmmaker known for his development of microcinematography. The films' subjects should be varied—never focused on a single discipline—and, above all, be satisfying *as films*: "Il s'agit de *cinéma* d'abord" (It's about *cinema* first). Painlevé's overall point is that too many documentaries were being made by nonspecialists of both film and the subject matter at hand. However, his call to action is not, as one might expect, a proposed overhauling of the subsidy system or a new emphasis on documentary pedagogy at IDHEC. Instead, he looks for the solution to this problem in the realm of exhibition—specifically, that of the welcoming community of cinephiles found in the ciné-club. Painlevé's call for an expansion in ciné-club programming of high-quality industrial and science documentaries made by those who are specialists in the subject matter and capable of making compelling films—a small community of which he was a part—might lead one to think that his essay smacked of self-promotion. As if anticipating such an objection, he asserts that his goals are to reveal the poetry in science, offer a breath of fresh air in programming, and provide a way to link film and culture.[25]

The second article in *Cinéma*'s inaugural issue was authored by Lotte Eisner, who wrote from her experience at a different institution of French film culture: the Cinémathèque française. Today, Eisner is remembered as a legendary curator who was instrumental in the creation of the Cinémathèque's archive and museum.[26] She was also a rigorous historian of German cinema, having published *The Haunted Screen* in 1952.[27] She begins her *Cinéma 55* article by reporting that the most frequented screenings at the Cinémathèque, other than those of Erich von Stroheim's films, were French avant-garde films and "German films known as 'Expressionist.'"[28] Regarding viewers' interest in German expressionism, she speculates that young people appreciate the films' "enigmatic" and "dreamlike" qualities, despite viewers' "tendency to be 'matter of fact' in the struggle of daily life."[29] Her main goal in the article, however, is to correct the misunderstanding that all German films of the classical period are works of expressionism.[30] Eisner notes that, ever since Siegfried Kracauer wrote of Max Reinhardt's 1917 theatrical production of Reinhard Sorge's *The Beggars* as "expressionist"—and due also, she concedes, to the subtitle of her own book (*Expressionism in the German Cinema and the Influence of Max Reinhardt*)—people have mistakenly categorized Reinhardt as an "expressionist" director. In fact, Eisner argues, Reinhardt also used impressionist techniques of lighting and, moreover, German cinema of the 1920s featured a mix of styles. *Cinéma* was thus from the beginning a space for nuanced arguments about film style and national cinema as well as a platform for one of the few women working in the realm of film criticism and history at this time.

Beyond such articles that supported programming initiatives or corrected the historical record on a given issue was the monthly "Guide du spectateur" (Spectator Guide), a recurring section of *Cinéma* featuring lengthy film reviews, overviews of national cinemas, and surveys of reviews from multiple publications. In that first issue, French, Soviet, and American films were reviewed, including Marcel Carné's *L'air de Paris* (The Air of Paris, 1954), Vsevolod Pudovkin's *Vasili's Return* (1953), Otto Preminger's *River of No Return* (1954), Luis Buñuel's *Robinson Crusoe* (1954), John Ford's *Mogambo* (1953), and two films by Robert Wise, *Executive Suite* (1954) and *Desert Rats* (1953). But most of the attention in the first "Guide du spectateur" was reserved for a re-release: Chaplin's *Modern Times* (1936), "the cinematic event of the month." There were extracts of reviews of *Modern Times* from other publications: a reprint of an article by Georges Sadoul from *Les Lettres françaises* along with admiring reviews from Claude Mauriac of *Le Figaro littéraire* and Jean de Baroncelli of *Le Monde*.

Beyond the "Guide du spectateur," the journal also published reports on films in progress. The first issue, for example, contained an article about the shooting of the first feature in the small port town of Sète, France, by then unknown director Agnès Varda. One Fernand Dufour of the Ciné-Club de Sète, who witnessed the

170   CHAPTER 9

shooting of the film, reports: "The experience that the making of *La Pointe Courte* represents is endearing in more ways than one. It has all the charms of an avant-garde attempt. Faith inspired each of the members of the 'crew' engaged in this exciting adventure: to produce a film, and a film which brings a message that is at once aesthetic, social, and human. This kind of admirable madness which consisted in shooting a major film with very limited financial means was brought to fruition, patiently, with a wise determination in a cleverly organized way."[31] Dufour notes the townspeople's engagement with the film's production and describes their enthusiastic participation in the scenes of jousting and dancing. He recognizes the director's and the crew's obvious and rare love of cinema "as a means of artistic expression" and expresses impatience to see the finished film.[32] *Cinéma* was thus invested in a wide range of films, including beloved classics by celebrated auteurs, Hollywood genre films, new releases from multiple nations, and even films in progress.

Attesting once again to *Cinéma*'s connection to ciné-clubs, the magazine's first issue devoted considerable space to a film education event held in July 1954 and sponsored by the Centre national d'éducation populaire (National Center for Popular Education).[33] Held at the Chateau de Marly in Val-Flory, west of Paris, the weeklong seminar was attended by more than sixty people, including directors and members of ciné-clubs from Germany, England, Belgium, Colombia, Denmark, Holland, Italy, Switzerland, and the US. At the event, production designer Max Douy spoke about set design and color; Jean Mitry, film theorist and cofounder of the Cinémathèque française, spoke about narrative and style in *The Magnificent Ambersons* (Orson Welles, 1942); and Lotte Eisner presented screenings of German expressionist films. The group also saw several Hollywood westerns, presented by a "specialist of the genre," Jean-Louis Rieupeyrout. The week's "*grande révélation*," however, was the session on Asian cinema presented by critic Georges Sadoul and Anne Philipe, writer, ethnographer, and wife of actor Gérard Philipe. Among the films screened were the Chinese *The White-Haired Girl* (Choui Khoua and Bin Wang, 1951), the Japanese *Okaasan/Mother* (Mikio Naruse, 1952), and the Indian *Do Bigha Zamin/Two Bighas of Land* (Bimal Roy, 1953). Finally, there were practical sessions designed to strengthen ciné-clubs, with discussions of how to program and introduce films and how to manage productive post-screening discussions.

The attention *Cinéma* devoted to the Marly event reflects an expansive vision of film culture, encompassing the education of viewers in workshops, the appreciation of cinema from around the world, the celebration of Hollywood genre films as well as the avant-garde, and the exposure of ciné-club members to legendary directors such as Jean Renoir, but also to craftsmen, theorists, archivists, and historians. The analysis, exploration, and celebration of film art should be cross-cultural, the article implies, and shared by professionals and nonprofessionals alike. Ciné-clubs, the pages of *Cinéma* reveal, were neither exclusive gatherings for insiders nor a forum for promoting a narrow range of films.

Subsequent issues featured an intriguing mix of material: in addition to reviews of films and accounts of ciné-club activities, there were excerpts of screenplays, interviews with directors, and calls to action on various issues concerning the French film industry. In the journal's second issue, for example, Marcel L'Herbier bemoans the decline of French film production and attendance and calls for stronger administrative coordination, a rethinking of France's export and import policies, better screenplays, and more resources devoted to developing the technical skills of directors.[34] Concluding on a nationalist and distinctly conservative note, L'Herbier advocates the creation of a "veritable national film production company . . . similar to that of the [prestigious state theater] Comédie-Française," which could compensate for the "denationalization caused by coproductions," "project to the world the true face of France," and "resuscitate the prestige of our cinematography."[35] Distinctly at odds with L'Herbier's call for a cinema of "prestige" is Renoir's astute prediction regarding low-budget films made by young people: "It is entirely possible that, in the future, great technical and industrial advances in cinema lead to the creation of an artisanal cinema, perhaps in the form of clubs, no doubt via 16mm, an artisanal cinema from which will emerge the most important works. There is every likelihood that the film that will amaze the people of the future will be a film made by young people, with no budget, working in 16mm."[36]

Without explicitly saying so, the second issue of *Cinéma* reflects a cleavage in attitude between those on the side of the Tradition of Quality and those anticipating the New Wave.[37]

CINÉMA 58 AND THE *NOUVELLE VAGUE*

In early 1958, *Cinéma* acknowledged the artistic and organizational crisis in the industry and celebrated new currents that might revitalize French cinema. The lead article by editor-in-chief Billard in the February issue of *Cinéma 58*, "40 Under 40," provides a snapshot of the rise of the New Wave (*La nouvelle vague*). Billard divides French filmmakers into two generations, those born before and after World War I.[38] The list of "old" directors contains many names still familiar to us today, including Marcel L'Herbier, Jean Renoir, Abel Gance, Raymond Bernard, Marcel Pagnol, Julien Duvivier, René Clair, Jacques Becker, Robert Bresson, Henri-Georges Clouzot, Jacques Tati, Marcel Carné, and Nicole Védrès. But the list of "new" directors contains the names of many directors who did not go on to enjoy lengthy and illustrious careers, reflecting the uncertainty of a transitional moment. Of those on the list, only Alexandre Astruc, Pierre Kast, Roger Vadim, Agnès Varda, Marcel Camus, and Louis Malle remain reasonably well known today. Alain Resnais, François Truffaut, Jean-Luc Godard, and Éric Rohmer had not yet made their first features and thus do not appear on the list. That Billard's list of promising directors includes Agnès Varda might seem surprising, given that *La Pointe Courte* (1955)

172   CHAPTER 9

received an extremely limited distribution, but the impact of ciné-club support and attention from the film press on a director's visibility was significant.[39]

The ever-shifting shape of the canon is made clear here. Just as we might be surprised by the inclusion of some directors on the list, there are conspicuous absences as well: Jacqueline Audry (1908–77), a commercially successful director of the 1950s—and one of the few female directors active in the French film industry before Varda emerged—is missing from the "old" list, and Jean-Pierre Melville (1917–73), whose dramas and thrillers are indisputably part of today's canon, is not among the "new." Billard concludes his overview by urging readers to keep their eyes on the films made by directors associated with *Cahiers du cinéma*: "a semi-aborted attempt by Rivette (*Le coup du berger*), a more successful one by Truffaut (*Les Mistons*), the next feature from Chabrol (*Le beau Serge*), all undertaken as independent productions . . . [and] liable to result in interesting discoveries."[40]

While Billard was in sync with many of his fellow critics in identifying the importance of a youthful rejuvenation of French film, he initially resisted describing the developments of this period as a "new wave." Billard protested the phrase itself:

> If a friend bores you with the "new wave," whether he sings its glories or curses its failings, simply tell him: Hiroshima. Art does not advance in waves, winds, and tides, against all odds: this reductive stormy metaphor for journalists scraping for column inches and filmmakers craving attention would have you applaud the emperor's new clothes, miss the forest for the trees, and deprive yourself of the crucial works of our time. The event in French cinema in 1959 is not the "new wave" (we'll revisit the adherents and victories of this mission in the autumn). The event of 1959 in French cinema is HIROSHIMA, MON AMOUR.[41]

Avoiding both Truffaut's polemics and the sometimes obscure references and breathy self-promotion in the pages of *Cahiers du cinéma*, *Cinéma* took its time in assessing the new currents of late-1950s cinema, offering in-depth reviews of individual films it deemed important and interviews of emerging directors, including Kast, Malle, Resnais, Truffaut, and Vadim.

By January 1960, however, Billard was willing to label the group of new films by young people a "new wave" and to defend it against its critics.[42] "The new wave, praised to the heavens only yesterday, is now the target of also-rans of every color and stripe, who tremble at the connection between youth and talent. The dogs may bark, but the caravan keeps rolling along."[43] He reports that 1960 will see even more new, young films than 1959 did. "As I write this, some fifteen-odd films have been completed, ready for release. Another twenty will be put into production during the next three months. The scale of the phenomenon, and the rapidity of its evolution, prompts us to postpone until next month the publication of our investigation of 'the new wave.'"[44] For the moment, in the January 1960 issue, *Cinéma 60* delved instead into the contemporary slate of exciting films by looking

FIGURE 9.3. *Cinéma 59*, July 1959, statement expressing resistance to the phrase "New Wave" and admiration for the film *Hiroshima, mon amour*.

FIGURE 9.4. *Cinéma 59*, July 1959, Emmanuelle Riva in *Hiroshima, mon amour*.

closely at Resnais's *Hiroshima, mon amour* (1959), Truffaut's *Les quatre cents coups/ The 400 Blows*, and Kast's *Le bel âge* (1960), works that combined a "maturity of thought," a "freedom of tone," and "formal invention." The journal would attempt to determine the New Wave's "real contributions on the aesthetic, technical, and financial levels" after a period of "oscillation between publicity campaign and a battle of generations."[45] Continuing its characteristic interest in screenplays, the magazine also featured in this issue excerpts of Marguerite Duras's screenplay for *Hiroshima, mon amour*, four character sketches written by Truffaut in preparation for making *The 400 Blows*, and dialogue from the scene in the latter between young Antoine Doinel and the psychologist. The issue also pays homage to Kast, a director who seemed central to the French New Wave in the late 1950s but who is less celebrated today. Commending *Le bel âge*, the magazine published excerpts from its screenplay, stills, and a filmography. The inclusion of such elements foregrounds the magazine's mission as a ciné-club publication; ciné-club *animateurs* around the country needed such information for their introductions and post-screening discussions.

In addition to publishing articles about New Wave directors and films, *Cinéma* documented the movement's production conditions. However, the magazine resisted the romanticization of low-budget filmmaking. In the February 1960 issue, Jean Cotet, Claude Chabrol's production director for *Le beau Serge* (1958), challenges the notion that New Wave filmmakers invariably sought reduced crews and low budgets. Yes, Cotet notes, New Wave filmmakers often relied on unorthodox sources of financing, shot on location, and sometimes made their films before securing a distributor. However, he adds, this mode of production was not necessarily what young filmmakers wanted. Instead, directors sought to "say what they want to say [and] express themselves as freely as possible with a restricted budget."[46] Asserting that the early profitability of New Wave films might not be sustainable, Cotet calls for additional government subsidy.[47]

In the following month, March 1960, *Cinéma* returned again to the subject of the New Wave. Marcel Martin, film critic and member of the magazine's editorial board, cautions against the "passion and mysticism" and "hasty generalizations" surrounding the New Wave. Moreover, Martin wants to avoid reducing the New Wave to individual directors because their ages, paths into the industry, narrative preoccupations, and styles were far too diverse.[48] Instead, and contrary to Cotet in the previous issue, he argues that the key characteristic of the New Wave is the shift in economic and material conditions under which films are being made. This shift in mode of production, he argues, is accompanied by a new tone: "modern, adult, lucid, disillusioned, pessimistic, willingly cynical and cruel, often amoral and libertine."[49] To his characterization of the New Wave, Martin adds cinephilia as a causal factor in the movement, noting that these filmmakers shared a passion for film history nourished by regular screenings at the Cinémathèque française.[50] For *Cinéma*, then, the New Wave was many things: first, a few films with a new tone and style; next, a new, low-budget mode of production; and, finally, a rise to prominence of a significantly large group of filmmakers making innovative films informed by a systematic exposure to global film history at the Cinémathèque française. Between 1958 and 1960, French film culture's understanding of the New Wave was in flux. Scrutiny of *Cinéma* reveals the month-by-month, on-the-ground development of perceptions about movements as they were emerging and shifting.

SADOUL AND THE WRITING OF FILM HISTORY

In addition to tracking the development of the New Wave as it emerged and documenting other trends in contemporary world cinema, *Cinéma* was invested in the writing of film history. Indeed, the magazine demonstrated a strong historiographic impulse as early as its second issue (December 1954), in which Georges Sadoul contemplates the task of writing film history in an article entitled

176   CHAPTER 9

"Paradoxes and Truths on the History of Cinema." Film scholars typically associate Sadoul only with his monumental, six-volume film history, *Histoire générale du cinéma* (1946–50), but he had multiple roles in French film culture in the postwar period. He served as secretary general of the FFCC, where he curated film programs that circulated through the federation's clubs; organized pedagogical sessions for ciné-club directors; wrote film criticism for multiple publications; and taught film courses at the Institut de filmologie and IDHEC.[51] Sadoul also served on the Commission de recherches historiques de la Cinémathèque française (Commission of Historical Research of the Cinémathèque Française) created by Henri Langlois in 1943 with the goal of "bringing together the pioneers and artisans of early cinema in order to collect their testimony and their memories."[52] In contemporary scholarship, Sadoul's multiple roles in French film culture have been forgotten, and synoptic accounts of world cinema by the likes of Robert Grau, Terry Ramsaye, Bardèche and Brasillach, and Jean Mitry have gone out of fashion. But Sadoul's 1954 essay in *Cinéma* provides fascinating clues to the nature of cinephilic anxiety at this moment in time.[53] How ironic that in 1954—the same year that his sixth volume of *Histoire générale du cinéma* was reprinted—Sadoul asserted that writing a history of film, or even a history of one director, was utterly impossible.

In "Paradoxes and Truths on the History of Cinema," Sadoul illustrates the historiographic challenges of writing film history, by first emphasizing the problem of access. Someone writing on Stendahl, he notes, can simply go to a library or a bookstore, acquire the novels, read, reread, annotate, and cite the text without risk of error.[54] In contrast, Sadoul asks us to contemplate the following situation: "I am writing a study in October 1954 on Orson Welles. . . . If I want to complete my study within three months, where will I rewatch and consult *The Magnificent Ambersons?* Perhaps *Citizen Kane* or *Lady of Shanghai* are still in distribution. But can I be sure to see them before January 1955?" He continues, enumerating the difficulties that arise even when a historian is writing about films that are still in distribution, noting that one cannot rely on one's memory of the films and certainly cannot ask the projectionist to pause during a screening so that one can take adequate notes. One might, he allows, rely on published screenplays for information. He reports, for example, that Jean George Auriol was able to publish in *La Revue du cinéma* a scene from the screenplay of *The Magnificent Ambersons* thanks to the support of RKO. But alas, he lamented, a screenplay is not the same as the finished film and cannot be relied upon to confirm details.

But even if one managed to locate a print of a film and create the viewing conditions that favor close analysis, there were other challenges. One could never be certain that the print on the Moviola had not been shortened, reordered, or altered in some way. Even if, by some miracle, one accessed a complete print whose elements conformed to the work's condition upon initial release, the film historian's work had scarcely begun. The writing of a complete film history, Sadoul asserted, required consultation of the screenplay, stills, posters, marketing materials, reviews of the film published in all of the countries in which it was shown, interviews of the director and actors, and reading of the source material, if the film had been adapted from a novel or a play.[55] Finally, film history cannot be written without an understanding of cameras, film stock, chemistry, physics and optics, and technical innovations.

Sadoul also argued that one must understand film financing and distribution and the history of film studios more generally. A full history of Welles, Sadoul insisted, must include the fact that RKO "mutilated" *The Magnificent Ambersons* and caused the director's unemployment for three or four years.[56] Even after conducting this research, the historian would still not be ready to write. Knowledge of film's industrial and technological contexts was insufficient. It was "impossible to speak of this art without studying its relationships with other arts or means of expression (ballet, the novel, architecture, radio, the press, television)."[57] Furthermore, the historian of film must undertake to understand the historical context in which a film was made, including the general history of cultures and people, relationships and social conflicts within various countries, and relationships between nations.

Next, his tone increasingly playful and faux-desperate, Sadoul imagines how a film historian might write an account of the year 1955 in cinema. The "ideal researcher" would need to begin by seeing the fifteen hundred or two thousand great films (*grands films*) produced that year by the seventy or eighty producing countries, read the worldwide film criticism written about this corpus of films, acquire their screenplays, and conduct an analysis (*analyse filmique*) of them. This researcher would also need to page through and absorb the information contained in the directories and trade publications published around the world, precious publicity materials, and the two to three hundred novels and plays from which the films were adapted. To conduct all of this research, the researcher would need to know many languages, including English, Arabic, Japanese, Chinese, Tamil, Telegu, Malay, Hungarian, and Bantu. "It would also be useful for him to visit these countries, not only to see films there, but to note the influence of a nineteenth-century painter from Prague (unknown in France) on a Czech cinematographer, of Balinese art on a Filipino set designer, or the behavior of the last Aztecs on the performances of Pedro Amendariz."[58]

Sadoul then reaches a "desperate conclusion": it is impossible to write not only a history of world cinema, but also the history of the films of a single nation, a single filmmaker, or even a single film. And yet, he concludes, we must try. Sadoul's humorously expansive vision of film history starts with one case study— *The Magnificent Ambersons*—and moves outward to an industrial, technological, and cultural history of global cinema. For Sadoul, then, the enterprise of writing film history requires both close analysis of individual films and large-scale economic, aesthetic, and social contextualization. The project was national and global, impossible and yet essential.

178   CHAPTER 9

In his insistence on the difficulty of providing an accurate and sufficiently expansive account of film history, it is possible that Sadoul was responding directly to Truffaut's critique of the latest volume of *Histoire générale du cinéma*.[59] Two months before Sadoul published his historiographical lament in *Cinéma*, Truffaut published a scathing article complaining of misremembered plot details and especially of the leftist Sadoul's ideological blind spots, notably his tendency to criticize Hollywood film.[60] Whether Sadoul was responding directly to Truffaut or not, his emphasis on completeness, his anxieties about gaps and missing sources, speak both to the ideological landscape of 1950s and to a vision of history that was already falling out of fashion. Indeed, in the years following Sadoul's fretting about film history's impossibility, the field of history moved away from what E. H. Carr in 1961 critiqued as the "ultimate view" of history—a belief that enough facts, words, and published pages could plausibly chronicle all of history's significant events.[61] Instead, the leading approaches to historiography took the incompleteness of sources, the subjectivity of the historian, and the need for critical interpretation as their starting points.

Sadoul further ensured the impossibility of his theory of film history through conceiving of it as the enterprise of an individual researcher. One person doesn't need to know twenty different languages and the nuances of every culture. Twenty people can know forty languages. Forty people speaking the same languages can form a research community, investigating small to mid-scale histories, what David Bordwell has described as the "piecemeal" approach to film history.[62] To his credit, Sadoul acknowledges the way that film history necessarily developed collaboratively over time, through mistakes along with discoveries. He notes that Lewis Jacobs made many erroneous assumptions in *The Rise of the American Film* (1939) about editing in a film he had not seen—Edwin S. Porter's *Life of an American Fireman* (1903)—which, in turn, were recirculated by Sadoul, much to Sadoul's chagrin.[63] But, Sadoul notes, if Lewis had not bothered to write about the film in 1939, it might have remained unknown by later historians.[64] Mistakes made by film historians can lead to fertile discussions and new discoveries. Sadoul recognized the longitudinal dimension of film history, but he struggled to envision it laterally: that a network of researchers (like the group of authors contributing to this book) could collectively produce histories spanning more nations, industries, languages, films, and animating questions than any individual working in isolation.

Although Sadoul wasn't thinking laterally, *Cinéma* certainly was. By the time the journal marked its first birthday in November 1955, it had become more self-conscious about its identity as a film journal. There were, as always, a startling array of topics covered, including the state of the contemporary French film industry; French film under the German occupation; ciné-club events; films from Mexico, the Netherlands, and Czechoslovakia; the works of Carl Theodor Dreyer and Vittorio De Sica; and *Boudu sauvé des eaux/Boudu Saved from Drowning* (Renoir, 1932) and *The Magnificent Ambersons*. The opening editorial announced a few changes: it would be "more varied, more current, better documented, and easier to read than in the past."[65] But the journal would continue to avoid publishing "pseudo-philosophical jargon that hides its lack of consistency under [the authors'] pretentious and bombastic style," and "bitter polemics in which wit and demonstrations of self-satisfaction take the place of argument."[66] The journal, they asserted, was not interested in the provocative formalism that existed in a certain sector of French film criticism, nor in discovering some misunderstood genius or the "metaphysical meaning of the work of the script-girl." This may seem like a not-so-veiled dig at *Cahiers du cinéma*, but it's worth recognizing how much cinematic material was being generated in postwar France, at every level of society—education, youth culture, popular press, lectures, discussions, radio broadcasts, production, adaptation, consumption, heritage, and legacy. It's clear just from this sampling of the pages of *Cinéma* that its contributors and editors were not operating in the hush of a rarefied cathedral, but rather in the roar of the marketplace, amid throngs of competing voices, wares bought and sold, traded and bartered, accessed and accessible—much like the landscape of commercial, popular cinema at the time. If nothing else, *Cinéma* reflects that wealth of material, the vitality of film culture at the center of French popular and intellectual discourse, and the scale of the exchanges between filmmakers, philosophers, historians, critics, and audiences. Clearly, resources such as this journal must be digitized and preserved for our continued contextual enquiry, as Sadoul would term it, to understand better the many layers of our cinephilia.

NOTES

1. *Cinéma 57*, no. 16 (March 1957). This journal is not yet available in the Media History Digital Library, but one can access its covers and tables of contents, as well as those of many other francophone film journals, here: https://calindex.eu/index.php.

2. *Cinéma 57*, no. 15 (February 1957).

3. François Truffaut, "Une certaine tendance du cinéma français," *Cahiers du cinéma* 31 (January 1954): 15–29. Essential starting points for understanding 1950s French films, the film industry, and film culture include Richard Neupert, *A History of the French New Wave* (Madison: University of Wisconsin Press, [2002] 2007); and Colin Crisp, *The Classic French Cinema, 1930–1960* (Bloomington: Indiana University Press, 1993).

5. For some useful steps in this direction, see Colin Burnett, *The Invention of Robert Bresson: The Auteur and His Market* (Bloomington: Indiana University Press, 2016); and Gwénaëlle Le Gras and Geneviève Sellier, eds., *Cinémas et cinéphiles populaires dans la France d'après guerre, 1945–1958* (Paris: Nouveau monde, 2015).

6. Henry Moret, "Petite histoire du festival de Tours," *Image et son*, no. 150–51 (April–May 1962), 37–38.

7. Laurent Mannoni, *Histoire de la Cinémathèque française* (Paris: Editions Gallimard, 2006), 136.

8. Léo Souillés-Debats, *La Culture cinématographique du mouvement ciné-club* (Paris: AFRHC, 2017).

9. Frédéric Gimello-Mesplomb, *Objectif 49: Cocteau et la Nouvelle Avant-Garde* (Paris: Séguier, 2014).

180   CHAPTER 9

10. Erika Noemi Badani Martinez, "Les revues françaises de cinéma entre 1950 et 1965," Rapport de recherche Bibliographique, Ecole Nationale Supérieure des Sciences de l'Information et des Bibliothèques, 2000, 17.

11. For an introduction to the major voices in French film criticism of the period, including Bazin, Georges Sadoul, François Truffaut, Roger Tailleur, and Bernard Dort, see Antoine de Baecque, *La cinéphilie: Invention d'un regard, histoire d'une culture, 1944–1968* (Paris: Fayard, 2003). For an in-depth study of one important journal, see Olivier Barrot, *L'écran français, 1943–1953: Histoire d'un journal et d'une époque* (Paris: Les Editeurs Français Réunis, 1979).

12. *L'Age classique du cinéma français: du cinéma parlant à la Nouvelle Vague* (Paris: Flammarion, 1995). Billard's son, Jean-Michel Frodon—also a well-known film critic and historian—authored the companion volume *L'Age Moderne du cinéma français: de la nouvelle Vague à nos jours* (Paris: Flammarion, 1995).

13. Léo Souillés-Debats, *La Culture cinématographique du movement ciné-club* (Paris: Association française de recherche sur l'histoire du cinema, 2017), 552–53.

14. Frédéric Gimello-Mesplomb, Pascal Laborderie, and Léo Souillés-Debats, eds., *La Ligue de l'enseignement et le cinéma: une histoire de l'éducation à l'image (1945–1989)* (Paris: AFRHC, 2016). *Cinéma* was actually the FFCC's longer-lived, second journal. Its predecessor, *Ciné-Club* (1947–54), was a large-format monthly that published articles by some of the most influential figures in mid-century French film culture, including Jean George Auriol, André Bazin, Jean Mitry, Georges Sadoul, and Jean Painlevé.

15. *Cinéma 55*, no. 1 (November 1954), 1. "La renaissance et l'expansion continue du mouvement ciné-club constituent sans doute un des événements marquants de la vie cinématographique française depuis la libération. Il manquait jusqu'alors à ce mouvement, un organe qui puisse approfondir encore, et davantage actualiser son action. C'est le but que se propose CINEMA 55."

16. *Cinéma 55*, no. 1, 1. ". . . prolongera auprès d'un public plus large l'effort collectif de réflexion et de critique des ciné-clubs."

17. *Cinéma 55*, no. 1, 1. "Revue de culture cinématographique, CINEMA 55 s'intéressera à tous les aspects culturels de la production et de la diffusion des films ainsi qu'à l'histoire et l'esthétique du cinéma."

18. *Cinéma 55*, no. 1, 2. ". . . s'attachera particulièrement à suivre de près le cinéma de notre pays: artistes et techniciens viendront dans ses colonnes exposer leurs réflexions sur leur métier, leurs projets et leurs problems. Ils contribueront ainsi à l'une des taches de CINEMA 55: la défense et l'illustration du cinéma français."

19. *Cinéma 55*, no. 1, 2. "CINEMA 55, enfin, constituera une tribune où spectateurs et specialists nourriront un fructueux dialogue qui aidera à mieux définir et à mieux faire apprécier les raisons de coeur et les raisons raisonnantes qu'ont les cinéphiles d'aimer le cinéma."

20. James Leo Cahill, *Zoological Surrealism: The Nonhuman Cinema of Jean Painlevé* (Minneapolis: University of Minnesota Press, 2019).

21. Roxane Hamery, "Jean Painlevé et l'esprit documentaire," in *Le Court Métrage Français de 1945 à 1968, de l'âge d'or aux contrebandiers*, ed. Dominique Bluher and François Thomas, 85–91 (Rennes, France: Presses Universitaires de Rennes, 2005).

22. Jean Painlevé, "Le bluff sur le toit," *Cinéma 55* (November 1954), 6.

23. Painlevé, 5. "Il faut dire que c'est ce qu'il y a de moins cher matériellement et mentalement que d'éclairer une toile, faire un travellingue sur un détail et d'assisoner d'un commentaire lyrico-fleur de peau dit par un spiqueur qui au fond s'en fout."

24. Painlevé, 7.

25. Painlevé, 8, ". . . permettre de susciter du point de vue cinégraphique pur une insufflation de vie nouvelle, la poésie étant incluse dans la science. Ce sera une manière supplémentaire de lier le cinéma et la culture."

26. Laurent Mannoni, "La 'Eisnerin' et les écrans démoniaques," *Sociétés & Représentations*, no. 32 (2011), 241–51. https://doi.org/10.3917/sr.032.0241.

CINÉMA AND FRENCH FILM CULTURE   181

27. Lotte H. Eisner, *L'écran démonique: Influence de Max Reinhardt et de l'expressionnisme* (Paris: Bonne, 1952, 1965). For the most recent translation of Eisner's work into English, see Lotte H. Eisner, *The Haunted Screen: Expressionism in the German Cinema and the Influence of Max Reinhardt*, trans. Roger Greaves (Berkeley: University of California Press, 2008).

28. Lotte Eisner, "L'Ecole Expressioniste, Mise en garde et mise au point," *Cinéma 55*, no. 1 (November 1954), 14.

29. Eisner, "L'Ecole Expressioniste," 14.

30. Naomi DeCelles explores Eisner's criticism, historiography, and archival work in *Recollecting Lotte Eisner: Cinema, Exile, and the Archive* (Oakland: University of California Press, 2022).

31. Fernand Dufour, "Agnès Varda tourne *La Pointe Courte*," *Cinéma 55*, no. 1 (November 1954), 80. "L'expérience que représente la réalisation de La Pointe Courte est attachante à plus d'un titre. Elle possède tous les charmes d'une tentative d'avant-garde. La foi a animé chacun des membres de 'l'équipe' engagée dans cette aventure excitante: produire un film, et un film qui apporte un message à la fois esthétique, social et humain. Cette espèce de folie admirable qui consistait à tourner un grand film avec des moyens financiers très réduits a été menée à bien, patiemment, avec une sage détermination d'une manière astucieusement organisée."

32. Dufour, "Agnès Varda tourne *La Pointe Courte*," 80.

33. René Gilson, "Marly: à l'école du spectateur," *Cinéma 55*, no. 1 (November 1954), 37.

34. Marcel L'Herbier, "Vers les Etats Généaux du Cinématographie," *Cinéma 55*, no. 2 (December 1954).

35. ". . . compense la dénationalisation qu'entraînent les coproductions, s'attacherait à produire les des films ambitieux, peu faits pour séduire le secteur privé, mais qui, projetant au monde le vrai visage de la France, ressusciteraient le prestige de notre cinématographie."

36. Jean Renoir, "A bâtons rompus," *Cinéma 55*, no. 2 (December 1954), 33. "Il est parfaitement possible que, demain, les très grands perfectionnements techniques et industriels du cinéma n'amènent la creation d'un cinéma artisanal, peut-être sous forme de clubs, probablement par le 16mm, cinéma artisanal d'où sortiront les oeuvres les plus importantes. Il y a de grandes chances pour que le film qui bouleversera les gens de l'avenir sera un film fait par de jenues gens, sans aucun moyen, et en 16mm."

37. For incisive analyses of the shifting notion of "quality" in 1950s French cinema, see Colin Burnett, "Cinema(s) of Quality," in *Dictionary of World Cinema: France*, ed. Tim Palmer and Charlie Michael, 140–48 (Chicago: Intellect Press, 2012); and Guillaume Vernet, "La 'qualité française' et la 'tradition de la qualité': arguments critiques d'une lutte politique," *1895* 98 (2022): 16–49.

38. Pierre Billard, "40 moins de 40," *Cinéma 58*, no. 24 (February 1958), 5–42. Cited in Richard Neupert, *A History of the French New Wave Cinema* (Madison: University of Wisconsin Press, 2007), xxii.

39. *La Pointe Courte* circulated in ciné-clubs and screened in January 1956 at the Paris art house Studio Parnasse. Kelley Conway, *Agnès Varda* (Champaign: University of Illinois Press, 2015), 25–26.

40. Billard, "40 moins de 40," *Cinéma 58*, no. 24 (February 1958), 34.

41. Pierre Billard, "Resnais: 'Non, tu n'as rien vu . . . ,'" *Cinéma 59*, no. 38 (July 1959), 1. "Si un ami vous importune avec la 'nouvelle vague,' qu'il vous en chante les mérites ou vous en dénonce les vices, répondez-lui: Hiroshima! L'art ne progresse point par vagues, vents et marées: cette dérisoire stratégie marine pour journalists en mal de copie et cinéastes en mal de publicité risque plutôt de vous faire prendre Le Pirée pour un homme, négliger l'essentiel pour l'accessoire, passer à côté des oeuvres capitales du moment. L'événement 1959 du cinéma français, ce n'est pas la 'nouvelle vague' (nous reviendrons en automne sur les tenants et les aboutissants de cette operation). L'Evénement 1959 du cinéma français, c'est HIROSHIMA, MON AMOUR."

42. Pierre Billard, "Introduction à la Nouvelle Vague," *Cinéma 60*, no. 42 (January 1960).

43. Billard, "Introduction à la Nouvelle Vague," 6.

44. Billard, 6.

45. Billard, 6.

46. Jean Cotet, "La 'nouvelle vague' a-t-elle révolutionné les méthodes de production?," *Cinéma 60*, no. 43, 79.

182   CHAPTER 9

47. Cotet, 80.

48. Marcel Martin, "Nouvelle Vague: Tentative de Bilan," *Cinéma 60*, no. 44 (March 1960), 5.

49. Martin, 11.

50. Martin, 11.

51. Valérie Vignaux, "Georges Sadoul et la Fédération française des ciné-clubs ou contribution à une histoire des usages non commerciaux du cinéma," *Cinémas* 27, no. 2–3 (2017): 179–94.

52. Commission de Recherche Historique and La Cinémathèque Française, *Fonds Commission de Recherche Historique* (Paris, 1896–1966), http://www.cineressources.net/repertoires/archives/fonds.php?id=crh.

53. Georges Sadoul, "Paradoxes et vérités sur l'histoire du cinéma," *Cinéma 55*, no. 2 (December 1954): 16–24.

54. Sadoul, "Paradoxes," 16.

55. Sadoul, 21.

56. Sadoul, 22.

57. Sadoul, 22.

58. Sadoul, 23. "Elles lui seront aussi utiles pour visiter ces pays, non seulement pour y voir les films, mais pour constater l'influence de tel peintre praguois du XIXe siècle (inconnue en France) sur tel opérateur tchèque, de l'art balinais sur un décorateur philippin ou du comportement des derniers Azthèques sur le jeu de Pedro Amendariz."

59. Georges Sadoul, *Le cinéma pendant la guerre (1939-1945)* (Paris: Denoël, 1954).

60. François Truffaut, "Georges Sadoul et la vérité historique," *La Parisienne*, no. 21 (October 1954), 1114–18. I am grateful to Bernard Bastide for drawing my attention to this source.

61. E. H. Carr, *What Is History?* (New York: Penguin, 1961). I am grateful to Eric Hoyt for sharing his ideas with me on the larger context of film historiography at this moment in time.

62. David Bordwell, *On the History of Film Style* (Cambridge, MA: Harvard University Press, 1997), 118.

63. Sadoul, "Paradoxes," 24.

64. Porter's editing would be scrutinized, of course, by many scholars who came after Jacobs and Sadoul. See André Gaudreault, "Detours in Film Narrative: The Development of Cross-Cutting," in *Early Cinema: Space, Frame, Narrative*, ed. Thomas Elsaesser, 133–44 (London: British Film Institute, 1990); Charles Musser, *Before the Nickelodeon: Edwin S. Porter and the Edison Manufacturing Company* (Berkeley: University of California Press, 1991); and Bordwell, *On the History of Film Style*, 118–39.

65. Editorial, *Cinéma 56*, no. 7 (November 1955), 1.

66. Editorial, *Cinéma 56*, no. 7, 2.

PUBLICATIONS REFERENCED

Cahiers du cinéma
Ciné-Club
Cinéma 56–60
La Revue du cinéma

BIBLIOGRAPHY

Baecque, Antoine de. *La cinéphilie: Invention d'un regard, histoire d'une culture, 1944–1968*. Paris: Fayard, 2003.

Barrot, Olivier. *L'écran français, 1943–1953: Histoire d'un journal et d'une époque*. Paris: Les Editeurs Français Réunis, 1979.

Billard, Pierre. *L'Age classique du cinéma français: du cinéma parlant à la Nouvelle Vague*. Paris: Flammarion, 1995.

CINÉMA AND FRENCH FILM CULTURE   183

Bordwell, David. *On the History of Film Style*. Cambridge, MA: Harvard University Press, 1997.

Burnett, Colin. "Cinema(s) of Quality." In *Dictionary of World Cinema: France*, edited by Tim Palmer and Charlie Michael, 140–48. Chicago: Intellect Press, 2012.

——. *The Invention of Robert Bresson: The Auteur and His Market*. Bloomington: Indiana University Press, 2016.

Cahill, James Leo. *Zoological Surrealism: The Nonhuman Cinema of Jean Painlevé*. Minneapolis: University of Minnesota Press, 2019.

Carr, E. H. *What Is History?* New York: Penguin, 1961.

Conway, Kelley. *Agnès Varda*. Champaign: University of Illinois Press, 2015.

Crisp, Colin. *The Classic French Cinema, 1930–1960*. Bloomington: Indiana University Press, 1993.

DeCelles, Naomi. *Recollecting Lotte Eisner: Cinema, Exile, and the Archive*. Oakland: University of California Press, 2022.

Eisner, Lotte H. *L'écran démonique: Influence de Max Reinhardt et de l'expressionisme*. Paris: Bonne, [1952] 1965.

——. *The Haunted Screen: Expressionism in the German Cinema and the Influence of Max Reinhardt*. Translated by Roger Greaves. Berkeley: University of California Press, 2008.

Frodon, Jean-Michel. *L'Age Moderne du cinéma français: de la nouvelle Vague à nos jours*. Paris: Flammarion, 1995.

Gaudreault, André. "Detours in Film Narrative: The Development of Cross-Cutting." In *Early Cinema: Space, Frame, Narrative*, edited by Thomas Elsaesser, 133–44. London: British Film Institute, 1990.

Gimello-Mesplomb, Frédéric. *Objectif 49: Cocteau et la Nouvelle Avant-Garde*. Paris: Séguier, 2014.

Hamery, Roxane. "Jean Painlevé et l'esprit documentaire." In *Le Court Métrage Français de 1945 à 1968, de l'âge d'or aux contrebandiers*, edited by Dominique Bluher and François Thomas, 85–91. Rennes, France: Presses Universitaires de Rennes, 2005.

Jacobs, Lewis. *The Rise of the American Film*. New York: Harcourt Brace, 1939.

Le Gras, Gwénaëlle, and Geneviève Sellier, eds. *Cinémas et cinéphiles populaires dans la France d'après guerre, 1945–1958*. Paris: Nouveau monde, 2015.

Ligue de l'enseignement et le cinéma: une histoire de l'éducation à l'image, La (1945–1989). Edited by Fréréric Gimello-Mesplomb, Pascal Laborderie, and Léo Souillés-Debats. Paris: AFRHC, 2016.

Mannoni, Laurent. *Histoire de la Cinémathèque française*. Paris: Editions Gallimard, 2006.

Martinez, Erika Noemi Badani. "Les revues françaises de cinéma entre 1950 et 1965." Rapport de recherche Bibliographique. Ecole Nationale Supérieure des Sciences de l'Information et des Bibliothèques, 2000.

Musser, Charles. *Before the Nickelodeon: Edwin S. Porter and the Edison Manufacturing Company*. Berkeley: University of California Press, 1991.

Neupert, Richard. *A History of the French New Wave*. Madison: University of Wisconsin Press, 2007 [2002].

Sadoul, Georges. *Le cinéma pendant la guerre (1939–1945)*. Paris: Denoël, 1954. [Volume 6 of *Histoire générale du cinéma*.]

Souillés-Debats, Léo. *La Culture cinématographique du mouvement ciné-club*. Paris: AFRHC, 2017.

Truffaut, François. "Une certaine tendance du cinéma français." *Cahiers du cinéma* 31 (1954): 15–29.

Vernet, Guillaume. "La 'qualité française' et la 'tradition de la qualité': arguments critiques d'une lutte politique." *1895* 98 (2022): 16–49.

Vignaux, Valérie. "Georges Sadoul et la Fédération française des ciné-clubs ou contribution à une histoire des usages non commerciaux du cinéma." *Cinémas* 27, 2–3 (2017): 179–94.

10

African Film Criticism in the Colonial Capital, 1957–1967

Rachel Gabara

Apart from a few films shot by African students in Europe in the mid- to late 1950s, sub-Saharan African cinema was born with political independence in the following decade, more than sixty years after the Lumière brothers' first moving images. A first generation of directors struggled to gain access to training and equipment; European funding came with strings attached, and new African nations manifested little interest in supporting their projects. Once a film was successfully completed, moreover, it was unlikely to be distributed or exhibited outside of European cultural centers in Africa and a few European festivals. As production gradually increased in a global media landscape without Africa-based film publications, only a small number of African films were reviewed or even mentioned in European magazines, be they prestigious, popular, or trade. Now as then, with production, distribution, and exhibition still a struggle sixty years after independence, a lack of magazines dedicated to African film and media leaves prospective African critics with a dearth of appropriate publication venues and African creators without a crucial link to potential spectators.

A return to the first years of Black African cinema, however, reveals the contemporaneous if comparably limited emergence of an accompanying film historical and critical framework. Within a span of ten years surrounding independence, Black African– and Black French–authored film history and criticism were born in the pages of three Paris-based and African owned and edited publications: *Présence Africaine, La Vie Africaine*, and *L'Afrique actuelle*.[1] In addition to members of a close-knit group of African students and filmmakers who wrote occasional articles, the first professional critics of African cinema made their mark in a series of calls for the promotion and development of a truly African cinema.

Paulin Soumanou Vieyra, in *Présence Africaine* beginning in the late 1950s, and D'dée, in *La Vie Africaine* and *L'Afrique actuelle* in the '60s, also accounted for and analyzed the rare African films that already existed.

Born in Dahomey in 1925, Paulin Soumanou Vieyra was sent by his family to attend school in France at the age of ten. While studying biology in Paris in 1947, he had his first contact with the French film industry when he was recruited to play the role of an African soldier in Claude Autant-Lara's *Le Diable au corps* (*Devil in the Flesh*). The same year, Alioune Diop established his now legendary journal *Présence Africaine*, with a Patronage Committee that featured white French intellectuals from the domains of literature and ethnography, including André Gide, Jean-Paul Sartre, Albert Camus, and Michel Leiris, and an Editorial Committee made up mostly of Black West and Central African intellectuals and authors such as Bernard Dadié, Mamadou Dia, and Abdoulaye Sadji. "Paris Dakar" appeared underneath the title and logo on the cover of the journal's first five issues, and its inaugural issue was released in both cities simultaneously.[2] This duality was also mirrored in the first issue's two prefatory essays, which spoke to different audiences. Gide's foreword addressed white French readers to state that "as rich and beautiful as is our civilization, our culture, we have finally accepted that it is not alone (not the only one?)."[3] Diop then presented the journal's primary raison d'être, to serve as a "window onto the world" for young Africans in need of "intellectual nourishment." The world they would see through this window, he clarified, was that of "the life of the mind in Europe."[4]

Présence Africaine was embedded in mainstream Parisian intellectual circles, then, while working to account for African and African diasporic cultural production in a mix of fiction, poetry, critical essays, and reviews by writers from France, sub-Saharan Africa, the Caribbean, and the United States. Those writing for the journal about cinema, however, were for years only French; in 1948, Georges Bataille reflected on the growing presence of Black actors in European and North American fiction films, and in 1951, Jean Caillens discussed a film shot by Claude Vermorel and his wife Claire Maffei in French Equatorial Africa.[5] Although Cameroonian journalist Iwiyé Kala-Lobe, a lifelong collaborator of Alioune Diop, attested to Diop's early interest in the creation of an African cinema, he recounted that an initiative undertaken in 1946 was eventually blocked by France's Ministry of the Colonies.[6]

Vieyra's experience as an extra convinced him of the potential importance of cinema to African independence; he changed the course of his studies and in 1953 became the first Black African student at the French Institute for Advanced Cinematographic Studies (IDHEC). After graduating, Vieyra and his friends and colleagues Jacques Mélo Kane, Mamadou Sarr, and Robert Caristan formed the African Cinema Group. Prevented from filming in French West Africa by the censorship that had been formalized by the 1934 Laval Decree, they instead shot *Afrique sur Seine* (1955), a black-and-white short depicting the lives of African students in Paris. When Diop's *Présence Africaine* entered its second series that same

FIGURE 10.1. Paulin Soumanou Vieyra and the African Cinema Group. Image courtesy of Stéphane Vieyra and PSV-Films.

year, the prominent French "Africanists" were removed from the masthead and the prior committees replaced with a single *Présence Africaine* Committee.[7] In the first issue of this new series, C. Ijdedem reviewed what was likely the first film shot by an African student in Europe, Mamadi Touré's now lost *Mouramani* (1953).[8] Vieyra had already authored several book reviews in *Présence Africaine*, and when he wrote his first article about the cinema, Black African film criticism was founded in the pages of a Paris publication.

Vieyra's "When French Cinema Speaks for Black Africa" appeared in 1957, with France's colonies in sub-Saharan Africa still several years away from political independence.[9] Only a few films had been made by sub-Saharan African directors, so Vieyra could not address the state of sub-Saharan African cinema; he instead critiqued a tradition of French filmic representations of sub-Saharan Africa and Africans. Although African artists and intellectuals had begun to respond to French characterizations of their continent during the interwar period, progress that culminated a decade after World War II with *Présence Africaine*'s Congress of Black Writers and Artists in Paris, Vieyra noted that "there are still domains in which Europe speaks and continues to speak exclusively in Africa's name, among others the cinematographic domain."[10] He divided those European directors still speaking for Africa into four categories—colonialists, ideologues, paternalists, and realists—finding only in the last and smallest group "our true friends," René Vautier, Alain Resnais, Chris Marker, and Jean Rouch. An African cinema must be born, Vieyra concluded, to allow Africans to tell their own stories, stories in which Africa would exist as more than just an exotic background. This would require the creation of scholarships in France to train future African directors and technicians, as well as cine clubs in Africa to train their future audience.[11]

Vieyra returned to West Africa the year this article was published, and he would be based in Dakar, Senegal, for the rest of his life. He was one of the most important figures of early sub-Saharan African cinema, his career combining many roles: civil servant, heading up the Cinema Sections of the High Commissariat of French West Africa and then the Mali Federation, the Newsreel Section of the Senegalese Ministry of Information, and the Senegalese Office of Radio Broadcasting and Television; director of newsreels and documentary films; producer of the early films of Senegalese director Ousmane Sembene; and film historian and critic. Recording, analyzing, and supporting efforts by Black Africans to reject and supplant Europe's cinematic paternalism, Vieyra published dozens of articles in *Présence Africaine*, the last of which appeared in 1987, the year of his untimely death. In addition to short reviews of European and African films and global film festivals, he set out a concrete program for the development of African cinema in a sequence of lengthier scholarly essays that began with "Remarks on African Cinema" (1958) and "Cinema and the African Revolution" (1961).[12] The first three of Vieyra's books about sub-Saharan African cinema—*Cinema and Africa* (*Le cinéma et l'Afrique*, 1969), *Sembene Ousmane, Filmmaker* (*Sembène Ousmane, cinéaste*, 1972), and *African Cinema, from Its Origins to 1973* (*Le Cinéma africain, des origines à 1973*, 1975)—appeared through *Présence Africaine*'s publishing company, which Diop had established just two years after the creation of the journal.

Vieyra was joined in the pages of *Présence Africaine* in the mid- to late 1960s by a group of filmmaker-critics that included Blaise Senghor from Senegal, Timité Bassori from Côte d'Ivoire, and Urbain Dia-Moukori from Cameroon. Occasional pieces also began to appear in news magazines, notably those of Cameroonian Félix Ewandé in *France Eurafrique*, with *Jeune Afrique*, apart from occasional reviews authored by Tunisian Férid Boughedir, most often publishing French journalists. Within a decade of Vieyra's first piece, special issues dedicated to independent Black African cinema appeared in two newer publications that, like *Présence Africaine*, were based in Paris but owned and edited by Africans. Less academic than Alioune Diop's journal if no less activist, the magazines *La Vie Africaine* and *L'Afrique actuelle* sought a wider audience, adding numerous photos and advertisements instead of footnotes to the words on the page.

La Vie Africaine was founded in 1959 by A. Baye Fall, during what scholars of early West African publishing Ruth Bush and Claire Ducournau identify as a "boom in magazine culture" in the years surrounding independence.[13] Produced and edited in Europe, it was distributed throughout West Africa—in Senegal, Mali, Upper Volta, and Guinea—by the Agence de Diffusion de Presse in Dakar.[14] Canadian-born journalist Georges Chaffard, who had reported on West Africa for Le Monde, took over the editorship from Baye Fall, then was himself succeeded by Dahomeyan writer Olympe Bhêly-Quenum. The last issue of La Vie Africaine appeared in 1965, and in the same year Bhêly-Quenum launched his own magazine, L'Afrique actuelle, which he described on the masthead as the first and only international African news magazine.[15] Responding in print to a letter from an African reader who had described the magazine as "foreign (étranger)," Bhêly-Quenum retorted angrily, "Foreign to whom and to what? One hundred percent Negro, but nobody else's Negro than my own and superbly Black, I more than many others have the right to found an African journal."[16]

The special sections of both La Vie Africaine and L'Afrique actuelle were put together by the fascinating and multitalented D'dée, whose pioneering contributions to Black African cinema and criticism have been forgotten even as those of Vieyra are at long last gaining wider recognition.[17] Almost exactly Vieyra's contemporary, D'dée was born André Trisot to Martinican parents in Paris in 1928. In the postwar years, he studied at France's national School of Fine Arts (Beaux-Arts) while working as a bebop dancer and choreographer in the Left Bank Paris nightclubs Tabou, Caveau des Lorientais, and Club Saint-Germain. It was in these clubs, where he was known as Hot D'dée, that he met French writer, singer, jazz musician, and inventor Boris Vian, who would become his close friend and collaborator. D'dée curated the illustrations for Vian's Handbook to St-Germain-des-Près, which includes an entry in his name. Together with Vian's widow Ursula, D'dée established the Boris Vian Foundation in 1981. Just a few years before his own death in 2016 at the age of eighty-seven, he authored a lengthy preface to an edition of two of Vian's previously unpublished works, here credited as Mr. D'dée.[18]

D'dée's first special issue, entitled "Cinema and Africa," was published in La Vie Africaine in June 1961, two years after Vian's death. It opens with a large photograph of an unidentified African man wearing a woolen Dogon hunter's bonnet and peering into the viewfinder of a movie camera that is mounted on a tripod. The photo is credited to Jean Suyeux, who along with Vian and D'dée had chronicled postwar Saint-Germain-des-Prés, and a lengthy quote attributed to Paulin Vieyra and Présence Africaine appears below. In this excerpt from the opening paragraph of his "Cinema and the African Revolution," Vieyra maintained the centrality of the cinema and television to modern life and culture. Following this claim of affiliation to both Vieyra and Diop, an editorial introduction extends Vieyra's assertion to the crucial role of the cinema in "the construction of a new Africa" while noting that not a single national African cinema had yet come into existence.[19]

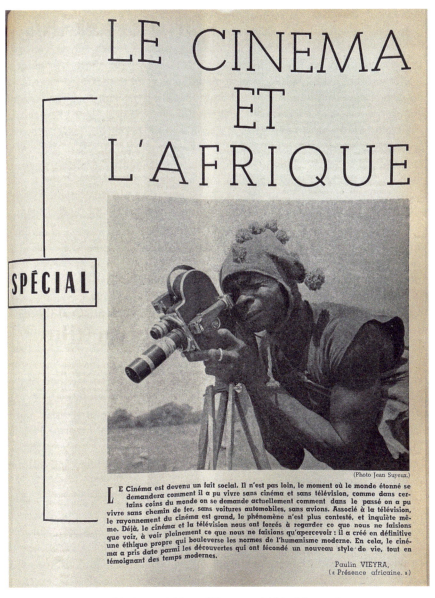

FIGURE 10.2. *La Vie Africaine* special issue, "Cinema and Africa," June 1961.

With virtually no films yet available to account for or analyze, the almost thirty-page special section of *La Vie Africaine* instead shared practical information on filmmaking for would-be African directors, relying on both African and French film historians and critics. D'dée, who was not African, was nonetheless strongly committed to an African cinema yet to come. A month earlier in the

190   CHAPTER 10

same magazine, he had argued that "too long deprived of the freedom to express themselves," it was time for Africans to "speak cinematographically in order to denounce real African problems."[20] D'dée now began his special issue with an article spread out over six pages, "The Cinema Is First an Industry and Technique: How Does One Make a Film?"[21] Detailing the steps of a filmmaking project from script to budget to fundraising to shooting to editing, he explained the roles of producer, director, and the various members of the technical crew. The instructional tone of D'dée's essay continued in a series of interspersed box texts reviewing "A Few Great Works of World Cinema" and "The Important Stages of the Invention of the Cinema," with additional information provided about advertising and about ticket sales in African movie theaters.[22]

Bhêly-Quenum's introduction had concluded by thanking the leadership of the French National Center for Cinema as well as Minister of Cultural Affairs André Malraux for unspecified support. His and D'dée's special issue was also concretely supported by preeminent French film historian and critic Georges Sadoul, with whom Vieyra had studied at the IDHEC, and renowned filmmaker and critic Jean Rouch, both of whom contributed short essays. Sadoul's "Africa Has Until Now Been the Country of 'Cinematographic Scarcity'" addressed Black characters in Hollywood films before moving on to French expedition and exotic films and the French documentarists Vieyra had earlier called "our true friends."[23] Rouch began with an American film about the Mau Mau rebellion in Kenya, Richard Brooks's *Carnival of the Gods* (1953), which Vieyra had reviewed for *Présence Africaine* three years prior. Affirming as had Sadoul that "since the invention of the Lumière brothers, we can say that no African has yet expressed himself via the intermediary of the camera," Rouch chose to retrace French ethnographic filmmaking in Africa from Jacques Dupont to Luc de Heusch.[24] In a third piece, French ethnographer Georges Bourdelon joined Rouch in notes from an interview likely conducted by D'dée, recounting his experience shooting educational films for the newly independent Central African Republic.[25]

We can see in D'dée's inclusion of Sadoul, Rouch, and Bourdelon a parallel to Alioune's Diop's "Patronage Committee" in the first series of *Présence Africaine*. And although all three supported the creation of an independent African cinema, none here acknowledged that its first steps had been taken—not even Rouch, who was undoubtedly aware of Vieyra's *Afrique sur Seine*.[26] It is perhaps for this reason that D'dée placed just after Sadoul's and Rouch's pieces two additional excerpts from Vieyra's "Cinema and the African Revolution," a couple of paragraphs praising Rouch's *Moi, un noir* (1958) and then a page about four additional films read as witnesses to African liberation. With Vieyra already an established figure—so much so, in fact, that he had not had time to write something new for the special issue—D'dée chose to conclude with a series of short pieces featuring African students from a variety of countries who were studying at the IDHEC. Ratovondrahona from Madagascar argued the importance of training African spectators to appreciate something other than foreign Westerns, and Honoré Dol from Mali the possibility of creating an African cinema that could prove its value to new independent governments by bringing in foreign currency.[27] A print debate brought these two together with Bassori, Ben Salem from Tunisia, Thomas Coulibaly from Upper Volta, and Jean-Paul Ngassa from Cameroon. And an inset set of quotes from recent IDHEC graduate Blaise Senghor, who was setting up his own production company in Senegal, then reinforced D'dée and Bhêly-Quenum's message about the cinema as an instrument of liberation, warning future filmmakers to "make Africa better known to Africans" and avoid "the flights of fancy of the 'New Wave.'"[28]

Toward the end of the section, writing as *La Vie Africaine*'s "special envoy" to the 1961 Cannes Film Festival, D'dée reported that "not a single African nation was represented."[29] He was therefore free to share information about less weighty matters, both the *folie* of the Croisette, particularly the arrival of Sophia Loren, and an interview he had conducted with the "ravishing" Miss America, whom he noted was Black. This piece made evident the difference between the magazine, which mixed accessible film history and criticism with chatty fan material, and its predecessor, scholarly journal *Présence Africaine*, a distinction accentuated by an interview with actress Juliette Greco about her impressions of shooting in Africa.[30] In its thirty pages, D'dée's section of *La Vie Africaine* included a total of twenty-three film stills and photos, some of which were added to the reprinted sections of Vieyra's article, unillustrated in the original. Pages of advertising images and text introduced prospective filmmakers to Brockliss-Simplex, producer of a range of production and projection equipment; I.C.A.M., manufacturer of flame-resistant fabric for theaters; and CAMECA, creator of the jukebox-like Scopitone projector, described as appropriate for both showing educational films to the African masses and enhancing the electoral campaigns of African politicians. The section's very last photo highlighted African interest in the cinema, showing three African teachers at Cannes wearing elegant boubous and being filmed by a French cameraman. If sub-Saharan Africa was arriving late to the cinema, it was doing so in style.

D'dée continued to write about cinema for *La Vie Africaine*, a year later setting Nigerien Mustapha Alassane's *Aouré* (*Marriage*, 1962) and Blaise Senghor's *Le grand Magal à Touba* (*Grand Magal in Touba*, 1962) against "films by 'Africanists'" to declare that "finally, True African Cinema" had arrived.[31] And, in February of 1967, Bhêly-Quenum's new journal *L'Afrique actuelle* published a special issue dedicated to "Young Black African Cinema," which, although it used the same opening photo as D'dée's first, bore a meaningfully different title. The progress made during the intervening six years had allowed for the transition from "cinema and Africa" to "African cinema," a shift that Vieyra himself would express in the same terms two years later.[32] And as had Diop for the second series of *Présence Africaine*, Bhêly-Quenum and D'dée removed their prior European collaborators, at least from print. D'dée alone was credited with the extraordinary effort of providing an

FIGURE 10.3. "Cinema Brings People Together; It Is Universal," *La Vie Africaine*, June 1961.

almost forty-page overview and assessment of the first seven years of sub-Saharan African cinema. With the support of the Cinémathèque française and the Ministry of Foreign Affairs, an accompanying "Week of Young Black African Cinema" was programmed in Paris for mid-April, with screenings at the Palais de Chaillot and the Rue d'Ulm.[33]

In D'dée's second special issue, the paragraph of Vieyra's article about cinema and revolution that had appeared underneath Suyeux's photograph in the first was replaced by Lenin's much earlier and more famous declaration that "of all the arts, the cinema is the most important for the revolution." In historical and critical work that was now almost exclusively his own, D'dée began by turning the tables on a history of European expedition films shot in Africa. Africans who had learned filmmaking while traveling in Europe, he claimed, could save a Western

FIGURE 10.4. "Africa to the Rescue of Western Cinema?," *L'Afrique Actuelle*, February 1967.

cinema that was no longer able to innovate.[34] In a second introductory essay, D'dée summarized the struggles of young African filmmakers who, returning home after official or unofficial training in Europe, discovered independent governments unwilling to support anything other than newsreel production. They could shoot footage only with funding from agencies in Europe, where they also had to return for editing and to show the resulting films in festivals. Only a dozen or so such heroic individuals existed, according to D'dée, constituting a generation after that of *Afrique sur Seine* and the first to create "a purely African cinematographic art."[35] Their work was presented in alphabetical order by *auteur* in the "*cahier technique*" that followed.

D'dée began his user manual to young African cinema, then, with its directors, from Alassane to Vieyra via the Brazzaville Camera Club, whose work he divided into three trends: social cinema, poetic fiction, and documentary. For each director, he provided a brief biography, a characterization of content and style, contact information, and a detailed filmography in which each film's funding, technical information, and cast were followed by a subjective critical evaluation of between a sentence and a few paragraphs. As in his first special issue, D'dée was highly aware that films were made not only by directors; a new cinema needed producers, screenwriters, actors, and technicians. His pages on directors were, therefore, followed by a list of African writers, along with their plays or novels that were apt for cinematic adaptation; a list of African technicians, including cameramen, sound technicians, and musicians, along with their basic qualifications and contact information; and a list of both African and Black Caribbean actors and actresses, along with their previous experience. A summary of funding agencies, both public and private, in Africa and in Europe, with their previously funded films, was followed by information on commercial and noncommercial distribution and exhibition in Africa, as well as festivals in Africa and Europe and film schools, including but not limited to the IDHEC. Prospective African filmmakers could find everything necessary to move forward in their careers, whether applying to film schools or looking for production funding, distributors, scripts, actors, or editors.

In a concluding essay entitled "For a Cinema of Quality," D'dée proposed a program for the development of African cinema, but also for cinema in Africa. Restating his conviction that the cinema was both art and industry, he urged African governments to support the training of both African creators and African spectators. More specifically, D'dée encouraged these governments to fund not the European productions shot in Africa that he called "Negro-and-white" films but African-authored productions to be distributed within Africa. Only then, he concluded, would the new African cinema "take the place in universal culture that the world has been awaiting."[36] The success of D'dée's boldly conceived practical handbook, his second initiative with regard to African filmmaking, was made clear just four months later in *L'Afrique actuelle*'s June 1967 issue. Editor Bhêly-Quenum published a lengthy interview with director and producer Blaise Senghor, which he prefaced by reminding readers of the special issue in which Senghor's first film had recently been catalogued. The subject of African cinema had never before been "seriously addressed by the African press, and even less so by the European or American newspapers," Bhêly-Quenum asserted. Of forty-five thousand copies printed, fewer than fifteen hundred remained unsold. A multitude of requests had arrived by mail at the magazine's offices where, for the previous several months, "crowds, both Black and White, had come to buy issue number 15."[37]

Like the special issue of *La Vie Africaine*, that of *L'Afrique actuelle* appealed to a readership wider than just Africans in Europe or current and future cineastes. And its ample illustrations, both film stills and photographs, now represented a cadre of African directors and their films. Still an important source of information about films, many of which have been lost, and filmmakers, many of whom have been forgotten, this special issue nonetheless reflects the research of one man with no access to print or film archives or reference books. A closing note repeated that it was "the first work of its kind in the global press," continuing that "as we wish to do better, we ask our readers to be kind enough to share with us any errors and omissions they notice."[38] *L'Afrique actuelle*, however, was even shorter lived than its predecessor, with only a thirty-seven-issue print run from 1965 to 1969, and D'dée never published a corrected and updated version. Interested readers had to wait almost a decade for Paulin Vieyra's *Le Cinéma Africain, des origines à 1973*, with its comprehensive and much lengthier handbook of filmmakers and films from around the entire continent, organized by country.[39]

It is not surprising that West and Central African film criticism began in French, although both *Présence Africaine* and *L'Afrique actuelle* gestured toward bilingualism with English, and in the pages of journals and magazines based in France. The same was true of filmmaking, with no training programs or facilities in sub-Saharan Africa during the decade before or two decades after independence from France and Great Britain, and with North America less accessible than Europe both linguistically and financially. And as both Vieyra and D'dée made sure to point out, those few early directors who obtained training and funding to shoot in Africa were obliged to return to Europe to complete and arrange to distribute their films. More noteworthy, in fact, than the origin of Black African film criticism in France is its origin in Black-owned and -edited publications. Only as the end of the first decade of independence approached did the most prestigious French film magazines such as *Cahiers du cinéma* and *Positif* slowly begin to recognize new African cinema, particularly after Ousmane Sembene won the Prix Jean Vigo for *La Noire de . . .* (*Black Girl*, 1966). The rare reviews and interviews in these publications were written only by white French critics, however, and Africa appeared in their pages for the most part via the films of Jean Rouch.

More surprising than this history, perhaps, is the continued scarcity of publications devoted to African film and media, even and especially in Africa. Only in the 1970s would a film magazine dedicated to African cinema be created, one that was based in West Africa but, in a paradoxical reversal from *La Vie Africaine* and *L'Afrique actuelle*, established and edited by a white Frenchman. Catholic priest and cinephile Father Jean Vast had come to Saint-Louis, Senegal, in 1950; in 1968 he created the Catholic Cinema Office of Senegal, and in 1973 he launched the decidedly not glossy *Unir Cinéma*, whose more than 150 typewritten issues appeared almost every other month through the 1990s.[40] Vast set up a cinema resource center, which served as a research library for the young African collaborators who joined him to write the publication's reviews, interviews, and short articles. Numerous additional pieces were reprinted from other sources, including French and Senegalese magazines *La Revue du cinéma*, *Afrique-Asie*, and *Waraango*, perhaps with or perhaps without permission, and Vieyra was a frequent partner, with much of his book *Le cinéma au Sénégal* (*Cinema in Senegal*) appearing in bits and pieces over the years.[41]

The short-lived *Écrans d'Afrique* (*African Screen*), founded in 1991 and discontinued in 1998, perhaps best exemplified D'dée's legacy. More consistently bilingual in French and English than *La Vie Africaine* and *L'Afrique actuelle*, *Écrans d'Afrique* was, unlike Alioune Diop's and Olympe Bhêly-Quenum's earlier publications, uniquely devoted to African film and media. Vibrantly designed and illustrated to reach a wide, global audience, it was a coproduction of the Pan-African Federation of Filmmakers (FEPACI) and Italian nongovernmental organization the Educational Orientation Center (COE), receiving financial support from Burkina Faso and the European Union. The magazine's editorial team was solely African, however; Burkinabé director Gaston Kaboré served as editor and Burkinabé journalist and film critic Clément Tapsoba as editor-in-chief. Both were a generation younger than Vieyra and D'dée; Kaboré had trained in France, whereas Tapsoba received his first of several diplomas from the African Institute of Cinematographic

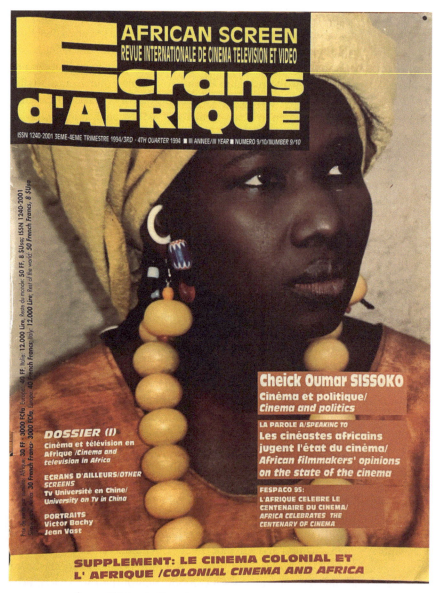

FIGURE 10.5. *Écrans d'Afrique/African Screen*, 1994.

Education (INAFEC), a film school that had opened in Burkina Faso in 1976 only to close its doors a decade later.

In France and its former colonies in West and Central Africa, a single print magazine devoted to African cinema and media circulates today. The Paris-based *Awotele*, created in 2015, times its triannual issues to coincide with pan-African film festivals held in Carthage, Tunisia; Ouagadougou, Burkina Faso; and Durban,

South Africa. *Awotele* launched a year after *Le Film Africain* (*African Film*), an industry publication created in 1993 by the Amiens International Film Festival, ceased publication. For African filmmakers based in France, *Le Film Africain* had furthered many of the goals of D'dée's earlier *cahier technique*, with additional funding from the French Ministry of Foreign Affairs in 2001 allowing for higher-quality paper and color photographs. On the African continent, the Senegalese Ministry of Culture and Communication released only a few issues of *Senciné*, a magazine promoting the Senegalese film industry, between 2014 and 2018. It is still possible to read African critics writing about African cinema in Africa, however, and not just in the academic *Journal of African Cinemas*, based at South Africa's University of Johannesburg.

Continuing in the model of *La Vie Africaine* and *L'Afrique actuelle*, a committed and eclectic film criticism has persisted in newspapers and in news, arts, and culture magazines. Senegal's Baba Diop, who has published in daily *Le Soleil* and biannual *Waraango* among other venues, recently stressed the importance of the role of African journalists as film critics, particularly at a time when African films may premiere in Africa instead of Europe or North America. "Before," Diop began in an interview with Bassirou Niang, "journalists and directors said there was no film criticism in Africa. I answered that this was because they didn't read the press."[42] Diop, who like Tapsoba served as president of the African Federation of Cinematographic Criticism (FACC), now teaches journalism to filmmaking students at the Université Gaston Berger in Saint-Louis. Working with Thierno Ibrahima Dia, he is the editor of *Africiné Magazine* at Africiné.org, which, with the stated goal of upholding African critical writing, has revived the Paulin Vieyra Film Prize, awarded by FACC critics at the biennial Pan-African Film Festival (FESPACO) in Ouagadougou, Burkina Faso. In what is likely the future of most film journalism, *Africiné* and the France-based online arts and culture review *Africultures*, both now almost exclusively online entities, more than any print publications serve as consistent guarantors of information about and analysis of sub-Saharan African film and media. French critic Olivier Barlet founded *Africultures* in 1997 and has since made Herculean efforts to maintain it; in addition to numerous reviews of films and festivals and interviews with filmmakers, partially digitized issues of *Écrans d'Afrique* are now available through the site.

Decrying the absence of "enlightening and provocative" African film criticism as the number of African films was finally increasing, Manthia Diawara in the late 1980s argued that European and North American film critics could only assess African films "through the prism of Western film language."[43] Highlighting this disconnect, Tapsoba recounted, soon after, a critical disagreement at FESPACO that nearly brought African and non-African critics to blows. At stake, according to Tapsoba, was an intimate connection between African filmmakers and their African spectators, who would reject any films that sought to satisfy a Western desire for exoticism.[44] Vieyra had been acutely aware of this problem and, remembering his beginnings at *Présence Africaine*, worked to match his interest in rigorous film

198   CHAPTER 10

criticism with his understanding of its relevance to and impact on African cinema. Directors must be critiqued by those "who know what they are talking about" but also have "a certain distance from the creator," Vieyra argued, and for this reason he had been working to train African journalists not just in the practical details of film production, but also in "the semiology and semantics of African cinema."[45] In D'dée's work for *La Vie Africaine* and *L'Afrique actuelle*, which built on Vieyra's more scholarly analyses, we find the beginnings of a popular Black African film criticism that has been constant work in creative progress. Global audiences rely on its attention not just to the political and cultural need for African cinema, not just to the European and North American cartels that have monopolized African movie theaters, but above all to the technique and signification of African media creations.

NOTES

1. These titles can be translated as "African Presence," "African Life," and "Contemporary Africa."

2. Bennetta Jules-Rosette, "Conjugating Cultural Realities: *Présence Africaine*," in *The Surreptitious Speech*: Présence Africaine *and the Politics of Otherness 1947–1987*, ed. V. Y. Mudimbe (Chicago: University of Chicago Press, 1992), 17. Mudimbe's edited volume is an invaluable resource with respect to *Présence Africaine*, yet cinema is mentioned not once in its more than four hundred pages, with Paulin Vieyra making just a single appearance.

3. André Gide, "Avant-propos," *Présence Africaine*, no. 1 (1947): 3. Unless otherwise noted, all translations are mine.

4. Alioune Diop, "Niam n'goura, ou les raisons d'être de *Présence Africaine*," *Présence Africaine*, no. 1 (1947): 8.

5. Georges Bataille, "Cinéma et acteurs noirs," *Présence Africaine*, no. 4 (1948): 690–96. Jean Caillens, "Sur le cinéma: la caméra se propose, mais l'Afrique dispose," *Présence Africaine*, no. 12 (1951): 233–34.

6. Iwiyé Kala-Lobe, "Alioune Diop et le cinéma africain," *Présence Africaine*, no. 125 (1983): 329.

7. For a history of the early years of *Présence Africaine* that includes a detailed discussion of the journal's more radical turn in the mid-1950s, see Salah Hassan, "Inaugural Issues: The Cultural Politics of the Early *Présence Africaine*, 1947–1955," *Research in African Literatures* 30, no. 2 (1999): 194–221. For an illustrated prehistory and early history, see Sarah Frioux-Salgas, "*Présence Africaine*. Une tribune, un mouvement, un réseau," *Gradhiva*, no. 10 (2009): 4–21. *Gradhiva*'s special issue devoted to *Présence Africaine* also features an excellent essay by Pap Ndiaye contextualizing the journal's intellectual origins in interwar Paris.

8. C. Ijdedem, "Mouramouni," *Présence Africaine*, no. 1/2 (1955): 159–60.

9. Paulin Soumanou Vieyra, "Quand le cinéma français parle au nom de l'Afrique noire," *Présence Africaine*, no. 11 (1956–1957): 142–45.

10. Vieyra, "Quand le cinéma français parle au nom de l'Afrique noire," 143.

11. Vieyra, "Quand le cinéma français parle au nom de l'Afrique noire," 143, 145.

12. Paulin Soumanou Vieyra, "Propos sur le cinéma africain," *Présence Africaine*, no. 22 (1958): 106–17; Paulin Soumanou Vieyra, "Le cinéma et la Révolution Africain," *Présence Africaine*, no. 34/35 (1961): 92–103.

13. Ruth Bush and Claire Ducournau, "'Small Readers' and Big Magazines: Reading Publics in *Bingo, La Vie Africaine,* and *Awa: la revue de la femme noire*," *Research in African Literatures* 51, no. 1 (Spring 2020): 48, 49. This boom does not appear to have included a single movie magazine.

AFRICAN FILM CRITICISM, 1957–1967 199

14. Bush and Ducournau, "'Small Readers' and Big Magazines," 65 n7.

15. Bhêly-Quenum also claimed that *L'Afrique actuelle* was "the only magazine of its kind owned and personally directed by an African." Reuben Musiker et al., "News and Notes," *African Studies Bulletin* 10, no. 2 (1967): 100.

16. O. B.-G. "Réponse à nos lecteurs," *L'Afrique actuelle*, no. 15 (1967): 3.

17. See my "Complex Realism: Paulin Soumanou Vieyra and the Emergence of West African Documentary Film," *Black Camera* 11, no. 2 (2020): 32–59; as well as Vincent Bouchard and Amadou Ouédraogo's coedited "Close-Up" section of *Black Camera* 13, no. 2 (2022): 295–499).

18. Boris Vian, *Manuel de St. Germain des Près* (Paris: Éditions du Chêne, 1974); Boris Vian, *Mademoiselle Bonsoir, suivi de La Reine des garces* (Paris: Librairie Général Française, 2009).

19. La Vie Africaine, "Pourquoi un numéro spécial sur le cinéma," *La Vie Africaine* (June 1961): 14.

20. D'dée, "Propositions pour une production cinématographique africaine," *La Vie Africaine* (May 1961): 25.

21. D'dée, "Le cinéma est d'abord une industrie et une technique: comment fabrique-t-on un film?," *La Vie Africaine* (June 1961): 14–19, 49.

22. "Quelques grandes oeuvres du cinéma mondiale," "Les grandes étapes de l'invention du cinéma," "La publicité et le cinéma," "Quelques statistiques sur la fréquentation des salles en Afrique," *La Vie Africaine* (June 1961): 17, 19, 24.

23. Georges Sadoul, "L'Afrique a été jusqu'à présent le pays de la 'disette cinématographique,'" *La Vie Africaine* (June 1961): 23, 25.

24. Jean Rouch, "A propos d'un débat sur le 'Carnaval des Dieux," *La Vie Africaine* (June 1961): 26. Rouch mistakenly referred to the director as Peter instead of Richard. See Paulin Vieyra's earlier review, "Le Carnaval des dieux," *Présence Africaine*, no 18/19 (1958): 244–46.

25. Georges Bourdelon, "Le cinéma au service du développement: une expérience de films éducatifs en République Centrafricaine," *La Vie Africaine* (June 1961): 31–32.

26. See Rouch's "Situation et tendances actuelles du cinéma africain," presented as a report to UNESCO in 1961, the same year as D'dée's special issue for *La Vie Africaine*, and republished as an appendix to UNESCO's 1967 *Premier catalogue sélectif international des films ethnographique sur l'Afrique noire*. In the new edition of his history of world cinema published two years after his article for *La Vie Africaine*, Sadoul added several pages addressing cinema in Africa while still proclaiming the lack of a single "truly African" film. Georges Sadoul, *Histoire du cinéma mondial, des origines à nos jours, 7e édition, revue et augmentée* (Paris: Flammarion, 1963), 499.

27. Ratovondrahona, "Cinéma commercial et loisirs populaires: voir quoi?," *La Vie Africaine* (June 1961): 33; Honoré Dol, "Construire le cinéma africain," *La Vie Africaine* (June 1961): 41.

28. "L'avenir du cinéma africain: un débat avec nos futurs cinéastes," *La Vie Africaine* (June 1961): 37–39; "Le point de vue d'un futur producteur africain: Blaise Senghor," *La Vie Africaine* (June 1961): 39.

29. D'dée, "Au festival de Cannes 1961: aucune nation Africaine n'était représentée," *La Vie Africaine* (June 1961): 36.

30. Colette Lacroix, "L'Actrice française qui a le plus tourné en Afrique: Juliette Graco," *La Vie Africaine* (June 1961): 34–35.

31. D'dée, "Enfin du vrai cinéma africain," *La Vie Africaine* (October 1962): 47.

32. Paulin Soumanou Vieyra, "Du Cinéma et l'Afrique au cinéma africain," in *Le Cinéma et l'Afrique* (Paris: Présence Africaine, 1969), 175–87.

33. Anonymous, "Semaine du jeune cinéma d'Afrique noire," *Combat* (April 18, 1967).

34. D'dée, "L'Afrique au secours du cinéma occidental?," *L'Afrique actuelle*, no. 15 (February 1967): 4.

35. D'dée, "Les jeunes réalisateurs africains," *L'Afrique actuelle*, no. 15 (February 1967): 5–6.

36. D'dée, "Pour un cinéma de qualité," *L'Afrique actuelle*, no. 15 (February 1967): 39–40.

37. Olympe Bhêly-Quenum, "Jeune cinéma d'Afrique noire, une chimère: interview exclusive de Blaise Senghor," *L'Afrique actuelle*, no. 19 (June 1967): 8.

38. *L'Afrique actuelle*, no. 15 (February 1967): 40.

200   CHAPTER 10

39. Paulin Soumanou Vieyra, *Le Cinéma Africain, des origines à 1973* (Paris: Présence Africaine, 1975), 21–225.

40. Olivier Barlet, "Au début des cinémas d'Afrique, la revue *Unir Cinéma* et le centre de documentation du Père Jean Vast," *Africultures* (2017), http://africultures.com/debut-cinemas-dafrique-revue-unir-cinema-centre-de-documentation-pere-jean-vast-14360/.

41. Paulin Soumanou Vieyra, *Le Cinéma au Sénégal* (Paris: OCIC/L'Harmattan, 1983).

42. Bassirou Niang, "JCC 2021–Entretien avec M. Baba Diop, Critique de cinéma," *Africiné* (2021), http://africine.org/entretien/jcc-2021-entretien-avec-m-baba-diop-critique-de-cinema/15237. Critic Jean Servais Bakyono published regularly in Abidjan daily *Le Jour* and other Ivorian newspapers and magazines from the 1980s until his death in 2006. Olivier Barlet, *Les Cinémas d'Afrique noire, le regard en question* (Paris: L'Harmattan, 1996), 237.

43. Manthia Diawara, "Popular Culture and Oral Traditions in African Film," *Film Quarterly* 41, no. 3 (1988): 6.

44. Clément Tapsoba, "De l'orientation de la critique du cinéma africain," in *L'Afrique et le Centenaire du Cinéma*, ed. FEPACI (Paris: Présence Africaine, 1995), 161–62.

45. Françoise Pfaff, "Paulin Soumanou Vieyra, pionnier de la critique et de la théorie du cinéma africain," *Présence Africaine*, no. 170 (2004): 31, 34.

PUBLICATIONS REFERENCED

Africiné Magazine
Africultures
Afrique-Asie
Awotele
Cahiers du cinéma
Écrans d'Afrique
France Eurafrique
Jeune Afrique
Journal of African Cinemas
L'Afrique actuelle
La Revue du cinéma
La Vie Africaine
Le Film Africain
Le Soleil
Positif
Présence Africaine
Senciné
Unir Cinéma
Waraango

BIBLIOGRAPHY

Barlet, Olivier. *Les Cinémas d'Afrique noire, le regard en question.* Paris: L'Harmattan, 1996.

Bouchard, Vincent, and Amadou Ouédraogo. "Paulin S. Vieyra, A Postcolonial Figure." *Black Camera* 13, no. 2 (2022): 295–499.

Bush, Ruth, and Claire Ducournau. "'Small Readers' and Big Magazines: Reading Publics in *Bingo, La Vie Africaine*, and *Awa: la revue de la femme noire*." *Research in African Literatures* 51, no. 1 (Spring 2020): 45–69.

Diawara, Manthia. "Popular Culture and Oral Traditions in African Film." *Film Quarterly* 41, no. 3 (1988): 6–14.

AFRICAN FILM CRITICISM, 1957–1967   201

Frioux-Salgas, Sarah. "*Présence Africaine.* Une tribune, un mouvement, un réseau." *Gradhiva*, no. 10 (2009): 4–21.

Gabara, Rachel. "Complex Realism: Paulin Soumanou Vieyra and the Emergence of West African Documentary Film." *Black Camera* 11, no. 2 (2020): 32–59.

Hassan, Salah. "Inaugural Issues: The Cultural Politics of the Early *Présence Africaine*, 1947–1955." *Research in African Literatures* 30, no. 2 (1999): 194–221.

Mudimbe, V. Y., ed. *The Surreptitious Speech*: Présence Africaine *and the Politics of Otherness 1947–1987.* Chicago: University of Chicago Press, 1992.

Niang, Bassirou. "JCC 2021–Entretien avec M. Baba Diop, Critique de cinéma." *Africiné* (2021). http://africine.org/entretien/jcc-2021-entretien-avec-m-baba-diop-critique-de-cinema/15237.

Pfaff, Françoise. "Paulin Soumanou Vieyra, pionnier de la critique et de la théorie du cinéma africain." *Présence Africaine*, no. 170 (2004): 27–34.

Rouch, Jean. "Situation et tendances actuelles du cinéma africain." In *Premier catalogue sélectif international des films ethnographique sur l'Afrique noire*, 374–408. Paris: Unesco, 1967.

Sadoul, Georges. *Histoire du cinéma mondial, des origines à nos jours, 7e édition, revue et augmentée.* Paris: Flammarion, 1963.

Tapsoba, Clément. "De l'orientation de la critique du cinéma africain." In *L'Afrique et le Centenaire du Cinéma*, edited by FEPACI, 157–165. Paris: Présence Africaine, 1995.

Vian, Boris. *Mademoiselle Bonsoir, suivi de La Reine des garces.* Paris: Librairie Général Française, 2009.

———. *Manuel de St. Germain des Près.* Paris: Éditions du Chêne, 1974.

Vieyra, Paulin Soumanou. *Le Cinéma africain, des origines à 1973.* Paris: Présence Africaine, 1975.

———. *Le Cinéma au Sénégal.* Paris: OCIC/L'Harmattan, 1983.

———. *Le Cinéma et l'Afrique.* Paris: Présence Africaine, 1969.

11

Japan's Post-1968: *Kikan firumu, Shinema 69,* and *Eiga hihyō*

Naoki Yamamoto

INTRODUCTION: JAPAN IN AND AFTER 1968

As in France and many other countries, Japan's 1968 was a year of political protests and social upheavals. Its main protagonists were college students who began occupying their classrooms and streets to protest oppression brought by US imperialism, the Japanese capitalist state, the "Old Left," and the Communist Party. With the help of these New Left radicals, even farmers, too, rose up to fight the construction of the newly planned Narita International Airport. Not surprisingly, this highly intense political situation led to a riot. On October 21, more than two thousand student protesters equipped with their iconic helmets and wooden *gewalt* sticks burned down the Shinjuku Station, the busiest train station in the Tokyo area, in an attempt to stop the transportation of jet fuel used for the ongoing US invasion of Vietnam. It is, however, misleading to treat the year 1968 as the single apex of the Japanese anti-establishment movement. From 1969 to 1970, local protests continued against the automatic renewal of the US-Japan Security Treaty, which was just about to happen at the end of 1970. Then, the real end point of Japan's long 1960s finally occurred in February 1972, when members of the far-left political faction United Red Army (Rengō sekigun, hereafter URA) were arrested after the Asama-Sansō incident, a spectacular, live-broadcast, nine-day-long shootout between URA members and the special police.

At the same time, the 1960s, especially the second half of the decade, were a turbulent period for the Japanese film industry. In 1958, there were 7,067 movie theaters in Japan, which sold 11.2 million tickets in total (this means every single Japanese citizen watched more than twelve films on average per year). In 1968, these numbers had rapidly declined to 3,814 theaters and to 3.1 million tickets sold.[1] This was due largely to the rise of the domestic TV industry, but thanks to the country's "high-speed" economic growth after World War II, Japanese people in general also became affluent enough to adopt other new forms of leisure activities such as playing golf for the adults and go-go dancing for the youth. Despite this unavoidable crisis, Japanese cinema remained productive in the late 1960s, releasing as many films—410 in 1967 and 494 in both 1968 and 1969—as in the 1950s.[2] But this perceived constancy was actually the product of the ongoing restructuring of the film industry, since a significant number of Japanese films of the period were now produced independently by such enterprising directors as Ōshima Nagisa, Wakamatsu Kōji, and Ogawa Shinsuke. In contrast, the five major Japanese film studios—Shōchiku, Tōhō, Daiei, Tōei, and Nikkatsu—could do little more than conserve their remaining properties. In particular, the situation hit Daiei and Nikkatsu much harder than others because they did not have their own theater chains. To secure their uncertain revenues, these two companies formed a new distribution company called Dainichi eihai as a joint venture, but it was only a drop in the bucket. Consequently, Daiei went bankrupt in 1971, while Nikkatsu managed to sustain its business by dedicating the company entirely to the production of softcore porn films.

Given such a radical restructuring of society and the industry, it comes as no surprise that Japan in the second half of the 1960s witnessed the emergence of a new critical discourse on film and its shifting functions. This chapter offers a comparative reading of the three independent Japanese film magazines published in and after 1968: *Kikan firumu* (*Film Quarterly*, 1968–72), *Shinema 69* (*Cinema 69*, 1969–71, which changed its title yearly as in *Shinema 70* and *71*), and *Eiga hihyō* (*Film Criticism*, 1970–73). Despite their short-lived existence, these magazines clearly demonstrate Japan's active participation in the ongoing global debates about how to revolutionize daily engagement with film and other mass communication media. Their informed focus on issues such as expanded cinema and video art (*Kikan firumu*), revised auteur theory and French poststructuralism (*Shinema 69*), and far-left radicalism and the liberation of the Third World (*Eiga hihyō*) quite convincingly testified to the emergence of a new global network that no longer based itself on the simple geopolitical divide between the West and the rest. Of many topics discussed there, this chapter pays special attention to the manner in which Japanese film critics' diligent search for alternative cinema ultimately led to a radical reconfiguration of film theory as such.

THREE MAGAZINES

Having appeared as the Japanese version of "post-1968" counter-discourse, *Kikan firumu, Shinema 69,* and *Eiga hihyō* all intended to establish a new form

204   CHAPTER 11

and meaning of "criticism" (*hihyō*) in the context of Japanese film criticism. As Hatano Tetsurō, the founder of *Shinema 69*, reminds us, the history of Japanese film criticism up to the late 1960s had been divided into two major tendencies, namely "impressionist criticism" (*inshō hihyō*) and "ideological criticism" (*ideorogii hihyō*).[3] While the former had long been a template for Japanese film criticism, frequently adopted by professional critics writing for *Kinema junpō* and other major commercial magazines, the latter also became very influential after the war, along with the legalization of the Japanese Communist Party (JCP) and its organizational support for "Old Left" filmmakers such as Imai Tadashi and Yamamoto Satsuo. But these two approaches were problematic because they seldom questioned the legitimacy of their own claims, as if they had some unflinching, well-nigh transcendental trust in their aesthetic sensibilities or political credos.

As a remedy for this long-standing problem, Hatano and editors of the other two magazines consciously adopted several strategies. First, they proactively solicited contributions from those who had not been contaminated with preexisting conventions of Japanese film criticism. Indeed, writers appearing in these magazines were mostly in their twenties and thirties and came from such diverse disciplines and backgrounds as art, literature, theater, music, TV, graphic design, guerrilla tactics, and computer science. Second, the editors also designed their magazines to be a site for direct and reciprocal communication. Besides asking the readers to submit their own film reviews and essays, they frequently organized workshop series, study groups, and film exhibitions in an effort to revitalize film criticism as a social practice. Third, because the editors were highly concerned with copious, profit-oriented restrictions imposed by print capitalism, they all decided to go independent by establishing their own publishing house and adopting the format of independent or coterie (*dōjin*) magazine. Though such a decision ultimately made these magazines financially unstable and short lived, it clearly testifies to their shared incentive to restructure Japanese film criticism from scratch, even by altering its very capitalist mode of production and distribution.[4]

The oldest of the three, *Kikan firumu* came out at first, in October 1968, as an organ of the Sōgestu Art Center. Originally founded in 1959 with family money by the film director Teshigahara Hiroshi (best known for *Woman in the Dunes*, 1964), this institution had already played a very important role in supporting burgeoning Japanese avant-garde art movements. It thus comes as no surprise that the magazine's main objective was to develop its own concept of "alternative cinema" (*mou hitotsu no eiga*) in collaboration with experimental filmmakers and video artists.[5] Thanks to very detailed reports provided by the New York–based filmmaker Iimura Takahiko and other foreign correspondents, the magazine was first of all very resourceful and cutting-edge in introducing some notable media experiments happening on the other side of the Pacific, including Jonas Mekas's FilmMaker's Cooperative, Stan VanDerBeek's expanded cinema, and Arthur Ginsberg's Video Free America.[6]

But the real contribution of *Kikan firumu* lies rather in its strong will to theorize this radical transformation of what people used to call "film" into something else, something that is more complicated and self-reflexive than a mere vehicle for storytelling. The magazine addressed this issue from a transnational perspective, frequently translating both interviews and theoretical essays retrieved from its exclusive editorial contract with *Cahiers du cinéma*, including Jean-Luc Godard's famous interview entitled "Struggle on Two Fronts" (1967).[7] It then adopted a very strict interdisciplinary approach, which was most succinctly represented in the magazine's editorial board consisting of Awazu Kiyoshi (graphic designer), Takemitsu Tōru (music composer), Nakahara Yūsuke (art critic), Yamada Kōichi (film critic), and the filmmakers Iimura Takahiko, Matsumoto Toshio, and Teshigahara Hiroshi. Of particular importance here is the participation of the graphic designer Awazu. As the film historian Yomota Inuhiko tells us, the impressive cover designs he created for each issue using "multiple layers of colors" and "bricolages of pre-modern Japanese signs and motifs" (see figure 11.1) compellingly visualize the magazine's conscious commitment to the practice of intermedial art as well as the carnivalesque atmosphere of late-1960s Japan.[8]

In comparison, *Shinema 69* embodies the "DIY" sprit widely shared among a younger generation of Japanese film critics of the time (see figure 11.2). According to the bibliographic record, it was active from January 1969 to October 1971 and was published by the publishing house Shinemasha. In reality, this company meant nothing more than the small family apartment of the founder Hatano, an ex–staff member at the Sōgestu Art Center. And although the editors—Hatano, Tejima Shūzō, and Yamane Sadao—originally intended their magazine to be a bimonthly, they were only able to publish three issues per year, even after they decided to reduce its circulation by half—from four thousand to two thousand copies—and to stop paying honoraria to their contributors from the January 1971 issue onward.[9] Despite such an unavoidable and persistent financial burden, the editors—especially Yamane as the writer of the magazine's editorial—always sought solutions at the grassroots level. In addition to frequently asking the reader to take part in their annual subscription program, Yamane went so far as to make his personal home address and phone number publicly available so that anyone who wished to support this magazine could talk or visit him in person.

Today, *Shinema 69* is remembered mostly for its discovery of Hasumi Shigehiko, who—with his distinctive writing style and up-to-date knowledge about French intellectual traditions, which he had obtained during his doctoral research at the Univesité de Paris from 1962 to 1965—became a towering figure in Japanese film criticism for the next two decades (I will come back to him in the next section). But the magazine itself also made a great contribution to the ongoing reform of Japanese film criticism by pursuing some fundamental questions, like "What is the main attraction of cinema?" and "What does it mean to write about this particular cinematic attraction, and how is it possible?" Despite their apparent naivete,

FIGURE 11.1. Front cover, *Kikan firumu*, no. 8, March 1971.

FIGURE 11.2. Front cover, *Shinema 69*, no. 1, January 1969.

these questions in effect reveal the magazine's strategic adoption of existentialist phenomenology as its own method. As if to follow Sartre's famous motto "Existence precedes essence," essays appearing in the magazine carefully tried to look at and describe film's own controversial state of being as experienced from each individual viewer's sensibility and understanding so that the very practice of "writing about cinema" could be more creative and autonomous.[10] Another important feature of *Shinema 69* was its renewed treatment of mainstream Japanese cinema. While the magazine kept track of the increasing visibility of "New Wave" directors like Ōshima Nagisa and Yoshida Kijū abroad, its main focus was placed rather on the work of studio-based genre film directors such as Suzuki Seijun, Katō Tai, and

208   CHAPTER 11

Makino Masahiro in a way similar to that of *Cahiers*'s famous appraisal of Howard Hawks and Alfred Hitchcock as film auteurs.[11]

Finally, we have *Eiga hihyō*, which was active from October 1970 to September 1973 under the editorship of Matsuda Masao (see figure 11.3). Besides being a film critic, Matsuda had been widely known as one of the major ideologues and organizers of the Japanese New Left movement in the late 1960s. This meant that the assessment of the magazine became contingent on the political climate of the specific historical period called "post-1968." Undoubtedly, *Eiga hihyō* was more visible and influential than the other two film magazines when it first came out, given its blatant call for liberating the world and our daily consumption of film and other mass communication media from the hands of capitalists qua neo-imperialists. But this meant that the magazine's historical importance—or more simply, what it actually discussed—rapidly faded into oblivion along with the society's general disillusionment with New Left radicalism. This sort of negative assessment could also be easily amplified by the presence of the film director Adachi Masao on the magazine's editorial board. As is well known, Adachi secretly left Japan for Palestine in 1974 to become a member of the Japanese Red Army (Nihon sekigun), a far-left political faction that throughout the 1970s and '80s committed a series of terrorist attacks both inside and outside the Arab world under the leadership of the Popular Front for the Liberation of Palestine. As a result, few written or spoken statements were made by Adachi during his "underground" years, which abruptly ended with his arrest and forced repatriation to Japan around 2000.[12] Meanwhile, *Eiga hihyō* came to be seen and dismissed as simply spreading dogmatic political visions provided by those presumably dangerous terrorist organizations.

Now, to change our perspective, we should first consider the fact that Matsuda, *Eiga hihyō*'s editor, was equally motivated to revitalize Japanese film criticism. Indeed, the official mission of *Eiga hihyō* was to transform the whole process of making, distributing, showing, watching, and writing about films into a new form of social engagement called "movement" (*undō*).[13] Interestingly, the term *movement* here meant less people's affiliation with actual political factions than an individual's critical decision to look at the world in its potentiality for change—a concept usually called *revolution*—and to apply this principle indiscriminately to the preexisting hierarchical divisions of labors between subject and object, mind and body, logic and emotion, theory and practice, producers and consumers, professionals and amateurs, and the everyday and political actions. To demonstrate this editorial policy even before the publication of the first issue, Matsuda and two other editorial members, Adachi and Sasaki Mamoru, had first produced an experimental film, *Ryakushō renzoku shasatsuma* (*A.K.A. Serial Killer*, 1969/75) together,[14] developing one of the most important concepts in 1960s Japanese film and media theory, *fūkeiron* (landscape theory),

FIGURE 11.3. Front cover, *Eiga hihyō* 4, no. 8, August 1973.

210 CHAPTER 11

as an open-ended discursive articulation of their collective engagement with independent filmmaking.[15]

DECENTERING FILM THEORY

In addition to these varying details, *Kikan firumu*, *Shinema 69*, and *Eiga hihyō* also shared a renewed sense of coevality with things happening outside Japan. Like *Kikan firumu*, *Shinema 69* made an editorial contract with the French film magazine of the same title (*Cinéma 69*, discussed in this volume by Kelley Conway) and, in every issue, organized a section titled "Situations of Cinema in the World" (*sekai no eiga jōkyō*) featuring a series of detailed firsthand reports from countries including Brazil, China, Cuba, Czechoslovakia, France, Germany, Italy, Poland, the Soviet Union, the UK, and the US. In contrast, *Eiga hihyō* selectively translated more political texts like Jean-Luc Godard and Jean-Pierre Gorin's "Dziga Vertov Group in America" (1970) or Fernando Solanas and Octavio Getino's "Toward a Third Cinema" (1969) as examples of contemporary attempts to revolutionize our daily commitment to film as both a medium and a social practice.[16] Nevertheless, a simple increase in numbers and amounts of translated text and transmitted information alone cannot differentiate these three magazines from their predecessors. As I have argued elsewhere, the history of Japanese film theory and criticism in the past century, especially during a period dubbed "classical" in our discipline, was always marked by a persistent desire to catch up with the latest discursive trends imported from abroad.[17] Correspondingly, all the major works of canonical film theorists—including Hugo Münsterberg, Béla Balázs, Jean Epstein, Rudolf Arnheim, Vsevolod Pudovkin, Sergei Eisenstein, André Bazin, Siegfried Kracauer, and Guido Aristarco—were available to the Japanese readers of the 1960s through translation.

Therefore, it is not quantity but quality that matters. What is crucial here is that the radical and self-reflective reform of Japanese film criticism put forward by those three post-1968 magazines ultimately led to a radical reconceptualization of what we scholars call *theory* and its application to a specific medium called *film*. Given its editorial focus on the legacy of avant-garde art movements, it seems natural that *Kikan firumu* addressed this issue by devising an "alternative" genealogy of theorizations of cinema from the perspective of experimental filmmaking. The result was the October 1971 special issue titled "Eiga sengenshū" (A Collection of Film Manifestos) which, just like P. Adams Sitney's *The Avant-Garde Film: A Reader of Film Theory and Criticism* (1978) or Scott MacKenzie's *Film Manifestos and Global Cinema Cultures* (2021), comprehensively compiled and translated key written texts by a variety of film practitioners qua theorists including Georges Méliès, Ricciotto Canudo, Filippo Tommaso Marinetti, Paul Wagner, Vsevolod Meyerhold, René Clair, Germaine Dulac, Alexandre Astruc, Cesare Zavattini, Orson Welles, Luis Buñuel, Maya Deren, Jonas Mekas, Glauber Rocha, and Robert

Kramer.[18] Equally notable was a collection of Dziga Vertov's written manifestos and essays, published in the March 1971 issue of the same magazine.[19] Directly translated from the 1966 Russian edition of Vertov's writings, this Japanese version appeared in full synchronicity with its English equivalent "The Writings of Dziga Vertov" (1970), included in Sitney's other anthology, *Film Culture Reader*.

However informative, this quasi-encyclopedic approach was problematic in that it acknowledged no substantial contributions from Japan or other non-Western countries, despite its conscious attempt to rewrite the history of film theory from a different and previously marginalized perspective. This was exactly the problem the film historian Satō Tadao squarely addressed in his book-length essay "Nihon no eiga riron" (Film Theory in Japan), published serially in *Shinema 69* from January 1969 to June 1971. To begin, Satō provocatively asked if there had been any film theory that one could distinctively call "Japanese." His answer was no, as long as readers uncritically accepted the traditional definition of *theory* and its unassailable monopoly by the West. "Individuals who have written in books on film theory in Japan," said Satō, "have mainly authored translations introducing foreign film theory," and therefore, "in Japan, unfortunately, very few individuals can be called film theorists."[20] Satō's polemic here was employed less to lament the absence of Japanese theorists with original insights than to illuminate a uniquely "Japanese" take on the definition of *film theory* as such. He thus went on to write: "It is not that Japan has no original film theory. . . . Unfortunately, however, Japanese film theory remains disorganized, buried in the word-of-mouth training at production studios, in the short essays and written interviews of directors and screenwriters, and in the film reviews written by critics."[21]

According to Satō, only a specific kind of local discourse developed and shared among practitioners working within the film industry in its largest sense could properly be called a Japanese film theory. This provocative statement, however, turned out to be less radical than it seemed, once he disclosed his own argument. First, Satō devoted a critical amount of his analysis to the work of Japanese writers with no professional experience in the industry, including Nakagawa Shigeaki (aesthetician), Terada Torahiko (poet and physicist), Sugiyama Heiichi (poet and film critic), Imamura Taihei (film critic), Ōtsuki Kenji (economist), Nakai Masakazu (philosopher), and Hanada Kiyoteru (writer and critic). Second, his strategic emphasis on a practical and vernacular local discourse cannot be a substantial point of reference to differentiate Japanese film theory from others. Indeed, D. N. Rodowick reminds us that quite a few examples of the texts we consider "canons" of classical film theory were equally developed, to a large extent, by means of filmmakers' self-reflection and published in a wide variety of "unorganized" and "non-academic" writing forms such as film reviews, written manifestos, and poetic or fictional prose.[22] Finally, Satō's counterargument unfortunately stopped before providing a more fundamental critique of theory as a specific mode of writing and knowledge production. This means that once he succeeded in expanding the geographic scope of film theory to include previously unrecognized Japanese contributions, he automatically applied the same evaluative criteria as before, only praising what one of his fellow Japanese critics rightly criticized as the "normative aesthetic" (*kihanteki bigaku*).

Importantly, it is Hasumi Shigehiko, another significant contributor to *Shinema 69*, who made this last criticism in his 1971 article titled "Eizō no riron kara riron no eizō e" (From a Theory of an Image to an Image of a Theory).[23] In this and other related essays published around the turn of the 1970s, Hasumi harshly criticized his fellow critics for failing to problematize their anachronistic acceptance of theory as a discourse of universal emancipation. This was because theory, he argued, especially in its current state, served as a discourse of oppression inasmuch as it violently integrates parts into the whole and mercilessly excludes any false or uncertain claims in its totalitarian pursuit of the so-called general truth. To liberate theory from such a reactionary state, Hasumi intentionally adopted a post-structuralist stance: rather than proposing "practical" or "anti-theoretical" discourse as an antidote, he first and foremost aimed to subvert the preexisting hierarchical relationship between word and image in his new conception of "film theory" in accordance with Jacques Derrida's contemporary attempt to deconstruct similar pairs of oppositional terms including mind and image, speech and writing, reason and experience, presence and absence, and the signifier and the signified.

This, however, does not mean that Hasumi totally denied the relevance of theory as a mode of critical inquiry. Indeed, he still employed the adjective *theoretical* time and again to designate his own "logical" attempt to clarify the ontological condition of an object or phenomenon under consideration. The difference was that people could now perform this practice through image, through their empirical commitment to both the making and viewing of film texts. It is in this context that Hasumi paid tribute to the work of a selected list of filmmakers who had consciously and persistently developed an internal critique of film as both a genuinely modern and institutionalized form of expression. One such director was Ozu Yasujirō, and Hasumi interpreted the director's constant violation of an imaginary line between the two on-screen characters in conversation as a highly self-reflective attempt to visualize what film *cannot* show us in principle— namely, the gaze that these two characters actually shared and exchanged.[24] In the end, Hasumi succinctly summarized his own intervention as an attempt not to establish a new film theory in its traditional sense, but rather to retrieve a theory of *the cinema* (*eiga to iumono*) that each individual film text embodies and speaks whenever it is both projected on screen *and* rightly interpreted by perceptive viewers like Hasumi himself.

Thanks to his provocative call for a "return" to films themselves, Hasumi soon came to be recognized as a gamechanger in post-1968 Japanese film criticism and remained influential for the next two decades. It is not difficult to criticize Hasumi for his apparently phenomenologist stance, his decision to put everything he deemed to be external to the autonomy of a film text—including social, financial, and ideological conditions of filmmaking—into brackets. As Aaron Gerow points out, however, Hasumi's apolitical intervention here should rather be seen as "a different politics, one that, stemming in part from a disillusionment with orthodoxies of 1960s radical politics and their claims of authority, struggled against universal abstractions, metanarratives, and other forms of categorical meaning that restricted the inherent creativity of criticism and film viewing."[25] Indeed, we should keep in mind that Hasumi addressed his critique not only to Satō's serialized essay but also to a series of debates presented by *Eiga hihyō* regarding terms such as *theory*, *criticism*, and *movement*. That said, my focus here does not go directly to the apparently political arguments posed by the magazine's main contributors like Hiraoka Masaaki and Ōta Ryū. Given their close relations with far-left political factions like the Japanese Red Army, their discussions tended to presume the existence of "Theory with a capital T"—a theory, of course, of world revolution. Instead, I illuminate how editor Matsuda dealt with the reconfiguration of "film theory" in his own terms.

Matsuda's critical engagement with theory had already started in the early 1950s, when he became a member of the JCP at the age of sixteen. Pursuing his career as a "professional" revolutionary, he soon realized the importance of theory as an indispensable tool to articulate and radicalize his daily (and physical) commitment to direct political actions taken under the JCP's 1951 militant line. However, Matsuda was always discontent with his colleagues' "unrevolutionary" treatment of theory—Marxist or otherwise—as a transcendental discourse that had always come from abroad (or above) to authorize their worldview a priori.[26] Notably, Matsuda argued that this was a problem rooted in Japan's belated experience of modernity, whereby generations of intellectuals had passively adopted a newly imported concept like *culture*, *theory*, or *revolution* only as a noun, a pure object of study to catch up with the West.[27] To depart from such a semi-colonized state, Matsuda went on to suggest that we treat those same imported concepts as verbs, deliberately challenging both the geopolitical and discursive conditions that had preemptively determined our epistemological judgments.

With his conscious attempt to verbalize theory, Matsuda brought about the following conversions. First, he liberated theory—or the very act of theorizing, to be more precise—from its contemporaneous domination by the West and Global North, with particular attention paid to the work of Third World Marxist revolutionaries like Frantz Fanon and Che Guevara. Second, he transformed theory into a discourse that corresponded to what he called "the voice-less consciousness" located at the bottom of our mind, a space including anger, emotion, feeling, affect, and violence. Consequently, emphasis was placed more on our sensory experience (perception and intuition) than on cognition (abstraction and reasoning). Finally, he treated theory as a site of collective thinking, thus always destined for eternal and unexpected changes, rather than as a finished product by a single author.

The last point is best represented in Matsuda's peculiar commitment to the debate on "landscape theory." Originally proposed by Matsuda through his participation in the production of *A.K.A. Serial Killer*, this theory suggested that we treat all the banal and standardized landscapes we encounter in our everyday life as a pure embodiment of state power.[28] But Matsuda quickly withdrew his commitment, even while the term *landscape* became a buzzword among his fellow critics working not only in film but also in photography, graphic design, music, city designs, and so on. This was partly because he was fully aware of the regressive (and unavoidable) transformation of his own concept into a commodity by print journalism and other industries. (For instance, the Japan National Railways ran an advertising campaign called "Discover Japan" with a marked emphasis on the beauty of Japanese rural landscapes.) But a more profound reason was that Matsuda, through a series of conversations with other commentators on his concept, came to realize that whatever he created—whether it be an independent film or a theoretical concept—remained a manifestation of antirevolutionary cultural capital as long as he was unmindful of the material conditions through which he produced and disseminated these products.[29] In other words, he now realized the importance of the *infrastructure* of theory and knowledge production.

This is why Matsuda decided to launch his own film magazine, *Eiga hihyō*, as an open and independent site for theoretical discussions of film and its sociopolitical use. As the founder and editor-in-chief, Matsuda made every effort to run the business without relying upon advertisements from major film companies and distributors. Consequently, he ended up publishing only a handful of articles with his signature in this magazine, while giving more space to young and upcoming contributors like Tsumura Takashi. Given the overtly militant, far-left-leaning atmosphere of the period in general and of the magazine in particular, whether this editorial policy yielded a successful outcome is open to discussion. But through his rare and admirable dedication to the infrastructure of theory, Matsuda still advanced his new dictum: "Media must transform themselves."[30] For Matsuda, the term *media* meant a device, a tool, or even a concept that generates "movements" among those who use or live with them, whereas the term *movement* in his lexicon meant the reciprocal traffic between sensual experience and intellectual reflection. Matsuda's intention was therefore to reinvent theory as one of those self-transforming media, along with film's own transformation into anything but the single privileged form of modern audiovisual experience.

Here, we can also rephrase Matsuda's dictum more simply as "Theory as a medium must transform itself." But how is this possible? This is exactly the question that we, as scholars of film and its global circulation, must address in earnest in our own historical context. Why, for instance, do we still hold on to the idea that what we call "theory" in our own discipline is, and continues to be, an exclusive domain of the West or Global North? How could we alter or update our notion of theory by deliberately integrating those long-forgotten but no less illuminative contributions from the rest of the world into our curricula? It goes without saying that Japanese film magazines, especially the ones I have discussed in this chapter, enable us to advance this urgent and unavoidable pedagogical mission from an inherently comparative and transnational perspective.

NOTES

1. Motion Picture Producers Association of Japan, "Statistics of Film Industry in Japan: 1955–2020," http://www.eiren.org/statistics_e/index.html (accessed December 20, 2023).

2. Ibid.

3. Hatano Tetsurō, "Sengo eiga hihyō e no tabi: Shiron," *Shinema 71*, no. 8 (June 1971): 38–43. Throughout this chapter, Japanese names appear in their original order unless otherwise specified.

4. In addition to sharing these editorial strategies, *Kikan firumu, Shinema 69*, and *Eiga hihyō* also appeared as part of the burgeoning "ciné-club" movement. On April 25, 1968, the film company Nikkatsu abruptly announced the dismissal of the veteran director Suzuki Seijun and refused to lend his films to the non-profitable screenings planned to be held between May and July of the same year, organized by the Ciné-Club Study Group (Shine kurabu kenkyūkai), the biggest among Japanese film societies with three thousand active members. Furious about this self-righteous business decision, members of the ciné-club held a mass demonstration in Tokyo's central Ginza district, asking for their own "right" to watch the films they wanted, rather than the ones imposed by the company. At the same time, a group of concerned directors, staff members, and film critics formed an alliance called the Joint Struggle Committee for the Suzuki Seijun Problem (Suzuki Seijun mondai kyōtō kaigi) to support Suzuki's lawsuit against Nikkatsu. This event clearly marked a watershed moment in the history of Japanese film criticism in that it captured the increasing concern about the autonomy of film viewers. Matsuda Masao, the editor of *Eiga hihyō*, served as the committee chair, and other active members also became main contributors to the other two new film magazines.

5. Yamada Kōichi and Awazu Kiyoshi, "Hakkan no kotoba," *Kikan firumu*, no. 1 (October 1968).

6. See, for example, Iimura Takahiko, "Chikaku ni okeru jikken," *Kikan firumu*, no. 1 (October 1968): 108–13; Ishizaki Kōichirō, "Kankaku no kakudai: Andāguraundo eiga no henbō," *Kikan firumu*, no. 1 (October 1968): 114–16; Konno Tsutomu, "Video seitaigaku to fukusha no shisō," *Kikan firumu*, no. 12 (July 1972): 103–22.

7. Jean-Luc Godard, "Futatsu no sensen no tōsō wo okonau," trans. Shibata Hayao and Yamada Kōichi, *Kikan firumu*, no. 1, 47–73.

8. Yomota Inuhiko, "Sekai no meiro no nakade," in *Geijutsu no yokgen: 60 nen-dai radikaru karuchua no kiseki*, ed. Yabuzaki Kyōko (Tokyo: Firumu ātosha, 2008), 12.

9. For the magazine's revenue and expenditure, see Yamane Sadao, "Media to shite no eiga to zasshi," *Shinema 71*, no. 7 (January 1971): 93–96.

10. See, for example, Hasumi Shigehiko, "Hihyō to firumu taiken," *Shinema 71*, no. 8 (June 1971): 2–14.

11. Indeed, the magazine frequently edited special issues dedicated to contemporary Japanese filmmakers such as Ōshima Nagisa (no. 4), Fukasaku Kinji (no. 5), Yoshidia Kijū (no. 6), and Imamura Shōhei (no. 7).

12. After his return to Japan, Adachi started making films again, and his recent films include *Yūheisha/Terorisuto* (*Prisoner/Terrorist*, 2007), *Danjiki geinin* (*Artist of Fasting*, 2016), and *Revolution+1* (2022).

13. See, for example, Matsuda Masao, "Hihyō no kasseika no tameni," *Chūō Daigaku Shinbun*, January 21, 1969, reprinted in Matsuda Masao, *Bara to mumeisha* (Tokyo: Haga shoten, 1970), 299–304.

216   CHAPTER 11

14. *A.K.A. Serial Killer* is an experimental documentary film about Nagayama Norio, a nineteen-year-old serial killer who murdered four random people using the gun he stole from the US Navy stationed in Yokosuka. Instead of telling a life story of this teenage murderer, the film is composed entirely of the "landscapes" he was supposed to see in his escape journey from Abashiri, Hokkaido, to Tokyo, Yokohama, Nagoya, Osaka, and Hong Kong. Although the film was completed in 1969, Matsuda and his collaborators decide not to screen it publicly, due to the ongoing shift in their own commitment to filmmaking and film criticism. The film was finally released in 1975.

15. For more on the "landscape theory," see Harry Harootunian and Sabu Kohso, "Message in a Bottle: An Interview with Adachi Masao," *boundary 2* 35, no. 3 (2008): 63–97; Yuriko Furuhata, *Cinema of Actuality: Japanese Avant-Garde Filmmaking in the Season of Image Politics* (Durham, NC: Duke University Press, 2013), 115–48; Rei Terada, "Repletion: Masao Adachi's Totality," *Qui Parle* 24, no. 2 (Spring/Summer 2016): 15–43.

16. Jean-Luc Godard and Jean-Pierre Gorin, "Jiga Verutofu shūdan no shisō," *Eiga hihyō* 2, no. 11 (November 1971), 14–25; O. Getino and F. Solanas, "Dai-san sekai no eiga ni mukatte," *Eiga hihyō* 4, no. 1 (January 1973), 116–27.

17. See my *Dialectics without Synthesis: Japanese Film Theory and Realism in a Global Frame* (Oakland: University of California Press, 2020).

18. "Eiga sengenshū," *Kikan firumu*, no. 10 (October 1971), 89–127.

19. Dziga Vertov, "Manifesuto to ronbun," trans. Fukushima Noriyuki, "Nikki to kōsō (shō)," trans. Moriyama Akira and Moriyama Kazuo, and "Kamera wo motta otoko," trans. Okada Kazuo, *Kikan firumu*, no. 8 (March 1971): 10–31, 32–44, and 45–47.

20. Satō Tadao, "Joshō: Nihon ni eiga riron wa attaka," *Shinema 69*, no. 1 (January 1969): 72.

21. Satō, "Joshō: Nihon ni eiga riron wa attaka," 73. An English translation is available as Satō Tadao, "Does Film Theory Exist in Japan?," trans. Joanne Bernardi, *Review of Japanese Culture and Society* 22 (December 2010): 14–23. Later, in 1977, Satō also published a monograph, *Nihon eiga rironshi* (Tokyo: Hyōronsha, 1977), based on the serialized essays he wrote for *Shinema 69*.

22. D. N. Rodowick, *Elegy for Theory* (Cambridge, MA: Harvard University Press, 2014), 54–80.

23. Hasumi Shigehiko, "Eizō no riron kara riron no eizō e," *Shinema 71*, no. 9 (October 1971), 73–96.

24. Hasumi, "Eizō no riron kara riron no eizō e," 78–80. See also Shiguéhiko Hasumi, *Directed by Ozu Yasujirō*, intro. Aaron Gerow, trans. Ryan Cook (Oakland: University of California Press, 2024).

25. Aaron Gerow, "Critical Reception: Historical Conceptions of Japanese Film Criticism," in *The Oxford Handbook of Japanese Cinema*, ed. Daisuke Miyao (Oxford: Oxford University Press, 2014), 74.

26. For Matsuda's early life, see Matsuda Masao, "Matsuda Masao ga kataru sengo shisō no 10-nin (1)," *Kikan Gendai no riron*, no. 8 (Summer 2006): 212–22.

27. Matsuda Masao, "Naraku no tabi e no tojō de," in *Fūkei no shimetsu*, rev. ed. (Tokyo: Kōshisha, 2013), 90–103.

28. See, for example, Matsuda Masao, "Misshitsu, Fūkei, kenryoku," in *Bara to mumeisha* (Tokyo: Haga Shoten, 1970), 123–26.

29. This critique was made by Tsumura Takashi, one of the most perceptive media theorists in post-1968 Japan. Though still in his early twenties and a student at Waseda University, Tsumura became a major contributor to *Eiga hihyō* and published several monographs, including *Warera no uchinaru sabetsu* (Tokyo: San'ichi shobō, 1970) and *Media no seiji* (Tokyo: Shōbunsha, 1974), before he abruptly stopped his contributions to media criticism and became a qigong (*kikō*) practitioner in the 1980s.

30. Matsuda Masao, "Media to gyaku ni media ni," in *Fukanōsei no media* (Tokyo: Tabata shoten, 1973), 300–313.

PUBLICATIONS REFERENCED

Cahiers du cinéma
Eiga hihyō (*Film Criticism*)

Kikan firumu (*Film Quarterly*)
Kinema junpō (*Movie Times*)
Shinema 69, 70, and *71* (*Cinema 69, 70,* and *71*)

BIBLIOGRAPHY

"Eiga sengenshū [A Collection of Film Manifestos]." *Kikan firumu*, no. 10 (October 1971): 89–127.

Furuhata, Yuriko. *Cinema of Actuality: Japanese Avant-Garde Filmmaking in the Season of Image Politics.* Durham, NC: Duke University Press, 2013.

Getino, Octavio, and Fernando, Solanas. "Dai-san sekai no eiga ni mukatte [Toward a Third Cinema]." *Eiga hihyō* 4, no. 1 (January 1973): 116–27.

Godard, Jean-Luc. "Futatsu no sensen no tōsō wo okonau [Struggle on Two Fronts]." Translated by Shibata Hayao and Yamada Kōichi. *Kikan firumu*, no. 1 (October 1968): 47–73.

Godard, Jean-Luc, and Jean-Pierre Gorin. "Jiga Verutohu shūdan no shiso [Thoughts of the Dziga Vertov Group]." *Eiga hihyō* 2, no. 11 (November 1971), 14–25.

Harootunian, Harry, and Sabu Kohso. "Message in a Bottle: An Interview with Adachi Masao." *Boundary 2* 35, no. 3 (2008): 63–97.

Hasumi, Shigehiko. *Directed by Ozu Yasujirō.* Introduction by Aaron Gerow. Translated by Ryan Cook. Oakland: University of California Press, 2024.

———. "Eizō no riron kara riron no eizō e [From a Theory of an Image to an Image of Theory]." *Shinema 71*, no. 9 (October 1971): 73–96.

———. "Hihyō to firumu taiken [Criticism and Film Experience]." *Shinema 71*, no. 8 (June 1971): 2–14.

Hatano, Tetsurō. "Sengo eiga hihyō e no tabi: Shiron [A Journey to Postwar Film Criticism]." *Shinema 71*, no. 8 (June 1971): 38–43.

Iimura, Takahiko. "Chikaku ni okeru jikken [An Experiment on Perception]." *Kikan firumu*, no. 1 (October 1968): 108–13.

Ishizaki, Kōichirō. "Kankaku no kakudai: Andāguraundo eiga no henbō [Expansion of the Senses: Transformation of Avant-Garde Film]." *Kikan firumu*, no. 1 (October 1968): 114–16.

Konno, Tsutomu. "Video seitaigaku to fukusha no shisō [Ideas of Video Ecology and Photocopy]." *Kikan firumu*, no. 12 (July 1972): 103–22.

Matsuda, Masao. *Bara to mumeisha* [Roses and the Nameless]. Tokyo: Haga shoten, 1970.

———. *Fukanōsei no media* [Media of Impossibility]. Tokyo: Tabata shoten, 1973.

———. *Fūkei no shimetsu* [Extinction of the Landscape], rev. ed. Tokyo: Kōshisha, 2013.

———. "Matsuda Masao ga kataru sengo shisō no 10-nin (1) [Matsuda Masao Speaks about Ten Key Figures in Postwar Japanese Thought]." Interview by Hirasawa Gō and Yabu Shirō. *Kikan Gendai no riron*, no. 8 (Summer 2006): 212–22.

Motion Picture Producers Association of Japan. "Statistics of Film Industry in Japan: 1955–2020." http://www.eiren.org/statistics_e/index.html (accessed December 20, 2023).

Satō, Tadao. "Does Film Theory Exist in Japan?" Translated by Joanne Bernardi. *Review of Japanese Culture and Society* 22 (December 2010): 14–23.

———. "Joshō: Nihon ni eiga riron wa attaka [Introduction: Does Film Theory Exist in Japan?]." *Shinema 69*, no. 1 (January 1969): 72–78.

———. *Nihon Eiga Rironshi* [A History of Japanese Film Theory]. Tokyo: Hyōronsha, 1977.

Terada, Rei. "Repletion: Masao Adachi's Totality." *Qui Parle* 24, no. 2 (Spring/Summer 2016): 15–43.

Tsumura, Takashi. *Media no seiji* [Politics of the Media]. Tokyo: Shōbunsha, 1974.

———. *Warera no uchinaru sabetsu* [Discrimination within Us]. Tokyo: San'ichi shobō, 1970.

Vertov, Dziga. "Kamera wo motta otoko [The Man with a Movie Camera]." Translated by Okada Kazuo. *Kikan firumu*, no. 8 (March 1971): 45–47.

———. "Manifesuto to ronbun [Manifestos and Essays]." Translated by Fukushima Noriyuki. *Kikan firumu*, no. 8 (March 1971): 10–31.

218 CHAPTER 11

———. "Nikki to kōsō (shō) [Journals and Plans (Excerpt)]." Translated by Moriyama Akira and Moriyama Kazuo. *Kikan firumu*, no. 8 (March 1971): 32–44.

Yamada, Kōichi, and Awazu Kiyoshi. "Hakkan no kotoba [Inaugural Remarks]." *Kikan firumu* 1 (October 1968).

Yamamoto, Naoki. *Dialectics without Synthesis: Japanese Film Theory and Realism in a Global Frame.* Oakland: University of California Press, 2020.

Yamane, Sadao. "Media to shite no eiga to zasshi [Film and Magazine as a Medium]." *Shinema 71*, no. 7 (January 1971): 93–96.

Yomota, Inuhiko. "Sekai no meiro no nakade [In a Maze of the World]." In *Geijutsu no yogen: 60 nendai radikaru karuchua no kiseki* [A Prediction of the Art: Traces of Radical Culture in the 1960s], edited by Yabuzaki Kyōko, 11–17. Tokyo: Firumu ātosha, 2008.

12

Film Appreciation

The Steady Rear Guard of Taiwanese Film Culture

James Udden

1983 was momentous for Taiwanese cinema. This was the first full year of the New Cinema movement in Taiwan, which saw the release of films such as the portmanteau work *The Sandwich Man*, which included the eponymous short by Hou Hsiao-hsien, and Edward Yang's feature-length masterpiece *That Day at the Beach*. In short order, this largely accidental movement would establish a permanent place for Taiwanese cinema in global film culture, creating a new film festival powerhouse by the end of the decade that would continue long thereafter.

The year 1983 was also marked by the first volume of a new film journal in Taiwan, *Film Appreciation* (電影欣賞), often referred to simply as *Fa*. Published by what was then officially the National Film Library—now the Taiwan Film and Audiovisual Institute—in 2021, the journal published its 185th volume. The longevity of the journal in what has always been a volatile publishing climate— film publications tend to come and go—can be explained by two factors: first, *Film Appreciation* has always had the stable institutional backing of the publicly funded national archives from which it emanates; and, second, this journal has always functioned as a published extension of that same archive, thus avoiding being at the forefront of the heated debates and controversies regarding Taiwanese cinema. As such, *Film Appreciation* serves as a much-needed rear guard of Taiwanese film culture, an indispensable source, for scholars who read Chinese, for understanding Taiwanese cinema over the past four decades. To fully

219

220 CHAPTER 12

appreciate this enduring cornerstone of Taiwan's film culture, we must explore not only what *Film Appreciation* is, but also what it is not.

WHAT *FILM APPRECIATION* IS NOT

There are three journals outside of Taiwan with which *Film Appreciation* should never be compared. This journal is categorically not Taiwan's version of *Cahiers du cinéma*, which began in France in 1951. This game-changing journal nurtured young critical talent such as Jean-Luc Godard and François Truffaut, who throughout the 1950s mercilessly attacked certain "tendencies" in French cinema while systematically developing the auteur theory that would soon spread across the globe, even laying the foundation for the emergence of academic film studies. Moreover, these same critics would eventually put these ideas regarding authorship into practice as core members of the French New Wave by the end of the 1950s, creating a global "model" for every new cinema ever since, including Taiwan's.[1] *Film Appreciation* has nothing resembling *Cahiers du cinéma*'s theoretical breakthrough, the *politique des auteurs*, that it can take credit for. Moreover, while there were members of the New Cinema who began as critics, such as Chen Guofu, none began as an employee of *Film Appreciation*.

Given its semiofficial imprimatur, one might be tempted to see *Film Appreciation* as Taiwan's equivalent of film journals that emerged under the Italian fascists, such as *Cinema* (nominally edited by Vittorio Mussolini, the son of "Il Duce," Benito Mussolini), *Bianco e Nero*, or *Film*. It is true that technically Taiwan was still a fascist one-party state under the nationalist Kuomintang (KMT) Party in 1983, although there were already clear signs of burgeoning democracy and localization even at that early stage. Yet we should remember that, under Italian fascism, *Cinema* was publishing articles by leftist writers such as Cesare Zavattini, who would prove to be a central figure in postwar Italian neorealism.[2] Likewise, nothing in the pages of *Film Appreciation* had the lasting impact of Umberto Barbaro's 1943 article on Visconti's *Ossessione* in *Film*, which is often credited for attaching the term *neorealism* to a new trend in Italian filmmaking, another global model that persists to this day.[3] *Fa* cannot claim to have coined an influential term describing a major film movement.

Even more surprising is how little *Film Appreciation* resembles Iran's *Film International*, which began in 1993. The parallels between Iranian and Taiwanese cinema are almost uncanny, but not when it comes to film journals. They were the birthplaces of two of the most distinctive "festival powerhouses" in the past few decades, and both followed almost identical tracks into the festival realm starting in the mid-1980s. Both cinemas originate from pariah states, albeit for very different reasons. Both places also stood to gain a great deal from any form of cultural dialogue, since they are arguably two of the most misunderstood places on the planet. Yet, in what is undoubtedly a much more difficult political climate, only Iran has a brash English-language vehicle for the rest of the world to read. Taiwan does not.

Film International is the English-language scion of the most significant film journal in Iran, *Mahndmeh-ye sinema'i-ye film* (*Film Monthly*). This Farsi-language progenitor was born in arguably even more difficult circumstances, having published its first issue in June 1981, when it was still far from clear what sort of cinema would be allowed in Iran. What is most surprising about *Film International* as the English-language counterpart is how much it airs all the "dirty laundry" of domestic issues regarding its cinema to the rest of the world. This includes detailed reports on films unknown outside of Iran that were highly controversial within Iran, continual reports of the failings of government policies regarding issues such as decrepit film theaters, and other articles often touting Iran's festival success even when such successes were not always welcomed by the clerical regime in Iran. This journal even used the term *McCarthyism* to describe the cultural policies of the mid-1990s.[4]

There is little of the English language to be found in *Film Appreciation* aside from abstracts and some of the wording of Kodak ads found consistently on its back covers. *Film Appreciation* does not even strive for a wide readership in mainland China, since it is published only in traditional Chinese characters, not simplified. (However, one can presume that better-educated readers on the mainland can handle traditional characters.) To wit, *Film Appreciation* is strictly for domestic consumption, bringing the entire gamut of world cinema to Taiwan, not Taiwanese cinema to the rest of the world.

Even within Taiwan, however, the editorial stance of *Film Appreciation* has historically been one of reticence. Since the 1980s the debates about Taiwanese cinema have been combative, even bitter at times. Yet the role of *Film Appreciation* has often been to monitor these debates rather than engender or inflame them. We can attribute this restraint to the genesis of the journal itself, since it originates from a government-run film archive.

The Film Library was operated initially by the KMT, which by the 1980s was treading on very uncertain ground after the Republic of China lost the recognition of the US government in 1979. The initial head of the Film Library was a KMT bureaucrat, Xu Ligong, who back then knew nothing about cinema. Yet, according to a later director of the film archive, Edmond Wong (who as a young critic defended the New Cinema movement in the 1980s), Xu Ligong wisely listened to young people who did know better. He did not dictate.[5] *Film Appreciation* was born in that climate.

For the most part, the debates themselves have centered around the political economy underpinning Taiwanese cinema. One central concern was the role of the KMT itself, which for decades had set the terms for Taiwanese cinema through censorship, government policies, and the guiding hand of the Central Motion Picture Company (CMPC). The CMPC was the leading studio in Taiwan for decades, operated directly by the Party. It often steered the direction not only of the more propagandistic fare in Taiwan but commercial trends as well. The New Cinema brought this issue to a head, since one of the defining features of the movement

222   CHAPTER 12

was its subtle suggestions that Taiwan was something distinct from China proper, even if these were never calls for outright Taiwanese independence. This went against the grain of how the KMT had justified ruling Taiwan since 1949. The culmination of these debates came with the triumph of Hou Hsiao-hsien's *City of Sadness* in 1989, which won the Golden Lion at the Venice Film Festival and enjoyed record-breaking box office success at home.

Yet the debates about Taiwanese cinema were never purely political; they were always as much about economics. Indeed, this became the more lasting debate, since once Taiwan democratized in the 1990s, the role of the KMT Party became less of an issue. This all stems from the severe economic crisis facing the Taiwanese film industry by the 1980s. It was the result of long-term policies that had favored Hong Kong films over local productions in Taiwan's market. It was also due to the CMPC now being on the verge of bankruptcy after a series of big-budget propaganda films designed to shore up the KMT's image after the loss of US recognition, a trend which simply proved to be unsustainable.

As a result, even before the emergence of the New Cinema and *Film Appreciation*, these issues were being addressed in daily publications in Taiwan. Most notable was a section called "Cinema Plaza" in the *United Daily News*, overseen by Peggy Chiao, now a famed writer, educator, and producer in Taiwan. Chiao's role was somewhat similar to Andre Bazin's in France in the 1950s, in that she was nurturing younger critics such as Chen Guofu, who would later become a director himself. These young critics were difficult to control, Chiao said, and merciless in their attacks on the flagging film industry. Before long, "Cinema Plaza" was closed down due to pressure on the newspaper from industry figures.[6]

The New Cinema was the unexpected byproduct of this crisis, and before long it became the convenient target for those casting blame about the sorry state of Taiwanese cinema. When it became clear by 1984 that the movement was not going to be the economic savior of the industry—something it was never designed to be to begin with—the New Cinema became the object of numerous attacks, deflecting blame from the actual failings of both the industry and the KMT that had led Taiwanese cinema to its lowly state. Once again, however, the heated debates occurred in the dailies, not in the pages of *Film Appreciation*. Even when a writer at *Fa* joined the fray, however, he found himself on the "wrong side" of these debates in retrospect. Liang Liang in 1985 published a multipart series in the journal called "A Preliminary Investigation into the Film Market." In part 5, he directly accused Hou Hsiao-hsien of indulging in his long-take style with little concern for either the story line or the audience, resulting in box office failures at home despite the festival accolades.[7]

Others were less willing to let the government itself off the hook, refusing to join this "Anti-Hou" (i.e., "Anti–New Cinema") faction. This included some short-lived film journals in the 1980s such as *400 Blows* and *Long Take*. One notable example in the latter is a scathing 1987 article by Edward Yang: after winning the

Silver Leopard at the Locarno International Film Festival, Yang blasted the KMT government for how poorly Taiwanese cinema was represented at film festivals compared to other nations.[8] In the same year, nearly every member of the movement and numerous critics published a joint declaration calling for the KMT government to clarify its film policies, since it never made clear where it truly stood on the cultural/commercial divide. Once again, however, this was published in most of the major newspapers in Taiwan, not in *Film Appreciation*. (To be perfectly fair, it was also published in the 1988 annual yearbook also published by the National Film Archives.)[9] A decade later, similar debates occurred over the *fudaojin*, the government's Assistance and Guidance Grant program for cinema that began in 1989. Once again, the raging polemics were to be found mostly in the daily press, such as *Dacheng Bao*[10] and *Ziyou Shibao*.[11]

There are even ways to numerically measure how much *Film Appreciation* was not at the front lines of the debates surrounding Taiwanese cinema: published anthologies. In 1988, Peggy Chiao edited a 430-plus-page anthology of articles and critical reviews from the 1980s about the New Cinema, which even included translations of reviews by the likes of Tony Rayns and J. Hoberman. This is the definitive collection of mostly Taiwanese writings when the movement was in its heyday. However, of the seventy-six items included in that volume, only two originated from *Film Appreciation*.[12] The most famous polemical volume came out in 1991 after the debates aroused by Hou's *City of Sadness*. Edited by Mi Zo and Liang Xinhua, *Death of the New Cinema* is a collection of thirty-three articles from 1987 to 1990. While it does include five works that originated from *Film Appreciation*, over a dozen of its selections are from a single newspaper in Taiwan, *The Independent Morning Post* (自立早報), a brash new journalistic voice that emerged in 1988 after the lifting of martial law in Taiwan. True to form, *Film Appreciation* was not dominating the conversation regarding Taiwanese cinema even when participating.

THE INSTITUTIONAL BACKDROP

To fully appreciate what *Film Appreciation* is (and not just what it is *not*) begins with understanding its institutional basis. This journal has always been published by a publicly funded film archive/library that has borne several different names over the years. In every issue, in fact, under the listing of the editorial staff is a listing of the staff of the entire archives as well. In 1975, the Government Information Office (GIO), which oversaw all film policies in Taiwan, formed the Motion Picture Development Foundation with the Taipei Film Business Association. In January 1979, the Film Library of this foundation was opened in Taipei and was funded by the GIO. The name of this body has changed over the years, becoming the National Film Archive in 1989, the Chinese Taipei Film Archives in 1995 (although its name in Chinese remained unchanged), then the Taiwan Film Institute in 2014, and finally the Taiwan Film and Audiovisual Institute (TFAI), which it has been known as since 2020. In 1991, this archive became its own foundation administered by the GIO. With the latest change, however, it is now its own administrative body.

Over the years, this single institution, the TFAI, was by far the most indispensable for my own research on Taiwanese cinema, carrying a collection of more than seventeen thousand film titles and nearly every film journal and newspaper article ever written about cinema in Taiwan. I have spoken with three different directors of this archive over the years: Edmond Wong, when I first explored the archive as a graduate student in the late 1990s applying for a Fulbright scholarship; Winston Lee, who was director when I did the Fulbright in 2000–01 (and later when I returned in 2005 for more research); and Zhang Qinpei, director when I returned for another research trip in late 2012. Edmond Wong and Zhang Qinpei were both notable critics in Taiwan before taking on this position; Winston Lee, on the other hand, was a government bureaucrat who had worked in the Film Office of the GIO in the early 1980s. Yet even Lee recounted a recurring nightmare for all three directors of the TFAI: it is always at the mercy of government coffers and those higher up who might suddenly question the value of subsidizing Taiwanese film culture.[13]

Yet, to date, these fears have never materialized. Moreover, this is a real plus for its flagship journal, *Film Appreciation*, since it does not have to rely on advertising to survive. The only exception was the back covers of *Fa*, which over the years had full-page color ads from Kodak. In the summer 2012 edition (no. 151), for example, there is an image of famed Taiwanese cinematographer Mark Lee Ping-Bing, with a quote in English: "HD doesn't hold the kind of fascination to me."[14] Otherwise, the only ads within the journal are mostly for various retrospectives and film festivals across the island and books published by the archives.

This is in stark contrast to another journal I recall from the 1990s named *Influence*. While living in Taiwan before I went to graduate school, I once mistakenly assumed this was the leading film journal in Taiwan due to its slick covers, its name's clever pun in Chinese, and its prominence as the most visible of all the film journals in Taiwanese bookstores at the time. Looking back at the issues still in my possession highlights how many ads lie within, everything from Chrysler cars to Kirin Beer. By the 2000s, however, this journal ceased to exist.

There is another built-in advantage for *Film Appreciation*: memberships. The TFAI is not dependent solely on taxpayers' money but also on membership dues. Every time I went to Taiwan for research at the archives (2000–01, 2005, 2012), I would apply for either a six-month or a yearlong membership to the archive and then would have access to all the films and publications in its collection. The prices were very reasonable, around US$30 for six months. Moreover, the archive always seemed to be used by numerous people every day—scholars, graduate students, and, presumably, industry figures and critics. While you are a member, you also receive every issue of *Film Appreciation* published during that period, which is how I came to be in possession of most of the fourteen volumes I still own. In two

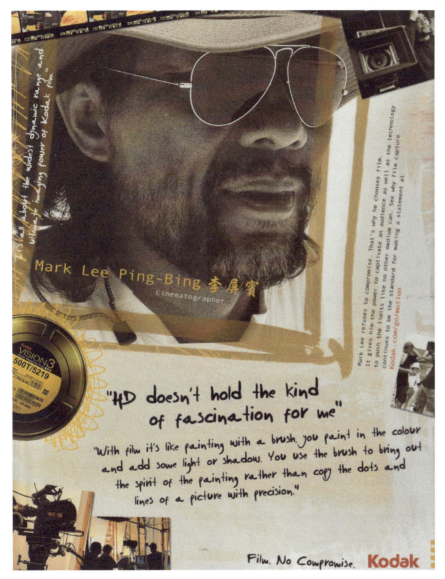

FIGURE 12.1. Kodak ad featuring cinematographer Mark Lee Ping-Bing, back cover of *Fa* issue 151, 2012.

cases I was not going to remain in Taiwan for six months, so they gave me some back issues just to be fair.

Despite the complaints of those working there, my sense has always been that this archive/film library is well funded as a result of steady membership dues in addition to government funding. The extent of other publishing done at the

Taiwan Film and Audiovisual Institute supports this; not only does the TFAI publish *Film Appreciation* (albeit now on a quarterly, not monthly basis), they have also published several books on a wide range of topics, plus their impressive annual yearbooks, the most indispensable source for my research over the years (I currently own twenty-two volumes of these yearbooks dating back to 1990).

The annual yearbooks are important for another reason. *Film Appreciation* operates seemingly in tandem with the yearbooks despite having different editors. The yearbooks are excellent sources for detailed information about the film industry and for summarizing the major issues of that year, compiling the most representative articles from various publications elsewhere. This frees *Film Appreciation* to explore whatever topics it may desire. What *Fa* seems to desire is to cover just about everything under the sun.

THE LAYOUT

The archival tenor of *Film Appreciation* is revealed through the lack of strong editorial statements—or oftentimes no editorial statements whatsoever. The majority of the editions of *Fa* that I own lack any foreword by any editor. When *Fa* does include them, they are not from the executive editor, but rather the editor-in-chief, who is also the head of the archives. Edmond Wong usually did not have a written statement, but in the January–February 1997 edition, he was compelled to respond to the recent deaths of two notable Chinese directors, Li Han-hsiang and King Hu, speculating about what the future would hold in a time of change.[15] Winston Lee seemingly avoided editorial statements altogether, based on my sample issues. Only Zhang Qinpei would open most of the editions during her tenure, but these are mainly introductions to the special topics being discussed in that issue. To this day, the heads of the archive seemingly have continued the tradition of its original head, Xu Ligong: be open, listen, and do not dictate.

The actual layout of the journal over the years has always depended on who is the executive editor of the journal itself, not the head of the archive. The newest editions I possess date from 2012 (nos. 151 and 152) and list Lin Yingzhi (林盈志) as executive editor. Both emphasize a single theme or two for that issue. Issue 151 is a collection of every conceivable article about King Hu to accompany a retrospective of his work at the archives, divided into three sections organized around three of his films.[16] The next issue focuses on key figures in the history of Taiwanese cinema such as Ming Ji (明驥—famed head of the CMPC who is often called the father of the New Cinema) and the star Zhang Meiyao (張美瑤).[17]

It is more common, however, for any issue of *Film Appreciation* to be more varied and less local. When I published an article in *Fa* in the 2000s, the editor I dealt with directly was Jady Long (龍傑娣). One striking change under her tenure was on the covers: a subtle alteration of the English acronym from *FA* to *Fa*, which continues to the present day. Another visual change on the covers is

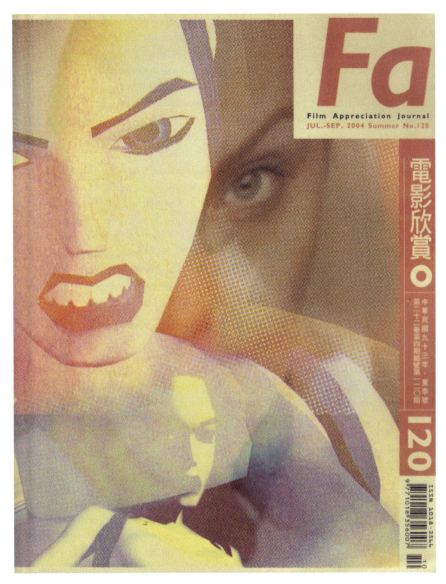

FIGURE 12.2. Streamlined front cover design for *Fa* issue 120, 2004.

captivating minimalist artworks original for each issue, with almost no linguistic encumbrances aside from the names and issue numbers on the righthand edge. More important, of course, are the contents within.

Long tended to break every issue into several sections. Usually, the first section was a special topic explored in depth with roughly three to five articles by several writers from anywhere. These topics could be a filmmaker such as Takeshi

228   CHAPTER 12

Kitano, Wong Kar-wai,[18] or Alexandr Sokurov,[19] or other sundry topics such as "What Is Chinese-Language Film Studies?,"[20] "8mm Cinema in the 21st Century,"[21] "Debates on Taiwanese Documentaries,"[22] or "Cinema and Video Games."[23] Usually, this section was followed by interviews of various key figures (including some translations from other languages), followed by other sections such as 新感官世介, which can be (very) roughly translated as "New Perspectives on the World" but is so broadly amorphous that it could include just about anything.

To show how wide a net *Film Appreciation* casts, around 2004 the journal began to ask a team of Taiwanese academics to edit a section devoted to more academic writings (學術版). Sometimes this section has been published separately from the regular journal. I was a direct beneficiary of this change, since one of the first articles I had ever published in English about Hou Hsiao-hsien was later translated into traditional Chinese characters and published in issue 124 of *Fa* in 2005.[24] To translate articles originally written in other languages is common practice at *Fa*, and unsurprisingly so. While the audience is decidedly local, even specialized, since it is primarily aimed at the more educated membership of the TFAI (Edmond Wong in his 1997 foreword addressed "members," not "readers"), the goal is to provide everyone in the Taiwanese film world—critics, scholars, students, filmmakers, industry figures, and more—a global perspective on cinema everywhere.

CONCLUSION

The former home page of the website for *Film Appreciation* included an English statement (a rarity) that contained this sentence: "With an average of 100,000 words per issue, the Journal is now a film archive of more than 15 million words and over 2,000 articles."[25] The use of the word *archive* is telling because that is what most defines this journal, the child of the government-funded-and-operated film archive in Taiwan since 1983. To take pride in sheer volume over any singular voice or vision is precisely what this journal is meant to do: to have not a voice, but "voices"; not a vision, but "visions" from every place and every time.

Since the 1980s, Taiwanese film culture has often been a heated battleground, and other film journals have come and gone. *Film Appreciation*, on the other hand, is a true survivor, a much-needed rear guard of film culture that has attempted to cover every topic of interest to the local film world over time and leave it for posterity. When the battles were most vehement over the New Cinema, *Fa* was more muted; when those passions had cooled, they would offer more in-depth retrospection. The goal of the journal is that of the archive within which it resides: to neither privilege nor preclude, to deem much as worthy of preservation, and in every case to provide some focus in due time. *Film Appreciation* may not have been a game-changer or a definer of sweeping debates, but it was and still is a necessity.

FILM APPRECIATION IN TAIWAN 229

NOTES

1. For more background, see Emilie Bickerton, *A Short History of Cahiers du Cinéma* (London: Verso, 2009).

2. Tag Gallagher, "NR = MC2: Rossellini, 'Neorealism' and Croce," *Film History* 2, no. 1 (Winter 1988): 87–97.

3. A good overview of the complicated origins and meanings of the term *neorealism* can be found in chapter 1 of Charles Leavitt, *Italian Neorealism: A Cultural History* (Toronto: University of Toronto Press, 2020).

4. James Udden, "The Other *Film International*: Iran's Journalistic Window in World Film Culture," *Film International* 12, no. 3 (September 2014): 96–105.

5. Edmond Wong in discussion with the author, Taipei, Taiwan, May 3, 2001.

6. Peggy Chiao in discussion with the author, Middleton, Wisconsin, March 10, 2002.

7. Liang Liang, "Daingying Shichangxue Chutan [wu] [A Preliminary Investigation into the Film Market, Pt. 5]," *Film Appreciation* 3, no. 2 (July 1985): 42–43.

8. Edward Yang, "Women shi godu de malasong changpao xuanshou [We Are Lonely Runners on a Marathon]," *Long Take*, no. 3 (October 1987): 17–19.

9. "Minguo qishiliunian Taiwan dianying xuanyan [1987 Declaration on Taiwanese Cinema]," *Cinema in the Republic of China Yearbook, 1988* (Taipei: National Film Archives, 1988): 37–38.

10. See Xian Ru, "Fudaojin Zhengyi: 2100 shuofenming [2100 Opinions in Debate over the Fudaojin]," *Dacheng Bao*, July 30, 1998, 2.

11. See Fan Qiongwen, "Dianying chuangzuo lianmeng lizheng guopian fudaojin [Film Creative League Debates the *Fudaojin*]," *Ziyou shibao*, July 21, 1998, 30; Zhong Mingfei, "Taiwan dianying zai haian zhong manwu [Taiwanese Cinema Is a Dancer in the Dark]," *Ziyou shibao*, September 25, 2001, 29; Zhu Yanping, "Fudaojin de misi: Baole tangyi de duyao [Confusion about the Fudaojin: Sugar-Coated Poison]," *Ziyou shibao*, December 6, 2001, 22.

12. Peggy Chiao, *Taiwan xin dianying [Taiwan's New Cinema]* (Taipei: China Times Publications, 1988).

13. Winston Lee in discussion with the author, Taipei, Taiwan, December 2012.

14. In December 2012, I was on set for Hou's *The Assassin* when Lee said this more pointedly in Chinese: "Being asked to use digital is like being asked to paint with a ballpoint pen."

15. Edmond Wong, "Biajishi baogao [A Report from the Editorial Room]," *Film Appreciation* 85 (January–February 1997): 2–3.

16. "Hu Jinchuan (King Hu)," *Film Appreciation* 151 (Summer 2012).

17. "Zuizhen—Ming Ji: huainian Tiwan xin dianying zhi fu [Most Real—Ming Ji: Remembering the Father of Taiwan's New Cinema]" and "Zuimei—Zhang Meiyao: Huainian Taiwan diyi meinu [Most Beautiful—Zhang Meiyao: Remembering Taiwan's Fist Beauty]," *Film Appreciation* 152 (Autumn 2012).

18. "Bei ye wu yu Wang Jiwei de yingxian shijian [The Incidental Imagery of Taekshi Kitano and Wong Kar-wai]," *Film Appreciation* 102 (December 1999–February 2000): 13–46.

19. "Sogunuofu: xianweiqiepian (Sokourov)," *Film Appreciation* 103 (March–May 2000): 19–40.

20. "Sheme shi zhongwen dianying yanjiu? [What Is Chinese-Language Film Studies?]," *Film Appreciation* 104 (June–August 2000): 11–47; "Sheme shi zhongwen dianying yanjiu? (*Xubian*) [What Is Chinese-Language Film Studies? (*Cont.*)]," *Film Appreciation* 105 (September–November 2000): 14–43.

21. "Yingge waiyan: xinshiji balimi dianying [Outside the Frame: 8mm Cinema in the 21st Century]," *Film Appreciation* 106 (January–March 2001): 12–57.

22. "Taiwan jilupian luntan [Debates on Taiwanese Cinema]," *Film Appreciation* 111 (April–June 2002): 11–34.

23. "Dianying yu dianwan [Cienma and Video Games]," *Film Appreciation* 120 (July–September 2004): 7–37.

230   CHAPTER 12

24. James Udden, "Hou Xiaoxian yu Zhongguo gengge wenti [Hou Hsiao-hsien and the Question of a Chinese Style]," *Film Appreciation* 124 (June–September 2005): 44–53.

25. For current information about the Taiwan Film & Audiovisual Institute, which publishes *Film Appreciation*, see https://www.tfai.org.tw/en/page/about-research.html.

PUBLICATIONS REFERENCED

400 Blows (Taiwan)
Bianco e Nero (Italy)
Cahiers du cinéma (France)
Dacheng Bao (Taiwan)
Film (Italy)
Film Appreciation (電影欣賞) (Taiwan)
Film International (Iran)
The Independent Morning Post (自立早報) (Taiwan)
Influence (Taiwan)
Long Take (Taiwan)
Mahndmeh-ye sinema'i-ye film (*Film Monthly*) (Iran)
United Daily News (Taiwan)
Ziyou Shibao (Taiwan)

BIBLIOGRAPHY

"Bei ye wu yu Wang Jiwei de yingxian shijian [The Incidental Imagery of Taekshi Kitano and Wong Kai-wai]." *Film Appreciation*, 102 (December 1999–February 2000): 13–46.

Bickerton, Emilie. *A Short History of Cahiers du Cinéma*. New York: Verso 2009.

Chiao, Peggy. Interview by author. Middleton, Wisconsin, March 10, 2002.

———. *Taiwan xin dianying* (*Taiwan's New Cinema*). Taipei: China Times Publications, 1988.

"Dianying yu dianwan [Cinema and Video Games]." *Film Appreciation* 120 (July–September 2004): 7–37.

Fan Qiongwen. "Dianying chuangzuo lianmeng lizheng guopian fudaojin [Film Creative League Debates the *Fudaojin*]." *Ziyou shibao*, July 21, 1998.

Gallagher, Tag. "NR = MC²: Rossellini, 'Neorealism' and Croce." *Film History* 2, no. 1 (Winter 1988): 87–97. http://www.jstor.org/stable/3814951.

"Hu Jinchuan (King Hu)." *Film Appreciation* 151 (Summer 2012).

Leavitt, Charles. *Italian Neorealism: A Cultural History*. Toronto: University of Toronto Press, 2020.

Lee, Winston. Interview by author. Taipei, Taiwan, December 2012.

Liang Liang. "Daingying Shichangxue Chutan [wu] [A Preliminary Investigation into the Film Market, Pt. 5]." *Film Appreciation* 3, no. 2 (July 1985): 42–43.

"Minguo qishiliunian Taiwan dianying xuanyan [1987 Declaration on Taiwanese Cinema]." In *Cinema in the Republic of China Yearbook, 1988*, 37–38 (Taipei: National Film Archives, 1988).

"Sheme shi zhongwen dianying yanjiu? [What Is Chinese-Language Film Studies?]." *Film Appreciation* 104 (June–August 2000): 11–47.

"Sheme shi zhongwen dianying yanjiu? (*Xubian*) [What Is Chinese-Language Film Studies? (*Cont.*)]." *Film Appreciation* 105 (September–November 2000): 14–43.

"Sogunuofu: xianweiqiepian (Sokourov)." *Film Appreciation* 103 (March–May 2000): 19–40.

"Taiwan jilupian luntan [Debates on Taiwanese Cinema]." *Film Appreciation* 111 (April–June 2002): 11–34.

FILM APPRECIATION IN TAIWAN   231

Udden, James. "Hou Xiaoxian yu Zhongguo gengge wenti [Hou Hsiao–hsien and the Question of a Chinese Style]." *Film Appreciation* 124, (June–September 2005): 44–53.

———. "The Other *Film International*: Iran's Journalistic Window in World Film Culture." *Film International* 12, no. 3 (September 2014): 96–105.

Wong, Edmond. "Biajishi baogao [A Report from the Editorial Room]." *Film Appreciation* 85 (January–February 1997): 2–3.

———. Interview by author. Taipei, Taiwan, May 3, 2001.

Xian Ru. "Fudaojin Zhengyi: 2100 shuofenming [2,100 Opinions in Debate over the Fudaojin]." *Dacheng Bao*, July 30, 1998.

Yang, Edward. "Women shi godu de malasong changpao xuanshou [We Are Lonely Runners on a Marathon]." *Long Take* 3 (October 1987): 17–19.

"Yingge waiyan: xinshiji balimi dianying [Outside the Frame: 8mm Cinema in the 21st Century]." *Film Appreciation* 106 (January–March 2001): 12–57.

Zhong Mingfei. "Taiwan dianying zai haian zhong manwu [Taiwanese Cinema Is a Dancer in the Dark]." *Ziyou shibao*, September 25, 2001.

Zhu Yanping. "Fudaojin de misi: Baole tangyi de duyao [Confusion about the Fudaojin: Sugar-Coated Poison]." *Ziyou shibao*, December 6, 2001.

"Zuimei—Zhang Meiyao: Huainian Taiwan diyi meinu [Most Beautiful—Zhang Meiyao: Remembering Taiwan's Fist Beauty]." *Film Appreciation* 152 (Autumn 2012).

"Zuizhen—Ming Ji: huainian Tiwan xin dianying zhi fu [Most Real—Ming Ji: Remembering the Father of Taiwan's New Cinema]." *Film Appreciation* 152 (Autumn 2012).

SECTION THREE

Intermediaries of State, Region, and Media

13

Kino

The Cinema Weekly of Stalin's Times

Maria Belodubrovskaya

The Moscow newspaper *Kino* circulated in Soviet Russia between 1923 and 1941. Its predecessor, *Kino-gazeta*, appeared briefly in 1918, and until March 1925 *Kino* too was called *Kino-gazeta* (literally, *Kino-newspaper*). Depending on the time period, the paper came out once every five, six, or seven days. It was the most significant and longest-running trade periodical focusing on cinema during the prewar period of Soviet film (1917–41). As such, it is an indispensable source of information for scholars of Russian film, history, and culture.

FUNCTION AND SCOPE

From March 1925, *Kino* was published by the Society of Friends of Soviet Cinema (ODSK, 1925–34), a voluntary film organization formed under the auspices of the People's Commissariat of Education, which counted among its members tens of thousands of cinema professionals and enthusiasts. From early 1932, the Central Committee of the Union for Workers in the Arts (RABIS) and Soiuzkino, the chief government agency in charge of cinema (later the Cinema Committee), published the newspaper jointly. From 1936 to 1937, *Kino* was put out by the umbrella Arts Committee, and from 1938 to 1941, when the Cinema Committee became independent from the Arts Committee, by the former agency alone. No other periodicals dealt with the film industry as such, and, as this lineage suggests, though the paper started as a venue to promote Soviet cinema, which was the mandate of ODSK, almost from the start *Kino* functioned as the official mouthpiece of Soviet state education and cinema authorities. As such, the focus of the paper was never just to deliver entertainment or entertainment news, but to deliberate and negotiate the program and practice of Soviet cinema under the Stalin regime.

236   CHAPTER 13

This does not mean that *Kino* was not a genuine trade periodical. On average, only one page in each issue was obligatorily devoted to official business, such as the Communist Party Central Committee's resolutions on cinema, the Cinema Committee's own decisions, programmatic editorials, and—in the late 1930s—reprints of speeches from the central party press. Though all published text in the Soviet Union was censored for political reasons and only subjects approved by the Party-affiliated editorial board ever appeared in print, much of *Kino*'s coverage dealt with actual problems of the industry, starting with feature-production planning and execution, followed by exhibition and distribution, and ending with technology, nonfiction film, film education, and the like. One of the paper's primary functions was to critique new screenplays and films. Its reviews provided early, less censored evaluations of new works, so much so that on occasion *Kino* had to contradict itself in subsequent reviews to match the assessment the work had received in the national press.

COVERAGE AND IMPORTANCE

While most of the coverage was "opinion" as opposed to objective news, one of *Kino*'s main offerings as a primary source is documentation of events. Although scholars of Soviet cinema have recently gained access to the extensive and highly reliable *Chronicles of Russian Cinema* compiled by Aleksandr Deriabin and colleagues,[1] *Kino* remains valuable to film historians because it gives us a different, more proximate access to what the film process really looked like week after week. The paper helps us understand why certain developments were discussed, avoided, or delayed, and who was working on what, and when. Some *Kino* articles were controversial when published, despite editorial supervision. The editorial board marked such risky articles with an asterisk and supplied a note, "For discussion purposes only." Just seeing what topics received an asterisk is useful to a historian. Some *Kino* articles were written in response to previous articles, and from issue to issue we can observe opposing views vigorously stated and refuted. For example, 1934 saw a genuine debate on whether "the thematic plan" was an appropriate designator for the Soviet studios' production programs. Thematic plans are now considered one of the fundamental features of Soviet filmmaking, but in 1934 there was still disagreement on whether production ought to be organized around content (the "themes" of the future films) or around practical considerations such as the availability of directors, stars, stories, and screenplays. The paper is also a source of screenplay versions. Occasionally, it featured excerpts from screenplay drafts or screenplay proposals. These are different from versions that appear in archives or in secondary sources and are excellent approximations of filmmakers' early intentions. Most importantly, names and activities of many uncredited individuals who made films—as well as critics, journalists, apparatchiks, and below-the-line personnel such as administrators, technicians, projectionists, and censors—can be found, usefully contextualized, in *Kino*'s pages. Some of these data are not retrievable elsewhere.

One simple historical trajectory that researchers can trace through the pages of *Kino* is which films mattered for the film industry at various points. The newspaper routinely reported on films: films planned, films under production, films delayed, films made, films released, and films banned. But these were typically discussed starting on page 3 in the four-page editions of the 1930s, and even later in the longer editions of the 1920s. However, some films also featured on pages 1 and 2, which meant that the Cinema Committee considered them particularly important. Which films were they? Take the year 1934, for example. Today's experts on Russian cinema would likely expect films like *Chapaev*, *Jolly Fellows*, *Peasants*, and *The Youth of Maxim* to be prominently profiled in *Kino* in 1934. These four films, all celebrating the Communist Party to an extent, are now considered canonical examples of Stalinist cinema. However, only one of these pictures, *Chapaev* (Georgii Vasil'ev and Sergei Vasil'ev, 1934), a heroic biopic about a legendary Russian Civil War commander, received notable front-page attention in 1934. The peasant comedy *Jolly Fellows* (Grigorii Aleksandrov, 1934), the communist biopic *The Youth of Maxim* (Grigorii Kozintsev and Leonid Trauberg, 1934), and *Peasants* (Fridrikh Ermler, 1934), a drama set on a collective farm and featuring an animated tribute to Stalin, were covered, but in short columns and under inconspicuous headlines.

Several films that did receive substantial front-page profiles are described below. On top of the list was *Chelyuskin* (Arkadii Shafran and Mark Troianovskii, 1934), a documentary about the rescue of the crew of the steamer *Chelyuskin* that had been crushed by ice in the Arctic in February 1934. The film got covered twice as prominently as *Chapaev* and three times as frequently as just about every other title, though this was likely because the *Chelyuskin* disaster was all over the front pages of all newspapers at the time.[2] The second most discussed film of 1934 was *Boule de suif* (Mikhail Romm, 1934), an adaptation of the story of a patriotic sex worker by Guy de Maupassant. Third and fourth in popularity were the now canonical *Aerograd* (Aleksandr Dovzhenko, 1935), about a new Socialist city, and *Chapaev*, respectively. These were closely followed by *Thunderstorm* (Vladimir Petrov, 1934), a classic nineteenth-century melodrama based on a play by Nikolai Ostrovskii, and Dziga Vertov's *Three Songs about Lenin* (1934), a eulogy to Vladimir Lenin. This is a surprising list, especially so because it includes two classic melodramas. We are used to associating 1934 in the history of Soviet cinema with the establishment of socialist realism, an aesthetic promoting the new socialist state, whose crowning achievement was *Chapaev*. Yet *Chapaev* only appears on the list due to the outsized attention the film received after its release in November 1934.[3] Besides, not one headline in *Kino* from 1934 contains the phrase *socialist realism* (*Bolshevik art*, yes, but not *socialist realism*).

Chapaev and socialist realism were not at the center of the Soviet film industry's agenda in 1934, and this is clear from the themes and debates contained in the

238   CHAPTER 13

pages of *Kino*. Instead, production planning was the key problem in 1934. January issues were devoted to production planning, or what kinds of films would be made that year and whether the studios or the Cinema Committee would decide which projects could move forward. The next problem was actors and genres: in March, *Kino* ran a series of articles on the role of the actor in the creative process, on science fiction film, and on literary adaptations. April was devoted to a scandal involving director Abram Room, who was accused of overspending on his production *Once over the Summer* (completed by a different team in 1936). At the same time, *Kino* published reports about the Cinema Committee's plans to reorganize filmmaking. The Room affair related to these plans, as overspending exemplified disorganization targeted by the reform. In May and June of 1934 the paper focused on the screenplay, and in June and July it revisited production planning in preparation for the industry-wide planning conference launched in Moscow on July 15. The coverage for the rest of 1934 is so diverse that it is hard to identify one topic emphasized over others.

Notwithstanding the fact that a portrait of Stalin appears on *Kino*'s front page about a dozen times in 1934, the paper continued to be a true trade periodical covering industry issues comprehensively, dynamically, and relatively openly. This is perhaps most clear from each issue's page 4, the last page of the paper, which contained ads for upcoming releases. The ads typically included a visual from the film, some information about the story, and the names of principal creators. But the centerpiece of the ad was the title, typically presented in a large, striking, dynamically positioned font. Once again, given what we think we know about the history of Soviet cinema in 1934, we would never guess which films' titles got printed in the boldest font in release ads. Ever heard of *The Royal Sailors* (1934)? This was a silent film about a revolt on a British ship made by a rather successful filmmaker, Vladimir Braun, who specialized in sea adventure. *The Royal Sailors* does not survive, but, judging by *Kino*'s design efforts, it was one of the most commercially viable films of 1934. The only film that compares, in terms of font size, is Vertov's *Three Songs about Lenin*—also a surprise, considering how unpopular Vertov and his entire brand of documentary filmmaking was supposed to have been by this time.[4] Three other films that get sizable-letter treatment are unpredictable too: *Revenge* (Evgenii Griaznov, Vostokfilm/Yalta Studio, 1933), *Jou* (Aleksandr Litvinov, Mosfilm, 1934), and *Gikor* (Amasi Martirosyan, Armenkino, 1934). All three are silent films, though about half of the films Russia produced by 1934 were sound films.[5] Two do not survive, even though most films from the 1930s are extant. Two are made by minority studios or focus on minority ethnic groups. And though all deal with Soviet topics—class struggle (*Revenge*), the exploitation of the Inuit in the Arctic (*Jou*), and the tragic life of a child under Armenian feudalism (*Gikor*)— all appear to be popular (melo)dramas rather than socialist-realist "masterpieces." Equally noncanonical films are advertised in some of the most striking ads: *Revolt of the Fishermen* (Erwin Piscator, 1934), *The Dreamers* (David Mar'an, 1934), and *The Last Ball* (Mikheil Chiaureli, 1934).

In terms of political repressions, 1934 was relatively peaceful. Yet in 1937, one of the most violent years in Soviet history, *Kino* looked very similar to its 1934 incarnation. Once again, it is impossible to pick out specific trends, since the paper reported on a wide variety of topics. As before, page 1 was dedicated to cinema's participation in the life of the country; pages 2 and 3 to types of features, plans, and productions; and page 4 to exhibition, minority forms and studios, and foreign and production news. Twice that year, however, the paper's normal look and character changed as Stalinist politics suddenly spilled all over its pages. This happened for the first time in issue 5, dated January 29, 1937. The front-page headlines of the issue read, "Hatred and Contempt for the Renegades of Humanity, Enemies of Socialist Culture, Enemies of the People!" and "Harshly Punish the Traitors!" With these headlines, the newspaper reported on the Second Moscow Show Trial, January 23–30, 1937. The trial falsely condemned leading figures in the Communist Party of participating in the made-up Trotskyite conspiracy against the Soviet state. It unleashed Stalin's Great Terror (1937–38), during which many highly talented and completely innocent people, including some in the film industry, were arrested and shot on suspicion of harboring foreign sympathies, which in Stalin's mind threatened disloyalty during the looming war in Europe. The message of the trial was so important for the authorities to communicate that every periodical had to report on it, and with appropriate vitriol.

The political upheaval created by the trial is visible in the scope of *Kino*'s content. After January 29, 1937, its overall coverage shrank. Issue 1 for 1937 contains a total of thirty-nine articles, and issue 2 contains thirty-two articles, while February issues 7, 8, and 9 contain just twenty-three, twenty-eight, and twenty-three articles, respectively. Only by issue 11, dated March 4, did the newspaper bounce back to its previous vigor. But then, another disaster struck. Sergei Eisenstein's highly anticipated *Bezhin Meadow* was banned by a Central Committee decree on March 5, 1937. We can tell that this event came as a total shock to the industry, because the newspaper said nothing about it until issue 14 on March 24, 1937. In that issue, a front-page article, "The Lessons of *Bezhin Meadow*," reported on the three-day conference held March 19–21 by the Cinema Committee to address the "suspension" of the film. The *Bezhin Meadow* affair took over the entire second page of issue 14 and came up again and again in subsequent issues. Then, as if to reinforce the rhetoric of the January Moscow Show Trial, issue 15 published Stalin's programmatic speech of March 3, 1937, "Defects of Party Work and Measures for Liquidating Trotskyite and Other Double Dealers." (The main Party newspaper *Pravda* also published the speech with a delay, on March 29, so there is nothing noteworthy about *Kino*'s timing here.) Stalin's speech painted a picture of the Soviet polity deeply infiltrated by traitors and enemies. Its text took three entire pages of issue 15, and page 4 featured articles illustrating the purported subversive activities in the film industry, naming the production of *Bezhin Meadow* among them. As a result, the total number of articles in this issue of *Kino* plummeted to four. Issue 16 contained another speech by Stalin and some concordant reactions

240 CHAPTER 13

from the film community on pages 2 and 3. But on pages 1 and 4, the paper defiantly returned to its normal groove. Issue 17 contained twenty-nine articles. When, in April 1937, the paper carried a speech about Trotskyite wreckers by the head of Soviet government Vyacheslav Molotov, that speech also appeared only on pages 2 and 3. The *Bezhin Meadow* affair moved down to page 4. Overall, though there is no denying that the language of the paper became more stilted in 1937 in the atmosphere of Stalin's attacks on the country, *Kino* continued to function as a trade periodical even then.

Only between January 1938 and May 1939 did the paper become so affected by the country's politics that it occasionally stopped reporting on cinema. In January 1938, Boris Shumiatskii, the longtime head of the Cinema Committee (1930–37) and an advocate of genre cinema and Hollywood production methods, was arrested and subsequently executed as a Trotskyite. His replacement, Semen Dukel'skii, came from the security services, supposedly to clean up the Trotskyite lair fostered by Shumiatskii at the Cinema Committee. Dukel'skii soon announced the closure of many films then under production that did not meet the political requirements of the day. The filmmakers, however, did not take to Dukel'skii, and in early June 1939 he was replaced by Ivan Bol'shakov, who was much closer to Shumiatskii in approach.

The change in *Kino*'s coverage in 1938 occurred gradually. Only a single issue of the paper (no. 11) is devoted entirely to the third and last Moscow Show Trial, the Trial of Twenty-One (March 2–13, 1938). For the rest of the year, the paper got away with dedicating only two pages per issue to Party-related business. And every time, such reporting was either motivated by a holiday (such as Red Army Day or the anniversary of Lenin's death) or clearly mandated from above, as when page 1 of issue 53 featured the article "On the Mounting of Party Propaganda in Connection with the Publication of *The Short Course on the History of VKP(b)*" (*The Short Course* was a new textbook on the history of the Communist Party edited by Stalin). Things got worse for cinema reporting in 1939. Between January and May 1939, *Kino* published twenty-five issues. Four of these issues said little about cinema, and two contained nothing about cinema at all. Issue 6, February 5, 1939, contained "the theses" of Chairman Molotov's upcoming report to the 18th Communist Party Congress, "The Third Five-Year Plan for the Development of National Economy of the USSR." The report covered the first two pages of the paper and spilled onto page 3. In issues 12, 13, and 14, the trade paper went numb. Issue 12 contained three articles: Molotov's opening address at the 18th Party Congress, Stalin's speech at the Congress, and a tiny piece at the bottom of page 4 reporting that Dukel'skii had been awarded an Order of Lenin "for his outstanding contribution to the development of Soviet cinema." Issue 13 comprised one article: Molotov's report on the Third Five-Year Plan. Issue 14 contained more speeches from the Congress and four tiny reports on the industry at the bottom left corner of the last page. The paper recovered somewhat by issue 15, in which page 3 led with a big, bold film title (Aleksandr Dovzhenko's *Shchors*), as if to signal that the paper was back, but the Congress and its resolutions tainted the coverage for some time, keeping the number of articles per issue low. By July 1939, however, likely encouraged by the departure of Dukel'skii, the paper was back, looking very much like itself. With the exception of one issue, number 59, entirely devoted to Stalin, no other issue in 1939 was dominated by official business. And, whereas only sixteen out of sixty issues in 1938 contained release ads, twenty-eight out of sixty did in 1939.

Remarkably, the nature of the films advertised in the paper did not change in the late 1930s. Though, as we just saw, not every issue contained advertisements, and the ads became less conspicuous over time (a seven-column footer in dark ink in 1935–37 became a box the width of two columns in 1939–41), the paper continued to promote new films. And, as before, hardly any officially recognized socialist-realist "masterpiece" was among these. About fifteen films received eye-catching ads on page 4 in 1937, for instance, but only one was an officially supported biopic: Mikhail Romm's *Lenin in October* (1937). The rest were either children's adventure films and literary adaptations (e.g., *Tom Sawyer*, Lazar' Frenkel' and Gleb Zatvornitskii, 1936) or melodramas (e.g., *Almas*, Grigorii Braginskii and Aga-Rza Kuliev, 1936). The vast majority were made at regional studios and by filmmakers we do not know today. This trend to advertise films that would have popular appeal rather than socialist-realist pedigree continued to the end of *Kino*'s run. Among about forty fiction titles advertised in 1940 (when nonfiction films also got ads), only three became official successes, two were later banned, and the others comprised non-prestige comedies, melodramas, and adventure movies. The conclusion that they were picked for their popular and even commercial prospects rather than their political value is supported by the fact that among them were two American musical films: *The Great Waltz* (Julien Duvivier, 1938) and *One Hundred Men and a Girl* (Henry Koster, 1937).

DESIGN AND EDITORS

The size of the paper changed somewhat initially but stabilized by the end of 1931. In 1928 and 1929, the paper looked similar to Hollywood trade periodicals such as *The Film Daily*. Each issue had eight pages with five columns of text each. Page 6 was devoted to letters to the editor and advertisements, and pages 7 and 8 were entirely assigned to boxed ads. The newspaper primarily advertised films about to be released, but there were also ads for books, periodicals, studios' release programs, and film stock and equipment. Important for exhibition research, the last page of every issue had a section detailing the repertory of Moscow's biggest cinemas. In the first half of 1930, the paper vacillated between a four-page format and an eight-page format, though both versions typically contained ads. With issue 37, the paper dropped the ads, and after that only the repertory section and one or two ads for new releases were printed in each issue. The film ads persisted to the end of *Kino*'s run in 1941, but the repertory section gradually disappeared between October and December of 1935, when the paper switched to profiling new releases

FIGURE 13.1. *Kino* title graphics in 1926–1930, early 1931, late 1931, and 1931–1934.

alone. In 1931, the five-column format with up to eight pages transformed into the seven-column width, and the paper settled on the four-page length.

The title design of the paper changed radically only twice between 1925 and 1941. The first transformation occurred in the early 1930s when the ornate Art Deco–ish title was replaced by a heavier and more industrial one (see figure 13.1). Shortly thereafter, this version of the lettering "KINO" appeared with an underline,

FIGURE 13.2. *Kino* title graphics in December 1934, in 1938, and in 1941.

a style which the periodical maintained for a while. The second change occurred in 1934, coinciding with a major political shift of the 1930s: the start of the Great Terror. Historians have always traced the origins of Stalin's persecution campaign to the assassination of the Leningrad Party boss Sergei Kirov, on December 1, 1934. The circumstances of this event remain mysterious to this day, but Kirov was an extremely popular leader. His assassination put Stalin on high alert or, if Stalin himself was involved, allowed Stalin to justify his subsequent witch hunt for internal enemies. *Kino* reported Kirov's death on the front page of issue 56 on December 4, 1934. That issue also had a new editor, to be discussed momentarily. Issue 59 of December 22, 1934, debuted new graphics for the paper's title, which are hard to describe other than to say that the lettering was more sophisticated and less industrial than the earlier version (see figure 13.2). This design persisted to the end of *Kino*'s existence, with minor modifications.

Who were the editors of *Kino*? This question requires additional research, as only one person on *Kino*'s editorial board was a celebrity. The celebrity was Sergei

244   CHAPTER 13

Eisenstein. Between October 1, 1930, and November 10, 1931, Eisenstein served on the editorial board, as listed on page 4 of every issue. This does not mean Eisenstein was closely involved: he was abroad this entire time. However, it tells us something about the orientation of the paper. During this span the paper replaced two pages of ads with two pages of articles on cinema. Perhaps Eisenstein or the presence of his name among the editors had something to do with this change.

While it might be tempting to ascribe the fortunes of *Kino* to the influence of its editor at any given moment, I contend that we cannot necessarily learn much about the periodical by researching the careers or commitments of its editors. The same person (Aron Mitlin), for example, was in charge from 1938 to 1941, so the publication dynamics I discussed above do not seem to have depended on the editor. All the editors had proven Party credentials—otherwise they would not have held this position. Konstantin Mal'tsev, for example, worked at the Central Committee Propaganda Department before becoming the editor of *Kino* as the chairman of the Society of Friends of Soviet Cinema (ODSK), the paper's initial publisher. He went on to head the Party Department at *Pravda*, the country's main newspaper, after leaving *Kino* in 1930. Mikhail Korol', who had literary ambitions and authored a screenplay, worked as a Soviet spy abroad between 1935 and 1938. Yet compare these credentials to those of Grigorii Vovsy, another editor, in charge in the mid-1930s. He was a Party man, too, but of a much milder variety. He had a literary education and never worked for either the Central Committee or security services. He was a career editor. Vovsy was arrested and killed as a "Trotskyite conspirator" during the Great Terror in 1938. Aron Mitlin, *Kino*'s last editor, was a similar type.

What is more telling are the periods of time in which the editors were stable and those in which they changed often. There were stretches of time when one person remained in charge for a long time: Mal'tsev for all of 1928 to January 1930; Korol' from August 1932 to December 1934; Vovsy from December 1935 to March 1937; and Mitlin from February 1938 to October 1941. These were indeed the periods of relative stability in the industry. In contrast, between January 1930 and the middle of 1932 the industry underwent a major restructuring (including the creation of one countrywide cinema agency, Soiuzkino), and during this time *Kino* was run by four different editors, jointly by the editor and the editorial board, and at times by only the editorial board without an editor. During the year between Kirov's murder, in December 1934, and December 1935, *Kino* had two "interim" editors, first Iosif Krinkin and then Nikolai Lebedev. Krinkin was reportedly close to cinema chief Shumiatskii and had worked for the secret police in the past. He was arrested in 1938 and spent five years in labor camps on false political charges. Lebedev was a film historian, critic, and editor who is best known today as an occasional director of the Moscow State Cinema Institute, VGIK.

Judging by the editorial reshuffling at *Kino*, the most uncertain period in prewar film history was the year 1937. That is, in fact, the case. In 1937, Eisenstein's

Bezhin Meadow was banned, and Shumiatskii's standing precipitously deteriorated in the lead-up to his arrest in January 1938. In less than one year, between issue 14 in March 1937, on *Bezhin Meadow*, and issue 9 in February 1938, *Kino* witnessed five editorial changes. Vovsy was succeeded by four "interim" editors in turn: Iogann Al'tman, a career editor; E. M. Tamarkin, a Central Committee Propaganda Department functionary; Pavel Bliakhin, a career art administrator, a playwright, and an editor of *Kino* back in 1926; and Iakov Boiarskii, another art functionary and a friend of Nikolai Ezhov, then chief executioner of the Great Terror. Ezhov, whose portrait appears prominently on the front page of *Kino* number 34 (July 22, 1937), was arrested in 1939 and shot in 1940 for "counterrevolution." Boiarskii was arrested and shot in connection with Ezhov, also in 1940. Mitlin's name appears in *Kino* for the first time on February 23, 1938.

As this analysis suggests, *Kino* was a resilient institution. Its editorial policy remained relatively consistent throughout its history, as the paper stubbornly attempted to keep a finger on the pulse of Soviet film culture. Though obviously self-censored and conforming to the politics of the day, as every news venue did under Stalin, the paper maintained its look, identity, readership, and even a sense of humor.[6]

DEAR BOY CINEMA

Speaking of humor, the paper is a source of visual material that goes beyond film ads and title graphics. It contains photographs of individuals and groups, film production stills, and caricatures. Caricatures in particular are a poignant indicator of the mood and morale of the film industry month by month. When I say caricatures, I mean two things: humorous drawings satirizing something (e.g., the screenplay shortage or production delays) and portraits. Though the latter often fulfill an informational function of supplying an image of an individual discussed in the text, the paper rarely presents the individual straight. The illustrations are often rendered in an exaggerated, grotesque style, sometimes subtly so and sometimes not. Who gets drawn this way and who does not reveals who was and was not taken seriously. For example, there are a few drawings of cinema chief Shumiatskii, some of which are satirical. His replacements, Dukel'skii and Bol'shakov, are featured only in photographs, though there is at least one caricature of Bol'shakov I have found (not in *Kino*, but in the popular satirical journal *Krokodil*). You could apparently lampoon Shumiatskii and Bol'shakov—but not Dukel'skii. This tells us something. In fact, one could write a history of Soviet cinema based on *Kino* caricatures alone.

Caricatures were not the only ludic feature of *Kino*. Though its language was often generic, the paper could also be entertaining and light. *Kino* accompanied some articles with spirited headlines and published verses and satirical pieces about industry developments. To give just one example, the issue of February 15,

246 CHAPTER 13

1940, was dedicated the twentieth anniversary of Soviet Cinema (Russian studios were nationalized in January 1920). The first page of this double issue was graced with the portraits of Lenin and Stalin, quotes about cinema by Lenin and Stalin, a greeting from Stalin, and an oversized graphic of a cameraman filming Red Square. Page 2 addressed the issue "Communism and Cinema." Page 5, however, featured three caricatures. A large one presented Sergei Eisenstein pirouetting in a tutu—Eisenstein was staging *Die Walküre* at the Bolshoi Theatre at the time. A smaller one featured Boris Chirkov playing the accordion in his title role in *The Youth of Maksim*. And next to it a grouping captioned "The Cherkasovs: Family Portrait" depicted five ghostly figures of Nikolai Cherkasov (Alexander Nevsky in Eisenstein's *Alexander Nevsky*, 1938) in his title roles. Page 7 included a piece by writer Evgenii Gabrilovich called "Dear Birthday Boy!," a loving reprimand to dear boy, cinema, in the form of birthday wishes. On page 8, a sketch of popular film characters marching in a parade supplemented a poetic panegyric by satirist Vil'gel'm Granov on the pinnacles of Soviet cinema to date.

DIGITIZATION

A large number of issues of *Kino* from 1924 to 1926 and a sampling of those from 1928 to 1930 are digitized by ElectroNekrasovka (http://electro.nekrasovka.ru/editions/), the site of the Central Nekrasov Library in Moscow. The rest of the issues are available both as unpreserved originals and electronically at major research libraries in Russia. In the US, the paper is available only on microfilm or as low-resolution scans in the collection of Soviet Newspapers distributed by Brill (https://brill.com/view/db/sco). It is crucial that the paper be made available more broadly, and this effort is currently underway (https://archive.org/details/mediahistory?query=kino). *Kino* is the most important primary source on Soviet film practice between 1923 and 1941, and no reliable historical research is possible without it. A rich and almost entirely unexplored repository of information on discourses, images, personalities, activities, institutions, and issues of the time, it has the potential to generate many new research questions about both Russian culture and transnational cinema.

NOTES

1. Aleksandr Deriabin, ed., *Letopis' rossiiskogo kino, 1863–1929* (Moscow: Materik, 2004), and *Letopis' rossiiskogo kino, 1930–1945* (Moscow: Materik, 2007).

2. Profiles of films on the front page are calculated using the total number of mentions, the kind of coverage received, and the size and number of accompanying visuals.

3. For more on the surprise of *Chapaev*, see Maria Belodubrovskaya, *Not According to Plan: Filmmaking under Stalin* (Ithaca, NY: Cornell University Press, 2017), 110–11. On *Chapaev*, see Julian Graffy, *Chapaev* (London: I.B. Tauris, 2010).

4. On *Three Songs about Lenin*, see John MacKay, "Allegory and Accommodation: Vertov's *Three Songs of Lenin* (1934) as a Stalinist Film," *Film History: An International Journal* 18, no. 4 (2006): 376–91.

KINO   247

5. Vincent Bohlinger, "The Development of Sound Technology in the Soviet Union during the First Five-Year Plan," *Studies in Russian and Soviet Cinema* 7, no. 2 (Summer 2013): 189–205. See also Valérie Pozner, "To Catch Up and Overtake Hollywood: Early Talking Pictures in the Soviet Union," in *Sound, Speech, Music in Soviet and Post-Soviet Cinema*, ed. Lilya Kaganovsky and Masha Salazkina, 60–80 (Bloomington: Indiana University Press, 2014); Lilya Kaganovsky, *The Voice of Technology: Soviet Cinema's Transition to Sound, 1928–1935* (Bloomington: Indiana University Press, 2018).

6. Between 1933 and 1939, *Kino*'s circulation expanded from 11,000 to 40,000. During the same period, the circulation of *Kino*'s only competitor, journal *Iskusstvo kino* (Cinema Art), grew only from 5,000 to 6,000.

PUBLICATIONS REFERENCED

The Film Daily
Kino (formerly *Kino-gazeta*)
Pravda

BIBLIOGRAPHY

Belodubrovskaya, Maria. *Not According to Plan: Filmmaking under Stalin.* Ithaca, NY: Cornell University Press, 2017.

Bohlinger, Vincent. "The Development of Sound Technology in the Soviet Union during the First Five-Year Plan." *Studies in Russian and Soviet Cinema* 7, no. 2 (Summer 2013): 189–205.

Deriabin, Aleksandr, ed. *Letopis' rossiiskogo kino, 1863–1929.* Moscow: Materik, 2004.

———. *Letopis' rossiiskogo kino, 1930–1945.* Moscow: Materik, 2007.

Graffy, Julian. *Chapaev.* London: I.B. Tauris, 2010.

Kaganovsky, Lilya. *The Voice of Technology: Soviet Cinema's Transition to Sound, 1928–1935.* Bloomington: Indiana University Press, 2018.

MacKay, John. "Allegory and Accommodation: Vertov's *Three Songs of Lenin* (1934) as a Stalinist Film." *Film History: An International Journal* 18, no. 4 (2006): 376–91.

Pozner, Valérie. "To Catch Up and Overtake Hollywood: Early Talking Pictures in the Soviet Union." In *Sound, Speech, Music in Soviet and Post-Soviet Cinema*, edited by Lilya Kaganovsky and Masha Salazkina, 60–80. Bloomington: Indiana University Press, 2014.

14

Cine-Mundial

Transatlantic and Hemispheric Cultural Circuits

Laura Isabel Serna

The most obvious use for film-related publications is to tell us something about the history of film and film culture. That is certainly the way I approached *Cine-Mundial*, a publication often described as the Spanish-language version of *Moving Picture World*. *Cine-Mundial* was published continuously by New York's Chalmers Publishing Company from 1916 to 1948, well after Chalmers had divested itself of its other motion picture–related publications.[1] When I turned to *Cine-Mundial*, I was hunting for clues about how films from the United States were received in Mexico. Though aimed at a general Latin American audience, reports (*crónicas*) that featured news from various capital cities and other locales provided fine-grained, if irregular, accounts of film culture. Those reports helped me trace a shift from the exhibition of mostly European films to what some referred to at the time as the "yanqui invasion."[2] In turn, recent scholarship by Rielle Navitski examines the way that *Cine-Mundial* and another Spanish-language fan magazine, *Cinelandia*, published in New York and Hollywood, respectively, worked to produce a Latin American audience comprised of film exhibitors, critics, moviegoers, and fans "linked by a common language" who could "imagine themselves part of a film culture meditated by but not limited to Hollywood cinema."[3] By the 1940s, Navitski observes, the audience imagined by *Cine-Mundial* was one that had learned to consume films from the United States as a marker of cultural progress, established a relationship with Hollywood stars, and welcomed Latin American film production in the 1930s and '40s while never abandoning Hollywood fare.[4]

As these two examples show, *Cine-Mundial*, a publication that might be seen as marginal in comparison to more widely circulated English-language trade and fan magazines published in the United States, sheds light on specific national histories of film exhibition and reception and on a broader, hemispheric story of what Navitski calls "an asymmetrical flow of cultural goods."[5] In this short essay, I explore other histories that *Cine-Mundial* might help us tell by delving deeper into the relationship between the magazine and consumer culture, thinking about the magazine's non-film-related content and the cultural geography it created, and, finally, considering how *Cine-Mundial* intersected with the transatlantic and hemispheric movement of intellectuals and journalists. Analyzing the magazine in these registers demonstrates the ways that film-related publications might help us see other cultural flows more clearly or in surprising ways.

Observing that cinema was both object and agent of consumer culture is not particularly novel. But *Cine-Mundial*, perhaps more so than other US-based, Spanish-language, film-related publications, puts this dual identity in sharp relief and demonstrates its adaptation to the contours of cinema's history in the hemisphere. The magazine's first issue boldly declared that its mission was to work "in favor of the film industry in the United States."[6] The labor of advocating for American film companies would, an unsigned article claimed, put "the North American seller in contact with the South American buyer," in hopes of nurturing "mutually beneficial" relationships.[7] Latin America was described as a "magnificent market" and the trade in films as a way of "tightening the bonds, that by natural law, should unite the two continents of the hemisphere."[8] *Cine-Mundial*'s declared purpose placed the publication amongst other trade journals, a type of publication defined in 1915 by John Claude Oswald, president of the Federation of Trade Press Associations, as "a periodical dealing with a field which concerns itself particularly with buying and selling of a commodity of some kind."[9] But *Cine-Mundial*'s explicit acknowledgment of the international work that commerce could perform aligned its promotion of American commerce with the discourse on Pan-American amity, the broader project of building harmonious international relations between the US and Latin American countries that took shape in the late nineteenth century and prompted the formation of the Pan-American Union, an institution dedicated to fomenting ties, chief among them commercial, between the various participant states.[10] This project dovetailed neatly with the opportunity for expansion into foreign markets that World War I created for the US film industry, as documented by Kristin Thompson.[11]

Hence, early issues of *Cine-Mundial* are more akin to a catalog than to a magazine. Film stills illustrated synopses and reviews of new films, full-page advertisements described slates of films soon to be available for distribution in Latin America, and film brokers in New York, the new center of global film distribution, offered their services. Lists of film production companies and their addresses were provided for the reader's convenience, and ads for every possible accessory a film exhibitor might need, from theater seats and projectors to novelty slides and postcards, filled the publication's back pages. Even early features focused on the business of film, sometimes recounting the history of American film production as a way of promoting the industry's wares or profiling the energetic businessmen who had built and were building a vibrant industry. Other features offered advice about the mechanics of film projection and theater design. Chalmers Publishing actively sought out advertising by placing announcements such as one in June 1917 that proclaimed, "*Cine-Mundial* reaches all the buyers and exhibitors of this territory [Latin America] each month," and asked, "Why not get *your* share of this business NOW?"[12] In other words, *Cine-Mundial* was conceived and promoted as a key interface between US film producers and ancillary interests and buyers and exhibitors in Latin America.

Though focused on motion pictures, *Cine-Mundial* was not unique in its goal of facilitating hemispheric commerce by providing industry-specific information. For example, *America e Industrias Americanas*, the official organ of the National Association of Manufacturers first published in 1912; *Revista Americana de Farmacia y Medicina*, the Spanish-language version of *American Druggist* established in 1911; and *Automovil Americana*, a Spanish-language class journal established in 1917 by the Class Journal Company in New York, which published a slate of auto-related journals in English, did for manufactured goods, pharmaceuticals, and cars what *Cine-Mundial* did for films. Other publications such as *Commerce in Latin America*, published out of New Orleans and sponsored by the fruit importers who docked their ships there, and *The South American*, a New York–based publication, offered readers articles sketching important moments in the history of various Latin American countries, accounts of major and growing industries and regional developments, and profiles of important public figures with the goal of easing business relationships. Unlike these publications, *Cine-Mundial* shed its primary identity as a trade publication to become one of the "magazines that reach the home."[13] With a reported circulation of thirty thousand in the early 1920s and fifty thousand in 1929, the magazine's subscription base had clearly extended beyond film entrepreneurs.[14] This shift reflects important changes in the global system of film distribution. As US film companies began to establish official exchanges and branch offices, *Cine-Mundial's* catalog function became less crucial.[15] While film companies continued to take out elaborate advertisements for new releases, *Cine-Mundial* increasingly focused on the most valuable film-related commodity of all: stars.

The publication's cover, which had originally featured a map of the hemisphere with markers indicating the location of major urban centers from New York to Buenos Aires, began to feature photographs, primarily of female stars. First set in stylized drawings that evoked the arts, and then on their own, these photographs grew bigger and bigger until, by the 1930s, the cover was dominated by individual stars' faces, which foregrounded the star image. Inside, profiles and accounts of film production featured numerous photographs and, as Navitski describes, regular features and columns worked to connect fans and stars via a range of practices

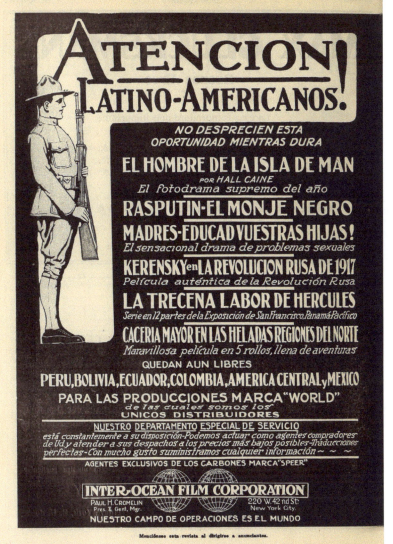

FIGURE 14.1. Advertisement for the New York–based film distributor Inter-Ocean Film Corporation, agent for World Films in parts of South America, Central America, and Mexico. They also provided Speer Carbons, which were used in film projection. *Cine-Mundial*, November 1917, 544.

FIGURE 14.2. A publicity photograph of Ramón Novarro. The accompanying text promotes his appearance in the film *Mata Hari* with Greta Garbo. *Cine-Mundial*, March 1932, 180.

that included acquiring biographical information, writing letters, and collecting the full-page portraits of stars that the magazine began publishing regularly.[16] In 1922, a multipage spread featuring photographs of correspondent José M. Sanchez García with various stars including Charlie Chaplin, Mae Murray, and Cecil B. De Mille encouraged readers to picture themselves as occupying the same social space, via their stand-in Sanchez García, as their favorite stars.[17]

While Hollywood stardom dominated the magazine, this fascination with famous people extended to both international and local celebrities, documenting a broader cultural fascination with celebrity and its image. In the 1920s, photographs illustrated features about figures ranging from Mussolini to opera composer Manuel Penella.[18] The monthly reports gathered in the *crónicas* section became photo heavy. Although they still touched on film-related news frequently, the accompanying photographs focused on local celebrities such as socialites, performers, athletes, and politicians. Photographs depicted everything from tennis club inaugurations and charity events to diplomatic receptions and parades. While these reports sometimes gestured toward politics, they primarily offered up images of the elite in various parts of Latin America participating in modern pursuits. In the mid-1920s, *Cine-Mundial* even featured a column devoted to graphological analysis that purported to give readers information about that key component of modern subjectivity—personality—while cultivating reader investment in buying future issues to see if their handwriting would be selected for analysis.

It was to this preoccupation with the modern self that advertising in the magazine was now directed. In 1926, a two-page ad in *Moving Picture World* featured a collage of brand names as proof that *Cine-Mundial*'s "advertisers are using Cine-Mundial in Latin-America the same way they are using the largest national magazines in the United States" and claimed that *Cine-Mundial* was an ideal vehicle for "establishing a name or trade-mark."[19] As historian Charles McGovern describes, this focus on advertising as a vehicle for conquering markets was part of a broader project of cultural imperialism. In the United States, he writes, advertising had "placed America at the pinnacle of world civilization . . . spreading civilization meant deploying advertising throughout the world."[20] This was a project that Chalmers Publishing cheerfully engaged. In one 1922 advertisement in *Printer's Ink, Cine-Mundial* touted its *paid* circulation and proffered a special booklet for advertisers that laid out its value vis-à-vis "export advertising dollar."[21] Readers could still find advertisements for films, of course, but advertisements for accessories and exhibition-related products had largely been replaced by advertisements for consumer goods produced in the United States. Products advertised ranged from razors, toothpaste, nail polish, and face cream to pens, typewriters, automobiles, batteries, folding chairs, and outboard motors. Ad copy promised clear skin, good digestion, a fashionable appearance, and social status. These were products that promised to help *Cine-Mundial*'s readers fashion themselves in the image of the glamorous stars whose photographs filled the magazine.

254   CHAPTER 14

This range of advertisements for products that, especially if imported, would be considered luxuries indicates the audience *Cine-Mundial* now hoped to reach. In Latin America, as opposed to the United States, this was a relatively thin slice of the population that transited urban spaces. As Steven Bunker and Victor Macias Gonzalez note of Mexico in the 1920s and '30s, although the government worked to improve the living standards of rural people and the urban working poor, the middle and upper-middle classes remained quite limited until the 1940s.[22] Argentina's middle class was growing, as Matthew Karush observes, but much of its consumption remained focused on domestically produced goods.[23] In Cuba, the "middle and upper classes enjoyed the amenities of modern life," but, as Mary Speck argues, their ability to consume was tempered by periodic economic downswings.[24] That is, these advertisements and the modern subjectivity they promised spoke to limited sectors of Latin America with the disposable income to purchase imported luxury goods or who might have wanted to dabble in luxury via an imported cream or beauty product. Although *Cine-Mundial* sought a pan-Latin audience, it spoke most clearly to those segments of Latin American readers who aspired to a middle-class lifestyle that included "appropriate apartments and houses, goods, and practices of domesticity."[25] As late as 1946, despite the publication's circulation having plummeted from a reported high of fifty thousand in 1929 to a mere twelve hundred copies per month, *Cine-Mundial* was still selling itself to potential advertisers as "the class magazine that does a special sales job in Latin America."[26] In this way, even though, as Navitski notes, its film-related coverage expanded to include the major national industries that emerged in Argentina and Mexico, *Cine-Mundial* continued to function as a mouthpiece for a consumer culture based on the consumption of goods produced in the United States.

Advertisements in conjunction with the coverage of stars and celebrities constituted one avenue of self-fashioning offered by *Cine-Mundial*. The magazine's non-film-related content comprised another way that readers could engage with modernity. In addition to features about stars and films and notes about production culture and studios, *Cine-Mundial* filled its pages with light reportage, short stories, lifestyle columns, advice columns, and humor. Favored topics included sports, particularly boxing; the arts, including literature; and news from Spain, Rome, and Paris. Short stories, though generally middlebrow (i.e., not particularly experimental), told tales of adventure in foreign lands, the dilemmas of the wealthy, or, in the 1940s, were novelizations of films. Numerous features showcased fashions often directly tied to recent films or to stars in multipage spreads. Lifestyle columns in the 1930s and '40s offered women (to whom they were insistently addressed) advice about beauty, housekeeping, and child rearing. These columns, penned by Elena de la Torre (the pseudonym of Elena Gomez de Zarraga), purported to draw on the most modern advances in domestic science and beauty culture. Regular columns that had begun as spaces for film entrepreneurs to receive answers to inquiries about the latest advances in projection morphed into places to ask questions about their favorite stars and film culture and then, in the 1930s, became sites for general inquiries about topics ranging from fashion and skin care to romance. Regular features such as *Baturillo Neoyorkino* (New York Mish Mash) combined droll observations about urban life with anecdotes about the city's entertainment culture, allowing readers to eavesdrop on life there.

Explaining the United States to *Cine-Mundial*'s readership constituted a central thread through the magazine's non-film-related content. Explanations included the fanciful fictional series about the life of a relatively well-off family from an unnamed Caribbean country, "Aventuras de La Familia Pérez en New York," penned by Costa Rican journalist and editor Modesto Martinez under the pseudonym Ramiro Pérez, as they socialized with their New York neighbors, participated in New York's night life, traveled, and—above all else—attempted to marry off their two daughters. The family's misadventures became the occasion for explanations of Irish maids, pets, dance academies, and the mismatch between the main character's tropical, provincial sensibilities and the United States. Other articles directly explained what Spaniards and Latin Americans might encounter in New York.[27] In the 1940s, topics had ranged from the zeal for contests to the complexities of marriage in the US.[28] In this way, *Cine-Mundial*'s editorial staff and contributors served as proxies for readers who, like them, were literate and educated and might have seen New York, with its communities of immigrants, expatriates, and exiles, as a central node in the hemisphere's cosmopolitan urban culture.

In addition to urban life in general, ideas and practices related to race were topics that received sustained attention. A November 1921 feature explained the Ku Klux Klan as both very US-American and very ridiculous.[29] A 1926 editorial, "Pigmentaciones," turned on a legal case involving a man married to a mixed-race woman who many believed to be "Spanish." Recounting this case allowed *Cine-Mundial* editor Francisco (Frank) García Ortega to unpack the practice of passing as a way of bypassing the color line. "Displaying one of our surnames," he wrote, "everything changes, and the gates are open."[30] Acknowledging that race played out differently in Latin America, García Ortega commented repeatedly that the so-called one-drop rule was an oddity of US culture. "There's no explaining [to white Americans]," he writes, "the Hispanic philosophy that tolerates intimacy between white men and black women."[31] At the same time, contributors echoed mainstream fascination and alarm about the popularity of African American culture. In 1926, Raymundo de la Veracruz reviewed *La noche negra* (*La revue nègre*) in Paris. De la Veracruz opined that African American music resonated with "the palpitations of our nervous and disordered life," attributing the public's fascination with jazz and other forms of African American performance to the "fact that as we advance in material progress we go backward spiritually and today, like in the ages of barbarism and savagery, instinct triumphs."[32] Rafael de Zayas Enriquez expanded on de la Veracruz's observations in an essay entitled "La Melanomania," which traced the emergence of African American music and performance culture in the United

256   CHAPTER 14

States. Noting links to the Caribbean, Zayas Enriquez called this fascination an "infirmity" that was caused by the moral decay of modernity.[33] Later, José Manuel Bada reviewed the ballet *Rascacielos* (*Skyscraper*) by John Carpenter, mounted at the Metropolitan Opera House in 1926. This coverage was complemented by Bada's 1927 profile of the arts scene in Harlem, in which he took the reader on a tour of the artistic vibrancy of the barrio he referred to as "Little Africa."[34] Even as contributors compared and contrasted the meaning and everyday experience of race in the United States, casual racism such as a description of a group of hopeful extras—"negros, negras, negritos, perros y gatas" (black men, black women, black children, dogs and cats)—implied that proximity to whiteness retained currency.[35] This somewhat convoluted and inconsistent discourse on race reflected the heterogeneity of the magazine's contributors.

For its entire run, *Cine-Mundial* was led by García Ortega, a Cuban national who came to the United States in the mid-1910s after briefly working in journalism on the island.[36] García Ortega maintained a low profile; he was only infrequently photographed at industry events.[37] Thus, his politics are difficult to ascertain. He was joined on the masthead by Francisco J. Ariza, who had come to New York from Mexico in 1902 and who also remains a political enigma. But later in the 1940s, García Ortega brought on J. M. Escuder, a Spanish journalist, who had worked in 20th Century Fox's foreign department briefly in 1936 before returning to Spain during the Spanish Civil War.[38] Upon his return to Spain, he directed *La Batalla*, the newspaper of the Partido Obrero de Unificación Marxista (POUM, or Workers' Party of Marxist Unification, an anti-Stalinist communist organization in Spain). He returned to the US after being brought up on what many saw as trumped-up charges in Valencia in 1937. His arrest was protested by various high-profile communists, including Mexican painter Diego Rivera. It was at this point that he returned to the United States and joined the staff of *Cine-Mundial*; he and his wife, a US citizen, remained in the sights of the House Un-American Activities Committee.

Though we have no direct evidence, it seems safe to say that García Ortega was known by and knew Spanish, Catalan, and Latin American journalists, writers, and artists in New York. Many of these contributors were well-known journalists or writers in their home countries or in other parts of Latin America, and many sought refuge in New York from political unrest in their home countries. For example, Mexican author and former poet laureate Rafael de Zayas Enriquez, a frequent contributor, had been a supporter of Mexican dictator Porfirio Díaz and of Victoriano Huerta, who had come to power via a coup against Francisco I. Madero in 1913. Catalan nationalist author J. Carner Ribalta worked in Spanish-language Hollywood before beginning to contribute to the magazine in the 1940s.[39] Argentine author and journalist Alejandro Sux, who began to contribute to the magazine in the 1940s at the same time that he was providing radio commentary for NBC's Pan-American radio program, had a long-standing association with anarchism, although his politics became more moderate over the course of his career.[40] The short stories of left-leaning Spanish editor and writer Eduardo Zamacois appeared with some regularity in *Cine-Mundial* in the 1940s, during the period he was in exile in New York.[41] And Cuban political cartoonist Ramón Arroyo Cisneros, who often signed his work Arroyito, was exiled numerous times from the Island.

Other contributors found themselves in the United States to work or to make professional connections in the world of journalism or the arts. For example, Catalan painter Josep Maria Recoder, whose pinup-style portraits of film stars gave *Cine-Mundial's* covers of the 1930s their distinctive look, lived in New York in the 1930s before returning to his native Barcelona.[42] Spaniard Miguel de Zárraga, a long-standing regular contributor, had moved around the Caribbean working as a correspondent and editor before he made his way to New York, where he connected with the city's Spanish-language newspapers, founded a weekly literary journal, and contributed editorials and prose to Spanish-language periodicals in other parts of the United States. Eventually, Zárraga and his wife, Elena de la Torre (Elena Gomez de Zárraga), found work in Hollywood.

These contributors' backgrounds and professional histories suggest the important place of Spanish-language periodicals for some currents of movement across the hemisphere. While it is difficult to ascertain how much contributors were paid, it seems reasonable to assume that their work was part of broader survival strategies during their sojourns or permanent settlement in the United States. A tantalizing hint at this dynamic can be found in correspondence dating from 1907 to 1908 between Rafael de Zayas Enríquez and Bernardo Reyes, then governor of the Mexican state of Nuevo Leon and a partisan of the Díaz regime, which would be overthrown by the revolution just years later. In his letters to Reyes, Zayas Enríquez, who was living in New York with his family, asks for his help securing freelance work with various periodicals based in Nuevo Leon. In his words, he sought opportunities to send "reviews and articles of general interest, daily if possible, in exchange for a salary."[43] In 1907, this sort of arrangement netted Zayas Enríquez a hundred dollars a month for an article a day. We can imagine then that in practical terms, *Cine-Mundial* provided paid work, occasional or regular, for exiles or sojourners who used their skills as authors and journalists to generate income that would support themselves and their families.

The magazine also brought modernist illustration to its readers across the continent, becoming a vehicle for the diffusion of the latest artistic innovations. Indeed, the artists who contributed to the magazine, whose illustrations and caricatures gave *Cine-Mundial* a distinct modernist aesthetic in the mid-1920s and '30s, included a significant number whose professional lives intersected with New York's cutting-edge literary and artistic circles. For example, Ramón Arroyo Cisneros worked with Harlem chronicler Lee Posner. Cuban modernist Enrique Riverón moved to the United States in 1930 and contributed to *Cine-Mundial* and *The New Yorker* while continuing to pursue his art career.[44] A young Miguel Covarrubias,

258   CHAPTER 14

in New York with the support of a grant from the Mexican government, also contributed numerous caricatures, including some that would be collected in his 1927 book *Negro Drawings*, to *Cine-Mundial, Vanity Fair,* and *The New Yorker*.[45] These working relationships suggest that beyond mere observation, artists who contributed to *Cine-Mundial* forged relationships not only with the Spanish-language press but also with modernist artists, writers, and cultural brokers.

Thus, although *Cine-Mundial* was "only tangentially linked to the most significant currents of the Spanish-language press in the United States" in terms of content, its contributors were deeply embedded in hemispheric literary and artistic circles.[46] As Nicolás Kanellos explains, the exile press sought to change conditions in their home country from abroad and the immigrant press sought to serve immigrant communities in the United States.[47] What, then, to make of *Cine-Mundial?* Its staunch commitment to advertising and marketing and its class-based address to the Latin American elite and aspiring middle classes would suggest a regressive politics. Yet a closer examination of its contributors hints at the magazine's function (and perhaps cinema's as well) as a refuge—not in intellectual but in material terms—for left-leaning and radical Latin American intellectuals and other sojourners traveling Pan-American circuits in the first half of the twentieth century.

NOTES

1. In 1927, *Moving Picture World* was purchased by Martin Quigley, publisher of *Exhibitors Herald*. Martin J. Quigley, "The Consolidated Publication!," *Exhibitors Herald and Moving Picture World*, January 7, 1928, 1. Eric Hoyt describes this merger, one of a few film trade publication mergers in the late 1920s, in *Ink-Stained Hollywood: The Triumph of American Cinema's Trade Press* (Oakland: University of California Press, 2022), 146–48.

2. This phrase, "Yankee invasion," was frequently used by Mexican journalists and film critics to describe the way that American films seemed to flood the Mexican market in the late 1910s. For example, see "El hijo de la loca: Película nacional," *Excelsior*, October 14, 1923.

3. Rielle Navitski, "Mediating the 'Conquering and Cosmopolitan Cinema': US Spanish-Language Film Magazines and Latin American Audiences, 1916–1948," in *Cosmopolitan Film Cultures in Latin America, 1896–1960,* ed. Rielle Navitski and Nicolas Poppe (Bloomington: Indiana University Press, 2017), 114.

4. Navitski, "Mediating," 116–17.

5. Navitski, 114.

6. "Nuestro programa," *Cine-Mundial,* January 1916, 10.

7. "Nuestro programa."

8. "Nuestro programa."

9. John Clyde Owen, "The Making of a Trade Paper," in *Lectures in the Forum in Industrial Journalism* (New York: Advertising and Selling, Inc., 1915), 114.

10. The term *Pan-Americanism* was first used in the press in reference to a series of inter-American conferences held to encourage political and economic cooperation between the various nations of the Americas. The Pan American Union, later the Organization of American States, was founded in 1910 out of the Commercial Bureau of the American Republics. In 1911, diplomat and early director John Barrett described the Union's mission as promoting "peace, good understanding, and exchange of commerce." John Barrett, *The Pan American Union* (Washington, DC: Pan American Union, 1911), 7.

CINE-MUNDIAL AND CULTURAL CIRCUITS 259

11. Kristin Thompson, *Exporting Entertainment: America in the World Film Market, 1907–1934* (London: British Film Institute, 1985), 72–73.

12. Advertisement for *Cine-Mundial*, June 9, 1917, 1682.

13. "Effective Publicity in Latin America," *Chicago Commerce*, October 7, 1922, 45.

14. The figure for 1922 is self-reported in "Effective Publicity in Latin America," but squares with Audit Bureau of Circulation figures published in *N. W. Ayer and Son's American Newspaper Annual and Directory*. The figure for 1929 is cited in Navitski, "Mediating," 142, n6.

15. On the early establishment of exchanges and agencies in South America, see Thompson, *Exporting Entertainment*, 72–73.

16. Navitski, "Mediating," 126–27. See also Laura Isabel Serna, *Making Cinelandia: American Films and Mexican Film Culture before the Golden Age* (Durham, NC: Duke University Press, 2014), 95–96.

17. "Cinemundial en Cinelandia," *Cine-Mundial*, June 1922, 304–5.

18. See, for example, two articles about Mussolini by W. Stephen Bush: "Jubileo-Benelli-Mussolini," *Cine-Mundial*, July 1925, 409; and "Mussolinizando," *Cine-Mundial*, October 1926, 666; an article about opera: Don José, "Alredador de la ópera 'El Gato de Montes' por Penella," *Cine-Mundial*, November 1921, 746–47; and others over the course of the magazine's run.

19. Advertisement, *Cine-Mundial, Moving Picture World*, February 13, 1926.

20. Charles F. McGovern, *Sold American: Consumption and Citizenship, 1890–1945* (Chapel Hill: University of North Carolina Press, 2006), 27.

21. Advertisement for *Cine-Mundial, Printer's Ink*, June 22, 1922, 111.

22. Steven J. Bunker and Victor Macias Gonzalez, "Consumption and Material Culture in the Twentieth Century," in *A Companion to Mexican History and Culture*, ed. William H. Beezley, 83–118 (Hoboken, NJ: Wiley-Blackwell, 2011), 87.

23. Matthew B. Karush, *Culture of Class: Radio and Cinema in the Making of a Divided Argentina, 1920–1940* (Durham, NC: Duke University Press, 2012), 32–33.

24. Mary Speck, "Prosperity, Progress, and Wealth: Cuban Enterprise during the Early Republic, 1902–1927," *Cuban Studies* 36 (2005): 51.

25. Bunker and Macias Gonzalez, "Consumption and Material Culture," 89.

26. Circulation figures are drawn from Navitski, "Mediating," 127, and the *Intercontinental Press Guide: A Directory*, 1947. The quotation is from the latter, on page 76.

27. See, for example, Julio Baronet, "Nueva York, prosa y romance," *Cine-Mundial*, May 1921, 328–29; José Manuel Bada, "Donde come New York," *Cine-Mundial*, December 1929, 1239; and Francisco J. Ariza, "Nueva York absurda," *Cine-Mundial*, June 1931, 441.

28. See, for example, J. Carner-Ribalata, "La fuerza del 'Ice Cream' o cómo se es americano," *Cine-Mundial*, August 1944, 389, and "La vida intima de los matrimonios norteamericanos," *Cine-Mundial*, June 1945, 287.

29. Luis G. Muñiz, "Una secta de zurradores," *Cine-Mundial*, November 1921, 749, 781.

30. "Pigmentaciones," [Editorial], *Cine-Mundial*, February 1926, 77.

31. "Baturillo Neoyorquino," *Cine-Mundial*, April 1921, 268.

32. Raymundo de la Veracruz, "La noche negra," *Cine-Mundial*, February 1926, 100.

33. R. de Zayas Enriquez, "La Melanomania," *Cine-Mundial*, January 1927, 10.

34. José Manuel Bada, "El barrio y el arte de los negros," *Cine-Mundial*, September 1927, 702.

35. "Los parias de Hollywood," *Cine-Mundial*, August 1927, 662.

36. García Ortega died in 1967. His obituary in *The New York Times* referred to him by his pseudonym, Jorge Hermida, and confused many of the details of his professional life, naming him founder of *The Moving Picture World*. "Jorge Hermida, 78, a Columnist Dies," *The New York Times*, November 2, 1967, 47. It is unclear, but it seems his parents were part of the wave of Spanish migration to Cuba in the late nineteenth century.

37. See, for example, "This Week in Pictures: Industry Secrets Revealed," *Motion Picture Herald*, November 27, 1937, 10, where he is pictured at a New York event hosted by producer Walter Wanger;

260 CHAPTER 14

and "This Week: The Camera Reports," *Moving Picture Herald*, July 12, 1947, 11, where he is pictured with representatives from studios in Cuba and Mexico.

38. "Escuder Formerly on 20th Fox Staff Here," *Motion Picture Daily*, August 4, 1937, 10. See "Journalist Faces Trail in Valencia," *The New York Times*, August 1, 1937, 29; and "Maxton Sees Escuder: Briton Eases Anxiety," *The New York Times*, August 28, 1937, 6. Escuder's name can be found in United States Congress Special Committee on Un-American Activities (1938–41), *Investigation of Un-American Propaganda Activities in the United States. Index to Hearings, vols. 1–14: Reports 1930–1941* (Washington, DC: Government Printing Office, 1942), 73.

39. Carner Ribalta was a Catalan nationalist who was exiled by Prime Minster Primo de Rivera in the 1920s, eventually landing in New York, where he worked for Paramount's foreign department and eventually wrote scripts for Spanish-language films. Pau Echauz, "Carner Ribalta, el catalanista que quiso crear un Hollywood en Sabadell," *La Vanguardia*, November 29, 2020, https://www.lavanguardia.com/cultura/20201129/49774909274/carner-ribalta-catalanista-hollywood-sabadell-secretario-macia.html.

40. Rana and Cappelletti note that Sux became less radical towards the end of his life (he died in 1959). Carlos Rana and Angel Cappelletti, eds., *El anarquismo en América Latina* (Buenos Aires: Editorial Ayacucho, 1990), xlix. On Sux's radio commentaries, see "Rockefeller Field Force Mustered: Latin Radio Campaign Is Surging Rapidly towards Its Peak," *Broadcasting*, August 31, 1942, 18.

41. Barbara Minesso, "Eduardo Zamacois: viajero, empresario, editor, periodista y escritor," *Belphégor* [En ligne], 18–2, published online December 11, 2020, http://journals.openedition.org/belphegor/3042 (accessed July 15, 2021).

42. Sources about Recoder are difficult to find. His paintings can be found for sale on websites such as artnet.com, and he is mentioned in a catalog documenting exhibitions by Catalan artists before 1938. Antònia Montmany, Montserrat Navarro, Narta Tort, and Francesc Fontbona, *Repertori d'exposicions individuals d'art a Catalunya (fins a l'any 1938)* (Barcelona, Spain: Institut d'Estudis Catalans, 1999), 290.

43. Rafael de Zayas Enríquez to Sr. General Bernardo Reyes, June 19, 1907, Correspondencia de Bernardo Reyes 1907–1908, Centro de Historia de Mexico, Condumex, Fondo DLI, carpeta 38, reprinted in Antonio Sabrit García Peña, "Rafael de Zayas Enríquez/Bernardo Reyes correspondencia 1907–1908," *Historia: Revista de la Dirección de Estudios Históricos* 59 (September–December 2008), 120. García Peña's concern in showcasing this correspondence is to trace how Zayas Enríquez fell out of favor with the Díaz regime after the publication of a book about Díaz, but it contains tantalizing hints about the material conditions of freelance journalism by expatriates who wrote for Spanish-language periodicals in the United States and other Spanish-speaking countries.

44. See https://www.aaa.si.edu/collections/enrique-rivern-papers-5433/biographical-note and https://www.lambiek.net/artists/r/riveron_enrique.htm.

45. Miguel Covarrubias, *Negro Drawings* (New York: Knopf, 1927). Carolyn Kastner's short article "The Cosmopolitan Circles of Miguel Covarrubias," *American Art* 30, no. 1 (Spring 2016): 11–15, overlooks the Spanish-language cultural elite in New York altogether when describing the connections he made there in the 1920s.

46. Navitski, "Mediating," 113.

47. Nicolás Kanellos and Helvetia Martell, *Hispanic Periodicials in the United States, Origins to 1960: A Brief History and Comprehensive Bibliography* (Houston, TX: Arte Público Press, 1999), 5–6.

PUBLICATIONS REFERENCED

America e Industrias Americanas
American Druggist
Automovil Americana

Cinelandia
Cine-Mundial
Commerce in Latin America
La Batalla
Moving Picture World
The New Yorker
Printer's Ink
Revista Americana de Farmacia y Medicina
The South American
Vanity Fair

BIBLIOGRAPHY

Barrett, John. *The Pan American Union*. Washington, DC: Pan American Union, 1911.

Bunker, Steven J., and Victor Macias Gonzalez. "Consumption and Material Culture in the Twentieth Century." In *A Companion to Mexican History and Culture*, edited by William H. Beezley, 83–118. Hoboken, NJ: Wiley-Blackwell, 2011.

Covarrubias, Miguel. *Negro Drawings*. New York: Knopf, 1927.

García Peña, Antonio Sabrit. "Rafael de Zayas Enríquez/Bernardo Reyes correspondencia 1907–1908." *Historia: Revista de la Dirección de Estudios Históricos* 59 (September–December 2008): 109–40.

Hoyt, Eric. *Ink-Stained Hollywood: The Triumph of American Cinema's Trade Press*. Oakland: University of California Press, 2022, https://doi.org/10.1525/luminos.122.

Kanellos, Nicolás, and Helvetia Martell. *Hispanic Periodicals in the United States, Origins to 1960: A Brief History and Comprehensive Bibliography*. Houston, TX: Arte Público Press, 1999.

Karush, Matthew B. *Culture of Class: Radio and Cinema in the Making of a Divided Argentina, 1920–1940*. Durham, NC: Duke University Press, 2012.

Kastner, Carolyn. "The Cosmopolitan Circles of Miguel Covarrubias." *American Art* 30, no. 1 (Spring 2016): 11–15.

McGovern, Charles F. *Sold American: Consumption and Citizenship, 1890–1945*. Chapel Hill: University of North Carolina Press, 2006.

Minesso, Barbara. "Eduardo Zamacois: viajero, empresario, editor, periodista y escritor." *Belphégor* [En ligne], 18–2. http://journals.openedition.org/belphegor/3042.

Navitski, Rielle. "Mediating the 'Conquering and Cosmopolitan Cinema': US Spanish-Language Film Magazines and Latin American Audiences, 1916–1948." In *Cosmopolitan Film Cultures in Latin America, 1896–1960*, edited by Rielle Navitski and Nicolas Poppe, 112–46. Bloomington: Indiana University Press, 2017.

Owen, John Clyde. "The Making of a Trade Paper." In *Lectures in the Forum in Industrial Journalism*. New York: Advertising and Selling, Inc., 1915.

Serna, Laura Isabel. *Making Cinelandia: American Films and Mexican Film Culture before the Golden Age*. Durham, NC: Duke University Press, 2014.

Speck, Mary. "Prosperity, Progress, and Wealth: Cuban Enterprise during the Early Republic, 1902–1927." *Cuban Studies* 36 (2005): 50–86.

Rana, Carlos, and Angel Cappelletti, eds. *El anarquismo en América Latina*. Buenos Aires: Editorial Ayacucho, 1990.

Thompson, Kristin. *Exporting Entertainment: America in the World Film Market, 1907–1934*. London: British Film Institute, 1985.

15

Radiolandia, Fan Magazines, and Stardom in 1930s and 1940s Argentina

Nicolas Poppe

On Wednesdays, Thursdays, and Sundays at 10:00 p.m. in mid-1940, nighttime radio listeners throughout Argentina were presented with actor Floren Delbene, *el cotizado galán de la pantalla* (the sought-after prince of the screen), in his latest program for Radio Belgrano, *El último estreno* (*The Latest Première*). Delbene, a star who had appeared in more than a dozen films in the late 1930s, including hits such as *Amalia* (dir. Luis Moglia Barth, 1936) and *Ayúdame a vivir* (*Help Me to Live*, dir. José A. Ferreyra, 1936), was a frequent presence on airwaves from Buenos Aires to well into the country's interior. Distinguishing him from other film stars such as Hugo del Carril and Libertad Lamarque, Delbene was one of the few dramatic crossover artists who was not a musician. Rather, in his programs, Delbene hosted and/or acted in *radioteatros* (radio dramas).

With scripts written by the Chileans Tito Davison and José Manteola, *El último estreno* also featured a constellation of actresses, some of whose lights burned brighter than others.[1] Among those performing in the program, Herminia Franco, Fanny Navarro, Mecha Ortiz, and Malisa Zini became stars whose afterimages persist to this day. Also on the program were Aída Alberti, Irma Córdoba, Elsa O'Connor, Alita Román, and Pepita Serrador, actresses perhaps less likely to be remembered today but who nevertheless enjoyed long careers on stage and set, as well as in broadcasting and, eventually, television studios. Never quite arriving to those levels were Rosita Contreras and Angelina Pagano. Nevertheless, a print advertisement for the program proclaimed, "Never has a radio program managed to gather so many stellar figures from our theater and cinema. All prestigious names, captivated by intense and lucid work."[2] Sponsored by Phillips' Milk of Magnesia, *El último estreno* not only sold the globally marketed antacid and laxative but also promoted sectors of the local entertainment industry through mass media. What little

FIGURE 15.1. Advertisement for Floren Delbene's radio program in *Radiolandia*, April 6, 1940, 47.

264   CHAPTER 15

we now know of *El último estreno*, which broadcast well-known figures of the movies and theater live on the radio, is found within the pages of the printed press (some of which have been digitized). In the pages of newspapers, trade publications, and fan magazines, the lives and labors of a wide range of entertainers were discussed and examined. As in other places, shining most intensely were movie stars. These stars allow us to better understand a wide range of issues, from media industry strategies to the aspirations of fans (which is to say everyday people), something especially important in places such as Argentina, which Beatriz Sarlo described as experiencing a culture of mixture, a peripheral modernity, thus receiving relatively little scholarly attention in comparison to the United States and Europe.[3]

By 1940, a national film industry had finally emerged in Argentina. Despite its vibrant local film culture, among the most active in the world in the 1920s and early 1930s, Argentina's film production had been unable to compete with imports from Hollywood and Europe until innovations in sound film technologies opened up domestic and, almost immediately, foreign markets. According to film historian Claudio España, "The industrial growth of Argentine cinema accompanied the process of widespread industrialization that happened in the country."[4] What was once unsustainable became an industrial practice as film production moved from the producer/director model of the silent era toward what España calls an "institutional model," a more studio-based production in the mold of Hollywood (and, to a lesser extent, European cinemas). Consequently, national film production saw its annual output grow from five movies in 1930 to nearly fifty by the end of the decade. As I have documented elsewhere, "Majors Argentina Sono Film and Lumiton were joined by new studios such as SIDE (Sociedad Impresora de Discos Electrofónicos), EFA (Establecimientos Filmadores Argentinos), and Estudios San Miguel, as well as fleeting independents such as Baires Film and Cinematografía Terra."[5] Ranging from new facilities to multipicture deals with in-demand stars, studios invested with the hope of hitting it big with audiences at home and abroad.

Stars such as Floren Delbene also found their way into the lives of everyday people in Buenos Aires and beyond through the radio. Throughout the 1920s and '30s, radio sets became more and more popular as experiments in broadcasting became increasingly professional. Unlike the public service model of the British Broadcasting Corporation (BBC) and other European broadcasters, Argentina saw radio follow the United States' commercial model. By the late 1930s, the radio had firmly cemented its place in Argentine culture, as well over a million sets had made their way into homes and other spaces, allowing listeners to enjoy varied regular programming on established stations such as LR1 Radio El Mundo (AM 1070). Christine Ehrick notes, "Newspapers tended to see radio as competition, and thus were [not] wont to give radio much press coverage (with exception of stations owned by or affiliated with a given newspaper). Thus, radio relied on separate radio and entertainment-themed publications to distribute programming schedules and to promote programs, celebrities, and radio listening generally." Like the cinema, which often appealed to the radio's popularity through what Ana M. López calls the "radiophonic imaginary," the radio was inextricably enmeshed with other media industries.[6]

Alongside the emergence of its national film industry and the consolidation of radio's place in society, a constellation of new popular magazines appeared in kiosks across Argentina. Joining an already active press, new fan magazines such as *Radiolandia* (*Radioland*), *Sintonía* (*In Tune*), *Cine Argentino* (*Argentine Cinema*), and *Astros* (*Stars*) set themselves apart by focusing on stars. In his foundational 1957 work *The Stars*, Edgar Morin argues that "their cult primarily subsists on specialized publications. Although there are no theater magazines, dance magazines, or even music magazines devoted entirely to actors, dancers, or singers, movie magazines are devoted essentially to the stars."[7] Even though this is certainly not the case today in Argentina (and was not wholly so even in the first half of the twentieth century), Morin's broader point resonates: at the time, Argentine fan magazines' interest in the stars was devout. In their pages, material written by correspondents abroad on Hollywood's stars, including those of its *colonia hispana*, increasingly lost column space to local stars. Such publications did more than diffuse information about the on- and off-screen trials and tribulations of local stars such as Libertad Lamarque and Luis Sandrini; these new fan magazines came to be the leading promoters of a national star system. As Mary Desjardins reminds us, "Fan magazines occasionally reported on actor labor issues and often referred to specific aspects of stars' contracts, but they most frequently focused on, and contributed to, the 'ideological work' of stars, or their status as figures constructed as both ordinary and extraordinary. Specifically, the fan magazine of the 1930s articulated a relation between the glamorous female star and the ordinary female fan." Extending Desjardins's work on Hollywood stars, I contend that periodicals such as *Cine Argentino* and *Sintonía* reflect and participate in the ideological work of Argentine stars.[8] In this essay, I trace how local stars came into sight in these magazines over the course of the 1930s. Stardom, if it could be defined as such, was much less systematic in Argentina than in other places, as it was more diffused among various media industries. Despite this, as Carolina González Centeno has pointed out, "following stars is, in turn, a way to accompany and promote the growth and consolidation of different local media: at first, radio, then cinema, and, finally, television."[9] Focusing my attention on *Radiolandia*, and more specifically on its coverage of Floren Delbene, an actor oscillating between the cinema and radio in 1940, I gesture toward some ways in which these magazines contributed to the formation of a local Argentine star system.

STARS IN THE PAGES OF *RADIOLANDIA*

With its energetic film culture centered in Buenos Aires, Latin America's largest city in 1940, it is of little surprise that Argentina had a rich history of film publications. Broadly of three types (newspapers, trade journals, and fan magazines), these publications were heavily influenced by foreign magazines, especially those from the United States, but they nonetheless catered to local readers whose interests and tastes differed from those in other places.[10] Earlier fan magazines such as *Cinema Chat, Cine Universal, Imparcial Film,* and *Magazine Cinematográfico* as well as fleeting, lesser-known ones like *Astros y Estrellas* (*Stars and Stars*) and *Sideral* (*Stellar*), focused largely on heavenly bodies from northern skies, but also directed some attention to local stars.[11] The emergence of a national film industry in the 1930s, as well as the increasing availability and popularity of the radio, also saw shifts in how Argentine magazines covered local entertainment culture. Some of the most notable transformations could be read within the pages of *Radiolandia*, which began its five-decade run as *La Canción Moderna* (*The Modern Song*). Lila Caimari notes: "With populist and anarchist resonances, *La Canción Moderna* was born in 1928 under the direction of Dante A. Linyera, partnered with the young Julio Korn, a future mass media magnate. The project briefly brought together the Jewish immigrant interested in cultural industries with the son of Italian immigrants determined to preserve a 'pure' and spontaneous popular culture."[12] Linyera, a tango composer, lyricist, and poet, had previously collaborated on the launch of the children's magazine *El Purrete* (*The Kid*) and the soccer magazine *La Cancha* (*The Pitch*), and, according to Matthew B. Karush, his decisions did not necessarily last: "Following Dante Linyera's brief term as editor, Korn would steer the magazine in a more mainstream direction."[13] Under Korn's direction, *La Canción Moderna* was a "precursor of a form of entertainment and escapist journalism [as it] compiled lyrics of fashionable songs, mixing them with stories of their authors and singers."[14] Centered on tango culture and music, the magazine also touched upon local entertainment culture from soccer to cinema, and it included diverse lyrics from American fox-trots, Mexican rancheras, and Peruvian waltzes. It would eventually broaden its interests to appeal to a larger readership.

Emerging out of the pages of *La Canción Moderna* as a supplement at the beginning of 1936, *Radiolandia* eventually displaced Korn's first entertainment publication and shifted its focus from radio to cinema.[15] Signaling its eventual transition away from a mere special section, the magazine used both titles in several issues. An important editorial was published in the first, which appeared on May 25, 1936, a national holiday in Argentina commemorating the May Revolution and the creation of the Primera Junta in 1810. In *Radiolandia*, the magazine claimed that both titles mark the same project: "*Radiolandia* is the materialization, in a name, of the current nature of LA CANCIÓN MODERNA. 'The world of the radio in a magazine,' our subtitle reads, and no one could deny that within our pages the outstanding current events of what radiotelephony does inside and outside our country are condensed."[16] Rebranding the magazine allowed Korn to adapt to new circumstances not only in the publishing world, but also in the media environment. In 1935, he launched his second title, the women's magazine *Vosotras* (the feminine second person plural subject pronoun in Spanish, equivalent to plural "you," "you all," or "y'all" in English). Soon, he would be among the major players in Argentine publishing.[17] "If there is one description that could define *Radiolandia*, as well as the rest of these publications, it would be popular. And popular, for Korn, [was] always synonymous with mass entertainment.

Both premises are thoroughly fulfilled in *Radiolandia*, which centers its focus on the entertainment world and its main protagonists."[18] *Radiolandia*'s rebranding also allowed Korn to more directly compete with two other important fan magazines: *Antena*, launched in 1931 by Jaime Yankelevich "in order to give Radio Belgrano an outlet for free publicity," and *Sintonía*, established in 1933 by Editorial Haynes (the publishing company that owned the station Radio El Mundo).[19] Like *Radiolandia*, *Antena* and *Sintonía* directed their attention to the entertainment world—usually, but not exclusively, to local activity. With the passage of time, information on the radio gave way to news on the cinema, but these magazines kept tabs on the characters, figures, stars, and workers of different entertainment sectors. Of the three, *Radiolandia* came to be the most successful. So successful was Korn's enterprise that it bought *Antena* in 1937 "with the intention of competing against itself" and it pushed *Sintonía* out of the market in 1941 (though it would later return).[20]

Like many other fan magazines, *Radiolandia* hooked readers with weekly updates about their favorite stars. From notes on the luxurious premiere of the latest local superproduction to information on the quotidian comings and goings of actors, the magazine brought attention to both marginal and major figures. Stars in the pages of *Radiolandia* were paradoxically at once ordinary and extraordinary, something Richard Dyer (among others) has noted as one of central contradictions of stardom.[21] *Radiolandia* offered its readers some of the few available glimpses into the lives of Argentine stars. Morin may have overlooked the importance of the radio in mediating the relationship between the stars and their public in *The Stars*, but, as the groundbreaking Argentine film historian Domingo Di Núbila (somewhat exaggeratingly) argues:

> Outside of the movies, they could only be seen in photographs in newspapers and magazines, and occasionally in fleeting newsreel snapshots. And they were only heard in rare radio interviews because portable recorders had not yet been invented. Journalism contributed to surrounding them with a mythical aura. The specialized magazine with the largest circulation, "Radiolandia" . . . never published anything that showed them as anything less than perfect beings. No slipups, no resignations, no sins, not even venial ones. Indiscreet gossip was confined to "telephone dialogues" and other benevolent columns. Changes in couples flaunted the rhetoric of fashionable novels.[22]

Similar to a newspaper like *La Nación* or a trade journal such as *Heraldo del Cinematografista*, *Radiolandia* provided a promotional feedback loop by regularly reporting on all stages of film production. Unlike those other kinds of film periodicals, which directed readers' attention to other niche aspects of the film industry, *Radiolandia*'s feedback loop primarily sold stars and the protagonists of local celebrity culture. Whether introducing readers to someone who is sure to make it, but almost certainly will not, in a regular column such as "Screen: News Broadcast of National Cinema" or reminding them of their favorite performances in an

268   CHAPTER 15

article such as "Does the Love They Feign On-Screen Leave Traces in the Hearts of Actors?," *Radiolandia* narrated a compelling version of the (working) lives of the characters of the Argentine entertainment industry.[23]

Among the stars about which *Radiolandia* kept readers up-to-date in 1940 were Charlo, Hugo del Carril, Delia Garcés, Libertad Lamarque, Amanda Ledesma, Niní Marshall, Luis Sandrini, Mercedes Simone, and Juan Carlos Thorry. Featured in anything from a brief note to the front cover, these stars were kept in the limelight by *Radiolandia*. The magazine's narrative about Floren Delbene, the host of *El último estreno*, is typical in its apparent contradictions: he lived an extraordinary life of which readers could only dream, but he was ordinary in that he was one of many working in the entertainment industry. For similar reasons, Delbene provides an intriguing case study to examine intermediality and stardom at a key moment in Argentine media history. Somewhat paradoxically, he is at once representative and unique. Today, Delbene is most often remembered, critically at least, in reference to a trilogy of films directed by José Agustín Ferreyra, produced by SIDE, and starring Lamarque; Delbene appeared as the male opposite her in two of the three films, *Ayúdame a vivir* and *Besos brujos* (*Bewitching Kisses*, 1937).[24] Delbene's career never reached the heights of other leading men such as Luis Sandrini, Hugo del Carril, and José Gola, but he played an important role in popularizing national cinema as a *galán* in the early sound period.[25]

Unlike most of his counterparts in the 1930s, however, Delbene's career started in silent cinema, as he appeared in a handful of films including *Muchachita de Chiclana* (*Chiclana Girl*, dir. Ferreyra, 1926) and *La quena de la muerte* (*The Quena of Death*, dir. Nelo Cosimi, 1928).[26] He then starred in the first Argentine film to use sound-on-disc, Ferreyra's 1931 *Muñequitas porteñas* (*Porteño Dolls*).[27] It took him some time to break into talkies, but he was extremely busy from 1936 to 1939.[28] With his film career slowing down significantly, especially after Mario Soffici's *Cita en la frontera* (*Date on the Border*, 1940), starring Lamarque, Delbene took refuge in other sectors of the entertainment industry, especially radio (where he had appeared for some time).[29] Unlike comics and musicians who (relatively easily) crossed over from radio to cinema and vice versa, Delbene hosted programs and/or acted in *radioteatros*. He also remained a constant presence in the press, especially fan magazines. As Richard deCordova reminds us, "Journalism provided the institutional setting for much, if not most, discourse on stars. The trade press, fan magazines, and newspapers all constituted specific positions from which to speak the star."[30] Consequently, as Janine Basinger succinctly argues, "You can trace a star's progress by tracking his or her plants, interviews, and photographs through these fan magazines."[31] (Increasingly, digital tools such as Lantern, the Media History Digital Library's search platform, allow us to trace these trajectories, although results are limited to their holdings.) Throughout this period, readers who loved, hated, or were indifferent toward Delbene could follow his place within the constellation of stars whose lights emanated from Argentina's various media industries.

FLOREN DELBENE IN CLOSE-UP

Even though he was not mentioned in *Radiolandia*'s "¿Quiénes son los astros 1940?" (Who Are the Stars 1940?), Floren Delbene appeared in the magazine regularly throughout the year.[32] Coverage on the star varied from reports on his latest professional activities to notes on his cultural impact to profiles to different kinds of gossip. Lamented in the gossip column "Como me lo contaron" (As They Told It to Me), Delbene was suffering a dry spell in the movies.[33] Beyond occasional news regarding *Cita en la frontera* that recalled Lamarque's and Delbene's popularity after *Ayúdame a vivir* and *Besos brujos* in Venezuela, Colombia, and other countries, reports were published about projects with two fleeting production companies (Platense Film and Artefilm) that never materialized.[34] Similarly, possible films with previous collaborators Leopoldo Torres Ríos, Lamarque, and Luis Moglia Barth failed to be produced.[35] If his work in the cinema stayed stagnant throughout the year, Delbene's participation on the radio picked up. Given a run-up similar to what he would have received during the promotion of a film, news of Delbene's work in radio drama began in preproduction. In a casting note that refers to his transnational popularity as a film star, "Floren Delbene a Radio Belgrano" (Floren Delbene to Radio Belgrano), *Radiolandia* notes, "The voice, well, of one of the actors who most relies on it among the best attributes of his success will be in contact with his female admirers starting next month."[36] More details are later given in "Comenzó una gran audición en LR3" (A Great Show Started on LR3).[37] *El último estreno*, of course, figured regularly among the pages of the "Programa radiotelefónico semanal" (Weekly Radio Program). Unlike its competitor *Sintonía*, which reviewed the program twice, *Radiolandia* did little to question the program's success.[38] Keeping in contact with his fans, Delbene continued to work in radio after *El último estreno* concluded. At the end of the year, *Radiolandia* commented that "Floren Delbene, the film star, is acting on Radio Belgrano" in the series *Sendero de dolor* (*Path of Pain*).[39] The photogenic Delbene was accompanied by fellow cast members perhaps better suited to the radio than the screen.

In addition to his professional existence in between media industries, *Radiolandia*'s readers were also treated to glimpses into Delbene's personal life. Figuring as one of many stars, his experiences in the limelight were related in columns such as "Dialoguitos telefónicos" (Telephone Chats) and stories such as "El cargo que se hace a nuestros galanes: ¿saben o no besar?" (The Charge Given to Our Leading Men: Do They Know How to Kiss?), "Sus momentos más felices" (Their Happiest Moments), and "¿Cuál ha sido el secreto de su éxito?" (What Has Been the Secret of Their Success?).[40] Delbene also featured in profiles highlighting professional

FIGURE 15.2 A short note in *Radiolandia*, December 14, 1940, 17.

and personals success. In "El triple triunfo de Floren Delbene" (Floren Delbene's Triple Success), *Radiolandia* congratulated the *galán* for his success in a contest held by a Venezuelan newspaper, in which Delbene figured in first, second, and third places in the category "most popular couple" with Libertad Lamarque, Herminia Franco, and Amanda Ledesma, respectively.[41] And "Floren Delbene es un viajero incansable" (Floren Delbene Is a Non-Stop Traveler) catches up with the star as he travels to Mar del Plata, a resort city not far from Buenos Aires.[42] The profile gives rare insight into Delbene's thoughts on his professional and private life. Beginning with an anecdote in which the handsome star flirts with a fellow traveler, it explains that Delbene's "great determination is to seek the unprecedented, not only in love, but everything." Delbene claims to not yet know love, but the profile argues that his wanderlust mirrors his professional experience. Delbene tells *Radiolandia*, "If I were to repeat myself when acting on screen, I do not think it would be me, but a copy of the character that I had just played in the previous production." The profile gives Delbene a measure of control of his career that he may or may not have possessed, as well as direct insight into the "philosophy of a star," according to a section heading. Ultimately, however, much of what readers learned of the star in *Radiolandia* was provided indirectly.

Delbene is also often the subject of inquiry of readers' letters. In the same issue in which a portrait of Delbene takes up an entire page, a not uncommon occurrence in the pages of Argentine fan magazines at the time, the actor is referenced in replies to readers' letters in "Chas de Cruz contesta" (Chas de Cruz Answers). The important film critic and editor of *Heraldo del Cinematografista* includes quick answers to three queries concerning Delbene (two regarding his roles opposite Libertad Lamarque and one about pipe smoking).[43] More biographical information regarding Delbene was often shared in the column "Preguntas y respuestas" (Questions and Answers). Two examples: "His name is Florentino Delbene. His relatives are well-known industrialists. But Floren has nothing to do with those establishments. He gave them up to act in the cinema,"[44] and "BLOND AND DARK-SKINNED [the letter writer's pseudonym].—Delbene is Argentine. Soulful more than romantic in all acts of life. He hardly frequents A-list parties. He runs away from everything that has to do with popularity."[45] Readers were interested not only in Delbene's origins but also in his current private life. Of special interest, unsurprisingly, was his love life. These issues and indiscretions, however, were generally divulged in gossip columns such as "Será cierto?" (Could It Be True?). Gossip was often threaded throughout the pages of *Radiolandia* to create a sustained narrative that readers could follow. In 1940, Delbene was reported to be involved with two actresses. In one issue, it is claimed "that nights ago the actress Herminia Franco, surprised to find Floren Delbene in the company of a beautiful blonde, could not help but shed some tears."[46] (Curiously, or perhaps not, featuring on the front cover of that issue of *Radiolandia* was Amanda Ledesma, a beautiful blonde with whom Delbene was connected.) *Radiolandia* also noted other comings and goings, such as hinting at the possibility that "the disagreements between a beautiful film actress and Floren Delbene arose because he twice lost his entire fortune on roulette?"[47] In sharing gossip of various kinds with its readers, *Radiolandia* demonstrates restraint and censorship. Although perhaps not to the extent intimated earlier by Di Núbila, *Radiolandia* sought to show glimpses into the real lives of the stars without bringing upon them undue pressure from advertisers, lobbying groups (e.g., direct or loose affiliates of the Catholic Church), and politicians. Like other fan magazines, *Radiolandia* not only wanted to steer clear of criticism, but its editors also did not want to lose the access that allowed them to mediate fans relationships with the stars.

RADIOLANDIA AND (INTERMEDIAL) STARDOM

Within its pages, *Radiolandia* kept readers up-to-date week by week with the stars of Argentina's increasingly developed and enmeshed media industries. Following figures such as Floren Delbene, who by no means was enjoying his prime in 1940, *Radiolandia* contributed to the growth and consolidation of the film industry and the radio by its focus on a local, intermedial star system. Much work is left to be done to better understand celebrity culture and stardom at this time in Argentina—significantly less systematic in the 1940s than in Hollywood, but nonetheless important socially—but it is clear it was expressed between media industries, including in different kinds of film publications such as the fan magazine *Radiolandia*. As Carolina González Centeno succinctly contends: "Singular coordination between the spectacular and the everyday, the special and the ordinary, the star promotes devotion and identification, fantasy. The magazine is aware of this power."[48] Captivating readers' attention, these stars were means through which readers became consumers. Not only did they consume the movies of the emerging national film industry as well as the radio (Di Núbila reminds us: "In sum, Argentine cinema sold. And the media of the time sold Argentine cinema"), but the ideological work of stars also sold *Radiolandia*'s readers on a wide range of values, products, and ideas, similar to the way in which *El último estreno* used Delbene's cinematic glamour to move an antacid/laxative into the homes of ordinary fans.[49]

272   CHAPTER 15

As Jesús Martín Barbero argues, "The new mass culture began not only as a culture directed to the popular classes but a culture in which the masses found synthesized in the music and in the narratives of radio and film some of the basic forms of their own way of perceiving, experiencing and expressing their world."[50] Through the consumption of different media industry products, often selling a singular star image, *Radiolandia*'s (primarily female) readership was allowed to see and be seen through consumption. Recalling these times, Aurora Alonso de Rocha writes in her work *Mujeres cotidianas (Everyday Women)* that the fan magazine "was so important for many women that I knew two girls whose given names were *Radiolandia*."[51]

NOTES

1. Similar to the performers, Davison's and Manteola's careers differed vastly. Even though he would have to wait some time, Davison eventually directed more than eighty feature films, largely in Mexico. Unlike his compatriot, little is known today of José Manteola. His illustrator brother Raúl, however, would gain renown for his Peronist propaganda.

2. "Jamás un programa radial conseguido reunir a tantas figuras estelares de nuestro teatro y cine. Nombres todos ellos de prestigio conquistado a través de una intensa y lucida labor." Advertisement for *El último estreno, Radiolandia*, April 6, 1940, 47.

3. Beatriz Sarlo, *Una modernidad periférica: Buenos Aires 1920 y 1930* (Buenos Aires: Nueva Visión, 1988).

4. "El crecimiento industrial del cine argentino acompañó al proceso de industrialización generalizada que se produjo en el país." Claudio España, "El modelo institucional," in *Cine argentino industria y clasicismo, 1933–1956, vol. 1,* ed. Claudio España (Buenos Aires: Fondo Nacional de las Artes, 2000), 34.

5. Nicolas Poppe, *Alton's Paradox: Foreign Film Workers and the Emergence of Industrial Cinema in Latin America* (Albany: SUNY Press, 2021), 170.

6. Ana M. López, "Film and Radio Intermedialities in Early Latin American Sound Cinema," in *The Routledge Companion to Latin American Cinema,* ed. Marvin D'Lugo, Ana M. López, and Laura Podalsky (Abingdon; New York: Routledge, 2018), 316–28. López also developed the idea in conference papers.

7. Edgar Morin, *The Stars* (Minneapolis: University of Minnesota Press, 2005 [1957]), 57.

8. See Mary Desjardins, "Not of Hollywood: Ruth Chatterton, Ann Harding, Constance Bennett, Kay Francis, and Nancy Carrol," in *Glamour in a Golden Age: Movie Stars of the 1930s,* ed. Adrienne L. McLean (London: Rutgers University Press, 2011), 24.

9. "El seguimiento de las estrellas es, a su vez, el camino para acompañar y promover el crecimiento y consolidación de los distintos medios locales: en un principio la radio, luego el cine y por último la televisión." Carolina González Centeno, "*Radiolandia*," in *Páginas de cine,* ed. Clara Kriger (Buenos Aires: Archivo General de la Nación, 2003), 149.

10. Published a few years later, a special Pan-American issue of *Revista del exhibidor* (October 1945) visually expresses these divisions through pastiches of the titles of newspapers ("Prensa argentina," 17), trade journals ("Prensa gremial," 21), and fan magazines ("Revistas porteñas," 22).

11. For more on these fan magazines, see Kriger, *Páginas de cine.*

12. "De resonancias populistas y anarquistas, *La Canción Moderna* nacía en 1928 bajo la dirección de Dante A. Linyera, asociado al joven Julio Korn, futuro mangante de los medios masivos. El proyecto reunió, por poco tiempo, al inmigrante judío interesado en las industrias culturales al hijo de inmigrantes italianos decidido a preservar una cultura popular 'pura' y espontánea." Lila Caimari, "Mezclas puras: Lunfardo y cultura urbana en Buenos Aires," in *Ciudades sudamericanas como arenas culturales,* ed. Adrián Gorelik and Fernanda Arêas de Peixoto (Buenos Aires: Siglo XXI, 2016), 169.

13. Matthew B. Karush, *Culture of Class: Radio and Cinema in the Making of a Divided Argentina* (Durham, NC: Duke University Press, 2012), 138. Karush rightly notes its editorial shift but errs in dating *La Canción Moderna*'s transition to *Radiolandia*.

14. "Precursora de una forma del periodismo de entretenimiento y evasión, *La Canción Moderna* recopilaba las letras de las canciones de moda, las mezclaba con historias de sus autores y cantantes." Carlos Ulanovsky, *Paren las rotativas* (Buenos Aires: Espasa, 1997), 38.

15. *Radiolandia* first appeared as a supplement on January 4, 1936.

16. "*Radiolandia* es la materialización, en un nombre, del carácter actual de LA CANCIÓN MODERNA. 'El mundo de la radio en una revista,' reza nuestro subtítulo, y nadie podría negar que en nuestras páginas, se compendia la actualidad sobresaliente de cuanto hace la radiotelefonía dentro y fuera de nuestro país." "Radiolandia," *Radiolandia*, May 23, 1936.

17. Korn's publications would eventually include *Radiolandia, Antena, Goles, Vosotras, TV Guía* (a collaboration with Editorial Abril), and *Anteojito* (*Specs*, a children's magazine). In 1965, the publishing company would have a circulation of seven million copies per month. Ulanovsky, *Paren las rotativas*, 168. At some point, Korn would also merge with Editorial Abril. Korn would sell the majority of his company in 1972 to Fabril Financiera and Celulosa Argentina. (By this time, the company also published *Labores* and *Chabela*.) Korn died on April 18, 1983.

18. "Si hay algún calificativo que pueda definir a *Radiolandia* así como al resto de estas publicaciones es el de popular. Y lo popular, para Korn, es siempre sinónimo de entretenimiento masivo. Ambas premisas se cumplen ampliamente en *Radiolandia*, que centra su enfoque en el mundo del espectáculo y sus principales protagonistas." González Centeno, "*Radiolandia*," 148–49.

19. Karush, *Culture of Class*, 138. Perhaps the most important figure in Argentine radio of the 1930s, Yankelevich's Radio Belgrano "dominated the market, charging the highest advertising rates and signing the biggest stars" (Karush, 64).

20. "Con el propósito de hacerse la competencia a sí mismo." Ulanovsky, *Paren las rotativas*, 51.

21. Richard Dyer, *Stars* (London: British Film Institute, 1998), 43.

22. "Fuera de las películas sólo podía verlas en fotos de diarios y revistas, y ocasionalmente en fugaces pantallazos de noticieros. Y sólo las escuchaba en escasas entrevistas radiofónicas porque aún no se habían inventado los grabadores portátiles. El periodismo contribuía a rodearlas de una aureola mítica. La revista especializada de mayor circulación, 'Radiolandia'—editada por Julio Korn, dirigida por Enzo Ardigó y con gente como Manzi, [Hugo] MacDougall [pseud. Hugo Mascías] y Floreal Fernández Raja en su redacción—jamás publicaba nada que las mostrara como algo menos que seres perfectos. Ningún desliz, ningún renuncio, ningún pecado, ni siquiera venial. Los chimentos indiscretos estaban confinados en 'dialoguitos telefónicos' y otras benévolas columnas. Los cambios de pareja ostentaban retórica de novelas de moda," quoted in Domingo Di Núbila, *La época de oro. Historia del cine argentino I* (Buenos Aires: Jilguero, 1998), 282–83.

23. "Pantalla: Noticiario del cine criollo"; "¿El amor que fingen en la pantalla deja huellas en el corazón de los artistas?, *Radiolandia*, November 2, 1940, 2–3.

24. Delbene did not appear in the trilogy's final film, *La ley que olvidaron* (*The Forgotten Law*, 1938).

25. Literally meaning "prince," *galán* is used to describe a leading man in Latin American cinema. A 1937 *Radiolandia* profile was entitled "Floren Delbene. First Argentine Film Leading Man. His Life—His Views—His Concerns—His Popularity." See "Floren Delbene. Primer galán cinematográfico argentino. Su vida—sus conceptos—sus inquietudes—su popularidad," March 6, 1937, 32–33. Sandrini, a comic star, did not fit neatly into the category of *galán*, even though his bumbling characters often had love interests. Not unlike Carlos Gardel, whom he played in the biopic *La vida de Carlos Gardel* (*The Life of Carlos Gardel*, dir. Alberto de Zavalía, 1939), Hugo del Carril was a tango singer whose musical performances were often used in relation to his role as protagonist and love interest. José Gola was never able to fully realize his potential to become the most important *galán* in Argentine cinema; he died suddenly in 1939 at the age of thirty-five.

26. In both films, he was credited under his full name, Florentino Delbene.

27. More specifically, *Muñequitas porteñas* used Vitaphone's system. The adjective "porteñas" and its related inflections refer to someone from the city of Buenos Aires.

28. In these years, he featured in *Amalia* (1936), *Ayúdame a vivir* (1936), *Santos Vega* (dir. Luis José Moglia Barth, 1936), *Lo que le pasó a Reynoso* (*What Happened to Reynoso*, dir. Leopoldo Torres Ríos, 1937), *Muchachos de la ciudad* (*City Boys*, dir. Ferreyra, 1937), *Besos brujos* (1937), *Sol de primavera* (*Spring Sun*, dir. Ferreyra, 1937), *Adiós Buenos Aires* (*Goodbye Buenos Aires*, dir. Torres Ríos, 1938), *El último encuentro* (*The Last Encounter*, dir. Luis Moglia Barth, 1938), *Senderos de fe* (*The Road of Faith*, dir. Moglia Barth, 1938), *Ambición* (*Ambition*, dir. Adelqui Millar, 1939), *Chimbela* (dir. Ferreyra, 1939), and *Cita en la frontera* (*Date on the Border*, dir. Soffici, 1940).

29. After an almost two-year period of inactivity, Delbene worked on six films for lesser-known production companies (1942–43). Gregorio Anchou suggested that "Floren Delbene's pilgrimage through this type of production forms the color palette of his first sunset" ("El peregrinaje de Floren Delbene por este tipo de producciones compone la paleta cromática de su primer ocaso"). "Veinticinco años de producción independiente. Las fronteras ignoradas," in *Cine argentino: industria y clasicismo, 1933–1956, vol. 1,* ed. Claudio España (Buenos Aires: Fondo Nacional de las Artes, 2000), 575. Subsequently, he spent another three-year period away from the silver screen. He would, however, return to more regular appearances on the screen from the late 1940s to the mid-1960s.

30. Richard deCordova, *Picture Personalities: The Emergence of the Star System in America* (Urbana: University of Illinois Press, 2001), 12.

31. Janine Basinger, *The Star Machine* (New York: Vintage, 2009), 58.

32. "¿Quiénes son los astros 1940?," *Radiolandia*, January 20, 1940, 30–31.

33. Elsa Pito Sordo, "Como me lo contaron," *Radiolandia*, June 22, 1940, 50. An aside reads:

'"Would you like me to point out unjust fact?'

'Come out with it.'

'Floren Delbene has just completed a year of movie inactivity. A high-earning, extremely popular *galán* that enjoys general affection goes for a year doing nothing in the cinema. What greater injustice is there?'

'Impossible. It must be assumed that our producers are a little blind . . . or one-eyed, at least.'"

"—Quiere que le señale un hecho injusto?

—Venga de ahí.

—Acaba de cumplir un año de inactividad cinematográfica a Floren Delbene. Galán cotizado, popularísimo, que goza de simpatías generales, va para un año que no hace nada en cine. ¿Quiere mayor injusticia?

—Imposible. Hay que suponer que nuestros productores están un poco ciegos . . . o tuertos por lo menos."

34. "Floren Delbene vuelve a la actividad," *Radiolandia*, April 13, 1940, 48. The note announces a project to be produced by Platense Film and directed by Juan Saracini. After the failure of *Yo hablo . . .* (*I Speak,* dir. Gándara, 1940), Platense vanished. "Floren Delbene en una nueva película," *Radiolandia*, February 3, 1940, n.p. *Heroes nuestros* (*Our Heroes*) was to be produced by Artefilm, a company that ended before it began.

35. "Floren Delbene actuará con Leopoldo Torres Ríos," *Radiolandia*, January 27, 1940, 45. Another film that failed to be produced was *Hogar, dulce hogar* (*Home Sweet Home*). Initially noted in "¿Floren Delbene con L. Lamarque?," *Radiolandia*, July 6, 1940, 49, the Argentina Sono Film project in development was to be directed by Moglia Barth. "Floren Delbene vuelve al 'set,'" *Radiolandia*, November 9, 1940, 49.

36. "La voz, pues, de uno de los actores que cuenta en ella con uno de los mejores atributos de su éxito, estará en contacto con sus admiradoras, a partir del mes próximo." "Floren Delbene a Radio Belgrano," *Radiolandia*, March 23, 1940, 19.

37. "Comenzó una gran audición en LR3," *Radiolandia*, June 8, 1940, 8.

38. "Sintonizando audiciones," *Sintonía*, April 10, 1940, 27. "Sintonizando audiciones," *Sintonía*, April 17, 1940, 23. Initially rating Delbene's show as a 36 percent, *Sintonía* improved its evaluation to a

RADIOLANDIA, FAN MAGAZINES, AND STARDOM 275

curious 68.4 percent a week later. In both, *El último estreno* is notably referred to as "LR3—Audición 'Leche de Magnesia Phillips.'"

39. "Floren Delbene, el astro cinematográfico, está actuando en Radio Belgrano." "Un astro en radio," *Radiolandia*, December 14, 1940, 17.

40. Delbene appears in several "Dialoguitos telefónicos." One example with love interest Herminia Franco: *Radiolandia*, September 21, 1940, 11. "El cargo que se hace a nuestros galanes: ¿saben o no besar?," *Radiolandia*, June 1, 1940, 2–3. "Sus momentos más felices," *Radiolandia*, June 8, 1940, 32–33; "¿Cuál ha sido el secreto de su éxito?," *Radiolandia*, September 28, 1940, 2–3.

41. "El triple triunfo de Floren Delbene," *Radiolandia*, February 24, 1940, 50.

42. "Floren Delbene es un viajero incansable," *Radiolandia*, June 22, 1940, 9–11.

43. Portrait of Floren Delbene, *Radiolandia*, October 12, 1940, 23; Chas de Cruz, "Chas de Cruz contesta," *Radiolandia*, October 12, 1940, 50.

44. "Se llama Florentino Delbene, Sus familiares son industriales muy conocidos. Pero Floren no tiene nada que ver con esos establecimientos. Renunció a ellos para actuar en cine." "Preguntas y respuestas," *Radiolandia*, September 28, 1940, 43.

45. "RUBIA Y MORENA.—Delbene es argentino. Sentimental, más que romántico, en todos los actos de su vida. No frecuenta casi las fiestas del ambiente. Huye de todo lo que sea popularidad." "Preguntas y respuestas," *Radiolandia*, July 27, 1940, 39.

46. "[Q]ue noches pasadas la actriz Herminia Franco al sorprender a Floren Delbene en compañía de una hermosa rubia no pudo evitar que se le escaparan algunas lágrimas." "Será cierto?," *Radiolandia*, August 17, 1940, 24.

47. "[Q]ue las desavenencias entre una bella actriz de cine y Floren Delbene surgieron porque éste en dos oportunidades perdió toda su fortuna en la ruleta?" "Será cierto?," *Radiolandia*, May 4, 1940, 24.

48. "Singular articulación entre lo espectacular y lo cotidiano, lo especial y lo ordinario, la estrella promueve la devoción e identificación, la fantasía. La revista es consciente de este poder." González Centeno, "*Radiolandia*," 149.

49. "En suma, el cine argentino vendía. Y los medios de la época vendían al cine argentino," quoted in Di Núbila, *La época de oro*, 283.

50. "La nueva cultura, la cultura de masa, empezó siendo una cultura no sólo dirigida a las masas, sino en la que las masas encontraron reasumidas, de la música a los relatos en la radio y el cine, algunas de sus formas básicas de ver el mundo, de sentirlo y de expresarlo." Jesús Martín Barbero, *De los medios a las mediaciones. Comunicación, cultura y hegemonía* (Mexico City: Ediciones G. Gili, 1991), 173. *Communication, Culture, and Hegemony: From the Media to Mediations*, trans. Elizabeth Fox and Robert A. White (London: SAGE, 1993), 159.

51. "[E]ra tan importante para muchas mujeres, que conocí a dos chicas que llevaban *Radiolandia* por nombre de pila." Aurora Alonso de Rocha, *Mujeres cotidianas* (Buenos Aires: Planeta, 1992), 200.

PUBLICATIONS REFERENCED

Antena (Antenna)
Anteojito (Specs)
Astros (Stars)
Astros y Estrellas (Celestial Bodies and Stars)
Chabela
Cine Argentino (Argentine Cinema)
Cine Universal (Universal Cinema)
Cinema Chat (Movie Chat)
El Purrete (The Kid)
Goles (Goals)
Heraldo del Cinematografista (Cinematographer's Herald)
Imparcial Film (Impartial Film)

La Cancha (*The Pitch*)
La Canción Moderna (*The Modern Song*), later *Radiolandia*
La Nación (*The Nation*)
Labores (*Labors*)
Magazine Cinematográfico (*Film Magazine*)
Radiolandia (*Radioland*)
Sideral (*Stellar*)
Sintonía (*In Tune*)
TV Guía (*TV Guide*)
Vosotras (*You*)

BIBLIOGRAPHY

Alonso de Rocha, Aurora. *Mujeres cotidianas*. Buenos Aires: Planeta, 1992.

Anchou, Gregorio. "Veinticinco años de producción independiente. Las fronteras ignoradas." In *Cine argentino: industria y clasicismo, 1933–1956, vol. 1*, edited by Claudio España. Buenos Aires: Fondo Nacional de las Artes, 2000.

Basinger, Janine. *The Star Machine*. New York: Vintage, 2009.

Caimari, Lila. "Mezclas puras: Lunfardo y cultura urbana en Buenos Aires." In *Ciudades sudamericanas como arenas culturales*, edited by Adrián Gorelik and Fernanda Arêas de Peixoto. Buenos Aires: Siglo XXI, 2016.

deCordova, Richard. *Picture Personalities: The Emergence of the Star System in America*. Urbana: University of Illinois Press, 2001.

Desjardins, Mary. "Not of Hollywood: Ruth Chatterton, Ann Harding, Constance Bennett, Kay Francis, and Nancy Carrol." In *Glamour in a Golden Age: Movie Stars of the 1930s*, edited by Adrienne L. McLean. New Brunswick, NJ: Rutgers University Press, 2011.

Di Núbila, Domingo. *La época de oro. Historia del cine argentino I*. Buenos Aires: Jilguero, 1998.

Dyer, Richard. *Stars*. London: British Film Institute, 1998.

España, Claudio. "El modelo institucional." In *Cine argentino industria y clasicismo, 1933–1956, vol. 1*, edited by Claudio España. Buenos Aires: Fondo Nacional de las Artes, 2000.

González Centeno, Carolina. "Radiolandia." In *Páginas de cine*, edited by Clara Kriger. Buenos Aires: Archivo General de la Nación, 2003.

Karush, Matthew B. *Culture of Class: Radio and Cinema in the Making of a Divided Argentina*. Durham, NC: Duke University Press, 2012.

Kriger, Clara, ed. *Páginas de cine*. Buenos Aires: Archivo General de la Nación, 2003.

López, Ana M. "Film and Radio Intermedialities in Early Latin American Sound Cinema." In *The Routledge Companion to Latin American Cinema*, edited by Marvin D'Lugo, Ana M. López, and Laura Podalsky. Abingdon, UK: Routledge, 2018.

Martín-Barbero, Jesús Martín. *Communication, Culture, and Hegemony: From the Media to Mediations*. Translated by Elizabeth Fox and Robert A. White. London: SAGE, 1993.

———. *De los medios a las mediaciones. Comunicación, cultura y hegemonía*. Mexico City: Ediciones G. Gili, 1991.

Morin, Edgar. *The Stars*. Minneapolis: University of Minnesota Press, 2005.

Poppe, Nicolas. *Alton's Paradox: Foreign Film Workers and the Emergence of Industrial Cinema in Latin America*. Albany: SUNY Press, 2021.

Sarlo, Beatriz. *Una modernidad periférica: Buenos Aires 1920 y 1930*. Buenos Aires: Nueva Visión, 1988.

Ulanovsky, Carlos. *Paren las rotativas*. Buenos Aires: Espasa, 1997.

16

The Illustrated Popular Film Magazine
Neue Filmwelt (1947–1953)

A Complex Stimulator of a New German Film Culture

Vincent Fröhlich

The *Neue Filmwelt (New Film World)*[1] was published in East Germany from 1947 to 1953. It was the first East German film magazine after World War II. Its founder and first editor was Karl Hans Bergmann, an important figure as cofounder of the recently established Deutsche Film AG (DEFA), which would be instrumental as a production facility for East German film until the fall of the Berlin Wall in 1989. Despite this, the *NFW* has not been mentioned in research, nor does it appear in the work of today's DEFA Foundation, which preserves and maintains the film heritage of DEFA. No question, this magazine seems to be a victim of "film studies' neglect of so many sources" and the unilateralism of the research field of film magazines, as Eric Hoyt points out.[2]

One possible corrective, of course, would be to use the *NFW* as a historical source and see what information can be extracted from it about DEFA, films or dubbed versions that are no longer extant,[3] the state of German film, film advertising, and so much more. This is how periodical publications that report on films and are aimed at a mass audience have been used in the past, such as movie magazines and newspapers; information about films, stars, and the industry has been gleaned from the pages of magazines without the "container" itself playing a major role in the analysis.[4] Alternatively, one could choose a path of analysis more commonly taken when film journals aimed at an intellectual audience are analyzed. The discourse of film theory has been analyzed this way in journals such as *Cahiers du cinéma, Positif, Cinethique, Filmkritik, Film Quarterly, Film Culture*, and *Screen*.[5]

However, I would like to argue for the existence of a special format, namely the popular illustrated film magazine, and for this specific format I suggest a third way to conduct an analysis, which I have already laid out in my essay "Where the

Film Has the (Visual) Word?"[6] This way of analysis, which weaves together quantitative methods, qualitative methods, and data visualizations, goes hand in hand with the following thesis: the self-consciously "intellectual" film magazines are not the only publications that form a discourse about film. Magazines like the *NFW*, the illustrated popular monthly movie magazine which supplies my case study, form a multi-voiced discourse and produce film knowledge, but they do so in a complex interplay of type text, visuality, issue structure, layout, and materiality. The particular mix of complex design elements (and signifying strategies) found in the popular illustrated film magazine has been much neglected. Perceived as too "light," popular illustrated film magazines have been more or less dismissed as mere advertising media or as beautifully designed publications hardly worthy of rigorous examination. Yet these very magazines, I would argue, had a strong influence on national and international film culture because of their popularity, their broader readership, and their multimodality. The launch of the *NFW* seems to me to be an ideal example for the pursuit of this thesis, since the period after World War II was essentially a new start for German film culture. The popular illustrated film magazines had an important role here as visual evangelists of a new national film culture.

In this essay, I will focus on the historical knowledge and information generated by the articles and pictures of the *NFW*. But this is always, in my opinion, bound to the magazine's design: the layout produces a discourse on its own. This chapter also pays attention to the multitude of aspects and actors that have had an impact on this knowledge production and the produced discourse.[7]

HISTORICAL AND POLITICAL CONTEXTS

When the first issue of the *NFW* was published on August 1, 1947, World War II was not even two years past—the East and West German film cultures were still in the process of reconstruction. The title *Neue Filmwelt (New Film World)* immediately suggested in two ways that this magazine was an expression of a relaunch of film culture and a relaunch of print-media film culture.

On the one hand, the title *Neue Filmwelt* was a sign of a relaunch, because it referred to a similarly titled film magazine published during World War II: the film magazine *Filmwelt* by the Scherl publishing house.[8] This magazine cooperated closely with the Universum-Film Aktiengesellschaft (the production conglomerate best known as Ufa) and was thus interwoven with the Nazis' film propaganda.[9] On the other hand, the title *Neue Filmwelt* refers to a new beginning, being open to "new film worlds" in terms of national film cultures. Both associations signify that print media texts surrounded film in Germany and formed a specific media culture of their own, before and after World War II. The *NFW* is thus also a reminder that films never stand alone: film magazines have constituted film culture significantly, for better or worse.

Although a differentiated description of German film during and after National Socialism is beyond the scope of this chapter, it is necessary to recall what the relationship between the national German film culture and other film cultures had been shortly before the publication of the *NFW*'s first issue.

Film was the central medium of propaganda for the National Socialists, who, as Thomas Hanna-Daoud emphasizes, were already intensively interested in film during the Weimar Republic.[10] Following Hitler's rise to power in 1933, the appointment of his confidant Joseph Goebbels as Reichsminister for National Education and Propaganda, the Gleichschaltung (the forced consolidation of all media corporations into one, the Ufa), and the unconditional alignment with the worldview of National Socialism, the National Socialist influence on and control over the production, distribution, and release of films in Germany was almost all-encompassing. As Klaus Kreimeier wrote, "A legend prevalent in film history is that the National Socialists succeeded in tainting with their ideological poison every cinematic genre, every film, and every subject, no matter how remote from politics."[11] But even if this is just a "legend," its existence shows in what a comprehensive way the films produced during the National Socialist regime were associated internationally and nationally with the National Socialist worldview, even if an analysis of many of these films produces a more differentiated result.

The fact that the National Socialist government had extensive control over German film presumably played a role in the creation of this legend. This control also meant that German cinemagoers were more or less cut off from other national film cultures. In his quantitative survey of film releases in Germany from 1933 to 1945, Klaus-Jürgen Maiwald demonstrates that no foreign productions were shown in the years 1943–45.[12] In the German-occupied territories, in turn, the extremely propagandistic newsreels were particularly hated—some German films were seen as a painful expression of a "cinematic" occupation in general. Moreover, and literally, some foreign cinemas were occupied; with the aim of "Germanizing" the film industry, more than one thousand cinemas were annexed in the occupied territories, showing German "required films."[13] Conversely, since Germany left the League of Nations in 1933, German films had been increasingly boycotted abroad.[14]

Moreover, cinema viewing—specifically during the last two years of the war, screening only German films—was extremely successful in the Greater German Reich; it held a central function of distraction and entertainment.[15] The fact that the German people had "fallen for" the seduction and propaganda of the Nazi regime also affected the reputation of the favorite medium of the Nazis[16] after the end of the war and subsequently put the popularity of German film and cinema attendance during the war to shame—which is still true today for the films of this period; Karsten Witte claims these are still seen as a "despicable heritage."[17]

A second central context is more political in nature: in the Soviet Union, film had an extraordinarily high status, which spilled over to the satellite states, especially the Soviet zone and the later German Democratic Republic (GDR). As

280   CHAPTER 16

David Bathrick states, "While the Western allies were primarily concerned with breaking up the existing cinematic monopoly of the UFA, for the Soviets the film was the central (political) medium of entertainment and education: One month after the German capitulation, the Soviet Military Administration in Germany . . . commissioned German technicians to refit a synchronization studio in Berlin for the purpose of dubbing Soviet films for German audiences."[18] Accordingly, the Soviet Military Administration in Germany (SMAD) aimed to begin East German film production as soon as possible, and as early as May 17, 1946, DEFA was founded. During June 6–9, 1947, many professionals in the field of culture met for the Film-Autoren-Kongreß (First Conference of Filmmakers). In this context, Alfred Lindemann, the driving force behind the founding of DEFA, pointed out an aspect that had arisen as a result of the film industry's cultural isolation: "It will not be easy for us to make our mark. We must be quite clear that our ten-year isolation from the rest of the world has led to a backlog of foreign films which will be dumped on the German market in the near future."[19]

Lindemann brought in Karl Hans Bergmann to replace the late Carl Haacker in DEFA's founding group. On June 9, 1947, one year after the founding of DEFA, the Deutsche Filmverlag was already established, which Bergmann ran in addition to his work as head of finance at DEFA. Bergmann had studied history, romance studies, and theater.[20] His main experience was as director and editor of communist cultural magazines. He was already head of the section "Film-Stage-Music" in the Revolutionary Trade Union Opposition (RGO) and had succeeded the theater director Hans Rodenberg as the editor in charge of the magazine *Der Ausweg* (until 1933). The RGO was declared illegal in 1934. In 1934 Bergmann became editor of the illegal magazine *Die Rampe* (*The Ramp*), dealing with cultural and political aspects, which in its subtitle described itself as the "Organ of the Communist Party for theaters and film companies."[21] In these positions, he also gained his first experiences in supervising advanced photomechanical image reproductions— methods that he could still describe in detail in his 2002 autobiography.[22] Even after fleeing to Switzerland in 1942, he produced a magazine there with other refugees: *Freies Deutschland* (*Free Germany*, with a first issue on September 3, 1943). In view of Bergmann's biography, it is hardly surprising that barely two months after the founding of the publishing house, on August 1, 1947, a magazine appeared as its first publication: *Neue Filmwelt*.

The question we must ask here is how much control, how much censorship affected the *Neue Filmwelt*. The magazine needed a license from the Russian authorities in order to be published (the license was SMAD 301 [2.VI. 47]), and each issue had to be presented to the respective Russian liaison officer; however, this was not a problem for the *NFW*, as Bergmann spoke generally of a "splendid cooperation" with the Russians—they were all apparently film enthusiasts and excited about new things being created.[23] From the eyewitness interview with Bergmann, his autobiography, and the surviving statements of Lindemann, who

NEUE FILMWELT, NEW GERMAN FILM CULTURE   281

had to resign from DEFA on March 31, 1948, the picture that emerges suggests that the magazine enjoyed a great deal of freedom with regard to the presentation of film in the first years under the Russian occupation. This freedom met constricting interference from the Socialist Unity Party of Eastern Germany (SED) and the accusation by Karl Klär and others from the party that the *NFW* was too Western, preferring film journalists instead of party members.[24]

THE EDITORIAL OF THE FIRST ISSUE

To what extent can the aspects mentioned so far also be observed within the first issue of the *NFW*? The issue begins with a powerful and multilayered editorial by Karl Hans Bergmann, from which the author continued to quote proudly in his memoirs. In the editorial, he describes both the educational mission and the way of producing film knowledge particular to an illustrated popular film magazine, proclaiming that the *NFW* is the product of a belief in the magic of film. Subsequently, the German film of National Socialism is harshly judged, and various aspects of this legacy are examined. German film, he claims, had recently been conveying the National Socialist "worldview";[25] film had even become part of that "herostratic propaganda machine . . . whose workings and results have plunged our people into a misery never known before." As a result, the German film industry had also been "turned into a ruinous site . . . not unlike the other industries in our country." Last but not least, Bergmann also mentions the popularity of film during the National Socialist regime; the annual revenues of Ufa had "increased to 250 million Reichsmarks by 1943." Bergmann's rather detailed reckoning with German film highlights the fact that the launch of this magazine could only be seen in light of the recent past. Indeed, it was the very result of it. This is also reflected in the focus Bergmann assigns to the magazine in the following humble sentences: "We want to hear and see, after the long years of being excluded, what the film art of the other nations has to say. We want to participate in the life and development beyond our borders, not as demanders or determiners, but as learners and experiencers." Only in the last paragraph of the editorial does Bergmann turn away from the past and basically summarize the format of the popular illustrated magazine and thus the targeted readership as well as the visual-typographical design: "So, a magazine for the man on the construction site? Quite right, but not for him alone. So for whom are we writing? For him, the human being among us, the witnessing, co-suffering and co-creating contemporary. The same person Rudolf Arnheim meant when he wrote a very personal preface to his wonderfully clear, completely factual book 'Film as Art': '. . . so that Ruth Vorpahl sometimes goes to the movies'. That's what we think, too, and with that we fade in. The film has the word." One could say Bergmann emphasizes that the illustrated magazine, as a visual medium, represents the film, "fades in," and thus invites "ordinary" people to go to the cinema; it is precisely this format, precisely this specific way of presentation, that could popularize film again among a broader segment of the population, like the mentioned "ordinary person," Ruth Vorpahl.[26]

Of course, editorials should always be taken with a grain of salt, as there may be too many differences between external and internal perceptions. Editorials should also be viewed as advertising for the launch of this specific magazine. What becomes clear, despite all caution, is how Bergmann wanted the magazine to be seen: as a popular illustrated film magazine that did not ignore the past and was open to foreign national film cultures. The picture he draws of the *NFW* thus contradicts common preconceptions of the format of the popular illustrated film magazine. For Bergmann, this is not a format that merely informs readers about upcoming movie premieres and promotes those films. Various lines of evidence tend to suggest that Bergmann, the founders of DEFA, and the Soviet licensors assigned the *NFW* a significant role in the project of restarting a German film culture. Those involved were most likely well aware that the production of German films alone was not enough to create a new, different German film culture. The impact of films, their appeal, and a "proper" understanding of them would increase with accompanying explanatory media to contextualize them. Not only was the *NFW* the first publication of the Deutscher Film-Verlag, but a large part of their later publications were also connected in one way or another with this very magazine.[27] And not only was the publication of the magazine close in time to the founding of DEFA—although DEFA had hardly completed any films—but Bergmann's expertise was also used in several ways. As one of DEFA's central figures, Bergmann was responsible for finances but had experience primarily as a magazine editor, and thus he became entrusted with this publication and wrote numerous texts for it.[28] The intention to reach a broader readership was so important, at least to Bergmann, that he procured paper for it on the black market, even at the risk of punishment. In this way, the circulation could be increased from the starting forty-five thousand to one hundred thousand.[29]

LAYOUT, DISCOURSE, AND NATIONAL FOCUS OF THE FIRST ISSUE

Which topics were predominant in the first issue? Did the contents live up to the claim of opening up to different national film cultures and the concern to "give film the floor" visually as well?

As can be seen in figure 16.1, different national film cultures are indeed covered in the first issue. German film (purple) receives the most print space with 14.5 pages, followed by Soviet film (red) with two essays and a total of four pages. The film cultures of the Western allies, the United States, France, and Great Britain receive somewhat less print space, with only three pages each, but the essays are prominently placed in the center of the magazine. The report on US film culture is the most critical, while the film cultures of the other three foreign countries are praised and national characteristics are highlighted.

The temporal orientation of the pages is shown in figure 16.2. If we correlate figures 16.1 and 16.2, it becomes clear that the *NFW*, especially in the pages devoted to German-language films or actors and actresses, is more focused on the past and the future. Only pages 22 and 23 (blue in the middle right) are devoted to the filmic past of a nation other than Germany (in this case, Soviet film history). Hence, the division and structure of the magazine issue can be seen, to some extent, as a reflection of the state of German film production and culture at the time, which was busy processing past and future productions, but had—in contrast to foreign film cultures—few titles to offer in the present.

Figure 16.3 shows that the impression (gained from figure 16.1) of an only slightly more intensive examination of Soviet film in terms of print area is substantially reinforced by comparing the numbers of films mentioned: 23 percent of films mentioned in the issue are of Soviet origin. The majority of films mentioned, 41 percent, are German. Of all the films mentioned, however, 20 percent are German films from earlier than 1933—that is, 49 percent of all German films mentioned in a 1947 German film magazine are at least fourteen years old. We can surmise that the intention was to evoke a positive German film tradition of the Weimar Republic (which is also reflected in the content of some of the essays).

The fact that many older films from abroad were now shown in Germany for the first time in 1947, as Lindemann had somewhat feared, is also reflected in the *NFW*, as figure 16.4 reveals.[30] Moreover, this shows how far back the evocation of a positive German film history goes. Five very early German films are mentioned: *Der Andere* (1913), *Student von Prag* (1913), *Engelein* (1914), *Der Liebesbrief der Königin* (1917), and *Der blonde Chauffeur* (1916). Early German film history up to 1920 and forthcoming productions in 1947 frame the list with five mentions each, while 1945 and 1946 (naturally) form a gap in mentions of German films.

Let us leave the structural and quantitative level and turn our attention to the individual articles. How is German film culture and the past dealt with there? My thesis here is that a pre–National Socialist past of German film culture is seen as an ideal that is remembered more strongly than the National Socialist film era.

As an example, due to the lack of space, I would like to concentrate only on the first three double-spread pages following the editorial. Thereafter, we encounter a double-page spread featuring the responses of ten people from the film industry, including Paul Wegener, Wolfgang Staudte, and Kurt Maetzig (cofounder of DEFA), to the question: "German Film—Where To?" The polyphony often identified as a core characteristic of magazines[31] is used here to map positions in the discourse surrounding the direction of German film. Half the authors explicitly refer to the National Socialist past. There seems to be agreement that "after the

FIGURE 16.1. National focus in *Neue Filmwelt*, no. 1, 1947.

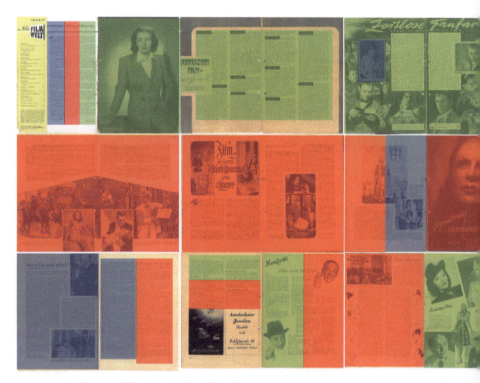

FIGURE 16.2. Temporal direction in *Neue Filmwelt*, no. 1, 1947.

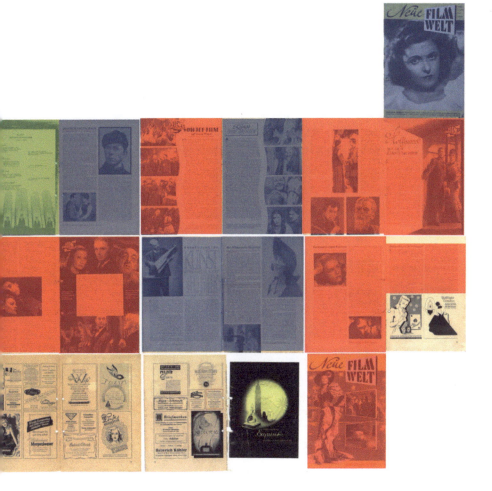

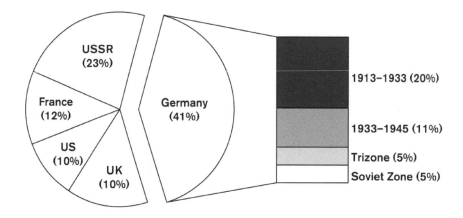

FIGURE 16.3. Mentioned films by country in *Neue Filmwelt*, no. 1, 1947.

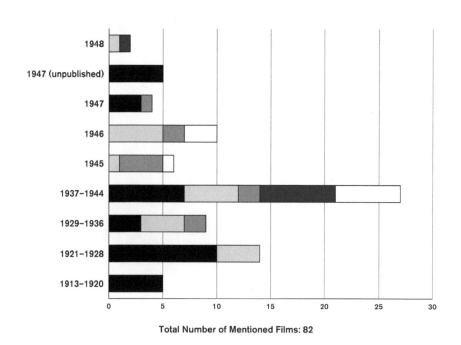

FIGURE 16.4. Mentioned films by country and year of premiere in *Neue Filmwelt*, no. 1, 1947.

NEUE *FILMWELT*, NEW GERMAN FILM CULTURE   289

substantive as well as tendentious hypertrophy of the Hitler era" (Paul Wegener), film is now taking "its first steps after the catastrophe" (Paul Bildt).

If visual elements are less important to this article on opinions about where German film should be heading, the two-page spread shown in figure 16.5 forms its own complex discourse precisely because of the interplay of script content, typography, and image—as I demonstrated in a previous essay.[32] This spread announces one of the first DEFA productions, the film *Wozzeck*, which would have its world premiere on December 17, 1947—more than four months after the publication of the *NFW*'s first issue. This is significant in several ways. First, consider how many and which films the director of *Wozzeck*, Georg C. Klaren (one of the voices on the direction of German film on the previous double-page spread), mentions as inspirations for his production: the French film *La Passion de Jeanne d'Arc* by Carl Theodor Dreyer (1928) and Fritz Lang's *Die Nibelungen* (1924) as well as "Russian masterpieces" and, somewhat more hidden, Gustav Gründgen's Effi Briest adaptation *Der Schritt vom Wege* (1939). The evocation of a positive German film tradition is thus combined with a reference to a relatively international selection of films. Second, Klaren points out that this acknowledgment sounds like a kind of defense,[33] noting "that under the Nazis it was all the more impossible to even suggest this material," referring to Georg Büchner's stage drama *Woyzeck*, "without becoming ripe for a concentration camp." The director thus emphasizes the contemporary nature of the historical material precisely by stressing that it is only now that a film adaptation is possible. Third, his statements about aesthetic aspects of his film adaptation are accompanied and complemented by an elaborate montage of film stills that are laid around the written text. This collage, as I detailed in the previous essay, exhibits precisely the aesthetic possibilities of a visual film presentation on the flat surface of a film magazine. And fourth, the textual connection to a positive German tradition is also supported by the images and layout. Albert Steinrück is shown in the middle of the verso page; he played the part of Woyzeck not in the film but in the 1913 world premiere of Büchner's play in Munich, staged by Eugen Kilian. By showing the actor of the theater role three decades earlier, the layout also refers in a visual manner to a "non-fascist, German national identity" and invokes a positive line of tradition.[34] These references correspond to the aesthetic style of the film: "Klaren employed a film style reminiscent of expressionist and progressive German cinema, re-establishing links to the film heritage of the Weimar Republic."[35] Finally, the two-page spread also brings out this line of tradition through effects of similarity typical for magazines, which are induced by the layout: the picture of the actor in the theater premiere of 1913 on the verso page is opposed almost symmetrically to the picture of the actor of the film adaptation on the recto page.[36] The two performances are placed on an equal footing visually— but without the written essay in any way commenting on this analogy.

After a short excerpt from the script of *Wozzeck* on the verso page, the following recto page is an obituary for the actor Joachim Gottschalk, who had died on

FIGURE 16.5. *Neue Filmwelt*, no. 1, 1947, 4–5. Halftone on stapled pulp paper, 41.2 × 28.6 cm, private collection.

November 6, 1941. He and his Jewish wife, seeing no way to escape the personal slander and official pressure on their marriage amid the National Socialist reign of terror, killed themselves and their son. Goebbels forbade any obituary or attendance at the funeral.[37] The obituary for Gottschalk, more than five years belated, shows once again the numerous possibilities the creators seem to have seen in the format of the illustrated popular film magazine—in the very first issue of a German film magazine after National Socialism, Joachim Gottschalk is honored as an actor and attention is drawn to his death. The nature of Gottschalk's acting, his "clear, unaccented sentences," is interpreted as an affront to the National Socialist way of speaking. The extent to which this obituary was part of a conscious programmatic approach is shown, among other things, by another obituary, for the actor Hans Meyer Hanno, in the fifth issue. Hanno was shot by National Socialists towards the end of the war while trying to escape. Once again, this page uses the visual possibilities to create relational structures. A film still is shown depicting Hanno together with Gottschalk; visually, he is placed in the company of another victim of the National Socialist regime—similar to the two-page spread for the film *Wozzeck* centering the actor in the theater premiere, the connection is made only visually, without any explicit comment through written text.

Of course, these mechanisms and discourses could be further examined, compared, and supplemented with other period documents, but that would take us too far here. Important for this essay is merely the observation that a complex, multimodal, and polyphonic discourse was emerging. The tendencies of the discourse are conspicuous in that, through the quantitative accumulation of films from the prewar period, through visual markers and explicit statements, there is an increased remembrance of a pre–National Socialist past, and National Socialism is mentioned as an immediate past catastrophe. As a media-specific type of concluding gesture, obituaries are retroactively written and the opening to other national cultures initialized.

THE FURTHER COURSE OF THE *NFW*

As has been shown, *Neue Filmwelt* started as an idealistic project that was intended to accompany, in its own way, the relaunch of the new German film culture, using complex layouts and passionate texts; this magazine was supposed to bring other national film cultures closer and, last but not least, to remind readers/viewers of a positive, pre–National Socialist German film culture. Within a few years, however, the magazine developed into a nationally biased film magazine, which in part carried out propaganda for the Soviets, had monotonous layouts, and finally ceased to exist. The following section will provide some explanations for these developments.

In an SED report of December 11, 1948, the *NFW* was reproached for the fact that "the mindset of the editors was essentially Western" and that "the emphasis of the magazine was along Western lines."[38] On April 14, 1949, two people from the Control Commission of the SED visited Bergmann.[39] Bergmann eventually fled (later to found a film club in West Berlin) and was replaced by Paul Letsch. From that point on, the magazine reported more intensively on national film cultures of the Eastern Bloc, praising Soviet film even more vehemently. In the final issue (figure 16.6) there was hardly any coverage of West German and Western film. However, later on, the field of Eastern film cultures presented by the *NFW* diversified considerably in return. In terms of the period covered, *Bicycle Thieves* (*Ladri di biciclette*) from 1948 was the oldest film mentioned, and the film premiering furthest in the future was *Cesta do pravěku* (1955). The time span from which the films originated shortened considerably.

In issue 9 of 1949, there was a change of printing technique, printing house, and layout, which enormously changed the look and discourse of the magazine. The number of pictures increased, extravagant typographies were used more often in the headlines, and picture sequences and montages increased somewhat. The publication design changed at the same time, with a tendency towards clearer political conformity. For example, especially during this period, the centerfold was used as a wide advertising space for Soviet film and its aesthetics. There was still a visual discourse, but it was now more politically pronounced and explicit. For example, in the centerfold shown in figure 16.7, a montage of film images was combined with a portrait of Stalin in the center headlined "30 Years of Soviet Film. A

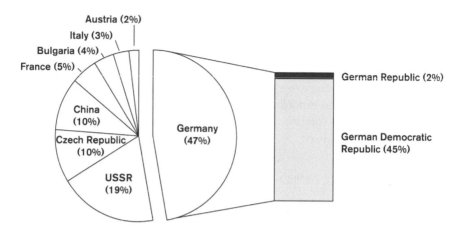

FIGURE 16.6. Mentioned films by country in *Neue Filmwelt*, no. 12, 1953.

Cross-Section in Pictures," while further down, the text reads: "The development and great importance of the Soviet film is unthinkable without J. V. Stalin [written in capital letters and spaced], whose 70th birthday all progressive people of the world celebrate on December 21." Film and politics flow into each other here, literally and figuratively.

The development of the more visual phase from issue 9 onwards can be related quite clearly to the change of publisher, the change of printing house, and the photomechanical reproduction method, as well as the SED report arriving beforehand and Bergmann's subsequent flight. The decline of the more visual phase, which began around issue 4 of 1950, cannot be explained by a change of publisher or printer. It seems plausible to me, as a hypothesis, that this change of direction can be seen as well in the simultaneous discontinuation of the illustrated program leaflet *Illustrierter Film-Spiegel*.[40] The *Illustrierter Film-Spiegel* bore in its title the name "Program leaflet of the magazine *Neue Filmwelt*." Typical for many postwar program leaflets, a single film was presented on four pages in terms of content, but mainly through the montage of numerous film stills. As a collector's item and as a kind of substitute for the cinematic reception that was still only partially possible due to the destruction caused by the war, this format was especially popular in Germany during the transitional postwar period. However, the *NFW* discontinued these leaflets and noticeably decreased the highly visual expression almost simultaneously; these changes to the layout continued with relative consistency until the magazine was terminated.

The leaflet also played another important role: as already mentioned, with issue 12 of 1953, the *NFW* was discontinued. In this last issue, however, it was announced that instead of the *NFW*, a successor magazine was being

FIGURE 16.7. *Neue Filmwelt*, no. 12, 1949, 18–19. Rotogravure on stapled pulp paper, 41.2 × 28.6 cm, private collection.

launched: *Der Filmspiegel*. This magazine was the country's definitive illustrated popular film magazine until the end of the GDR, so it played a major role in shaping the GDR's film culture. Its origin, however, lies in the *NFW* (which in turn had taken up the title of the *Filmwelt*). One can also assume it is not by chance that the title *Filmspiegel* is reminiscent of the *NFW*'s illustrated supplement with the similar title *Illustrierter Film-Spiegel*.

PANORAMA

A multi-perspective analysis of the *NFW* reveals a complex multimodal and polyphonic discourse. This discourse, moreover, turns out to be extremely volatile over the course of the *NFW*. The *NFW* shows itself here very clearly as a product of a transitional period; the expression of the multimodal discourse presents itself as particularly susceptible to the effects of the numerous actors involved.

The intermedial relationship to film particularly complicates the matter, as this relationship encompasses links to the print media associated with film and to the actors who belong to both media worlds. For example, the "genealogical" lines of titles, from *Filmwelt* to *Neue Filmwelt*, from the leaflet *Illustrierter Film-Spiegel* to *Filmspiegel*, show that the relationships of popular illustrated film magazines can be better assessed if other print products such as program leaflets are also taken

294 CHAPTER 16

into account because they, like the illustrated popular film magazine, are also part of a historical popular accompaniment and promotion of film.

Looking forward, I propose four theses that point beyond the object and can be discussed in further research on the format of the popular illustrated film magazine:

1. Popular illustrated film magazines initiate and accompany the conversation about individual films as well as about film as such. It is especially in times of transition that this function becomes particularly evident.
2. Popular illustrated film magazines produce their own multimodal knowledge about film. They need to be further contoured as formats of their own with their own media logics.
3. Popular illustrated film magazines, because of their target-group orientation, have a considerable, hitherto rather neglected, share in the creation of a national as well as international film culture.
4. The three aspects mentioned above, however, are dependent on a complex field of tensions among personal, technical, material, historical, political, and intermedial aspects of the medium of film and its related print products.

Popular illustrated film magazines can easily be underestimated because of their multimodal presentation style, their supposedly easy-to-understand manner, and their targeting of a broad audience. Yet this multimodal manner, the particularly intensive embedding in print media as well as cinematic culture, and consideration of the resulting complex relationships pose challenges to analysis. In the future, the influence of these relationships on the popular illustrated film magazine must be taken into account in order to better grasp this format in its multimodal complexity and its mode of participation in national and international film cultures.

NOTES

1. Abbreviated *NFW* hereafter.
2. Eric Hoyt, "Lenses for Lantern: Data Mining, Visualization, and Excavating Film History's Neglected Sources," *Film History* 26, no. 2 (2014), 150.
3. Because a dubbing studio was established in the Soviet zone almost immediately after the end of the war, extensive information about no-longer-extant dubbed versions of films from the Eastern Bloc can be drawn precisely from the *NFW*. For example, a Czechoslovak film entitled *Mr. Habetin* is reviewed in detail in issue 10 of 1949, pages 8–9, and film stills are staged in an elaborate manner. The presentation suggests that there was a dubbed version under this title—there is nothing about it in the DFF archives or on the internet. In all likelihood, it is the film *Pan Habetín odchází* (ČSSR 1949).
4. For similar observations on the description of film magazines, see the following analyses: Tamar Jeffers McDonald and Lies Lanckman, "Introduction," in *Star Attractions*, ed. Tamar Jeffers McDonald and Lies Lanckman, 1–10 (Iowa City: University of Iowa Press, 2019); Patrick Rössler, "Die Zeitschriften des Stummfilms als transmediale 'kleine Archive,'" *Jahrbuch für Internationale Germanistik* 50, no. 2 (2018): 211–45; Daniel Biltereyst and Lies van de Vijver, "Introduction: Movie Magazines,

Digitization and New Cinema History," in *Mapping Movie Magazines: Digitization, Periodicals and Cinema History*, ed. Daniel Biltereyst and Lies van de Vijver, 1–13 (London: Palgrave Macmillan, 2020).

5. See, for example, Malte Hagener, *Moving Forward, Looking Back: The European Avant-Garde and the Invention of Film Culture, 1919–1939* (Amsterdam: Amsterdam University Press, 2007).

6. Vincent Fröhlich, "Where the Film Has the (Visual) Word? On the Visuality and Materiality of Illustrated Film Magazines Exemplified by *Neue Filmwelt* (1947–1953)," *periodICON* 1, no. 1 (2021).

7. Following the holistic ideal, I have chosen a methodological mix of production studies, actor media theory, material philology, layout analysis, and film historiography. For an explanation of a holistic approach to magazines, also see Penny Tinkler, "Fragmentation and Inclusivity: Methods for Working with Girls' and Women's Magazines," in *Women in Magazines: Research, Representation, Production, and Consumption*, ed. Rachel Ritchie et al., 25–39 (New York: Routledge, 2016).

8. Patrick Rössler, *Filmfieber. Deutsche Kinopublizistik 1917–1937* (Erfurt, Germany: Universität Erfurt, 2017), 217; Rössler even concludes, "Whether, in view of these interconnections [with the Ufa], it is still possible to speak of an independent press organ or whether the *Filmwelt* thus already has to be considered as a PR organ of the Ufa, can hardly be decided anymore."

9. Michael Töteberg, "Reklame! Reklame! Reklame!," in *Das Ufa-Plakat. Filmpremieren 1918 bis 1943*, ed. Peter Mänz and Christian Maryška, 12–16 (Heidelberg, Germany: Edition Braus, 1998).

10. Thomas Hanna-Daoud, *Die NSDAP und der Film bis zur Machtergreifung* (Köln, Germany: Böhlau, 1996), 259.

11. Klaus Kreimeier, *The Ufa Story: A History of Germany's Greatest Film Company, 1918–1945* (Berkeley: University of California Press, 1999), 283.

12. Klaus-Jürgen Maiwald, *Filmzensur im NS-Staat* (Dortmund, Germany: Nowotny, 1983), 137–38.

13. Kreimeier, *Ufa Story*, 336.

14. Kreimeier, 225.

15. "Almost 1.12 billion people went to the movies in 1943 in the 'Greater German Reich' (including Luxembourg, Alsace-Lorraine, and the Warthegau but not the Czech areas). Statistically, that meant more than fourteen film attendances per person, a record not even approached in any other war year, much less any peacetime year." Kreimeier, *Ufa Story*, 344.

16. This is not only in terms of politics and propaganda but also on a rather personal level. For instance, Koop describes Adolf Hitler as a "cinephile." Volker Koop, *Warum Hitler King Kong liebte, aber den Deutschen Micky Maus verbot. Die geheimen Lieblingsfilme der Nazi-Elite* (Berlin: be.bra verlag, 2015), 11.

17. Karsten Witte, "Film im Nationalsozialismus," in *Geschichte des deutschen Films*, ed. Wolfgang Jacobsen, Anton Kaes, and Hans H. Prinzler (Stuttgart, Germany: Metzler, 1993), 119.

18. David Bathrick, "From Soviet Zone to Volksdemokratie: The Politics of Film Culture in the GDR, 1945–1960," in *Cinema in Service of the State: Perspectives on Film Culture in the GDR and Czechoslovakia, 1945–1960*, ed. Lars Karl and Pavel Skopal (New York: Berghahn, 2015), 18.

19. Alfred Lindemann, quoted in Seán Allan, "DEFA: An Historical Overview," in *DEFA: East German Cinema, 1946–1992*, ed. Seán Allan and John Sandford (New York: Berghahn, 2010 [reprint]), 5.

20. For information on Bergmann, see also his filmed interview by Ralf Schenk, *Zeitzeugengespräch: Karl Hans Bergmann DEFA-Stiftung*, TC 1:30.

21. Schenk, *Zeitzeugengespräch: Karl Hans Bergmann DEFA-Stiftung*, TC 4:02.

22. Karl Hans Bergmann, *Der Schlaf vor dem Erwachen. Stationen der Jahre 1931–1949* (Berlin: DEFA-Stiftung, 2002), 55–56. *Die Rampe* had already drawn attention to "ideologically suspect films such as *Hitlerjunge Quex*" (D 1933) (57).

23. Schenk, *Zeitzeugengespräch: Karl Hans Bergmann DEFA-Stiftung*, TC 31:10.

24. Schenk, TC 24:14.

25. My own translation of Karl Hans Bergmann, "Vorwort—Klein Geschrieben," *Neue Filmwelt* 1, no. 1 (1947), I.

296   CHAPTER 16

26. As far as our research goes, no one knows who Ruth Vorpahl was or why Arnheim dedicated the book to her. In an email from July 24, 2022, Helmut H. Diederichs explained that, during his several meetings with Rudolf Arnheim, he did ask him about Ruth Vorpahl once or twice but never got an answer.

27. The other publications of the publishing house appeared later and a large part of them were related to the magazine. The film calendar was clearly marked as belonging to *NFW*, and visual material was deliberately used in it that is not found in the magazine. The program leaflets, presumably published monthly, bore the title *Illustrierter Film-Spiegel, Programmblätter der Zeitschrift 'Neue Filmwelt.'*

28. Even in his autobiography, Bergmann quotes exclusively from the editorial of his passion project.

29. Bergmann, *Schlaf vor dem Erwachen*, 386.

30. Based on the outlined contexts, the time span of the release of films was initially divided into eight-year intervals and, starting in 1945, into one-year intervals. The bars of the two different intervals can thus only be compared to a limited extent—but national comparability, which is the main concern here, is maintained within one block.

31. Tinkler, "Fragmentation and Inclusivity," 32.

32. Fröhlich, "Where the Film Has the (Visual) Word?"

33. Georg C. Klaren continued to write screenplays during the National Socialist regime and is listed, among other things, as the originator author of the propaganda film *Achtung! Feind hört mit! (Attention! The Enemy Is Listening!)* (G 1940).

34. The director states in newspapers that his film "is indebted to Expressionism." Georg C. Klaren, "Transzendentaler Film," in *Aufbau* 9 (1949): 956.

35. Jan-Christopher Horak, "Postwar Traumas in Klaren's *Wozzeck* (1947)," in *German Film and Literature: Adaptations and Transformations*, ed. Eric Rentschler (New York: Methuen, 1986), 133.

36. Vincent Fröhlich, "Viewing Illustrated Magazines with Wittgenstein: Methodological Approaches to the Visual Seriality of Illustrated Magazines (1880–1910)," in *Periodical Studies Today: Multidisciplinary Analyses*, ed. Jutta Ernst, Dagmar von Hoff, and Oliver Scheiding, 54–88 (Boston: Brill, 2022). On the importance of symmetry in illustrated journals, see Vincent Fröhlich, "A/Symmetry and Dis/Order: Data-Based Reflections on Balancing Stability and Change in Illustrated Magazines from 1906–1910," in *Visuelles Design: die Journalseite als gestaltete Fläche/Visual Design: The Periodical Page as a Designed Surface*, ed. Andreas Beck, Nicola Kaminski, Volker Mergenthaler, and Jens Ruchatz, 85–117 (Hannover, Germany: Wehrhahn, 2019).

37. Kay Weniger, *Das große Personenlexikon des Films. Die Schauspieler, Regisseure, Kameraleute, Produzenten, Komponisten, Drehbuchautoren, Filmarchitekten, Ausstatter, Kostümbildner, Cutter, Tontechniker, Maskenbildner und Special Effects Designer des 20. Jahrhunderts. Band 3: F—H. Barry Fitzgerald—Ernst Hofbauer* (Berlin: Schwarzkopf & Schwarzkopf, 2001), 336ff.

38. Quoted in Bergmann, *Schlaf vor dem Erwachen*, 389–90.

39. Schenk, *Zeitzeugengespräch: Karl Hans Bergmann DEFA-Stiftung*, TC 23:30.

40. It must be added, however, that the individual leaflets are not dated and can therefore only be assigned an approximate date, something that is at least made possible by the common numbering of the leaflets and the premiere date of the film depicted.

PUBLICATIONS REFERENCED

Cahiers du cinéma
Cinethique
Der Ausweg
Der Filmspiegel

Die Rampe
Film Culture
Film Quarterly
Filmkritik
Filmwelt
Freies Deutschland
Illustrierter Film-Spiegel
Neue Filmwelt
Positif
Screen

FILMS REFERENCED

Gajer, Václav, dir. *Pan Habetín odchází*. Československý státní film, 1949. 1 hr, 33 min.

Klaren, Georg C., dir. *Wozzeck*. DEFA-Studio für Spielfilme, 1947. 1 hr, 41 min.

Schenk, Ralf, dir. *Zeitzeugengespräch: Karl Hans Bergmann*. À jour Film- und Fernsehproduktion, 2001. 112 min.

BIBLIOGRAPHY

Allan, Seán. "DEFA: An Historical Overview." In *DEFA: East German Cinema, 1946–1992*, edited by Seán Allan and John Sandford, 1–21. New York: Berghahn, 2010 [repr.].

Bathrick, David. "From Soviet Zone to Volksdemokratie: The Politics of Film Culture in the GDR, 1945–1960." In *Cinema in Service of the State: Perspectives on Film Culture in the GDR and Czechoslovakia, 1945–1960*, edited by Lars Karl and Pavel Skopal, 15–38. New York: Berghahn, 2015.

Bergmann, Karl Hans. *Der Schlaf vor dem Erwachen. Stationen der Jahre 1931–1949*. Berlin: DEFA-Stiftung, 2002.

Biltereyst, Daniel, and Lies van de Vijver. "Introduction: Movie Magazines, Digitization and New Cinema History." In *Mapping Movie Magazines: Digitization, Periodicals and Cinema History*, edited by Daniel Biltereyst and Lies van de Vijver, 1–13. London: Palgrave Macmillan, 2020.

Fröhlich, Vincent. "A/Symmetry and Dis/Order: Data-Based Reflections on Balancing Stability and Change in Illustrated Magazines from 1906–1910." In *Visuelles Design: die Journalseite als gestaltete Fläche/Visual Design: The Page as a Designed Surface*, edited by Andreas Beck, Nicola Kaminski, Volker Mergenthaler, and and Jens Ruchatz, 85–117. Hannover, Germany: Wehrhahn, 2019.

———. "Viewing Illustrated Magazines with Wittgenstein: Methodological Approaches to the Visual Seriality of Illustrated Magazines (1880–1910)." In *Periodical Studies Today: Multidisciplinary Analyses*, edited by Jutta Ernst, Dagmar von Hoff, and Oliver Scheiding, 54–88. Boston: Brill, 2022.

———. "Where the Film Has the (Visual) Word? On the Visuality and Materiality of Illustrated Film Magazines Exemplified by *Neue Filmwelt* (1947–1953)." *periodICON* 1, no. 1 (2022): 21–48.

Hagener, Malte. *Moving Forward, Looking Back: The European Avant-Garde and the Invention of Film Culture, 1919–1939*. Amsterdam: Amsterdam University Press, 2007.

Hanna-Daoud, Thomas. *Die NSDAP und der Film bis zur Machtergreifung*. Köln, Germany: Böhlau, 1996.

Horak, Jan-Christopher. "Postwar Traumas in Klaren's *Wozzeck* (1947)." In *German Film and Literature: Adaptations and Transformations*, edited by Eric Rentschler, 132–45. New York: Methuen, 1986.

Hoyt, Eric. "Lenses for Lantern: Data Mining, Visualization, and Excavating Film History's Neglected Sources." *Film History* 26, no. 2 (2014): 146–68.

Klaren, Georg C. "Transzendentaler Film." *Aufbau* 9 (1949): 956.

CHAPTER 16

Koop, Volker. *Warum Hitler King Kong liebte, aber den Deutschen Micky Maus verbot. Die geheimen Lieblingsfilme der Nazi-Elite*. Berlin: be.bra verlag, 2015.

Kreimeier, Klaus. *The Ufa Story: A History of Germany's Greatest Film Company, 1918–1945*. Berkeley: University of California Press, 1999.

Maiwald, Klaus-Jürgen. *Filmzensur im NS-Staat*. Dortmund: Nowotny, 1983.

McDonald, Tamar Jeffers, and Lies Lanckman. "Introduction." In *Star Attractions*, edited by Tamar Jeffers McDonald and Lies Lanckman, 1–10. Iowa City: University of Iowa Press, 2019.

Rössler, Patrick. "Die Zeitschriften des Stummfilms als transmediale 'kleine Archive.'" *Jahrbuch für Internationale Germanistik* 50, no. 2 (2018): 211–45.

———. *Filmfieber. Deutsche Kinopublizistik 1917–1937*. Erfurt, Germany: Universität Erfurt, 2017.

Thielmann, Tristan, and Jens Schröter. "Akteur-Medien-Theorie." In *Handbuch Medienwissenschaft*, edited by Jens Schröter, 148–58. Stuttgart, Germany: Metzler, 2014.

Tinkler, Penny. "Fragmentation and Inclusivity: Methods for Working with Girls' and Women's Magazines." In *Women in Magazines: Research, Representation, Production, and Consumption*, edited by Rachel Ritchie et al., 25–39. New York: Routledge, 2016.

Töteberg, Michael. "Reklame! Reklame! Reklame!" In *Das Ufa-Plakat. Filmpremieren 1918 bis 1943*, edited by Peter Mänz and Christian Maryška, 12–16. Heidelberg, Germany: Edition Braus, 1998.

Weniger, Kay. *Das große Personenlexikon des Films. Die Schauspieler, Regisseure, Kameraleute, Produzenten, Komponisten, Drehbuchautoren, Filmarchitekten, Ausstatter, Kostümbildner, Cutter, Tontechniker, Maskenbildner und Special Effects Designer des 20. Jahrhunderts. Band 3: F—H. Barry Fitzgerald—Ernst Hofbauer*. Berlin: Schwarzkopf & Schwarzkopf, 2001.

Witte, Karsten. "Film im Nationalsozialismus." In *Geschichte des deutschen Films*, edited by Wolfgang Jacobsen, Anton Kaes, and Hans H. Prinzler, 119–70. Stuttgart, Germany: Metzler, 1993.

SECTION FOUR

Data, Curation, and Historiography

17

Chronicling a National History

Hye Bossin's Canadian Film Weekly *and* Year Book

Paul S. Moore

"Canada's motion picture history began outside Canada," Hye Bossin (1906–64) stated in a foundational primer on the subject.[1] That statement is as true for today's historians of the Canadian film industry as it was when Bossin published a chronicle of the nation's film history in the first *Year Book of the Canadian Motion Picture Industry* (1951–70). The effort was an offshoot of *Canadian Film Weekly* (1942–70), one of Canada's two pioneering film trade publications. *Film Weekly* later incorporated its rival, *Canadian Moving Picture Digest* (1917–57), bringing both branches of Canadian film trade press under a single umbrella, edited by Bossin. For too long, *Canadian Film Weekly* and *Canadian Moving Picture Digest* remained stranded outside the Media History Digital Library (MHDL). Earliest editions were not collected by Canadian libraries in the first place, and microfilmed copies of early volumes relied upon orphaned issues archived in the New York Public Library. These copies were digitized in 2015 and deposited to HathiTrust via Google Books. For almost a decade they have been available to researchers in the United States, but, in a cruel paradox, they are geo-blocked from access by researchers in Canada in an overreach of copyright precaution. The global task force of the MHDL has thankfully liberated some of those volumes and we have recently digitized several privately held partial collections. Thankfully, the Canadian branch of the MHDL is no longer only a hypothetical entity. Nonetheless, relying on US institutions to tell our own stories is a lamentably familiar tale.[2]

As I have argued elsewhere, Hollywood consistently viewed Canada as just another US regional exchange territory, treating Toronto the same as Cleveland or Dallas.[3] Routines in film distribution followed established circuits for stage, vaudeville, and music, which integrated Canadian theaters into US

FIGURE 17.1. Nameplate of *Canadian Film Weekly*.

touring circuits. Radio and TV networks easily crossed the border, too; even the hallowed public channels of the Canadian Broadcasting Corporation largely programmed simulcasts of US networks until the 1950s for radio and the 1990s for television.[4] A significant majority of the Canadian population lived in towns and cities just north of the US border, scattered from coast to coast, and not least in the cities where our six exchange territory "film rows" were located: Vancouver, Calgary, Winnipeg, Toronto, Montréal, and Saint John (all are just a short ride or drive from a border crossing). Even today, Canada is considered part of the US "domestic" box office. From 1920 to 2005, our largest chain of movie theaters was directly owned by Paramount, operated as a branch plant of Hollywood and an easy scapegoat for the tepid appetite of Canadian audiences who failed to attend the few Canadian feature films that got made.[5] Similarly, Canada's film trade news was also routinely integrated into US entertainment trade papers (even a surprising amount of news about French media in Quebec). Above, I bemoaned delays in adding Canadian magazines to the MHDL, but there was admittedly no urgent need to log our film trade papers. In another irony of the digital age, online US sources have made research about Canadian film industries far more accessible, convenient, and reliable than local, analog searches of our own domestic periodicals. My research for this very chapter was *entirely* limited to online sources during pandemic lockdowns, and my own work demonstrates perfectly that using US journals for research on Canadian cinema often suffices.

This situation would have embittered and saddened the two editors of our twinned historic film trade papers, but neither would have been surprised. The first of the two journals, *Canadian Moving Picture Digest* (1917–57), was edited for almost its entire existence by Ray Lewis, a strident bullhorn for national independence from US control in Hollywood. My prior research with Louis Pelletier and Jessica Whitehead has focused on the *Digest* largely because of Lewis's high profile and eccentric personality.[6] She was a rare woman in the field, whom *Variety*'s Sime Silverman labeled "the Girl-Friend in Canada." In the 1930s, she testified before antitrust commissions and courtrooms and lobbied in corporate and political offices, all the while editorializing at length and spotlighting hope and possibility for a uniquely Canadian film business that was equally British, US-American, and homegrown.

For this brief essay, I will give long-overdue attention to the other journal's editor, Hye Bossin, who helmed *Canadian Film Weekly* from its first issue in 1942 until he died at fifty-eight in 1964. We have perhaps ignored Bossin because he had a less enthralling persona than that of Ray Lewis, and left a quieter, less dramatic rhetorical wake. But Bossin, too, was a stalwart defender of the particularity and unique character of the Canadian film business, while recognizing how his trade magazine relied almost entirely on the goodwill of Hollywood distributors for advertising revenue. An extensive, personal appreciation of Bossin explained how he "fought constantly for advertising from the American companies who saw no reason why they should support a Canadian trade paper ('let them read Box Office')."[7] US purse strings tightly bound nearly all aspects of English Canadian popular culture, especially in the realm of movies, which were almost by definition a wholly US phenomenon. This meant that Bossin, editing and publishing a Canadian film trade paper, "was painfully aware that his loyalty was being given to an enterprise that for the most part was not Canadian, did not concern itself with anything Canadian, took millions of dollars out of the country each year, and spent as little as possible in Canada. He was also well aware that the distributors and theater owners could put him out of business overnight if he dared to write a word of criticism about their American ownership."[8] Despite these constraints, his legacies are remarkable.

Crucially, Bossin documented, reported, and published histories of Canadian film, reaching back to the beginnings of cinema, that are still often cited today. Bossin's editing of the *Canadian Film Weekly* grew tentacles across maturing institutions of the Canadian cinema business in the late 1940s and '50s, as the film industry shifted from being a mere branch of Hollywood distribution to also being a center of independent domestic production for animation, documentary, and television. As the National Film Board began garnering Oscar nominations, and Canadian producers began releasing occasional award-winning feature films, Bossin was instrumental in creating our own national film awards, still given annually under a new moniker. He launched a Canadian film critics' poll and printed Canadian box office reports to spotlight how our tastes for Hollywood films were different, if only slightly, from the elephant in the room to the south. His legacy continued after his death, as the *Weekly* continued with new names; its *Year Book* lasted into the new millennium.

Canadian Film Weekly was created early in 1942, soon after an independent chain exhibitor, Nat Taylor, bought the remnants of an existing trade paper, *The Canadian Independent*. That paper had been edited by Stella Falk since it began in 1936 as an organ of the Canadian Independent Theatre Association but Falk found herself in an extended libel lawsuit with Ray Lewis. The magazine was briefly rebranded *The Canadian Motion Picture Exhibitor* in 1940 before Falk stepped down.[9] Perhaps the lawsuit put the publication in danger, either financially or reputationally, but perhaps Taylor also recognized it was a good moment to rebrand the paper because his own chain, Twinex ("Twentieth Century") Theatres, was no longer independent. Indeed, a new era had just begun across all Canadian exhibition, with the formation of Canadian Odeon as a national chain in 1941, cobbled together from a string of independent regional chains to compete against the dominant Paramount-owned Famous Players Canadian Corporation.[10] Taylor had negotiated to affiliate with Odeon but ultimately signed with Famous Players, apparently leveraging one against the other to obtain a greater degree of autonomy in booking and promotion.[11] Lewis's *Digest* published all the details as well as many speculative questions about Taylor's dealings, and he must have been irate to have his business aired while negotiations were still underway. Enter: Hye Bossin, managing editor of the *Exhibitor* from June 1941, soon under its new name, *Canadian Film Weekly*.

Bossin was a lifelong bachelor, although known to be a lady's man, handsome and athletic.[12] He was the same age as Taylor, both born in 1906 in Toronto's tight-knit Jewish community. Bossin's family was significantly poorer, however, living together above their father's secondhand store, initially in the heart of the working-class "ward" downtown. The family moved twice but stayed under one roof even as adult siblings with careers. For more than two decades editing *Film Weekly*, Bossin lived with his unmarried sisters, long after their parents died.[13] Bossin's older brother left school early and made a career working for the wealthy owner of a horse racetrack, then a business publishing race results, and later still a service through which dozens of telephone operators would give live results from races straight across the continent.[14] Second oldest, Hye left school early to support the family. For his first twenty years' working life, he labored in the same print shop, starting as a messenger and rising to fully apprenticed journeyman compositor. The job allowed him to become "a voracious reader and a scholar. . . . 'In those days,' he once remarked, 'the print shops were a poor man's university.' There, he developed an urge to write."[15] He was surely inspired by his younger brother, Arthur, who wrote movie reviews for *The Toronto Star* and other papers and became a protégé of Walter Winchell in 1929. Under the pen name Art Arthur, he wrote for *The Brooklyn Eagle* starting in 1932.[16] Arthur began selling screenplays in Hollywood, and his name was sometimes spotlighted as a local boy when movies he wrote played at home in Canada.[17] He later wrote the Oscar-winning 1946 documentary *Seeds of Destiny*.

Perhaps spurred by his younger brother's success as a journalist and writer, Hye Bossin also began to work as a freelance journalist in the 1930s. When Emma Goldman lectured in Toronto in 1934, he published an interview in *The Jewish Standard*, where he had a regular column, "Even as You and Hye."[18] In 1938, he finally quit the print shop and tried his hand in the "publicity mills" of Hollywood for a year, but soon returned to Toronto with some fanfare by launching a column in *The Star Weekly*, "Tattler's Tales," which was collected into a book.[19] His background of printing, journalism, weekly columns, and entertainment reporting was a perfect combination for Taylor's new trade paper. *Canadian Film Weekly* provided Bossin with "a writing-editing job in which he was his own boss. He proceeded to publish with efficiency and determination . . . in a constant state of frenzied disorder, with papers, letters, and books piled around him on a desk

FIGURE 17.2. A family photo of Hye Bossin with his sister, Celia. Courtesy of Allen Bossin.

covered with notes and material. He had no patience with people who made mistakes or who failed to carry out his instructions, and he would fly into rages when things went wrong, were lost, late, or left undone."[20] This meticulous attention to quality produced "a highly professional, highly readable paper that faithfully chronicled the daily events of Canadians in the business of films."[21]

From his 1941 start as editor, Bossin acted for the mutual profit and benefit of the Canadian film trade, including its US owners. For the previous decade, Lewis's *Digest* had been a central character in antitrust commissions, lawsuits, and libel allegations and had reported openly about head office resignations and machinations. In contrast, under Taylor's patronage, Bossin established a worthy rival to Lewis's *Digest* in the form of a less charismatic and rhetorical, more impartial trade paper. Bossin offered a crisp, professional style. He gave *Canadian Film Weekly* a modern front page, crammed with all the week's headlines and ledes, akin to the US trade paper *The Film Daily*, whereas Lewis was still using a dated, newsletter style that spotlighted her full-page editorials, with news reporting buried well inside. The *Weekly* was well positioned to exploit the newly competitive situation of having two national cinema chains, reporting news about Famous, Odeon, and independents alike without infighting, intrigue, or speculation. Bossin gained esteem among fellow entertainment journalists and film industry players across Canada and beyond. His sharp wit and humorous stories were widely quoted, even in the US.[22] His editorial column was entitled "On the Square," for his first office on Dundas Square, overlooking Toronto's film row. But "he never used

FIGURE 17.3. Hye Bossin (far right) next to Ray Lewis, with Martin Quigley (second from left) and two Canadian advertising executives judging a showmanship competition. *Motion Picture Herald*, September 26, 1953.

it to air his views editorially. . . . In this column he wrote of the theater and of books he enjoyed, of writers he admired, and of events and people that interested him. He seldom said an unkind word about anyone, although privately he denounced those who talked loudly of things they knew little about."[23] Bossin's generosity was especially clear for his rival editor, Lewis. The pair often worked alongside each other for special industry events, and Bossin offered sincere congratulations when Lewis was awarded the Canadian Picture Pioneer of the Year in 1953, just a year before she died.[24] Her son and managing editor, Jay Smith, eventually sold the *Digest* to Bossin in 1957, and her legacy was honored on the amalgamated masthead that stated *Canadian Film Weekly* was "incorporating *Canadian Moving Picture Digest*."[25]

Bossin's role in reporting on the Canadian film industry was vital in the post–World War II years, when a major building spree of new, sleek modern cinemas were constructed, coast to coast. Movie attendance and box office hit all-time highs in the early 1950s, after dozens of neon signs were installed in downtowns across the country, flashing the Paramount and Odeon brand names of the competing chains.[26] Drive-ins opened outside every city and many towns, and art cinemas, film societies and film festivals were launched across Canada. The National Film Board spotlighted Canada's innovative, award-winning filmmaking talent, and Marshall McLuhan achieved global renown for new theories of communication and culture. Reflecting this mid-century flourishing of national media in Canada, Bossin began a *Film Weekly* Canadian critics' poll in 1943, ranking best Hollywood films released the previous year, but from a uniquely Canadian perspective. The results each March were paired with a list of top box office in Canada, a rare moment such figures were separated from their US counterparts. Much was made annually by the very same critics submitting their choices about the disparity or overlap between the Critics' Poll list and Canadian box office annual reports. They constantly weighed the problem of delayed releases of major Hollywood pictures, noting how ranked films were sometimes nearly two years out of sync with Oscar nominees.[27] Bossin was also among the key actors who helped launch an annual Canadian Film Awards, established in 1949 by the Canadian Association for Adult Education, under a steering committee that included officers of the National Film Board, the Canadian Foundation, and the National Gallery of Canada. Bossin served on the initial jury with an important Toronto film critic and cinephile, Gerald Pratley, among others. The first awards ceremony featured a presentation by Prime Minister Louis St. Laurent.[28] This effort had its pitfalls, because some years there was no Canadian feature production worthy to award "film of the year." In one form or other, however, the annual awards continue today, and the nominations stand for posterity as an important inventory of achievement.

The 1950s were Bossin's heyday, and he embraced his extracurricular role as steward for our own Canadian national film history. His concern was to build a reputation for Canada, starting within its own borders, by compiling the news and histories of Hollywood film and media industries in Canada as if they mattered for Canadian culture. Bossin used the *Film Weekly* to offer commemorations and extend appreciation on a weekly basis alongside the news. He conducted interviews with pioneers and gathered photographs and documents towards a first authoritative account of the earliest days of cinema exhibition and filmmaking in Canada. Over the years, he published several entries for a planned book, *Canada and the Film*, to be copublished with the National Film Board of Canada.[29] Short histories Bossin had published in *Canadian Film Weekly* since 1943 were drawn upon for the inaugural *Year Book* in 1951, which included a seventeen-page, extensively illustrated essay, "Canada and the Film: The Story of the Canadian Motion Picture Industry."[30] No less than Terry Ramsaye reviewed the first yearbook admiringly as "primarily a book of the Now . . . substantially a one-man job, done at the other end of a desk engaged in the race with the publication of deadlines of a weekly journal. That helps with keeping in touch with the present."[31] And yet, it was the historical essay that drew special notice from Ramsaye for its reprinted "discovery and presentation of that letter in which Thomas A. Edison, in May 1894, thanked the Holland Brothers at Ottawa in Canada for the first public exhibition of his initial motion picture device, the Kinetoscope." Bossin's stature as an industry insider opened access to pioneers for interviews and donations of documents. US film "yearbooks and almanacs helped to solve the industry's information management problems," including the constant need to work across the northern border.[32] Lists of Canadian cinemas and contacts for Toronto film exchanges had long been part of Jack Alicoate's editing of *Film Daily Year Book* as a copious database. From 1951, Canada would have its own annual directory and movie theater database, but Bossin's editorial spin laced early volumes with his own essays of historical research, adding a dash of Ramsaye's style of editing the *Motion Picture Almanac* with an emphasis on biographies of key figures in the industry.[33]

In 1949, the same year the Canadian Film Awards began, Bossin offered "A Plea for a Canadian Film Archive," in a *Film Weekly* editorial, an explanation of

308   CHAPTER 17

a real effort underway in collaboration with members of the Toronto branch of the National Film Society, which again included movie critic Gerald Pratley. The proposal was to establish a Canadian Film Archive in Ottawa, an equivalent to the Museum of Modern Art Film Library or the British Film Institute, "to trace, catalogue, assemble, exhibit and circulate a library of film programmes so that the motion picture may be studied and enjoyed as any other of the arts is studied and enjoyed."[34] Bossin noted wryly how Canadian institutions had entirely neglected moving pictures as a crucial part of heritage worth preserving, both within the film industry and in government and civic society. He wrote how "strange that such a powerful industry and art as the moving picture should be without historic records in places designed to house them. How ridiculous will it seem several generations from now?"[35]

Bossin was central to creating the Canadian Film Archive, admiringly cheered on by Terry Ramsaye again, who lamented that

> genuine institutional interest is too often entirely external to the business. The surviving pioneers and their successors, wherever you find them, are interested in the yesterdays more for occasions of socializing than for preserving the tradition. . . . Meanwhile if the story of the motion picture is to be kept straight it will have to be continuously protected from the extravagant and retroactive memories of so many of the alleged records and current recollections of those who did not do all those important things they talk about.[36]

The fledgling effort was hatched in an Ottawa meeting with Walter Herbert, director of the Canada Foundation.[37] Bossin occasionally published important "chapters" in the planned book-length treatise, in subsequent numbers of the *Year Book* as well as in multiple contributions to the *Journal of the Screen Producers Guild*.[38] Over the previous decades, several biographical and anecdotal pieces had been published in *Canadian Moving Picture Digest*, including an extensive recollection of dozens of key early figures in an inaugural celebration of Canadian Moving Picture Pioneers in 1940, but the task of stewardship over a more concerted documentation of Canadian film history fell to Bossin.

One outcome of Bossin's efforts ended in disaster. In 1963, the volunteer effort of the Canadian Film Archive was transferred formally to become a division of the Canadian Film Institute in Ottawa and partnered with the National Film Board of Canada in Montréal. Concerted efforts "without any federal Government subsidy" escalated pleas for donations, both of funds and film prints. The work quickly paid off and the group began public exhibitions of historically important films.[39] In a tragic twist of fate, the success of Bossin's efforts to rally contributions of early and historically important films to the Canadian Film Archive ended up destroyed. In 1965, a *Globe and Mail* article sketched how plans were "being made for a permanent vault where all the film can be kept under ideal humidity and temperature conditions. The collecting and preserving of film is an urgent project," the journalist explained to its public readership, "because the conditions under which film

FIGURE 17.4. Hye Bossin (left) receiving a citation for his historical writing from Walter Herbert, chairman of the Canadian Film Awards. *Ottawa Journal*, November 12, 1955.

is kept govern its lifetime. This is particularly true of the nitrate stock film used in early movie making, a highly volatile material."[40] As if predicting rather than warning, almost all of the collected one million feet of film went up in flames in a July 1967 fire in suburban Montréal at a "hangar" being used by the National Film Board to store the Canadian Film Archive collection, which was uninsured because the nitrate films were both irreplaceable and inflammable.[41] Were Bossin still alive, perhaps he would have found the catastrophe a bitterly ironic twist of fate, sadly befitting the sorry saga of the struggle to create a uniquely Canadian film culture.

Bossin's role in establishing the very idea of Canadian film history was recognized almost immediately, a testament to how urgent and innovative it was simply to have a film archive in Canada. In 1955, he received a special citation from the Canadian Film Awards, "in recognition of his contribution to motion pictures in Canada and particularly his promotion of a Canadian Film Archive."[42] The same year, he was named Honorary Canadian Picture Pioneer of the year "for his research and historical work."[43] An offshoot of this work appeared in 1957 in book form as *Stars of David*, which told the history of Jewish theater in Toronto and the work on stage and in radio and movies of Jewish people from Toronto.[44] Bossin included an extensive chapter about the many Jewish men and women who were central to the establishment of the moving picture business in Canada. These historical interests were transformed into a temporary "Canadian Film History Museum" display in 1963 at The Little Cinema, a 16mm dual auditorium–art house

310   CHAPTER 17

that Nat Taylor briefly opened in downtown Toronto.[45] A collaboration with the National Film Board, the museum presented "an array of old time movies, one-sheets, cameras and equipment of yesteryear."[46] Bossin's historical work sometimes included strange permutations, such as his being the contact for fans of Mary Pickford in 1963 when Walter Winchell asked readers of *Photoplay* to loan her old pictures from her Biograph days.[47] Bossin's histories remained central to others' research, even after his death. Not least of these researchers was Peter Morris, who was head of the Canadian Film Institute in Ottawa in the late 1960s and head of the Film Archives during the fire. As professor of film studies at Queen's University in the 1970s, Morris would publish *Embattled Shadows*, a first comprehensive study of the kind Bossin had long promised.[48] After Bossin died in 1964, Nat Taylor hired a new editor and later changed the name of the *Weekly* to *Canadian Film Digest*, which continued to 1976. The *Year Book* continued for decades longer, under new owners and editors, until 2007.[49] When Bossin died, accolades were fulsome, recognizing that he was among the most respected and best-liked people in Canadian showbusiness. One person was quoted pointedly saying that "he was the face of the industry; he was synonymous with it."[50] This continues to be true, in terms of lasting influence over institutions that continue today, however much his name has faded from memory.

Bossin's importance in forging a national film industry history in Canada is crucial to spotlight for global scholars of the film trade and its periodical press. The day-to-day of advertising sales and transforming studio publicity into articles might predominate, even within film papers edited with the most high-minded of journalistic intentions. Yet, even when unintended, the work of chronicling the film trade is truly the first rough draft of film history. Indeed, this is the guiding principle behind the compiled internet archives of the MHDL. Not always as deliberately as Bossin—because rarely does a country need it so direly—other nations' film editors and journalists worked with similar reflexivity about their roles chronicling the industry. Their work is so rarely cynical and often ends up valorizing the film industry uncritically. Bossin is not alone in using his pages nostalgically to look back upon the history of the movies and the film business, to honor pioneers and contribute biographies of friends and foes alike upon their passing. On the one hand, Bossin alone in Canada compiled a weekly paper and an annual yearbook and forged other enduring ways to chronicle our national film history. On the other hand, within a global film history, his achievements are a yardstick that can be used to measure the parallel work happening in every nation's film press.

NOTES

1. Hyman (Hye) Bossin, born March 30, 1906, died September 12, 1964. Hye Bossin, "Canada and the Film: The Story of the Canadian Motion Picture Industry," *Year Book of the Canadian*

CHRONICLING A NATIONAL HISTORY IN CANADA 311

Motion Picture Industry (Toronto: Film Publications of Canada, 1951), 21. Bossin's point was that the first Kinetoscope parlor in New York in April 1894 was opened by Canadians, Andrew and George Holland, licensed Edison agents.

2. The lamentations are fulsome in the string of titles, both popular histories and film scholarship: Pierre Burton, *Hollywood's Canada: The Americanization of Our National Image* (Toronto: McClelland and Stewart, 1975); Peter Morris, *Embattled Shadows: A History of Canadian Cinema, 1895–1939* (Montreal: McGill–Queen's University Press, 1978); Gerald Pratley, *Torn Sprockets: The Uncertain Projection of the Canadian Film* (Toronto: Associated University Presses, 1987); Manjunath Pendakur, *Canadian Dreams and American Control: The Political Economy of the Canadian Film Industry* (Toronto: Garamond Press, 1990).

3. Paul S. Moore, *Now Playing: Early Moviegoing and the Regulation of Fun* (Albany: State University of New York Press, 2008), 4–6.

4. Anne F. MacLennan, "American Network Broadcasting, the CBC, and Canadian Radio Stations During the 1930s: A Content Analysis," *Journal of Radio Studies* 12, no. 1 (2005): 85–103.

5. In addition to Morris, *Embattled Shadows*, and Pendakur, *Canadian Dreams and American Control*, other studies of the struggle to support Canadian feature film production include Ted Magder, *Canada's Hollywood: The Canadian State and Feature Films* (Toronto: University of Toronto Press, 1993), and Michael Dorland, *So Close to the State(s): The Emergence of Canadian Feature Film Policy* (Toronto: University of Toronto Press, 1998).

6. Jessica L. Whitehead, Louis Pelletier, and Paul S. Moore, "'The Girl Friend in Canada': Ray Lewis and *Canadian Moving Picture Digest* (1915–1957)," in *Mapping Movie Magazines: Digitization, Periodicals and Cinema History*, ed. Daniel Biltereyst and Lies Van de Vijver, 127–52 (London: Palgrave Macmillan, 2020). See also Louis Pelletier and Paul S. Moore, "Une excentrique au coeur de l'industrie: Ray Lewis et le *Canadian Moving Picture Digest*," *Cinémas* 16, no. 1 (2005): 59–90.

7. Pratley, *Torn Sprockets*, 77.

8. Ibid., 78.

9. Whitehead, Pelletier, and Moore, "'The Girl Friend in Canada,'" 141–43; "Coper Replaces Mrs. Falk," *Film Daily*, March 19, 1941, 3.

10. Paul S. Moore, "Nathan L. Nathanson Introduces Canadian Odeon: Producing National Competition in Film Exhibition," *Canadian Journal of Film Studies* 12, no. 2 (2003): 22–45.

11. Paul Corupe, "Taking Off 'The Mask': Rediscovering Nat Taylor and the B-Movies of Canada's Past," *Take One* 12, no. 44 (2003): 17–21.

12. Bossin played on Famous Players Toronto Hockey and Softball teams in 1926, which were meant for employees, so perhaps his company was printing programs for the company? See "Canada," *Motion Picture News*, February 13, 1926, 818, and October 2, 1926, 1297. Soon after, Bossin is noted among organizers of a local Jewish softball league. See "Softball Champions Honored," *Toronto Star*, November 25, 1929, 8; "Jewish Community League Opens May 18," *Toronto Star*, April 7, 1931, 13.

13. Allen Bossin, "The Bossin Story: One Hundred Years in the Making," online family history of the Bossin Cousin Club, www.bossincousins.wordpress.com.

14. Bob Bossin, *Davy the Punk: A Story of Bookies, Toronto the Good, the Mob and My Dad* (Toronto: Porcupine's Quill, 2014).

15. "Film Weekly Editor Hye Bossin Dies," *Toronto Star*, September 14, 1964, 29.

16. Walter Winchell began quoting humor from Arthur Bossin's Toronto journalism as early as "Variety," *Akron Beacon-Journal*, August 15, 1929, 26. Art Bossin's stories were sometimes syndicated across the US by the Consolidated Press Association, as early as "Ban on Liquor Import to US Hurts Canada," *Santa Rosa Republican*, August 9, 1930, 8. As "Art Arthur," his brief turn on CKGW Toronto radio began in September 1932. His column in *The Brooklyn Eagle*, "Reverting to Type," was written "Walter Winchell" style, as if transcribing a flurry of radio announcements, and began December 27, 1932, the same day that Arthur also wrote a review of the opening of Radio City Music Hall, "Roxy's Wand Guides Miracle Music Hall."

312   CHAPTER 17

17. "Art Arthur, Movie Writer, Is Successful Torontonian," *Toronto Star*, January 14, 1938, 3. See also ads for *Love and Hisses* in *Windsor Star*, January 22, 1938, 20, and *Edmonton Journal*, February 8, 1939, 11.

18. Theresa and Albert Moritz, *The World's Most Dangerous Woman: A New Biography of Emma Goldman* (Toronto: University of Toronto Press, 2001), quoting Hye Bossin, "A Rebel Speaks," *Toronto Jewish Standard*, June 29, 1934, 6.

19. The column debuted with Hye Bossin, "Tattler's Tales of Toronto," *Toronto Star Weekly*, January 21, 1939, 2; "Six Columnists in Star Weekly," *Toronto Star*, January 27, 1939, 21. A single copy of the book that compiled Bossin's columns, *A Tattler's Tale of Toronto* (1940), is archived at the Thomas Fisher Rare Book Room, University of Toronto. In 1939, the three Toronto daily papers commissioned Bossin to write a book, *A Saint in Street Clothes*, to commemorate the founder of the local newsboys' clubhouse. See "Life Story of Frankel Aids Newspaper Boys," *Toronto Globe and Mail*, April 29, 1939, 8.

20. Pratley, *Torn Sprockets*, 77.

21. Ibid.

22. Quips, puns, and clever jokes from Hye Bossin were quoted, for example, in Jack Karr, "Movie-Go-Round," *Toronto Star*, April 7, 1943, 26, and January 26, 1946, 10; Phil M. Daly, "Along the Rialto," *Film Daily*, December 8, 1944, 5; and Roly Young, "Rambling with Roly," *Toronto Globe and Mail*, September 30, 1946, 11.

23. Pratley, *Torn Sprockets*, 78.

24. "Ray Lewis, Industry Leader, Passes," *Canadian Film Weekly*, July 14, 1954, 3.

25. "'The Digest' Will Stop Publishing," *Canadian Film Weekly*, February 27, 1957, 1, 3.

26. Canadian box office admissions peaked at 261 million in 1952; receipts had a maximum of $108 million in 1953, and the number of theaters reached a pinnacle of 2,813 in 1954, before all three measures dropped sharply in the late 1950s. See "Box Office Statistics," *Year Book of the Canadian Motion Picture Industry* (Toronto: Film Publications of Canada, 1963), 25.

27. Roly Young, "Rambling with Roly," *Toronto Star*, March 13, 1944, 18, and February 17, 1948, 11; and "Sinatra, Ingrid Voted Screen's Top Performers," *Toronto Star*, March 8, 1958, 23.

28. Jack Karr, "Showplace, 29 Films Entered," *Toronto Star*, March 30, 1949, 13; Mona Purser, "The Homemaker, St. Laurent to Make Canadian Film Awards," *Toronto Globe and Mail*, April 23, 1949, 15. See also "The Canadian Film Awards," *Year Book of the Canadian Motion Picture Industry* (Toronto: Film Publications of Canada, 1951), 157–59.

29. Pratley, *Torn Sprockets*, 79, concluded his discussion of Bossin by noting how, "sadly, like Canadian cinema as a whole, much of the unpublished material seems to have been lost since his death since the manuscript passed to several individuals and the National Film Board, with no one even knowing if it all still exists as a whole."

30. Bossin, "Canada and the Film," expanded and corrected "Fifty Years of the Motion Picture in Canada," *Canadian Film Weekly*, December 22, 1943, 6 and 31, and a series of "Flashbacks" that began in *Canadian Film Weekly* on March 15, 1944.

31. Terry Ramsaye, review of *Year Book of the Canadian Motion Picture Industry*, *Motion Picture Herald*, December 15, 1951, 38.

32. Eric Hoyt, *Ink-Stained Hollywood: The Triumph of American Cinema's Trade Press* (Oakland: University of California Press, 2022), 54, https://doi.org/10.1525/luminos.122.

33. Ibid., 156–58.

34. Hye Bossin, "A Plea for a Canadian Film Archive," *Canadian Film Weekly*, January 26, 1949, 9.

35. Ibid. Bossin noted that the Canadian Picture Pioneers, created in 1940, "already has much material in its archives."

36. Terry Ramsaye, "Canada Remembering," *Motion Picture Herald*, November 15, 1952, 20.

37. Will McLauglin, "Twixt Studio, Screen," *Ottawa Journal*, November 14, 1953, 35, quoting Bossin's recollection in a recent issue of *Canadian Film Weekly*.

CHRONICLING A NATIONAL HISTORY IN CANADA   313

38. Other historical essays by Bossin include the following: "The Story of L. Ernest Ouimet, Pioneer," *Year Book of the Canadian Motion Picture Industry* (Toronto: Film Publications of Canada, 1952), 23–43; "At the Very Beginning, The Holland Brothers of Ottawa Ushered in the World Motion Picture Industry," *Year Book of the Canadian Motion Picture Industry* (Toronto: Film Publications of Canada, 1952), 45–49; "They Led the Way: The Motion Picture Industry Marks the Golden Anniversary of the Silver Screen," *Year Book of the Canadian Motion Picture Industry* (Toronto: Film Publications of Canada, 1953), 17–23; " 'To Them: Honor': The Canadian Picture Pioneers Notes the Work of the Worthy," *Year Book of the Canadian Motion Picture Industry* (Toronto: Film Publications of Canada, 1954), 24–29; "Production in Canada," *Journal of Screen Producers Guild* (December 1959), 28–29; "Over-Censored Canada," *Journal of the Screen Producers Guild* (December 1963), 25–28.

39. Eileen Pettigrew, "Film Enthusiasts Hunt for Relics of Movies," *Toronto Globe and Mail*, April 22, 1965, W6.

40. Ibid.

41. "A Million Feet Lost, Vintage Canadian Film Destroyed by Blaze," *Toronto Globe and Mail*, July 26, 1967, 1; "Film Loss Blamed on Government," *Ottawa Citizen*, July 26, 1967, 2. This news item did not appear until three days after the catastrophic fire, only after Peter Morris was interviewed by the Canadian Press as archivist for the Canadian Film Institute.

42. "Hye Bossin, Former Printer Became Editor of Film Weekly," *Toronto Globe and Mail*, September 14, 1964, 11.

43. "Canada MPEA Asks Distributor Meeting; Rosenfeld Honored," *Motion Picture Daily*, November 2, 1955, 1 and 5.

44. Hye Bossin, *Stars of David: Toronto, 1856–1956* (Toronto: Canadian Jewish Congress, 1957).

45. "Interesting Things to Do and See in Metropolitan Toronto Area during Weekend," *Toronto Globe and Mail*, January 25, 1963, 35.

46. "Film History Museum Wins Patrons for Little Theatre Up Escalator," *Boxoffice*, April 1, 1963, 49.

47. Walter Winchell, "The Midnight World of Walter Winchell," *Photoplay*, August 1963, 72.

48. Morris, *Embattled Shadows*. One important oversight Morris inherited from Bossin was the boast by exhibitor John C. Green that he gave the first projected cinema exhibition in Canada for the Holland Brothers' Vitascope in Ottawa on July 21, 1896. A Lumière Cinématographe had, in fact, begun exhibiting in Montreal earlier, on June 27, 1896, and another Vitascope had begun earlier, in Winnipeg on July 18, 1896. See Germain Lacasse, "Cultural Amnesia and the Birth of Film in Canada," *Cinema Canada* 108 (June 1984), 6–7; Paul S. Moore, "Mapping the Mass Circulation of Early Cinema: Film Debuts Coast-to-Coast in Canada in 1896 and 1897," *Canadian Journal of Film Studies* 21, no. 1 (2012): 58–80.

49. Stan Helleur was editor from 1964 to 1969, with a slightly new title, *Canadian Film and TV Bi-Weekly*. See G. J. "Fitz" FitzGerald, "On and Off the Record," *Montreal Gazette*, December 1, 1964, 4; and "Stanley Heller (sic) Is Editor, Canadian Film Weekly," *Box Office*, November 30, 1964, 8. Taylor's later partner in creating Cineplex in 1979, Garth Drabinsky, was editor from 1972 to 1976 of the newly named *Canadian Film Digest*. The yearbooks continued with two new owners and publishers; in the 1980s, still as *Canadian Film Digest Yearbook*, edited and published by Patricia Thompson; and in the 1990s until 2007, as *Film Canada Yearbook*, edited and published by Deborah Tiffin.

50. "Film Weekly Editor Hye Bossin Dies," *Toronto Star*, September 14, 1964, 29.

PUBLICATIONS REFERENCED

Brooklyn Eagle
Canadian Film Digest

CHAPTER 17

Canadian Film Digest Year Book
Canadian Film Weekly
Canadian Film Weekly Year Book of the Canadian Motion Picture Industry
Canadian Film & TV Bi-Weekly
Canadian Film & TV Bi-Weekly Year Book of the Canadian Entertainment Industry
Canadian Independent
Canadian Motion Picture Exhibitor
Canadian Moving Picture Digest
Film Canada Yearbook
Film Daily
Film Daily Year Book
Globe and Mail (Toronto)
Star Weekly (Toronto)
Toronto Star
Variety

BIBLIOGRAPHY

Bossin, Bob. *Davy the Punk: A Story of Bookies, Toronto the Good, the Mob and My Dad.* Toronto: Porcupine's Quill, 2014.

Bossin, Hye. "At the Very Beginning, The Holland Brothers of Ottawa Ushered in the World Motion Picture Industry." In *Year Book of the Canadian Motion Picture Industry*, 45–49. Toronto: Film Publications of Canada, 1952.

———. "Canada and the Film: The Story of the Canadian Motion Picture Industry." In *Year Book of the Canadian Motion Picture Industry*, 21–41. Toronto: Film Publications of Canada, 1951.

———. "Over-Censored Canada." *Journal of the Screen Producers Guild* (December 1963), 25–28.

———. "Production in Canada." *Journal of Screen Producers Guild* (December 1959), 28–29.

———. *Stars of David: Toronto, 1856–1956.* Toronto: Canadian Jewish Congress, 1957.

———. "The Story of L. Ernest Ouimet, Pioneer." In *Year Book of the Canadian Motion Picture Industry*, 23–43. Toronto: Film Publications of Canada, 1952.

———. "They Led the Way: The Motion Picture Industry Marks the Golden Anniversary of the Silver Screen." In *Year Book of the Canadian Motion Picture Industry*, 17–23. Toronto: Film Publications of Canada, 1953.

———. "'To Them: Honor': The Canadian Picture Pioneers Notes the Work of the Worthy." In *Year Book of the Canadian Motion Picture Industry*, 24–29. Toronto: Film Publications of Canada, 1954.

Burton, Pierre. *Hollywood's Canada: The Americanization of our National Image.* Toronto: McClelland and Stewart, 1975.

Corupe, Paul. "Taking Off 'The Mask': Rediscovering Nat Taylor and the B-Movies of Canada's Past." *Take One* 12, no. 44 (2003): 17–21.

Dorland, Michael. *So Close to the State(s): The Emergence of Canadian Feature Film Policy.* Toronto: University of Toronto Press, 1998.

Hoyt, Eric. *Ink-Stained Hollywood: The Triumph of American Cinema's Trade Press.* Oakland: University of California Press, 2022, https://doi.org/10.1525/luminos.122.

Lacasse, Germain. "Cultural Amnesia and the Birth of Film in Canada." *Cinema Canada* 108 (June 1984): 6–7.

MacLennan, Anne F. "American Network Broadcasting, the CBC, and Canadian Radio Stations During the 1930s: A Content Analysis." *Journal of Radio Studies* 12, no. 1 (2005): 85–103.

Magder, Ted. *Canada's Hollywood: The Canadian State and Feature Films.* Toronto: University of Toronto Press, 1993.

Moore, Paul S. "Mapping the Mass Circulation of Early Cinema: Film Debuts Coast-to-Coast in Canada in 1896 and 1897." *Canadian Journal of Film Studies* 21, no. 1 (2012): 58–80.

———. "Nathan L. Nathanson Introduces Canadian Odeon: Producing National Competition in Film Exhibition." *Canadian Journal of Film Studies* 12, no. 2 (2003): 22–45.

———. *Now Playing: Early Moviegoing and the Regulation of Fun.* Albany: State University of New York Press, 2008.

Moritz, Theresa, and Albert Moritz. *The World's Most Dangerous Woman: A New Biography of Emma Goldman.* Toronto: University of Toronto Press, 2001.

Morris, Peter. *Embattled Shadows: A History of Canadian Cinema, 1895–1939.* Montreal: McGill-Queen's University Press, 1978.

Pelletier, Louis, and Paul S. Moore. "Une excentrique au coeur de l'industrie: Ray Lewis et le Canadian Moving Picture Digest." *Cinémas* 16, no. 1 (2005): 59–90.

Pendakur, Manjunath. *Canadian Dreams and American Control: The Political Economy of the Canadian Film Industry.* Toronto: Garamond Press, 1990.

Pratley, Gerald. *Torn Sprockets: The Uncertain Projection of the Canadian Film.* Toronto: Associated University Presses, 1987.

Ramsaye, Terry. Review of *Year Book of the Canadian Motion Picture Industry. Motion Picture Herald,* December 15, 1951, 38.

Whitehead, Jessica L., Louis Pelletier, and Paul S. Moore. "'The Girl Friend in Canada': Ray Lewis and *Canadian Moving Picture Digest* (1915–1957)." In *Mapping Movie Magazines: Digitization, Periodicals and Cinema History,* edited by Daniel Biltereyst and Lies Van de Vijver, 127–52. London: Palgrave Macmillan, 2020.

18

Cinema Theaters from Within

Giornale dello Spettacolo's *Success, Longevity, and Data Abundance*

Daniela Treveri Gennari

In 1945, the Associazione Generale Italiana dello Spettacolo (General Italian Association for Entertainment, or AGIS) was established in Italy with the aim of uniting national cinema, theater, music, opera, and dance associations in order to represent their needs and interests. Simultaneously, the association's biweekly trade journal, *Bollettino di informazione*, emerged, and it continues to represent the perspective of the entertainment industry today. Focusing on the editorial commitments of the journal, whose name became *Il Giornale dello Spettacolo* in 1957, this essay aims to investigate its audience, circulation, emergence, and strategies. A unique wealth of information for researchers investigating the history of cinema and the film industry, the *Giornale dello Spettacolo* (*GdS*) is now available online. This chapter will first appraise the emergence of the journal in the historical context of postwar Italy, the most significant period of modernization of the national cultural industry. It will then briefly provide an overview of the different phases of the journal from 1945 to today, highlighting the significant changes it went through and the ways in which the cultural sectors engaged with it. Lastly, it will present the 1950s cinema section as a case study to investigate the journal's unique traits in the mediascape of that time and to finally explore what resources it has provided today to scholars interested in analyzing and commenting on the figures of the film industry in Italy.

INTRODUCTION

Movie magazines and film trade journals as a source and field of research in film and cinema studies have stimulated a wealth of research projects and publications over the years. From using the film press to explore the representation of specific topics to investigations into marketing, reception, and audiences, as well as methodological analyses of these sources and of processes of archival and audiovisual preservation, this subfield is constantly generating new and inspiring research.[1] One of the most recent examples—Biltereyst and Van de Vijver's *Mapping Movie Magazines*—brings together a wide range of contributions that make use of several methods to explore the significance of movie magazines for the study of films, their reception, and their social and aesthetic values, decentralizing the role of films themselves by giving paratexts in their own right the central role in research.[2] However, while this volume reaffirms the opportunity film journals and popular magazines offer for the study of film and cinema more broadly, the editors are keen to declare the limitations of the field, echoing Hoyt's concern that scholars tend to focus only on a few journals like *Variety* while "many other cinema-related periodicals largely remain untouched" and that the bulk of research is still limited to the US, the UK, and a few other countries.[3]

When looking at the Italian context, the literature on film journals and magazines similarly reflects a variety of approaches and methodologies but a symmetrically significant limitation in its investigation due to a scholarly reliance on relatively few publications. Scholars of Italian cinema have used movie magazines for overviews of the history of film publishing and in-depth analyses of film criticism in the popular and specialized presses, as well as for inquiries into fan letters and audience responses. By looking at film periodicals as "an inexhaustible reservoir of materials to be interrogated for research,"[4] this field has developed across several lines of inquiry, exploring movie magazines as part of broader studies on mass culture,[5] on the relationship between Italian intellectuals and film criticism,[6] on the role of the popular press in guiding audiences toward models of stardom, genres, and key figures in cinema history,[7] and on how certain specific themes emerged from movie magazines.[8] Other works have explored how cinema magazines were "capable of orienting and shaping cinema consumption, actively participating in the creation of meaning of film from an aesthetic perspective and of cinema from a social one, in a continuous process of negotiation with other institutions or instances, such as production and the audience."[9] Furthermore, projects have investigated the importance of the paratext in relation to film consumption, film taste, and memories of cinemas by exploring surveys, interviews, and fan letters published in movie magazines.[10]

The body of scholarly work under this particular field developed, from the 1970s, at a slow pace, predominantly due to fragmented and incomplete collections of magazines scattered across Italy in private and public archives that were often under-resourced and not easily accessible. The recent digitization process that several Italian institutions started undergoing, following success-ful examples from abroad, has certainly facilitated the research of magazines and journals buried until now in remote and unreachable libraries and archives. For instance, the Digital Library Luigi Chiarini at the Centro Sperimentale di Cinematografia in Rome[11] has since 2001 digitized a wide range of film maga-zines, press materials, and trade journals with the aim of preserving the most valuable collections from deterioration, guaranteeing their interoperability across different projects, safeguarding intellectual property rights, and ultimately ensuring greater accessibility of the material.[12] The library has successfully coop-erated with other international projects (such as the Periodical Indexing Project and the Federation Internationale des Archives du Film, as well as more recently the Globalizing and Enhancing the Media History Digital Library initiative), securing immediate access to resources on a very large scale.[13] However, this has not accelerated the study of many magazines, and so—as De Luna Freire affirms for the Brazilian case—there are a significant number of Italian cinema journals and publications available digitally which "still await the deeper interest of researchers."[14]

What is missing in this landscape of research on movie magazines and journals is a thorough analysis of the Italian film trade press.[15] While scholars have extensively explored the scholarly content of *Cinema, Cinema Nuovo,* and equally the various sections of more popular magazines such as *Oggi, Famiglia Cristiana,* and the film-specific *Hollywood* and *La Rivista del Cinematografo,* more specialized film trade journals such as *Cinespettacolo* have had less atten-tion from researchers. Within this category, perhaps the case to highlight most urgently is that of *Giornale dello Spettacolo.*[16] From the postwar period onward, the *GdS* has kept researchers informed on the entertainment industry with data so granular that it has no equal across the rest of Europe. The journal is key to understanding the development of exhibition and distribution across the coun-try from the most successful years in Italian cinema to today. Its patchy analy-sis within scholarly research does not depend—as Hoyt suggests in the context of US film periodicals—on the fact that "certain magazines have existed longer than others," as the *GdS*'s longevity exceeds that of any other film trade maga-zine in Italy.[17] It may depend more on the lack of "reference aids" that allow a proper search and investigation into such a rich trove of material.[18] Unlike many other magazines kept in the hands of private collections, found sold in local markets, and scattered in public and private institutions, the *GdS* is present in several public libraries as well as in the AGIS headquarters—where, however, it is only made available to researchers thanks to the kindness of AGIS staff, often unaware of the significance of their collection's value as a window into the indus-trial strategies of Italian cinema both across the national territory and abroad. The *GdS,* therefore, requires an urgent action of digitization to facilitate and expand not only its access, but a fully searchable functionality that would allow scholars to thoroughly explore its content.

GIORNALE DELLO SPETTACOLO: HISTORY AND BACKGROUND

Film magazines started to appear in Italy at the beginning of the 1900s, initially as a publicity vehicle for production and distribution companies. However, beginning in the 1930s some significant changes are evident, turning them into a prolific industry: printed images became cheaper, magazines were "more to be seen than read,"[19] several more titles appeared in print, and the audience for these publications gradually diversified. Furthermore, film criticism was becoming a regular presence in the Italian press through the voices of eminent writers such as Alberto Savinio, Alberto Moravia, and Massimo Bontempelli.[20] However, one had to wait until the 1950s for the arrival of the most prestigious film journals (such as *Cinema, Cinema Nuovo,* and *Filmcritica*) and for the full development of a critical theoretical debate. The 1950s, as Paolo Noto states, witnessed a clear stratification of the editorial system, in which "relatively disengaged magazines, publications dedicated to 'high' popularization, militant magazines[,] and periodicals analyzing cinema as an artistic and social expression" coexisted and even shared collaborators and readers.[21] An incomplete inventory of the movie magazines available in the country reported by Pellizzari indicates that sixty-five new magazines were published during 1930–43, compared to 102 for 1944–48 and 289 for 1949–71, suggesting an exponential growth of the specialized film publishing industry and a burgeoning audience for this wide range of publications.[22]

The postwar period was significant from the film industry perspective, as it was the time when cinema had started reemerging after the end of the war, rebuilding its infrastructure, formulating its laws, and organizing its representative institutions. It is within this context that the *GdS* was born (August 15, 1945), first as *Bollettino di Informazioni,* a biweekly publication of the Lombardy Association of Cinema and Theatre Exhibitors, and since 1952 as *Bollettino dello Spettacolo,* officially affiliated with AGIS (Associazione Generale Italiana dello Spettacolo),[23] the association representing employers in the entertainment sector. AGIS brought together trade associations, federations, and foundations and is still present throughout the country today, with regional and interregional branches. The association represents entrepreneurs in the sectors of cinema exhibition and public and private activities, including theater, music, dance, and popular entertainment, circus, traveling shows, and contemporary popular music. It fulfills the dual function of a body representing the interests of the entertainment industry and a trade union organization offering its members technical, administrative, trade union, fiscal, legal, and communications services.[24]

320   CHAPTER 18

The association was promoted by the heads of the above-mentioned categories first in Lombardy, Piedmont, Veneto, and Liguria, and then across the rest of the country. Its trade journal was ultimately renamed *Il Giornale dello Spettacolo* in 1957 and the headquarters of the association was transferred from Milan to Rome, where it remains. The *GdS* presented several articles updating the members about various categories of information (programming, exhibition, distribution, audiences, etc.), along with broader film industry–related topics and a section of quantitative and qualitative data on films produced and exhibited in cinemas across the country.

The history of the trade journal is obviously intertwined with the various phases of the history of AGIS, which from its birth until the 1980s operated in close relationship with the state and its representatives, especially during the period in which Giulio Andreotti was under secretary of state (1947–53), playing a decisive role within the film industry. Later, AGIS took on its own distinct and clear role as "a counterpart to political, administrative and state power."[25]

The trade journal has lasted until today, updating its layout and becoming a color publication in 2004, with fourteen thousand copies distributed by subscription in Italy and abroad.[26] The journal's print edition was suspended in November 2013 in order to respond to the "very rapid evolution of the world of communication and the difficulties of the printed paper," as explained by Roberto Ferrari, director of Edizioni GdS, the publishing company that prints the journal.[27]

A CASE STUDY: THE *GDS* IN THE 1950s

As Francesco Di Chiara and Paolo Noto observe, "The 1950s are in many ways a crucial decade for understanding postwar Italian cinema."[28] This period was, in fact, a moment of film industrial reconstruction, legislative changes, and successful national productions that managed at times to stand up to the Hollywood invasion of Italian cinema that had characterized the immediate postwar period.[29] It was also a time in which the proliferation of the number of cinemas was "a sign of the general prosperity of the exhibition business, which was not to be repeated at any other time in the 20th century."[30] In this period, more than thirty film magazines and several monographs on film were published, and the film industry drew significant scrutiny in the trade press.[31]

The *GdS* covered developments in the exhibition and distribution sectors useful to those working in the industry, as well as legislation concerning cinema. Additionally, the trade journal offered quantitative data on film programming, box office metrics, and circulation, which allowed exhibitors to fully understand the current industrial state of their category and which still gives scholars the opportunity to evaluate and develop a film industrial history of postwar Italian cinema. The different sections of the journal offered a platform to illustrate new legislative, economic, technological, and political challenges to the exhibition sectors, as well

FIGURE 18.1. A new theater is profiled in *Giornale dello Spettacolo*, May 4, 1957.

as an opportunity for dialogue between exhibitors and the association representing them through the letters to the journal and an all-embracing display of data on exhibition and programming.

Within these broad areas were several topics AGIS members were keen to be updated on, including legislative or procedural changes relevant to them: ticket price amendments;[32] trade union employment laws;[33] agreements between exhibitors and distributors;[34] technological innovation and updates from abroad, like the experimental 3-D glasses developed in the US;[35] world cinema industry reports;[36] information on audience behavior, attendance figures, and programming trends;[37] and surveys on audience preferences.[38]

The journal also devoted a page to letters, a brief section called "Il Gazzettino/ Il Bollettino delle Grane" (The Gazette of Grievances), which allowed exhibitors to openly vent their frustrations and share their concerns with other members on a wide range of topics (from irregular building of cinemas exceeding the approved seating capacity[39] to the new practice of kissing inside cinemas).[40] Lastly, but not irrelevant to a comprehensive research project on cinema exhibition, is the publicity for films and for technical equipment and accessories needed to make cinemas more attractive to audiences. Film advertising is particularly relevant to scholars interested in comparing, for instance, how distributors and exhibitors classified films according to genre and how this might depart from audiences' categorizations.[41] However, any advertising is insightful, as it provides a full picture of how the theaters were attempting to keep up with technologies, resolve their financial challenges, and engage with loyal and new audiences.

All these sections are highly relevant to those investigating postwar exhibition, distribution, and programming strategies, as official accounts are patchy and limited. These sections are also extremely valuable for better comprehending the dynamics between the exhibitors' association and other key players in postwar Italian culture. For example, the Catholic film exhibition circuit, developed in Italy under the tight regulations of the Cinema Catholic Centre, at times represented a threat to the commercial sector, as parish venues often operated as commercial enterprises, infringing several of the strict protocols instructed by the complex agreements between the Associazione Cattolica Esercenti Cinema (Catholic Association of Cinema Exhibitors, or ACEC) and AGIS. In 2018, I conducted a close investigation of the *GdS* that offers a multifaceted picture of the relationship between commercial and religious institutions, highlighting both the "apprehensions of commercial exhibitors about parish cinemas overstepping their boundaries" and the attempt of the parish cinemas "to assert themselves as proper exhibitors."[42] During the 1950s, when the Catholic cinema exhibition circuit was at its peak, the *GdS* became "the arena for industrial exhibitors to express their dissatisfaction about the publicity, programming and types of films shown in parish cinemas, as well as issues around lay management." It also gave commercial exhibitors a platform to express their frustrations with the "high volume of applications to transform parish cinemas into commercial ones," constituting real competition for the sector, as the religious venues were significantly cheaper than the commercial ones and had the strong support of the Catholic Church, extremely powerful at the time.[43] The disputes between commercial and parish cinemas, which characterized the entire decade of the 1950s, exemplify the significant role the journal played in displaying tensions within the sector and offering the reader a better understanding of practices and dynamics not often visible or recorded.

Moreover, from a scholarly perspective, the pages of the *GdS* dedicated to the exhibition figures and programming are extremely valuable, as they provide an account of the programming procedures, the geographic trajectories of the films, the films' popularity, and the audiences' responses at a granular level that allows a highly detailed reconstruction of the postwar cinema industry. At the very beginning of the *GdS*'s history, few data were given. The section "Le cifre parlano chiaro" (The Figures Speak for Themselves) gave the box office intakes of films shown in Rome in first-run cinemas, while the section "Rubrica Film" (Film Section)

FIGURE 18.2. "Borsa Film," *Giornale dello Spettacolo* year 1, no. 25, April 11, 1959.

provided information only on films screened in Milan, with dates, specific cinemas, and numbers of spectators. However, in 1947 the journal started offering more detailed box office figures: for example, it provided information on all Italian films screened in first-run cinemas, including release dates.[44] From 1952, the journal began presenting more regular box office data. The section "Borsa Film" appeared for the first time in September 1952[45] with data for first-, second-, and third-run cinemas in Milan, sharing information on films, production companies, days of screenings, numbers of cinemas, numbers of spectators, and total box office revenues.

The editors explained that this new biweekly section was meant to satisfy readers' requests—especially those of regional exhibitors—by providing insight into the data of first- and second-run cinemas in Milan.[46] On November 30 of the same year, a short explanatory note informed readers that, because of the success of "Borsa Film," the section would also start providing data on other Italian cities, starting with Turin (first run)[47] and then Rome[48] and Genoa,[49] as well as a yearly summary of major successes classified by production company.[50] From May 15, 1953, together with those of Rome, Genoa, Turin, and Milan, several other cities'[51] first-run cinemas' box office intakes and numbers of screening days were published.[52] And beginning on November 30, 1953, a new section entitled "Statistiche istruttive" (Instructive Statistics) reported the average gross revenue achieved on each day of programming in major Italian cities.[53] Starting in 1955, several additional sections contained box office data. From January 27, 1955, "Borsa Film" changed and the reading of the box office was divided as follows: films according to nationality, box office figures for first-run cinemas in the sixteen main cities, and cities where the films had been screened. "Tirando le somme" (Summing Up), written by the journalist Alessandro Ferraù with the intention of filling the gap of essential box office analysis, is a section that became a regular presence in the trade journal, analyzing successes and failures in the country (such as films generating more than 100 million lire or less than 50 million lire at the box office), as well as detailed box office evaluation amongst the main cities according to film nationalities (Italian, US, European, and others) and a comparative analysis of Italian films in cinemas around the country, according to genre, stars, and locations.

324   CHAPTER 18

Ferraù's insightful analyses are still invaluable today for their information on film consumption and popularity across the country. They also reflect on key aspects of the development of cinema in those years, from Cinemascope and color to geographic differences in relation to art cinema and documentaries, genre, nationality, and stardom. Ultimately, they not only offer a portrait of the industrial dynamics at play in film exhibition and the means by which this is reflected in film consumption, but also allow researchers to explore the Italian film industry in a longitudinal way, mapping changes and developments across time that would not otherwise be possible.

CONCLUSION

Hoyt's suggestion to "reevaluate the ways we are selecting, using, and interpreting motion-picture trade papers and fan magazines" is still very pertinent today for the Italian context.[54] Several trade journals and popular magazines remain unexplored as sources of data and of case studies for investigations of publishing practices within the film industry. Digitization and accessibility play a crucial part in integrating these materials with others already in the scholarly domain. However, collaborations across libraries, archival institutions, universities, and digital humanities centers are key to providing the most fruitful opportunity to ensure that funding is made available and resources are properly integrated to facilitate further research and comparative work. For the case of *Il Giornale dello Spettacolo*, a comprehensive process of computational analysis would guarantee cross-examination of the rich data available in the journal and promote new findings across cinema exhibition practices, film consumption, and the distribution industry.

NOTES

1. Martin Levin, *Hollywood and the Great Fan Magazines* (New York: William Morrow, 1977); Kathryn H. Fuller-Seeley, *At the Picture Show: Small-Town Audiences and the Creation of Movie Fan Culture* (Charlottesville: University Press of Virginia, 1996); Samantha Barbas, *Movie Crazy: Fans, Stars, and the Cult of Celebrity* (New York: Palgrave Macmillan, 2002); Adrienne L. McLean, "'New Films in Story Form': Movie Story Magazines and Spectatorship," *Cinema Journal* 42, no. 3 (2003): 3–26; Marsha Orgeron, "'You Are Invited to Participate': Interactive Fandom in the Age of Movie Magazine," *Journal of Film and Video* 61, no. 3 (2009): 3–23; Anthony Slide, *Inside the Hollywood Fan Magazine: A History of Star Makers, Fabricators, and Gossip Mongers* (Jackson: University Press of Mississippi, 2010); Mark Glancy, "*Picturegoer*: The Fan Magazine and Popular Film Culture in Britain During the Second World War," *Historical Journal of Film, Radio and Television* 31, no. 4 (2011): 453–78; Michael Cowan, "Learning to Love the Movies: Puzzles, Participation, and Cinephilia in Interwar European Film Magazines," *Film History* 27, no. 4 (2015): 1–45; Rafael De Luna Freire, "Investigation and Preservation of Old Brazilian Cinema Newspapers," *Mercosul Audiovisual* 1, no. 1 (2018): 51–61.

2. Daniel Biltereyst and Lies Van de Vijver, eds., *Mapping Movie Magazines: Digitization, Periodicals and Cinema History* (London: Palgrave Macmillan, 2020).

3. Biltereyst and Van de Vijver, *Mapping Movie Magazines*, 1. See also Eric Hoyt, "Lenses for Lantern: Data Mining, Visualization, and Excavating Film History's Neglected Sources," *Film History* 26, no. 2 (2014): 146–68.

4. Raffaele De Berti, *Dallo schermo alla carta. Romanzi, fotoromanzi, rotocalchi cinematografici: il film e i suoi paratesti* (Milan, Italy: Vita e Pensiero, 2000), 4. See also Cristina Bragaglia, "Le riviste di cinema," in *Materiali sul cinema italiano degli anni '50, vol. 1: Quaderni di documentazione della Mostra Internazionale del Nuovo Cinema, no. 74* (Pesaro, Italy: 1978); see also Davide Turconi and Camillo Bassotto, eds., *Il cinema nelle riviste italiane dalle origini ad oggi* (Venice: Edizioni Mostracinema, 1972).

5. See David Forgacs, *L'industrializzazione della cultura italiana (1880–2000)* (Bologna, Italy: Il Mulino, 2000). See also Raffaele De Berti, "La stampa popolare e il cinema," in *Il prodotto culturale*, ed. Fausto Colombo and Ruggero Eugeni, 73–92 (Rome: Carocci, 2001).

6. Paolo Noto, "Quale 'mestiere del critico'? Un'intrusione nella corrispondenza di Guido Aristarco," *Cinergie* 8, no. 15 (2019): 55–67.

7. See, for example, De Berti, *Dallo schermo alla carta*; Raffaele De Berti, "Il cinema fuori dallo schermo," in *Storia del cinema italiano 1949–1953, vol. 8: Edizioni di Bianco & Nero*, ed. Luciano De Giusti, 116–29 (Venice: Marsilio, 2003); Emiliano Morreale, ed., *Lo schermo di carta. Storia e storie dei cineromanzi* (Milan, Italy: Il Castoro, 2007); Raffaele De Berti and Irene Piazzoni, eds., *Forme e modelli del rotocalco italiano tra fascismo e guerra*, Quaderni di Acme, 115 (Milan, Italy: Cisalpino, October 2–3, 2008); Claudio Bisoni, *La critica cinematografica. Un'introduzione* (Bologna, Italy: CLUEB, Cooperativa Libraria Universitaria Editrice Bologna, 2013); Diego Cavallotti, "To the Anonymous Video-Maker: Subjectivity Construction in Italian Amateur Photo-Film-Video Magazines between 1975 and 1985," in *A History of Cinema without Names: A Research Project*, ed. Diego Cavallotti, Federico Giordano, and Leonardo Quaresima (Milan, Italy: Mimesis, 2016), 263–71; Paolo Noto, "Immagini del pubblico nella stampa cinematografica italiana degli anni Cinquanta," *Cinema e Storia* 7, no. 1 (2018): 31–46; Alfonso Venturini, "Lettere a Nostromo. La corrispondenza con i lettori della rivista 'Cinema' dal 1937 al 1943," *L'avventura: International Journal of Italian Film and Media Landscapes* 4, no. 1 (2018): 93–108; Mariapia Comand and Andrea Mariani, *Ephemera. Scrapbooks, fan mail e diari delle spettatrici nell'Italia del Regime*, ricerche (Venice: Marsilio, 2020).

8. Andrea Minuz, "I 'valori spirituali del cinema italiano.' Antisemitismo e politica della razza nelle riviste cinematografiche degli anni trenta," *Trauma and Memory* 5, no. 3 (2017): 96–102; Mauro Giori, "La fotografia nelle riviste di cinema italiane (1907–1918)," in *Moltiplicare l'istante. Beltrami, Comerio e Pacchioni tra fotografia e cinema*, ed. Elena Dagrada, Elena Mosconi, and Silvia Paoli (Milan, Italy: Il Castoro, 2007), 125–38.

9. Francesco Di Chiara and Paolo Noto, "I padroni del cinema italiano: il rapporto tra critica e produzione nella stampa cinematografica degli anni Cinquanta," in *Atti critici in luoghi pubblici: scrivere di cinema, tv e media dal dopoguerra al web, vol. 7: Pandora comunicazione, Cinema*, ed. Michele Guerra and Sara Martin (Parma, Italy: Diabasis, 2019), 499.

10. Daniela Treveri Gennari et al., *Italian Cinema Audiences: Histories and Memories of Cinema-Going in Post-war Italy* (New York: Bloomsbury Academic, 2020).

11. "Biblioteca digitale," *Fondazione Centro Sperimentale di Cinematografia*, https://www.fondazionecsc.it/biblioteca-digitale-biblioteca-luigi-chiarini/ (accessed December 3, 2020).

12. Laura Ceccarelli and Laura Pompei, "Biblioteca digitale," in *Viaggio tra le stelle del cinema con la rivista STAR*, Quaderni della Biblioteca Luigi Chiarini (Rome: Fondazione Centro Sperimentale di Cinematografia, 2009), 9.

13. Ibid.; Debora Demontis and Stefania Tuveri, "Spoglio periodici," in *Viaggio tra le stelle del cinema con la rivista STAR*, Quaderni della Biblioteca Luigi Chiarini (Rome: Fondazione Centro Sperimentale di Cinematografia, 2009), 13.

14. De Luna Freire, "Investigation and Preservation," 55.

326   CHAPTER 18

15. Di Chiara and Noto, *I padroni del cinema italiano*, 509–10.

16. Abbreviated *GdS* hereafter.

17. Hoyt, "Lenses for Lantern," 154.

18. Ibid.

19. De Berti, *Dallo schermo alla carta*, 110.

20. Ibid., 5–6; Lorenzo Pellizzari, "Il cinema pensato: tra liberazione e colonizzazione," in *Storia del cinema italiano 1945–1948, vol. 7: Edizioni di Bianco & Nero*, ed. Callisto Cosulich (Venice: Marsilio, 2003), 467; Giori, "La fotografia nelle riviste," 127; Bisoni, *La critica cinematografica*, 34. For a comprehensive list of cinema magazines of the period 1907–44, see Riccardo Redi, ed., *Cinema scritto. Il catalogo delle riviste italiane di cinema 1907–1944* (Rome: Associazione italiana per le ricerche di storia del cinema, 1992).

21. Noto, "Immagini del pubblico," 32.

22. Pellizzari, "Il cinema pensato," 468.

23. AGIS was established on December 7, 1945.

24. AGIS, "Mission," https://www.agisweb.it/chi-siamo/ (accessed December 4, 2020).

25. Gian Piero Brunetta, *Storia del cinema italiano. Dal neorealismo al miracolo economico 1945–1959* (Rome: Editori Riuniti); "AGIS," *Treccani*, https://www.treccani.it/enciclopedia/agis_%28Enciclopedia-del-Cinema%29/ (accessed December 10, 2020).

26. "I 60 anni del Giornale dello Spettacolo," *GDM*, https://www.giornaledellamusica.it/news/i-60-anni-del-giornale-dello-spettacolo (last modified February 11, 2004).

27. "Il Giornale dello Spettacolo termina le pubblicazioni," *E-Duesse.it*, http://www.e-duesse.it/News/Cinema/Il-Giornale-dello-Spettacolo-termina-le-pubblicazioni-163108 (last modified December 2, 2013).

28. Di Chiara and Noto, "I padroni del cinema italiano," 499.

29. Vito Zagarrio, "L'industria italiana tra crisi della produzione e boom dell'esercizio," in *Storia del cinema italiano 1945–1948, vol. 7: Edizioni di Bianco & Nero*, ed. Callisto Cosulich, 363–87 (Venice: Marsilio, 2003).

30. Elena Mosconi, "Tanti punti di proiezione," in *Storia del cinema italiano 1949–1953, vol. 8: Edizioni di Bianco & Nero*, ed. Luciano De Giusti (Venice: Marsilio, 2003), 177.

31. Bisoni, *La critica cinematografica*, 43.

32. B, "Il Sovrapprezzo Invernale," *Bollettino di informazioni* year 6, no. 10, October 1–15, 1950, 1.

33. "In Sintesi le Assunzioni Obbligatorie," *Bollettino di informazioni* year 7, no. 116, February 15, 1951, 2.

34. "Disciplina Legale al Noleggio di Film," *Bollettino dello Spettacolo* year 8, no. 151–52, August 15–31, 1952, 1.

35. Angiolo Maros Dell'Oro, "Tre-dimensioni con Cine-occhiali," *Bollettino dello Spettacolo* year 7, no. 15, October 15, 1952, 2.

36. "Qua e là per il Mondo del Cinema," *Bollettino dello Spettacolo* year 9, no. 161, January 15, 1953, 3.

37. De Luca, "Il Rapporto Contrattuale tra l'Esercente e lo Spettatore," *Bollettino dello Spettacolo* year 10, no. 199, May 10, 1954, 1.

38. Alessandro Ferraù, "Dall'Indagine del Centro per la Cinematografia Utili Indicazioni sulle Tendenze del Pubblico," *Bollettino dello Spettacolo* year 11, no. 220, January 13, 1955, 3.

39. Bru, "Posto più Posto meno," *Bollettino dello Spettacolo* year 8, no. 155, October 15, 1952, 3.

40. "Processo al Bacio," *Bollettino dello Spettacolo* year 11, no. 221, January 20, 1955, 1.

41. Treveri Gennari et al., *Italian Cinema Audiences*.

42. Daniela Treveri Gennari, "'L'esercente industriale non scocci': Mapping exhibition tensions between commercial and parish cinemas in post-war Italy," *Schermi* 2, no. 3 (January–June 2018): 150.

43. Ibid.

44. "Incassi di Film Italiani," *Bollettino di informazioni*, 1947, 3.

GIORNALE DELLO SPETTACOLO'S SUCCESS   327

45. "Borsa Film," *Bollettino dello Spettacolo* year 7, no. 154, September 30, 1952, 4.
46. Ibid.
47. "Borsa Film," *Bollettino dello Spettacolo* year 8, no. 158, November 30, 1952, 2.
48. "Borsa Film," *Bollettino dello Spettacolo* year 8, no. 159, December 15, 1952, 2.
49. "Borsa Film," *Bollettino dello Spettacolo* year 8, no. 160, December 31, 1952, 5.
50. In this year (1952) a new name was also given to the journal, *Bollettino dello spettacolo, quindicinale AGIS d'informazioni* (a weekly from 1955).
51. Naples, Catania, Palermo, Bologna, Trieste, Firenze, Venice, and Padova.
52. "Borsa Film," *Bollettino dello Spettacolo* year 9, no. 170, May 15, 1953, 2.
53. "Statistiche Istruttive," *Bollettino dello Spettacolo* year 9, no. 184, November 30, 1953, 5.
54. Hoyt, "Lenses for Lantern," 148.

PUBLICATIONS REFERENCED

Cinema
Cinema Nuovo
Cinespettacolo
Famiglia Cristiana
Filmcritica
Hollywood
Il Giornale dello Spettacolo (formerly *Bollettino di informazione* and then *Bollettino dello Spettacolo*)
La Rivista del Cinematografo
Oggi

BIBLIOGRAPHY

AGIS. "Mission." https://www.agisweb.it/chi-siamo/. Accessed December 4, 2020.
"Agis." *Treccani.* https://www.treccani.it/enciclopedia/agis_%28Enciclopedia-del-Cinema%29/. Accessed December 10, 2020.
B. "Il sovrapprezzo invernale." *Bollettino di informazioni* year 6, no. 10 (October 1–15, 1950).
Barbas, Samantha. *Movie Crazy: Fans, Stars, and the Cult of Celebrity.* New York: Palgrave Macmillan, 2002.
Biltereyst, Daniel, and Lies Van de Vijver, eds. *Mapping Movie Magazines: Digitization, Periodicals and Cinema History.* New York: Palgrave Macmillan, 2020.
Bisoni, Claudio. *La critica cinematografica. Un'introduzione.* Bologna, Italy: CLUEB, Cooperativa Libraria Universitaria Editrice Bologna, 2013.
"Borsa Film." *Bollettino dello Spettacolo* year 7, no. 154 (September 30, 1952), 4.
———. *Bollettino dello Spettacolo* year 8, no. 158 (November 30, 1952), 2.
———. *Bollettino dello Spettacolo* year 8, no. 159 (December 15, 1952), 2.
———. *Bollettino dello Spettacolo* year 8, no. 160 (December 31, 1952), 5.
———. *Bollettino dello Spettacolo* year 9, no. 184 (November 30, 1953), 5.
Bragaglia, Cristina. "Le riviste di cinema." In *Materiali sul cinema italiano degli anni '50, vol. 1.* Quaderni di documentazione della Mostra Internazionale del Nuovo Cinema, no. 74. Pesaro, Italy, 1978.
Bru. "Posto più posto meno." *Bollettino dello Spettacolo* year 8, no. 155 (October 15, 1952).
Brunetta, Gian Piero. *Storia del cinema italiano. Dal neorealismo al miracolo economico 1945–1959.* Rome: Editori Riuniti, 2000.
Cavallotti, Diego. "To the Anonymous Video-Maker: Subjectivity Construction in Italian Amateur Photo-Film-Video Magazines between 1975 and 1985." In *A History of Cinema Without Names:*

328 CHAPTER 18

A Research Project, ed. Diego Cavallotti, Federico Giordano, and Leonardo Quaresima, 263–71. Milan, Italy: Mimesis, 2016.

Ceccarelli, Laura, and Laura Pompei. "Biblioteca digitale." In *Viaggio tra le stelle del cinema con la rivista STAR*, Quaderni della Biblioteca Luigi Chiarini, 9. Rome: Fondazione Centro Sperimentale di Cinematografia, 2009.

Centro Sperimentale di Cinematografia. "Biblioteca digitale." *Fondazione Centro Sperimentale di Cinematografia.* https://www.fondazionecsc.it/biblioteca-digitale-biblioteca-luigi-chiarini/. Accessed December 3, 2020.

Comand, Mariapia, and Andrea Mariani. *Ephemera. Scrapbooks, fan mail e diari delle spettatrici nell'Italia del Regime*, ricerche. Venice: Marsilio, 2020.

Cowan, Michael. "Learning to Love the Movies: Puzzles, Participation, and Cinephilia in Interwar European Film Magazines." *Film History* 27, no. 4 (2015): 1–45.

De Berti, Raffaele. *Dallo schermo alla carta. Romanzi, fotoromanzi, rotocalchi cinematografici: il film e i suoi paratesti*. Milan, Italy: Vita e Pensiero, 2000.

———. "Il cinema fuori dallo schermo." In *Storia del cinema italiano 1949–1953, vol. 8, Edizioni di Bianco & Nero*, edited by Luciano De Giusti, 116–29. Venice: Marsilio, 2003.

———. "La stampa popolare e il cinema." In *Il prodotto culturale*, edited by Fausto Colombo and Ruggero Eugeni, 73–92. Rome: Carocci, 2001.

De Berti, Raffaele, and Irene Piazzoni, eds. *Forme e modelli del rotocalco italiano tra fascismo e guerra*. Quaderni di Acme, 115. Milan, Italy: Cisalpino, October 2–3, 2008.

De Luca. "Il rapporto contrattuale tra l'esercente e lo spettatore." *Bollettino dello Spettacolo* year 10, no. 199 (May 10, 1954), 1.

De Luna Freire, Rafael. "Investigation and Preservation of Old Brazilian Cinema Newspapers." *Mercosul Audiovisual* 1, no. 1 (2018): 51–61.

Dell'Oro, Angiolo Maros. "Tre-dimensioni con cine-occhiali." *Bollettino dello Spettacolo* year 7, no. 15 (October 15, 1952), 2.

Demontis, Debora, and Stefania Tuveri. "Spoglio periodici." In *Viaggio tra le stelle del cinema con la rivista STAR*, Quaderni della Biblioteca Luigi Chiarini, 13. Rome: Fondazione Centro Sperimentale di Cinematografia, 2009.

Di Chiara, Francesco, and Paolo Noto. "I padroni del cinema italiano: il rapporto tra critica e produzione nella stampa cinematografica degli anni Cinquanta." In *Atti critici in luoghi pubblici: scrivere di cinema, tv e media dal dopoguerra al web, vol. 7*, edited by Michele Guerra and Sara Martin, 499–510. *Pandora comunicazione. Cinema.* Parma, Italy: Diabasis, 2019.

"Disciplina legale al noleggio di film." *Bollettino dello Spettacolo* year 8, no. 151–52 (August 15–31, 1952), 1.

Ferraù, Alessandro. "Dall'indagine del Centro per la Cinematografia utili indicazioni sulle tendenze del pubblico." *Bollettino dello Spettacolo* year 11, no. 220 (January 13, 1955).

Forgacs, David. *L'industrializzazione della cultura italiana (1880–2000)*. Bologna, Italy: Il Mulino, 2000.

Fuller-Seeley, Kathryn H. *At the Picture Show: Small-Town Audiences and the Creation of Movie Fan Culture*. Charlottesville: University Press of Virginia, 1996.

GDM. "I 60 anni del *Giornale dello Spettacolo*." *GDM.* Last modified February 11, 2004. https://www.giornaledellamusica.it/news/i-60-anni-del-giornale-dello-spettacolo.

Giori, Mauro. "La fotografia nelle riviste di cinema italiane (1907–1918)." In *Moltiplicare l'istante. Beltrami, Comerio e Pacchioni tra fotografia e cinema*, edited by Elena Dagrada, Elena Mosconi, and Silvia Paoli, 125–38. Milan, Italy: Il Castoro, 2007.

Glancy, Mark. "*Picturegoer*: The Fan Magazine and Popular Film Culture in Britain during the Second World War." *Historical Journal of Film, Radio and Television* 31, no. 4 (2011): 453–78.

Hoyt, Eric. "Lenses for Lantern: Data Mining, Visualization, and Excavating Film History's Neglected Sources." *Film History* 26, no. 2 (2014): 146–68.

"Il Giornale dello Spettacolo termina le pubblicazioni." *E-Duesse.it.* Last modified December 2, 2013. http://www.e-duesse.it/News/Cinema/Il-Giornale-dello-Spettacolo-termina-le-pubblicazioni-163108.

"In sintesi le assunzioni obbligatorie." *Bollettino di informazioni* year 7, no. 116 (February 15, 1951).

"Incassi di film italiani." *Bollettino di informazioni.* 1947.

Levin, Martin. *Hollywood and the Great Fan Magazines.* New York: William Morrow, 1977.

McLean, Adrienne L. "'New Films in Story Form': Movie Story Magazines and Spectatorship." *Cinema Journal* 42, no. 3 (2003): 3–26.

Minuz, Andrea. "I 'valori spirituali del cinema italiano.' Antisemitismo e politica della razza nelle riviste cinematografiche degli anni trenta." *Trauma and Memory* 5, no. 3 (2017): 96–102.

Morreale, Emiliano, ed. *Lo schermo di carta. Storia e storie dei cineromanzi.* Milan, Italy: Il Castoro, 2007.

Mosconi, Elena. "Tanti punti di proiezione." In *Storia del cinema italiano 1949-1953, vol. 8: Edizioni di Bianco & Nero,* edited by Luciano De Giusti, 177–187. Venice: Marsilio, 2003.

Noto, Paolo. "Immagini del pubblico nella stampa cinematografica italiana degli anni Cinquanta." *Cinema e Storia* 7, no. 1 (2018): 31–46.

———. "Quale 'mestiere del critico'? Un'intrusione nella corrispondenza di Guido Aristarco." *Cinergie* 8, no. 15 (2019): 55–67.

Orgeron, Marsha. "'You Are Invited to Participate': Interactive Fandom in the Age of the Movie Magazine." *Journal of Film and Video* 61, no. 3 (2009): 3–23.

Pellizzari, Lorenzo. "Il cinema pensato: tra liberazione e colonizzazione." In *Storia del cinema italiano 1945-1948, vol. 7: Edizioni di Bianco & Nero,* edited by Callisto Cosulich. Venice: Marsilio, 2003.

"Processo al bacio." *Bollettino dello Spettacolo* year 11, no. 221 (January 20, 1955), 1.

"Qua e là per il mondo del cinema." *Bollettino dello Spettacolo* year 9, no. 161 (January 15, 1953), 3.

Redi, Riccardo, ed. *Cinema scritto. Il catalogo delle riviste italiane di cinema 1907-1944.* Rome: Associazione italiana per le ricerche di storia del cinema, 1992.

Slide, Anthony. *Inside the Hollywood Fan Magazine: A History of Star Makers, Fabricators, and Gossip Mongers.* Jackson: University Press of Mississippi, 2010.

"Statistiche Istruttive." *Bollettino dello Spettacolo* year 9, no. 184 (November 30, 1953), 4.

Treveri Gennari, Daniela. "'L'esercente industriale non scocci': Mapping exhibition tensions between commercial and parish cinemas in post-war Italy." *Schermi* 2, no. 3 (January–June 2018): 137–54.

Treveri Gennari, Daniela, Catherine O'Rawe, Danielle Hipkins, Silvia Dibeltulo, and Sarah Culhane. *Italian Cinema Audiences: Histories and Memories of Cinema-Going in Post-war Italy.* New York: Bloomsbury Academic, 2020.

Turconi, Davide, and Camillo Bassotto, eds. *Il cinema nelle riviste italiane dalle origini ad oggi.* Venice: Edizioni Mostracinema, 1972.

Venturini, Alfonso. "Lettere a Nostromo. La corrispondenza con i lettori della rivista *Cinema* dal 1937 al 1943." *L'avventura. International Journal of Italian Film and Media Landscapes* 4, no. 1 (2018): 93–108.

Zagarrio, Vito. "L'industria italiana tra crisi della produzione e boom dell'esercizio." In *Storia del cinema italiano 1945-1948, vol. 7: Edizioni di Bianco & Nero,* edited by Callisto Cosulich, 363–87. Venice: Marsilio, 2003.

19

Searching for Similarity

Computational Analysis and the US Film Industry Trade Press of the Early 1920s

Eric Hoyt, Ben Pettis, Lesley Stevenson, and Sam Hansen

During the early 1920s, few niche businesses were more crowded than the trade press of the US film industry. *Moving Picture World, Motion Picture News*, and *Exhibitor's Trade Review* published in New York City and competed for dominance among a nationwide readership. Many more regional papers sprang up in the nation's distribution hubs, such as Atlanta, Chicago, Kansas City, and Minneapolis, to serve their local industry communities. And yet still more trade papers covered the movies: *Camera!* published in Los Angeles for the production community; *Harrison's Reports* issued weekly reviews that were "free from the influence of film advertising"; and the most famous entertainment trade paper of all, *Variety*, reported on the movies alongside vaudeville and "legitimate theatre."

How unique were these trade papers? This is a question relevant to today's researchers, who encounter all of the above-mentioned trade papers (and more) when running searches within the Media History Digital Library's search platform, Lantern. Is a review in *Exhibitor's Trade Review* interchangeable with a review in *Exhibitors Herald*? Should a news item that appears in *Motion Picture News* be interpreted any differently than one that appears in *Moving Picture World*?

Questions of similarity (and its inverse, distinctiveness) were also on the minds of the publications' original readers and editors more than a century ago. Exhibitors "are watching the motion picture journals more or less critically," observed W. Stephen Bush in 1917, who had recently left his position editing *Moving Picture World* to take a leadership role at *Exhibitor's Trade Review*.[1] The motion picture distributors purchased large amounts of advertising within the same trade papers that reviewed their products. Could the reviews be trusted? How much of the new content was the work of the papers' own writers, editors, and correspondents? And how much of it was barely edited reprints of press releases, the work of studio publicists? "The reading pages of the motion picture trade papers are loaded with press matter from the various manufacturers," alleged one industry executive at the time.[2]

Within this environment of mistrust, the trade papers competed for readers and subscribers by emphasizing their independence, originality, and distinctiveness. In *Ink-Stained Hollywood: The Triumph of American Cinema's Trade Press*, one-quarter of our team (Eric Hoyt) chronicled the rivalries among trade papers and their significance to communities within the industry.[3] His research utilized a range of sources and methods, including investigating court archives, performing quantitative content analysis, and reading countless issues of the trades. But one question lingers: Just how much overlap and similarity were there among the trade papers in using the same press releases and language?

This question matters not simply for assessing each publication's claim to a singular identity but also for understanding the early cultural norms that shaped an industry that now dominates global media, communication, and culture. If these papers truly offered unique insights and stories, then we can view the landscape of contemporary Hollywood as emerging from a genuine dialogue that represented the widely varying perspectives of people with different roles in the industry. Conversely, if the papers promoted themselves as distinct but merely parroted the same information and even spoke in similar styles, should we instead understand early industry workers as cogs in a machine that has never recognized their labor as distinctive or agential?

We turn to these questions with computational analysis methods. Text similarity measurement algorithms are widely used throughout the internet, for purposes as varied as purchasing concert tickets and flagging papers for plagiarism. If we ran similar algorithms on a corpus of trade papers from the year 1922, what patterns might emerge? Many publications carefully crafted distinct identities and claims to individuality, but how unique was the content that appeared within their pages? How might the results confirm, complicate, or complement what we already know? The nuances of the language in each publication would have helped create in-groups and out-groups that not only segmented groups within the film industry but also defined the boundaries of the industry itself. Understanding the relative similarities and differences among publications allows us to assess these publications' claims to individuality. Even more significantly for scholars of film, journalism, and media industry history, these measurements also help us understand the environment in which individual laborers were producing, distributing, and exhibiting films.

In this chapter, we discuss the process and outcomes of an exploratory study on the use of computational methods to assess large volumes of motion picture trade papers. We begin by introducing our corpus—twenty-one digitized volumes of trade papers and fan magazines. We briefly discuss the publications' backgrounds and industry profiles, including the ways they presented themselves and the ways in which they were perceived by readers. Second, we explain the computational methods that we used for measuring text similarity. We try to keep our descriptions clear and succinct while pointing readers who want to dive deeper into the specific techniques and suggestions for where to turn next. Finally, we share the results of our research study and reflect on the process and its potential broader utility for film history research. We contend that computational methods like text similarity measurement are a useful complement to traditional research methods of archival research and close reading, enabling research questions that might otherwise not be feasible for human researchers to investigate alone, particularly when working with large corpora.

UNDERSTANDING THE CORPUS: FILM INDUSTRY TRADE PRESS OF 1922

We began this project, quite naively, with the idea to run similarity measurements across the nearly three million pages available online in the Media History Digital Library (MHDL).[4] However, this proved unfeasible due to the computational processing power and time that would be required.[5] Moreover, we realized there would be advantages to narrowing our focus to a single year. We selected the year 1922, with an emphasis on July 1922, for two chief reasons. First, the MHDL had already digitized a wide cross section of trade papers from that year, including— appropriately for this book—several published outside of the United States. Second, we knew from Eric's earlier research that there was a great deal of competition within the American film industry's trade press during this period.

In 1922, *Variety* and the Chicago-based *Exhibitors Herald* were pursuing strategies to grow their readership and influence within the industry, emphasizing independence, integrity, and uniqueness as distinguishing factors. During the following year, *Exhibitors Herald* created the "'Herald Only' Club," emphasizing the loyalty of subscribers who exclusively wrote into *Exhibitors Herald* and read that paper at the exclusion of its rivals.[6] Given the competitive bent of the 1920s trade press, how distinct was each publication? Would the "'Herald Only' Club" have any factual grounding once the word patterns, sentences, and page structures were analyzed at scale?

In addition to the above-mentioned trade papers, we included sixteen additional unique journals. Our corpus included fan magazines (*Photoplay, Shadowland,* and *The Picturegoer*), a technical journal (*American Cinematographer*), English-language trade papers published outside the US (*Canadian Moving Picture Digest* and *The Film Renter and Moving Picture News*), and studio-generated publicity (*Universal Weekly* and *Paramount Pep*). When subjected to computational analysis, this mix of film publications held the potential for both expected and surprising similarities to emerge (see table 19.1). [tabref 19.1]

TABLE 19.1 Corpus of Selected 1922 Trade Papers

Publication	Location	Dates	URL
American Cinematographer, The	Los Angeles, US	July 1922	http://archive.org/details/americancinemato00amer
Camera	Los Angeles, US	April 1922–April 1923	http://archive.org/details/camera05unse
Canadian Moving Picture Digest	Toronto, CA	May–October 1922	https://archive.org/details/canadian-moving-picture-digest-1922-05
Cine-Mundial	New York, US	1922	http://archive.org/details/cinemundial07unse
Cinéa	Paris, FR	1922	http://archive.org/details/cina22pari
Exhibitor's Trade Review	New York, US	June–August 1922	http://archive.org/details/exhibitorstra00newy
Exhibitors Herald	Chicago, US	July–September 1922	http://archive.org/details/exhibitorsherald15exhi
Exhibitors Herald	Chicago, US	October–December 1922	http://archive.org/details/exhibitorsherald15exhi_0
Film Daily, The	New York, US	1922	http://www.archive.org/details/filmdaily2122newy
Film Renter and Moving Picture News, The	London, UK	July–August 1922	https://archive.org/details/film-renter-and-moving-picture-news-1922-07
Great Selection: "First National First" Season 1922–1923, The	New York, US	1922	http://archive.org/details/greatsel00firs
Kinematograph, Der	Düsseldorf, DE	July 1922	https://archive.org/details/kinematograph-1922-07
Motion Picture News	New York, US	July–August 1922	http://archive.org/details/motionpicturenew26july
Motion Picture Studio, The	London, UK	June 1922–February 1923	http://archive.org/details/motionpicturestu02unse
Moving Picture World	New York, US	July–August 1922	http://archive.org/details/movingpicturewor57july
Paramount Pep	New York, US	July–December 1922	http://archive.org/details/paramountpepjuld07unse
Photoplay	Chicago, US	July–December 1922	http://www.archive.org/details/photoplayvolume222chic
Picturegoer	London, UK	1922	http://archive.org/details/picturegoer34odha
Shadowland	New York, US	January–May 1922	http://archive.org/details/shadowland192200brew

(*Continued*)

334 CHAPTER 19

TABLE 19.1 (*Continued*)

Publication	Location	Dates	URL
Tess of the Storm Country (United Artists Pressbook)	Los Angeles, US	1922	http://archive.org/details/pressbook-ua-tess
Universal Weekly	New York, US	1922	http://archive.org/details/universal1516univ
Variety	New York, US	July 1922	https://archive.org/details/variety67-1922-07

NOTE: The date range varies between publications depending on how each was compiled and digitized. Each volume may contain multiple issues of a given publication.

TABLE 19.2 Top Volume Pairings Arranged by Set Distance

Pairing	Set distance	Volume A	Volume B
1	94.3168875	*The Great Selection*	*Motion Picture News* (July–August 1922)
2	92.6631758	*Exhibitors Herald* (July–September 1922)	*The Great Selection*
3	92.2992333	*Film Daily* (1922)	*The Great Selection*
4	91.8996811	*The Great Selection*	*Exhibitors Herald* (October–December 1922)
5	91.7403586	*Exhibitor's Trade Review* (June–August 1922)	*The Great Selection*

For all of the strengths of this corpus, though, we acknowledge that it is nevertheless an incomplete cross section of the 1920s trade press. Due to the limited availability of digitized scans, there were many journals that we were unable to include. The Philadelphia-based *Harrison's Reports*, for example, featured film reviews, a fiery editorial page, and no advertisements; editor P. S. Harrison's proclaimed independence from outside interests and allegiance to independent exhibitors would make this publication a valuable point of comparison to other trade papers of the time. Unfortunately, the MHDL's thirty-four-year digitized run of *Harrison's Reports* does not begin until 1928—nine years after it began publishing—due to the MHDL's inability to access print originals for scanning. We also lacked digitized copies of the once numerous, now rare-to-find, regional trade papers that sprang up in the late 1910s and early 1920s to serve distribution exchange cities and territories such as Atlanta, Kansas City, and Minneapolis. The two papers in our corpus that were sometimes classified as regionals—Chicago's *Exhibitors Herald* and Toronto's *Canadian Moving Picture Digest*—both vigorously resented and pushed back against the "regional" designation by the early 1920s.

Despite these limitations, the 1922 corpus features many significant US trade papers of that era plus many other publications that could potentially serve as litmus tests for the process as a whole. If, for example, our computational methods indicated that the German-language *Der Kinematograph* is highly similar to *The Film Daily* or *Photoplay*, then something about the process must be inaccurate. But if our various similarity tests could reliably identify high-level similarities and significant differences between publications, it would enable us to select specific texts from the larger corpus to perform traditional close readings on.

The use of computational methods alongside traditional humanities approaches can help researchers work with enormous volumes of content. If, after analysis by a computer and close reading by a researcher, the discourse among these publications registers substantial differences, then we have an indication that robust conversation gave early industrial figures opportunities to make choices about the direction of the business. If, conversely, all publications were to receive high similarity scores across these metrics, then we would have an indication that certain topics, events, and even actual content repeats across the industrial ecosystem. The ability to perform close readings across a large corpus of text is a valuable tool for assessing not just a single publication, but broader industrial trends as well.

COMPUTATIONAL METHODS
FOR SIMILARITY DETECTION

Our project situates computational methods as a complement to traditional methods of reading and analysis. Automation and scripting cannot, and should not, fully replace the role of the human researcher who interprets and synthesizes meaning from a text. Computers are highly efficient when working with enormous volumes of data, but they lack the precision and ability to interpret nuance within a text. A human researcher works more slowly but can understand that nuance in context. The text similarity algorithms that we discuss below, therefore, are not a replacement for the role of a human researcher but instead function as an assistant that can help us by processing a large set of input text and directing our time and attention toward the close readings that are most likely to yield interesting similarities. Though it is not necessary for all humanities scholars to become experts in mathematics or computer science, a working familiarity with the processes and key concepts was useful to inform our analyses of text similarity across motion picture trade papers.

Large-scale computational analyses require us to reframe how we conceptualize what the text *is*. Most humanities scholars are used to thinking of a document in a holistic sense—it contains numerous words, which are placed in a particular order to convey meaning. For many computational methods, however, the order of words in a document is entirely ignored. Instead, we construct numerical representations of written text to mathematically assess similarity by measuring the distance between numbers. For our exploratory analysis, we use the "bag-of-words" model, which understands a document as a "collection of words that are used in differing proportions."[7] Instead of treating a document as words in a particular order with meanings, we simply count the frequency of words in a given document and compare these frequencies to those of other texts. Large language models (LLMs) such as OpenAI's ChatGPT software use more advanced "embeddings" to represent text mathematically, but the underlying principle of representing text in a numerical form is similar. The transformation methods used by many LLMs can be more accurate at evaluating written text but are slow and computationally expensive; for our initial exploratory analysis, we used simpler methods such as term frequencies and calculating Levenshtein distances. These computational approaches are gross oversimplifications of textual meaning and overlook important nuance, but they also make it feasible to quickly process large volumes of text.

There are many additional caveats to our computational method, as well as several possible types of preprocessing work to address them. First, many computational methods for processing text are sensitive to differences in the lengths of documents. Texts within the MHDL corpus are not of a consistent length; some volumes contain multiple issues of a single publication, while other volumes may be separated into individual issues. Furthermore, each issue of a publication contains separate articles and sections. Separating these parts into individual documents beforehand can improve the accuracy of the calculations but at the expense of requiring more manual preparation. But standardizing page counts and sections is just one kind of significant preprocessing work that can be performed on a corpus before running similarity comparisons. For example, many projects remove stop words—common words such as *the*, *a*, or *and*—from input texts to avoid overrepresenting them in results. In addition, all MHDL files are processed using optical character recognition (OCR), which identifies text within a scanned image and provides data in a format that is usable in a computer script. While OCR technologies have been continually improving, it is an unavoidable fact that errors will occur. Many factors influence the accuracy of OCR text: the quality of scans, varying page layouts, differing typefaces, and even something as seemingly simple as an image appearing on a page.[8]

These are the kinds of tradeoffs that must be considered when using computational approaches, and they are an important reminder that such methods will never fully replace the role of the human researcher. For our initial exploratory analysis, we did not perform any preprocessing and instead sought to assess the effectiveness of using raw data directly from the MHDL. We selected a variety of text similarity algorithms that balance these caveats with the utility of processing large volumes of text and used their resulting similarity measures as guides to shape our ongoing research process.

EUCLIDEAN AND COSINE DISTANCE

The most basic measurements of text similarity that we used were the Euclidean distance and cosine distance between each volume of the selected corpus. Both methods measure the relative frequency of words that appear within each text and provide a numeric representation of how "far" each document is from each other.[9] They are quick to calculate and offer a general approximation of similarity but are not well suited for representing context.

To demonstrate how these distances are measured, let's consider a smaller example: two short strings of text, rather than an entire volume. Here are two sentences that regularly appear in *Exhibitors Herald* in its "What the Picture Did for Me" section:

Sentence A: "TELL US WHAT THE PICTURE DID FOR YOU and read in the HERALD every week what the picture did for the other fellow, thereby getting the only possible guide to box office values."

Sentence B: "Join in This Co-operative Service Report Regularly on Pictures You Exhibit and Read in The Herald Every Week What Pictures Are Doing for Other Exhibitors"

The first step in calculating Euclidean and Cosine distances is to identify each unique word that appears in the two texts and count its frequency in each. For example, the word *exhibit* appears zero times in sentence A and one time in sentence B. Words that may appear similar to a human reader—such as *picture* and *pictures*—are considered entirely different to the computational model. We take these word frequencies and plot them, using each word as an axis and the number of occurrences represented as the point's distance from the origin. This results in Euclidean cosine distances, which are determined by measuring the distance between plotted points. The Euclidean distance is the length of the line segment directly between the plotted points. The cosine distance is determined by drawing a line from (0,0) to each plotted point, and then measuring the angle between the two lines.[10] When working by hand, it is only feasible to compare two or three words at a time; after all, what would a graph with four or more dimensions even look like? But the underlying mathematics is the same, even with additional axes. Computers can plot points across greater numbers of dimensions, effectively comparing the relative frequencies of any given number of words.

When applied to entire volumes, these distances provide a useful overview of general similarity between texts and are a useful starting point for comparisons and analysis. Euclidean distance can range anywhere from zero to much larger values in the hundreds or thousands, with smaller values representing texts that are more similar. When comparing texts of a similar length, Euclidean distance is useful for revealing minute differences. Cosine distance, however, is more effective for comparing texts of different lengths. This measurement ranges from 0 to 1, with lower numbers being more similar.

338   CHAPTER 19

Because these distance measures ignore the *order* of words and only consider their frequencies, they are of limited utility on their own. They are useful for providing a zoomed-out view of many texts within a corpus but (as we discuss later) yielded limited insight when applied to the MHDL corpus. Other text similarity methods were better suited for assessing motion picture trade papers.

LEVENSHTEIN DISTANCE

The other methods we used to test for similarity between texts in our corpus are variations of Levenshtein distance, a measure first proposed by mathematician Vladimir Levenshtein in the 1960s.[11] In general, Levenshtein distance is a measure of the number of edits it takes to turn one string into another. An edit can be inserting a new letter, deleting a letter, or replacing one letter with another. Accordingly, the order of the words matters, unlike in the calculation of Euclidean and cosine distances.[12] For Levenshtein distance, lower numbers of edits indicate that the two texts are more similar.

For example, consider the following words:

Word A: *color*
Word B: *colour*

To go from word A to word B, only a *u* needs to be inserted, and to go from word B to word A, only a *u* must be deleted, so they have a Levenshtein distance of 1 (out of a maximum of 6) and a normalized distance of 1/6, or about 16.67 percent. If measured using cosine distance, they would have a cosine difference of 1, or 100 percent different texts. Though technically accurate for tallying the instances of the two words, the cosine difference does not reflect the actual similarity of these terms.

When analyzing millions of words, this may mislead us into thinking two texts are more different than they actually are. Levenshtein distances help mitigate this concern by showing the similarities *within* the words themselves. Since its introduction, mathematicians have developed a number of variants of Levenshtein distance:

- *InDel distance*: Only insertions and deletions are allowed as edits.
- *Normalized distance*: The calculated Levenshtein distance is divided by the maximum possible value. By representing all distance measures between zero and one, it becomes more feasible to compare different text pairings.
- *Sorted distance*: The words from each text are alphabetized before calculating the distance. The order of the words no longer matters.
- *Set distance*: Each unique word in a string is only listed once before the sorted distance is measured.

Levenshtein distance and its variants are very useful for finding similarity where there may be regional spelling variations (e.g., *theater* and *theatre*) or where text is slightly changed during its reuse. For example, consider the following sentences:

Sentence A: The park sees hundreds of visitors a day.

Sentence B: Hundreds of visitors a day see the park.

The original Levenshtein distance is 28. Using sorted distance instead, sentences A and B have a distance of 1; only the *s* at the end of *sees* would need to be deleted since all the other words are identical. Sorting the words alphabetically first and negating the impact of their order in the sentence results in very few changes between the sets of words, suggesting that it is very likely the two sentences are highly similar.

Each of these variants can suggest distinct—and even conflicting!—interpretations of the relative similarity among texts. Using multiple measurements in combination can offer greater insight into the results. In our analyses, we used the InDel distance and sorted distance variants.

WORKFLOW

One important consideration when selecting an algorithm to use for calculating text similarity is the computational complexity and time requirements. We had to wait more than twenty-four hours for the algorithm to process each pair of texts and deliver results with multiple variants of Levenshtein distance. Current understandings of computer science suggest that it is not possible to significantly reduce this computational complexity or decrease processing time.[13] While calculating only Euclidean and cosine distances was significantly quicker, it is still not a "plug and play" process. We provide an overview of our workflow not as a step-by-step tutorial but rather to give a sense of the work that is still required even when using "automated" computational methods.

First, we downloaded raw text files of each document from the MHDL. For tracking purposes, we ensured that each file maintained the volume's unique ID.[14] Recent upgrades to the MHDL and Lantern websites have made large-scale querying and downloading possible.[15] We did not perform further preprocessing steps for our initial analysis. Assessing OCR accuracy, removing stop words, and conducting consistent stemming and tokenization may improve our process.

After preparing the text files, we used a series of Python scripts to run each comparison algorithm. We used the "pandas" and "rapidfuzz" libraries to assist with processing our text files.[16] Three different distance metrics were generated with rapidfuzz and then normalized: InDel distance (called a ratio score in the rapidfuzz library), sort score, and set score. In all three cases, higher values indicated higher similarity.

340   CHAPTER 19

Our Python scripts created two kinds of output files: CSV files with specific similarity values for each "candidate text" and summary text files listing the top similarity values for each measurement. The text similarity algorithms helped us focus our time and attention on where we were most likely to find interesting similarities, particularly among texts that registered as similar across multiple measurements of distance.

ANALYZING THE RESULTS

Though we highlight only a few findings here due to limited space, we encourage interested readers to download the compiled data sets, available on the Media History Digital Library, and explore the calculated distances and rankings for themselves.[17]

The volumes that were most similar to one another were *Exhibitors Herald* (July–September 2022) and *Exhibitors Herald* (October–December 2022). This pair had an InDel distance of 47.96/100 and a sorted distance of 91.69/100. This finding is unsurprising; two consecutive volumes of *Exhibitors Herald* were viewed as being most similar to each other. Many structural components of a publication, such as mastheads and section headings, are likely to appear in *all* volumes, regardless of the actual content and topics included within a given issue.

The next highest sorted distances were between pairs of New York weekly trade papers:

- *Motion Picture News* (July–August 1922) and *Moving Picture World* (July–August 1922) with a sorted distance of 86.239513; and
- *Motion Picture News* (July–August 1922) and *Exhibitor's Trade Review* (June–August 1922) with a sorted distance of 85.8518859.

At face value, this would seem to support the perceptions of the aforementioned "'Herald Only' Club" members who viewed the Chicago-based *Exhibitors Herald* as distinctively different from its rivals based in New York.[18] However, further highly ranked pairings suggest that *Exhibitors Herald* had similar text to *Exhibitor's Trade Review* and *Motion Picture News* (with sort distances ranging from 85.3 to 83.8). Whether published in New York or Chicago, the sorted distances suggest that weekly US film trade papers are more similar to each other than to monthly fan magazines, non-US weekly trade papers, or even a daily trade paper from the US like *The Film Daily*.

If we use set distance scores, the results change significantly. As previously mentioned, set distance is the calculation taken when duplicate words in a string are eliminated before the sorted distance is measured—in other words, the frequency of the words does not matter. Using this calculation can be helpful for comparing volumes of different lengths. We noticed that the volume *The Great Selection:*

"First National First" Season 1922–1923 appeared in the five highest-scoring pairs of volumes according to the sorted distance (see table 19.2). This was a promotional booklet generated by First National to market its upcoming productions to exhibitors, and it contained titles, names, advertising copy, and publicity text that appeared throughout US film industry trade papers.[19] When we looked at the volume that ranked as most similar to *The Great Selection, Motion Picture News* (July–August 1922), we saw that it contained twenty consecutive pages of the same promotional material contained in *The Great Selection*, including a full-page ad for a canine star, "Strongheart the Wonderdog in 'Brawn of the North'" (see figure 19.1).[20]

The next four highest-ranked set distances paired *The Great Selection* with other US trade papers: *Exhibitors Herald* [92.66], *The Film Daily* [92.3], *Exhibitors Herald* [91.9], and *Exhibitor's Trade Review* [91.74]. Blanketing the field to promote its films to exhibitors, First National produced its own promotional booklet in house and paid leading trade papers to carry the same promotions as advertisements. The set distance measurement helped us identify this same promotional text reappearing across multiple publications. [tabref 19.2]

Which publications scored the lowest? That is, which publications were the *least* similar to anything else in the corpus? Among the least similar pairings, we found that one text dominated the list across each of our measures. Our only Spanish-language magazine in the corpus, *Cine-Mundial*, appeared in all ten of the highest Euclidean distance pairings—signaling a lack of similarity. Similarly, the German-language trade paper *Der Kinematograph* was in eight of the lowest Levenshtein pairs and six of the highest cosine distances. All of this makes sense: the algorithms, just like a human reader, recognize that the patterns of language are different in those non-English language magazines.

For this reason, the most intriguing low scoring result was *Camera!*, an English-language US trade paper, which appeared in all the lowest-scoring pairs among the Levenshtein variants we computed. Founded in 1918, *Camera!* was the film industry's first weekly trade paper to consistently publish from Los Angeles.[21] *Camera!* cultivated creative workers on the West Coast as both its primary readers and advertisers; the paper provided industry news alongside ads taken out by aspiring writers and actors seeking employment on such productions.[22] While *Camera!* covered industry news related to First National in 1922, First National did not purchase advertising for its movies in *Camera!* since the customers it sought to reach (exhibitors) did not subscribe to the paper. The editors of *Camera!* addressed its readers as in-group members of a creative community and industry who were different from the exhibitor community and non-showbusiness people living in Los Angeles (see figure 19.2).[23] Over the next few years, several other film industry trade papers emerged in Los Angeles, competing against *Camera!* and eventually succeeding it. In 1922, though, *Camera!* occupied a unique position within the

FIGURE 19.1. Advertisement for "Strongheart the Wonderdog in 'Brawn of the North,'" *Motion Picture News*, 1922, https://lantern.mediahist.org/catalog/motionpicturenew26july_1003. The same ad was shared in *The Great Selection: "First National First" Season 1922–1923*.

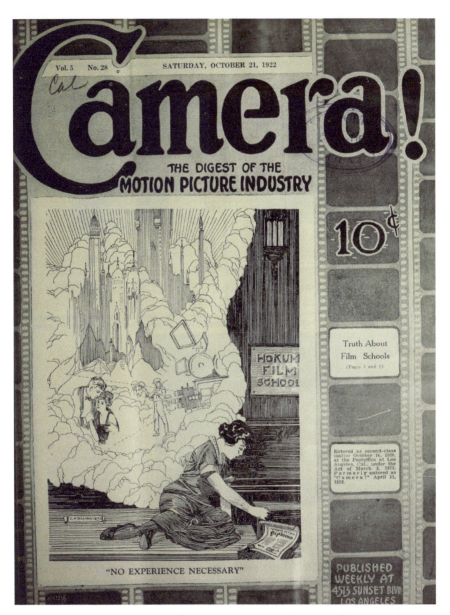

FIGURE 19.2. Cover of a 1922 issue of *Camera!*, criticizing profit-seeking film schools that misled the students who enrolled. https://lantern.mediahist.org/catalog/camera05unse_0571.

industry—one that, a full century later, our computer algorithms identified as distinct among other magazines that year.

CONCLUSIONS

Our algorithmic analyses suggest that there was a great deal of similarity among the four top weekly US trade papers oriented toward exhibitor readers (*Moving Picture World, Motion Picture News, Exhibitor's Trade Review,* and *Exhibitors Herald*). Despite *Exhibitors Herald's* emphasis on its uniqueness and midwestern location, the paper's structure, use of language, and overlaps in advertising had much more in common with the New York weeklies than with the fan magazines, LA trade paper, and non-US publications in our corpus. Ultimately, *Exhibitors Herald* publisher Martin Quigley would acquire all three of those competing trade papers, rebranding the consolidated publication at the end of 1930 as *Motion Picture Herald*. Our computational analyses indicate a great deal of similarity across the papers in 1922. While these findings do not come as great surprises, they have enriched our understanding of both the historic magazines and the use of computational methods for large-scale text analysis.

What the computational results cannot tell us is what the trade papers meant to the people who originally created them, read them, and used them. The editors of *Motion Picture News* and *Exhibitors Herald*, William A. Johnston and Martin Quigley, respectively, each cultivated distinctive personas within the industry. They competed with one another for influence, power, and reader loyalty. Quigley emphasized his independence and integrity at every turn. Johnston successfully sued the editors of *Exhibitor's Trade Review* for libel when they attacked him in print. These aspects of the trade papers' histories require close reading of the magazines, as well as locating and analyzing sources outside of the papers themselves (e.g., court documents, private correspondences, audit bureau circulation reports). Algorithms are no substitute.

Yet computational methods do let us find and see things differently. Without the search indexing algorithms within Lantern, we would never have found many of the relevant pages that we read and analyzed closely with our eyes. The text similarity testing algorithms described in this chapter are, in part, attempts to achieve an even wider form of search—querying advertisements and strings of publicity text that reoccur across multiple publications, even when the specific words, phrases, and occurrences are not yet known. The promising results from the set distance rankings, with *The Great Selection: "First National First" Season 1922–1923* scoring highest, have informed the work we are now undertaking in researching the reuse of text and graphics from Hollywood pressbooks across trade papers, fan magazines, and US newspapers. As we move forward, we are approaching the work with curiosity, humility, and the knowledge that no algorithmic results or score ranking will ever tell the whole story. We invite others to do the same, with the hope of locating many more stories to tell.

NOTES

1. W. Stephen Bush, "Looking Forward," *Exhibitor's Trade Review*, June 16, 1917, 91.

2. Leander Richardson to William A. Johnston (open letter), "One Trade Paper Enough," *Variety*, December 28, 1917, 239, https://lantern.mediahist.org/catalog/variety49-1917-12_0400.

3. Eric Hoyt, *Ink-Stained Hollywood: The Triumph of American Cinema's Trade Press* (Oakland: University of California Press, 2022). Open access publication: https://doi.org/10.1525/luminos.122.

4. For more on using distant reading to explore the MHDL, see Charles R. Acland and Eric Hoyt, eds., *The Arclight Guidebook to Media History and the Digital Humanities* (Falmer, UK: REFRAME/ Project Arclight, 2016). Open access publication: http://projectarclight.org/book.

5. We estimated that even the most basic algorithms could require several months of computing time to calculate. Although it may have been possible to decrease this time through code optimization and distributed computing strategies, we chose to select a much smaller corpus for our initial exploratory analyses.

6. C. M. Hartman, quoted in "'Herald Only' Club Gains Six; Veteran and Newcomer Give Reasons for Joining," *Exhibitors Herald*, March 29, 1924, 63, http://lantern.mediahist.org/catalog/exhibi torsherald18exhi_o_0073; George Rea letter to Exhibitors Herald, *Exhibitors Herald*, May 26, 1923, 69, http://lantern.mediahist.org/catalog/exhibitorsherald16exhi_o_0869.

7. Shawn Graham, Ian Milligan, and Scott B. Weingart, *Exploring Big Historical Data* (London: Imperial College Press, 2015), 114.

8. Ryan Cordell, "'Q i-Jtb the Raven': Taking Dirty OCR Seriously," January 7, 2016. https://ryan cordell.org/research/qijtb-the-raven-mla/.

9. John R. Ladd, "Understanding and Using Common Similarity Measures for Text Analysis," *Programming Historian* 9 (2020), https://doi.org/10.46430/phen0089.

10. Michel Marie Deza, *Encyclopedia of Distances* (New York: Springer, 2014), 335–36.

11. Vladimir I. Levenshtein, "Binary Codes Capable of Correcting Deletions, Insertions, and Reversals," *Soviet Physics Doklady* 10, no. 8 (February 1966): 707–10.

12. Gonzalo Navarro, "A Guided Tour to Approximate String Matching," *ACM Computing Surveys* 33, no. 1 (March 1, 2001): 31–88, https://doi.org/10.1145/375360.375365.

13. Arturs Backurs and Piotr Indyk, "Edit Distance Cannot Be Computed in Strongly Subquadratic Time (Unless SETH Is False)," *arXiv*, August 15, 2017, https://doi.org/10.48550/arXiv.1412.0348.

14. See table 19.1 for publication names and IDs.

15. For more information on using application programming interfaces (APIs) to programmatically search and retrieve data from the Media History Digital Library, see https://lantern.mediahist.org/api.

16. For pandas, see https://pandas.pydata.org/; for rapidfuzz, see https://maxbachmann.github.io/ RapidFuzz/index.html.

17. The compiled data sets are available for download at https://doi.org/10.5061/dryad.gtht76htc.

18. C. M. Hartman, quoted in "'Herald Only' Club Gains Six; Veteran and Newcomer Give Reasons for Joining," *Exhibitors Herald*, March 29, 1924, 63, http://lantern.mediahist.org/catalog/exhibi torsherald18exhi_o_0073; George Rea letter to Exhibitors Herald, *Exhibitors Herald*, May 26, 1923, 69, http://lantern.mediahist.org/catalog/exhibitorsherald16exhi_o_0869.

19. Associated First National Pictures, Inc., *The Great Selection: "First National First" Season 1922–1923*, ca. 1922, https://lantern.mediahist.org/catalog/greatseloofirs_0005.

20. "Associated First National Pictures, Inc. presents the first group of its Great Selection of Incomparable Fall Attractions" [advertisement], *Motion Picture News*, August 26, 1922, 961, https:// lantern.mediahist.org/catalog/motionpicturenew26july_0987.

21. Hoyt, *Ink-Stained Hollywood*, 111–13.

22. "The Pulse of the Studio," *Camera!*, April 13, 1919, 8, http://lantern.mediahist.org/catalog/ camera1919losa_0034; "Where to Sell Your Scenarios," *Camera!*, April 13, 1919, 13, http://lantern. mediahist.org/catalog/camera1919losa_0039.

23. Hoyt, *Ink-Stained Hollywood*, 113.

PUBLICATIONS REFERENCED

The American Cinematographer
Camera!
Canadian Moving Picture Digest
Cine-Mundial
Cinéa
Der Kinematograph
Exhibitors Herald
Exhibitor's Trade Review
The Film Daily
The Film Renter and Moving Picture News
The Great Selection: "First National First" Season 1922–1923
Harrison's Reports
Motion Picture News
The Motion Picture Studio
Moving Picture World
Paramount Pep
Photoplay
The Picturegoer
Shadowland
Tess of the Storm Country (United Artists Pressbook)
Universal Weekly
Variety

BIBLIOGRAPHY

Acland, Charles R., and Eric Hoyt, eds. *The Arclight Guidebook to Media History and the Digital Humanities.* Falmer, UK: REFRAME/Project Arclight, 2016. Open access publication: http://projectarclight.org/book.

Backurs, Arturs, and Piotr Indyk. "Edit Distance Cannot Be Computed in Strongly Subquadratic Time (Unless SETH Is False)." *arXiv*, August 15, 2017. https://doi.org/10.48550/arXiv.1412.0348.

Cordell, Ryan. "'Q i-Jtb the Raven': Taking Dirty OCR Seriously." January 7, 2016. https://ryancordell.org/research/qijtb-the-raven-mla/.

Deza, Michel Marie. *Encyclopedia of Distances.* New York: Springer, 2014.

Graham, Shawn, Ian Milligan, and Scott B. Weingart. *Exploring Big Historical Data.* London: Imperial College Press, 2015.

Hoyt, Eric. *Ink-Stained Hollywood: The Triumph of American Cinema's Trade Press.* Oakland: University of California Press, 2022. Open access publication: https://doi.org/10.1525/luminos.122.

Ladd, John R. "Understanding and Using Common Similarity Measures for Text Analysis." *Programming Historian* 9 (2020). https://doi.org/10.46430/phen0089.

Levenshtein, Vladimir I. "Binary Codes Capable of Correcting Deletions, Insertions, and Reversals." *Soviet Physics Doklady* 10, no. 8 (February 1966): 707–10.

Navarro, Gonzalo. "A Guided Tour to Approximate String Matching." *ACM Computing Surveys* 33, no. 1 (March 1, 2001): 31–88. https://doi.org/10.1145/375360.375365.

20

Provenance of Early Chinese Movie Publications

Emilie Yueh-yu Yeh and Darrell William Davis

Researching the past often depends on chance and serendipity. Sometimes an incidental discovery can unexpectedly fill a missing piece in a puzzle; often, a relentless search may result in nothing. A film historian's task is not always rewarding, and frustration abounds when the work needed is to seek materials of the early twentieth century, an era before there was a notion of a film library or archive. In the case of Chinese film, it is especially challenging, as many films before the 1930s did not survive, and many print sources such as handbills, posters, scripts, and company records were destroyed or scattered around the world. In working with the Media History Digital Library (MHDL) and curating books and periodicals for digitization, we find revisiting early Chinese film history an uneven path, though it sometimes seems miraculous or, more often, quotidian.

This chapter details the process of choosing, searching, and introducing key sources in early Chinese-language film history, including artifacts from China, Hong Kong, and, to some extent, Taiwan, while also balancing among three distinct sources of film history: periodicals, catalogs, and book-length publications. In every case, there were important influences from abroad, via Hollywood, Japanese, and European film industries. We single out the period before 1930 in this study, as it is less familiar to global researchers.[1] This phase is normally called "early cinema" by Chinese historians; that term is defined differently from its use in European and US film scholarship. Due to the scarcity of surviving films predating 1930, the "early" phase of cinema in China and Hong Kong usually refers to the period from the 1900s to early 1930s (rather than the period between the 1890s and 1910s). This periodization follows the time line of films made by the first Chinese producers to the advent of sound and the rise of left-wing cinema, two concurrent

348   CHAPTER 20

developments in the early 1930s.[2] Recently this early phase has been extended to the 1890s, with growing interest in exhibition history and audience reception before the twentieth century. Not only must we acknowledge differences in periodization, but we should also emphasize the provenance of sources online, offline, and between the lines. What we call "historic" sources have their own background or derivation, not only their original creation and circulation but also the routes they may have taken to their online, virtual forms. And there are other materials that may be at least as important that were not or could not become available for digital scanning and upload. Even so, we can profit from dead ends, also-rans, and sources that may not arrive in the digitized forms of canonical history. Hence, we envision the personification of this process as a form of biography, a record of the recovery of the materials in their digital afterlives.

Following the focus on early cinema, our original proposed items for digitization in the MHDL were three of the earliest film periodicals published in Shanghai and Hong Kong, along with two authoritative sources on the industry and filmmaking techniques. These works all appeared in the 1920s, during the Republican era that commenced with the 1911 Revolution led by Dr. Sun Yat-sen, founder of the Nationalist Party (Kuomintang or KMT). This period corresponded with the formative, exuberant era of film exhibition, joined by an ardent production culture inspired by nationalism. Getting access to these materials was not always straightforward; often, under current copyright regimes, they could be consulted but not reproduced. Our tale is not triumphant, but partial, accidental, and provisional. In many cases, there were setbacks due to bureaucracy, the COVID-19 pandemic, and even avarice.

Our original plan was to digitize two very early film magazines in China—*The Motion Picture Review* (*Yingxi zazhi*, 1921) and *Movies Magazine* (*Dianying zazhi*, 1924–25). (All Chinese names in this chapter are rendered in the Hanyu Pinyin system, and the order of Chinese proper names follows the norm in Chinese, surname preceding first name.) *The Motion Picture Review*, allegedly the first film magazine circulated in Shanghai, released just three issues before it closed. It was put out by the Shanghai Photoplay Society, organized by a group of professional English translators and connoisseurs of Hollywood pictures. The cover image of its first issue features Harold Lloyd, indicating the international popularity of the US comedian and his slapstick turns. More vividly, the image foregrounds the magazine's selling point: the stars of Hollywood, who constituted the silver screen's main appeal for the middle-class audiences in China.[3] *Movies Magazine* was launched in 1924, with a total of thirteen issues. Compared to *The Motion Picture Review*, which devoted most of its pages to portraits of movie actors, *Movies Magazine* covers more theories, film reviews, and filmmaking techniques, representing the rising importance of motion pictures as a major sphere of technical craft, aesthetic pursuit, and cultural consumption in China. These two magazines are held in the Shanghai Library and the China Film Archive, in both print and microfilm. They, along with many other surviving film periodicals to date, were reprinted in *Republican Film Magazine Compilation* (2013), a 167-volume series of film periodicals between 1921 and 1949, a conservation milestone undertaken by the National Library of China.[4] There was no copyright issue in selecting these two titles for the MHDL to begin with, as the original publishers no longer exist. And as mentioned, these magazines now have been restored and reproduced in hardcopy form for public use. We discussed the prospect of digitizing the items with one of the editors, who advised us that permission to create a digital copy of these two magazines must be cleared with the authorities of the National Library and that the layers of clearance would be forbidding.

We then discovered that the National Library produces microfilm originals of these two magazines for the use of researchers.[5] We inquired about purchase but were told an antipandemic measure issued in Beijing prohibited any staff to enter the storeroom to retrieve any stock. After several rounds of inquiries—with staff in various divisions, including the microfilm office, circulation, and, eventually, reader services—we were referred to the bookstore of the National Library to check if there were copies available for sale. The bookstore staff told us that the government had just suspended all such sales until further notice. Due to COVID-19 travel restrictions, we were prevented from going to Beijing or Shanghai to personally negotiate with the authorities there to obtain usable materials, as the originals were not to be used by non-library staff and the printouts from the existent microfilms are usually hard to read. As a result, we had to abandon our attempt to secure these two items, either in person or by remote access.

Our third selection is the 1924 monograph *On Photoplay* (*Yingxi xue*) by Xu Zhuodai (1881–1958). More than two hundred pages long, it was among the first film books published in China, taking a systematic approach to film production, from scriptwriting to directing and other aspects of filmmaking. The title *On Photoplay* may not be the best translation, as there is *xue* in the title, meaning "learning," "studying," or "science."[6] Hence it could also be translated as *Photoplay Studies* or *The Science of Photoplay* to highlight the concept of *xue*, a form of pedagogy as well as a system of knowledge and techniques.[7] The original copy of *On Photoplay* was held in Shanghai Library;[8] a photocopy of the book is available in the holdings of the Chinese University of Hong Kong library, which we used to offer the digital scan to the MHDL. There was no issue with copyright, as the author Xu Zhuodai died in 1958 and the publishing firm Huaxian Commercial Press has since closed. More details on this book will follow in the next section.

Our next selection is *China Cinema Year Book 1927* (*Zhonghua yingyue nianjian*), edited by Cheng Shuren, Gan Yazi, and Chen Dingxiu. At over 200 pages, this was among the first formal publications on the Chinese film industry. A print

350   CHAPTER 20

version is held in the Shanghai Library, and a digital copy is available open access on Duxiu Academic Search, the world's largest online database for Chinese-language academic publications.[9] Registered users can access only fifty pages at a time. We followed this path and offered the scanned copy to the MHDL.[10]

The last item in our curation is the first film periodical published in Hong Kong, *Silver Light* (*Yin Guang*). Five issues were published, beginning from the first issue in 1926 and closing with the fifth issue in 1927.[11] Launched by Hong Kong Chinese writers, *Silver Light* represents a key page in the indigenous film writing of Hong Kong.[12] In many respects, it resembles its Shanghai counterparts in layout, structure, and rhetoric. The inaugural issue foregrounds the need to create a local Hong Kong response to the new medium of the twentieth century, not letting those writers up north dominate the national cinematic discourse. Despite the mild regional competitive tone, most of the writers shared a similar agenda with their counterparts in Shanghai in their concern for the future of Chinese cinema and their vision of the role of motion pictures to propel social and cultural advancement. Seizing on screen performance as an effective vehicle for prompting spectators into a socially conscious position, writers of *Silver Light* put an emphasis on acting as cinema's "enlightening" function (echoing the title of the magazine, light on the silver screen). In its last two issues, cosmopolitanism was on the rise, marking the unique Hong Kong perspective in how Chinese cinema should be fashioned to be on par with its European and US counterparts.[13] *Silver Light* is available to view in the library of the University of Hong Kong, in both print and microfilm, and digital versions of the five extant issues are also available in the MHDL.

With our failure to secure digital copies of *The Motion Picture Review* and *Movies Magazine*, we turned to the most important source on prewar Taiwan cinema, *A History of Cinema and Drama in Taiwan*, penned by Lü Su-Shang, published in 1961. This, too, was a failed endeavor, for financial reasons.[14] *A History of Cinema and Drama in Taiwan* was self-published by the author, who was himself an actor, dramatist, and critic and had intimate knowledge of and connections with different sectors in Taiwan's performing arts, including cinema. His account took in the beginning of the Japanese colonial period to postwar Taiwan and remains to date the most comprehensive local chronicle of Taiwan performing arts. It has been used as the key reference for writing early Taiwan film history, especially the colonial Japanese era, which lasted until 1945.[15] The 580-page volume is very thorough and well illustrated, with chapters on cinema, radio broadcasts, and performing arts, including Taiwanese opera, dramaturgy, music, and puppetry.[16] We were pleased to have chosen this source, as its print quality is decent and the sheer volume of its coverage is impressive, a rare and valuable book on the history of media archaeology of Taiwan. Nevertheless, the rights holder's reluctance to share it with global readers embodies reverberations of the suppressed history of local culture in Taiwan. The resentment felt by the author's descendant and others like him might take years to resolve. In the following, we provide more detailed accounts of the two book-length publications in our selection.

ON PHOTOPLAY (1924)

Adapted and translated by Xu Zhuodai from Kaeriyama Norimasa's *The Production and Photography of Moving Picture Drama* (1917), this primer is an introduction to screenplays, stagecraft, camerawork, lighting, editing, film stock, and other subjects. Film was a new medium, different from drama, according to Xu. It was something modern, taken from abroad, and needed to be handled with knowledge and special attention. The book is divided into eight chapters and an appendix:

1. Elements [or Essence] of Photoplay
2. Forms and Classifications of Photoplay
3. Making Meaning and Original Storywriters
4. Methods of Writing Screenplays and Role of Scriptwriters
5. Staging Directors [i.e., film directors]
6. Actors
7. Shooting Studios and Settings
8. Methods of Cinematography, Tricks [or Techniques] and Technicians

Appendix [a technical vocabulary of Japanese and Chinese translations of English-language terms about film stock, lenses, focal length, and even color]

In all chapters, following his Japanese source, Xu points to the materiality of making movies, the cinematic techniques, "tricks," and many technical details. His second chapter, "Forms and Classifications of Photoplay," provides genre classifications, including drama, comedy, slapstick, historical drama, fairy tale, social drama, action thriller, detective story, military, war, spectacle, education, philosophical, literary and art film such as the screen adaptations of Tolstoy's novels, and, finally, fine arts.[17] These classifications are thorough and correspond to directions taken in studio filmmaking and criticism in later decades. Nearly all his chapters emphasize the uniqueness and novelty of photoplay creation, reminding readers to observe the special techniques required for making motion pictures; this is striking, as Xu Zhuodai propagated the concept of what we call "medium specificity" today. This specificity was noted by writers who were his contemporaries but never advocated as strongly as Xu did in this book. This, of course, could just reflect the sources that he adapted or translated from. Nonetheless, Xu's intent to introduce filmmaking as a craft to the Chinese audience is evident.

As a humorist in the popular fiction known as Mandarin Ducks and Butterfly School, Xu directed, wrote, and starred in at least fifteen films. He was a key

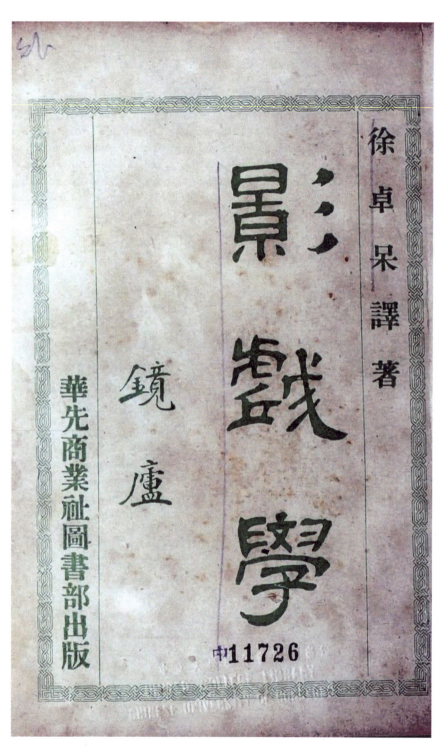

FIGURE 20.1. Title page, *On Photoplay*.

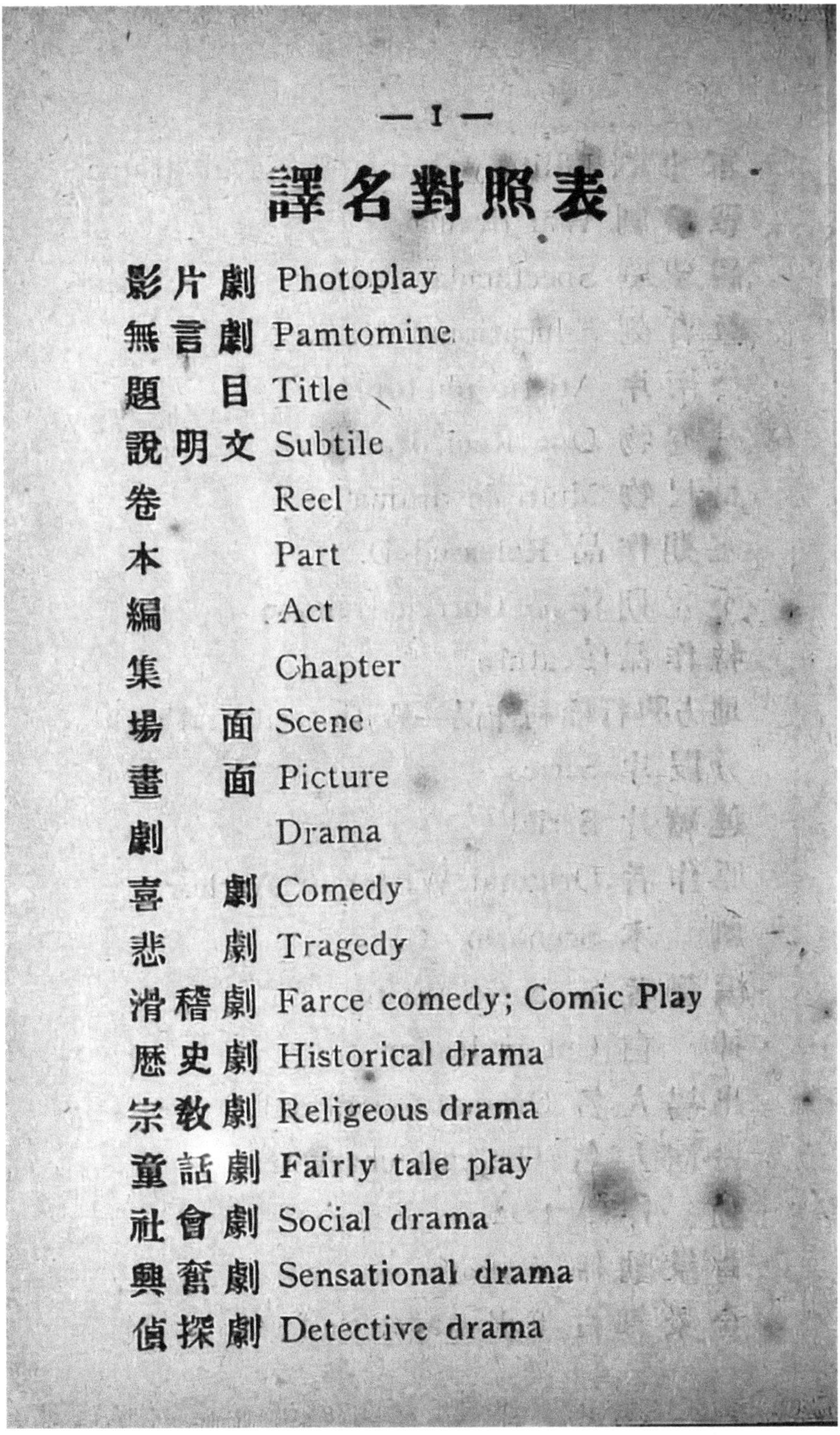

譯名對照表

— I —

影	片	劇	Photoplay
無	言	劇	Pamtomine
題		目	Title
說	明	文	Subtile
卷			Reel
本			Part
編			Act
集			Chapter
場		面	Scene
畫		面	Picture
劇			Drama
喜		劇	Comedy
悲		劇	Tragedy
滑	稽	劇	Farce comedy; Comic Play
歷	史	劇	Historical drama
宗	敎	劇	Religeous drama
童	話	劇	Fairly tale play
社	會	劇	Social drama
興	奮	劇	Sensational drama
偵	探	劇	Detective drama

FIGURE 20.2. Bilingual glossary of film terms, *On Photoplay*.

354   CHAPTER 20

representative from the Butterfly School in outlining the symbiosis between popular fiction and filmmaking. Like many of his Butterfly colleagues, Xu published widely in relation to cinema. He was also co-owner of a small production house, Kaixin (Happy), that specialized in slapstick and other comedies. At the peak of his film career, he was called the "Charlie Chaplin of the East."[18] In several of his slapstick productions, Xu employed "tricks" in creating comic effects, suspense, and surprise, indicating Xu's practice of his preaching.[19] Tricks are highlighted in his eighth chapter, "Methods of Cinematography, Tricks (or Techniques) and Technicians," in a special section where Xu describes the mechanisms involved and the impressions made by careful setups and timing. It is interesting to speculate on where his knack for such tricks originated. Xu studied in Japan around 1902, majoring in industrial technology. But having visited a local gymnastics school, he decided to change his major to gymnastics. Upon returning to China, he set up a gymnastics school and, later, a film company, while pursuing a career writing popular fiction. From industrial technology to gymnastics, from fiction to slapstick, Xu was able to leverage his skills into film writing and filmmaking, exemplifying a "cultural entrepreneur," a multitalented figure capable of sparking synergy between different registers, media, and platforms.[20]

CHINA CINEMA YEAR BOOK 1927

Yearbooks are commonly known as annual publications prepared by graduating classes to commemorate their activities and achievements. They celebrate the community of students, teachers, staff, and parents, as well as myriad cultural pursuits, athletics, and special events. Yearbooks are a standard record for liberal arts institutions and high schools, to represent and remember a given class. The MHDL, on the other hand, describes "year books" as annual catalogs that provide directories of personnel, products, and services. They have a distinct industry purpose, especially their provision of space for advertisement and promotion.[21] In Hollywood, year books were "issued annually by the leading trade paper publishers [and were used] in the 1920s to structure data" (i.e., annual records outlining and praising activities of the film industry).[22] The *China Cinema Year Book* is an interesting mix of commemoration and industry catalog, serving chiefly to introduce readers to the top companies and people in Chinese cinema. *China Cinema Year Book* and other year books might be called the databases of their time, given their purpose of compiling, organizing, and making information "searchable."

China Cinema Year Book was edited by three authors: Cheng Shuren (S. J. Benjamin Cheng), Gan Yazi (Atsu Kann), and Chen Dingxiu (D. S. Chen). This 1927 volume prepares a comprehensive view of Chinese film history, production, distribution, exhibition, performance, writers, directors, designers, projectionists, and censorship. It comprises forty-seven sections, surveying the filmscape in

FIGURE 20.3. Front cover, *China Cinema Year Book 1927*.

356 CHAPTER 20

Republican China circa the mid-1920s, including a brief on the formation of the industry in the 1910s. The information collected is impressive. Since its publication, this book has provided primary materials and information for researchers working on Chinese film history.[23] For those who are serious about this topic, it is a must read. Below is an abridged list of the forty-seven sections, in which the catalog format is quite clear:

1. Foreword
2. The History of the Motion Picture Industry in China
3. Chinese Producers
4. Chinese Feature Productions
5. Chinese Comedy Productions
6. Foreign Producers
7. Productions Made by Foreign Producers
8. Supervisors of Productions [Signed picture of Anna May Wong, "Orientally Yours"]
9. Photoplay Writers and Their Productions
10. Scenario Writers and Their Productions
11. Chinese Title Writers and Their Productions
12. English Title Writers and Their Productions
[...]
17. Laboratorymen [*sic*] and Their Products
[...]
23. Title Card Writers
24. Specialists Trained Abroad
25. Makeup Directors
26. Stars and Their Productions
27. Actors and Actresses [Picture of Wu Bongfan, along with his character's name Mr. Weiwei, from *The Stormy Night*]
28. Chinese Productions (Arranged Chronologically) [Picture of G.E. Weiss] [Picture of J. Bendorf]
29. Theater Companies (Chinese Management)
30. Theater Companies (Foreign Management)
31. Agencies for Foreign Pictures
[...]
33. List of Theaters
[...]

China Cinema Year Book gives a clear view of the types of pictures, division of labor, and technical work involved in making, distributing, and exhibiting films, both domestic and foreign. In sections 4 and 5, we see the listings of Chinese Features and Chinese Comedies. Is this a distinction between feature-length films and shorts? Not necessarily, though many of the comedies produced at this time in China are in fact shorts with two or three reels. The difference here is based mainly on their subject matters. The term *features* (*Zhuang ju*) is a translation of Italian *opera*, which has a connotation of serious drama, rather than light fare (such as *opera buffa*), hence a separate category is used for such light entertainment as "comedies." Is there a difference between photoplay writers and scenario writers (sections 9 and 10)? Scenario writers work scene by scene, while photoplays span the whole work. The "Laboratorymen" who are listed in section 17 undertook the processing of negatives, making prints, so these were most likely employees of studios. Title writers (sections 11 and 12, Chinese and English) are distinguished from title card writers (section 23). Title cards are titles at the beginning of the film, whereas title writers are those who write or translate the many intertitles that help carry the story, a standard feature in the silent diegesis. The title writers enjoyed a high status in the early film industry, since their bilingualism and writing skills were instrumental in setting up the film business, first in exhibition and promotion and later in production. The film career of Cheng Shuren, one of the volume's coauthors, exemplifies such a trajectory. Though written in Chinese, the *Year Book*'s basic format is bilingual, in Chinese and English, and so are the ads for products from Shanghai and environs. The international, cosmopolitan mode reflects the extraterritoriality of the foreign settlements in Shanghai where many of the production companies were located; similarly, in many other treaty port cities, it was common to see listings of foreign distributors and exhibitors. The dominance of foreign players in the film industry[24] is aptly represented in section 2, "The History of the Motion Picture Industry in China," in which Cheng and his coauthors identified Benjamin Brodsky as the person who shot the first two films in China.[25] Sections 6 and 7 are lists of foreign producers and their films, while sections 30 and 31 catalogue foreign-owned theaters and agencies that distributed foreign pictures.

If school yearbooks look back, *China Cinema Year Book* looks ahead by casting a net for investors, talent, and leaders and inviting potential stakeholders to read about the pursuits of Chinese filmmakers and, perhaps, consider joining the game. It addresses itself to potential investors and players in the Chinese film industry, which explains its directory-like structure, a who's who or calling card of people and companies active in this new business. They were anticipating big business blossoming in China's film industry, and indeed, 1925 saw a significant rise in feature-length film production. It was the year when "film-making in China transitioned from an artisanal mode to an industrial output dominated by a few

358   CHAPTER 20

big companies."[26] For instance, *The Stormy Night*, directed in 1925 by Zhu Shouju, cofounder of the Grand China Lilium Film Company, is a sophisticated romantic comedy about a famous writer who almost falls into an affair. The writer goes to the country to rest and compose. He finds trouble in his involvement with a local woman, while his wife and children remain in Shanghai. This film is mentioned several times in the *Year Book* (sections 4, 28, and 46), as it had been released in the recent past.[27] The design of the *Year Book* volume is very much like a press kit, while the presentation is similar to advertisement, although the illustrations do not always align well with the section headings. For instance, there is an autographed photo of Anna May Wong in the list of production supervisors, and several pictures of foreigners appear in section 8 on Chinese productions. These photos boast movie star glamour and hyperbole typical of Shanghai show-business swagger, displaying what would now be called the Republican China sensibility: mature, worldly, and opulent—in sum, the Roaring Twenties.[28] There is consistency between ad copy and design in detailing the successes of talent, directors, and technicians; the ad copy uses the rhetoric of advanced, cultured connoisseurs. Cheng and his coauthors were insiders who knew the community, the equipment, and the business.

Cheng's film book has a nationalist bent in its rhetoric. In the prelude to the volume, a calligraphy couplet appears: "Our film enterprise is yet to prosper, we should all continue to endeavor." This is striking, as it rephrases Dr. Sun Yat-sen's last words enjoining his comrades to unify China by ridding it of imperialist powers when he died in 1925. This nationalist overtone returns in the foreword to the directory of movie theaters (section 33), and the zeal is pronounced. While applauding the promise and energy of China's film industry, Cheng calls for more of it to be held in domestic hands, rather than by foreign owners from concession areas in many parts of China (e.g., Shanghai, Tientsin, Canton, Hankow, Harbin, and many more). In effect, the latter arrangement put China's film industry in thrall to foreign entities, whether British, Russian, French, German, Japanese, or Spanish. The extraterritoriality policy allowed regulation of large businesses by foreign governments. While a movie palace might be doing huge business in Shanghai, its owner, manager, and programs were mostly foreign. Cheng writes: "Our Republican Chinese industry is on the wax, although we still work in a piecemeal fashion. Until now, we lack a bird's-eye view of the movie landscape, and cannot command movement in the industry as a whole. In production we are doing well, but of the 156 cinemas running in our country, 90 percent of those are controlled by foreign merchants. This is a risk, as movie theaters can be places that uplift our people and give expression to ancient country values. We need to rise up and exert control over our Republican cinema industry."[29]

Given Cheng's later movement, detailed below, it is odd that *China Cinema Year Book* does not mention the industry in Taiwan, which was then a Japanese colony. But it lists film enterprises in Hong Kong, Macao, Manila, Bangkok, Singapore,

Tokyo, Vietnam, Jamaica, and even the United States (in New York, Chicago, San Francisco, and Honolulu) that traded in Chinese films, labor, and craft. The Chinese diaspora is apparent in Cheng's mapping of his "China Film World."

Cheng Shuren exemplifies study-abroad returnees of the early twentieth century, in helping China rebuild itself in the modern world.[30] But it is Cheng's liberal arts education, rather than science and engineering, that facilitated his entry into the film industry, a nascent field ripe for cultivation. At age sixteen in 1911, he enrolled in Tsinghua, the liberal arts college founded by US expatriates in Beijing, by means of the reparations from the Boxer Indemnity.[31] Besides academic subjects, he undertook extracurricular activities, including debate, drama, sports, music, and photography.[32]

In the early 1920s, Cheng continued his education in the US, enjoying a government scholarship at Lawrence College in Appleton, Wisconsin, where he majored in education. After graduating from Lawrence he did not return home, but went to New York, where he earned a master of arts in education at Columbia University and a certificate in cinematography at New York Film School. Cheng then interned as a cameraman at the Famous Players studio, Long Island.[33] In New York, Cheng met Zhou Ziqi (Chow Tse-chi), a Chinese diplomat in the US who turned a page in his life. At this time Zhou, a former premier as well as the first president of Tsinghua and a Columbia alumnus, was looking for study-abroad graduates to help him run Peacock Motion Picture Corporation, a Sino-American joint venture that he cofounded with US businessmen in 1922. Registered as a US company, Peacock was a transnational enterprise backed by US capital and the former head of the British American Tobacco Company. Its main purpose, like many others before it, was to tap into the growing film market as well as the cut-rate labor force of China. Hence, Zhou invited Cheng to help propagate US imports distributed by Peacock.[34] For this, Cheng proposed to put translated intertitles (from English to Chinese) on screen to ease the viewing of foreign pictures.[35] During this time, Chinese moviegoers relied on handbills with detailed synopses to follow the story. Cheng's idea of projecting Chinese intertitles on screen would allow patrons to better grasp the story while watching the film.[36] He devoted himself to this task and translated the intertitles of twenty-one Hollywood pictures into Chinese, including most of the films distributed by Peacock, according to the number of works listed under his name in *China Cinema Year Book*.[37] This led Peacock to great success financially.

Cheng's ambition went beyond intertitle translation; he shot his first film, *Love's Sacrifice*, in 1925. But his further plan was shattered when Zhou Ziqi passed away. In 1927, Cheng finally completed his second feature, an adaptation of the classic *Dream of the Red Chamber*. Unfortunately, the film's poor reception pushed Cheng out of film production and Peacock altogether.[38] After Peacock, he managed two second-run cinemas and invested in restaurants and a department store. When the war broke out in 1937, Cheng accepted a job offer from the KMT to build railways

First National Pictures
LEAD-OTHERS FOLLOW

LEADING EXHIBITORS SHOW
First National Attractions
BECAUSE THEY GET THE MAXIMUM REVENUE
AT THE BOX OFFICE

美國第一國家影片公司出品
確為世界最名貴之影片由

中國孔雀電影公司獨家經理
總經理朱錫年謹白

SOLE AGENTS IN CHINA
PEACOCK MOTION PICTURE CORPORATION
LUTHER M. JEE – GENERAL MANAGER
116 SINZA ROAD   SHANGHAI

FIGURE 20.4. Peacock Motion Picture Corporation was sole agent for First National Pictures, boasting a full-page English-language announcement.

EARLY CHINESE MOVIE PUBLICATIONS   361

in southwestern China,[39] where the government set up its temporary capital in Chungking to continue its war with Japan. He remained there until the end of the war. After the ensuing civil war between the KMT and the Communist Party concluded in 1949, Cheng moved to Taiwan, following the retreat of the KMT from the mainland. He became manager of the Taipei branch of China Travel Agency, a KMT government office.[40] In Taiwan, he quit film completely and kept a low profile the rest of his life.

China Cinema Year Book was published nearly a century ago. Despite the long duration, Cheng's image as a mover and shaker is clear, to the extent that his visibility eclipsed the contributions of the other two editors, Chen Dingxiu and Gan Yazi. Gan was a key staff member and scriptwriter at Peacock while Chen was Cheng's spouse and business partner. Chen Dingxiu (1900–52) was one of the first female college graduates in China and a celebrated student leader in the 1919 May Fourth movement, a massive student and worker protest that fought for national autonomy and equality. Chen was a versatile and prolific writer; she composed fiction and was active on stage. She married Cheng in 1924 and helped him realize his film ambitions, including coediting the first-ever cinema year book. She also worked on the titles of their first production, Love's Sacrifice (1925). But their marriage became estranged as Cheng had extramarital relationships. When Cheng followed the KMT to Taiwan, Chen remained in China with their four daughters.

The careers of Cheng Shuren and Xu Zhuodai, author of On Photoplay, are representative of study-abroad students returning to China who later made their mark on the country's developing cinema industry and culture.[41] Such figures played a key role in the formation of the early Chinese film industry. These study-abroad returnees helped build the institution of cinema in China.[42] Cheng studied education and film in the States while Xu went to Japan to learn science and sports. Together with many others who shared similar paths, they built up the transnational network of the Chinese film industry during this time, even though this network seemed limited in scope because they were study-abroad students who became cultural brokers upon repatriation. They were energetic but did not transform themselves into industrialists, unlike the Shaw brothers, who started their studio Tianyi in 1925, making low-budget costume dramas and growing into the vertically integrated Shaws Movietown after World War II. The kind of circuits and work the student returnees started were provisional and short term, lacking staying power in most instances. Everything Cheng and Xu did tended to be short lived. In the case of Cheng, he would settle down as a government employee, leaving his film dream and his family completely behind.

On Photoplay and China Cinema Year Book 1927 are foundational texts for the formation of China's film industry. They are conscious of their transnational status, given the authors' foreign education and linguistic skills. Yet they intend to establish a solid national platform for the film industry in China, to meld the

FIGURE 20.5. From left: Cheng Shuren, Chen Dingxiu, and Gan Yazi.

technology, craft, and business models of filmmaking with the stories and values of Chinese tradition. These two works have an extendable status, in that they could be transformed to a digital existence and become known far beyond their former intended audience. It would be nice to think that this fortuitous transition comes from their historical importance, but as mentioned above, this is just serendipitous good luck. Other periodicals and books published in the 1920s or earlier are at least as important, but they could not be digitized for various reasons. This indicates the unevenness of digital availability, which, in the case of our subject,

EARLY CHINESE MOVIE PUBLICATIONS   363

early Chinese cinema, remains precarious and unpredictable, especially given the strong possibility that there are "historic" sources that have not yet even been discovered. We must be open to the chance of encountering new materials, and more sensitive to the provenance of materials we already have.

Our own experiences with digitizing newspaper sources to databases is rich, however fitful. In reconstructing the Chinese filmscape in the first part of the twentieth century, Emilie Yueh-yu Yeh and her research partners targeted coverage of film exhibition in both Chinese and English newspapers and subsequently published two open-access online databases for movies and film criticism, one in Chinese and the other in English.[43] This was rewarding, in that press coverage in Hong Kong and three other Chinese cities, including Guangzhou, Hangzhou, and Tianjin, is now accessible worldwide. However, in numerous instances, relevant figures and coverage were not included in these databases. These missing links sometimes are crucial in filling the gaps and lapses in our historical narrative. Due to inevitable flaws in ocular scanning by humans, search keywords, or language renderings, it is possible and likely that key developments have fallen between the cracks. As Ramona Curry writes, we must have "a willingness to accept that despite recently much broadened access to historical resources, some knowledge gaps must remain unfilled."[44] This is a remark Curry made about her "detective" work on the enigmatic Benjamin Brodsky, one of the major producers in early Chinese cinema, who sometimes deliberately exaggerated and attenuated names, dates, and places to tell a taller tale. We must bear this acceptance in mind when we decide what to write into the story and how to curate the vagaries of an ever elongated, diffused past of the medium. There will always be new materials to be excavated and old facts to be expanded, if not amended. A digital library for world cinema history is a good starting point.

NOTES

The authors thank Yongchun Fu, Wenchi Lin, Enoch Yee Lok Tam, Snowie Wong, the late Zhang Wei (1959–2023), and the staff at the National Library of China for their assistance in this project.

1. There are only a few complete surviving prints from the 1920s or before; therefore, Chinese film history's introduction to the world concentrated on the films made in the 1930s, the so-called "classics of Chinese cinema." Zhen Zhang's *An Amorous History of the Silver Screen* (Chicago: University of Chicago Press, 2005) is the first in-depth study on early cinema in China.

2. See Wong Ain-ling, "Foreword" [Qianyan], in *Chinese Cinema: Tracing the Origins* [*Zhongguo dianying zuo yuan*], ed. Wong Ain-ling (Hong Kong: Hong Kong Film Archive, 2011), 4–5; Li Daoxin, *The Cultural History of Chinese Cinema (1905–2004)* [*Zhongguo dianying wenhua shi (1905–2004)*] (Beijing: Beijing University Press, 2004).

3. Stardom was the main focus in the film industry at the time. Stars, male and female, foreign and domestic, always occupied center stage in film news and reviews. China's star power was invested in Ruan Lingyu (1910–35), whose premature death resulted in nationwide mourning. See the feature-length biopic of Ruan, *Center Stage* (dir. Stanley Kwan, 1992), and Richard J. Meyer, *Ruan Ling-Yu: The Goddess of Shanghai* (Hong Kong University Press, 2005).

364   CHAPTER 20

4. Shanghai Library, Zhou Deming, and Zhang Wei, eds., *Republican Film Magazine Compilation* (Beijing: National Library Press, 2013).

5. Thanks to Yongchun Fu for providing this information.

6. Note that the other term *yingxi* in the title *Yingxi xue* is the same as that in the title of *Motion Picture Review, Yingxi zazhi*. In the 1920s, both *yingxi* and *dianying* were used to name motion pictures. Some scholars translated *yingxi* as "shadowplay," an attempt to establish an indigenous provenance for motion pictures. Yeh has contested the translated term *shadowplay* by offering *photoplay* as an alternative, taking into account the exhibition histories in Hong Kong and South China. See Emilie Yueh-yu Yeh, "Translating *Yingxi*: Chinese Film Genealogy and Early Cinema in Hong Kong," in *Early Film Culture in Hong Kong, Taiwan, and Republican China: Kaleidoscopic Histories*, ed. Emilie Yueh-yu Yeh, 19–50 (Ann Arbor: University of Michigan Press, 2018).

7. Zhang Yingjin calls it *film studies* in his *Chinese National Cinema* (New York: Routledge, 2004), 50.

8. A photocopy of *On Photoplay* was reprinted in 2018, along with a few other volumes in a series called "Historical Materials of Chinese Cinema" published in 2018. See Xu Zhuodai, *On Photoplay* (Beijing: Dongfong chuban she, 2018). This series is available in the library of Princeton University.

9. Duxiu is a database of Chinese academic materials including books, journals, newspapers, dissertations, conference papers, and other formats of documents in multiple disciplines from the 1930s to the present. Millions of e-resources are available in full text at https://www.duxiu.com/.

10. See https://archive.org/details/chinese-cinema-year-book-1927-01.

11. See the digitized December 1926 issue of *Silver Light* at https://archive.org/details/SliverLight-1926-12.

12. Formal Chinese writing on film in Hong Kong began as early as in 1924 in a weekly column called "Film Corner" (*Ying Hei Ho*) in *The Chinese Mail* (est. 1872). *The Chinese Mail* is the Chinese edition of *The China Mail* (1845–1974), one of the earliest English papers published in Hong Kong. Between 1923 and 1925, to satisfy the booming exhibition business in Hong Kong, *The China Mail* had a film column under three different names: "The Films," "Cinema Chatter," and "Screenland." "Film Corner" was added to correspond to the film column in the English-language *China Mail*. It ran a total of thirty-eight issues before it was closed down in 1925. From then on, *Silver Light* filled the gap to become the leading voice in local film criticism. For a detailed analysis of "Film Corner," see Ting-yan Cheung and Pablo Sze-pang Tsoi, "Indigenized Practice: Hong Kong Cinema in the 1920s," in Yeh, *Early Film Culture*, 71–100. All thirty-eight articles can be previewed in Emilie Yueh-yu Yeh, Feng Xiaocai, Liu Hui, and Poshek Fu, eds., *Early Chinese Film Database* (Hong Kong: Hong Kong Baptist University Library, 2015), http://digital.lib.hkbu.edu.hk/chinesefilms/.

13. Courtesy of Enoch Yee Lok Tam's observation.

14. The rights holder Lü Xianguang, the author's son, asked for a price beyond reason, complaining that his father's work has been underappreciated and never received due recognition.

15. For more coverage on early cinema in Taiwan during the colonial era (1900–1940s), please see Lee Daw-Ming and Emilie Yueh-yu Yeh, eds., *Historical Source Database of Cinema Studies on Taiwan Film History* (Taipei: Taipei National University of the Arts, 2016).

16. Like Cheng Shuren, Lü Su-shang attempted to provide a complete record of cinema since its first introduction to Taiwan, almost the same time as it became Japan's colony in 1895.

17. Xu Zhuodai, *On Photoplay* (Shanghai: Hua Xian Shang Ye She Tu Shu Bu, 1924), 15–16. See also https://archive.org/details/photoplay-1924-12.

18. Fan Boqun, ed., *Hua ji da shi, Xu Zhuodai* [*The Master of Comedy, Xu Zhuodai*] (Taipei: Yeqiang, 1993). His pen name "Zhuo Fuling" (similar to Zhuo Bielin, a sinified pronunciation of "Chaplin") pays respect to the comedy giant.

19. See Emilie Yueh-yu Yeh and Enoch Yee Lok Tam, "Forming the Movie Field: Film Literati in Republican China," in Yeh, *Early Film Culture*, 244–76. A good example of Chinese slapstick is *Laborer's Love* (dir. Zhang Shichuan, 1922), a clever burlesque involving traditional Chinese medicine. This film was recently restored by Bologna Cinema Ritrovato to 4K standard, as a signpost of centennial development.

20. Christopher Rea writes of "'cultural entrepreneurship,' a multifaceted approach to culture as business, embodied by inventive and entrepreneurial figures who actively engaged in multiple forms of cultural production, from fiction writing and translation to drama, filmmaking, radio broadcasting, and consumer product manufacturing." Christopher G. Rea, "Comedy and Cultural Entrepreneurship in Xu Zhuodai's *Huaji* Shanghai," *Modern Chinese Literature and Culture* 20, no. 2 (Fall 2008): 40–91.

21. David Pierce writes for the MHDL, "The Year Books were published by industry trade magazines, and there was a tacit understanding that the purchase of ads would help ensure that no negative coverage would appear"—a quid pro quo between the industry and the publisher, a win-win outcome. See https://mediahist.org/collections/yearbooks/.

22. Eric Hoyt, "Arclights and Zoom Lenses: Searching for Influential Exhibitors in Film History's Big Data," in Daniel Biltereyst, Richard Maltby, and Philippe Meers, eds., *The Routledge Companion to New Cinema History* (New York: Routedge, 2019), 88. See also Eric Hoyt, *Ink-Stained Hollywood: The Triumph of American Cinema's Trade Press* (Oakland: University of California Press, 2022), https://doi.org/10.1525/luminos.122.

23. For instance, Yoshino Sugawara in her book on Republican Shanghai's film culture offers a thorough socioeconomic guide to the film industry, including its business models, technological advancements, and ownership of the movie theaters. Sugawara, *Eigakan no nakano kindai: eiga kankyaku no Shanghai shi* [*Modernity in the Space of Cinema: A History of Film Spectators in Shanghai*] (Kyoto: Koyoshobo, 2019). Yongchun Fu also relied on the source materials in *China Cinema Year Book* when he studied the contributions of foreigners to the Shanghai film industry, in Yongchun Fu, *The Early Transnational Chinese Film Industry* (London: Routledge, 2019).

24. Fu, *Early Transnational Chinese Film Industry*.

25. Cheng Shuren, Gan Yazi, and Chen Dingxiu, eds., *China Cinema Year Book 1927* (Shanghai: The China Year Book, 1927), 17.

26. Emilie Yueh-yu Yeh, "*Wenyi* and the Branding of Early Chinese Film," *Journal of Chinese Cinemas* 6, no. 1 (2012): 66.

27. For decades, *The Stormy Night* was believed to be lost. But in 2011, a print was discovered in the storage of the late Japanese director Kinugasa Teinosuke, who was presented with a copy of the film as a gift by Zhu Shouju when he visited Shanghai in the late 1920s. It is now in the collection of the National Film Center, Tokyo.

28. Yingjin Zhang, ed., *Cinema and Urban Culture in Shanghai, 1922–1943* (Stanford, CA: Stanford University Press, 1999); Leo Ou-fan Lee, *Shanghai Modern: The Flowering of a New Urban Culture in China* (Cambridge, MA: Harvard University Press, 1999).

29. "List of Pictures" section 33, in Cheng et al., *China Cinema Year Book 1927*. Other sections from the *Year Book* are as follows:

13. Casting Directors

14. Directors and Their Productions

15. Assistant Directors

16. Cameramen and Their Productions

[. . .]

18. Foreign Producers

19. Productions Made by Foreign Producers

20. Supervisors of Productions [Signed picture of Anna May Wong, "Orientally Yours"]

21. Photoplay Writers and Their Productions

22. Cartoonists

[. . .]

32. Translators and Pictures Retitled

366 CHAPTER 20

[. . .]

34. Offices of Different Companies

35. Reports of Chinese Pictures from Foreign Markets

36. Theaters in Foreign Countries

37. Buyers of Chinese Pictures for Domestic Markets

38. Buyers of Chinese Pictures for Foreign Markets

39. Motion Picture Organizations

40. Schools of Acting

41. Motion Picture Publications

42. Chinese Censorship

43. Local and Police Regulations

44. Past and Present Legal Advisors of Producers

45. Dealers in Motion Picture Equipments and Appratus [sic]

46. Chinese Productions (Arranged According to Producers)

47. Projectionists

30. The literature on Chinese study-abroad returnees is wide. See Yung Wing, *My Life in China and America* (New York: Henry Holt, 1909). This is cited in Barbara Austen's "Yung Wing's Dream: The Chinese Educational Mission, 1872–1881" with a wonderful picture of the first group of Chinese students arriving in Connecticut in 1872. Connecticut History.org, 2019. See also Chen Yun-Chung, "The Limits of Brain Circulation: Chinese Returnees and Technological Development in Beijing," *Pacific Affairs* 81, no. 2 (2008): 195–215. A broad view can be found in Teresa Brawner Bevis and Christopher Lucas, *International Students in American Colleges and Universities: A History* (New York: Palgrave Macmillan, 2007).

31. The Boxer Indemnity resulted from the Eight-Powers' war with Qing to tackle the Boxer Rebellion in 1899. It was one of the many "unequal treaties" between China and the world. It bound the Qing court to pay 450 million taels, or 67.5 million pounds, to the eight foreign powers at an interest rate of 4 percent for repayment over forty years. In 1908, the US decided to use its share to fund education, including scholarships for Chinese students in the US, as well as the building of Tsinghua University, Beijing.

32. According to Zhang Wei, in his fifth year in Tsinghua, Cheng was impressed by a Hollywood movie and decided to pursue a career in filmmaking. Zhang Wei, "Cheng Shuren: The First Generation of Overseas Professional Returnees in the Republican Film Field" [Minguo yingtan de diyi dai 'zhuanye haigue'—Cheng Shuren qi ren qi shi], in *A Collection of Film Essays: A Dusty Corner of Modern Chinese Films* [*Tanying xiaoji—Zhongguo xiandai yingtan de shenfeng yi yu*] (Taipei: Xiuwei chuban, 2009), 3–5.

33. Zhang Wei, "Cheng Shuren," 6–7.

34. Liu Lu and Kong Lingqi, "Ershi shiji ershi niandai Kongque dianying gongci chutan" [A Brief Study on Peacock Motion Pictures Corporation in the 1920s], *Dandai dianying* (*Contemporary Cinema*), no. 9 (2019): 119–20. According to a news report, Zhou was invited to this joint venture to help US manufacturers (e.g., American Textile Company and others) and the Dragon Film Corporation sell products in China; see "Big China Companies: Financed with American Gold," *South China Morning Post*, January 3, 1923, 7.

35. In January 1923, Zhou and Cheng returned to China and put Peacock on track by importing Hollywood movies. Zhang Wei, "Cheng Shuren," 8.

36. Ibid.

37. "Translators and Pictures Retitled," Section 32, in Cheng et al., *China Cinema Year Book 1927*.

38. Zhang Wei, "Cheng Shuren," 16–19. Peacock was still active when Cheng quit. It signed an exclusive deal with RKO on distributing RKO sound pictures. Courtesy of Yongchun Fu.

39. Zhang Wei, "Cheng Shuren," 20–21.

40. *Who's Who in Taiwan* (Taipei: Guoguang Press, 1947), 196.

41. Japan was one of the most popular destinations for study-abroad students in the late Qing and early Republican period. Lu Xun, the most eminent modern Chinese writer, was a study-abroad medical student in Sendai, Japan.

42. See Ramona Curry, "Benjamin Brodsky (1877–1960): The Transpacific American Film Entrepreneur—Part One, Making *A Trip thru China*," *Journal of American-East Asian Relations* 18 (2011): 58–94. Brodsky had many Chinese study-abroad friends among his contacts in Hong Kong, Shanghai, and the US. See especially fig. 20.2 on p. 71, "Directors of the China Cinema Company," image originally published in *The Moving Picture World*, vol. 24, no. 2 (April 10, 1913): 224, https://lantern.mediahist.org/catalog/movingpicturewor24newy_0238.

43. Emilie Yueh-yu Yeh, Feng Xiaocai, Liu Hui, and Poshek Fu, eds., *Early Chinese Film Database* (Hong Kong: Hong Kong Baptist University Library, 2015), http://digital.lib.hkbu.edu.hk/chinesefilms/; Emilie Yueh-yu Yeh, ed., *A History of Film Exhibition and Reception in Colonial Hong Kong (1897 to 1925)* (Hong Kong: Lingnan University, 2021), https://digital.library.ln.edu.hk/en/projects/flim/.

44. Curry, "Benjamin Brodsky," 63.

PUBLICATIONS REFERENCED

China Cinema Year Book 1927
The China Mail
The Chinese Mail
A History of Cinema and Drama in Taiwan
The Motion Picture Review (Yingxi zazhi, 1921)
Movies Magazine (Dianying zazhi, 1924–1925)
On Photoplay (Yingxi xue)
Silver Light (Yin Guang)
South China Morning Post

BIBLIOGRAPHY

Austen, Barbara. "Yung Wing's Dream: The Chinese Educational Mission, 1872–1881." Connecticut History, October 26, 2021. https://connecticuthistory.org/yung-wings-dream-the-chinese-educational-mission-1872-1881/.

Bevis, Teresa Brawner, and Christopher Lucas. *International Students in American Colleges and Universities: A History*. New York: Palgrave Macmillan, 2007.

Chen, Yun-Chung. "The Limits of Brain Circulation: Chinese Returnees and Technological Development in Beijing." *Pacific Affairs* 81, no, 2 (2008): 195–215.

Cheng, Shuren, Gan Yazi, and Chen Dingxiu, eds. *China Cinema Year Book 1927*. Shanghai: The China Year Book, 1927. https://archive.org/details/chinese-cinema-year-book-1927-01.

Curry, Ramona. "Benjamin Brodsky (1877–1960): The Transpacific American Film Entrepreneur—Part One, Making *A Trip thru China*." *Journal of American-East Asian Relations* 18 (2011): 58–94.

Daoxin, Li. *The Cultural History of Chinese Cinema (1905–2004)* [*Zhongguo dianying wenhua shi (1905–2004)*]. Beijing: Beijing University Press, 2004.

Duxiu Academic Search. https://www.duxiu.com/.

Fan, Boqun, ed. *Hua ji da shi, Xu Zhuodai* [*The Master of Comedy, Xu Zhuodai*]. Taipei: Yeqiang, 1993.

368   CHAPTER 20

Fu, Yongchun. *The Early Transnational Chinese Film Industry*. London: Routledge, 2019.

Hoyt, Eric. "Arclights and Zoom Lenses: Searching for Influential Exhibitors in Film History's Big Data." In *The Routledge Companion to New Cinema History*, edited by Daniel Biltereyst, Richard Maltby, and Philippe Meers, 83–95. New York: Routledge, 2019.

———. *Ink-Stained Hollywood: The Triumph of American Cinema's Trade Press*. Oakland: University of California Press, 2022, https://doi.org/10.1525/luminos.122.

Janes, Samantha, and David Pierce. "Yearbooks." https://mediahist.org/collections/yearbooks/. Accessed December 13, 2023.

Lee, Daw-Ming, and Emilie Yueh-yu Yeh, eds. *Historical Source Database of Cinema Studies on Taiwan Film History*. Taipei: Taipei National University of the Arts, 2016. https://www.ln.edu.hk/daci/research_and_projects_details?pkey=19&cat=Film+Studies&keywords=.

Lee, Leo Ou-fan. *Shanghai Modern: The Flowering of a New Urban Culture in China*. Cambridge, MA: Harvard University Press, 1999.

Liu, Lu, and Kong Lingqi. "Ershi shiji ershi niandai Kongque dianying gongci chutan" [A Brief Study on Peacock Motion Pictures Corporation in the 1920s]. *Dandai dianying* (*Contemporary Cinema*), no. 9 (2019): 118–32.

Meyer, Richard J. *Ruan Ling-Yu: The Goddess of Shanghai*. Hong Kong University Press, 2005.

Rea, Christopher G. "Comedy and Cultural Entrepreneurship in Xu Zhuodai's *Huaji* Shanghai." *Modern Chinese Literature and Culture* 20, no. 2 (Fall 2008): 40–91.

Shanghai Library, Zhou Deming, and Zhang Wei, eds. *Republican Film Magazine Compilation*. Beijing: National Library Press, 2013.

Sugawara, Yoshino. *Eigakan no nakano kindai: eiga kankyaku no Shanghai shi* [Modernity in the Space of Cinema: A History of Film Spectators in Shanghai]. Kyoto: Koyoshobo, 2019.

Who's Who in Taiwan. Taipei: Guoguang Press, 1947.

Wong, Ain-ling. "Foreword" [Qianyan]. In *Chinese Cinema: Tracing the Origins* [Zhongguo dianying zuo yuan], edited by Wong Ain-ling, 4–7. Hong Kong: Hong Kong Film Archive, 2011.

Xu, Zhuodai. *On Photoplay*. Shanghai: Hua Xian Shang Ye She Tu Shu Bu, 1924. https://archive.org/details/photoplay-1924-12.

———. *On Photoplay*. Beijing: Dongfong chuban she, 2018.

Yeh, Emilie Yueh-yu. "Translating *Yingxi*: Chinese Film Genealogy and Early Cinema in Hong Kong." In *Early Film Culture in Hong Kong, Taiwan, and Republican China: Kaleidoscopic Histories*, edited by Emilie Yueh-yu Yeh, 19–50. Ann Arbor: University of Michigan Press, 2018.

———. "*Wenyi* and the Branding of Early Chinese Film." *Journal of Chinese Cinemas* 6, no. 1 (2012): 65–94.

———, ed. *A History of Film Exhibition and Reception in Colonial Hong Kong (1897 to 1925)*. Hong Kong: Lingnan University, 2021. https://digital.library.ln.edu.hk/en/projects/.

Yeh, Emilie Yueh-yu, Feng Xiaocai, Liu Hui, and Poshek Fu, eds. *Early Chinese Film Database*. Hong Kong: Hong Kong Baptist University Library, 2015. http://digital.lib.hkbu.edu.hk/newsclipping/.

Yeh, Emilie Yueh-yu, and Enoch Yee Lok Tam. "Forming the Movie Field: Film Literati in Republican China." In *Early Film Culture in Hong Kong, Taiwan and Republican China*, edited by Emilie Yueh-yu Yeh, 244–76. Ann Arbor: University of Michigan Press, 2018.

Yung, Wing. *My Life in China and America*. New York: Henry Holt, 1909.

Zhang, Wei. "Cheng Shuren: The First Generation of Overseas Professional Returnees in the Republican Film Field" [Minguo yingtan de diyi dai 'zhuanye haigue'—Cheng Shuren qi ren qi shi]. In *A Collection of Film Essays: A Dusty Corner of Modern Chinese Films* [Tanying xiaoji—Zhongguo xiandai yingtan de shenfeng yi yu], 1–24. Taipei: Xiuwei chuban, 2009.

Zhang, Yingjin. *Chinese National Cinema*. New York: Routledge, 2004.

———, ed. *Cinema and Urban Culture in Shanghai, 1922–1943*. Stanford, CA: Stanford University Press, 1999.

Zhang, Zhen. *An Amorous History of the Silver Screen*. Chicago: University of Chicago Press, 2005.

APPENDIX

This appendix reflects the broad array of magazines available online via the Media History Digital Library. Here, we have listed several titles from outside the United States that are available at the time of publishing, as well as relevant publications from the United States that are mentioned in the book's chapters.

Note: Date spans are approximate and not comprehensive.

TABLE A.1 Magazines Available Online in the Media History Digital Library

Title	Publisher	Number of items	Nation	Date span	URL
American Cinematographer, The	A.S.C. Agency, Inc.	388	United States	1921–63	https://mediahist. org/pub/american cinematographer
Bioscope, The	Archibald Hunter; Games Ltd; Bioscope Publishing Co Ltd	15	United Kingdom	1912–32	https://mediahist. org/pub/the bioscope
Box Office Digest Annual, The	Robert E. Welsh; National Box Office Digest; The Box Office Digest	4	United States	1938–48	https://mediahist. org/pub/the boxoffice digestannual
Boxoffice	Ben Shlyen	121	United States	1937–48, 1961–63	https://mediahist.org/ pub/boxoffice

(Continued)

370 APPENDIX

TABLE A.1 *(Continued)*

Title	Publisher	Number of items	Nation	Date span	URL
British Kinematography	British Kinematograph Society	7	United Kingdom	1947–53	https://mediahist.org/pub/britishkinematography
Canadian Film Digest	Film Publications of Canada, Ltd.	9	Canada	1971–76	https://mediahist.org/pub/canadianfilmdigest
Canadian Film Weekly	Film Publications of Canada, Ltd.	272	Canada	1942–70	https://mediahist.org/pub/canadianfilmweekly
Canadian Film Weekly Year Book of the Canadian Motion Picture Industry	Film Publications of Canada, Ltd.	20	Canada	1951–70	https://mediahist.org/pub/canadianfilmweeklyyearbook
Canadian Moving Picture Digest	Canadian Moving Picture Digest	110	Canada	1918–57	https://mediahist.org/pub/canadianmovingpicturedigest
Chin Chin Screen	Shanghai: Chin Chin Press 上海：青青出版社	30	China	1935–49	https://mediahist.org/pub/chinchinscreen
Chinese Cinema Year Book 中華影業年鑑 January 1927	Chinese Cinema Year Book	1	China	1927	https://mediahist.org/pub/chinesecinemayearbook
Cine-Journal	Dureau, Georges	19	France	1908–14, 1926	https://mediahist.org/pub/cinejournal
Cine-Mundial	Chalmers Publishing Company	28	United States	1916–46	https://mediahist.org/pub/cinemundial
Cine-Technician, The	Association of Cine-Technicians	5	United Kingdom	1935–39, 1943–45, 1953–56	https://mediahist.org/pub/thecinetechnician
Cinéa	Deluc, L. and Roumanoff, A.	3	France	1921–23	https://mediahist.org/pub/cinea
Cinelandia	Spanish-American Pub. Co.	224	United States	1926–47	https://mediahist.org/pub/cinelandia
Cinema (Rome)	Cinema	1	Italy	1939–40	https://mediahist.org/pub/cinemarome
Cinema en Theater	Leiden, NL: Cinema en Theater	5	Netherlands	1921–22	https://mediahist.org/pub/cinemaentheater

MAGAZINES AVAILABLE IN THE MHDL 371

TABLE A.1 *(Continued)*

Title	Publisher	Number of items	Nation	Date span	URL
Cinema Illustrazione	Cinema Illustrazione	310	Italy	1930–39	https://mediahist.org/pub/cinemaillustrazione
Cinema News and Property Gazette	Cinema News	2	United Kingdom	1912–13	https://mediahist.org/pub/cinemanewsandpropertygazette
Cinema News and Property Gazette Technical Supplement	Cinema News	1	United Kingdom	1924–25, 1943, 1946	https://mediahist.org/pub/cinemanewsandpropertygazettets
Cinema Quarterly	G.D. Robinson	2	United Kingdom	1933–35	https://mediahist.org/pub/cinemaquarterly
Cinema Year Book of Japan	The International Cinema Association of Japan	1	Japan	1937	https://mediahist.org/pub/cinemayearbookofjapan
Cinema Year Book of Japan 1938	The International Cinema Association of Japan	1	Japan	1938	https://mediahist.org/pub/cinemayearbookofjapan38
Cinématographie française, La	Revue Hebdomadaire	2	France	1937	https://mediahist.org/pub/lacinematographiefrancaise
Close-Up	Kenneth Macpherson	12	Switzerland	1920–30	https://mediahist.org/pub/closeup
Courrier cinématographique, Le	Charles Le Fraper	249	France	1911–23	https://mediahist.org/pub/lecourriercinematographique
Critica cinematografica, La	La Critica Cinematografica	9	Italy	1946–48	https://mediahist.org/collections/lacriticacinematografica
Documentary News Letter	Film Centre	5	United Kingdom	1940–45, 1947–49	https://mediahist.org/pub/documentarynewsletter
Exhibitor's Trade Review	Exhibitor's Trade Review, Inc.	18	United States	1919, 1921–26	https://mediahist.org/pub/exhibitorstradereview
Exhibitors Herald	Exhibitors Herald Co.	42	United States	1917–27	https://mediahist.org/pub/exhibitorsherald
Famous News	Famous Players Canada, Ltd.	11	Canada	1981–82, 1990–91	https://mediahist.org/pub/famousnews

(Continued)

372 APPENDIX

TABLE A.1 *(Continued)*

Title	Publisher	Number of items	Nation	Date span	URL
Film Daily	The Film Daily	86	United States	1918–48	https://mediahist.org/pub/filmdaily
Film Renter and Moving Picture News, The	The Film Renter and Moving Picture News	4	United Kingdom	1922	https://mediahist.org/pub/thefilmrenterandmovingpicturenews
Film Revue	Film Revue	1	Germany	1947	https://mediahist.org/pub/filmrevue
Film Daily Year Book	The Film Daily	24	United States	1925–51	https://mediahist.org/pub/filmyearbook
Film-Magazin Vereinigt Mit Filmwelt	Verlag Illustrierte Filmwoche GmbH	1	Germany	1929	https://mediahist.org/pub/film-magazinvereingtmitfilmwelt
Film-Photos Wie Noch Nie	Kindt & Bucher Verlag	1	Germany	1921	https://mediahist.org/pub/film-photoswienoochnie
Filmindia	Filmindia Publications, Ltd.	11	India	1937–49	https://mediahist.org/pub/filmindia
Filmkünstler; wir über uns selbst	Sibyllen Verlag	1	Germany	1928	https://mediahist.org/pub/filmkunstler
Filmland: deutsche Monatschrift	Paul Ickes	1	Germany	1924–25	https://mediahist.org/pub/filmland
Harrison's Reports	Harrison's Reports, Inc.	36	United States	1928–62	https://mediahist.org/pub/harrisonsreports
Hua Pei Movie, The	Beijing: Movie Press 北京:電影報社	2	China	1943–44	https://mediahist.org/pub/thehuapeimovie
Illustrated Films Monthly	F.F.W. Oldfield	2	United Kingdom	1913–14	https://mediahist.org/pub/illustratedfilmsmonthly
Kinematograph, Der	E. Lintz	292	Germany	1907–32	https://mediahist.org/pub/derkinematograph
Kinematograph Year Book	Kinematograph Publications, Ltd.	16	United Kingdom	1927–50	https://mediahist.org/pub/kinematographyearbook
Kino	Committee for Cinema Affairs of the USSR Council of People's Commissars	88	Soviet Union	1934, 1936	https://mediahist.org/pub/kino

MAGAZINES AVAILABLE IN THE MHDL 373

TABLE A.1 *(Continued)*

Title	Publisher	Number of items	Nation	Date span	URL
Kulturfilme UFA	UFA	1	Germany	1925	https://mediahist.org/pub/kulturefilmeufa
Lichtbild-Bühne, Die	Lichtbild-Bühne	81	Germany	1911–18	https://mediahist.org/pub/dielichtbildbuhne
Mensajero Paramount	Paramount Pictures, Inc.	3	United States	1927–38	https://mediahist.org/pub/mensajeroparamount
Motion-Play	National Gravure Circuit	10	United States	1920–22	https://mediahist.org/pub/motion-play
Movie Life	Shanghai: Movie Books 上海：電影圖書出版社	8	China	1935–40	https://mediahist.org/pub/movielife
Movie Mirror	Macfadden Group	8	United States	1932–36	https://mediahist.org/pub/moviemirror
Movie Monthly	Shanghai: Wen Hua Art Books Printing Co. 上海:文華美術圖書印刷公司	11	China	1932	https://mediahist.org/pub/moviemonthly
Movie Monthly—China	Shanghai: Liu He Movie Company 上海:六合影片營業公司	10	China	1928–29	https://mediahist.org/pub/moviemonthlychina
Movie News	Shanghai: Phenomenon Book Press 上海:現象圖書刊行社	4	China	1935	https://mediahist.org/pub/movienews
Movie News Weekly	Shanghai: Movie News Weekly Book Press 上海:電影新聞圖畫週刊社	3	China	1939	https://mediahist.org/pub/movienewsweekly
Movie Sketch	Shanghai: Man Lu Publishing Co. 上海:漫廬圖書公司	12	China	1935	https://mediahist.org/pub/moviesketch
Movie World	Shanghai: Movie World Press 上海:電影世界社	8	China	1934–35	https://mediahist.org/pub/movieworld

(Continued)

374 APPENDIX

TABLE A.1 *(Continued)*

Title	Publisher	Number of items	Nation	Date span	URL
Movietone	Shanghai: Movietone 上海:電聲周刊社	61	China	1934–41	https://mediahist.org/pub/movietone
Moving Picture World	Chalmers Publishing Company	90	United States	1907–27	https://mediahist.org/pub/movingpictureworld
New Movie Magazine, The	Hugh C. Weir	11	United States	1930–35	https://mediahist.org/pub/thenewmoviemagazine
New York Clipper, The	Frank Queen Publishing Company	132	United States	1903–20	https://mediahist.org/pub/thenewyorkclipper
On Photoplay	Hua Xian Shang Ye She Tu Shu Bu 華先	1	China	1924	https://mediahist.org/pub/onphotoplay
Optical Lantern and Cinematograph Journal, The	E.T. Heron	1	United Kingdom	1904–05	https://mediahist.org/pub/opticallanternandcinematographjournal
Optical Magic Lantern Journal, The	Optical Magic Lantern Journal Co.	148	United Kingdom	1889–1903	https://mediahist.org/pub/theopticalmagiclanternjournal
Paramount Pep-O-Grams	Paramount Pep Club	5	United States	1925–30	https://mediahist.org/pub/paramountpepograms
Phonogram, The	Herbert A. Shattuck	32	United States	1900–12	https://mediahist.org/pub/thephonogram
Photoplay	Photoplay Magazine Publishing Company; MacFadden Publications, Inc.	102	United States	1916–63	https://mediahist.org/pub/photoplay
Picture Play Magazine	Street & Smith	36	United States	1915–38	https://mediahist.org/pub/pictureplaymagazine
Picture Show	Amalgamated Press/Fleetway Publications	4	United Kingdom	1919–20	https://mediahist.org/pub/pictureshow

MAGAZINES AVAILABLE IN THE MHDL   375

TABLE A.1 *(Continued)*

Title	Publisher	Number of items	Nation	Date span	URL
Picture Show Annual, The	Amalgamated Press, Ltd.	33	United Kingdom	1926–61	https://mediahist.org/pub/thepictureshowannual
Picturegoer	Odham's Press	8	United Kingdom	1921–23, 1934–38	https://mediahist.org/pub/picturegoer
Pictures and the Picturegoer	Odham's Press	4	United Kingdom	1915–16, 1924–25	https://mediahist.org/pub/picturesandpicturegoer
Revue du cinéma, La	Gallimard	3	France	1928–29, 1931, 1947–48	https://mediahist.org/pub/larevueducinema
Screen Stage Monthly	Shanghai: Screen and Theater Press 上海:電影戲劇社	3	China	1936	https://mediahist.org/pub/screenstagemonthly
Screen & Radio Weekly	Des Moines Register and Tribune Syndicate	10	United States	1934–39	https://mediahist.org/pub/screen-and-radio-weekly
Screen Weekly	Beijing: The Peking Gazette Movie Weekly Press 北京:京報電影週刊社	2	China	1924–25	https://mediahist.org/pub/screenweekly
Setāreh-ye Sinemā (Cinema Star)		311	Iran	1954–78	https://mediahist.org/pub/cinemastar
Silver Light	Zhonghua Yingye Nianjian She中華影業	1	China	1926	https://mediahist.org/pub/silverlight
UFA -Magazin	Pressabteilung der UFA	2	Germany	1926–27	https://mediahist.org/pub/ufamagazin
UFA Verleih-Programme	Pressabteilung der UFA	1	Germany	1924	https://mediahist.org/pub/ufaverleihprogramme
Universal Weekly	Motion Picture Weekly Publishing Co.	15	United States	1912–36	https://mediahist.org/pub/universalweekly
Variety	Sime Silverman	715	United States	1905–64	https://mediahist.org/pub/variety

(Continued)

376 APPENDIX

TABLE A.1 *(Continued)*

Title	Publisher	Number of items	Nation	Date span	URL
Weekly Kinema Guide: London Suburban Reviews and Programmes	K.G. Publ. Co., Ltd.	1	United Kingdom	1930	https://mediahist.org/pub/weekly kinemaguide
What's New?	Famous Players Canada, Ltd.	29	Canada	1949–74	https://mediahist.org/pub/whatsnew
Who's Who on the Screen	Charles Donald Fox and Milton L. Silver	2	United States	1920	https://mediahist.org/pub/whoswhoon thescreen

CONTRIBUTOR BIOS

KAVEH ASKARI is associate professor and director of film studies at Michigan State University. He is the author of *Making Movies into Art* (2014) and *Relaying Cinema in Midcentury Iran: Material Cultures in Transit* (2022) as well as coeditor of *Performing New Media, 1890–1915* (2014).

MARIA BELODUBROVSKAYA is associate professor in the Department of Cinema and Media Studies at the University of Chicago. She is the author of *Not According to Plan: Filmmaking under Stalin* (2017) and has published articles on film aesthetics, history, theory, and Russian cinema in *Cinema Journal, Film History, Projections, Slavic Review, Studies in Russian and Soviet Cinema, KinoKultura*, and several edited volumes.

KELLEY CONWAY is professor in the Department of Communication Arts at the University of Wisconsin–Madison. Her research focuses on French film history and aesthetics. She is the author of *Agnès Varda* (2015), *Chanteuse in the City* (2004), and essays on the films of Chantal Akerman, Catherine Breillat, Jacques Demy, Jean-Luc Godard, and Jean Renoir.

MICHAEL COWAN is professor and chair in the Department of Cinematic Arts at the University of Iowa. He has written and edited numerous books on German cinema, including most recently *Film Societies in Germany and Austria: Tracing the Social Life of Cinema* (2023).

DARRELL WILLIAM DAVIS is honorary professor at Digital Arts and Creative Industries, Lingnan University, Hong Kong. He specializes in East Asian cinema and media industries. He is the author of *Picturing Japaneseness: Monumental Style, National Identity, Japanese Film* (1996) and coauthor, with Emilie Yueh-yu Yeh, of *East Asian Screen Industries* (2019) and *Taiwan Film Directors: A Treasure Island* (2005).

VINCENT FRÖHLICH is a postdoctoral researcher at the Institute for Media Studies in Marburg, Germany. He heads a research project on illustrated film magazines ("Seeing Film between the Lines") and is founder and editor of the open access journal *periodICON: Studies in the Visual Culture of Journals.*

RACHEL GABARA is the Nancy Gillespie Brinning Professor in French at the University of Georgia and the author of a series of essays on African cinema in its global context. Her recent work includes *Reclaiming Realism: From Documentary Film in Africa to African Documentary Film* (forthcoming, Indiana University Press).

SAM HANSEN is a database developer at the University of Wisconsin–Madison. They have worked on the Media History Digital Library and PodcastRE, among other projects. Their research interests include text and data mining and bibliometrics.

BELINDA QIAN HE is an assistant professor in East Asian and Cinema & Media Studies and an affiliate faculty member in the Department of Women, Gender, and Sexuality Studies at the University of Maryland, College Park. She is currently completing a book manuscript titled "Expose and Punish: Trial by Moving Images in Chinese Revolutionary Times."

ERIC HOYT is the Kahl Family Professor of Media Production at the University of Wisconsin–Madison. He is the author of *Hollywood Vault: Film Libraries before Home Video* (2014) and *Ink-Stained Hollywood: The Triumph of American Cinema's Trade Press* (2022), and director of the Media History Digital Library and the Wisconsin Center for Film and Theater Research.

CHUNG-KANG KIM is associate professor in the Department of Theater and Film at Hanyang University, Seoul, South Korea. She edited a book, *ReFocus: The Films of Kim Ki-young* (2023), and is completing a book manuscript entitled "Attractive Nation: Popular Cinema in Trans-War Korea (1937–1971)." She is the coauthor of *Rediscovering Korean Cinema* (2019) and *Queer Korea* (2020).

DARSHANA SREEDHAR MINI is an assistant professor in the Department of Communication Arts, University of Wisconsin–Madison. She is the author of *Rated A: Soft-Porn Cinema and Mediations of Desire in India* (University of California Press, 2024) and coeditor of "South Asian Pornographies: Vernacular Formations of the Permissible and the Obscene," published in *Porn Studies* in 2020.

PAUL S. MOORE is a professor of sociology at Toronto Metropolitan University. His media histories of cinema publicity have appeared in *Film History, Canadian Journal of Film Studies*, and, with Sandra Gabriele, *The Sunday Paper: A Media History* (2022).

RIELLE NAVITSKI is associate professor in the Department of Theatre and Film Studies at the University of Georgia. She is the author of *Transatlantic Cinephilia: Film Culture between Latin America and France, 1945–1965* (2023) and *Public Spectacles of Violence: Sensational Cinema and Journalism in Early Twentieth-Century Mexico and Brazil* (2017).

BEN PETTIS is a PhD candidate in media and cultural studies at the University of Wisconsin–Madison. He studies internet platforms and web histories, and develops computational tools for analyzing large collections of audiovisual content.

NICOLAS POPPE is associate professor of Luso-Hispanic studies at Middlebury College. Among other scholarly works, he is the author of *Alton's Paradox: Foreign Film Workers and the Emergence of Industrial Sound Cinema in Latin America* (2021).

LAURA ISABEL SERNA is associate professor of cinema and media studies and history at the University of Southern California. She is the author of *Making Cinelandia: American*

CONTRIBUTOR BIOS   379

Films and Mexican Film Culture before the Golden Age (2014) and coeditor and cotranslator with Colin Gunckel of *"There Are No Hispanic Stars!" Collected Writings of a Latino Film Critic in Hollywood, 1921–1939* (2023).

ERIC SMOODIN is professor emeritus of American studies at the University of California, Davis. He is the author, most recently, of *Paris in the Dark: Going to the Movies in the City of Light, 1930–1950* (2020).

LESLEY STEVENSON is a PhD candidate in media and cultural studies at the University of Wisconsin–Madison. Her research explores the intersections of identity, labor, and power in the media and entertainment industries, particularly at the early-career level.

BABAK TABARRAEE is an assistant professor of instruction and the coordinator of the Persian program at the University of Texas at Austin. His writings have appeared in *Mashriq and Mahjar, Dibur, Iranian Studies, The Soundtrack, Cinephile, Film Quarterly, Journal of Islam and Muslim Studies,* and *The Routledge Companion to Cult Cinema.*

DANIELA TREVERI GENNARI is professor of cinema studies at Oxford Brookes University with an interest in audiences, popular cinema, film exhibition, and programming. Daniela has led the AHRC-funded projects "Italian Cinema Audiences" and "European Cinema Audiences: Entangled Histories and Shared Memories." Her latest publication is the edited volume *The Palgrave Handbook of Comparative New Cinema Histories* (with Lies Van de Vijver and Pierluigi Ercole, 2024).

JAMES UDDEN is professor and chair of cinema and media studies at Gettysburg College. He has published extensively on Asian cinema, including *No Man an Island: The Cinema of Hou Hsiao-hsien* (2nd ed., 2017), and coedited *The Poetics of Chinese Cinema* (2016) with Gary Bettinson.

NAOKI YAMAMOTO is an associate professor of film and media studies at the University of California Santa Barbara. He is the author of *Dialectics without Synthesis: Japanese Film Theory and Realism in a Global Frame* (2020) and coeditor of *Tenkeiki no Mediologī* (2019), a Japanese anthology on media theory and practice in 1950s Japan.

EMILIE YUEH-YU YEH is Lam Wong Yiu Wah Chair Professor of Visual Studies and Dean of Arts at Lingnan University, Hong Kong. She is coeditor of *32 New Takes on Taiwan Cinema* (2022) and editor of *Early Film Culture in Hong Kong, Taiwan, and Republican China* (2018).

INDEX

Abbas, K. A., 37, 41, 53–54
Abel, Richard, 87, 88
Abend, Hallett, 94, 103n36
Academy Company *(Hakwŏnsa)*, 59
ACEC (Catholic Association of Cinema
    Exhibitors), 322
Achard, Marcel, 30
Adachi Masao, 208, 215n12
Adventures of Kathlyn (film serial), 89
advertising: *Cine-Mundial* and transnational
    cultural influence, 250, 251*fig.*, 253–54;
    computational analysis of United States
    film industry trade press (early 1920s), 341,
    342*fig.*, 344; in *Film Appreciation*, 221, 224,
    225*fig.*; in *filmindia*, 43–50, 44*fig.*, 47*fig.*,
    49*fig.*; *Harrison's Reports*, lack of advertising,
    1–5, 2*fig.*, 3*fig.*, 9, 18–19, 39, 330, 334, 373*fig.*; *Il*
    Giornale dello Spettacolo in 1950s, 322; in *Kino*,
    238, 241, 244, 249; *Neue Filmwelt (New Film*
    World) and post-World War II German film
    culture, 291–92; newspapers and syndicated
    movie sections, 88, 89, 91–92, 95, 98–99, 101
Aerograd (film), 237
Afaq, film reviews in, 43
African Cinema, from Its Origins to 1973 (Le
    Cinéma africain, des origines à 1973, Vieyra),
    187, 194
African Cinema Group, 185, 186
African Federation of Cinematographic
    Criticism (FACC), 197

African film criticism in Paris: African-owned/
    Paris-based and -edited publications
    (1957–67), overview, 15–16; D'dée's influence,
    16, 188–93, 193*fig.*, 194–95, 197–98; *L'Afrique*
    actuelle, 15–16, 184, 185, 187, 188, 191, 194–95,
    197–98, 199n15; *La Vie Africaine*, 15–16,
    184, 185, 187–90, 189*fig.*, 191–94, 192*fig.*, 195,
    197–98; *Présence Africaine*, 15–16, 184–88,
    190, 191, 194, 197–98, 198n2; sub-Saharan
    African cinema promotion and development
    calls, 184–85; Vieyra's influence, 16, 185–88,
    186*fig.*, 190–95, 197–98
African Institute of Cinematographic Education
    (INAFEC), 195–96
Africiné Magazine, and African film criticism, 197
Africultures, and African film criticism, 197
Afrique-Asie, and African film criticism, 195
Afrique sur Seine (film), 185, 190
Afshari, Jahangir, 84n37
Agence de Diffusion de Presse, 188
The Age of New Waves: Art Cinema and the
    Staging of Globalization (Tweedie), 9
AGIS (Associazione generale italiana dello
    spettacolo, General Italian Association for
    Entertainment), 316, 318, 320–22, 326n23
Ai Xia, 114
A.K.A. Serial Killer (film), 208, 214, 216n14
'Ālam-e Sinemā (The World of Art), and Iranian
    editorial content, 82n9
Alassane, Mustapha, 191, 193

381

382 INDEX

Alberti, Aída, 262
ALCo Gravure/Gravure Service Corp., 92, 103n26
Aleksandrov, Grigorii, 237
Alexander Nevsky (film), 246
Alicoate, Jack, 307
Allégret, Marc, 30
All India Tour (G.I.P. Railway), 43, 44*fig.*
Almas (film), 241
Alonso de Rocha, Aurora, 272
alternative cinema, *Kikan Firumu* on, 204
Al'tman, Iogann, 245
Amalia (film), 262
Amar Jyoti (film), 37
amateur science. See *Film und Lichtbild*
    and amateur science
America e Industrias Americanas, and
    transnational cultural influence, 250
American Cinematographer, computational
    analysis of United States film industry trade
    press, 332, 333*fig.*
American Council of Learned Societies
    (ACLS), 10
American Druggist, and transnational cultural
    influence, 250
Amiens International Film Festival, 197
Amrit Manthan (film), 37
Anchou, Gregorio, 273n29
Andreotti, Giulio, 320
Anita Louise's Life (film), 116*fig.*
Annecy International Animation Festival, 166
Antena (Antenna), and Argentine celebrity
    culture, 267, 273n17
antisemitism and Nazi propaganda, 289–90
Aouré/Marriage (film), 191
April Revolution (South Korea), 64–65, 69n22
Arche, Alto, 153
Archenhold, Friedrich Simon, 158n7
archival preservation: of Canadian films, Bossin's
    proposal for, 307–10; *Film Appreciation*
    (*Fa*, 電影欣賞) and Taiwanese film culture,
    228; Internet Archive, 5, 10; *Kino* (Soviet
    Union), digitization of, 246. See also data,
    curation, and historiography; Media History
    Digital Library (MHDL); *individual names
    of archives*
Archivo Histórico de Revistas Argentinas
    (Universidad de la República, Uruguay), 131
Argentina: celebrity culture in, 265–71, 272n10,
    273n17; *Heraldo del cinematografista*,
    MHDL accessibility of, 4, 5. See also Latin
    American cine club magazines; *Radiolandia
    (Radioland)*, fan magazines, and celebrity
    culture

Arirang, generalist content of, 59
Aristarco, Guido, 140, 210
Ariza, Francisco J., 256
Arnheim, Rudolf, 139, 210, 281–82, 296n26
Arnoux, Alexandre, 26–28
Arroyo Cisneros, Ramón (Arroyito), 257
Artefilm, 269, 274n34
Arthur, Art (Arthur Bossin), 304, 311n16
artificial intelligence (AI), 336
Arzoo (film), 52
Askari, Kaveh, 14
Associazione generale italiana dello spettacolo
    (AGIS, General Italian Association for
    Entertainment), 316, 318, 320–22, 326n23
Astros (Stars), and Argentine celebrity culture, 265
Astros y Estrellas (Celestial Bodies and Stars), and
    Argentine celebrity culture, 266
Astruc, Alexandre, 139, 171, 210
Atlanta Constitution, newspapers and syndicated
    movie sections, 99
Atsu Kann (Gan Yazi), 349
audience and reader participation: in *Cine-
    Mundial*, 253–55; *Cine-Mundial* and United
    States culture explained to readership,
    255–56; *filmindia*, hybrid audience and
    identity, 14, 37–38, 48, 53–54; *Film und
    Lichtbild*, letters column, 153; and "Herald
    Only" Club (*Exhibitors Herald*), 332; *Il
    Giornale dello Spettacolo* in 1950s, 321–22;
    of Latin American cine club magazines,
    136–38; Latin American readers' connection
    to film culture, 136–38; *Neue Filmwelt
    (New Film World)* and post-World War II
    German film culture, 281; *Radiolandia* and
    Argentine celebrity culture, 270–71; readers
    during Japan's post-1968, 204; readers' letters
    and cine-news, 113–14; *Setāreh-ye Sinemā
    (Cinema Star)*, film criticism respect vs.
    fan service disparagement, 14, 71–82, 74*fig.*,
    77*fig.*, 78*fig.*
Audry, Jacqueline, 172
Aurenche, Jean, 34n3
Auric, Georges, 29
Auriol, Jean George, 176
Autant en emporte le vent (Gone with the Wind,
    film), 32
Autant-Lara, Claude, 185
auteur theory: *Cinéma* and mid-century French
    film industry, 163, 170; and *Film Appreciation*
    (電影欣賞, Taiwan), 220; and Japan's
    post-1968, 203, 208; and *Pour Vous*, 29; and
    Setāreh-ye Sinemā, 78, 80–82. See also *Kikan
    firumu (Film Quarterly)*, Japan's post-1968

INDEX   383

Automovil Americana, and transnational cultural influence, 250

The Avant-Garde Film (Sitney), 210

"Aventuras de La Familia Pérez en New York" (Martinez), 255

Awazu Kiyoshi, 205

Awotele, and African film criticism, 196–97

Ayúdame a vivir/Help Me to Live (film), 262, 268, 269

Bada, José Manuel, 256

Bailby, Léon, 26, 32

Bakyono, Jean Servais, 200n42

Balázs, Béla, 210

Bara, Theda, 89

Barbaro, Umberto, 220

Bardèche, Maurice, 176

Baroncelli, Jean de, 169

Barrett, John, 258n10

Barry, Iris, 168

Basinger, Janine, 268

Bassori, Timité, 187, 191

Bataille, Georges, 185

Bathrick, David, 280

The Battle at Elderbush Gulch (film), 120

Baye Fall, A., 188

Bazin, André, 163, 166, 210, 222

B.B. Samant & Company, 37–38

Becker, Jacques, 171

The Beggars (play), 169

Belodubrovskaya, Maria, 9, 16

Bénac, Gaston, 32

Benson-Allott, Caetlin, 120

Bergmann, Karl Hans, 277, 280, 281–82, 291

Bernard, Raymond, 171

Berndt, Wilhelm, 149, 155, 157n5

Besos brujos/Bewitching Kisses (film), 268, 269

Bezhin Meadow (film), 239–40, 245

Bhabi (film), 38

Bhêly-Quenum, Olympe, 188, 190, 191, 194, 199n15

Bianco e Nero (Italy): and Latin American cine club publications, 135, 139; study of, 11; and Taiwanese film culture, 220

Biblioteca Luigi Chiarini del Centro Sperimentale di Cinematografia, 11

Bicycle Thieves/Ladri di biciclette (film), 291

Bildt, Paul, 289

Bild und Film, amateur science interest in film (Germany, pre-World War I), 144, 147, 148, 148nn7–8

Billard, Pierre, 166, 171, 172

Biltereyst, Daniel, 6, 7–8, 317

Binghua Gao, 107, 108*fig.*

Bin Wang, 170

Birmingham (AL) News, newspapers and syndicated movie sections, 88

"The Birth of an Avant-Garde: *La caméra-stylo*" (Astruc), 139

Bliakhin, Pavel, 245

The Blood of a Poet (film), 120

Boiarskii, Iakov, 245

Boileau-Narcejac, 79

Bölsche, Wilhelm, 150

Bol'shakov, Ivan, 240, 245

Bombay Chronicle (India), film criticism in, 41

Bontempelli, Massimo, 319

Bordwell, David, 178

"Borsa Film" (*Il Giornale dello Spettacolo, GdS*), 323–24

Bossin, Celia, 305*fig.*

Bossin, Hye, 17, 301–10, 305*fig.*, 306*fig.*, 309*fig.*, 310n1, 311n12, 312n19

Bost, Pierre, 26, 34n3

Boston Globe, newspapers and syndicated movie sections, 99

Boston Post, newspapers and syndicated movie sections, 91

Boudu sauvé des eaux/Boudu Saved from Drowning (film), 178

Bougedir, Férid, 187

Boule de suif (film), 237

Bourdelon, Georges, 190

Boxer Indemnity (China), 366n31

Boxoffice, study of, 1

box office analysis, *Il Giornale dello Spettacolo* on, 322–24, 323*fig.*

Braginskii, Grigorii, 241

Brasillach, Robert, 176

Braun, Vladimir, 238

Brawn of the North (film), 342*fig.*, 344

Brazzaville Camera Club, 193

Bresson, Robert, 171

Brill, 246

British American Tobacco Company, 359

British Broadcasting Company (BBC), 264

British Distributors, India, 50

British filmmaking, 42–43, 50

Brockliss-Simplex, 191

Brodsky, Benjamin, 357, 363

Brooklyn Eagle, Art Arthur's writing in, 304

Brooklyn Times-Union, newspapers and syndicated movie sections, 99

Brooks, Richard, 190

"The Brother Overseas" (*filmindia*, Patel), 1, 18–19

384   INDEX

Büchner, Georg, 289
Buek, G. H., 92
Bukhsh Ellahie & Co., 46
Bunker, Steven, 254
Buñuel, Luis, 169, 210
Burkina Faso, and African film criticism, 195–97
Bush, Ruth, 188
Bush, W. Stephen, 330
Bushman, Francis X., 89

Cagney, James, 97
Cahiers du Cinéma: and African film criticism, 195; vs. *Cinéma* and mid-century French film industry, 163, 166, 172, 179; and editorial content of Iranian publications, 71, 80, 82n2; film studies analysis of, 277; and Japan's post-1968, 205; and Latin American cine club publications, 135, 139, 140; and Taiwanese film culture, 220; "Une Certaine tendance du cinéma français" in, 26
Caillens, Jean, 185
Caimari, Lila, 266
Camera!, computational analysis of United States film industry trade press, 330, 333*fig.*, 341–44, 343*fig.*
Campany, David, 116
Camus, Albert, 185
Camus, Marcel, 171
"Canada and the Film: The Story of the Canadian Motion Picture Industry" (*Canadian Film Weekly Year Book*), 307
Canada and the Film (Bossin), 307
Canadian Association for Adult Education, 307
Canadian Broadcasting Corporation, 302
Canadian Film Archive, 308
Canadian Film Awards, 307
Canadian Film Digest, and Canadian film industry, 310, 313n49
Canadian Film Institute, 310
Canadian film journals, 301–15; archival preservation proposal and eventual fire, 307–10; box office admissions, 312n26; and Canada's film industry history, 301–2, 310; *Canadian Film Weekly* and Bossin, 17, 301–10, 302*fig.*, 305*fig.*, 306*fig.*, 309*fig.*, 310n1, 311n12, 312n19; *Canadian Film Weekly Year Book*, 307; *Canadian Moving Picture Digest*, 302–6, 306*fig.*, 308; and *Film Daily* (United States trade paper), 305
Canadian Film & TV Bi-Weekly Year Book of the Canadian Entertainment Industry, 313n49

Canadian Film Weekly: and Canadian film industry, 301–10, 302*fig.*, 305*fig.*, 306*fig.*, 309*fig.*, 310n1, 311n12, 312n19; study of, 17
Canadian Film Weekly Year Book of the Canadian Motion Picture Industry (Bossin), 17, 301, 303, 308, 310
Canadian Foundation, 307
Canadian Independent, and Canadian film industry, 303
The Canadian Motion Picture Exhibitor, and Canadian film industry, 303
Canadian Moving Picture Digest: and Canadian film industry, 301–6, 306*fig.*, 308; computational analysis of United States film industry trade press, 332, 333*fig.*, 334; and film criticism, 50
Cannes Film Festival, 191
Canudo, Ricciotto, 210
Caristan, Robert, 185
Carlyle, Rita, 40
Carné, Marcel, 26, 169, 171
Carnival of the Gods (film), 190
Carpenter, John, 256
Carr, E. H., 178
Carril, Hugo del, 262, 268, 273n25
cartoons, comics, and illustration: caricatures in *Kino* (Soviet Union), 245–46; *Cine-Mundial* and transnational cultural influence, 257–58; in *Delight*, 62; in newspapers, 98. *See also* visual design and layout
Casablanca (film), 120
Catholic Association of Cinema Exhibitors (ACEC), 322
Catholic film exhibition, postwar Italy, 322
celebrity culture and gossip: and Chinese film history, 363n3; in *Cine-Mundial*, 250–53, 252*fig.*; in *filmindia*, 41; study of, 7–8. *See also* audience and reader participation; *Radiolandia (Radioland)*, fan magazines, and celebrity culture
Cendrars, Blaise, 26
censorship: and crime thriller genre, 80–82; Laval Decree (1934), 185; National Board of Review (United States), 80, 84n42; and sexual content of *Delight*, 61, 65–66
Centipede (film), 71
Central Committee of the Union for Workers in the Arts (RABIS, Soviet Union), 236–36, 239, 244, 245
Central Motion Picture Company (CMPC), 221–22, 226
Central Nekrasov Library (Moscow), 246

Centro Sperimentale di Cinematografia, 319
"A Certain Tendency of the French Cinema"
(Truffaut), 163
Cesta do pravěku (film), 291
Chabrol, Claude, 172, 175
Chaffard, Georges, 188
Chalmers Publishing Company, 17, 248, 250, 253.
See also *Cine-Mundial* and transnational
cultural influence
Chand Ka Tukda (film), 38
Chandrasena (film), 38
Chapaev (film), 237
Chaplin, Charlie, 89, 169, 253
Chaplin Club (Rio de Janeiro), 133
Charlo, 268
Chateau de Marly event (1954), 170
ChatGPT software (OpenAI), 336
Chelyuskin (film), 237
Chen Dingxiu (D. S. Chen), 349, 354, 361, 362*fig.*
Cheng Shuren (S. J. Benjamin Cheng), 349, 354,
357, 358–59, 361, 362*fig.*
Chen Guofu, 220, 222
Chen Yanyan, 114
Cherkasov, Nikolai, 246
Chez les mangeurs d'hommes (hoax
documentary), 31
Chiao, Peggy, 222, 223
Chiaureli, Mikheil, 238
Chicago Record-Herald, newspapers and
syndicated movie sections, 90
Chicago Tribune, newspapers and syndicated
movie sections, 88–89, 90*fig.*
*China Cinema Year Book 1927 (Zhonghua
yingyue nianian)*, and understanding
Chinese film history, 349, 354–63, 355*fig.*,
361n21, 361n23
China Film Archive, 349
Chin Chin Screen (Qingqing dianying 青青電影),
intermediality in film publications, 113–14
Chinese film history (1920s), 347–68; *China
Cinema Year Book 1927 (Zhonghua yingyue
nianian)*, 349, 354–63, 355*fig.*, 361n21,
361n23; curating sources of, overview, 18,
347–51; *Motion Picture Review (Yingxi zazhi)*,
348–50, 364n6; *Movies Magazine (Dianying
zazhi)*, 348–50; *On Photoplay (Yingxi xue)*,
349, 351–54, 352*fig.*, 353*fig.*, 361, 364n8; *Silver
Light (Yin Guang)*, 350, 364n12
Chinese film publications, intermediality of,
107–27; cinemascapes and cine-news in,
110–15, 117, 121; cine-news, defined,
113–14; film periodicals concept, 108–9;

film periodical types, 112–13; intermedial
dynamic in, 14–15, 107–10, 108*fig.*, 120–22;
intermediality, defined, 109–10; material
and discursive elements, overview, 14–15; as
paper cinema and cinematic *lianhuanhua*,
110, 114–21, 116*fig.*, 118*fig.*, 119*fig.*
Chinese Film Research Society, 111–12, 123n7
Chinese Library Press, 124n14
Chinese Mail (China Mail), 364n12
Chinese University of Hong Kong, 349, 350
Chirkov, Boris, 246
Choui Khoua, 170
Chow Tse-chi (Zhou Ziqi), 359
Chronicles of Russian Cinema (Deriabin), 236
Chugtai, Ismat, 52
Chun Doo Hwan, 68n4
Churchill, Douglas W., 97, 99
Cinéa, computational analysis of United States
film industry trade press, 333*fig.*
Cine Argentino (Argentine Cinema), and
Argentine celebrity culture, 265
ciné-club, of *Pour Vous*, 29
Cineclub (Brazil), and Latin American cine club
publications, 135
Ciné-Club (Cinéma predecessor), and
mid-century French film industry, 180n14
Cine Club (Colombia), and Latin American cine
club publications, 133–34
cine club magazines of Latin America. *See* Latin
American cine club magazines
Cine Club (Mexico), and Latin American cine
club publications, 133
ciné-club movement: *Cinéma* and mid-century
French film industry, 166–71; and Japan's
post-1968 magazines, 215n4
Cine Club Núcleo (publishing company), 132
cine clubs, defined, 133
Cine Club Universitario (Santiago de Chile), 134
Cine Club (Uruguay), study of, 15. See also
*Cuadernos de Cine Club; Cuadernos de Cine
Club* (Uruguay, previously *Cine Club*)
Cine Foro (Chile), and Latin American cine club
publications, 135
Ciné France (France), and *Pour Vous* as
contemporary publication, 29, 30
Cine-Kodak, 51
Cinelandia: Harrison's influence on, 4;
modern-day accessibility of, 5; study of, 11;
and transnational cultural influence, 248
Ciné-Liberté (France), and *Pour Vous* as
contemporary publication, 30
Cinema, and postwar Italian film industry, 318

386 INDEX

"Cinema and Africa" (*La Vie Africaine*), 188, 189*fig.*

Cinema and Africa (*Le cinéma et l'Afrique*, Vieyra), 187

Cinema and Nation (Hjort and MacKenzie), 8

"Cinema and the African Revolution" (*La Vie Africaine*), 188, 190

Cinema Catholic Centre, 322

Cinema Chat (*Movie Chat*), and Argentine celebrity culture, 265

Cinema Committee (Soviet Union), 235–40

Cinéma (France): and Latin American cine club publications, 132, 139; study of, 15. See also *Cinéma* (France) and mid-century French film industry

Cinéma (France) and mid-century French film industry, 163–83; and ciné-club movement, 166–71; *Cinéma* and year-to-year title change, 163; *Cinéma 57* cover, 164*fig.*; *Cinéma* mission and identity, 166, 178–79; *Cinéma 57* table of contents, 165*fig.*; "Guide du spectateur" (Spectator Guide), 160; and the New Wave (La nouvelle vague), 171–75, 173*fig.*, 174*fig.*; and Sadoul on writing of film history, 175–79; and *Shinema 69*, 210; understanding film culture in post-World War II France, 15, 163–66

Cinema illustrazione, study of, 11

Cinema Nuovo (Italy): and Latin American cine club publications, 132, 139; and postwar Italian film industry, 318

"Cinema Plaza" section (*United Daily News*, Taiwan), 222

cinema reform movement, 147–48

Cinema Rex, 84n36

Cinema Samachar (India), Patel's early career at, 38

cinemascapes, defined, 110–11, 123n5. See also Chinese film publications

Cinema Star (Iran). See *Setāreh-ye Sinemā* (*Cinema Star*)

Cinémathèque française, 11, 166, 168–70, 175, 176

cinematic *lianhuanhua* of Chinese film publications, 114–21, 116*fig.*, 118*fig.*, 119*fig.*

cinematography. See film industry

Cinema World (*Yŏnghwa segye*), publication duration of, 58, 67n3

Ciné Miroir (France), and *Pour Vous* as contemporary publication, 29

Cinémonde (France), and Latin American cine club publications, 139

Ciné-Mondial (Vichy France), political view of, 32

Cine-Mundial and transnational cultural influence, 248–61; and advertising, 250, 251*fig.*, 253–54; and celebrity culture, 250–53, 252*fig.*; computational analysis of United States film industry trade press, 333*fig.*, 341; design of magazine, 249; and film's role in North and South America relationships, 17, 248–50; Harrison's influence on, 4; hemispheric commerce facilitated by magazine, 250; illustration used by magazine, 257–58; modern-day accessibility of, 5; non-film content of magazine, 254–56; and political events, 256–57; study of, 17

cine-news, defined, 113–14. See also Chinese film publications

Ciné Pour Tous (France), and *Pour Vous* as contemporary publication, 29

Ciné Revue (France), and *Pour Vous* as contemporary publication, 29

Cinespettacolo, and postwar Italian film industry, 319

Cinethique, film studies analysis of, 277

Cine Universal (*Universal Cinema*), and Argentine celebrity culture, 265

Cine Universitario (Montevideo), 132, 141n4

circulation. See subscription pricing and circulation

Cita en la frontera/Date on the Border (film), 268, 269

Citizen Kane (film), 176

City of Sadness (film), 222, 223

Clair, René, 26, 171, 210

classical film theory, 139, 166, 169, 210–11

Cleveland Leader, newspapers and syndicated movie sections, 88–90

Clift, Montgomery, 78

Clouzot, Henri-Georges, 171

Clubman (Britain), and Iranian editorial content, 76

Cocteau, Jean, 29, 120, 166

Cologne Society of Natural Scientists, 148

Comandon, Jean, 149, 168

Commerce in Latin America, and transnational cultural influence, 250

Commercial Bureau of the American Republic, 258n10

Commission de recherches historiques de la Cinémathèque française (Commission of Historical Research of the Cinémathèque Française), 176

Communist Party (China), 361. See also Chinese film history (1920s)

INDEX 387

Communist Party (Soviet Union), 236–40. See also *Kino*
"Compilation of Movies Magazines from the Republican Era" (Shanghai Library), 123–24n14
Complete Catalog of Chinese Modern Film Periodicals, 113
computational analysis of United States film industry trade press (early 1920s), 330–46; analysis of results, 340–44, 342*fig.*, 343*fig.*; to find patterns and trends, 18, 330–32, 344; identifying publications for study, 332–35, 333–34*fig.*; methods, 335–39, 345n5; workflow of research, 339–40
Congress of Black Writers and Artists (Paris), 187
Consolidated Press Association, 311n16
Contreras, Rosita, 262
Conway, Kelley, 15, 210
copyright: *Delight* and photography, 61; and geo-blocking of research, 301
Córdoba, Irma, 262
Cosimi, Nelo, 268
cosine distance, 337–39, 341. See also computational analysis of United States film industry trade press (early 1920s)
Cotet, Jean, 175
Coulibaly, Thomas, 191
Covarrubias, Miguel, 257–58
Cowan, Michael, 11, 15
crime thriller genre, 80–82
Critics' Poll list (*Canadian Film Weekly*), 306
Cuadernos de Cine Club (Uruguay, previously *Cine Club*), and Latin American cine club publications, 133, 135, 139, 140, 143n38
cultural entrepreneurship, 365n20
Curry, Ramona, 363

D. S. Chen (Chen Dingxiu), 349, 354
Dacheng Bao, and Taiwanese film culture, 223
Dadié, Bernard, 185
Daiei film studio, 203
Daily Film Renter, news-sharing agreement of, 9
Dainichi eihai film distribution company, 203
Damita, Lili, 32, 74
Dariush, Hajir, 78, 84n40
Das Bild im Dienst der Schule und Volksbildung, amateur science interest in film (Germany, pre–World War I), 157
data, curation, and historiography, 299–368; Canadian film journals, 301–15; Chinese film history (1920s), 347–68; computational

analysis of United States film industry trade press (early 1920s), 347–68; Italian film industry trade publications, 316–29; overview, 17–18. See also Canadian film journals; Chinese film history (1920s); computational analysis of United States film industry trade press (early 1920s)
Davai, Parviz, 82n2
Davis, Darrell, 11, 13, 18
Davison, Tito, 262, 272n1
Davoodi, Abolhassan, 71
The Dawn (film), 118*fig.*
Day, Sara, 97
Dayton (OH) News, newspapers and syndicated movie sections, 91
D'dée (André Trisot), 16, 188–93, 193*fig.*, 194–95, 197–98
"Dear Birthday Boy!" (Gabrilovich), 246
deCordova, Richard, 268
de Cruz, Chas, 4
DEFA Foundation, 277. See also Deutsche Film AG (DEFA)
de Havilland, Olivia, 12*fig.*, 32
De la Torre, Elena, 254, 257
De la Veracruz, Raymundo, 255
Delbene, Floren (Florentino), 17, 262–65, 263*fig.*, 268–71, 273n26, 273n29, 273n33
Delight, 57–70; and "delight" slogan, 65; entertainment content and visual strategy, 58–64, 60–64*fig.*, 67; hybrid identity of, 14; Korean War and publishing industry growth, 57–58; political propaganda of, 58, 64–67, 66*fig.*; postwar role of, overview, 14; pricing and circulation of, 59; publication duration of, 58, 68n4; study of, 14
Delluc, Louis, 133
Del Ruth, Roy, 26
De Luna Freire, Rafael, 317, 318
DeMille, Cecil B., 31, 253
D'entre les morts (Boileau-Narcejac), 79
Der Andere (film), 283
Der Ausweg, and post–World War II German film culture, 280
Der blonde Chauffeur (film), 283
Deren, Maya, 210
Der Filmspiegel, and post–World War II German film culture, 293
Deriabin, Aleksandr, 236
Der Kinematograph: amateur science interest in film (Germany, pre–World War I), 157; computational analysis of United States film industry trade press, 333*fig.*, 341; study of, 11

388 INDEX

Der Lehrfilm, amateur science interest in film (Germany, pre-World War I), 157, 161n61
Der Liebesbrief der Königin (film), 283
Derrida, Jacques, 212
Der Schritt vom Wege (film), 289
Desert Rats (film), 169
De Sica, Vittorio, 178
Desjardins, Mary, 265
Des Moines Register and Tribune Syndicate, 98, 105
Detroit Free Press, newspapers and syndicated movie sections, 95–99, 96*fig.*, 98*fig.*, 104n67
Deutsche Film AG (DEFA), 277, 280–83
Deutsche Filmverlag (publishing house), 280, 282
de Zavalía, Alberto, 273n25
Dharma Patni (film), 48, 49*fig.*
Dia, Mamadou, 185
Dia, Thierno Ibrahima, 197
Dia-Moukori, Urbain, 187
dianying huabao periodicals, 122n1
Diawara, Manthia, 197
Díaz, Porfirio, 256, 260n43
Di Chiara, Francesco, 320
Die Büchse der Pandora (film), 133
Diederichs, Helmut H., 296n26
Die Lichtbild-Bühne: amateur science interest in film (Germany, pre-World War I), 145; news-sharing agreement of, 9; study of, 11
Die Nibelungen, 289
Die Rampe, and post-World War II German film culture, 280
Dietrich, Marlene, 29, 97
Dietz, Edith, 95, 97
Dietz, George, 95
Digital Library Luigi Chiarini (Centro Sperimentale di Cinematografia), 319
Di Núbila, Domingo, 267, 271
Diop, Alioune, 185, 187, 188, 190, 191, 197
Director (India), film reviews in, 43
Do Bigha Zamin/Two Bighas of Land (film), 170
Dol, Honoré, 191
D'Orsay, Fifi, 32
Dostoevsky, Fyodor, 138
Douy, Max, 170
Dovzhenko, Aleksandr, 237, 240
Draupadi (film), 50
The Dreamers (film), 238
Dream of the Red Chamber (film), 359
Dreyer, Carl Theodor, 178, 289
Duca, Lo, 31
Ducournau, Claire, 188

Dufour, Fernand, 169–70
Dukel'skii, Semen, 240, 241, 245
Dulac, Germaine, 210
Duniya Kya Hai (film), 47–48
Dupont, Jacques, 190
Duras, Marguerite, 174
Durbin, Deanna, 74
Ďurovičová, Nataša, 8
Duvivier, Julien, 171, 241
Duxiu Academic Search database, 350
Dyer, Richard, 267

East German film culture. See *Neue Filmwelt (New Film World)* and post-World War II German film culture
Ecksan, K. L. (pseudonym), 100
Écrans d'Afrique/African Screen, African film criticism, 196*fig.*
Edison, Thomas A., 307
Editor and Publisher, newspapers and syndicated movie sections, 92, 99
editorial content: advice columns in *Delight*, 64; contributors' pay, *Cine-Mundial*, 257; of *Film Appreciation* (Taiwan), 221, 226; honoraria for writers, Japanese publications, 205; *Il Giornale dello Spettacolo* in 1950s, 320–24, 321*fig.*, 323*fig.*; of Iranian publications, 74, 75; *Kino* and Stalinist Soviet Union, 236–41, 243–45; of Latin American cine club magazines, 134–35; *Pour Vous* and French film culture (1928–40), 26, 31–32. See also *Neue Filmwelt (New Film World)* and post-World War II German film culture; newspapers and syndicated movie sections
Editorial Haynes, 267
Ehrick, Christine, 264
Eiga hihyō (Film Criticism): Japan's post-1968, 16, 203–4, 208–10, 209*fig.*, 213, 214, 215n4; study of, 16
"Eiga sengenshū" (A Collection of Film Manifestos, *Kikan firumu*), 210
Eisenstein, Sergei, 78, 210, 239, 244–45, 246
Eisner, Lotte, 169, 170
El crimen de Oribe/The Crime of Oribe (film), 138
"The Electric Human" (Günther), 156*fig.*
ElectroNekrasovka, 246
"Elektrotechnisches Beiheft" (*Film und Lichtbild* supplement), 154
El muro (The Wall, film), 138
El Purrete (The Kid), and Argentine celebrity culture, 266

El último estreno (Radio Belgrano), 262–64, 263*fig.*, 268–71, 270*fig.*, 275n38

Embattled Shadows (Morris), 310

Emmer, Luciano, 168

Empresario Internacional, study of, 11, 12

Engelein (film), 283

Epstein, Jean, 210

Ermler, Fridrikh, 237

Escuder, J. M., 256

España, Claudio, 264

Euclidean and cosine distance, 337–39, 341. *See also* computational analysis of United States film industry trade press (early 1920s)

"Even as You and Hye" *(Jewish Standard)*, 304

Ewandé, Félix, 187

Executive Suite (film), 169

exhibitors: in Canada, 301–6; "discovery" of film and cinema by amateur science communities, 145–49, 157–58nn6–8, 158n12; Japan's post-1968 and theaters of 1958–68, 202–3; of postwar Italy, 319–20, 321*fig.*, 322

Exhibitors Herald: computational analysis of United States film industry trade press, 330, 332, 333*fig.*, 334, 337–38, 340–44; study of, 18

Exhibitor's Trade Review: computational analysis of United States film industry trade press, 330, 333*fig.*, 334*fig.*, 340–44; study of, 18

Experimentierbuch (experiment book), 155

Experimentierbuch für die Jugend, amateur science interest in film (Germany, pre-World War I), 156*fig.*

Ezhov, Nikolai, 245

Ezra, Elizabeth, 9

Fa. See *Film Appreciation (Fa*, 電影欣賞*)* and Taiwanese film culture

Falk, Stella, 303

Famiglia Cristiana, and postwar Italian film industry, 318

Famous Cine Laboratory (Bombay), 43, 46*fig.*

Famous Films, 48

Famous Pictures, 37

Famous Players Canadian Corporation, 304, 305, 311n12

Famous Players studio (United States), 359

fan magazines. *See* celebrity culture and gossip

fan magazines as newspaper supplements. *See* newspapers and syndicated movie sections

Fanon, Frantz, 213

far-left radicalism, Japan. See *Eiga hihyō (Film Criticism)*, Japan's post-1968

Farmanara, Bahman, 78

Fédération française des ciné-clubs, 133, 137, 141n6

Federation Internationale des Archives du Film, 318

Felix, Friederich, 149

Fellini, Federico, 139

Fenin, George N., 140

Ferdowsi (Iran), as intellectual journal, 73

Ferrari, Roberto, 320

Ferraù, Alessandro, 320–21

Ferreyra, José Agustín, 268

Feyder, Jacques, 25, 27*fig.*

Film Advisory Board (Britain), 42–43

Film and Image Syndicate of Viennese Teachers, 157

Film and Radio (Dianying yu boyin 電影與播音*)*, 109

Film Appreciation (Fa, 電影欣賞*)* and Taiwanese film culture: as archive, 228; design and layout of, 226–28, 227*fig.*; and lack of influence, 220–23; and New Cinema movement, 16, 219, 220–23, 226, 228; study of magazine, 16; and Taiwan Film and Audiovisual Institute (TFAI) as institutional basis, 16, 219–21, 223–26, 228

Film Art (Dianying yishu 電影藝術*)*, 112

Film Artistes' Association of India, 51

Film as Art (Arnheim), 281–82, 296n26

Film-Autoren-Kongreß (First Conference of Filmmakers), 280

Film Canada Yearbook, and Canadian film industry, 313n49

Filmcritica, and postwar Italian film industry, 319

film criticism: Critics' Poll list *(Canadian Film Weekly)*, 306; *filmindia*, film criticism and film trade, 50–52; *filmindia*, film critics as experts, 40–43; *hihyō* (Japanese film criticism), 204; Latin American cine club magazines and politicization of Latin American film culture, 138–41; *Setāreh-ye Sinemā (Cinema Star)*, film criticism respect vs. fan service disparagement, 14, 71–82, 74*fig.*, 77*fig.*, 78*fig. See also* African film criticism in Paris; Canadian film journals

Film Culture Reader (Sitney), 211

film cultures, critics, and circuits: African film criticism in Paris, 184–201 (*See also* African film criticism in Paris); *Cinéma* and mid-century French film culture, 163–83; *Film Appreciation* and Taiwanese film culture, 219–31; *Film und Lichtbild* and amateur science, 145–62; Japan's post-1968 and *Kikan*

390 INDEX

film cultures (*continued*)
   firumu, Shinema 69, and *Eiga hihyō*, 202–18;
   Latin American cine club magazines, 131–44;
   overview, 15–16. See also *Cinéma* (France)
   and mid-century French film industry; *Film
   Appreciation* (*Fa*, 電影欣賞) and Taiwanese
   film culture; *Film und Lichtbild* and amateur
   science; Japan's post-1968; Latin American
   cine club magazines
Film Culture (United States): film studies
   analysis of, 277; and Latin American cine
   club publications, 132, 139, 140
Film Daily (India), on *filmindia*, 41
Film Daily (United States trade paper): and
   Canadian film industry, 305; computational
   analysis of United States film industry trade
   press, 333*fig.*; news-sharing agreement of, 9;
   study of, 9
Film Daily Year Book, and Canadian film
   industry, 307
Film d'oggi: and postwar Italian film industry,
   318; study of, 11
Film Enquiry Committee (India), 51
filmfārsi (Iranian popular films), 72, 73.
   See also *Setāreh-ye Sinemā (Cinema Star)*
Film für Alle, and amateur film, 157
filmindia, 37–56; advertising, 43–50, 44*fig.*, 47*fig.*,
   49*fig.*; "The Brother Overseas" (Patel), 1,
   18–19; cover images, 38–40, 43–46, 46*fig.*,
   47*fig.*; "Editor's Mail" column, 40, 48, 54; film
   criticism and film trade, 50–52; film critics
   as experts in, 40–43; hybrid audience and
   identity of, 14, 37–38, 48, 53–54; as *Mother
   India*, 38, 52–53; subscription pricing and
   circulation of, 38, 39, 43–44, 48, 53
film industry: of Argentina, 264–65, 268; and
   Japan's post-1968, 202–3; nitrate film, 308–9;
   and professionalization of scientific film,
   155–57; Soviet Cinema nationalization (1920),
   246; Taiwan and economic nature of, 222. *See
   also* Canadian film journals; celebrity culture
   and gossip; exhibitors; *Film Appreciation*
   (*Fa*, 電影欣賞) and Taiwanese film culture;
   New Wave (*La nouvelle vague); Radiolandia
   (Radioland)*, fan magazines, and celebrity
   culture; *individual country names*
Filmistan Studios, 51
Film (Italy), and Taiwanese film culture, 220
Film Journal (*Dianying zazhi* 電影雜志), 112
Film Journalists Association of India, 37
Filmkritik, film studies analysis of, 277
film magazines as intermediaries of state,
   region, and media, 233–99; *Cine-Mundial*

and transnational cultural influence,
   248–61; intermediality, defined, 109–10;
   intermediality, study of, 7–8; *Kino* and
   Stalinist Soviet Union, 235–47; *Neue Filmwelt*
   and post-World War II German film culture,
   277–99; overview, 16–17; *Radiolandia
   (Radioland)*, fan magazines, and celebrity
   culture, 262–76. See also *Kino; Neue Filmwelt
   (New Film World)* and post-World War II
   German film culture
Film Manifestos and Global Cinema Cultures
   (MacKenzie), 210
Film Monthly (Iran), editorial content, 71–72
Film News (*Dianying xinwen* 電影新聞), 109, 115
Film Quarterly, film studies analysis of, 277
Film Renter and Moving Picture News,
   computational analysis of United States film
   industry trade press, 332, 333*fig.*
Films in Review (United States), and Latin
   American cine club publications, 139
film society movement (Latin America), 131–33,
   141n6. *See also* Latin American cine club
   magazines
film study as scholarly field: classical film theory,
   139, 166, 169, 210–11; collaboration for study of,
   5–6; *Neue Filmwelt* analysis, overview, 277–88,
   295n7; new cinema history discipline, 6–7
Film und Lichtbild and amateur science, 145–62;
   amateur film as outgrowth of amateur
   science, 151–57, 152*fig.*; amateur scientific
   publishing and self-determination, 149–51;
   cultural links between cinema and amateur
   science, 15, 145–49; *Film und Lichtbild*, study
   of magazine, 15; *Film und Lichtbild* and
   film as experiential science, 154–55, 156*fig.*;
   Film und Lichtbild cover, 146*fig.*; *Film und
   Lichtbild* inception and content, 151–54; and
   professionalization of scientific film, 155–57
Film und Wissen, film and science, 157
Film (Uruguay, later *Nuevo Film* Uruguay), and
   Latin American cine club publications, 132,
   141n4
Film Weekly (*Dianying zhoukan* 電影周刊), 112
Filmwelt, and post-World War II German film
   culture, 278. See also *Neue Filmwelt (New
   Film World)* and post-World War II German
   film culture
Five-Year Plan for Compulsory Education
   (South Korea), 57
Flaherty, Robert, 168
Fonda, Henry, 78
Ford, John, 169
Forfaiture (The Cheat, film), 31

Foucault, Michel, 67
400 Blows (Taiwan), 174, 222
France. *See* African film criticism in Paris; New Wave *(La nouvelle vague); Pour Vous* and French film culture (1928–40)
Francé, Raoul Heinrich, 150
France Eurafrique, African film criticism, 187
Franck'sche Verlag, 146, 150, 151, 154. See also *Film und Lichtbild* and amateur science
Franco, Herminia, 262, 270, 271
Frank, Nino, 29–30
Frankfurter Zeitung (Germany), Kracauer's articles in, 35n19
Franklin, Sidney, 31
Freies Deutschland, and post-World War II German film culture, 280
French Ciné-Club Federation (FFCC), 166–68, 176, 180n14. See also *Cinéma* (France) and mid-century French film industry
French Federation of Ciné-Clubs, 15
French National Center for Cinema, 190
French poststructuralism. See *Shinema 69, 70, and 71 (Cinema 69, 70, and 71)*, Japan's post-1968
Frenkel', Lazar', 241
Fröhlich, Vincent, 9, 17, 277–78
Fu, Yongchun, 365n23
fūkeiron (landscape theory), 2 16n14, 208–10, 214
Fuller-Seeley, Kathryn, 7
Fustiñana, Andrés José Rolando (Roland), 137
"The Future Kingdom of Silver (Screen)" (Binghua Gao), 107, 108*fig.*

Gabara, Rachel, 15–16
Gabin, Jean, 163
Gable, Clark, 97
Gabriele, Sandra, 87
Gabrilovich, Evgenii, 246
galán, defined, 273n24
Galestian, Paruir, 72–73, 76, 82n12, 83n14
Galt, Rosalind, 9
Gance, Abel, 133, 166, 171
Gan Yazi (Atsu Kann), 349, 354, 361, 362*fig.*
Garbo, Greta, 74
Garcés, Delia, 268
García Ortega, Francisco (Frank), 255, 259n36
García Peña, Antonio Sabrit, 260n43
Gardner, Ava, 75
Gauhar be Baha (Bukhsh Ellahie & Co.), 46
"Geheimnisse der belebten Natur" (Secrets of Living Nature, Berndt), 149
Gennari, Daniela Treveri, 11, 13, 18

Gente de Cine: and Latin American cine club publications, 131–32, 134, 137, 139, 141nn7–8; study of, 15
Gente de Cine club, 131
German Democratic Republic (GDR), 278–79. See also *Neue Filmwelt (New Film World)* and post-World War II German film culture
German film culture: Eisner on, 169; *Pour Vous* on, 30–31. See also *Film und Lichtbild* and amateur science; *Neue Filmwelt (New Film World)* and post-World War II German film culture
Gerow, Aaron, 213
Getino, Octavio, 210
Gide, André, 185
Gikor (film), 238
Ginsberg, Arthur, 204
Giovacchini, Saverio, 9
G.I.P. Railway, 43, 44*fig.*
Giraudoux, Jean, 26
Glamour, photography of, 61
Global Art Cinema: New Theories and Histories (Galt and Schoonover), 9
Global Cinema History Task Force, 10–11
Globalizing and Enhancing the Media History Digital Library, 318
global movie magazine networks: data, curation, and historiography, overview, 17–18; film cultures, critics, and circuits, overview, 15–16; and globalizing MHDL, 10–13, 12*fig.*; *Harrison's Reports*, influence on other publications, 1–5, 2*fig.*, 3*fig.*, 9, 18–19, 39, 330, 334, 373*fig.*); hybrid journals, overview, 13–15; importance of study of, 6–10, 18–19; intermediaries of state, region, and media, overview, 16–17; MHDL, magazines available in, 11, 18, 369–76*fig. See also* data, curation, and historiography; film cultures, critics, and circuits; film magazines as intermediaries of state, region, and media
Global Neorealism: The Transnational History of a Film Style (Giovacchini and Sklar), 9
Globe and Mail (Toronto), and Canadian film industry, 308
Godard, Jean-Luc, 139, 171, 205, 210, 220
Goddard, Paulette, 100*fig.*
Goebbels, Joseph, 279, 290
Goerke, Franz, 158n7
Gola, José, 268, 273n25
Golden Tobacco Company, 45, 47*fig.*
Goldman, Emma, 304
Gomez de Zarraga, Elena (pseudonym), 255, 257
González Centeno, Carolina, 265, 271

392 INDEX

Gorin, Jean-Pierre, 210
gossip columns. *See* newspapers and syndicated movie sections
Gottschalk, Joachim, 289–90
Government Information Office (GIO, Taiwan), 223
Gow, Gordon, 77, 83n33
Gramophone, 51
Grand China Lilium Film Company, 358
Grandville, Grace, 97
Granov, Vil'gel'm, 246
Gras, Enrico, 168
Grau, Robert, 176
The Great Selection: "First National First" Season 1922–1923 (promotional booklet), 333*fig.*, 334*fig.*, 340–42, 344
Great Terror (Soviet Union, 1937–38), 239–40, 243–45
The Great Waltz (film), 241
Greco, Juliette, 191
Green, John C., 313n48
Grémillon, Jean, 168
Griaznov, Evgenii, 238
Grierson, John, 168
Griffith, D. W., 120
Gross, Benjamin S., 88
Groupe des Trentes (Group of Thirty), 167
Gründgen, Gustav, 289
Guevara, Che, 213
Gunga Din (film), 41
Günther, Hanns, 155, 156*fig.*
Gwalan (film), 50

Haacker, Carl, 280
Hablemos de Cine (Peru), and Latin American cine club publications, 135
Haeckel, Ernst, 150
Hanada Kiyoteru, 211
Hanna-Daoud, Thomas, 279
Hanno, Hans Meyer, 290
Hansen, Sam, 18
Harrison, Peter S., 1, 2*fig.*, 3*fig.*, 4, 9, 18–19
Harrison's Reports: computational analysis of United States film industry trade press, 330, 334; influence on other publications, 1–5, 2*fig.*, 3*fig.*, 9, 18–19, 39, 330, 334, 373*fig.*
Hasumi Shigehiko, 205, 212–13
Hatano Tetsurō, 204, 205
HathiTrust Digital Library, 17, 301
Hauff, Wilhelm, 150
The Haunted Screen (Eisner), 169
Hayakawa, Sessue, 31

Hays Office Production Code, 41, 100–101
He, Belinda Qian, 11, 14–15
Heibon, and content of *Delight,* 58, 62, 68n4
Helleur, Stan, 313n49
Hellwig, Albert, 147
Heraldo del Cinematografista (Cinematographer's Herald): and Argentine celebrity culture, 267, 270; Harrison's influence on, 4; modern-day accessibility of, 5
"Herald Only" Club *(Exhibitors Herald)*, 332
Herbert, Walter, 308, 309*fig.*
Hermida, Jorge (García Ortega), 255, 259n36
Heusch, Luc de, 190
High Commissariat of French West Africa, 187
Hiraoka Masaaki, 213
Hiroshima mon amour (film), 139, 143n38, 172, 173*fig.*, 174, 174*fig.*
Histoire générale du cinéma (Sadoul), 176, 178
A History of Cinema and Drama in Taiwan (Lü Su-Shang), 350–51
Hitchcock, Alfred, 78–81, 79*fig.*, 84nn36–40, 208
Hitler, Adolf, 279, 289–90, 295n16
Hjort, Mette, 8
Hoberman, J., 223
Hoffmann, E. T. A., 150
Holland Brothers, 307, 313n38, 313n48
Hollywood, la Mecque du cinéma (Cendrars), 26
Hollywood (magazine): and editorial content of Iranian publications, 74, 82n6; and postwar Italian film industry, 318; readers' letters, 113–14
"Hollywood Reporter" (column), newspapers and syndicated movie sections, 97, 98*fig.*
Hollywood Reporter (magazine): *filmindia's* similarity to, 37, 40; newspapers and syndicated movie sections, 101
Holmes, Tim, 101
Honar va Sinemā (Art and Cinema), and Iranian editorial content, 78
Hope (Hope Company/*Hŭimangsa*), generalist content of, 59
Hou Hsiao-hsien, 219, 222, 223, 228
Hoyt, Eric, 7, 18, 39, 110, 277, 318, 324, 331
huabao (pictorial magazine genre), 114
Huerta, Victoriano, 256
Humboldt, Alexander von, 150, 159n26
hybrid journals, 23–127; Chinese film publications, intermediality of, 107–27; *Delight,* 57–70; *filmindia,* 37–56; newspapers and syndicated movie sections, 86–106; overview, 13–14; *Pour Vous,* 25–36; *Setāreh-ye Sinemā (Cinema Star),* 71–85. *See also*

Chinese film publications, intermediality of; *Delight; filmindia;* newspapers and syndicated movie sections; *Pour Vous; Setāreh-ye Sinemā (Cinema Star)*

I Confess (film), 78, 79*fig.*, 84n36

Iimura Takahiko, 204, 205

Ijdedem, C., 186

Il Giornale dello Spettacolo (GdS, formerly *Bollettino di informazione* and then *Bollettino dello Spettacolo)*: Associazione generale italiana dello spettacolo (AGIS, General Italian Association for Entertainment), 316, 318, 320–22, 326n23; omission from digitization, 18, 318–19

illustration. *See* cartoons, comics, and illustration; visual design and layout

Illustrierter Film-Spiegel (Program leaflet of the magazine Neue Filmwelt, leaflet), 292–94, 296n27

Imai Tadashi, 204

Imamura Taihei, 211

Imparcial Film (Impartial Film), and Argentine celebrity culture, 265

Independent Morning Post, and Taiwanese film culture, 223

India. See *filmindia*

Indianapolis Star, newspapers and syndicated movie sections, 92–94

Indianapolis Sunday Star, newspapers and syndicated movie sections, 93*fig.*

Indian Motion Picture Association, 51

Indian Motion Picture Congress, 41

Influence, and Taiwan film culture, 224

Ink-Stained Hollywood: The Triumph of American Cinema's Trade Press (Hoyt), 7, 331

Institut des hautes études cinématographiques (IDHEC): and African film criticism in Paris, 185, 190, 191, 194; *Cinéma* and mid-century French film industry, 163, 168, 176

intermediality: defined, 109–10; study of, 7–8. *See also* Chinese film publications; film magazines as intermediaries of state, region, and media

International Film (Kukche yŏnghwa), publication duration of, 58, 67n3

Internet Archive, 5, 10

Inter-Ocean Film Corporation, 251*fig.*

Iran: film industry of, 71; *Film International* and *Mahndmeh-ye sinema'i-ye film (Film Monthly),* 220–21; *Iran Film,* and

Iranian editorial content, 82n9; *Iranian Cosmopolitanism* (Rekabtalaei), 83n20; and Pahlavi (Shah of Iran), 73. See also *Setāreh-ye Sinemā (Cinema Star)*

"Iraq agitation," *filmindia* on, 48–50

Italian film industry trade publications, 316–29; Associazione generale italiana dello spettacolo (AGIS, General Italian Association for Entertainment), 316, 318, 320–22, 326n23; film journals under fascist Italy, 220; *Il Giornale dello Spettacolo* history and background, 319–20; *Il Giornale dello Spettacolo* in 1950s, 320–24, 321*fig.*, 323*fig.*; *Il Giornale dello Spettacolo* omission from digitation, 18, 318–19; research importance of, 316–18

It Magazine, newspapers and syndicated movie sections, 95

Ivens, Joris, 168

Jacobs, Lewis, 178

Jahān-e Sinemā (The World of Cinema), and editorial content of Iranian publications, 72, 82n6

Japan: *Heibon* and content of *Delight,* 58, 62, 68n4; Japanese materials in *On Photoplay (Yingxi xue),* 351; South Korea and diplomatic relations, 68n14; and South Korean government, 65; as study-abroad destination, 367n41; Taiwan as Japanese colony, 358. *See also* Japan's post-1968

Japan's post-1968, 202–18; *Eiga hihyō (Film Criticism),* 16, 203–4, 208–10, 209*fig.*, 213, 214, 215n4; film industry and theaters of 1958–68, 202–3; *Kikan firumu (Film Quarterly),* 16, 203–4, 206*fig.*, 210, 215n4; and political unrest, 202; *Shinema 69, 70, and 71 (Cinema 69, 70, and 71),* 16, 203–7, 207*fig.*, 210–12, 215n4

Jayashree, 37

Jeune Afrique, and African film criticism, 187

Jewish Standard, "Even as You and Hye," 304

Jinnah, Muhammad Ali, 52

Johnston, William A., 344

Joint Struggle Committee for the Suzuki Seijun Problem (Suzuki Seijun mondai kyōtō kaigi), 215n4

Jolly Fellows (film), 237

Jou (film), 238

Journal of African Cinemas, and African film criticism, 197

"Judas" (Sushila Rani Patel), 38, 50

Kaboré, Gaston, 195
Kaixin (Happy) production house, 354
Kala-Lobe, Iwiyé, 185
Kane, Jacques Mélo, 185
Kanellos, Nicolás, 258
Kansas City Journal-Post, newspapers and syndicated movie sections, 99
Kansas City Star, newspapers and syndicated movie sections, 99
kan xinwen (beauty of theatrical experiences), 125n28
Karush, Matthew, 254, 266
Karwan, film reviews in, 43
Kast, Pierre, 171, 172, 174
Kastalia, amateur science interest in film (Germany, pre-World War I), 161
Katō Tai, 207
Kaur, Rajkumari Amrit, 51
Kessler, Frank, 147
Khachikian, Samuel, 73, 74*fig.*
Khandekar, Vishnu Sakharam, 48
Kikan firumu (Film Quarterly): Japan's post-1968, 16, 203–4, 206*fig.*, 210, 215n4; study of, 16
Kilian, Eugen, 289
Kim, Chung-kang, 14
Kim Chi-yǒng, 66
Kim Hye-chǒng, 61, 63*fig.*
Kimiavi, Parviz, 71, 72
Kim Yǒn-suk, 68n20
Kinema junpō (Movie Times), Japan's post-1968, 204
Kinematographie Klub (Vienna), 153
Kinematographische Monatshefte, amateur science interest in film (Germany, pre-World War I), 161n61
Kinetoscope, 307
King Hu, 226
Kino, 235–47; caricatures used by, 245–46; circulation, 235, 247n6; coverage and importance, 236–41; design, 241–43, 242*fig.*, 243*fig.*; digitization, 246; editorial decision making, 243–45; function and scope, 16, 235–36; *Kino-gazeta*, duration of, 235; Stalinist Soviet Union, overview, 235–36; study of, 16
Kinsey Reports, 66
Kirov, Sergei, 243
Kismet (film), 38
Kitano, Takeshi, 227–28
Klär, Karl, 281
Klaren, Georg C., 289
Knapp, Joseph P., 91

Kodak, 221, 224, 225*fig.*
Koop, Volker, 295n16
Korean War, and South Korea's publishing industry growth, 57–58
Korn, Julio, 266–67, 273n17
Korol', Mikhail, 244
Kosmos. Entwurf einer physischen Weltbeschreibung (Cosmos: A Sketch of a Physical Description of the Universe, Humboldt), 150, 159n26
Kosmos: Handweiser für Naturfreunde, amateur science interest in film (Germany, pre-World War I), 150–53, 160n43
Kosmos Bändchen (Kosmos Booklets), amateur science interest in film (Germany, pre-World War I), 151
Kosmos Klub für wissenschaftliche und künstleriche Kinematographie (Kosmos Club for Scientific and Artistic Cinematography), 153
Koster, Henry, 241
Kozintsev, Grigorii, 237
Kracauer, Siegfried, 30, 35n19, 169, 210
Kramer, Robert, 210–11
Kreimeier, Klaus, 279
Krinkin, Iosif, 244
Ku Klux Klan, 255
Kuliev, Aga-Rza, 241
Kulturfilm movement, 155–57
Kuomintang (KMT) Party (Taiwan), 220–23

La Batalla, and transnational cultural influence, 256
La Cancha (The Pitch), and Argentine celebrity culture, 266
La Canción Moderna (The Modern Song, later *Radiolandia)*, and Argentine celebrity culture, 266. See also *Radiolandia (Radioland)*, fan magazines, and celebrity culture
La Cinématographie française: news-sharing agreement of, 9; study of, 9
La Conquête de l'air (La conquista dell'aria, film), 28
La critica cinematografica, study of, 9
La dolce vita (film), 139, 143n38
Lady of Shanghai (film), 176
L'Afrique actuelle, African film criticism in Paris, 15–16, 184, 185, 187, 188, 191, 194–95, 197–98, 199n15
L'air de Paris/The Air of Paris (film), 169
Lall, Chuni, 51

Lamarque, Libertad, 262, 265, 268, 269, 270
Lamarr, Hedy, 74
Lambrecht, Friedrich, 159
"La Melanomania" (Zayas Enriquez), 255–56
La Nación (The Nation), and Argentine celebrity culture, 267
Lanckman, Lies, 7–8
landscape theory, 208–10, 214, 216n14
Lang, Fritz, 289
L'Ange bleu (The Blue Angel, film), 29
Langlois, Henri, 166, 168, 176
language, similarity in publications. *See* computational analysis of United States film industry trade press (early 1920s)
La Noire de . . . /Black Girl (film), 195
Lantern (search platform), 5, 10, 330, 339, 344. *See also* Media History Digital Library (MHDL)
La Passion de Jeanne d'Arc (film), 289
La Pointe Courte (film), 169, 171–72
La quena de la muerte/The Queen of Death (film), 268
La Revue du cinéma (France): and African film criticism, 195; and Latin American cine club publications, 195; and mid-century French film industry, 176
large language models (LLMs), 336
La Rivista del Cinematografo, and postwar Italian film industry, 318
The Last Ball (film), 238
Lateef, Shahid, 52
Latin American cine club magazines, 131–44; cine clubs, defined, 133; content of, 134–35; film critics and politicization of Latin American film culture, 136, 138–41; and film society movement, 131–33, 141n6; popularity of, 15, 133; readers' connection to film culture, 136–38; transnational fostering of cinephilia, 15; visual design of, 133–34, 134*fig.*, 135*fig.* See also *Cine-Mundial* and transnational cultural influence
Laughter Stage (Xiaowutai 笑舞台), intermediality in film publications, 125n28
Laurencin, Marie, 26
Laval Decree (1934), 185
La vida de Carlos Gardel (The Life of Carlos Gardel, film), 273n25
La Vie Africaine: African film criticism in Paris, 15–16, 184, 185, 187–90, 189*fig.*, 191–94, 192*fig.*, 195, 197–98; study of, 15
Le beau Serge (film), 172, 175
Lebedev, Nikolai, 244

Le bel âge (film), 174
Le coup du berger (film), 172
Le Courrier cinématographique, study of, 11
L'Écran français (France), and Latin American cine club publications, 139
Ledesma, Amanda, 268, 270, 271
Le Diable au corps/Devil in the Flesh (film), 185
Lee, Winston, 224, 226
Leenhardt, Roger, 166
Lee Ping-Bing, Mark, 224, 225*fig.*
Le Film Africain, and African film criticism, 197
Le grand Magal à Touba/Grand Magal in Touba (film), 191
Leiris, Michel, 185
Le Journal du Ciné-club (France), and Latin American cine club publications, 133
Lenin, Vladimir, 192, 237, 246
Lenin in October (film), 241
Lenk, Sabine, 147
Le Quai des brumes (film), 26
Les Miracles (cinema), 26
Les Mistons (film), 172
Les Nouveaux Messieurs (film), 25
Le Soleil, and African film criticism, 197
Les quatre cents coups/The 400 Blows (film), 174
Les Statues meurent aussi (Statues Also Die) (film), 163
Letsch, Paul, 291
Levenshtein, Vladimir, 338
Levenshtein distances, 336, 338–39. *See also* computational analysis of United States film industry trade press (early 1920s)
Lever Brothers, 101
Lewis, Ray, 50, 302–6, 306*fig.*
L'Herbier, Marcel, 163, 171
Liang Liang, 222
Liang Xinhua, 223
Library of Congress, 5
Lichtbilderei GmbH, 148
Lichtbildkunst, amateur science interest in film (Germany, pre-World War I), 158n7
Life (magazine): photography by, 68n5; and *The Wrong Man* (film), 84n37
Life of an American Fireman (film), 178
Li Han-hsiang, 226
Lindemann, Alfred, 280–81, 283
L'Intransigeant (France): Bailby's ownership of, 26; political slant of, 31
Linyera, Dante A., 266
Lin Yingzhi, 226
literacy: in Iran, 73, 82n3, 82n7, 83n15; in South Korea, 57, 59

396 INDEX

Litvinov, Aleksandr, 238
Liu-He Film Company, 112
Lloyd, Harold, 348
Lombardy Association of Cinema and Theatre Exhibitors, 319
Long, Jady, 226–27
Long Take, and Taiwanese film culture, 220
Look, photography by, 68n5
Looking Past the Screen (Smoodin), 7
López, Ana M., 264
Loren, Sophia, 191
Los Angeles Illustrated Daily News, newspapers and syndicated movie sections, 97
Los Angeles-Tehran (film), 71
Los Angeles Times (Pre-View), newspapers and syndicated movie sections, 94–95
Lo schermo, study of, 11
Los Tigres Voladores (The Flying Tigers), Harrison's influence on, 4
Love's Sacrifice (film), 359, 361
LR1 Radio El Mundo (AM 1070, Argentina), and celebrity culture, 264
Lumière Cinématographe, 313n48
Lü Su-Shang, 350–51

Macias Gonzalez, Victor, 254
MacKenzie, Scott, 8, 210
Madero, Francisco I., 256
Maetzig, Kurt, 283
Maffei, Claire, 185
The Magnificent Ambersons (film), 170, 176, 177, 178
Mahndmeh-ye sinema'i-ye film (*Film Monthly*, Iran), and Taiwanese film culture, 220–21
Maiwald, Klaus-Jürgen, 279
Makino Masahiro, 208
Mali Federation, 187
Malle, Louis, 171, 172
Mal'tsev, Konstantin, 244
Mandarin Ducks and Butterflies School, 115, 351–54
Manteola, José, 262, 272n1
Manto, Saadat Hasan, 52
Mao Jianpei, 114
Mapping Movie Magazines: Digitization, Periodicals and Cinema History (Biltereyst and Van de Vijver, eds.), 7–8
Mapping Movie Magazines (Biltereyst and Van de Vijver), 317
Mar'an, David, 238
Marcellini, Romolo, 28
Marcha (Uruguay), and Latin American cine club publications, 139

Marinetti, Filippo Tommaso, 210
Marion, Denis, 30
Marker, Chris, 163, 187
Marly event (1954), 170
Marshall, Niní, 268
Martin, Douglas, 95, 97
Martin, Mabel Brown, 91
Martin, Marcel, 175
Martín Barbero, Jesús, 272
Martinez, Modesto, 255
Martínez Carril, Manuel, 140
Mass Cinema (*Dazhong dianying* 大眾電影), intermediality in film publications, 122
Mata Hari (film), 252fig.
Match L'Intran (France), Bailby's ownership of, 26
Matsuda Masao, 208, 213–14
Matsumoto Toshio, 205
Maupassant, Guy de, 237
Mauriac, Claude, 169
Maxwell, Reginald, 42
May Fourth movement (1919, China), 361
McAvoy, May, 26
McDonald, Tamar Jeffers, 7–8, 101
McElwee, John, 5
McGovern, Charles, 253
McLuhan, Marshall, 306
Media History Digital Library (MHDL): and Canadian film industry documentation, 301, 302, 310; for computational analysis of United States film industry trade press (early 1920s), 330, 332, 334, 336, 338–40; *filmindia* and availability in, 53; globalizing effort for, 10–13, 12fig.; Lantern (search platform), 5, 10, 330, 339, 344; magazines available in, 11, 18, 369–76fig.; magazine types in, 86; for understanding Chinese film history, 347–50, 354, 365n21
Medizinisch-Kinematographisches Institut, 157
Medizin und Film, amateur science interest in film (Germany, pre-World War I), 157
Mehrabi, Massoud, 71–73
Mekas, Jonas, 204, 210
Mekas, Jonas & Adolfas, 139
Méliès, Georges, 120, 210
Melville, Jean-Pierre, 172
Mexico. See *Cine-Mundial* and transnational cultural influence
Meyer, Max Wilhelm, 150
Meyerhold, Vsevolod, 210
Micron XIB, 51
Mikrofilmarchiv der deutschsprachigen Presse, 11
Mikrokosmos, amateur science interest in film (Germany, pre-World War I), 151

Milk of Magnesia (Phillips), 262

Milwaukee Journal, newspapers and syndicated movie sections, 89, 100

Ming Ji, 226

Mingxing Film Company, 112

Mingxing Monthly (*Mingxing yuebao* 明星月報), intermediality in film publications, 113

Mini, Darshana, 5, 14

Mitchell, Margaret, 32

Mitlin, Aron, 244, 245

Mitry, Jean, 170, 176

Mi Zo, 223

Modern Cinema (*Xiandai dianying* 現代電影), intermediality in film publications, 113

Modern Screen, newspapers and syndicated movie sections, 101

Modern Times (film), 169

Mogambo (film), 169

Moglia Barth, Luis, 262, 269

Moi, un noir (film), 190

Molotov, Vyacheslav, 240

Mon Film (France), 30

Mon Film (Paramount Pictures' journal), 29

Monroe, Marilyn, 59, 60*fig.*

Moore, Paul, 14, 17

Moravia, Alberto, 319

Morgan, Gene, 88

Morin, Edgar, 265, 267

Morlay, Gaby, 25, 27*fig.*

Morning Star (*Chenxing* 晨星), intermediality in film publications, 112

Morris, Peter, 310, 313n48

Moscow State Cinema Institute (VGIK), 244

Mother India (formerly *filmindia*), 38, 52–53. See also *filmindia*

Motion Picture Almanac, and Canadian film industry, 307

Motion Picture Herald, study of, 1

Motion Picture Mail (*New York Mail and Express*), newspapers and syndicated movie sections, 89

Motion Picture News: computational analysis of United States film industry trade press, 330, 333*fig.*, 334*fig.*, 340–44; study of, 18

Motion Picture Review (*Yingxi zazhi* 影戲雜志): intermediality in film publications, 112; and understanding Chinese film history, 348–50, 364n6

Motion Picture Studio, computational analysis of United States film industry trade press, 333*fig.*

Motion-Play Magazine, newspapers and syndicated movie sections, 91–94, 93*fig.*

Mouramani (film), 186

Movie & Dance News (*Wuying xinwen* 舞影新聞), intermediality in film publications, 109

Movie Monthly (*Dianying yuebao* 電影月報), intermediality in film publications, 112

Movie News Weekly (*Dianying xinwen* 電影新聞), intermediality in film publications, 116*fig.*

Movie Pictorial (*Dianying huabao* 電影畫報), intermediality in film publications, 107, 108*fig.*, 109, 122n1

movie sections in newspapers. *See* newspapers and syndicated movie sections

Movie Sketch (*Dianying manhua* 電影漫畫), intermediality in film publications, 114

Movies Magazine (*Dianying zazhi*), and understanding Chinese film history, 348–50

Movietone (*Diansheng* 電聲), intermediality in film publications, 113, 115, 122

Moving Picture World: and *Cine-Mundial*, 248; computational analysis of United States film industry trade press, 330, 333*fig.*, 340–44; and Quigley, 258n1; study of, 18

Mr. Habetin (film), 294n3

Muchachita de Chiclana/Chiclana Girl (film), 268

Mudimbe, V. Y., 198n2

Mukherjee, Debashree, 50

Muñequitas porteñas/Porteño Dolls (film), 268

Münsterberg, Hugo, 210

Murray, Mae, 253

Museum of Modern Art Library, 5

Mussawar (India), film reviews in, 43

Mussolini, Benito, 220, 253

Mussolini, Vittorio, 220

N. W. Ayer and Son's American Newspaper Annual and Directory, 86–87, 103n38

Nadia, Fearless, 48

Nagayama Norio, 216n14

Nakagawa Shigeaki, 211

Nakahara Yūsuke, 205

Nakai Masakazu, 211

Napoléon (film), 133

Naruse, Mikio, 170

National Board of Review (United States), 80, 84n42

National Ethics Committee for Magazines, 63

National Film Board of Canada, 303, 306–10

National Film Library (Taiwan Film and Audiovisual Institute, TFAI), 16, 219–21, 223–26, 228

National Film Society (Canada), 308

National Gallery of Canada, 307

398 INDEX

Nationalist Party (Kuomintang or KMT, China), 348, 359

National Socialism (Germany)/Nazism and film propaganda, 279, 283–90. See also *Neue Filmwelt (New Film World)* and post-World War II German film culture

Navarro, Fanny, 262

Navitski, Rielle, 9, 15, 112, 248–49, 250, 254

NBC, 256

Negin (Iran), as intellectual journal, 73

Negro Drawings (Covarrubia), 258

Nehru, Jawaharlal, 52

Neroy, D. B., 38

network, defined, 8

Neuburger, Albert, 155

Neue Filmwelt (New Film World) and post-World War II German film culture, 277–99; analysis of, overview, 277–88, 295n7; and *Der Filmspiegel* inception, 293; historical and political context of, 17, 278–81; and *Illustrierter Film-Spiegel* (*Program leaflet of the magazine* Neue Filmwelt, leaflet), 292–94, 296n27; magazine's evolution, propaganda and editorial stance, 291–93, 292*fig.*, 293*fig.*; magazine's first issue, Bergmann's editorial, 281–82; magazine's first issue and layout, editorial stance, national focus, 282–91, 284–88*fig.*, 290*fig.*, 296n30; *Neue Filmwelt*, study of magazine, 9, 17

Neue Photographische Gesellschaft, 149

Nevsky, Alexander, 246

new cinema history discipline, 6–7

New Cinema movement (Taiwan), 16, 219, 220–23, 226, 228

New Jack Printing Press, 37

Newman, Kathleen, 8

New Movie Songs (*Dianying xinge ji* 電影新歌集), intermediality in film publications, 109

New Orleans Item, newspapers and syndicated movie sections, 91

newspapers, and Argentine celebrity culture, 264

newspapers, digitizing, 363. See also Chinese film history (1920s)

newspapers and syndicated movie sections, 86–106; "Cinema Plaza" section (*United Daily News*, Taiwan), 222; as hybrid film journalism, 14; magazines, defining, 86, 101–2; *Motion-Play Magazine*, 91–94, 93*fig.*; newspaper supplements and novelties, inception of, 87–91; *Pre-View (Los Angeles Times)*, 94–95; pricing, 87, 89, 94, 95, 101;

rotogravure sections, inception of, 89, 90*fig.*; *Screen & Radio Weekly*, 95–101, 96*fig.*, 98*fig.*, 100*fig.*; subscription pricing and circulation of, 86–87, 89, 94, 95, 101, 103n48, 104n67; Sunday newspaper supplement format of, 86–87; syndicated, rotogravure Sunday fan magazines, 91–92; syndicated, rotogravure Sunday fan magazines, inception of, 91–92

news through cinema. *See* Chinese film publications

New Sun Company (*Sint'aeyangsa*), 59, 60, 68n9

New Sun (Sint'aeyang), publication of, 68n9

New Wave (*La nouvelle vague*): *Cinéma* (France) and mid-century French film industry, 171–75, 173*fig.*, 174*fig.*; and Latin American cine club magazines, 135, 139, 171; and magazines of Japan's post-1968, 207; study of, 9

New York Daily News, newspapers and syndicated movie sections, 86, 97, 99

New Yorker, and transnational cultural influence, 257–58

New York Evening Mail, newspapers and syndicated movie sections, 89

New York Mail and Express, newspapers and syndicated movie sections, 91

New York Morning Journal, newspapers and syndicated movie sections, 91

New York Public Library, 5, 11, 12*fig.*

New York Sun, newspapers and syndicated movie sections, 89

New York Times, newspapers and syndicated movie sections, 91, 97, 99, 103n36

New York Tribune, newspapers and syndicated movie sections, 89

New York World, newspapers and syndicated movie sections, 87

Ngassa, Jean-Paul, 191

Niang, Bassirou, 197

"Nihon no eiga riron" (Film Theory in Japan, Satō), 211–13

Nikkatsu film studio, 203, 215n4

nitrate film, 308–9

Normalization Act (1965), 68n14

Normand, Mabel, 74

Noto, Paolo, 320

Novarro, Ramón, 252*fig.*

Nuevo Film (Uruguay, previously *Film*), and Latin American cine club publications, 132, 141n4

Oakland Tribune, newspapers and syndicated movie sections, 95, 99–100

O'Connor, Elsa, 262
Odeon, 303–6
O Fan (Brazil), and Latin American cine club publications, 133
Office catholique international du cinéma, 136–37
Ogawa Shinsuke, 203
Okaasan/Mother (film), 170
Omid, Jamal, 73
Once over the Summer (film), 238
One Hundred Men and a Girl (film), 241
On Photoplay (Yingxi xue), and understanding Chinese film history, 349, 351–54, 352*fig.*, 353*fig.*, 361, 364n8
OpenAI, 336
Ophüls, Max, 31
optical character recognition (OCR), 5, 336. *See also* computational analysis of United States film industry trade press (early 1920s)
Organization of American States, 258n10
Orlan, Pierre Mac, 26
Ortega, García, 256
Ortiz, Mecha, 262
Ōshima Nagisa, 203, 207
Ossessione (film), 220
Ostādān-e jenāyat (Masters of Crime, Gow), 83n33
Osten, Franz, 39
Ostrovskii, Nikolai, 237
Oswald, John Claude, 249
Ōta Ryū, 213
Ōtsuki Kenji, 211
Ozu Yasujirō, 212

Pabst, Georg Wilhelm, 133
Pagano, Angelina, 262
Pagnol, Marcel, 171
Pahlavi, Mohammad Reza (Shah of Iran), 73
Painlevé, Jean, 166, 167–69
Pakistan, *filmindia (Mother India)* and anti-Muslim sentiment, 52–53
Pakravan, Tina, 71
Pan-African Federation of Filmmakers (FEPACI), 195
Panama cigarettes (Golden Tobacco Company), 45, 47*fig.*
Pan-Americanism, 249, 258n10
Pan-American Union, 249, 258n10
Pandit, Sambanand Monappa, 39
Pan Habetín odchází (film), 294n3
paper cinema of Chinese film publications, 110, 114–21, 116*fig.*, 118*fig.*, 119*fig.*

"Paradoxes and Truths on the History of Cinema" (Sadoul), 175–79
Paramount, Canadian theaters owned by, 302, 304, 306
Paramount Pep, computational analysis of United States film industry trade press, 332, 333*fig.*
Paramount Pictures, 29
Park Chung Hee, 65–66
Parker, D. N., 37, 38
Parsons, Louella, 90
Partido Obrero de Unificación Marxista (POUM, Workers' Party of Marxist Unification), 256
Patel, Baburao, 1–3, 14, 37–39, 40–43, 44, 48, 50–51, 52–53
Patel, Sushila Rani ("Judas"), 38, 50
Pathé KOK projector, 159n23
Paul Kendel Fonoroff Collection for Chinese Film Studies (University of California, Berkeley), 125n35
pausing mechanisms for projectors, 159n23
Pawar, G. P., 48
Pawar, Lalita, 48
Peacock Motion Picture Corporation, 359, 360*fig.*
Pearson, Virginia, 90
Peasants (film), 237
Pelletier, Louis, 302
Pellizzari, Lorenzo, 319
Penella, Manuel, 253
Pérez, Ramiro (pseud.), 254
Periodical Indexing Project, 318
Petrov, Vladimir, 237
Pettis, Ben, 18
Pfizer, Ina, 149, 150
P for Pelican (film), 71
Philadelphia Record, newspapers and syndicated movie sections, 91–92
Philipe, Anne, 170
Phillips' Milk of Magnesia, 262
photography: photographic content of *Delight* (South Korea), 58–64, 60–64*fig.*, 67, 68n5; still images and moving images, intersection of, 123n4. *See also* visual design and layout
Photoplay: computational analysis of United States film industry trade press, 332, 332*fig.*; and content of *Delight*, 58, 63; newspapers and syndicated movie sections, 105
Pickford, Mary, 74, 89, 90*fig.*, 310
Picturegoer, computational analysis of United States film industry trade press, 332, 333*fig.*

400 INDEX

Picture News (Dianying zazhi), intermediality in film publications, 118*fig.*

Pierce, David, 365n21

Piscator, Erwin, 238

Platense Film, 269, 274n34

political content: and Chinese film history, 347–48, 358–59; *Cine-Mundial* and transnational cultural influence, 256–57; colonialism, *filmindia* on, 42–43; of *Delight* (South Korea), 58, 64–67, 66*fig.*; *filmindia (Mother India)* and anti-Muslim sentiment, 52–53; and Iran's film industry, 71–72; "Iraq agitation," *filmindia* on, 48–50; Japan's post-1968, 202–18; Latin American cine club magazines and politicization of Latin American film culture, 138–41; of *Mother India* (formerly *filmindia*), 38, 52–53. See also *Film Appreciation (Fa,* 電影欣賞*)* and Taiwanese film culture; film magazines as intermediaries of state, region, and media; Japan's post-1968; *individual names of countries*

Ponce de León, Julio, 139

Pope, Vernon, 98

Poppe, Nicolas, 5, 17

Porter, Edwin S., 178

Positif: and African film criticism, 197; film studies analysis of, 277

Posner, Lee, 257

post-World War II German film culture. See *Neue Filmwelt (New Film World)* and post-World War II German film culture

Poulenc, Francis, 166

Pour Vous and French film culture (1928–40), 25–36; audience of, 25, 32–33; closure of, 14, 32–34; content of, 13–14, 25–33, 27*fig.*, 33*fig.*; Des Amis de *Pour Vous*, 29; editorial board of, 26, 31–32; study of magazine, 9, 17; subscription cost of, 26

Prabhat Film Company/Studios, 37–39

Pradhan, Snehapradha, 51

Pratley, Gerald, 307, 308, 312n29

Pravda (Soviet Communist Party), Stalin's speech (March 3, 1937) in, 239

Preminger, Otto, 169

Présence Africaine: African film criticism in Paris, 15–16, 184–88, 190, 191, 194, 197–98, 198n2; study of magazine, 15

Pre-View (Los Angeles Times), newspapers and syndicated movie sections, 94–95

Price, Gertrude M., 88

print and cinema, intermediality in. See Chinese film publications

Printer's Ink: and syndicated movie sections, 91; and transnational cultural influence, 253

printing: of *filmindia*, 37–38; Japan's post-1968 and magazine publishing, 204; of *Mother India* (formerly *filmindia*), 52–53; rotogravure material, 89, 91–92, 94, 98. See also newspapers and syndicated movie sections

Programme der medizinischen Woche, amateur science interest in film (Germany, pre-World War I), 157

"Propaganda as Documentary" (Shaw), 42

Pudovkin, Vsevolod, 139, 169, 210

Pullaiah, P., 48

Punjab Mail (film), 48, 50

Quarterly of Film Radio and Television, and Latin American cine club publications, 141n8

Quigley, Martin, 258n1, 306*fig.*, 344

Radio Belgrano, *Radiolandia* and celebrity culture, 262–64, 263*fig.*, 268–71, 270*fig.*, 275n38

Radio El Mundo, ownership of, 267

Radiolandia (Radioland), fan magazines, and celebrity culture, 262–76; and advertising, 262, 263*fig.*, 272; and Delbene, 17, 262–65, 263*fig.*, 268–71, 273n26, 273n29, 273n33; and *El último estreno* (Radio Belgrano), 262–64, 263*fig.*, 268–71, 270*fig.*, 275n38; *galán*, defined, 273n24; movie magazine influence on Argentine film culture, 17; *Radiolandia*, study of, 17; *Radiolandia* and promotion of celebrity culture, 265–72, 270*fig.*

Ramsaye, Terry, 176, 307, 308

Ranjit Cinetone, 43

Rascacielos (Skyscraper, ballet), 256

Ratovondrahona, 190

Rawling, Judy, 61

Rayns, Tony, 223

RCA Photophone, 51

Rea, Christopher, 365n20

readers' letters. See audience and reader participation

Reardon, G. F., 50

Rear Window (film), 79, 84n37

Recoder, Josep Maria, 257

Reinhardt, Max, 169

Rekabtalaei, Golbarg, 83n20

Renoir, Jean, 170, 171, 178

Ren Pengnian, 111

Resnais, Alain, 139, 163, 168, 171, 172, 174, 187

Revenge (film), 238

Revista Americana de Farmacia y Medicina, and transnational cultural influence, 250

Revista de Cinema (Brazil), and Latin American cine club publications, 135
Revista del exhibidor, and Argentine celebrity culture, 272n10
Revolt of the Fishermen (film), 238
Revolutionary Trade Union Opposition (RGO), 280
"Revolution Promise" (Park), 65
Reyes, Bernardo, 257
Rhee, Syngman, 65, 69n22
Ribalta, J. Carner, 256, 260n39
Rieupeyrout, Jean-Louis, 170
Río de la Plata region (Argentina and Uruguay). *See* Latin American cine club magazines
Rivera, Diego, 256
River of No Return (film), 169
Riverón, Enrique, 257
Rivette, Jacques, 172
RKO studio, 41, 177
Robert, Bernes, 97
Robinson Crusoe (film), 169
Rocha, Glauber, 210
Rochester Democrat and Chronicle, newspapers and syndicated movie sections, 99
Rodenberg, Hans, 280
Rodowick, D. N., 211
Rohmer, Éric, 171
Roland (Andrés José Rolando Fustiñana), 137
Román, Alita, 262
Romm, Mikhail, 237, 241
Room, Abram, 238
Roosevelt, Franklin D., 28
Rotha, Paul, 168
rotogravure material, 89, 91–92, 94, 98. *See also* newspapers and syndicated movie sections
Rouch, Jean, 187, 190, 195
Rowden, Terry, 9
Rowshanfekr (Iran), as intellectual journal, 73
The Royal Sailors (film), 238
Ruan Lingyu, 114
Ryakushō renzoku shasatsuma/A.K.A. Serial Killer (film), 208, 214, 216n14

S. J. Benjamin Cheng (Cheng Shuren), 349, 354
Sadaf (Iran), as intellectual journal, 73
Sadji, Abdoulaye, 185
Sadoul, Georges, 169, 170, 175–79, 190
A Saint in Street Clothes (Bossin), 312n19
Sala, Leo, 137–38
Salem, Ben, 191
Sales, Sohrab Shahid, 71, 72
Samjungdang, 59
Sanchez García, José M., 253

Sandrini, Luis, 265, 268
The Sandwich Man (film), 219
Sant Tukaram (film), 37
Saracini, Juan, 274n34
Sarlo, Beatriz, 264
Sarr, Mamadou, 185
Sartre, Jean-Paul, 185, 205
Sasaki Mamoru, 208
Satie, Erik, 19
Sati Mahananda (film), 38
Satō Tadao, 211–12, 213
Sauvy, Élisabeth (Titaÿna), 31–32
Savinio, Alberto, 319
Scherl publishing house, 278
Schoonover, Karl, 9
Scott, Claude, 42–43
Scott, Walter, 150
Screen: film studies analysis of, 277; study of, 7
Screen & Radio Weekly, newspapers and syndicated movie sections, 95–101, 96*fig.*, 98*fig.*, 100*fig.*
Screen Stage Monthly (Dianying xiju 電影戲劇), intermediality in film publications, 109
Second Moscow Show Trial (Great Terror, Soviet Union, 1937–38), 239–40
Seeds of Destiny (documentary), 304
Seitz, Fritz (Friederich), 146, 151
Sembene, Ousmane, 187, 195
Sembene Ousmane, Filmmaker (Sembène Ousmane, cinéaste, Vieyra), 187
Senciné, and African film criticism, 197
Senegal, sub-Saharan African cinema, 187–88, 191, 195, 197–98. *See also* African film criticism in Paris
Senghor, Blaise, 187, 191, 194
Séptimo Arte (Chile), and Latin American cine club publications, 134, 134*fig.*
Sequence (United Kingdom), and Latin American cine club publications, 139
Serna, Laura Isabel, 17
Serrador, Pepita, 262
Setāreh-ye Sinemā (Cinema Star), 71–85; collage design of, 14, 72, 78–80, 79*fig.*; and editorial content of Iranian publications, 14, 75, 77*fig.*, 82n6; film criticism respect vs. fan service disparagement for, 14, 71–82, 74*fig.*, 77*fig.*, 78*fig.*; study of, 14
sexual content: *Delight* on, 58–64, 60–64*fig.*, 67; *filmindia* on, 43, 45*fig.*; Hays Office Production Code, 41, 100–101; *yuejing* (Chinese film publication sections), 114
Shadowland, computational analysis of United States film industry trade press, 332, 333*fig.*

402 INDEX

Shafran, Arkadii, 237
Shakuntala (film), 37
Shalini Cinetone Kolhapur, 48
Shallert, Edwin, 95
Shanghai Library, 123–24n14, 349
Shanghai Photoplay Society, 348
Shantaram, V., 37
Shaw, Alexander, 42–43
Shaw brothers, 361
Shaws Movietown, 361
Shchors (film), 240
Shenbao 申報, *intermediality in film publications, 111*
Sher, Jack, 97
Shibao Pictorial Weekly (*Shibao tuhuazhoukan* 時報圖畫周刊), intermediality in film publications, 111, 117, 119*fig.*
Shinema 69, 70, and 71 (*Cinema 69, 70, and 71*): Japan's post-1968, 16, 203–7, 207*fig.*, 210–12, 215n4; *Shinema 69*, study of, 16
Shinemasha, 205
Shirdel, Kamran, 78
Shōchiku film studio, 203
The Short Course on the History of VKP(b) (Stalin), 240
Shumiatskii, Boris, 240, 244, 245
Sideral (*Stellar*), and Argentine celebrity culture, 266
SIDE (Sociedad Impresora de Discos Electrofónicos), 264, 268
Sight and Sound (Iran), editorial content, 71, 82n2
Sight and Sound (United Kingdom), and Latin American cine club publications, 139, 140
Silver City (*Yindu* 銀都), intermediality in film publications, 109
Silver Flower Monthly (*Yinhua ji* 銀花記), intermediality in film publications, 109
Silver Light (*Yin Guang*), and understanding Chinese film history, 350, 364n12
Silverman, Sime, 302
Silver Screen Singing (*Yinmu gesheng* 銀幕歌聲), intermediality in film publications, 109
Simone, Mercedes, 268
A Simple Event (film), 71
Sinemā Teātr (*Cinema & Theater*), and editorial content of Iranian publications, 72, 82n6
Sinemā va Namāyeshāt (*Cinema and Spectacle*), and editorial content of Iranian publications, 74
Singh, Debi, 50
Sintonía (*In Tune*), and Argentine celebrity culture, 265, 267, 269

Sitney, P. Adams, 210, 211
"Situations of Cinema in the World" (*Shinema 69*), 210
Sklar, Robert, 9
Skolsky, Sidney, 99
Smith, Jay, 305
Smoodin, Eric, 7, 13–14
Soanes, Wood, 99
Socialist Unity Party of Eastern Germany (SED), 281, 291
Society of Friends of Soviet Cinema (ODSK), 235, 244
Soffici, Mario, 268
Sōgestu Art Center, 204
Sokhan (Iran), as intellectual journal, 73
Sokurov, Alexandr, 228
Solanas, Fernando, 210
Sorge, Reinhard, 169
sound film inception: in Chinese film, 347–48; *Pour Vous* on, 25–29
South American, and transnational cultural influence, 250
South Bend Tribune, newspapers and syndicated movie sections, 99, 100*fig.*
South India, *filmindia* on, 40, 48–49, 49*fig.*
South Korea: April Revolution, 64–65, 69n22–23; Golden Age of Cinema, 68n12; Japan and diplomatic relations, 68n14. See also *Delight; individual names of political leaders*
Soviet Military Administration in Germany (SMAD), 280
Soviet Union. See *Kino; Neue Filmwelt (New Film World)* and post-World War II German film culture
Speck, Mary, 254
St. Laurent, Louis, 307
St. Louis Globe-Democrat, newspapers and syndicated movie sections, 90
St. Louis Republic, newspapers and syndicated movie sections, 91
Stage and Screen (*Wutai yinmu* 舞台銀幕), intermediality in film publications, 113
Stalin, Joseph, 238, 239–41, 243–45, 246, 291–92. See also *Kino*
Star Attractions: Twentieth-Century Movie Magazines and Global Fandom (McDonald and Lanckman, eds.), 7–8
Starlight (*Xingguang* 星光), intermediality in film publications, 115
Star (magazine), study of, 11
The Stars (Morin), 265
Stars of David (book), 309
Star Weekly (Toronto), "Tattler's Tales," 304

Staudte, Wolfgang, 283
Stein, Otto Theodor, 148
Steinrück, Albert, 289
Stevens, George, 41
Stevenson, Lesley, 18
Stoddard, Ralph, 88
Storck, Henri, 168
The Stormy Night (film), 358, 365n27
Stroheim, Erich von, 163, 169
Stromgren, Richard L., 7
"Strongheart the Wonderdog in *Brawn of the North*" (advertisement), 342*fig.*, 344
Student von Prag (film), 283
subscription pricing and circulation: circulation of *Kino* (Soviet Union), 235, 247n6; of *Delight* (South Korea), 59; of *Film Appreciation* (Taiwan), 224; of *filmindia*, 38, 39, 43–44, 48, 53; *Film und Lichtbild*, 151; of newspapers with syndicated movie sections, 86–87, 89, 94, 95, 101, 103n48, 104n67
Sugiyama Heiichi, 211
Sunday newspapers and movie sections. *See* newspapers and syndicated movie sections
Sun Yat-sen, 348, 358
The Surreptitious Speech (Mudimbe), 198n2
Sux, Alejandro, 256–57, 260n39
Suyeux, Jean, 188, 192
Suzuki Seijun, 207
Sylvia, Gaby, 25

Tabarraee, Babak, 14
T'ae Hyŏn-sil, 63
Taipei Film Business Association, 223
Taiwan: Film and Audiovisual Institute (formerly National Film Library), 16, 219–21, 223–26; *A History of Cinema and Drama in Taiwan* (Lü Su-Shang), 350–51; as Japanese colony, 358. *See also Film Appreciation* (*Fa*, 電影欣賞) and Taiwanese film culture
Takemitsu Tōru, 205
Tam, Enoch Yee-lok, 123n5
Tamarkin, E. M., 245
Tapsoba, Clément, 195, 197
Tarkhad, Nalini, 38
Taschwer, Klaus, 149
Tati, Jacques, 171
"Tattler's Tales" (*Star Weekly, Toronto*), 304
Taylor, Nat, 303–5, 310
Teatro al día, study of, 11
technology: and accessibility for study of movie magazines, 5–10; and African film criticism, 191; Canadian exhibition of, 307, 313n48; *filmindia* and film/equipment manufacturing

companies, 51–52; *Il Giornale dello Spettacolo* on, in 1950s, 322; of postwar Italy, 322. *See also Film und Lichtbild* and amateur science
Teinosuke, Kinugasa, 365n27
Tejima Shūzō, 205
Telegu language film, 48, 49*fig.*
Temple, Shirley, 96*fig.*
temporal analysis: of *Il Giornale dello Spettacolo* in 1950s, 324; time span of film releases and post-World War II German film culture, 282–91, 284–88*fig.*, 290*fig.*, 296n30
Terada Torahiko, 211
The Terror (film), 26
Teshigahara Hiroshi, 204, 205
Tess of the Storm Country (United Artists Pressbook), computational analysis of United States film industry trade press, 334*fig.*
Thackeray, Bal, 39
That Day at the Beach (film), 219
The Rise of the American Film (Jacobs), 178
Third Moscow Show Trial (Great Terror, Soviet Union, 1937–38), 240
Thorry, Juan Carlos, 268
Thought Company (*Sasanggyesa*), 59
Three Songs overview Lenin (film), 237, 238
Thunderstorm (film), 237
Tianyi studio, 361
Tiempo de Cine (Argentina), and Latin American cine club publications, 132, 135, 136*fig.*, 137, 140, 143n38
The Times of India, film reviews in, 50
Titaÿna (Élisabeth Sauvy), 31–32
Tōei film studio, 203
Toeplitz, Jerzy, 140
Tōhō film studio, 203
Tolstoy, Leo, 48, 351
Tom Sawyer (film), 241
Torn Sprockets (Pratley), 312n29
Toronto Star, and Canadian film industry, 304
Torre Nilsson, Leopoldo, 137–38
Torres Ríos, Leopoldo, 138, 269
Touré, Mamadi, 186
Transnational Cinema: The Film Reader (Ezra and Rowden), 9
Trauberg, Leonid, 237
trends, detecting. *See* computational analysis of United States film industry trade press (early 1920s)
Trisot, André. *See* D'dée
Troianovskii, Mark, 237
True Story (*Silhwa*), publication of, 68n9
Truffaut, François, 26, 34n3, 163, 166, 171, 172, 174, 178, 220

404　INDEX

Tsumura Takashi, 216n29
Tufān dar shahr-e mā (*Storm in Our City*, film), 73, 74*fig.*
Turner, Lana, 76, 77*fig.*
Tweedie, James, 9
Twinex ("Twentieth Century") Theatres, 303

Udden, James, 16
Ufa (Universum-Film Aktiengesellschaft), 278–81, 295n8
Union mondiale du documentaire (World Documentary Union), 167
Unir Cinéma, and African film criticism, 195
United Artists, 4
United Daily News (Taiwan), "Cinema Plaza" section, 222
United Nations Educational, Scientific and Cultural Organization, 136–37
United Red Army (Japan), 202, 208, 213
United States: and Canadian film industry documentation, 301–2; and celebrity culture influence in Argentina, 265; *Cine-Mundial* and United States culture explained to readership, 255–56; influence of/on Latin American cine club publications, 131–44; *Neue Filmwelt* (*New Film World*), post-World War II German film culture, and influence of, 282–83. See also *Cine-Mundial* and transnational cultural influence; newspapers and syndicated movie sections
Universal Weekly, computational analysis of United States film industry trade press, 332, 334*fig.*
Universidad de la República (Uruguay), 131
University of California, Berkeley, 125n35
University of Hong Kong, 349, 350
Universum-Film Aktiengesellschaft (Ufa), 278–81, 295n8
Unterrichtsfilmgesellschaft GmbH, 157
Urania Institute (Berlin), 147, 149, 150, 155, 157n5, 158n7
Urban, Charles, 155
Uruguay. *See* Latin American cine club magazines

Vadim, Roger, 171, 172
VanDerBeek, Stan, 204
Van de Vijver, Lies, 6, 7–8, 317
Vanity Fair, and transnational cultural influence, 258
Varda, Agnès, 169, 171

Variety: computational analysis of United States film industry trade press, 332, 334*fig.*; content of, 330; and Silverman, 302; study of, 317; and Winchell, 311n16
Vasil'ev, Georgii, 237
Vasil'ev, Sergei, 237
Vasili's Return (film), 169
Vast, Jean, 195
Vautier, René, 187
Védrès, Nicole, 171
Verma, Raja Ravi, 39
Vermorel, Claude, 185
Vertigo (film), 79
Vertov, Dziga, 211, 237, 238
Vian, Boris, 188
Vian, Ursula, 188
Vieyra, Paulin Soumanou, 16, 185–88, 186*fig.*, 190–95, 197–98
Vigo, Jean, 168
Visages d'Orient (*The Good Earth*, film), 31
Visconti, Luchino, 220
visual design and layout: cartoons, comics, and illustration, 62, 98, 245–46, 257–58; *Cinéma 57* cover, 164*fig.*; *Delight* (South Korea), visual strategy, 58–64, 60–64*fig.*, 67; *Film Appreciation* (Taiwan), 226–28, 227*fig.*; *filmindia* cover images, 38–40, 43–46, 46*fig.*, 47*fig.*; *Film und Lichtbild* cover, 146*fig.*; *Kino* and Stalinist Soviet Union, caricatures, 245–46; *Kino* and Stalinist Soviet Union, design, 241–43, 242*fig.*, 243*fig.*; of Latin American cine club magazines, 133–34, 134*fig.*, 135*fig.*; *Neue Filmwelt* (*New Film World*) and post-World War II German film culture, 282–91, 284–88*fig.*, 290*fig.*; photography, 58–64, 60–64*fig.*, 67, 68n5; *Setāreh-ye Sinemā* (*Cinema Star*), collage design, 14, 72, 78–80, 79*fig.*
Vitascope (Holland Brothers), 313n48
Vivre sa vie (film), 139, 143n38
von Sternberg, Josef, 29
Vorpahl, Ruth, 282, 296n26
Vosotras (*You*), and Argentine celebrity culture, 266, 273n17
Vovsy, Grigorii, 244, 245

Wadia, Homi, 48
Wagner, Paul, 210
Wakamatsu Kōji, 203
Wales, Clarke, 97
Waller, Greg, 7, 145

Wang Lianying, 111
Waraango, and African film criticism, 195, 197
Warner Bros., 12, 26, 76
Washington Herald, newspapers and syndicated
   movie sections, 92
Wegener, Paul, 283, 289
Welles, Orson, 170, 176, 177, 210
West, Mae, 97
"When French Cinema Speaks for Black Africa"
   (Vieyra), 186–87
"Where the Film Has the (Visual) Word?"
   (Fröhlich), 277–78
The White-Haired Girl (film), 170
Whitehead, Jessica, 302
Wilcox, Grace, 95, 97, 98*fig.*
Wilkerson, W. R., 37, 41
Williams, Whitney, 97
Winchell, Walter, 304, 310, 311n16
Wisconsin Center for Film and Theater
   Research, 10
Wise, Robert, 169
Witte, Karsten, 279
Woman in the Dunes (film), 204
Wong, Anna May, 95, 358
Wong, Edmond, 221, 224, 226, 228
Wong Kar-wai, 228
World Cinemas, Transnational Perspectives
   (Ďurovičová and Newman, eds.), 8
World War I, and Kulturfilm movement, 155–57
World War II: Canadian film industry following,
   306; Germany's occupation of France, 14, 25,
   31–34; postwar France, 15, 163–66. *See also*
   Italian film industry trade publications; *Neue
   Filmwelt (New Film World)* and post-World
   War II German film culture
Wozzeck (film), 289, 290
The Wrong Man (film), 78, 79

Xiaoyu Xia, 123n13
Xinwen bao 新聞報, intermediality in film
   publications, 111
Xu Ligong, 221, 226
Xu Zhuodai, 348, 351, 354, 361

Yamada Kōichi, 205
Yamamoto Naoki, 16
Yamamoto Satsuo, 204
Yamane Sadao, 205
Yang, Edward, 219, 222–23
Yang Xiaozhong, 114
"Yankee invasion," 248, 258n2
Yankelevich, Jaime, 267
Yan Ruisheng, 111
Yan Ruisheng (film), 111–12, 114, 117, 119*fig.*
*Year Book of the Canadian Motion Picture
   Industry.* See *Canadian Film Weekly Year
   Book of the Canadian Motion Picture
   Industry*
year books, defined, 354. See also *Canadian
   Film Weekly Year Book of the Canadian
   Motion Picture Industry*; *China Cinema
   Year Book 1927 (Zhonghua yingyue
   nianian)*, and understanding Chinese film
   history
Yeh, Emilie Yueh-yu, 11, 13, 18, 123n5, 363
yingxi ("shadowplay"), 364n6
yingxi xiaoshuo (paper cinema subgenre), 115
yinmu ("silver screen"), 109
yin (silver), 109
Yomota Inuhiko, 205
Yoshida Kijū, 207
Yoshiwara (film), 31
The Youth of Maxim (film), 237, 246
yuejing (Chinese film publication sections), 114

Zamacois, Eduardo, 257
Zani, Giselda, 139
Zárraga, Miguel de, 257
Zatvornitskii, Gleb, 241
Zavattini, Cesare, 139, 210, 220
Zayas Enriquez, Rafael de, 255–56, 257, 260n43
Zhang Meiyao, 226
Zhang Qinpei, 224, 226
Zhou Ziqi (Chow Tse-chi), 359
Zhu Shouju, 358
Zini, Malisa, 262
Ziyou Shibao, and Taiwanese film culture, 223

Founded in 1893,
UNIVERSITY OF CALIFORNIA PRESS
publishes bold, progressive books and journals
on topics in the arts, humanities, social sciences,
and natural sciences—with a focus on social
justice issues—that inspire thought and action
among readers worldwide.

The UC PRESS FOUNDATION
raises funds to uphold the press's vital role
as an independent, nonprofit publisher, and
receives philanthropic support from a wide
range of individuals and institutions—and from
committed readers like you. To learn more, visit
ucpress.edu/supportus.